LOOSENING
THE GRIP

LOOSENING THE GRIP

A Handbook of Alcohol Information

JEAN KINNEY, M.S.W.
Assistant Professor of Clinical Psychiatry
Executive Director, Project Cork Institute
Dartmouth Medical School
Hanover, New Hampshire

GWEN LEATON
Formerly Director of Education
Edgehill Newport, Inc.
Newport, Rhode Island

FIFTH EDITION

Illustrations by
Stuart Copans, M.D.

 Mosby

St. Louis Baltimore Berlin Boston Carlsbad Chicago London Madrid
Naples New York Philadelphia Sydney Tokyo Toronto

Dedicated to Publishing Excellence

Publisher: James M. Smith
Editor: Vicki Malinee
Developmental Editor: Catherine Schwent
Project Manager: Carol Sullivan Weis
Manufacturing Supervisor: Tim Stringham
Design Manager: Sheilah Barrett

FIFTH EDITION

Printed in the United States of America
Composition by Top Graphics
Printing/binding by R.R. Donnelly

Previous editions copyrighted 1978, 1983, 1987, 1991

Mosby–Year Book, Inc.
11830 Westline Industrial Drive
St. Louis, MO 63146

International Standard Book Number 0-8151-5071-7

Contributors

Chapter 10, Adolescents
ROBERT J. BIDWELL, M.D.

Dr. Bidwell is Associate Professor of Pediatrics at the University of Hawaii John A. Burns School of Medicine and Director of Adolescent Medicine at the Kapiolani Medical Center for Women and Children. Dr. Bidwell is a member of the Board of Directors of the *Coalition for a Drug-Free Hawaii,* an agency working on the prevention of substance abuse statewide.

JEAN KINNEY, M.S.W.

Jean Kinney, Assistant Professor of Psychiatry at Dartmouth Medical School, was the Associate Director of the Alcohol Counselor Training Program at Dartmouth from 1972-1978, the program that was the impetus for this text. Upon the completion of the Alcohol Counselor Training Program, she joined Project Cork, a program established to develop and implement a model curriculum for medical student education. The program has expanded to serve as a resource for medical educators nationally.

GWEN LEATON

Gwen Leaton was involved in the Alcohol Counselor Training Program as a Research Assistant. With its completion she held several positions as Director of Education and Training in both academic and treatment settings, most recently at Edgehill Newport. At present her interest in alcohol and alcoholism remains, although she is no longer professionally involved in the field.

Chapter 10, Psychiatric Illness
FRED C. OSHER, M.D.

Dr. Osher, entered the field of psychiatry after serving as the Medical Director of a Detoxification Center in Detroit, a setting which sparked his continuing interest in substance abuse issues. Following his training in Psychiatry he became a staff psychiatrist and clinical researcher with a community mental health center, with a special interest in those with psychiatric illness and substance abuse problems. Following a stint with the Substance Abuse and Mental Health Services Administration (SAMHSA), he has recently joined the Institute of Psychiatry and Human Behavior at the University of Maryland in Baltimore, as the Director of Community Psychiatry.

Chapter 2, Alcohol and the Body
Chapter 5, Medical Complications
TREVOR R.P. PRICE, M.D.

Dr. Price is Chairman of the Department of Psychiatry, Professor and Chairman of Psychiatry, at the Medical College of Pennsylvania, and Chair of the Council overseeing Project Cork Institute at Dartmouth, a program to promote medical education on alcohol and alcoholism. He entered psychiatry after training in internal medicine. His interest in alcohol was sparked during his tenure at Dartmouth Medical School when he was a member of the faculty for the Alcohol Counselor Training Program.

Chapter 11, Psychiatric Medications
DONALD A. WEST, M.D.

Dr. West, Associate Professor of Psychiatry at Dartmouth Medical School, is actively involved in coordinating Substance Abuse Services at the Dartmouth Hitchcock Medical Center and Medical Director of the short term psychiatric unit at the Medical Center. He originally came to Dartmouth on a half-year sabbatical from the University of New Mexico, which he spent with the substance abuse treatment team, and the area apparently began to look like home.

By the time a text has reached its Fifth Edition it becomes difficult to sort out and separate the particular contributions of individual people. Those listed above assumed responsibility for revising and updating of material for this edition. Much of what remains incorporated here is, however, the product of others who contributed to earlier editions, whose work remains, and who also need to be mentioned.

Chapter 10
Adolescents
FREDERICK BURKLE, JR., M.D., M.P.H., FAAP, FACEP

Dr. Burkle came to a psychiatry residency program at Dartmouth Medical School after a practice in pediatrics. He has since left chilly New England and is a Professor of Pediatrics and Surgery at the University of Hawaii John A. Burns School of Medicine and Professor of Public Health at the University of Hawaii School of Public Health.

Illustrator
Chapter 7, Effects of Alcohol Problems on the Family
STUART COPANS, M.D.

Dr. Copans was formerly a Fellow in Child Psychiatry at Dartmouth Medical School. During that period, he was a lecturer in the alcohol counselor training program, discussing the effects of alcohol abuse on the family—the early signs of what has since become a major professional interest. He presently is Program Medical Director, Tyler Adolescent Residential Treatment Center, Brattleboro Retreat, a Dartmouth-affiliated teaching hospital.

Chapter 10, The Elderly
Chapter 11, Suicide Evaluation and Prevention
RICHARD GOODSTEIN, M.D.
Dr. Goodstein formerly Vice President of Medical Education at the Carrier Foundation and Clinical Associate Professor of Psychiatry at Rutgers Medical School, is currently Senior Director of Medical Partnerships at Merck & Co. in Pennsylvania.

Chapter 10
Adolescents
HUGH MACNAMEE, M.D.
Dr. MacNamee was an Associate Professor of Clinical Psychiatry in the Division of Child Psychiatry at Dartmouth until his death in 1984. Much of the material on adolescents incorporated here reflects lectures he gave to the alcohol counselor trainees. His eminently practical stance and uncommon common sense were always much in evidence. Some things really cannot be improved on.

Chapter 5
Sleep Disturbances
PETER HAURI, PH.D.
Dr. Hauri is presently Professor of Psychology at the Mayo Medical School, Administrative Director of the Sleep Disorders Center at The Mayo Clinic and a Consultant to the Division of Behavioral Medicine in the Department of Psychology and Psychiatry at the Mayo Clinic.

Chapter 1
Alcohol
Susan McGrath Morgan, MSW, CADC
Susan Morgan was a member of the Alcohol Counselor Training Program staff. Her efforts are reflected here in the discussion of alcohol's history. After her tenure with the counselor trainees, she completed her MSW and is now working in the mental health system in Vermont and also has a private practice.

God of Compassion, if anyone has come to Thine altar troubled in spirit, depressed and apprehensive, expecting to go away as he came, with the same haunting heaviness of heart; if anyone is deeply wounded of soul, hardly daring to hope that anything can afford him the relief he seeks, so surprised by the ill that life can do that he is half afraid to pray; O God, surprise him, we beseech Thee, by the graciousness of Thy help; and enable him to take from thy bounty as ungrudgingly as Thou givest, that he may leave his sorrow and take a song away.

Author Unknown

Preface

Material on alcohol and alcoholism is mushrooming. Books, articles, scientific reports, pamphlets. On present use, past use, abuse. Around prevention, efforts at early detection, effects on the family, effects on the body. When, where, why . . .

And yet, if you are in the helping business and reasonably bright and conscientious and can find an occasional half hour to read but don't have all day to search library stacks, then it's probably hard for you to lay your hands on the information you need when it would be most helpful.

This handbook is an attempt to partially remedy the situation. It contains what we believe is the basic information an alcohol counselor or other professional confronted with alcohol problems needs to know and would like to have handy. The work here isn't original. It is an effort to synthesize, organize and sometimes "translate" the information from medicine, psychology, psychiatry, anthropology, sociology, and counseling that applies to alcohol use and alcoholism treatment. This handbook isn't the last word. But we hope it is a starting point.

Preface, *Loosening the Grip*, First Edition, 1978.

RECENT DEVELOPMENTS

In the period since the publication of the first edition of this handbook, what was then described as rapid growth in the literature has become a veritable deluge. Consequently, the demands upon those in the helping professions are even greater. To be current would entail not only scanning the literature from the disciplines mentioned, but also the many new journals of the alcohol and substance abuse fields.

The alcohol field has grown since the first edition of *Loosening the Grip* was published. In the process of undertaking this revision, we could not help but appreciate the many changes that have taken place. Landmarks that have caught our attention include the following:

CAUSES OF DEPENDENCE

- Alcoholism's having a genetic basis was no longer a "recent" finding, nor a controversial notion. Furthermore, in early 1990, biological researchers reported having identified a gene that appeared to play a role in making some individuals more

vulnerable to dependence upon alcohol. While its proven not
as simple as may have appeared at first blush, nonetheless
considerably more is known about the physical factors that
underpin addiction.

- Psychological problems that accompany alcohol dependence
  are now recognized as symptoms of the disease and secondary
  to it. The belief that these precede the onset of the disease and
  thereby cause alcoholism has been largely discredited.

TREATMENT

- Early intervention has replaced "the need to hit bottom" as a
  means of initiating treatment.
- Outpatient treatment has become as widely available as inpatient care.
- Treatment personnel are more commonly being identified, not
  as alcohol "counselors" viewed as paraprofessionals, but they
  are being referred to as alcohol or substance abuse therapists
  and recognized as a full-fledged professionals.
- Alcohol issues are no longer viewed as solely the concern of
  those in the alcohol and substance abuse fields. All helping
  professionals are recognizing the need to master basic clinical
  skills in this arena.

THE FAMILY

- Addressing the family as part of the alcoholic's treatment is no
  longer seen as optional or merely a "nice touch." It has come
  to be viewed as an essential element.
- Beyond incorporating the family into the treatment plan of
  those who are alcoholic, they are seen as warranting and are
  being offered treatment as clients in their own right.
- The negative consequences of being a child in an alcoholic
  family—negative consequences that can reach into adulthood—have been recognized.
- Beyond formal treatment there has emerged a self-help movement for adult children of alcoholics.

THE SCOPE OF THE FIELD

- The alcohol field has enlarged its concerns to alcohol problems and alcohol abuse, not just frank alcoholism.
- The physical effects of "moderate" alcohol use and its impact
  upon health for the nonalcoholic have clearly gained attention. Research is no longer being directed primarily to the
  obvious physical toll that accompanies long-term heavy alcohol use. Of equal importance is the impact of "social" drinking on health.

THE GENERAL PUBLIC

- Attitudes of the general public have changed dramatically.
- Intoxication and drunkenness are far less tolerated, particularly in areas of public safety.
- Per capita alcohol use has declined to the lowest level in over a decade.

CHANGES IN THIS EDITION

Beyond expanding the information that touches on each of the above topics and is woven throughout this edition, some changes introduced warrant comment.

- Increasingly, attention is being paid to differences and special issues that confront particular segments of the population. In this edition, you will find a new chapter devoted to special populations. The groups that are specifically addressed include adolescents, women, the elderly, as well as alcohol issues in the workplace. While dealing with the special considerations that apply in treatment of each of these special populations, we have tried as well to highlight general principles that would pertain to working with any special populations, be they defined by race, ethnicity, sexual orientation, or disability.
- The changes in diagnostic criteria introduced by the publication of the fourth edition of the Diagnostic and Statistical Manual, referred to as DSM-IV, are incorporated.
- While not having a crystal ball and not being able to see into the future, this edition nonetheless touches on the issues being raised in respect to alcohol treatment in relation to health care reform.
- Along with changes in treatment being dictated by changes in health care delivery, there is growing pressure on clinicians in the alcohol field. This edition addresses the pressures for greater professionalism, as well as the issue of certification or licensure. As part of this discussion of alcohol professionals, the material on ethics has been expanded.

Despite all the changes in the field, we still appreciate how well the bulk of the principles underpinning alcohol treatment have stood the test of time, despite new knowledge. In large measure the challenge for the field is in learning how to apply the old truths to new situations.

There are more changes on the horizon. Increasingly, the alcohol and drug fields are no longer seen as wholly separate and distinctive, but as coming together. The notion of "alcoholics" and "addicts" as being different populations is recognized in this day and age as a myth. Multiple substance use has become the rule. In light of this, we struggled with the question of whether this edition should be changed to reflect this clinical reality. Should we give equal weight to different substances and move away from giving the major attention to alcohol?

As will become evident, we decided not to transform this handbook into one directed at substance use generally. The decision in part may have been guided by the old New England wisdom that "If it ain't broke, don't fix it." But there is also a strong clinical rationale for maintaining an alcohol focus. In our national concern with the problems of "substance use," it must be kept clearly in mind that overwhelmingly the problem, in terms of sheer numbers of people affected, has been, and continues to be, alcohol. While polysubstance use has become the rule, the common denominator is virtually always alcohol. By identifying problems of alcohol use, you'll simultaneously identify those at greatest risk for other drug use. (For example, studies of those dependent on cocaine have found that over 90% are simultaneously dependent on alcohol!) Furthermore, the advice commonly heard within AA circles, "keep it simple," seems to have some relevance. Those attempting to master the basics, those to whom this handbook is primarily addressed, do have to start somewhere. Clearly that somewhere should be alcohol. Later, having become comfortable and skilled in handling alcohol use, clinicians will be able to pick up the additional, special points pertaining to other drugs with relative ease.

Since the first edition was published, we received comments on the title. Yes, there is a story behind it. When we were preparing the original text, an apt title did not leap forth. Somewhere along the line, in casual conversation someone recounted the comment of an alcoholic struggling to get sober. This alcoholic, discussing her drinking in a rather defiant and belligerent fashion said, "If God didn't want me to drink, He'd knock the glass out of my hand!" One of us jokingly commented that we hoped whoever was present had supplied the obviously perfect retort, "He will, all you have to do is loosen your grip." Somehow that metaphor caught the simplicity and the complexity, the ease and the difficulty, the "holding on" and "being held" that are a part of alcohol problems.

An almost mandatory conclusion for book prefaces is an exhaustive listing of "all persons whose support and assistance . . ." Trusting that our families, friends, and professional colleagues know who they are, we wish to depart from that tradition. In fact the most significant contribution to this work has been made by individuals whose names and identities, such as the woman in the example just given, are in many instances unknown to us—alcohol therapists, those in the fellowship of AA, members of the clergy, school counselors, the medical profession—all those who have been responsible for the strides in our collective understanding and clinical practice—all those whose efforts in their professional and private lives make loosening the grip possible.

Jean Kinney
Gwen Leaton

Contents

9 Treatment techniques and approaches 239

LOOSENING
THE GRIP

Alcohol

ALCOHOL

Ramses III distributed beer to his subjects and then told them the tingling they felt radiated from him.

ONCE UPON A TIME . . .

Imagine yourself in what is now Clairvoux, high in the Swiss hills. Stone pots dating from the Old Stone Age have been found that once contained a mild beer or wine. The beverage probably was discovered very much like fire—nature plus curiosity. If any watery mixture of vegetable sugars or starches, such as berries or barley, is allowed to stand long enough in a warm place, alcohol will make itself.

No one knows what kind of liquor came first—wine, beer, or mead—but by the Neolithic Age it was *everywhere*. Tales of liquor abound in folklore. One story relates that at the beginning of time the forces of good and evil contested with each other for domination of the earth. Eventually the forces for good won out. But a great many of them had been killed in the process, and wherever they fell, a vine sprouted from the ground. So it seems some felt wine to be a good force. Other myths depict the powers of alcohol as gifts from their gods. Some civilizations worshipped specific gods of wine. The Egyptians' god was Osiris; the Greeks', Dionysius; and the Romans', Bacchus. Wine was used in early rituals as libations (poured out on the ground, altar, etc.). Priests often drank it as part of the rituals. The Bible, too, is full of references to sacrifices including wine.

From ritual uses it spread to convivial uses, and customs developed. Alcohol was a regular part of meals, viewed as a staple in the diet, even before ovens were invented for baking bread. The Assyrians received a daily portion from their masters of a "gallon" of bread and a gallon of fermented brew (probably a barley beer). Bread and wine were offered by the Hebrews on their successful return from battle. In Greece and Rome wine was essential at every kind of gathering. Alcohol was found to contribute to fun and games at a party, for example, the Roman orgies. Certainly, its safety over water was a factor, but the effects had something to do with it. It is hard to imagine an orgy where everyone drank water or welcoming a victorious army with lemonade. By the Middle Ages alcohol permeated everything, accompanying birth, marriage, death, the crowning of kings, diplomatic exchanges, signing treaties, and councils. The monasteries became the taverns and inns of the times, and travelers received the benefit of the grape.

The ancients figured that what was good in these instances might be good in others, and alcohol came into use as a medicine. It was an antiseptic and an anesthetic and was used in combinations to form salves and tonics. As a cure it ran the gamut from black jaundice to knee pain and even hiccups. St. Paul advised Timothy, "No longer drink only water, but use a little wine for the sake of your stomach and your frequent ailments." Liquor was a recognized mood changer, nature's tranquilizer. The biblical King Lemuel's mother advises, "Give wine to them that be of heavy hearts." The

Bible also refers to wine as stimulating and cheering: "Praise to God, that He hath brought forth fruit out of the earth, and wine that maketh glad the heart of man."

FERMENTATION AND DISCOVERY OF DISTILLATION

Nature alone cannot produce stronger stuff than 14% alcohol. Fermentation is a natural process which occurs when yeasts combine with plants, be it potatoes, fruit, or grains. The sugar in the plants, exposed either to wild yeasts from the air or commercial yeasts, produces an enzyme, which in turn, converts sugar into alcohol. Fermentive yeast cannot survive in solutions stronger than 14% alcohol. When that level is reached, the yeast, which is a living thing, ceases to produce and dies.

In the tenth century an Arabian physician, Rhazes, discovered distilled spirits. Actually, he was looking for a way to release "the spirit of the wine." It was welcomed at the time as the "true water of life." European scientists rejoiced in their long-sought "philosopher's stone," or perfect element. A mystique developed, and alcohol was called "the fountain of youth," *eau-de-vie, aqua vitae. Usequebaugh* from the Gaelic *usige beath,* meaning breath of life, is the source of the word "whiskey." The word "alcohol" itself is derived from the Arabic *al kohl.* It originally referred to a fine powder of antimony used for staining the eyelids and gives rise to speculation on the expression, "Here's mud in your eye!" The word evolved to describe any finely ground substance, then the essence of a thing, and eventually came to mean "finely divided spirit," or the essential spirit of the wine. Nineteenth-century temperance advocates tried to prove that the word "alcohol" is derived from the Arabic *alghul,* meaning ghost or evil spirit.

Distilled liquor wasn't a popular drink until about the sixteenth century. Before that it was used as *the* basic medicine and cure for all human ailments. Distillation is a simple process that can produce an alcohol content of almost 93% if it is refined enough times. Remember, nature stops at 14%. Start with a fermented brew. When it is boiled, the alcohol separates from the juice or whatever as steam. Alcohol boils at a lower temperature than the other liquid. The escaping steam is caught in a cooling tube and turns into a liquid again, leaving the juice, water, etc. behind. Voila! Stronger stuff—about 50% alcohol.

Proof as a way of measuring the strength of a given liquor came from a practice used by the early American settlers to test their brews. They saturated gunpowder with alcohol and ignited it: too strong, it flared up; too weak, it sputtered. A strong blue flame was considered the sign of proper strength. Almost straight alcohol was diluted with water to gain the desired flame. Half and half was considered 100 proof. Thus 86-proof bourbon is 43% alcohol. Because alcohol dilutes itself with water from the air, 200-proof, or 100%,

Persia. Malcolm, in his "History of Persia," relates that wine was discovered in that kingdom in the reign of Janisheed. He attempted to preserve grapes in a large vessel. Fermentation occurred and the king believed that the juice was poison and labeled it as such. A lady of the palace, wishing to commit suicide, drank from it. She was pleased with the stupor that followed and repeated the experiment until supply was exhausted. She imparted the secret to the king and a new quantity was made. Hence wine in Persia is called "delightful poison."

SPOONER, WALTER, W.
The Cyclopaedia of Temperance and Prohibition, 1891.

can you find the anachronism in this picture?

Rhazes discovers distilled spirits

alcohol is not possible. The U.S. standards for spirits are between 195 and 198 proof.

ALCOHOL USE IN AMERICA

Alcohol came to America with the explorers and colonists. In 1620, the *Mayflower* landed at Plymouth because, as it says in the ship's log, "We could not now take time for further search or consideration, our victuals having been much spent, especially our bere." The Spanish missionaries brought grapevines, and before the United States was yet a nation, there was wine making in California. The Dutch opened the first distillery on Staten Island in 1640. In the Massachusetts Bay Colony brewing ranked new in importance after milling and baking. The Puritans did not disdain the use of alcohol as is sometimes supposed. A federal law passed in 1790 gave provisions for each soldier to receive a ration of one-fourth pint of brandy, rum, or whiskey. The colonists imported wine and malt beverages and planted vineyards, but it was Jamaican rum that became the answer to the thirst of the new nation. For its sake, New Englanders became the bankers of the slave trade that supplied the molasses needed to produce rum. Eventually whiskey, the backwoods substitute for rum introduced to America by land, superseded rum in popularity. Sour-mash bourbon became the great American drink.

This is a very brief view of alcohol's history. The extent of its uses, the ways in which it has been viewed, and even the amount of writing about it that survives give witness to the value placed on this strange substance. Alcohol has been everywhere, connected to everything that is a part of everyday life. Growing the grapes or grains to produce it is even suspected as the reason for the development of agriculture. Whether making it, using it as a medicine, drinking it, or writing about it, people from early times have devoted much time and energy to alcohol.

WHY BOTHER?

So alcohol happened. Why didn't it go the way of the dinosaurs? Think about the first time you ever tasted alcohol. . . . Some people were exposed early and don't remember the experience of a little sherry in their bottle or rubbed on their gums when they were teething. Some were allowed a taste of Dad's beer or the Christmas Day champagne at a tender age. Some sneaked sips at the first big wedding or party they were around. Some never even saw it until junior or senior high school. Still others were taught from infancy that it was evil and may not have touched it until college or the army took them away from home. And there are some who, for one reason or another, have never touched the stuff. If you are in the majority, however, you probably encountered it in a variation on one of the above themes.

In vino veritas.

PLINY

Maybe you didn't like that first sip of Dad's beer or Aunt Tillie's sherry. Rather than admit it, you decided they must know what was good. So you took a sip every time it was offered. *As you're fighting your way to the top, it helps to have a taste of what's up there.*

Perhaps you were around for the preparations for a big party at your house. Ice, soda, and funny-colored stuff in big bottles were lined up with neat things like cherries, oranges, lemons, and sugar. The atmosphere was busy and exciting. When the guests began to arrive, the first thing they got was something from those bottles. Everyone seemed to talk and laugh quite a bit, and after a while no one seemed to see you. Mom left her drink in the kitchen while she served some of those tasty cheese things she let you try earlier. One quick sip. *To keep the party going, keep the best on hand.*

Perhaps people in your home drank on weekends, but not you. Mom and Dad said things like, "When you're of age" or "Wouldn't want to stunt your growth" or "This is a big people's drink." Anyway, you weren't getting any tastes. Somewhere along the school trail, you wound up at a party you had expected to be like all the others you'd been to. Not this time. Someone brought some beer, and everyone else was having some. There might have been a brief flash of guilt when you thought of the folks, but who wants to stick out in a crowd? So you kept up with the gang. Soon you felt as grown-up as you'd ever been. *On your night of nights, add that sophisticated touch.*

Or perhaps your folks never touched the stuff. They were really opposed to alcohol. They gave you lots of reasons: "It's evil," "People who drink get into terrible trouble," "Vile stuff, it just eats you up" or even, "God's against it." Well, you admired your folks, or were scared of them, or you really believed that part about God's stand. Anyway, no one pushed you too much. Then came the army or college. It seemed as though everyone drank something, sometime, somewhere. They weren't dropping dead at the first sip or getting into too much trouble that you could see. Even if there was a little trouble, someone said, "Oh, well, he was just drunk—sowing some wild oats." Lightning didn't strike. You didn't see the devil popping out of glasses. Just the opposite, most of your friends seemed to be having a lot of fun. *When the gang gets together* . . . bowling, fishing, sailing, hiking, swimming, everywhere.

It could be that you grew up with wine being served at meals. At some time you were initiated into the process as a matter of course. You never gave it a second thought. You might have had a religious background that introduced you to wine as a part of your ritual acceptance into adulthood or as a part of your particular church's worship.

We take a drink only for the sake of the benediction.

PERETZ

With time, age, and social mobility, the reasons for continuing to drink become more complex. It is not unusual to drink a bit more than one can handle at some point. After one experience of being drunk, sick, or hung over, some people decide never to touch the stuff again. For most, however, something they are getting or think they are getting out of alcohol makes them try it again. Despite liquor's real effects on us, most of us search for an experience we have had with it, or want to have with it, or have been led to believe that we can have with its use. *As an essential part of the Good Life, _____ cannot be excelled.*

If all be true that I do think,
There are five reasons we should drink;
Good wine—a friend—or being dry—
Or lest we should be by and by—
Or any other reason why.

HENRY ALDRICH, DEAN OF CHRIST CHURCH, OXFORD
'Reasons for Drinking' (1689)

Theories to explain alcohol use

Those trying to explain drinking behavior have always been more interested in alcohol*ism* than in explaining alcohol *use* per se. Nonetheless, various theories have been advanced to explain the basic why behind alcohol use. Probably all contain some truth. They are included for historical perspective. They resurface from time to time as "new" ideas and may also be assumed by the uninformed to explain alcoholism.

"It calms me down, helps my nerves. It helps me unwind after a hard day." This explanation can be thought of as the *anxiety thesis*. In part it is derived from Freud's work. Freud had concluded that in times of anxiety and stress, people fall back on things that have worked for them in the past. In theory, the things you will choose to relieve anxiety are those you did when you last felt most secure. That lovely, secure time might last have been at Mom's breast. It has been downhill ever since. In this case, use of the mouth (eating, smoking, drinking) would be chosen to ease stressful situations.

Another version of the anxiety thesis came from Donald Horton's anthropological studies. He observed that alcohol was used by primitive societies either ritually or socially to relieve the anxiety caused by an unstable environment. Drunken acts are acceptable and not punished. The greater the environmental stress, the heavier the drinking. Therefore in this view, alcohol's anxiety-reducing property is the one universal key to why people drink alcohol. This theory has by and large been rejected as the sole reason for drinking. Indeed, as biological research advances are made and more is learned of the actual effects of the drug alcohol, it can no longer even be said that alcohol reduces anxiety. At best it partially masks anxiety.

Another theory that surfaced was based on the need for a feeling of power over oneself or one's environment. Most people don't talk about this, but take a look at the heavy reliance of the liquor industry on he-man models, executive types, and beautiful women surrounded by adoring males. People in ads celebrate winning anything with a drink of some sort.

The *power theory* was explored by researchers in the early 1970s, under the direction of David McClelland. They examined folk tales from both heavy- and light-drinking societies. Their research indicated that there was no greater concern with relief from tension or anxiety in heavy-drinking societies than in those that consumed less. To look at this further they conducted a study with college men over a period of 10 years. Without revealing the reasons for the study, they asked the students to write down their fantasies before, during, and after the consumption of liquor. The stories revealed that the students felt bigger, stronger, more influential, more aggressive, and more capable of great sexual conquest the more they drank. The conclusion was that people drink to experience a feeling of power. This power feeling was seen as having two different patterns, depending on the personality of the drinker. What was called *p-power* is a personal powerfulness, uninhibited and carried out at the expense of others. Social power, or *s-power*, is a more altruistic powerfulness, power to help others. This s-power was found to predominate after two or three drinks; heavier drinking produced a predominance of p-power.

Another theory arose during the late 1960s at the height of the "counterculture" with the wave of drug use, particularly psychedelic drugs. This approach, as discussed by Andrew Weil, claimed that every human being has some need to reach out toward some larger experience. People will try anything that suggests itself as a way to do that, for instance, alcohol, drugs, yoga, or meditation. Some drugs are commonly known to "blow your mind" or are even designated as "mind-expanding drugs." Evidence cited for seeking altered states of consciousness begins with very young children who whirl, or hyperventilate, or attempt in other ways to produce a change in their experience. When older, people learn that chemicals can produce different states. In pursuit of these states, alcohol is often used because it is the one intoxicant we make legally available. The "drug scene" was viewed as another answer to the same search. Weil suggested that this search arises from the "innate psychological drive arising out of the neurological structure of the human brain." His conclusion was that we have put the cart before the horse in focusing attention on drugs rather than on the states people seek from them. Thus he suggested that society acknowledge the need itself for an altered state of consciousness and cope with it in a positive rather than a negative way.

Another perspective on factors that may contribute to alcohol use focuses on stresses associated with modern everyday life—be it in the pressures of making it in the corporate world, the declining economy, or the changes in family structure. Use of alcohol is seen as one response to stress. Other responses to stress include hypertension, ulcer disease, and migraine headaches. Accordingly, "stress management" became popular as a technique to helping people develop alternative, less destructive means of coping with stress.

Current research efforts are less interested in identifying factors within the individual that motivate alcohol use. Instead, the focus has turned to the social settings in which people find themselves, in order to identify factors associated with patterns of use. Accordingly, for example, attention is turning to the roles of peers in determining adolescents' decisions to use alcohol, or the influence of parental standards in setting norms for their teenagers' drinking, or the impact of legislative approaches.

In general, the accepted stance now seems to be a "combination of factors" approach. One inescapable fact is that from the very earliest recorded times alcohol has been important to people. Seldon Bacon, former head of the Rutgers School of Alcohol Studies, made a point worth keeping in mind. He called attention to the original needs that alcohol might have served: satisfaction of hunger and thirst, medication or anesthetic, fostering of religious ecstasy. Our modern, complex society has virtually eliminated all these earlier functions. Now all that is left is alcohol the depressant, the mood-altering drug, the possible, or believed, reliever of tension, inhibition, and guilt. Contemporary society has had to create new "needs" that alcohol can meet.

Myths

In thinking about alcohol use, remember that myths are equally important to people. Many think that alcohol makes them warm when they are cold (not so), sexier (in the courting, maybe; in the execution, not so), manlier, womanlier, cured of their ills (not usually), less scared of people (possibly), and better able to function (only if very little is taken). An exercise in asking a lot of people what a drink does for them will expose a heavy reliance on myths for their reasons. Whether factually based or not, myths often influence people's experience of alcohol use, a phenomenon referred to as the "influence of expectancies." Whatever the truth in the mixture of theory and myth, enough people in the United States rely on the use of alcohol to accomplish something for them to support a $92,000,000,000 industry in 1992. Americans spent more in 1992 on alcohol than on all non-alcoholic beverages combined.

ALCOHOL PROBLEMS: THE FLY IN THE OINTMENT

Alcohol is many faceted. With its ritual, medicinal, dietary, and pleasurable uses, alcohol can leave in its wake confusion, pain, disorder, and tragedy. The use and abuse of alcohol have gone hand in hand in all cultures. With the notable exceptions of the Muslims and Buddhists, whose religions forbid drinking, temperance and abstinence have been the exception rather than the rule in most of the world.

As sin or moral failing

Societies have come to grips with alcohol problems in a variety of ways. One of these regards drunkenness as a sin, a moral failing, and the drunk as a moral weakling. The Greek word for drunk, for example, means literally to "misbehave at the wine." An Egyptian writer

Did you know that Budweiser offered Carrie Nation $500 if she would smash only their bottles?

The Moslem and Buddist tradition Completely supports prohibition. But they lack the elation Of Miss Carrie Nation when she fought to uphold her position.

All excess is ill, but drunkenness is the worst sort.

WILLIAM PENN

admonished his friend with the slightly contemptuous "thou art like a little child." Noah, who undoubtedly had reason to seek relief in drunkenness after getting all those creatures safely through the flood, was not looked on kindly by his children as he lay in his drunken stupor. The complaints have continued through time. A Dutch physician of the sixteenth century criticized the heavy use of alcohol in Germany and Flanders by saying "that freelier than is profitable to health, they take it and drink it." Some of the most forceful sanctions have come from the temperance movements. An early temperance leader wrote that "alcohol is preeminently a destroyer in every department of life." As late as March 1974, the New Hampshire Christian Civic League devoted an entire issue of its monthly newspaper to a polemic against the idea that alcoholism is a disease. In its view the disease concept gives reprieve to the "odious alcohol sinner."

As a legal issue

Many see the use of liquor as a legislative issue and believe misuse can be solved by laws. Total prohibition is one of the methods used by those who believe that legislation can sober people up. Most legal approaches through history have been piecemeal affairs invoked to deal with specific situations. Excessive drinking was so bad in ancient Greece that "drinking captains" were appointed to supervise drinking. Elaborate rules were devised for drinking at parties. A perennial favorite has been control of supply. In 81 AD, a Roman emperor ordered the destruction of half the British vineyards.

Bacchus has drowned more men than Neptune.
THOMAS FULLER

The sin and legal views of drunkenness often go hand in hand. They have as a common denominator the idea that the drunk chooses to be drunk. He is therefore either a sinner or a ne'er-do-well who can be handled by making it illegal to drink. In 1606 intoxication was made a statutory offense in England by an "Act for Repressing the Odious and Loathsome Sin of Drunkenness." In the

*Temperate temperance is best.
Intemperate temperance injures the
cause of temperance.*

MARK TWAIN

*Equal Suffrage. The probable
influence of Women's Suffrage upon
the temperance reform can be no
better indicated than by the
following words of the Brewer's
Congress held in Chicago in 1881:
Resolved, That we oppose always
and everywhere the ballot in the
hands of woman, for woman's vote
is the last hope of the
prohibitionists.*

SPOONER, WALTER, W.
The Cyclopaedia of Temperance and
Prohibition, 1891.

reign of Charles I, laws were passed to suppress liquor altogether. Settling a new world did not dispense with the problems resulting from alcohol use. The traditional methods of dealing with these problems continued. From the 1600s to the 1800s, attitudes toward alcohol were low key. Laws were passed in various colonies and states to deal with liquor use, such as an early Connecticut law forbidding drinking for more than half an hour at a time. Another law in Virginia in 1760 prohibited ministers from "drinking to excess and inciting riot." But there were no temperance societies, no large-scale prohibitions, and no religious bodies fighting.

America's response to alcohol problems

Drinking in the colonies was largely a family affair and remained so until the beginning of the nineteenth century. With increasing immigration, industrialization, and greater social freedoms, drinking became less a family affair. Alcohol abuse became more open and more destructive. The opening of the West brought the saloon into prominence. The old, stable social and family patterns began to change. The frontier hero took to gulping his drinks with his foot on the bar rail. Attitudes began to intensify regarding the use of alcohol. These developments hold the key to many modern attitudes toward alcohol, the stigma of alcoholism, and the wet-dry controversy. Differing views of alcohol began to polarize America. The legal and moral approaches reached their apex in the United States with the growth of the temperance movement and the Prohibition amendment in 1919.

Temperance and prohibition. The traditional American temperance movement did not begin as a prohibition movement. The temperance movement coincided with the rise of social consciousness, a belief in the efficacy of law to resolve human problems. It was part and parcel of the humanitarian movement, which included child labor and prison reform, women's rights, abolition, and social welfare and poverty legislation. Originally it condemned only excessive drinking and the drinking of distilled liquor, *not all liquor or all drinking*. It was believed that the evils connected with the abuse of alcohol could be remedied through proper legislation. The aims of the original temperance movement were largely moral, uplifting, rehabilitative. Passions grew, however, and before long those who had condemned only the excessive use of distilled liquor were condemning all liquor. Those genial, well-meaning physicians, businessmen, and farmers began to organize their social life around their crusade. Fraternal orders, such as the Independent Order of Good Templars of 1850, grew and proliferated. In a short span of time it had branches all over the United States with churches, missions, and hospitals—all dedicated to the idea that society's evils were caused by liquor. This particular group influenced the growth of the Women's Christian Temperance Union (WCTU) and the Anti-Saloon League. By 1869 it had become The National

Prohibition Party, the spearhead of political action, which advocated complete suppression of liquor by law.

People who had no experience at all with drinking got involved in the crusade. In 1874 Frances Willard founded the WCTU in Cleveland. Women became interested in the movement, which simultaneously advocated social reform, prayer, prevention, education, and legislation in the field of alcohol. Mass meetings were organized to which thousands came. Journals were published; children's programs taught fear and hatred of alcohol; libraries were established. The WCTU was responsible for the first laws requiring alcohol education in the schools, some of which remain on the books. All alcohol use—moderate, light, heavy, excessive—was condemned. All users were one and the same. Bacon, in describing the classic temperance movement, says there was "one word for the action— DRINK. One word for the category of people—DRINKER."

By 1895, many smaller local groups had joined the Anti-Saloon League, which had become the most influential of the temperance groups. It was nonpartisan politically and supported any prohibitionist candidate. It pressured Congress and state legislatures and was backed by church groups in "action against the saloon." Political pressure mounted. The major thrust of all these activities was that the only real problem was alcohol and the only real solution was prohibition.

In 1919, Congress passed the Eighteenth Amendment, making it illegal to manufacture or sell alcoholic beverages. The Volstead Act had 60 provisions to implement Prohibition. The Act was messy and complicated, and no precedent had been set to force the public cooperation required to make it work. Prohibition remained in effect from 1920 to 1933.

Prohibition shaped much of the economic, social, and underground life. The repeal under the Twenty-first Amendment in 1933 did not remedy the situation. While there was a decline in alcoholism under Prohibition, as indicated by a decline in deaths from cirrhosis, it had failed nonetheless. The real problems created by alcohol were obscured or ignored by the false wet-dry controversy. The quarrel raged between the manufacturers, retailers, and consumers on one side and the temperance people, many churches, and women on the other. Those with alcohol problems or dependent on alcohol were ignored in the furor. When Prohibition was repealed the problem of abuse was still there, and those with dependence upon alcohol were still there along with the stigma of alcoholism.

Another approach to alcohol problems is that of the "ostrich." The ostrich stance became popular after the failure of Prohibition and is still not totally out of fashion. Problems arising from conflicting values and beliefs are often handled with euphemisms, humor, ridicule, and delegation of responsibility.

Our inconsistent attitudes toward alcohol are reinforced in subtle ways. For example, consider the hard-drinking movie heroes. There's the guy who drinks and drinks and then calls for more,

The front door of the Boston Licensing Board was ripped down by the crush to get beer licenses the day Prohibition ended.

never gets drunk, out-drinks the bad guys, kills off the rustlers, and gets the girl in the end. Then there's Humphrey Bogart, who is a drunken mess wallowing in the suffering of humanity until the pure and beautiful heroine appears, at which point he washes up, shaves, and gets a new suit, and they live happily ever after.

DRUNKENNESS VERSUS ALCOHOLISM

It is important to see that alcohol dependence is not separate from alcohol. Dependence does not spring full blown from somewhere. It is generally a condition that develops over time. Alcohol is available everywhere. A person really has to make a choice *not* to drink in our society. In some sets of circumstances one could drink for the better part of a day and never seem out of place at all. Some brunches have wine punch, Bloody Marys, or café brulêt as their accompaniment. Sherry, beer, or a mixed drink is quite appropriate at lunchtime. Helping a friend with an afternoon painting project or even raking your own lawn is a reasonable time to have a beer. Then, after a long day, comes the pre-dinner cocktail, maybe some wine with the meal. Later, watching a tape with friends, drinks are offered. And surely, some romantic candlelight and a nightcap go hand in hand. For most people this would not be their daily or even weekend fare. The point is that none of the above would cause most people to raise an eyebrow. The accepted times for drinking can be all the time, anywhere. Given enough of the kind of days we described, the person who chooses to drink may develop problems because alcohol is a drug and does have effects on the body.

Is alcoholism, which is now termed alcohol dependence, a purely modern phenomenon, a product of our times? There are no references to alcoholics as such in historical writing. The word *alcoholism* was first introduced in 1849. Magnus Huss, a prominent Swedish physician, wrote a book on the physical problems associated with drinking distilled spirits titled *Chronic Alcoholic Illness: A Contribution to the Study of Dyscasias Based on my Personal Experience and the Experience of Others.* (The term *dyscasias* is no longer used. Even then, the meaning of the term was a bit vague, covering a combination of maladies and generally used to describe those thought to have a "poor constitution.") In using the term alcohol-*ism*, Huss was following the common scientific practice of using "ism" as a description of a disease, especially those associated with poisonings. While recognizing the host of medical complications, he thought that the culprit was distilled spirits and not associated with fermented beverages.

While the word alcoholism is a relatively modern one, there are vague references as far back in time as the third century that distinguish between being merely intoxicated and being a drunkard. In a commentary on imperial law, a Roman jurist of that era suggests that inveterate drunkenness be considered a medical matter rather

Food without drink is like a wound without a plaster.

BRULL

than a legal one. In the thirteenth century James I of Aragon issued an edict providing for hospitalization of conspicuously active drunks. In 1655 a man named Younge, an English journalist, wrote a pamphlet in which he seemed to discern the difference between one who drinks and one who has a chronic condition related to alcohol. He says, "He that will be drawn to drink when he hath neither need of it nor mind to it is a drunkard."

History of alcohol treatment efforts

The first serious considerations of the problem of inebriety, as it was called, came in the eighteenth and nineteenth centuries. Two famous writings addressed the problem in what seemed to be a new light. Although their work on the physical aspects of alcohol became fodder for the temperance zealots, both Dr. Benjamin Rush and Dr. Thomas Trotter seriously considered the effects of alcohol in a scientific way. Rush, a signer of the Declaration of Independence and the first Surgeon General, wrote a lengthy treatise with an equally lengthy title, *An Inquiry into the Effects of Ardent Spirits on the Human Body and Mind, with an Account of the Means of Preventing and the Remedies of Curing Them.* Rush's book is a compendium of the attitudes of the time, given weight by scholarly treatment. The more important of the two, and the first scientific formulation of drunkenness on record, is the classic work of Trotter, an Edinburgh physician. In 1804 he wrote *An Essay, Medical, Philosophical, and Chemical, on Drunkenness and Its Effects on the Human Body.* He states: "In the writings of medicine, we find drunkenness only cursorily mentioned among the powers that injure health. The priesthood hath poured forth its anathemas from the pulpit; and the moralist, no less severe, hath declaimed against it as a vice degrading to our nature." He then gets down to the heart of the matter: "In medical language, I consider drunkenness, strictly speaking, to be a disease, produced by a remote cause, and giving birth to actions and movements in the living body that disorder the functions of health." Trotter did not gain many adherents to his position, but small efforts were also being made in the United States at that time and elsewhere.

Around the 1830s, in Massachusetts, Connecticut, and New York, small groups were forming to reform "intemperate persons" by hospitalizing them, instead of sending them to jail or the workhouse. The new groups, started by the medical superintendent of Worcester, Massachusetts, Dr. Samuel Woodward, and a Dr. Eli Todd, did not see inebriates in the same class with criminals, the indigent, or the insane. Between 1841 and 1874, 11 nonprofit hospitals and houses were set up. In 1876 the *Journal of Inebriety* started publication to advance their views and findings. These efforts were taking place against the background of the temperance movement. Consequently, there was tremendous popular opposition from both the church and

Wine is a bad thing,
It makes you quarrel with your neighbor.
It makes you shoot at your landlord,
It makes you—miss him.

PORTRAIT OF A MAN WHO SWEARS HE WILL NEVER HAVE another drink

the legislative chambers. The *Journal* was not prestigious by the standards of the medical journals of that time, and before Prohibition the hospitals were closed and the *Journal* had folded.

Another group also briefly flourished. The Washington Temperance Society began in Chase's Tavern in Baltimore in 1840. Six drinking buddies were the founders, and they each agreed to bring a friend to the next meeting. In a few months parades and public meetings were being held to spread the message: "Drunkard! Come up here! You can reform. We don't slight the drunkard. We love him!" At the peak of its success in 1844, the membership consisted of 100,000 "reformed common drunkards" and 300,000 "common tipplers." A women's auxiliary group, the Martha Washington Society, was dedicated to feeding and clothing the poor. Based on the promise of religious salvation, the Washington Temperance Society was organized in much the same way as the ordinary temperance groups, but with one difference. It was founded on the basis of one drunkard helping another, of drunks telling their story in public. The society prospered all over the East Coast as far north as New Hampshire. A hospital, the Home for the Fallen, was established in Boston and still exists under a different name. There are many similarities between the Washington Society and Alcoholics Anonymous (AA): alcoholics helping each other, regular meetings, sharing experiences, fellowship, reliance on a Higher Power, and total abstention from alcohol. The Society was, however, caught up in the frenzies of the total temperance movement: the controversies, power struggles, religious fights, and competition among the leaders. By 1848, just 8 short years after being founded, it was absorbed into the total prohibition movement. The treatment of the alcoholic became unimportant in the heat of the argument.

Recognition of the alcoholic as a sick person did not reemerge until comparatively recently. The gathering of a group of scientists at Yale's Laboratory of Applied Psychology (later the Laboratory of Applied Biodynamics) and the Fellowship of Alcoholics Anonymous, both begun in the 1930s, were instrumental in bringing this about. Also in the 1930s a recovering Bostonian, Richard Peabody, first began to apply psychological methods to the treatment of those with alcoholism. He replaced the terms "drunk" and "drunkenness" with the more scientific and less judgmental "alcoholic" and "alcoholism." At Yale, Yandell Henderson, Howard Haggard, Leon Greenberg, and later E. M. Jellinek founded the *Quarterly Journal of Studies on Alcohol (QJSA)*—since 1975 known as the *Journal of Studies on Alcohol.* Unlike the earlier *Journal of Inebriety*, the *QJSA* had a sound scientific footing and became the mouthpiece for alcohol information. Starting with Haggard's work on alcohol metabolism, these efforts marked the first attempt to put the study of alcohol and alcohol problems in a respectable up-to-date framework. Jellinek's masterwork, *The Disease Concept of Alcoholism,* was a product of the Yale experience. The Yale Center of Alcohol Studies and the Classified Abstract Archive of Alcohol Literature were established. The Yale Plan Clinic was also set up to diagnose and treat alcoholism. The Yale Summer School of Alcohol Studies, now the Rutgers School, educated professionals and lay people from all walks of life. Yale's prestigious influence had far-reaching effects. The National Council on Alcoholism (NCA), a volunteer organization, also grew out of the Yale School. It was founded in 1944 to provide public information and education about alcohol, through the joint efforts of Jellinek and Marty Mann, a recovering individual who became the NCA's first president.

On the other side of the coin, Alcoholics Anonymous was having more success in treating alcoholics than any other group. AA grew, and in 1983 it estimated a membership of 1 million in both America and abroad. Its members became influential in removing the stigma that had so long been an accompaniment of alcoholism. Lawyers, business people, teachers, people from every sector of society began to recover. They could be seen leading useful, normal lives without alcohol. (More will be said in Chapter 9 on the origins and program of AA itself.) The successful recoveries of its members unquestionably influenced the course of later developments.

Alcohol is a very necessary article . . . It makes life bearable to millions of people who could not endure their existence if they were quite sober. It enables Parliament to do things at eleven at night that no sane person would do at eleven in the morning.

GEORGE BERNARD SHAW, 1907

Public policy and alcohol

Changing perceptions of alcoholism have become the foundation for public policy. Alcoholism is increasingly being recognized as a major public health problem. At the center of the federal efforts has been the National Institute of Alcohol Abuse and Alcoholism (NIAAA), established in 1971. The NIAAA at its founding became a major sponsor of research, training, public education, and treatment programs. The legislation creating NIAAA was a landmark in our societal response to alcoholism. This bill, the Comprehensive Alcohol Abuse and Alcoholism Prevention, Treatment, and Rehabilitation Act of 1970, was sponsored by former Senator Harold Hughes, himself a recovering person. Beyond creating the NIAAA, the legislation created what might be called a "bill of rights" for those with alcoholism. It recognized that they suffer from a "disease that requires treatment"; it provided some protections against discrimination in hiring of recovering alcoholics. (That protection was further extended through the much more recent passage of the American with Disabilities Act, to protect those with handicaps from discrimination.)

In a similar vein, the Uniform Alcoholism and Intoxication Treatment Act, also passed in 1971, dealing with the issue of public intoxication, was recommended for enactment by the states. This Act mandated treatment rather than punishment. With it public inebriation was no longer a crime. These legislative acts incorporated the emerging new views of alcoholism and alcohol abuse: it is a problem; it is treatable.

On the heels of this legislation, there was a rapid increase during the 1970s in alcoholism treatment services, both public and private, both residential and outpatient. In addition, each state mandated alcohol (and drug abuse) services that focused on public information and education as well as treatment. Similarly, community mental health centers that received federal support were required to provide alcohol services. Also health insurance coverage began to include rather than exclude alcoholism treatment services for its subscribers.

However, the recent concern about rising health care costs, increases that have consistently exceeded the rate of inflation, has now brought about efforts to limit coverage for many treatment services. Alcohol and drug abuse, being the newest services covered, have disproportionately felt the ax. Insurance providers are increasingly reluctant to cover residential care. Thus the earlier most common form of treatment, the "28-day residential program," is no longer the dominant treatment model. All facilities are required to document patient status to justify the continuing need for treatment. The result has been much more outpatient care and the closing of many inpatient treatment programs because there were an inadequate number of patients to cover operating costs. Many professionals recognize that inpatient care need not be the universal standard. However, it is critically important for some patients.

Alcohol treatment professionals. With the increase in alcohol services, a new professional emerged, the *alcohol counselor*. These professionals formed the backbone of treatment efforts. With the increasing professionalism, the term *counselor* is more commonly being replaced by *therapist*. Alcohol counselors' associations were formed in many states. In some instances these groups certify alcohol counselors; in others, state licensing boards were established.

The concern with credentialing of alcohol counselors began in the mid-1970s. A decade later, physicians in the alcohol and substance abuse fields began to examine the same questions. What qualifications should a physician have to work in the field? Is personal experience the primary route by which many physicians initially entered, sufficient? The question was answered, as for alcohol counselors, with a clear *No*. Thus first steps were taken among physicians to establish a physicians' credentialing process. At this time there are several different physician groups for those professionally involved in the alcohol and drug fields. The largest of these organizations, The American Medical Society on Alcoholism and Other Drug Dependencies (AMSAODD) currently has approximately 5000 members. In 1986, AMSAODD began to offer a certification examination for members in the treatment of chemical dependency. Other efforts have been launched to create a medical specialty in "addiction medicine," which would be analogous to other medical specialties, such as orthopedics, pediatrics, or family practice, and which would by definition entail a standardized training sequence and a process to award certification. The Society of Addiction Medicine has been in the forefront of this effort. The creation of a new medical specialty is a long process. It requires the approval and sanction of the Board of Medical Specialties, the national group that oversees the component member boards. Similarly there are credentials for nurses in the substance abuse field. In combination these efforts testify to the concern for creating standards, the recognition of a core knowledge base and associated clinical skills, and represents an effort to bring those medical personnel engaged in the care of alcohol and drug abuse patients fully into the medical mainstream.

Education for all helping professionals on alcohol problems has become more common, with a proliferation of workshops, special conferences, and courses. Concern about professional education and standards has not been restricted to those whose primary professional involvement is with alcohol and substance abuse. It has been increasingly recognized that a core knowledge base and associated clinical skills need to be part of virtually any helping professional's training. Thus the federal Alcohol and Drug Institutes and the Office of Substance Abuse Prevention have initiated programs to improve professional education among physicians, nurses, and social workers. These efforts have included designing model curriculum, preparing curriculum materials, and working with the associated professional societies to promote the inclusion of education on alcohol and other drugs by these professions.

With the emergence of alcohol treatment as a new health care program, efforts were initiated to develop standards, not only for treatment personnel, but also for treatment agencies. In 1984, the Joint Committee on the Accreditation of Health Care Organizations first established minimal standards for alcohol rehabilitation programs. These efforts have resulted from, and at the same time contributed to our society's response to alcoholism as a major public health problem.

The focus on alcohol*ism* during the 1980s broadened to include the larger issues of alcohol problems and alcohol use. Previously, the public's attitude could have been summarized as "the only *real* alcohol problem is alcoholism and that wouldn't happen to me." Now alcohol problems are not seen as so far removed from the average person. Drunken driving has captured public attention. This alcohol-related problem can potentially touch anyone. The concern about driving while intoxicated seems to have spilled over to intoxication in general. Intoxication has become less acceptable and is as likely to elicit disgust as to be considered funny or amusing. Other alcohol-related issues also have hit the public policy agenda. The lobby for warning labels on alcoholic beverages saw its efforts succeed in 1989. Some are now calling for the labeling of contents of alcoholic beverages, as is required for other foodstuffs or household products.

An alcoholic is someone you don't like who drinks as much as you do.
DYLAN THOMAS

Questions are being raised about alcohol advertising. Special concerns are the apparent targeting of alcohol beverage advertisements to young people, women, and minority groups. The suspicion is that advertising is not simply directed at capturing a larger share of the existing market for individual companies by encouraging drinkers to try other brands. Rather it is viewed as also directed to increasing the market size, i.e., promote use among those who are nondrinkers or very light drinkers. Another concern is not only about the targets of advertising, but their content as well. There has been some concerted lobbying in response to ads which have—even by advertising standards—been blatantly sexist, depicting women in a demeaning manner, and promoting the stereotypes of male behavior that contribute to sexual harassment.

Another concern has been directed at the alcohol beverage industry's (especially the distillers) sales promotion in developing countries. With a declining domestic market, one way to maintain profits would be through foreign sales. As they industrialize, developing countries are already experiencing significant increases in alcohol-related problems. Western patterns of alcohol use, which are being introduced, are often very different from traditional practices. The basic question raised from efforts to increase sales in the developing countries is essentially an ethical one. Is there any justification for introducing alcohol problems into countries already struggling with the problems of poverty, malnutrition, inadequate health care, high rates of maternal and infant mortality, and illiteracy?

Health and fitness. Alcohol use in relation to health and fitness has received considerable attention. An ironic twist is the fact that the alcohol manufacturers are spending undisclosed amounts of the $1 billion plus advertising budgets to sell lower alcohol content beverages! Alongside "lite" and near beers and wine coolers, there has been a dramatic growth in sales of sparkling waters and nonalcoholic wines and beers.

Another window on public attitudes is the way in which alcohol use is portrayed in the media, especially television programming. Within the past year, several network feature films with alcoholics as major characters aired in prime time. And on the soap operas, several of the major characters are active alcoholics but also some are recovering. Overall, from soaps to cop shows, drinking behavior is portrayed less glamorously, more realistically, and far less frequently than in the past. A major public educational campaign conducted out of the Harvard School of Public Health in collaboration with the media has selected specific alcohol-related themes for attention. For example, the designated driver was incorporated into prime-time television shows.

Significant changes are underway in respect to our view on alcohol's problems and what constitutes appropriate alcohol use. To our knowledge a book published in the mid-1980s, *How to Control Your*

Social Drinking, was a first. Its introduction noted that it was not intended for alcoholics, for whom controlled drinking is not recommended, but was directed to the social drinker, who, in our drinking society, may find that it is easy to drink more than is intended or healthy. Basically, it offered a compilation of tips for hosts, partygoers, and top-level business executives on techniques to keep consumption down, while discussing the benefits of moderation. Its significance is not that it contained any startling or new information, simply that it was published and presumably seen as a topic of sufficient general interest to generate book sales.

ALCOHOL COSTS: PAYING THE PIPER

In the United States, statistics on who drinks—what, where, and when—have been kept since 1850. However, many comparisons between different historical periods is difficult. One reason is that statistics have only been gathered methodically and impartially since 1950. Another reason is that there have been changes in the way the basic information is organized and reported. A century ago, reports included numbers of "inebriates" or "drunkards." In the 1940s through the 1960s, "alcoholics" were often a designated subgroup. Then came the 1970s and another change. "Heavy drinkers" or "heavy drinkers with a high problem index" began to replace "alcoholics" as a category in reporting statistical information. In 1980 alcohol dependence syndrome emerged as another category. So the task of identifying changes in drinking practices is not an easy one.

Who drinks what, when, and where

Nonetheless, out of the maze of statistics available on how much Americans drink, where they drink it, and with what consequences, some are important to note. It is now estimated that 68% of men and 47% of women are drinkers. They comprise about 60%% of the adult population. Per capita consumption during the 1960s rose 32%. In the 1970s, despite some ups and downs, consumption basically leveled off, then became to decline. In 1989 the consumption was the lowest since 1967. In 1991 the statistically average American consumed the equivalent of 2.31 gallons of pure ethanol. Annually, the average American drinks 0.9 gallons of liquor, 3.4 gallons of wine, and 21.8 gallons of beer. Because the alcohol content of each varies in terms of absolute alcohol, 31% of the alcohol comes from liquor, 13% from wine, and 56% from beer. Not only has there been a decline in total alcohol consumption, over the past few years there has also been a major shift in beverage preference. Since 1978 liquor consumption has dropped about 25%. Wine has grown more popular but the rise in its consumption has leveled off.

How do the changes in drinking patterns compare to that of other countries? Since the mid-1970s alcohol consumption in

Drinking patterns

Patterns of alcohol consumption vary according to a number of demographic factors. Among the key factors are the following:

Sex   Women are far more likely to be nondrinkers than men. Among those women who do drink, they consume significantly less than men. Men are more than 4 times more likely to be heavier drinkers than women, with respective rates of 19% and 7%.

Age   Persons over 44 years of age are more likely to be abstainers than those under 44. Again, for men and women the proportion of heavier drinkers is relatively constant across all age groups.

Race   Whites have the highest proportion of members who consume alcohol. Only one third of African-American women and women of Hispanic origin use alcohol.

Education   Alcohol use increases for both men and women with higher levels of education. Those with more than 12 years of education are virtually twice as likely to be drinkers as those with less. The rates of heavier drinking are not influenced by educational level.

Family income   The proportion of drinkers rises with family income. However, the proportion of heaviest drinking is highest for both men and women with the highest and lowest household incomes.

Geographic region   The South has a third more abstainers than other regions. The heaviest levels of alcohol consumption are in the New England, Mid-Atlantic, North Central, and Pacific Coast states. However, if the numbers who abstain are not included in calculating consumption, then, of those who actually do drink, consumption is highest in the South and lowest in the Northeast.

A Tale of 10 Beers and 10 People

3 drink none

5 share 2

1 drinks 2

1 drinks 6

industrialized countries began to level and showed a decline in the earlier part of this decade. Of 25 countries surveyed, nearly two thirds have had a decline in consumption. The increase in half of the others was limited to 1%. In contrast, the consumption of alcoholic beverages is increasing in developing countries.

A word of caution: all of these figures describe the statistically average American. However, it is important to realize that the average American is a statistical myth. The typical American does not in fact drink his or her "statistical quota." First of all, recall that approximately one third do not use alcohol at all. The remaining two thirds show a wide variation in alcohol use. Thus 70% of the drinking population consumes only 20% of all the alcohol. The remaining 30% of the drinkers consumes 80% of the alcohol. Most significantly, one third of that heavy-drinking 30%, or less than 7% of the total population, consumes 50% of all alcohol. Picture what that means. Imagine having 10 beers to serve to a group of 10 people. If you served these to represent the actual consumption pattern described, you'd have the following: Three people would sit there empty handed. Five people would share two beers. That leaves two people to divide up eight beers. Of those two people, one person would take two and the other person would get a whole six pack!

The federal government has estimated that 10% of the total adult population are problem drinkers. (This percentage is derived not from consumption figures but independently determined by the presence of problems attendant to alcohol use.) The similar proportions of very heavy drinkers and problem drinkers are striking. Extrapolating from the most recent census figures, we find that 17.6 million persons age 18 and over are problem drinkers. It is also estimated that 1 out of 5 adolescents 14- to 17-years old has a serious drinking problem, which is 2.8 million teenagers. Thus in the United States an estimated 20.4 million people have drinking problems. For every person with an alcohol problem, it is estimated that four family members are directly affected. Thus approximately 81.6 million family members are touched by alcohol problems.

Over the past two decades, national polls have included questions about alcohol problems. An ever-increasing number of those interviewed have indicated an alcohol problem in their immediate family. In 1972 the figure was less than 1 out of every 10 people (12%). Six years later, 1 person in 4 (24%) said that an alcohol problem had adversely affected his or her family life. In 1983 that figure rose to 1 out of every 3. Only 1 year later, the figure reported by a Harris poll was that 38% of all households reported being beset by alcohol problems. In 1988, a survey conducted for NIAAA, found that 43% of the population reported having a family member with alcoholism. In terms of which families are affected, those who are separated or divorced are more likely to report a family member with an alcohol problem. Those separated or divorced are three times more likely to report having had an alcoholic spouse. Younger adults were also more likely to report having an alcoholic family member, than were older adults. The proportions are 42% for those under age 45 versus 26% of those over age 65. In any of these figures there is not much precision in distinguishing between alcoholics and those who are nonalcoholic but abuse alcohol and are problem drinkers. These nonalcoholic problem drinkers might include the one-time drunken traffic offender who appears in court or the person who, when drunk for the one and only time in his life, puts his foot through a window and ends up in a hospital emergency room. But we suspect that when reporting "troubles" people are not referring to those who miss work after a particularly festive New Year's Eve!

Among those with alcoholism, under 5% are among the homeless, the modern counterpart of what was one time termed skid row. At least 95% of problem drinkers are employed or employable; they are estimated to comprise 10% of the nation's work force. Most of them are living with their families. The vast majority live in respectable neighborhoods and are homemakers, bankers, physicians, sales people, farmers, teachers, and clergy. They try to raise decent children, go to football games, shop for their groceries, go to work, and rake the leaves.

Work is the curse of the drinking classes.

OSCAR WILDE, 1946

Economic costs versus economic benefits

Although they constitute only a small portion of the drinking population, alcohol abusers and alcoholics combined cost the

United States a huge amount of time and money each year. In assessing these costs, government statistics rely heavily on the most recent census, conducted every 10 years. The quantity of information generated may take several years to analyze. When dealing with national counts of anything, from population figures, to the numbers of licensed drivers, to the quantity of alcohol sold, the data are almost always an estimate. The figures are derived from the most recent data available or inferred from other numbers. From time to time, the federal government, revises the manner in which it may calculate particular figures. In respect to the economic costs related to alcohol use these costs were reported in the *8th Special Report to the U.S. Congress* as being $85.8 billion. These costs are comparable to the cost of all cancers and respiratory diseases *combined*. The figures ignore family costs, such as battered wives, abused or neglected children, or the economic impact of divorce on the family unit. However, the earlier *7th Special Report to the U.S. Congress on Alcohol and Health* had predicted the cost of $136.3 billion in 1990 and a rise to $150 billion by 1995. The changes do not reflect a decline in alcohol problems and their costs, but reflect a different way of gathering the data.

Using the figures from the *7th Report*, as these are the figures that break down the components of costs, the proportion of alcohol-related social costs are summarized in Table 1.

TABLE 1

Social costs

	$ (in billions)	%
Reduced productivity in the workplace	55.3	47.3
Reduced productivity in the home	9.4	8.1
Motor vehicle crashes	13.2	11.3
Comorbidities (related illnesses)	9.9	8.5
Unintentional injuries (excluding auto)	8.3	7.1
Crime	8.1	6.9
Fetal alcohol syndrome	4.2	3.6
Treatment for alcoholism	4.4	3.8
Other	3.9	3.4
TOTAL SOCIAL COSTS	$116.7	100.0

The other side of the cost coin is economic revenues. The total tax revenues on alcohol raised by federal and state authorities in 1987 was $13.3 billion. The federal tax rates on distilled spirits was raised for the first time in 34 years. The tax on liquor was then raised 20%. Nonetheless, alcohol, especially distilled spirits, is a true bargain. Because inflation has outstripped any federal and state tax increases, the real price of distilled spirits has been cut by nearly half. The real costs of beer dropped 20%, and the cost of wine dropped by almost 25%. Alcoholic beverages have become so inexpensive that their prices are now within the range of many nonalcoholic beverages. While the costs of soda have tripled in that period, the costs of alcoholic beverages have not quite doubled, so both are now in the same price range. The net effect of all this is that the typical American can drink more but spend less of the total family income to do it.

How do the social benefits of alcohol use compare to its social costs? Social benefits, in terms of tax revenues, wages, salaries, and income generated directly by the manufacture and sales of alcohol or indirectly via the hospitality industry or philanthropic contributions by the alcohol beverage industry have not been similarly systematically calculated nor reported on an annual basis. Nor has there been any effort to translate the benefits to individuals from alcohol consumption into dollars.

A rough calculation of the cost-benefits of alcohol can be made simply by taking the totals for both economic costs and benefits and dividing each by the same standard unit. If all of the alcohol sold in the US (1985)—which was 499,268,000 gallons of ethanol—were treated as if it had all been marketed as fifths of 80 proof liquor, that would have been equivalent to 6,240,850,000 fifths. Now, if we divide the total numbers of fifths of alcohol consumed by the bill to society, the social costs, the social cost per each fifth is $18.73. Similarly calculated the social benefit would be $10.11. Thus for every $1.00 in tax revenues, there is $1.90 spent to deal with the problems associated with use.

Other attempts have been made to consider the social costs of alcohol use, especially in respect to health care costs. One study with the provocative title "The taxes of sin: Do smokers and drinkers pay their way?" was concerned with just that question. A variety of costs related to drinking and smoking were examined, for example, things such as the impact of early mortality attributable to smoking and heavy drinking. One result would be that if smokers and drinkers die early, what they have paid into retirement plans or social security in part becomes available to subsidize the benefits of others. The conclusion was that smokers do pay their way. However, those with alcoholism do not. Taxes on alcohol were found to cover about a half of the expenses generated by those who drink heavily.

How does alcohol consumption compare to use of other beverages? The expenditures for alcoholic beverages hit a record 96.2 bil-

Roughly 100 beer cans per man, woman, and child were manufactured in the United States in 1972.

lion in 1992. All together, what Americans paid out for alcoholic beverages has generally tended to match or exceed spending for all other beverages.

Recent sales for different beverages are summarized in Table 2. However, the rate of increase is smaller than for non-alcoholic beverages.

TABLE 2
Beverage retail sales in millions of dollars

Beverage	1988	1989	1990	1991	1992	% change
	($)	($)	($)	($)	($)	
Soft drinks	43,042	45,822	47,290	52,251	53,933	+25.3
Beer	42,863	44,586	45,580	49,082	50,197	+17.1
Distilled spirits	28,869	29,093	29,397	30,890	33,925	+17.5
Milk	13,996	15,144	16,780	16,394	16,764	+20.0
Juices	9,930	10,726	11,127	11,706	12,650	+27.3
Wine	12,016	11,651	11,681	12,082	12,195	+1.5
Coffee	7,728	7,687	7,751	7,094	6,889	-10.9
Bottled water	2,821	3,330	3,450	3,480	3,535	+25.3
Tea	1,194	1,185	1,208	1,211	1,251	-5.8
Powdered drinks	781	759	816	897	828	+6.0
All alcoholic beverages	83,721	85,830	86,658	92,054	96,317	+15.0
All nonalcoholic beverages	79,492	84,653	88,422	93,033	95,850	+20.5

Personal costs

The personal cost of alcoholism is tremendous. It is estimated that alcohol-related deaths may run as high as 10% of all deaths annually. The alcoholic's life expectancy is shortened by 15 years. The mortality rate is two and a half times greater than that of non-alcoholics. Those with alcoholism also have a higher rate of violent deaths. Drinking figures prominently into both accidental death and violent death, for alcoholics and nonalcoholics alike. Alcohol use has been associated with the major causes of accidental death in the United States—motor fatalities, falls, drownings, fires, and burns.

Motor-vehicle fatalities. The number of fatalities involving alcohol has been declining. Between 1982 and 1989, the proportion of accidents involving an intoxicated driver declined from 46.3% to 39.2%. Furthermore, though the absolute number of fatal motor accidents involving teenage drivers has continues to increase, the proportion involving alcohol has declined. Nonetheless, motor vehicle fatalities remain the single leading cause of death in the United States, particularly for those between the ages 5 and 34. It has been estimated that per mile driven, the chances for a fatal accident are 8 times greater for an individual with a blood alcohol concentration of 0.10

Best while you have it use your breath,
There is no drinking after death.

C.1616, JOHN FLETCHER, ENGLISH PLAYWRIGHT

or higher (the legal level for intoxication) than for a nondrinking driver. In fatal motor vehicle accidents involving a pedestrian or bicyclist, the odds are greater that it will be they and not the motorist who has been drinking. The severity of injuries and associated length of a hospital stay were also related to alcohol consumption at levels of 0.10 or above.

Alcohol consumption and the outcome of an accident are related in several other ways. Drinking is likely to decrease the use of protective devices, such as seat belts and, for motorcyclists, safety helmets. For the latter, with intoxicating levels of alcohol, the use of helmets declines by one third. Also, for those who have been drinking and sustain injuries, emergency medical care may be made more difficult. For accident victims with similar severity of injuries, those who had been drinking had lower blood pressure and lower P_{CO_2}, (the latter is a measure of blood gases and both are indexes for shock). Thus their medical condition was more fragile and likely to lead to problems if resuscitation and/or emergency care were delayed.

Falls. Drinking increases the risk of both death and injury from falls. A review of all studies of deaths from falls showed alcohol involved in 17% to 73% of the groups studied. As blood alcohol rises, the greater the risk of falls. Compared to those who have not been drinking, those with a 0.10 blood alcohol content (BAC) have a 3 times greater risk of a fall; with a BAC of 0.16 or above the risk is 60 times higher. Of the injuries commonly associated with falls, fractures of the ribs and vertebrae are 16 times higher for people who are heavy chronic drinkers than for nonproblematic or "social" drinkers. One study following people over a decade found that the likelihood of a fatal fall increased in proportion to the number of drinks an individual had reportedly consumed on a "typical" drinking occasion.

Other accidents. This is the fourth leading cause of accidental death in the United States. Drinking has been shown in a number of studies to significantly increase the risk of injury and death by burns and fire. Alcohol was determined to be involved in between 37% to 73% of all fatalities, and a BAC above the legal levels of intoxication was found in 50% of all cases. For home fires involving cigarette smoking, the proportion involving alcohol increases. Alcohol is believed to be involved in approximately 38% of deaths from drowning.

Suicide. Alcohol plays a significant role in suicide. Studies indicate that in 4 out of 5 suicide attempts, the individual had been drinking, and that 35% to 40% of all successful suicides of nonalcoholics are alcohol related. Half of all successful suicides are alcoholics. Drinking is also associated with more lethal means of suicide, particularly the use of firearms. Alcohol is associated more often with impulsive suicides than it is with premeditated suicides.

THE SCREAMER ...Experience the ups and downs of Problem drinking.

Violence. Alcohol use is a significant factor in cases of homicide and family violence. In as many as 67% of all homicides either the victim, the assailant, or both had been drinking. Similarly, drinking is seen as a precipitating factor in child abuse, wife beatings, and other family violence. Though the data on family violence remain limited, estimates of the role of intoxication vary from 30% to over 70%, depending on the particular population studied. It has been estimated that alcohol is implicated in two thirds of incidents of family violence.

As discussed in both the *7th* and *8th Special Reports to the U.S. Congress on Alcohol and Health,* there are many variations on a theme. The incidence of violence differs with drinking patterns, binge drinkers vs. steady heavy drinkers, and the acceptance or nonacceptance of violence in families. Similarly, in work on violence and children, what is being discussed as "violence" can encompass or refer to only some of the following: physical abuse, sexual abuse, psychological abuse, neglect, maltreatment, and abandonment.

Crime. Alcohol is reflected in national crime statistics. As noted already, drinking is part of the picture in over half of all homicides and figures prominently in family violence. It is a significant factor in assaults in general. For 72% of the perpetrators and 79% of the victims alcohol was seen as playing a role. In attempted and completed rapes, alcohol again is involved. For 50% of the rapists and for 30% of the victims alcohol was a prominent feature. In cases of robbery up to 22% of the offenders had been drinking. The current estimate of the total national bill for alcohol-related crimes and misdemeanors is over $3 billion. The relationship between crime and alcohol use is not wholly clear. For example, are those who have been drinking more likely to be apprehended? Or, does it reflect patterns of law enforcement?

Health care and alcohol

Alcohol has a significant impact both on health care delivery and health care costs. The following summarizes some significant points:

- Studies have consistently shown that a minimum of 20% of all hospitalized persons have a significant alcohol problem, whatever the presenting problem or admitting diagnosis. That is an absolute minimum. In some institutions, the proportion is apt to be higher. Veterans Administration estimates that 50% of all VA hospital beds are filled by veterans with alcohol problems.
- In terms of health care costs, the American Medical Association in 1993 issued a report stating that of the annual $666 billion that Americans spend on health care annually, one of every 4 dollars is related to caring for those who are victim of alcohol or other addictions and related problems.
- In thinking about health care expenses, some people incur a disproportionate share of these costs. One large-scale study of

If once a man indulges himself in murder, very soon he comes to think little of robbing; and from robbing he comes next to drinking and sabbath-breaking, and from that to incivility and procrastination.

THOMAS DE QUINCEY, 1839

hospital costs found that a small proportion of patients, only 13%, had hospital bills equal to the remaining 87%. The distinguishing characteristic of the high-cost group was not age, sex, economic status, or ethnicity. It was that those people were heavy drinkers and/or heavy smokers. A follow-up study found that high-cost users also had multiple hospitalizations. Patients with a history of alcoholism have significantly more repeated hospitalizations than those without such a history.

- When health care costs for untreated alcoholics and their families are compared to families without alcoholism, the difference is striking. The families with alcohol dependence have 100% greater medical costs. If one looks at the 1-year period prior to treatment for alcoholism, the health care costs for untreated alcoholism increases to over 300% of those of the general public. Such a pattern of increasing medical care immediately prior to diagnosis is true for many chronic diseases, including diabetes, hypertension, heart disease, and respiratory illnesses.
- It is not only the family unit but also children of those with alcoholism who have higher than anticipated health care costs. A study conducted by the Children of Alcoholics Foundation found that children of alcoholics had a 24.9% greater rate of health care utilization than their peers. Furthermore, if hospitalized, their stay in a hospital was 29% longer; the hospital bill for their care were 36% greater.
- *Following* alcohol treatment, there is a rapid decline in the total family's health care costs.

It is unfortunate and ironic that of all these health care costs, only a small proportion—approximately 13%—represents expenditures for rehabilitation or treatment of the primary alcohol problem. The bulk of the costs are for treatments of alcohol-induced illness and trauma. Equally disturbing is that the NIAAA estimates that approximately 85% of the nation's alcoholics and problem drinkers are not receiving any formal treatment. Even if one were to factor in the members of AA, who enter without involvement in formal treatment (approximately sixty percent of the 2 million members of AA), that only reduces the "untreated" portion by another 5%.

Another recently recognized health care cost is that which accompanies fetal alcohol syndrome (FAS) and fetal alcohol effects (FAE). It was estimated in 1987 that the annual costs for treatment and the special education, training, and the support services required add another $2.4 billion to the costs for our nation's health care. These infants grow to become children and eventually adults who will continue to require care.

If one considers the federal dollars spent on health research, alcohol is a health concern that has been getting short shrift. When compared to other diseases such as heart disease and cancer, the amount of federal research dollars spent on alcohol research is not proportional to the economic costs or to the numbers of those affect-

ed. In the early part of the last decade, 15 times more was spent on heart disease research than on alcoholism and alcohol abuse research. And the amount spent on cancer research was 35 times greater, although the associated costs are only three quarters of those associated with alcohol abuse and alcoholism.

One of the big questions is how alcohol and other drug use problems will fare under health care reform. Despite numerous studies that demonstrate that treating alcoholism is cost effective and that any treatment is better than no treatment, alcoholism remains the only major disease not routinely covered by health insurance. There is more awareness of the toll that alcoholism and alcohol abuse can take in our public and private lives. Yet at the same time there remains the bias that such problems are "different" than other medical illnesses. Many national groups prepared and submitted papers to Congress to influence health care reform. There are two main points which these policy statements address. One is the importance of not have a dual standard of care, one for traditional medical problems and a different one for substance abuse, as if the latter was not a "real" or "legitimate" medical condition. The other point is to emphasize the potential savings which can result if substance abuse is treated, rather than waiting for the emergence of its medical complications. How substance abuse fares under health care reform will dictate the patterns of care that will prevail in the next years. The fate of substance abuse treatment under health care reform will also testify to the extent to which we have come to recognize alcohol and other drug problems as health concerns, rather than moral issues.

RESOURCES AND FURTHER READING

History and overview

Alcoholics Anonymous: *Alcoholics Anonymous comes of age,* New York: AA World Service, 1957.

Bacon S: The classical temperance movement in the U.S.A., *British Journal of Addiction* 62:5-18, 1967.

Chafetz M: *Liquor, The Servant of Man,* Boston: Little, Brown & Co Inc., 1965.

DP: The Washingtonians, *AA Grapevine* 27(9):16-22, 1971.

Lender ME, Kamchanappe KR: Temperance tales, antiliquor fiction and American attitudes toward alcoholics in the late 19th and early 20th centuries, *Journal of Studies on Alcohol* 38(7):1347-1370, 1979.

Rorabaugh W: *The alcohol republic: An american tradition,* New York: Oxford University Press, 1979.

Sournia JC: *A history of alcoholism.* Cambridge MA, Basil Blackwell 1990.
    This is a translation of the French work *Histoire de l'alcoolisme.* It chronicles the history of alcoholism in Western societies.

Why people drink

Horton D. Alcohol use in primitive societies. In Pittman DJ; White HR, eds: *Society, culture, and drinking patterns reexamined,* New Brunswick NJ: Rutgers Center of Alcohol Studies, 1991.

> This chapter an edited version of a classical study of the functions of alcohol in preliterate societies. It concludes that levels of alcohol use are correlated with levels of societal anxiety, such as might be induced by the adequacy of food supplies or presence of external dangers. This data was later reexamined by others using newer cross-cultural measures, and alternative explanations suggested which did not see drinking as a response to the cultural conditions cited by Horton, but as related instead to the nature of social structures. (See Field, same volume.)

MacAndrew C, Edgerton R: *Drunken comportment,* Chicago: Aldine, 1969.

McClelland D, et al: *The drinking man,* New York: The Free Press, 1972.

Weil A: Man's innate need: Getting high. In *Dealing with drug abuse,* Ford Foundation Report: New York, 1972.

Social costs and social policy

American Medical Association: *Factors contributing to the health care cost problem,* Chicago IL: AMA, 1993.

> Health care costs and the rate of growth of those costs in the 1990s have reached levels regarded with great concern by consumers, health care providers, insurers, the government, and others. Many studies have been conducted as to the causes of growth or have estimated those parts of overall growth attributable to specific factors. The inspiration for this volume was the identification of a need for a single reference containing a concise presentation of the essential statistical facts across many disparate studies. (Author abstract.)

Baldwin WA, Rosenfeld BA, Breslow MJ, Buchman TG, Deutschman CS, Moore RD: Substance abuse-related admissions to adult intensive care, *Chest* 103(1):21-25, 1993.

> The frequency of intensive care unit (ICU) admissions related to substance abuse was examined. Of 435 ICU admissions, 14% were tobacco related and generated 16% of costs, 9% were alcohol related generating 13% of costs, and 5% were illicit drug related generating 10% of costs. In all, 28% of ICU admissions generating 39% of costs were substance abuse related. Substance abuse-related admissions were significantly longer and more costly than admissions not related to substance abuse (4.2 days versus 2.8 days; $9,610 vs. $5,890. Frequency of substance abuse-related admission was linked with the patient's insurance status (Medicare, private insurance, uninsured). In the uninsured group, 44% of admissions were substance abuse related (35% to 52%), significantly higher than in the private insurance and Medicare groups, and generating 61% of all ICU costs in the uninsured group. Large fractions of adult ICU admissions and costs are substance-abuse related, particularly in uninsured patients. (Authors' abstract.)

Butynski W, Canova D, Reda JL, eds: *State resources and services related to alcohol and other drug abuse problems: Fiscal year 1989. An analysis of state alcohol and drug abuse profile data,* Rockville, MD: NIAAA and NIDA, 1990.

> This 1989 report provides a wealth of data on alcohol and drug use programs and problems on a state-by-state and national level. An introduction with highlights a discussion of the purpose of the study and methodology is provided. Following are 8 major subject areas addressed, with detailed data. These major areas include funding sources; characteristics of clients served; the availability of state models; the major policy issues as defined by state agencies; programmatic needs for which there were insufficient resources; and trends and changes identified in 1989 in prevention and treatment services. The 23 tables provided a wealth of data, generally on a state-by-state basis.

Centers for Disease Control and Prevention: Years of potential life lost before age 65:United States, 1990 and 1991. *Morbidity and Mortality Weekly Report* 42(13):251-253, 1993.

Years of potential life lost (YPLL) is a public health measure that reflects the impact of deaths occurring in years preceding a conventional cut-off year of age, usually 65 years. This report summarizes YPLL data for 1990 and provisional data for 1991. During 1990, YPLL before age 65 years (YPLL-65) totaled 12,237,379 in the United States. Unintentional injuries accounted for the largest proportion of YPLL-65 from all causes (17.5%), followed by malignant neoplasms (15.1%), suicide/homicide (12.2%), diseases of the heart (11.2%), congenital anomalies (5.4%), and human immunodeficiency virus infection including acquired immunodeficiency syndrome (HIV/AIDS) (5.4%). Deaths from chronic liver disease or cirrhosis declined from 1989 to 1990 by -3.9%. Public Domain.

Cheung YW: Ethnicity and alcohol/drug use revisited: A framework for future research (review), *International Journal of the Addictions* 25(5A-6A):581-605, 1991.

Despite the large pool of research findings pertaining to ethnic and racial variations in the use of drugs (including alcohol), the relationship between ethnicity and drug use has not been thoroughly examined. This paper describes some of the major findings regarding ethnic and racial variations in drug use, examines the methodological limitations of such studies, and addresses the problem of shortage of theoretical explanations for ethnic variations in drug use. (Author abstract.)

Children of Alcoholics Foundation. *Children of alcoholics in the medical system: Hidden problems, hidden costs.*, New York: Children of Alcoholics Foundation, 1990.

The Children of Alcoholics Foundation launched the first major study of the effects of parents' alcohol abuse on their youngsters' health care patterns, utilization rates and costs of their medical care. The Foundation hypothesized that children from alcoholic families as compared with other children, would have greater health care usage, including more frequent admissions to hospitals, longer hospital stays and higher health care costs. The study population consisted of dependent children of adults who were in treatment for alcoholism or related disorders between 1984-1986 and youngsters from other families. The data was based on claims filed by 1.6 million subscribers under group policies carried by Independence Blue Cross and included analysis by admission rates, length of hospitalizations and financial costs of inpatient, short procedure unit and home health care.

Cook PJ, Moore MJ: Violence reduction through restrictions on alcohol availability, *Alcohol Health and Research World* 17(2):151-156, 1993.

Strong associations have been shown between alcohol use and violence and between restrictions on alcohol availability and per capita alcohol consumption. This work reviews studies showing these relationships and explore their effects on rates of violence. Analysis demonstrates that increases in beer excise taxes are associated with reductions in per capita alcohol consumption and decreases in the incidence of violent crime, particularly rape and robbery.

Greenfield TK, Graves KL, Kaskutas LA: Alcohol warning labels for prevention: National survey findings, *Alcohol Health and Research World* 17(1):67-75, 1993.

After November 1989, Federal law required health warning labels on all alcoholic beverage containers sold in the United States. The authors examined the effectiveness of warning labels as a reminder of the hazards of drinking. They found little evidence to indicate changes in behavior attributable to warning labels, except for limiting drinking when about to drive and an increase in conversations about drinking and pregnancy among women of childbearing age.

Gruenewald PJ: Alcohol problems and the control of availability: Theoretical and empirical issues. In Hilton ME, Bloss G, eds: *Economics and the prevention of alcohol-related problems. NIAAA research monograph 25,* Rockville MD: National Institute on Alcohol Abuse and Alcoholism, 1993.

This chapter reviews the theoretical and empirical basis of knowledge about alcohol availability and its effects on alcohol consumption and alcohol-related problems. Theoretical approaches considered include those based on: social norms, the distribution of consumption model, consumer demand and the full price of alcoholic beverages, subjective availability, and a theory of routine activities. The empirical literature reviewed includes studies of monopoly versus license systems for the distribution of alcoholic beverages, the geographical density of outlets, hours and days of sale, and laws governing the forms of availability (the principal forms being on-premise and off-premise availability). The author concludes with a discussion of a number of fundamental problems, both theoretical and empirical, be resolved by future studies of the relationship between alcohol availability and alcohol-related problems.

Hoffmann NG, DeHart SS, Fulkerson JA: Medical care utilization as a function of recovery status, *Journal of Addictive Diseases* 12(1):97-108, 1993.

A sample of 3,572 chemical dependency inpatients aged 25 to 82 years were the subjects of a study to evaluate whether observed reductions in health care costs are associated with successful recovery from alcoholism and other drug dependence, a function of regression to the mean, or ancillary health care during alcoholism/drug abuse treatment. The total number of hospital days were calculated for the year prior to treatment, and one and two years post-treatment. Utilization rates are not significantly different between recovering and relapsed patients prior to treatment; however, the differences between the two groups for the first and second year post-treatment are significant. The recovery patients showed a continued low utilization rate while the relapsed group had considerably higher utilization in both years. Recovery status is an essential factor to consider when determining valid cost-offsets for medical care utilization after alcoholism/drug treatment. (Copyright 1993, The Haworth Press.)

Holder HD: Changes in access to and availability of alcohol in the United States: Research and policy implications, *Addiction* 88(Supplement):67S-74S, 1993.

Recent changes in alcohol availability and access in the United States are reviewed and the role public policy research played in such changes are discussed. The paper finds that there are two concurrent trends, i.e. increased alcohol availability through changes in wine and spirits structural availability, lower prices and increased outlet densities, and decreased availability and access through higher minimum drinking ages, server intervention and training, server liability, low- and no-alcohol beverages, and warning labels on alcohol containers. This paper discusses these trends and the implications for policy development to which research is an input. (Author abstract.)

Institute for Health Policy, Brandeis University: *Substance abuse: The nation's number one health problem,* Robert Wood Johnson Foundation: Princeton, NJ, 1993.

This manual is one in a series published by the Foundation. This volume addresses alcohol and substance use, and assembles basic data of interest to policy makers. It is organized into 3 major sections, plus an introductory overview which deals with historical trends and indices of societal cost. Section One addresses patterns of use, including implications of early use, trends in heavy use, and demographics in respect to use. Section Two deals with consequences of use and addresses morbidity, mortality, implications for the health care system, families, the workplace, and the impact on the criminal justice system. Section Three deals with efforts to address the problem, including treatment, control policies, laws, and community action. For each major topical area, charts and graphs are used to summarize the material in the brief narrative.

Jones NE, Pieper CF, Robertson LS: The effect of legal drinking age on fatal injuries of adolescents and young adults, *American Journal of Public Health* 82(1):112-115, 1992.

> This study examined the effect of legal drinking age (LDA) on fatal injuries in persons aged 15 to 24 years in the United States between 1979 and 1984. Effects on pre-LDA teens, adolescents targeted by LDA, initiation at LDA, and post-LDA drinking experience were assessed. A higher LDA was associated with reduced death rates for motor vehicle drivers, pedestrians, unintentional injuries excluding motor vehicle injuries, and suicide. An initiation effect on homicides was identified. Reductions in injury deaths related to drinking experience were not found. In general, a higher LDA reduced deaths among adolescents and young adults for various categories of violent death. (Authors' abstract.)

Manning WG, Keeler EB, Newhouse JP, Sloss EM, Wasserman J: The taxes of sin: Do smokers and drinkers pay their way? *Journal of the American Medical Association* 261(11):1604-1609, 1989.

> We estimate the lifetime, discounted costs that smokers and drinkers impose on others through collectively financed health insurance, pensions, disability insurance, group life insurance, fires, motor-vehicle accidents, and the criminal justice system. Although nonsmokers subsidize smokers' medical care and group life insurance, smokers subsidize nonsmokers' pensions and nursing home payments. On balance, smokers probably pay their way at the current level of excise taxes on cigarettes; but one may, nonetheless, wish to raise those taxes to reduce the number of adolescent smokers. In contrast, drinkers do not pay their way; current excise taxes on alcohol cover only about half the costs imposed on others. (Authors' abstract.)

Mosher JF; Jernigan DH. New directions in alcohol policy, *Annual Review of Public Health* 10:245-279, 1989.

> Changes and reform in alcohol policy over the past decade are reviewed. The role of the beverage industry in blocking policy change is analyzed. Strategies are presented to overcome these impediments, including regulatory actions, legal liability, interventions with servers, and creation of coalitions at the community and state level. (Author abstract.)

National Institute on Alcohol Abuse and Alcoholism: *1st Special Report to U.S. Congress on Alcohol and Health,* Washington DC: U.S. Government Printing Office, 1971.

> This is the first of a series of reports, mandated by the legislation that created the NIAAA requiring reports to Congress on a regular basis.. This and subsequent Reports offer an update of material from previous reports, and summarizes new findings. The areas covered typically include, the demographics of alcohol use and alcohol problems, the etiology of alcohol problems and alcoholism, as well as treatment, and public policy issues.

National Institute on Alcohol Abuse and Alcoholism: *2nd Special Report to U.S. Congress on Alcohol and Health,* Washington DC: U.S. Government Printing Office, 1974.

National Institute on Alcohol Abuse and Alcoholism: *3rd Special Report to U.S. Congress on Alcohol and Health,* Washington DC: U.S. Government Printing Office, 1978.

National Institute on Alcohol Abuse and Alcoholism: *4th Special Report to U.S. Congress on Alcohol and Health,* Washington DC: U.S. Government Printing Office, 1981.

National Institute on Alcohol Abuse and Alcoholism: *5th Special Report to U.S. Congress on Alcohol and Health,* Washington DC: U.S. Government Printing Office, 1983.

National Institute on Alcohol Abuse and Alcoholism: *6th Special Report to U.S. Congress on Alcohol and Health,* Washington DC: U.S. Government Printing Office, 1987.

National Institute on Alcohol Abuse and Alcoholism: *7th Special Report to U.S. Congress on Alcohol and Health,* Washington DC: U.S. Government Printing Office, 1990.

Sinclair JD; Sillanaukee P. The preventive paradox: A critical examination. (commentary), *Addiction* 88(5):591-595, 1993.

    This commentary reexamines the "prevention paradox" which suggests that even were there an effective "cure" for alcoholism and the numbers of alcoholics in the population greatly diminished that this would have at best a slight impact upon societal costs. In contrast, even a slight decrease in consumption by light and moderate drinkers, inasmuch as they are for more numerous, would prove a much more effective means of reducing total societal costs attributable to alcohol use. The authors point out what they consider to be significant flaws in this perception and re-examine some of the data presented elsewhere in support of their view. (Authors' abstract.)

Smith GR, Burns BJ: Recommendations of the Little Rock Working Group on Mental and Substance Abuse Disorders in Health-Care Reform, *Journal of Mental Health Administration* 20(3):247-353.

    This article reports the recommendations of a nonpartisan group of academicians and clinicians to consider plans for mental health and substance abuse disorders in health care reform. The recommendations are based on the assumption that it is vital to include mental health and substance abuse benefits in any health care reform. The eight recommendations made and outlined in this paper include the following: (1) universal access and inclusion of these benefits is essential; (2) mental health and substance abuse benefits must be mainstreamed rather than perpetuating the fragmented present system; (3) coverage for health care should not be denied on the basis or prior substance abuse and/or mental health services; (4) special incentives are required to provide adequate coverage for those with severe and persistent chronic mental or substance abuse disorders; (5) a comprehensive array of services is needed; (6) unreasonable limits should not be placed upon these benefits; (7) methods to assess quality and assure access to needed services are required; and (8) health reform must support ongoing research on cost-effectiveness, treatment outcomes around mental health and substance abuse services.

Weisner C: The merging of alcohol and drug treatment: A policy review. *Journal of Public Health Policy* 13(1):66-80, 1992.

    Alcohol and drug treatment have separate histories in the United States. The large public treatment systems were established as separate institutions in the early 1970s and have developed separate research traditions and treatment programs. However, as a response to current treatment financing policy and epidemiologic descriptions of combined alcohol and other drug use in the population, the two treatment systems are merging at the state and local levels. This large structural change is taking place without the development and evaluation of treatment methods for combined problems and without discussion of overall health service or policy implications. This paper describes the changes occurring, examines the literature for its contributions in providing direction, and discusses current patterns of treatment. (Author's abstract.)

Windom RE, ed: Perspectives on alcohol abuse, *Public Health Report* 103(6):557-723 (entire issue), 1988.

    This issue, devoted entirely to alcohol issues, is composed of invited papers by nationally recognized experts, in areas ranging from the economic impact of problems of alcohol use to research findings in programmatic, social, and biological research. It serves as an excellent update and overview of the field.

Policy statements on health care reform

American Academy of Psychiatrists in Alcoholism & Addictions. Addressing substance abuse: A priority in health care reform, *American Journal on Addiction* 3(1):87, 1994.

Bigby JA, Butynski W, Elam LC, et al: *Statement to the President's Task Force on National Health Care Reform,* Hanover NH: Project Cork Institute, 1993.

Center on Addiction and Substance Abuse, Columbia University; Brown University Center for Alcohol and Addiction Studies: *Recommendations on substance abuse coverage and health care reform,* New York: Center on Addiction and Substance Abuse, 1993.

Special Report: Health Care Reform, *SAMHSA News* 1(4):1-8 (entire issue), 1993.

Alcohol and the body

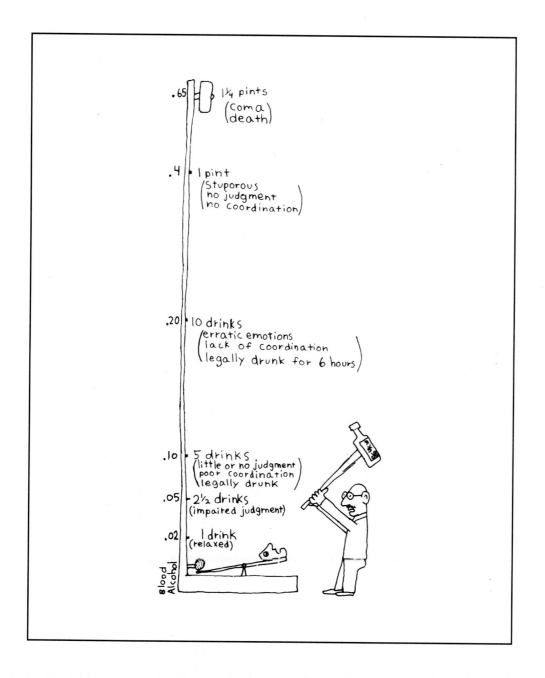

Alcohol is a drug. When ingested, it has specific and predictable physiological effects on the body—any body, every body. Usually attention is paid to the physical impact of chronic use or what happens with excessive use. Often overlooked are the normal, routine effects on anyone who uses alcohol. Let us examine what happens to alcohol in the body—how it is taken up, broken down, and how it thereby alters body functioning.

DIGESTION

The human body is well engineered to take the foods ingested and change them into substances needed to maintain life and provide energy. Despite occasional upsets from too much spice or too much food, this process goes on without a hitch. The first part of this transformation is called digestion. Digestion is like a carpenter who dismantles an old building, salvages the materials, and uses them in new construction. Digestion is the body's way of dismantling food to get raw materials required by the body. Whether alcohol can be called a food was at one time a big point of controversy. Alcohol does have calories. One ounce of pure alcohol contains 210 calories. To translate that into drinks, an ounce of whiskey contains 75 calories or a 12-ounce can of beer contains 150 calories. Alcohol's usefulness as a food is limited, however. Sometimes alcohol is described as providing "empty calories." It does not contain vitamins, minerals, or other essential nutrients. Also, alcohol can interfere with the body's ability to use other sources of energy. As a food, alcohol is unique in that it requires no digestion. Since alcohol is a liquid, no mechanical action by the teeth is required to break it down. No digestive juices need be added to transform it into a form that can be absorbed by the bloodstream and transported to all parts of the body.

	Calories
Beer, 12-oz can	*173*
Martini, 3 oz, 3:1	*145*
Olive, 1 large	*20*
Rum, 1 oz	*73*
Sherry, sweet, 3 oz	*150*
Fortified wines	*120-160*
Scotch, 1 oz	*73*
Cola, 8 oz	*105*
Pretzels, 5 small sticks	*20*

THE JOY OF COOKING

ABSORPTION

What happens to alcohol in the body? Surprisingly, absorption of alcohol begins almost immediately with a very small amount taken up into the bloodstream through the tiny blood vessels in the mouth. But the majority goes the route of all food when swallowed—into the stomach. If other food is present in the stomach, the alcohol mixes with it. Here too some alcohol seeps into the bloodstream. Up to 20% can be absorbed directly from the stomach. The remainder passes into the small intestine to be absorbed. The amount of food in the stomach when drinking takes place has important ramifications. Alcohol is an irritant. It increases the flow of hydrochloric acid, a digestive juice secreted by cells of the stomach lining. Anyone who has an ulcer and takes a drink can readily confirm this. This phenomenon explains the feeling of warmth as the drink goes down. The presence of food serves to dilute the alcohol and diminish its irritant properties.

The amount of food in the stomach is a big factor in determining the speed with which the alcohol is absorbed by the bloodstream. The rate of absorption is largely responsible for the feeling of intoxication—thus the basis for the advice "Don't drink on an empty stomach." The presence of food slows absorption. How much and how quickly alcohol is absorbed depends both on the total amount of alcohol in the stomach contents and the relative proportion of alcohol to food. The greater the amount of alcohol and the smaller the amount of food in the stomach, the more rapidly it is absorbed into the bloodstream and the higher the resulting blood alcohol level. A sex-based difference also seems to influence blood alcohol levels. This is related to differing amounts of an enzyme produced by the stomach lining that promotes the breakdown of alcohol (more on this later). Because women have significantly lower levels of this enzyme, more of the alcohol they drink remains available to enter the small intestine and be taken up by the blood. Therefore if women and men consume equivalent amounts of alcohol, women will have a higher blood alcohol concentration.

In addition to the impact of food in the stomach, the rate of absorption varies with the type of beverage. The higher the concentration of alcohol in a beverage (up to 50%, or 100 proof), the more quickly it is absorbed. This partially explains why distilled spirits have more apparent "kick" than wine or beer. In addition, beer contains some food substances that slow absorption. Carbon dioxide, which hastens the passage of alcohol from the stomach, has the effect of increasing the speed of absorption. Champagne, sparkling wines, or drinks mixed with carbonated soda give a sense of "bubbles in the head."

Now, on from the stomach to the pyloric valve. This valve controls the passage of the stomach's contents into the small intestine. It is sensitive to the presence of alcohol. With large concentrations of alcohol, it tends to get "stuck" in the closed position—a condition called pylorospasm. When pylorospasm occurs, the alcohol trapped in the stomach may cause sufficient irritation and distress to induce vomiting. This is what accounts for much of the nausea and vomiting that may accompany too much drinking. A "stuck" pylorus also may serve as a self-protective mechanism. It may prevent the passage into the small intestine of what might otherwise be life-threatening doses of alcohol.

BLOOD ALCOHOL CONCENTRATION (BAC)

In considering the effects of alcohol, several questions come to mind. How much alcohol? And, in how large a person? How fast did the alcohol get there? Is the blood alcohol level rising or declining? Let us consider each of these in turn.

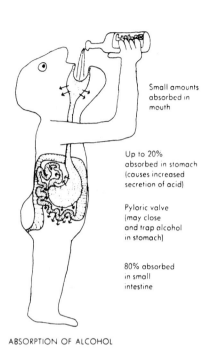

Small amounts absorbed in mouth

Up to 20% absorbed in stomach (causes increased secretion of acid)

Pyloric valve (may close and trap alcohol in stomach)

80% absorbed in small intestine

ABSORPTION OF ALCOHOL

The concentration of alcohol in the blood is the first concern. One tablespoon of sugar mixed in a cup of water yields a much sweeter solution than a tablespoon diluted in a gallon of water. Similarly, a drink with 1 ounce of alcohol will give a higher blood alcohol level in a 100-pound woman than in a 200-pound man. In fact, it will be virtually twice as high. Her body contains less water than his. The second factor is rate of absorption, which depends both on the amount and concentration of alcohol in the stomach and how rapidly it is ingested. So quickly drink a scotch on the rocks on an empty stomach and you will probably be more giddy than if you drink more alcohol more slowly, say in the form of beer after a meal. Even with a given blood alcohol level, there is greater impairment the faster the level has been achieved. Impairment is based on both the amount absorbed and the rate of absorption. Finally, on any drinking occasion, there are different effects for a particular blood alcohol level depending on whether the blood alcohol level is going up or coming down.

Once in the small intestine, the remainder of the alcohol (at least 80%) is very rapidly absorbed into the bloodstream. The bloodstream is the body's transportation system. It delivers nutrients that the cells require for energy and picks up wastes produced by cell metabolism. By this route, too, alcohol is carried to all parts of the body.

Although blood alcohol levels are almost universally used as the measure of alcohol in the body, this does not mean that alcohol merely rides around in the bloodstream until the liver is able to break it down. Alcohol is both highly soluble in water and able to pass rapidly through cell walls. Therefore it is distributed uniformly throughout the water content of all body tissues and cells. For a given blood alcohol level, the alcohol content in the tissues and cells varies in proportion to their amount of water. The alcohol content of liver tissue is 64% of that in the blood; of muscle tissue, 84%; of brain tissue, 75%. It takes very little time for the tissues to absorb the alcohol circulating in the blood. Within 2 minutes brain tissues will accurately reflect the blood alcohol level.

BREAKDOWN AND REMOVAL

The removal of alcohol from the body begins as soon as the alcohol is absorbed by the bloodstream. Small amounts leave unmetabolized through sweat, urine, and breath. The proportion of alcohol in exhaled air has a constant and predictable relationship to the blood alcohol concentration—which is the basis for the use of breathalyzers. These routes, at most, only account for the elimination of 5% of the alcohol consumed. The rest has to be changed chemically and metabolized to be removed from the body.

In 1990, a joint Italian-United States research group, headed by Mario Frezza and Charles Lieber, published new findings on metabolism. These were front page news, particularly because they identified differences between men and women. The breakdown, or metabolism, of alcohol occurs in a multistep process. The first step is its change to acetaldehyde. The enzyme that accomplishes this is called alcohol dehydrogenase, referred to as ADH. Before Frezza and Lieber's work this enzyme was thought to be present and active only in the liver. They, however, identified a gastric form of ADH (alcohol dehydrogenase), that is, ADH produced by the stomach.

The acetaldehyde that is formed is itself acted on in the second step of metabolism, by still another enzyme called acetaldehyde dehydrogenase. Acetaldehyde dehydrogenase too is present both in the stomach and liver. Then, *very* rapidly the acetaldehyde produced is metabolized into acetic acid. The acetic acid formed by the metabolism of the alcohol is dispersed throughout the body, where it is broken down in cells and tissues to become carbon dioxide and water. The following diagram illustrates the chain of events:

Alcohol -> acetaldehyde* -> acetic acid -> carbon dioxide and water

Frezza and Lieber's work indicates that rather than the liver being solely responsible for alcohol's breakdown, some metabolism of alcohol takes place in the stomach because of the presence of gastric alcohol dehydrogenase. The breakdown of alcohol that occurs in the stomach they termed "first-pass metabolism." For nonalcoholic men, the amount of alcohol that can be metabolized by the stomach may be as great as 30% of the alcohol consumed. Nonalcoholic women will metabolize only half that amount in the stomach. Therefore greater proportions of alcohol enter the bloodstream of women. For both sexes, a history of chronic heavy alcohol use leads to a significant decrease in first-pass metabolism.

Almost any cell or organ can break down the acetic acid that is formed. But only the liver or the stomach can handle the first steps. These first steps depend upon the availability of a substance known as NAD^+, which is essential for the enzyme ADH to act. This substance, or cofactor, is present only in the liver and stomach. The rate of metabolism, that is, how fast it takes place, is determined by the availability of this cofactor. It is not in infinite supply nor immediately present in sufficient quantities to accomplish the metabolism of alcohol in one fell swoop.

---

*It is at this point that disulfiram (Antabuse), a drug used in alcoholism treatment, acts. Antabuse stops the breakdown of acetaldehyde by blocking acetaldehyde dehydrogenase. Thus acetaldehyde starts to accumulate in the system. It is very toxic, and its effects are those associated with an Antabuse reaction. A better term would be *acetaldehyde reaction*. The toxicity of acetaldehyde usually isn't a problem. It breaks down faster than it is formed. But Antabuse does not allow this to take place so rapidly—thus the nausea, flushing, and heart palpitations. It has been observed that Orientals often have such symptoms when drinking. These are probably based on biochemical differences resulting from genetic differences. In effect, some Orientals may have a built-in Antabuse-like response.

As alcohol is oxidized to acetaldehyde, this cofactor NAD^+ is changed. With alcohol's metabolism, NAD^+ is converted to NADH. As this occurs, the proportion of NADH to NAD^+ increases. The change in the relative amounts of these two substances has a number of important biochemical ramifications, which are discussed in Chapter 5.

Generally the rate at which food is metabolized depends on the energy requirements of the body. Experience will confirm this, especially for anyone who has taken a stab at dieting. Chopping wood burns up more calories than watching the VCR. Eat too much food and a storehouse of fat begins to accumulate around the middle. By balancing our calorie intake with exercise, we can avoid accumulating a fat roll. Again, as a food, alcohol is unique. It is metabolized at a constant rate. The liver does not have a variable-rate set point for alcohol. The presence of large amounts at a particular moment does not prompt the liver to work faster. Despite alcohol's potential as a fine source of calories, increased exercise (and hence raising the body's need for calories) does not increase the speed of metabolism. This is probably not news to anyone who has tried to sober up someone who's drunk. It is simply a matter of time. Exercise may only mean that you have to contend with a wide-awake drunk rather than a sleeping one. He or she is still intoxicated. The rate at which alcohol is metabolized may vary a little between people. It will also increase somewhat after an extended drinking career. Yet the average rate is around 0.5 ounce of pure alcohol per hour—roughly equivalent to one mixed drink of 86-proof whiskey, or a 4-ounce glass of wine, or one 12-ounce can of beer. The unmetabolized alcohol remains circulating in the bloodstream, "waiting in line." The presence of alcohol in the blood, and hence the brain, is responsible for its intoxicating effects.

I'm on an 1800 calorie diet... 10 beers and 25 pretzel sticks.

ALCOHOL'S ACUTE EFFECTS ON THE BODY

What is the immediate effect of alcohol on the various body organs and functions?

Digestive system

As already noted, alcohol is an irritant. This explains the burning sensation as it goes down. Alcohol in the stomach promotes the flow of gastric juices. A glass of wine before dinner may thereby promote digestion by "priming" the stomach for food. But with intoxicating amounts, alcohol impedes or stops digestion.

Circulatory system

In general, acute use of alcohol has relatively minor effects on the circulatory system in healthy individuals. In moderate amounts, alcohol is a vasodilator of the surface blood vessels. The vessels near the skin surface expand, which accounts for the sensation of warmth and flush to the skin that accompanies drinking. Despite the feeling of warmth, body heat is lost. Thus whoever sends out the St. Bernard with a brandy cask to the aid of the snow-stranded traveler is misguided. Despite the illusion of warmth, a good belt of alcohol will likely further cool off the body.

Kidneys

Anyone who has had a couple of drinks may well spend some time traipsing back and forth to the bathroom. The increased urine output is not caused by alcohol's direct action on the kidneys, nor is it due simply to the amount of liquid consumed. This phenomenon is related to the effect of alcohol on the posterior portion of the pituitary gland located at the base of the brain. The pituitary secretes a hormone that regulates the amount of urine produced. When the pituitary is affected by alcohol, its functioning is depressed. Therefore too little of the hormone is released and the kidneys form a larger-than-normal amount of dilute urine. This effect is most pronounced when alcohol is being absorbed and the blood alcohol level is rising.

Liver

The liver is very sensitive to the acute effects of alcohol. (See Chapter 5 for more information about the long-term effects of alcohol on the liver.) It has been demonstrated that for any drinker, not just heavy drinkers, even relatively small amounts of alcohol (1 to 2 ounces) can lead to accumulation of fat in liver cells.

The liver performs an incredible number of different functions—a very important one is its role in maintaining a proper blood sugar level. Sugar (the body's variety, called glucose) is the only source of energy that brain cells can use. Because the brain is the master control center of the body, an inadequate supply of food has far-reaching consequences. When alcohol is present in the system, the liver devotes all of its "attention," so to speak, to metabolizing it. This may well interfere with the normal liver function of maintaining a steady adequate supply of blood sugar. In the liver there is a stored form of glucose (glycogen) that usually is readily available. However, because of an inadequate diet, or fasting for a day or two, it may not be present. At such times the liver normally would use a more complicated biochemical process to transform other nutrients such as protein into glucose. This process is called gluconeogenesis. However, in the presence of alcohol this complicated maneuver is blocked. In such cases *hypoglycemia* can result. In a hypoglycemic state there is a below-normal concentration of blood sugar. The brain is deprived of its proper nourishment. Symptoms include hunger, weakness, nervousness, sweating, headache, and tremor. If the level is sufficiently depressed, coma can occur. Hypoglycemia may be more likely to occur and may be more severe in individuals who already have liver damage from chronic alcohol use. But it can occur in otherwise normal people with healthy livers who have been drinking heavily and have not been eating properly for as little as 48 to 72 hours.

In individuals with adequate diets, other metabolic effects of alcohol may cause abnormally high levels of blood glucose. This is called *hyperglycemia,* which is a state similar to that occurring in diabetics. In view of its potentially significant effect on blood sugar levels, the danger posed by alcohol for the diabetic is obvious.

The liver also plays an important role in the metabolism of other drugs. The presence of alcohol can interfere with this role and be responsible for some alcohol-drug interactions. As mentioned before, the liver enzyme ADH is essential to the metabolism of alcohol. Quantitatively, it is the liver's major means of metabolizing alcohol. The liver does have a "backup" system, however. This secondary system is called MEOS (short for *m*icrosomal *e*thanol *o*xidizing *s*ystem), and it is located in intracellular structures called microsomes. While termed a backup system for metabolizing alcohol, it is believed that this secondary system only begins to help out significantly in removing alcohol after long-term heavy drinking. Yet it is mentioned here because it is a major system in metabolizing other drugs.

Acutely, the MEOS activity is inhibited dramatically by the presence of alcohol. Therefore other drugs are not broken down at the usual rate. If other drugs in the system have a depressant effect similar to that of alcohol, the central nervous system will be subjected to both simultaneously. However, with some drugs there are additional potential problems. Suppose someone is taking a prescription drug, such as phenytoin (Dilantin) or warfarin sodium (Coumadin), at set intervals and also drinks. The presence of alcohol acutely interferes with the metabolism of the medication; thus when the next scheduled dose is taken substantial amounts of the earlier dose remain, and cumulative toxic effects may occur.*

Central nervous system

Precisely how alcohol affects the brain and thereby influences behavior is not fully understood. Research indicates that alcohol exerts a major effect on the physical structure of nerve cell membranes, which in turn alters their functioning. These changes may

I have very poor and unhappy brains for drinking: I could well wish courtesy would invent some other custom of entertainment.

OTHELLO (1602-4) ACT 2, SC. 3, 1. [34]

---

*With chronic long-term alcohol use the activity of the MEOS is speeded up. In this instance the drugs are broken down faster, so higher doses must be administered to achieve a given therapeutic effect. (See Chapter 5 for more about alcohol-drug interactions.)

be transient with acute alcohol intake, may persist with chronic use, or may lead to other changes in the structure and function of nerve cells as they compensate and adapt to the continued presence of high levels of alcohol. These effects on nerve cells, directly caused by the presence of alcohol, are presumed to play a major role in causing the behaviors seen with acute intoxication and also are believed to be the basis for the phenomena of tolerance. In addition, they are believed to be tied to the phenomenon of withdrawal, when analogous but opposite changes occur with the sudden discontinuation of alcohol.

Alcohol is viewed as significantly affecting the production and activity of neurotransmitters, which are chemical substances in the brain. They transmit messages from one nerve cell to another by crossing the synapses, the spaces between the cells, and activating the receptors on the "receiving" nerve cell. Specifically, alcohol is known to affect three different neurotransmitters. Alcohol decreases the levels of an inhibitory transmitter (GABA). It hastens the breakdown and removal from the body of the neurotransmitter norepinephrine. Also, alcohol depresses the over-all activity of serotonin in the central nervous system (CNS). Interestingly, decreased levels of the neurotransmitter serotonin have been linked through other research to behaviors associated with intoxicated states, depression, anxiety, poor impulse control, aggressiveness, and suicidal behavior. Possibly there may be inherited differences in the way alcohol is metabolized or in how it influences the central nervous system (CNS). Such differences could be the biochemical basis for a genetic predisposition to alcoholism, which may be a significant factor in as many as 50% of all cases. (The genetic basis for alcohol problems and alcohol dependence is discussed in Chapter 3.)

Without question, the central nervous system, particularly the brain, is the organ system most sensitive to the presence of alcohol. This sensitivity is what being "high," drunk, intoxicated, or impaired is all about. The neurophysiological basis for intoxication is not fully understood, but the intensity of the effect is directly related to the concentration of alcohol in the blood and hence the brain. The degree of intoxication is also dependent on whether the blood alcohol level is rising, falling, or constant. It is known that the central nervous system and behavioral effects of a given *blood alcohol* concentration (BAC) are greater when the blood alcohol level is rising. This is called the *Mellanby effect*. It is as if there were a small "practice effect," or short-term adaptation by the nervous system to alcohol's presence. Thus for a given blood alcohol level, there is more impairment if the blood level is rising than is found with the same BAC when the level of alcohol in the blood is falling.

The drug alcohol is a CNS depressant. It interferes with the activity of various brain centers and neurochemical systems—sometimes with seemingly paradoxical results. A high BAC can suppress CNS function across the board, even to the point of causing respiratory arrest and death. At lower doses it may lead to the activated, giddy, poorly controlled, and disinhibited behaviors that are typical of intoxication. This is not due to stimulation of CNS centers that mediate such behavior. Rather it is attributable to the indirect effect of selective suppression of inhibitory systems that normally keep such behavior in check.

Watch or recall someone becoming intoxicated and see the progression of effects. The following examples refer to the CNS effects in a hypothetical "average" male. Of course the observed effects of differing numbers of drinks over an hour in any given person may vary considerably. However, the type and severity of behavioral effects that do occur are a direct function of the amount of alcohol consumed; they progress in a fairly predictable fashion.

The "drinks" used in the following examples are a little under one-half ounce of pure alcohol, the equivalent of a 12-ounce beer, a 4-ounce glass of wine, or an ounce of 86-proof whiskey. Many generous hosts and hostesses mix drinks with more than 1 ounce of booze. So, as you read on, don't shrug off the "ten-drink" section as an impossibility. Five generous ones could easily have as much alcohol.

One drink. With 1 drink, the drinker will be a bit more relaxed, possibly loosened up a little. Unless he chugged it rapidly, thus getting a rapid rise in blood alcohol, his behavior will be little changed. If he is of average height and weighs 160 pounds, by the end of an hour his blood alcohol level will be 0.02. (The actual measurement is grams %, or grams/100 milliliters. For example, 0.02 g% = 200 mg%.) An hour later all traces of alcohol will be gone.

Two and one-half drinks. With 2½ drinks in an hour's time, your party-goer will have a 0.05–blood alcohol level. He's high. The "newer" parts of the brain, those controlling judgment, have been affected. That our friend has been drinking is apparent. He may be loud, boisterous, making passes. Disinhibited, he is saying and doing things he might usually censor. These are the effects that mistakenly cause people to think of alcohol as a stimulant. The system isn't really hyped up. Rather the inhibitions have been suspended, due to the depression by alcohol of the parts of the brain that normally give rise to them. At this time our friend is entering the danger zone for driving. With 2½ drinks in an hour, 2.5 hours will be required to completely metabolize the alcohol.

Five drinks. With 5 drinks in an hour, there is no question you have a drunk on your hands, and the law would agree. A blood alcohol level of 0.10 is sufficient to issue a DWI in any state. It is more than enough for states with a lower legal limit for intoxication. By this time the drinker's judgment is nil. ("Off coursh I can drive!") In addition to the parts of the brain controlling judgment, the centers controlling muscle coordination are depressed. There's a stagger to the walk and a slur to the speech. Even though the loss of dexterity and reaction time can be measured, the drinker, now with altered perception and judgment, will claim he has never functioned better. For all traces of alcohol to disappear from the system, 5 hours will be required.

Ten drinks. This quantity of alcohol in the system yields a blood alcohol content of 0.20. More of the brain than just the judgment, perceptual, and motor centers are affected. Emotions are probably very erratic—rapidly ranging from laughter to tears to rage. Even if your guest could remember he had a coat—which he may not because of memory impairment—he'd never be able to put it on. For all the alcohol to be metabolized, 10 hours will be required. He'll still be legally drunk after 6 hours.

Sixteen drinks—2 six-packs + 4 beers. With this amount of alcohol, the drinker is stuporous. Though not passed out, nothing the senses take in actually registers. Judgment is gone, coordination wiped out, and sensory perception almost nil. With the liver handling roughly 1 ounce of alcohol per hour, it will be 16 hours, well into tomorrow, before all the alcohol is gone.

Twenty drinks—not quite a fifth of whiskey. At this point, the person is in a coma and dangerously close to death. The vital brain centers that send out instructions to the heart and breathing apparatus are partially anesthetized. At a blood alcohol level of 0.40 to 0.50, a person is in a coma; at 0.60 to 0.70, death occurs.

Acute overdose and toxicity

With alcohol as with many other drugs, an acute overdose may be fatal. Usually this occurs when very large doses of alcohol are consumed within a very short period of time. Rapid absorption of the ingested alcohol leads to a rapid and steep rise in BAC. In a relatively brief period, this may lead to loss of consciousness, coma, progressive respiratory depression, and death. Thus a "chug-a-lug" contest can be a fatal game.

In general, the acute lethal dose of alcohol is considered to be from 5 to 8 mg/kg of body weight—the equivalent of about a fifth to a fifth and a half of 86-proof liquor for the typical 155-pound male. Acute doses of this amount of alcohol can be expected to result in BACs in the range of 0.35 to 0.70. Alcohol overdoses with fatal outcomes are consistently associated with BACs in this range, which is not at all surprising. It is known that a BAC above 0.40 will severely, and all too likely, lethally depress respiratory function.

Of course, the exact lethal dose and BAC in any individual will vary with age, sex, general physical health, and the degree of prior tolerance to alcohol. All things being equal, a very large, healthy, young adult male will tolerate a dose of alcohol that might well be fatal for a small, medically ill, elderly female. This is true, only more so, for the alcohol-dependent person, who has established toler-

A drunken night makes a cloudy morning.

SIR WILLIAM CORNWALLIS

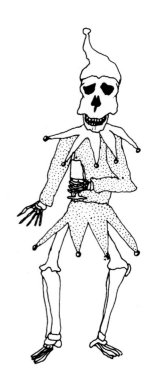

ance, compared with the alcohol-naive novice drinker. Thus the alcoholic person may tolerate an acute dose of alcohol that would kill an otherwise comparable nonalcoholic individual. Although chronic heavy drinking and a high tolerance to alcohol may provide the alcoholic individual with some margin of safety, this protection is finite. Even the most severely dependent person may do himself in by consuming enough alcohol in one drinking bout to raise the BAC to the upper end of the lethal range. Therefore it is probably fair to say that a BAC of 0.70 or higher is certain to be lethal to anyone. The higher the level within the 0.35- to 0.70-range, the greater the risk of death.

Differences in women

Substitute a 120-pound woman in the previous examples, and the weight differential would dramatically speed up the process. A woman and a man who have identical body weights and who both drink the same amounts of alcohol will have different blood alcohol levels. Hers will be higher. Women and men differ in their relative amounts of body fat and water. Women have a higher proportion of fat and correspondingly lower amounts of water. This difference is significant since alcohol is not very fat-soluble. Her body contains less water than his body in which to dilute alcohol.

Simply on that basis, let's contrast a 120-pound woman to our hypothetical 160-pound male drinker. With 1 drink in 1 hour, she would have a BAC of 0.04; 2½ drinks, and her BAC would be up slightly over 0.10. By 5 drinks, she'd have a 0.21 reading. Should she make it through 11 drinks, she'd be in a coma with a blood alcohol level of 0.45.

Beyond body weight and differences in the proportions of fat and water, there are other important differences between men and women with respect to how they handle alcohol. A woman's menstrual cycle significantly influences her rate of absorption and/or metabolism of alcohol. This difference presumably relates to the changing balance of sex hormones and appears to be the result of several interacting factors. During the premenstrual phase of her cycle, a woman absorbs alcohol more rapidly. The absorption rate is significantly faster than in other phases of the menstrual cycle. So, premenstrually, a women will get a higher blood alcohol level than she would get from drinking an equivalent amount at other times. In practical terms, a woman may find herself getting high or becoming drunk faster right before her menstrual period. Also evidence exists that women taking birth-control pills absorb alcohol faster and consequently have higher blood alcohol levels.

The differences between men and women in the levels of gastric acetaldehyde also are significant. Gastric acetaldehyde may account for the metabolism of up to 30% of alcohol in males. This means that for men, nearly one third of the alcohol consumed will be metabolized in the stomach and never pass into the small intestine to be absorbed into the bloodstream. This is not true for women. Women have lower levels of gastric ADH. Because of this, significantly less alcohol is metabolized in the stomach and, consequently, more alcohol is available to enter their circulation when the alcohol passes from the stomach to the small intestine. When consuming identical amounts of alcohol, women will have higher blood alcohol concentrations than men, even if one accounts for differences in their weight and relative proportion of body fat and water.

There are also apparent differences in the metabolism of male and female chronic heavy drinkers. For both men and women with a history of heavy drinking, there is less gastric ADH. Since women have less gastric ADH to start with, and because it declines with heavy alcohol use, there is a veritable absence of gastric ADH. Thus for women who have a history of heavy drinking, the amount of alcohol that reaches the bloodstream will be virtually identical to having a dose administered intravenously. The difference in metabolism and the increased demands upon the liver to metabolize alcohol may be one of the mechanisms accounting for women's recognized greater vulnerability to liver disease.

Quite possibly, other important biological differences may exist between men and women in alcohol's effects. Virtually all the physiological research has been conducted on men, and researchers have assumed their findings to be equally true for women. Though the basic differences between absorption rates of men and women were reported as early as 1932, they were forgotten or ignored until the mid-1970s. The impact of the menstrual cycle was not recognized or reported until 1976! With this failure to examine the effects of the primary and obvious difference between men and women, who knows what more subtle areas have not been considered. Women have been getting short shrift not only in terms of alcohol research. It is equally true in all areas of medical investigation. In light of this the National Institutes of Health is making efforts to promote equal inclusion of women as subjects of biomedical research and in investigations of trials of new drugs.

Despite biological differences between people, every human body reacts to alcohol in basically the same way. This is true despite the fact that for a given blood alcohol level, a very heavy drinker who has developed tolerance to alcohol may show somewhat less impairment in function than an inexperienced drinker would. This uniform, well-documented response enables the law to set a specific blood alcohol level for defining intoxication. The blood alcohol level can be easily measured by blood samples or a breathalyzer. The breathalyzer is able to measure blood alcohol levels because just as carbon dioxide in the blood diffuses across small capillaries in the lungs to be eliminated as exhaled air, so does alcohol. The amount of carbon dioxide in exhaled air is directly proportionate to that circulating in the bloodstream. The same is true for alcohol. The breathalyzer

measures the concentration of alcohol in the exhaled air. From that measurement the exact concentration of alcohol in the blood can be determined.

Tolerance

The immediate effects of consumption of the drug alcohol have been described. With continued regular alcohol use over an extended period, changes take place. Tolerance develops, and any drinker, not only the alcohol-dependent individual, can testify to this. The first few times someone tries alcohol, one drink is enough to feel tipsy. With some drinking experience, one drink no longer has that effect. In part this may reflect greater wisdom. The veteran drinker has learned "how to drink" to avoid feeling intoxicated. The experienced drinker has learned to sip, not gulp, a drink and avoids drinking on an empty stomach. The other reason is that with repeated exposures to alcohol, the CNS adapts to its presence. It can tolerate more alcohol and still maintain normal functioning. This is one of the properties that defines alcohol as an addictive drug. Over the long haul the body requires a larger dose to induce the effects previously produced by smaller doses.

Not only does tolerance develop over relatively long spans of time, there are also rapid adaptive changes in the CNS on each drinking occasion. A drinker is more out of commission when the blood alcohol level is climbing than when it is falling. In a testing situation, if someone is given alcohol to drink and then asked to perform certain tasks, the results are predictable. Impairment is greater on the ascending limb—the rising blood level, or absorption, phase. As the blood alcohol level drops in the elimination phase, the individual, when similarly tested, will be able to function better with the same blood alcohol content. It is as if one learns to function better with the presence of alcohol after "practice." In fact what probably has happened is that the brain has made some subtle adjustments in the way it functions. Here too there are differences between men and women. Both show greater impairment as alcohol levels rise, but there are differences in the kinds of impairment. When intoxicated, women appear to have greater impairment than men for tasks that require motor coordination. Yet, they are superior to men in tasks that require attention. Since driving requires both skills, neither appears the better bet on the highway.

Alcohol as an anesthetic

Alcohol is an anesthetic, just as depicted in all the old Western movies. By modern standards, it is not a very good one. The dose required to produce anesthesia is very close to the lethal amount.

When the vital centers have been depressed enough by alcohol to produce unconsciousness, it only takes a wee bit more to put someone permanently to sleep. Sadly, several times a year almost any newspaper obituary column documents a death from alcohol. Usually the tragedy involves young people chugging a fifth of liquor on a dare or as a prank, or coerced drinking as part of a college fraternity initiation.

OTHER TYPES OF ALCOHOL

In this discussion of alcohol, it is clear that we have been referring to "booze," "suds," "the sauce," "hooch," or any of the other colloquial terms for beverage alcohol. To be scientifically accurate, the kind of alcohol discussed is called ethanol, ethyl alcohol, or grain alcohol. Alcohol, if one is precise, is a term used to refer to a family of substances. What all alcohols have in common is a particular grouping of carbon, hydrogen, and oxygen atoms arranged in a similar fashion. They differ only in the number of carbon atoms and the associated hydrogen atoms. Each alcohol is named according to the number of carbons it has. Ethanol has two carbon atoms.

The other kinds of alcohol with which everyone is familiar are wood alcohol (methyl alcohol) with one carbon and rubbing alcohol (isopropyl) with three carbons. Because of their different chemical makeup, these other alcohols cause big problems if taken into the body. The difficulty lies in differences in rates of metabolism and the kinds of by-products formed. For example, it takes 9 times longer for methanol to be eliminated than it does ethanol. Although methanol itself is not especially toxic, when the liver enzyme ADH acts on it, formaldehyde instead of acetaldehyde is formed. Formaldehyde causes tissue damage, especially to the eyes. The formaldehyde then breaks down into formic acid, which is also not as innocent as the acetic acid produced by ethanol metabolism and can cause severe states of acidosis. Ingestion of methyl alcohol can lead to blindness and can be fatal; it requires prompt medical attention.

As an interesting aside, the treatment of acute methanol poisoning is one of a handful of situations in clinical medicine where ethanol has a legitimate and important therapeutic role. Then, administering ethanol slows the rate of methanol metabolism, which results in a reduction of the levels of toxic by-products formed. Why? Because, ethanol successfully competes with methanol for the limited amount of liver enzyme ADH required for the metabolism of either variety of alcohol. The rapid administration of ethyl alcohol, while at the same time treating acidosis to correct the body's acid-base imbalance, may ameliorate or entirely eliminate serious complications. Poisonings from nonbeverage alcohols don't happen only to those alcohol-dependent persons who in desperation will drink anything. Several years ago there was an Italian wine scandal. Table wines were laced with methanol, resulting in more than 100 deaths. A far more common accident involves the toddler who gets into the medicine cabinet or the teenager or adult who doesn't know that all alcohols are not the same and have different effects.

The influence of expectations

The focus in this chapter has been on the pharmacological properties of alcohol. The physical changes described, especially alcohol's effects upon the CNS, are directly tied to the amount of alcohol consumed. Pharmacologists refer to this phenomenon as "dose-related" effects. However, our psyche also enters into the equation. Although one's beliefs, wishes, or attitudes cannot negate alcohol's actions, they do have an impact. A person's expectations influence the experience of drinking and how a drinking episode is interpreted. There is increasing literature on this alcohol "expectancy" effect, which examines how beliefs about alcohol's effects influence drinking behavior. Some of these studies involve research situations in which people think they are getting alcohol when, in fact, the drink they consume has none. The explanation for this interaction between pharmacological effects and beliefs is that beliefs are likely to influence what in your surroundings you notice and tune in to while drinking. Thus the person who expects that drinking makes people more aggressive is likely to see others as "asking" for a fight, whereas the person who thinks that drinking enhances sexuality will be attuned to "invitations" for intimacy.

Anything taken into the body has effects. All too often we are discovering these effects to be more harmful than had been previously thought. Chemical additives, fertilizers, pesticides, antibiotics given to livestock destined for the table, and coloring agents—all are being recognized as less benign than were supposed. In some instances the federal Food and Drug Administration (FDA) has outlawed or severely restricted use. Let us hope caution with the use of alcohol will become as widespread. Many of the acute problems our society encounters with alcohol use may be lessened as uninformed and unconsidered use is replaced by knowledge about the drug we drink.

RESOURCES AND FURTHER READING

Agency for Toxic Substances and Disease Registry: Methanol toxicity, *American Family Physician* 47(1):163-171, 1993.

> Methanol is used in a variety of commercial and consumer products. Increased use of methanol as a motor fuel may lead to higher ambient air levels and a greater potential for ingestion from siphoning accidents. Methanol toxicity initially is not characterized by severe toxic manifestations. It represents a classic example of "lethal synthesis," in which toxic metabolites can cause fatality after a characteristic latent period. Methanol is well absorbed following inhalation, ingestion or cutaneous exposure. It is oxidized in the liver to formaldehyde, then to formic acid, which contributes to the profound metabolic acidosis occurring in acute methanol poisoning. The metabolic products of methanol can produce a syndrome of delayed-onset acidosis, obtundation, visual disturbance and death. Intravenous sodium bicarbonate therapy should be considered if the patient's blood pH is below 7.2. Treatment is discussed. (Author abstract.)

Browning MD, Hoffer BJ, Dunwiddie TV: Alcohol, memory, and molecules, *Alcohol Health and Research World* 16(4):280-284, 1992.

> Although the molecular mechanism of memory has long eluded researchers, recent discoveries have shed light on this mechanism. The authors present an overview of memory formation and examine a hypothesis for alcohol's well-known ability to disrupt the formation of short-term memory. Public Domain.

Earleywine M, Martin CS: Anticipated stimulant and sedative effects of alcohol vary with dosage and limb of the blood alcohol curve, *Alcoholism: Clinical and Experimental Research* 17(1):135-139, 1993.

> Anticipations of alcohol's effects reportedly covary with the amount consumed. Alcohol's stimulant and sedative properties also may contribute to alcohol consumption. Anticipations of stimulant and sedative effects have not been investigated extensively. The present study examined the stimulant and sedative effects subjects anticipated experiencing if they were on the ascending or descending limb of the blood alcohol curve after consuming two or four standard drinks. The subjects reported anticipating greater stimulant effects than sedative effects on the ascending limb of the blood alcohol curve, and greater sedative effects than stimulant effects on the descending limb. Subjects also reported anticipating larger effects with larger doses. Men tended to anticipate smaller effects than women. (Author abstract.)

Earnest MP: The neurotoxic effects of ethanol and other common alcohols (review), *Current Opinion in Neurology and Neurosurgery* 4(3):453-457, 1991.

> Recent literature on the neurotoxicology of ethanol is summarized, emphasizing clinical features, specifically seizures, movement disorders, peripheral neuropathy, stroke, and the fetal alcohol syndrome. Findings on the pathology, neuropsychology and basic mechanisms of ethanol toxicity are described, neurotoxicity of methanol and isopropyl alcohol are also discussed. (Author abstract.)

Gibbons B: Alcohol: The legal drug, *National Geographic* 181(Feb):2-35, 1992.

> Directed toward the lay public, this is a very clear, lucid, and authoritative discussion of alcohol the drug and its effects.

Loke WH: Physiological and psychological effects of alcohol (review), *Psychologia* 35(3):133-146, 1992.

> The effects of alcohol on human physiological and psychological processes are reviewed. Among the physiological processes discussed are the effects on the skin, gastrointestinal tract, and the cardiovascular system. The absorption and distribution pathways of alcohol are also discussed. Psychological effects include vision, muscular co-ordination, and memory processes. Research indicates that alcohol impairs vision and muscular co-ordination. It is also noted that no standard system to test the effects of alcohol on reaction time has been developed. (Author abstract.)

Martin CS, Moss HB: Measurement of acute tolerance to alcohol in human subjects, *Alcoholism: Clinical and Experimental Research* 17(2):211-216, 1993.

Acute tolerance can be defined as a decrease in response to alcohol within a single exposure to the drug, which occurs independently of changes in blood alcohol concentrations (BACs). BACs change over time in most human alcohol administration studies, and computational techniques that account for these changes must be used to measure the rate of acute tolerance development. The most widely used acute tolerance measure in human research is often called the Mellanby effect, and involves the comparison of responses at the same BAC on the ascending and descending limbs of the blood alcohol curve. The authors compared the Mellanby measure with two other measures of acute tolerance: a conceptually similar area under the curve measure, and a slope function approach that used data only from the descending limb of the blood alcohol curve. The measures were intercorrelated and discussed with regard to empirical and conceptual issues. Exploratory comparisons of those with and without a family history of alcoholism are reported. Methodological recommendations for the computation of acute tolerance are made. The results suggest new methods for measuring the rate of acquisition of acute tolerance, and suggest areas for future research on tolerance-proneness and risk for alcoholism. (Author abstract.)

Alcohol dependence

DEFINITIONS

The social problems associated with alcohol use have been described in the first two chapters. Even if there were no such phenomenon as alcohol dependence, the mere presence of the beverage, alcohol, would lead to social disruption and considerable social costs. This is now being recognized. For too long the statistics on dented fenders caused by impaired drivers, or the dollars lost by industry, or even the percentage of alcohol-related hospital admissions had been overlooked. Seen merely as the product of many people's single, uninformed encounters with alcohol, they were dismissed as the cost a drinking culture has to pay.

Attitudes, however, have changed dramatically. Those who choose to drink are no longer seen as potentially endangering only themselves. Drinkers no longer are accepted as having a right to "let loose," "to celebrate," to "unwind," or indiscriminately "to tie one on" or "get smashed" from time to time. Drinkers no longer are viewed as not accountable for things that occur while they are under the influence. Having come to recognize the impact of these individual decisions upon the public safety, society has significantly changed its attitudes as to what constitutes acceptable and unacceptable drinking. Though still not universally true, in more and more quarters individuals are not considered free to drink in a manner that endangers others. Increasingly, intoxicated behavior is not overlooked, is far less tolerated, and is likely to be met with direct expressions of disapproval.

There are, however, those whose drinking behavior will not be touched by admonitions to "Drink responsibly." There are those whose behavior will not be altered by TV ads that urge friends to select a designated driver to see that all return home safely after an evening that includes drinking. There are those whose behavior will not respond to friends' suggestions to "take it easy" or friends' expressions of disapproval. The special problem that besets these 24.8 million individuals is that for them alcohol is no longer the servant, but the master. The chances are quite good that this concern is individualized with the faces of people we know or have known. There are also the estimated 99.2 million family members who live directly in the shadow of someone's dependence on alcohol.

What is alcohol dependence? Who has alcoholism? These questions will confront the alcohol therapist daily. A physician may request assistance in determining if an alcohol problem exists. A client or a spouse may challenge, "Why, she can't be an alcoholic because . . . " Even in nonworking hours the question crops up during conversation with good friends or casual acquaintances. A number of definitions have been provided. As a starting point, consider the word *alcoholic.* This continues to be the term most commonly used for those with alcohol dependence. The word itself provides some clues. The suffix *-ic* has a special meaning. According to *Webster's New Collegiate Dictionary:*

> *-ic* n suffix: One having the character or nature of; one belonging to or associated with: one exhibiting or affected by.

Attaching *-ic* to alcohol, we form a word that denotes the person linked with alcohol. Okay, that's a start. Clearly, not all drinkers are linked with alcohol, just as all baseball players are not linked with the Boston Red Sox. Why the link or association? The basis is probably frequency of alcohol use, pattern of use, quantity used, or frequency of indications that the person has been tippling. "Belonging to" has several connotations, including "an individual being possessed by or under the control of." The Chinese have a saying that goes: "The man takes a drink, the drink takes a drink, and then the drink takes the man." This final step closely approximates what the word "alcoholic" means. It offers a good picture of the progression of alcohol*ism,* or alcohol dependence.

It is worth noting that the discussion or debate on who is an alcoholic and what is alcoholism is relatively recent. This doesn't mean that society before had not noticed those we now think of as suffering from alcoholism. Certainly, those deeply in trouble with alcohol have been recognized for centuries, but their existence was accepted as a fact, without question or any particular thought about the matter. To the extent that there was debate, it centered on why, as well as how the person should be handled. Essentially two basic approaches prevailed. One was that "obviously" these individuals were morally inferior. The evidence cited was that of the vast majority of people who drank moderately without presenting problems for themselves or their communities. The other view has been that "obviously" such individuals were possessed; would those in their right mind drink like that of their own volition?

With increasing scientific study and understanding of "the drink taking the man" phenomenon, the more complicated the task of definition became. In addition to the awareness that some people are distinctly different from many who drink moderately, the other clear discovery was that those with alcoholism are not alike. Not all develop DTs (delirium tremens) upon cessation of drinking. There are big differences in the quantity of alcohol consumed or the number of years of drinking before family problems arise. Many chronic heavy drinkers develop cirrhosis but more do not. Given the range of differences among those with alcoholism, what is the basic core, the essential features that are common to all cases of alcoholism? An answer to this question is fundamental to any attempt to define the condition.

One swallow doesn't make a summer but too many swallows make a fall.

G.D. PRENTICE

Early definitions

Over the past half century, as alcoholism increasingly was viewed as a disease, a number of attempts were made to define the condition. What follows is a cross section of the early definitions that were put forth:

1940s, Alcoholics Anonymous. AA has never had an "official" definition. The concept of Dr. William Silkworth, one of AA's early friends, is sometimes cited by AA members: . . .an obsession of the mind and an allergy of the body. The obsession or compulsion guarantees that the sufferer will drink against his own will and interest. The allergy guarantees that the sufferer will either die or go insane.

Another operative definition frequently heard among AA members is: "An alcoholic is a person who cannot predict with accuracy what will happen when he takes a drink."

1946, E.M. Jellinek, a pioneer in modern alcohol studies. "Alcoholism is any use of alcoholic beverages that causes any damage to the individual or to society or both."

1950s, Marty Mann, a founding member of the National Council on Alcoholism (now known as the National Council on Alcoholism and Drug Dependence). "An alcoholic is a very sick person, victim of an insidious, progressive disease, which all too often ends fatally. An alcoholic can be recognized, diagnosed, and treated successfully."

1950, World Health Organization. The Alcoholism Subcommittee defined alcoholism as: "Any form of drinking which in extent goes beyond the tradition and customary 'dietary' use, or the ordinary compliance with the social drinking customs of the community concerned, irrespective of etiological factors leading to such behavior, and irrespective also of the extent to which such etiological factors are dependent upon heredity, constitution, or acquired physiopathological and metabolic influences." This initial formulation has since been substantially revised as the following definitions demonstrate.

1960, Mark Keller, former editor of the *Journal of Studies on Alcohol.* "Alcoholism is a chronic disease manifested by repeated implicative drinking so as to cause injury to the drinker's health or to his social or economic functioning."

1968, American Psychiatric Association. According to the Committee on Nomenclature and Statistics: "Alcoholism: this category is for patients whose alcohol intake is great enough to damage their physical health, or their personal or social functioning, or when it has become a prerequisite to normal functioning." Three types of alcoholism were further identified: episodic excessive drinking, habitual excessive drinking, and alcohol addiction.

1977, American Medical Association. From the *Manual on Alcoholism,* edited by the AMA Panel on Alcoholism: "Alcoholism is an illness characterized by significant impairment that is directly associated with persistent and excessive use of alcohol. Impairment may involve physiological, psychological, or social dysfunction."

In examining the early definitions, we find that each, although not necessarily conflicting, tended to have a different focus or emphasis. Some were purely descriptive. Others attempted to speak to the origins of the condition. Several concentrated on the unfortunate consequences associated with alcohol use. Others zeroed in on hallmark signs or symptoms, especially loss of control or frequency of intoxication.

Add to these expert definitions all of the definitions that have been used casually by each of us and our neighbors. These have varied from "alcoholism is an illness," to "it's the number one drug problem," to "when someone's drunk all the time," to "someone down on skid row," to "those who can't hold their liquor." Note that generally, lay people have had far more permissive criteria and have adopted definitions that would exclude themselves as candidates for the condition!

Actions taken by the World Health Organization (WHO) in 1977 and the American Psychiatric Association (APA) three years later were important in clarifying and promoting greater consensus as to the definition of alcoholism. The changes instituted by these groups were important in introducing more consistency between alcoholism and conditions related to other psychoactive substance use. (The World Health Organization prepares and publishes the *International Classification of Diseases,* known as ICD. It provides a comprehensive list of all injuries, diseases, and disorders, and is used worldwide. The American Psychiatric Association publishes a manual restricted to mental disorders, known as the *Diagnostic and Statistical Manual.*) Ironically, for the sake of clarification both groups abandoned use of the term "alcoholism." Neither group disputed the existence of the phenomenon of alcoholism. For medical and scientific purposes, however, both the WHO and APA substituted *alcohol dependence syndrome* for what heretofore had been discussed as *alcoholism.* This was done because of the multiple definitions abounding in the professional community. This change also was necessitated by the general public's widespread everyday use of "alcoholic" and the variants that were being coined, such as "workaholic." When the same term is shared by lay people and medical scientists, but used differently, confusion is likely. So, paradoxically, it was in part the very success in educating the public about alcoholism as a disease that necessitated the change in terminology.

Uniform terminology is essential. When it comes to clinical interactions with colleagues and other professionals, the day is past when each clinician has the luxury of defining the disease according to individual biases and preferences. In the United States, the APA's *Diagnostic and Statistical Manual* provides the approved terminology. The 1980 version of the *Diagnostic and Statistical Manual,* the third edition *(DSM-III)* distinguished between two separate alcohol-related syndromes: alcohol abuse and alcohol dependence. Both conditions entailed impairment in social and occupa-

'Tis not the drinking that is to be blamed, but the excess.

JOHN SELDON, 1689

tional functioning. The essential distinguishing feature of dependence was the presence of tolerance and withdrawal. There is always room to quibble with definitions, and that particular operational definition did have its critics. The major criticism of the definition had been that physical dependence was required to make the diagnosis of dependence. This is never a black-and-white situation. There are those who may not show marked physical dependence but whose lives are in utter chaos because of alcohol use. However, this was an instance when living with imperfections was preferable to the alternative, which would have been everyone's continuing to feel free to define the condition for themselves. In subsequent revisions of the *Manual,* the *DSM-III-R* in 1987 and the *DSM-IV* in 1994, changes were made in response to these concerns.

With the growing acceptance of alcoholism as a disease, there was a corresponding drop-off in the number of formal definitions. Attention had turned to efforts to specify the conditions which need to be met to make a diagnosis of the condition. Then suddenly, what seemingly had been settled—that alcohol dependence was a disease—was called into question. The prospect of health care reform and the need to make decisions about what would and would not be covered by any mandated health insurance rekindled the debate. Within this context, a policy statement defining alcoholism was issued by the American Society of Addiction Medicine (ASAM), a professional association of physician specialists in the alcohol and drug field.

1993, American Society of Addiction Medicine. "Alcoholism is a *primary,* chronic *disease* with genetic, psychological and environmental factors influencing its development and manifestations. The disease is *often progressive* and *fatal.* It is characterized by continuous or periodic: *impaired control over* drinking, preoccupation with the drug alcohol, use of alcohol despite *adverse consequences,* and distortions in thinking, most notably *denial. . .* "

The statement then proceeds to elaborate on each of the words in italics. Interestingly, the society makes an explicit statement about the meaning of the word "disease." It emphasizes that a disease represents an "involuntary disability."

A DISEASE?

The remainder of this chapter will be devoted to the evolution of the understanding of alcoholism as a disease and the major pieces of work that have led to our present formulation of what alcohol dependence is, its complexity, and how to recognize it. First, we turn to the work of E.M. Jellinek, who has been called the father of alcohol studies not only in the United States but internationally. Next discussed is the guidelines established by a Committee of the National Council on Alcoholism and published in 1972. The guidelines represented the first effort to set forth explicit signs and symptoms to be used in diagnosing alcoholism. Following this, in 1980, there was the publication of the APA's first diagnostic criteria for alcohol dependence. Then, in 1983, a landmark study by George Vaillant was published outlining the natural history of alcoholism and its recovery. Finally, there are the most recent revisions to the APA's Diagnostic and Statistic Manual, and the research and thinking that shaped them.

Anyone who is sufficiently interested in alcohol problems to have read this far is probably accustomed to hearing alcoholism referred to as an illness, disease, or sickness. As noted repeatedly, this has not always been the case. Alcoholism—alcohol dependence—has not always been distinguished from drunkenness. Alternatively, it has been seen as a lot of drunkenness and categorized as a sin or character defect. The work of E.M. Jellinek was largely responsible for the shift from a defect to an illness model. In essence, through his research and writings he said, "Hey, world, you folks mislabeled this thing. You put it in the sin bin, and it really belongs in the disease pile."

Implications of disease classification

How we label something is very important. It provides clues to how to feel and think, what to expect, and how to act. Whether a particular bulb is tagged as a tulip or garlic will make a big difference. Depending on which I think it is, I'll either chop and sauté or plant and water. Very different behaviors are associated with each. An error may lead to strangely flavored spaghetti sauce and a less colorful flower bed next spring.

For both lay people and professionals the recognition that alcoholism belongs properly in the category of disease has had a dramatic impact. Sick people generally are awarded sympathy. The accepted notion is that sick people do not choose to be sick. Being sick is not pleasant. It is agreed that care should be provided to restore health. During the period of sickness, people are not expected to fill their usual roles or meet their responsibilities. A special designation is given to them—that of patient. Furthermore, sick people are not to be criticized for manifesting the symptoms of their illness. To demand that a person with flu stop running a fever would be pointless and unkind. Accompanying the perception of alcoholism as an illness, the individual with the disease—the alcoholic—came to be viewed as a sufferer and victim. Much of the bizarre behavior displayed came to be recognized as unwillful and symptomatic. No longer the object of scorn, the individual with alcoholism was seen as requiring care. The logical place to send the alcoholic was a hospital or some type of rehabilitation facility instead of jail. Since the 1940s there has been a gradual shift in public perceptions. Nationwide polls now find that over 80% of the respondents say they believe alcoholism to be an illness.

Although Jellinek's efforts may have triggered this shift, a number of other events added impetus. The National Council on

I do Not drink

More Than
a Sponge. –Rabelais

Alcoholism put its efforts into lobbying and public education. The American Medical Association and American Hospital Association published various committee reports. State agencies created treatment programs. Medical societies and other professional associations assumed responsibility for their members' education and addressed the ethical responsibility to treat alcohol problems. We suspect that the single biggest push has come from recovering alcoholics, especially through the work of AA. Virtually everyone today has personal knowledge of an apparently hopeless alcoholic who has stopped drinking and now seems a new, different person.

The formulation of alcoholism as a disease opened up possibilities for treatment that were formerly nonexistent. It brought into the helping arena the resources of medicine, nursing, social work, and other professions that before had no mandate to be involved. Also it is gradually removing the stigma associated with the condition of alcoholism. This improved the likelihood that individuals and families would seek help rather than be encumbered by shame or burdened by a sense of hopelessness trying to keep the condition a family secret. Finally, the resources of the federal government were focused on alcohol problems as a major public health issue, and a host of treatment and educational programs were created.

Criticisms of the disease concept

The disease concept of alcoholism has had its critics. One former criticism arose in academic circles. Over a decade ago, a rash of articles were published setting forth different models or frameworks for viewing alcoholism. The different models were described as the *moral* model, *disease* model, *AA* model, *learning* model, *self-medication* model, and *social* model. The writers described these different models as if they were mutually exclusive, conflicting, and as if an either/or choice was required. Such narrow thinking is now discredited. The current view is that models representing differing approaches are not in opposition; they might be compared to the "blind-men-describing-the-elephant" phenomenon. They complement one another and highlight differing points of emphasis. To view alcoholism as a disease does not mean that one discounts the role of learning, disregards the influence of society, or fails to recognize that some drinking is self medication. Similarly the views of AA on alcoholism don't require that one discount alcoholism as a disease. Certainly its members don't!

Other objections to the disease concept have come from the treatment community. One is that it possibly can put too much emphasis on the physician as the major helper. While doctors certainly have a role to play in diagnosis and physical treatment, medical training has not necessarily prepared them for counseling. Even if it has, a physician alone does not have available all the time needed to offer counseling, support, and education to both patient and family. This requires a team of professionals. Yet the disease concept may imply that the doctor alone is qualified to provide or direct treatment. Criticism frequently has been leveled at MDs for being uninterested in or unconcerned with the problem of alcohol dependence. Possibly the misuse of the disease concept also may foster unrealistic expectations of, and place undue burdens on, doctors.

Another criticism with some merit is that the disease label implies the possibility of a cure through the wonders of modern medicine worked on a passive patient. Emphasis on alcoholism as a chronic illness requiring the active participation of the patient in rehabilitation should remove this reservation. Characteristically the management of chronic disease involves five elements. There is treatment of acute flare-ups. Emotional support is a necessity; after all, no one likes having a chronic illness! Education is needed, so that the individual can be well informed about the illness and assist in self-care. Rehabilitative measures are initiated to prompt the life changes necessary to live with the limitations imposed by the illness. Family involvement is critical so the family can be informed and can deal with the impact that the chronic illness has on their lives, which is a prerequisite for their being supportive.

A noteworthy characteristic of a chronic illness is that it tends to develop slowly. Quite conceivably, with an acute illness such as flu, one can go to bed feeling chipper and wake up the next morning sick. It literally happens overnight. However, one does not become diabetic, arthritic, or alcoholic overnight. The disease state develops slowly. There will be warning signs and symptoms before the point at which it is unequivocally present. We have E.M. Jellinek to thank for beginning to sketch out this progression in alcoholism.

Another criticism levied at the disease concept is that it can be used as an excuse. "Don't look at me, I'm not responsible. I'm sick. Poor me (sigh, sigh)." But this criticism overlooks a significant point. A drinking alcoholic is expected to try shooting holes into any definition. Some who would criticize the disease concept on this basis are possibly those who have run headlong into the denial that characterizes alcohol dependence. If denial goes unrecognized as a symptom of the disease, it can only cause frustration. And, even then, alcohol-dependent individuals are very sensitive to what will immobilize those around them so that their drinking can continue undisturbed. As you acquire more information about alcohol dependence, you will begin to recognize these maneuvers—the first step in gaining skill to effectively counter disarming tactics. A one-liner that seems to cover the situation fairly well comes from a once-prominent billboard on the Boston skyline: *There's nothing wrong with being an alcoholic, if you're doing something about it.*

Another recent variant of this criticism is less concerned with the particular individual who is alcohol-dependent than with the larger social trend. People have questioned whether or not, as a society, we have become too accepting of the notion of "disease" or "vic-

tim" and willing to excuse behaviors for which people do need to be held accountable. Certainly court cases such as that of the now-infamous Menendez brothers come to mind. There are other examples cited by critics. One piece of evidence is the large market of "recovery literature." In it everyone is seemingly a victim of some sort, as witnessed by the proliferation of information on codependency, adult children, and dysfunctional families. Many of the terms and constructs were borrowed from the addictions field and applied to other areas. Upon first hearing of the notion of sexual addiction, someone commented, "Whatever happened to bad judgment, immorality, sin, and the notion of personal responsibility for choices?" Indeed, that question does need to be asked. Although we are probably more sympathetic to self-help efforts generally than others may be, and appreciative of their contributions—especially AA—there is a danger of not drawing lines where they need to be drawn. In overextending concepts such as the disease model to areas further afield, there is the danger of trivializing and diminishing the usefulness of the model when it is very much needed.

NATURAL HISTORY

The natural history of an illness refers to the typical progression of signs and symptoms as the disease unfolds if it goes untreated. Jellinek was one of the first to speak of alcoholism as a disease and of its progression. Thus he was seeing the condition in what was wholly a new light and considering it from a perspective that was quite different from the views that then prevailed. An appreciation of this early work is important. Those in any profession need to be knowledgeable about its history. As in our personal lives our family history casts a long shadow and partially determines how we see the world, so history molds the thought and theory of our professions and occupations. We may not always be fully aware of the influences in our personal lives; the same is true of our professional practice. Much of how we view alcohol dependence today is clearly derived from the work of Jellinek. Those involved in alcohol counseling need to be familiar with the work that marked the evolution of the field.

Jellinek's phases of alcoholism

How did Jellinek arrive at his disease formulation of alcoholism? A trained biostatistician, he was understandably fascinated by statistics, the pictures they portray, and the questions they raise. Much of his work was descriptive, defining the turf of alcoholism: who, when, where. One of his first studies, published in 1952, charted the signs and symptoms associated with alcohol addiction. This work was based on a survey of over 2000 members of AA. Although differences certainly existed between persons, the similarities were, to him, striking. There was a definite pattern to the appearance of the symptoms. Also there was a progression of the disease in terms of increasing dysfunction. The symptoms and signs tended to go together in clusters. On the basis of these observations, Jellinek developed the idea of four different phases of alcohol addiction: *prealcoholic, prodromal, crucial,* and *chronic.* Although many may not be aware of the origins, these phases have been widely used in alcohol treatment circles. The four phases are portrayed graphically on p. 64.

In the *prealcoholic phase,* according to Jellinek's formulation, the individual's use of alcohol is socially motivated. However, the prospective alcoholic soon experiences psychological relief in the drinking situation. Possibly his or her tensions are greater than other people's, or possibly the individual has no other way of handling tensions that arise. It does not matter. Either way, the individual learns to seek out occasions at which drinking will occur. At some point the connection is perceived. Drinking then becomes the standard means of handling stress. But the drinking behavior will not look different to the outsider. This phase can extend from several months to 2 years or more. An increase in tolerance gradually develops.

Suddenly the prealcoholic will enter the *prodromal phase.* Prodromal means warning or signaling disease. According to Jellinek, the behavior that heralds the change is the occurrence of "alcoholic palimpsests" or blackouts.* Blackouts are amnesia-like periods during drinking. The person seems to be functioning normally but later has no memory of what happened. Other behaviors emerge during this phase that testify to alcohol's no longer being just "a beverage," but a "need." Among these warning signs are: sneaking extra drinks before or during parties, gulping the first drink or two, and guilt about the drinking behavior. At this point consumption is heavy, yet not necessarily conspicuous. To look "okay" requires conscious effort by the drinker. This period can last from 6 months to 4 or 5 years, depending on the drinker's circumstances.

The third phase is the *crucial phase.* The key symptom that ushers in this phase is loss of control. Now taking a drink sets up a chain reaction. The drinker can no longer control the amount consumed after taking the first drink. Yet the drinker can control whether or not to take a drink. So, it is possible to go on the wagon for a time. With loss of control, the drinker's coverup is blown. The drinking is now clearly different. It requires explanation, so rationalizations begin. Simultaneously, the alcoholic attempts a sequence of strategies to regain control. The thinking of the alcoholic goes as follows: "If I just _____, then it will be okay." Solutions commonly adopted by the alcoholic are: "going on the wagon," i.e., deliberate periods of abstinence, changing drinking patterns, or geographical changes to escape/avoid/be relieved of _____; similarly job changes occur. All these attempted solutions are doomed to failure. The alcoholic

I really don't need alcohol. I'd just rather have a glass of sherry than a tranquilizer.

---

*This is a description of Jellinek's work. A discussion of blackouts and the more recent findings is covered in Chapter 5.

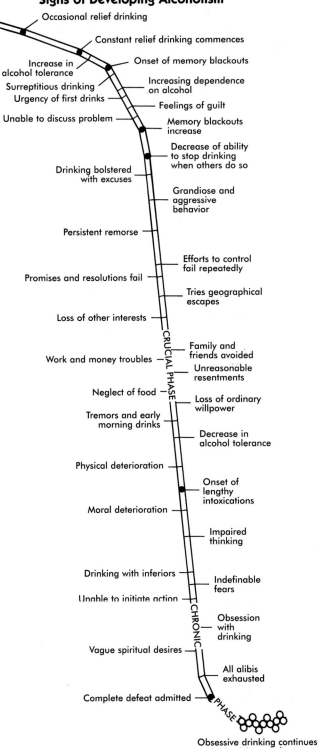

Signs of Developing Alcoholism

Occasional relief drinking

Constant relief drinking commences

Onset of memory blackouts

Increase in alcohol tolerance

Increasing dependence on alcohol

Surreptitious drinking

Urgency of first drinks

Feelings of guilt

Unable to discuss problem

Memory blackouts increase

Decrease of ability to stop drinking when others do so

Drinking bolstered with excuses

Grandiose and aggressive behavior

Persistent remorse

Efforts to control fail repeatedly

Promises and resolutions fail

Tries geographical escapes

Loss of other interests

CRUCIAL PHASE

Family and friends avoided

Work and money troubles

Unreasonable resentments

Neglect of food

Loss of ordinary willpower

Tremors and early morning drinks

Decrease in alcohol tolerance

Physical deterioration

Onset of lengthy intoxications

Moral deterioration

Impaired thinking

Drinking with inferiors

Indefinable fears

Unable to initiate action

CHRONIC

Obsession with drinking

Vague spiritual desires

All alibis exhausted

Complete defeat admitted

PHASE

Obsessive drinking continues in vicious circles

responds to these failures—alternately resentful, remorseful, and aggressive. Life has become alcohol-centered. Family life and friendships deteriorate. The first alcohol-related hospitalization is now likely to occur. Morning drinking may begin to creep in, foreshadowing the next stage.

The final stage in the process as outlined by Jellinek is the *chronic phase*. In the preceding crucial phase, drinkers may have been somewhat successful in maintaining a job and their social footing. Now, as drinking begins earlier in the day, intoxication is an almost daily–day long phenomenon. "Benders" are more frequent. The individual may also go to dives and drink with persons outside his normal peer group. Not unexpectedly, the alcoholic finds himself on the fringes of society. When ethanol is unavailable, poisonous substitutes are the alternative. During this phase, marked physical changes occur. Tolerance for alcohol drops sharply. No longer able to hold the liquor, the alcoholic becomes stuporous after a few drinks. Tremors develop. Many simple tasks are impossible in the sober state. The individual is beset by indefinable fears. Finally, the rationalization system fails. The long-used excuses are revealed as just that—excuses. The alcoholic is seen as spontaneously open to treatment. Often, however, drinking is likely to continue because the alcoholic can imagine no way out of these circumstances. Jellinek did emphasize that alcoholics do not have to go through all four stages before successful treatment can occur.

Types of alcoholism: Jellinek's species

The pattern described above refers to the stages of alcohol addiction. Jellinek continued his study of alcoholism, focusing on alcohol problems in other countries. The differences he found could not be accounted for simply by the phases of alcohol addiction. They seemed to be differences of kind rather than simply of degree of addiction. This led to his formulation of species, or categories, of alcoholism. Each of these types he named after a Greek letter.

Alpha alcoholism. This type represents a purely psychological dependence on alcohol. There is neither loss of control nor an inability to abstain. What is evident is the reliance on alcohol to weather any or all discomforts or problems in life, which may lead to interpersonal, family, or work problems. A progression is not inevitable. Jellinek noted that other writers may call this species *problem drinking*.

Beta alcoholism. This is present when physical problems such as cirrhosis or gastritis develop from alcohol use but the individual is not psychologically or physically dependent. Beta alcoholism is likely to occur in persons from cultures where there is widespread heavy drinking and inadequate diet.

Gamma alcoholism. This variant is marked by a change in tolerance, physiological changes leading to withdrawal symptoms, and a

Prealcoholic

Prodromal

Crucial

Chronic

loss of control. In this species there is a progression from psychological to physical dependence. It is the most devastating species in terms of physical health *and* social disruption. This is the species Jellinek originally studied. It progresses in the four phases discussed: prealcoholic, prodromal, crucial, and chronic. The gamma alcoholic appeared to be the most prominent type in the United States. This species was the type most common among the members of AA that Jellinek studied. Characteristics of this species alone are often seen as synonymous with alcoholism.

Delta alcoholism. Delta alcoholism is very similar to the *gamma* variety of alcoholism. There is psychological and physical dependence, but there is no loss of control. Therefore on any particular occasion the drinker can control the amount consumed. The individual, however, cannot go on the wagon for even a day without suffering withdrawal.

Epsilon alcoholism. While not studied in depth, this type appeared to be significantly different from the others. Jellinek called this *periodic alcoholism*, a type marked by binge drinking. Though not elaborating, he felt this was a species by itself, not to be confused with relapses of *gamma* alcoholics.

Having described these various species in *The Disease Concept of Alcoholism,* Jellinek concluded that possibly not all of the species identified are properly categorized as diseases. There was no question in his mind that *gamma* and *delta* varieties, each involving physiological changes and a progression of symptoms, were diseases. He speculated that maybe *alpha* and *epsilon* varieties are, however, symptoms of other disorders. By more adequately classifying and categorizing the phenomena of alcoholism, he brought scientific order to a field that formerly had been dominated by beliefs. That was no modest contribution.

Species reexamined

In many respects a considerable portion of the research now being undertaken is addressing the same question that concerned Jellinek. As noted earlier, although there are common features in alcoholism, there are differences too. Because of this, alcohol dependence is sometimes described as a "heterogeneous" disease. Differences need to be explained. They may represent factors that may have important implications for treatment, prevention, or early diagnosis. By way of comparison, it is recognized that there are different types of pneumonia or different types of diabetes. Distinguishing between them is necessary to determine appropriate treatment; in the case of pneumonia the type dictates the type of antibiotic that will be prescribed.

In respect to types of alcoholism, several possible subgroups are now being suggested. People involved with genetics research believe it is possible and useful to distinguish between *familial* and *nonfa-*

milial alcoholism. Familial alcoholism is marked by a positive family history of alcoholism, has an earlier age of onset, has no increased presence of other psychiatric disorders, and has more severe symptoms that necessitate early treatment. Jellinek too had recognized a possible subgroup of alcoholics. In 1940, he had proposed a diagnostic category termed *familial alcoholism.*

Another set of distinctions sometimes made is between *primary* alcoholism and *secondary* or reactive alcoholism. The secondary or reactive type is seen as alcoholism that grows out of or is superimposed on a psychiatric illness or major psychological problem. This is not to imply that such researchers think that this alcoholism need not be treated in its own right. It does mean that in such cases the individual may require active treatment for more than alcoholism, i.e., treatment for the condition(s) that spawned or facilitated its development.

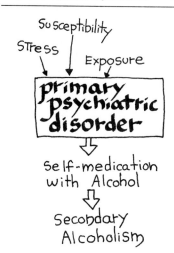

GUIDES FOR DIAGNOSIS
NCA criteria

Having introduced the perspective of alcoholism as a disease, the next major task was to establish guidelines for diagnosis. This step was taken in 1972 with the publication of a paper entitled "Criteria for the Diagnosis of Alcoholism." The article was prepared by a special committee of the National Council on Alcoholism and published in two different medical journals. The Committee's charge was to set forth guidelines to be used by physicians in diagnosing alcoholism. Physicians were provided thereby with an explicit, firm set of standards to use in making a diagnosis. In undertaking this endeavor the Committee collected all the signs and symptoms of alcoholism that could be ascertained through physical examination, medical history, social history, laboratory tests, and clinical observations. These signs and symptoms were then organized into two categories, or "tracks," of data. The first track consisted of *Physiological and Clinical Data.* Included within that track were the facts a physician can discover either through physical examination, laboratory tests, or medical history. The second track was termed the *Behavioral, Psychological, and Attitudinal Data.* It was composed of information that the patient or family might report about the patient's life situation, the social history, and those things the physician can observe directly about the patient's involvement with alcohol.

Within each of the two data tracks, the criteria were further divided into subgroups of major or minor criteria. That means exactly what you would expect: major criteria were the "biggies"; the presence of only one was sufficient to make the diagnosis. However, several minor criteria, from both tracks, were needed to support a diagnosis. Finally, each of the potential signposts was weighted as to whether or not it "definitely," "probably," or "possibly" indicated alcoholism.

Table 1 summarizes some of the key criteria set forth by the Criteria Committee.

Many similarities existed between the symptoms of alcohol addiction developed by Jellinek in 1952 and the criteria published 20 years later. However, Jellinek composed his list based on the self-reports of recovering alcoholics, so the signs were from *their* point of view. A good number of the symptoms Jellinek included involved efforts to deceive and the attempts of the alcoholic individuals to appear normal. This provided little assistance to the physician or helper interviewing an active alcoholic. In those situations, the physician is unable to rely on his or her usual instincts to believe the client. To further complicate the process of making a diagnosis based on Jellinek's list, many of the behaviors included are not the kinds of things a physician can easily detect. So the NCA criteria were a marked improvement.

TABLE 1

Criteria for diagnosis of alcoholism

Physiological data	Diagnostic significance*	Behavioral data	Diagnostic significance*
Major criteria		**Major criteria**	
Physiological dependence evidenced by withdrawal syndromes when alcohol is interrupted or decreased	1	Continued drinking, despite strong medical indications known to patient	1
Evidence of tolerance, by blood alcohol level of 0.15 without gross evidence of intoxication or consumption of equivalent of fifth of whiskey for more than one day by 180-lb man	1	Drinking despite serious social problems	1
		Patient's complaint of loss of control	2
Alcoholic blackouts	2		
Major alcohol-related illnesses in person who drinks regularly			
Fatty Liver	2		
Alcoholic hepatitis	1		
Cirrhosis	2		
Pancreatitis	2		
Chronic gastritis	3		
Minor criteria		**Minor criteria** (very similar to Jellinek's symptoms of phases of alcohol addiction)	
Laboratory tests		Repeated attempts at abstinence	2
Blood alcohol level of 0.3 or more at any time	1†	Unexplained changes in family, social, or business relationships	3
Blood alcohol level of 0.1 in routine examination	1†	Spouse's complaints about drinking	2
Odor of alcohol on breath at time of medical appointment	2		

Modified from Criteria Committee, National Council on Alcoholism. Criteria for the diagnosis of alcoholism, American Journal of Psychiatry, August 1979, pp. 41-49.

*1, Must diagnose alcoholism; 2, probably indicates alcoholism; 3, possibly due to alcoholism.

†1There seems to be some discrepancy between 1 meaning a must diagnose alcoholism and the committee's statement that more than one must be in evidence. We note this out, have no explanation.

The Committee that developed the Criteria for Diagnosis also addressed the nature of alcoholism and commented on its treatment. Alcoholism was characterized as a *chronic progressive disease*. It was noted that although it is incurable, it is highly treatable. Because it is a chronic disease, the diagnosis once made never can be dropped. Therefore an individual successfully involved in a treatment program would have his or her diagnosis amended to "alcoholism: arrested" or "alcoholism: in remission." Criteria were set forth to determine when this change in diagnosis was appropriate. The Committee recommended that factors other than the length of sobriety be taken into account. Among the items listed as signs of recovery were full, active participation in AA, active use of other treatments, use of Antabuse-like preparations, no substitution of other drugs, and returning to work. The committee was primarily interested in diagnosis, not treatment. Yet implicit in the standards suggested for diagnosing "alcoholism: arrested" is a view that alcoholism requires a variety of treatment and rehabilitative efforts.

DSM-III criteria

Although definitely on the right track and more useful to clinicians than Jellinek's formulations, the NCA criteria were nonetheless very cumbersome. With the publication in 1980 of the APA's Diagnostic and Statistical Manual, Edition 3, these criteria were taken a step forward. Known as *DSM-III*, the *Diagnostic and Statistical Manual* was a milestone not only for alcoholism, but for other psychiatric conditions as well. It provided a major departure from previous diagnostic schemes in several ways. For one, it set forth very specific diagnostic criteria, explicitly stating what signs and symptoms must be present to make a diagnosis for a specific condition. The purpose for this was to make diagnosis of psychiatric conditions more uniform. Thus diagnosis was no longer based on what the clinician thought was the underlying reason for the condition, for example, whether it was psychological maladjustment or a physiological abnormality.

In this third edition of manual there was also significant revision, reorganization, and renaming of major groups of psychiatric illnesses. Thus for the first time *substance use disorders,* which includes alcohol dependence and alcohol abuse, became a separate major diagnostic category. Previously these different addictions had been assigned to the category of *personality disorders*. This earlier assignment reflected the common notion that substance abuse was the result of psychological problems. With the creation of the new category, the manual no longer implied any particular etiology.

The diagnostic manual and its counterpart, the *International Classification of Diseases (ICD)*, are routinely updated and revised to reflect new knowledge. In response to clinicians' concerns, in 1987 when the third edition was revised—the version known as *DSM-*

III-R—changes were made in the way alcohol dependence was defined.

One of the criticisms of the third edition had been that alcohol dependence was tied to the presence of physical evidence of addiction. The third edition required the presence of tolerance and/or withdrawal symptoms. Thus in the *DSM-III* formulation, those whose lives were in utter disarray as the result of their drinking, but who were without these physical manifestations, could not be diagnosed as alcohol-dependent. This was the case even though their drinking pattern was not that of a "social drinker" and included those for whom the consequences of use were clearly destructive. In response to this concern modifications were introduced in the *DSM-III-R*. In that edition, nine symptoms were listed. A diagnosis was to be made when any three were positive for a period of at least one month. This revised version of the third edition was intended to be exactly what its title suggested: a revision, an interim document until the fourth edition was prepared. The fourth edition was published in 1994.

DSM-IV criteria

Revision of the diagnostic manual is a complex process. It entails convening study groups of experts who not only review the literature but also promote pilot testing to determine the impact of any changes being considered. In developing the fourth edition there were several issues of particular importance to those involved in preparing the section on substance use. The group felt it was important to devise a single set of criteria that would be applicable to all psychoactive substances. For example, evidence of withdrawal might be such a common feature of dependence, even though the particular symptoms would depend on the particular substance. Another area of concern was the relationship of any proposed criteria to the World Health Organization's classification system, ICD-10. Indeed, pilot research showed that there was a high degree of overlap between the two classification systems. If a person is diagnosed as alcohol-dependent by one standard, there is high likelihood that he will be diagnosed as dependent by the other criteria.

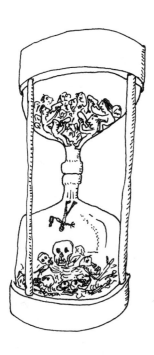

One of the biggest issues with which the task force drafting the Substance-Related Disorders section struggled was whether to keep or whether to drop the category of abuse. There were those who questioned whether abuse really was a separate condition, or whether it was really just "early" dependence. Because some of the same criteria are used to diagnose either condition, e.g. "use despite negative social consequences," the issue was further confused. In making diagnoses, the idea is to find the things which distinguish between illnesses, not the features which are common. Here research findings were able to offer some guidance. A follow-up study was conducted of individuals who had been diagnosed as having alcohol abuse four years previously. The results showed that alcohol abuse did not inevitably blossom into dependence. That was true of only 30% of those reexamined. For the remaining 70%, either their problems remitted, or a pattern of abuse continued without escalating. Thus the natural history of alcohol abuse appears to differ from that of alcohol dependence. For the latter, the likelihood that dependence will "go away" without treatment is very low. The more common pattern is continued and worsening symptoms. The task force decided to retain abuse as a distinct category from dependence. The counterpart to abuse in the ICD-10 schema is "harmful use."

Finally, the task force also was aware that in some sections the *DSM-III-R* was not as specific as was desirable. For example, severity for dependence was to be noted as mild, moderate, or severe, with the latter being when "many criteria" beyond the minimum number required were positive.

Thus in the *DSM-IV* edition, the number of criteria for dependence has been reduced from nine, not by deletions but by combining two previously separate items. Beyond the diagnosis, there is other information that clinicians are requested to note in a medical or clinical record. They are asked to indicate if dependence occurs with or without physiological dependence (items 1 and 2 above). For those who are alcohol-dependent but no longer actively drinking, and in recovery, some description of their current status is important. Several options are provided to denote the extent of recovery, whether there is full or partial remission, and the duration, either early or sustained. The time interval suggested for determining that someone has achieved full sustained remission is a 12-month period. Other information to be noted in a medical or clinical record is whether the patient is living in a controlled environment, be it a half-way house or a correctional facility, and whether the patient is using specific medications that interfere with or deter intoxication. Such medications are more common in the treatment of narcotics addiction. However, disulfiram (Antabuse) would apply for those with alcohol dependence. Both of these latter situations are important because they may well have implications for the patient's ability to maintain sobriety independently.

Criteria for abuse that do not overlap those for dependence were selected. However, it may seem a fine line to distinguish between continued use that causes physical or psychological problems (dependence) and continued use that leads to social or interpersonal problems (abuse). But there is a difference. Drinking qualifies as abuse if it leads to problems with other people, even if there is no particular distress for the drinking person.

In addition to standards for diagnosing substance abuse and substance dependence, other substance-related conditions are addressed. These include intoxication and withdrawal, as well as several conditions that are substance-induced, such as sleep disorders and delirium (mental confusion), which are handled in other sections of the Manual.

DSM-IV criteria for alcohol dependence

The *DSM-IV* describes *alcohol dependence* as a maladaptive pattern of use leading to significant impairment or distress, when three or more of the following seven items occur in the same 12-month period:

1. Tolerance can be evidenced either as (a) a need for increased amounts of alcohol to achieve intoxication or the desired effect, or (b) diminished effect with continued use of the same amount
2. Withdrawal is the presence of characteristic signs of alcohol withdrawal, or the use of the same or closely related substance to relieve or avoid withdrawal
3. Drinking in larger amounts or over a longer period than was intended
4. A persistent desire or unsuccessful efforts to cut down or control drinking
5. Considerable time spent in activities related to drinking, or recovering from drinking episodes
6. Important social, occupational, or recreational activities given up or reduced due to drinking
7. Drinking continues even when it is known that physical or psychological problems are caused by or aggravated by continued use

---

DSM-IV criteria for alcohol abuse

The *DSM-IV* describes *alcohol abuse* as a maladaptive pattern of use leading to significant impairment or distress, when one or more of the following have occurred in a 12-month period:

1. Recurrent drinking that results in a failure to fulfill major role obligations at work, school, or home
2. Recurrent drinking when it is physically hazardous, such as while driving, or when involved with risky recreational activities
3. Recurrent alcohol-related legal problems
4. Continued drinking despite persistent social or interpersonal problems caused or aggravated by use

---

NATURAL HISTORY OF ALCOHOLISM: JELLINEK REVISITED

In 1983 George Vaillant published *The Natural History of Alcoholism*. This book set forth the results of several studies that have been invaluable in confirming, and in many instances amplifying, our understanding of alcoholism as a disease. This work can be seen as representing an update of the work initiated more than 30 years earlier by Jellinek, when he outlined the stages of alcohol addiction. Vaillant's work is based upon two groups of men who have been followed for approximately 50 years, from their adolescence into their sixties. The major goal of the research was to study adult development through the life cycle. There was an interesting side benefit for the alcohol field. Not unexpectedly during the course of the study, members from both groups developed alcoholism. Thus for the first time it became possible to begin to separate "the chicken from the egg." The question could be asked, "What are the factors that distinguish those who develop alcoholism from those who do not?"

One group in the study, the college sample, has been officially described as "students from an Eastern university." In fact it is composed of Harvard undergraduates from the classes of 1942 to 1944. The other group, referred to as "the core city sample," is comprised of men who were from high-crime, inner-city neighborhoods. They were initially selected to participate in the study when they were about 14 years old, primarily because they were not known to be seriously delinquent. At the beginning of study, those in both groups were extensively interviewed. A variety of psychological tests were administered, detailed family histories were obtained, and measures of the subjects' personal functioning were made. Since that time these men have been periodically recontacted to collect detailed information on the progress of their lives.

In brief, Vaillant determined that those who became alcoholic were not more likely to have had impoverished childhoods or to have had preexisting personality or psychological problems. Therefore it was his conclusion that such problems, which are often cited as evidence of an "alcoholic personality," do not predate the emergence of the disease. On the contrary, they are the symptoms or consequences of alcohol dependence. As for predictors of alcoholism, the significant determinants were found to be a family history of alcoholism or having been raised in a culture with a high rate of alcoholism.

Several other findings are worth noting. Vaillant compared the various diagnostic classifications or diagnostic approaches. He discovered a high overlap between those diagnosed as alcoholic (using *DSM-III* criteria) and those identified as "problem drinkers" with a high "problem index"—a sociological classification system. The specific negative consequences seemed to be of little importance. However, by the time the individual had experienced four or more negative consequences as the result of drinking, it was almost assured that a formal diagnosis of alcohol dependence could be made. Virtually no one had four or more alcohol-related problems through mere "bad luck."

Also, as alcoholism progressed over time, the number of problems tended to increase and the overall life situation—psychological adjustment, economic functioning, social and family relationships—deteriorated. Vaillant observed that studies that have pointed to the contrary usually were reporting on persons who went for treatment and were recontacted at a single point. He speculates that these studies have not followed up the individuals for a sufficient length of time. While active alcoholism has a downward course, there will be, during the slide, both ups and downs. Presumably, people who

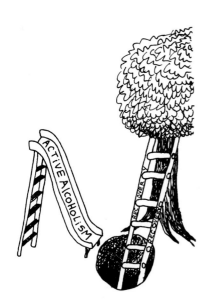

enter treatment facilities do so at a low point. Therefore at follow-up, even if they continue as active alcoholics, it should not be surprising to find their situation somewhat improved. However, if follow-up were conducted at several times, the full ravages of untreated alcoholism would become apparent. As Vaillant notes, paraphrasing an AA saying, "Alcoholism is baffling, cunning, powerful, . . . and patient."

Vaillant concluded that there is indeed a progression in alcoholism. (However, there is not the orderliness in symptoms' emergence that Jellinek had described.) As a result of the progression, there are only two likely outcomes. The men in the study either died or recovered through abstinence. The proportion who either returned to nonproblematic drinking or whose alcoholism stabilized was very small. Again, over time, with increasing incidence of follow-up, this small middle ground continued to shrink.

In his book, *The Disease Concept of Alcoholism,* Jellinek had noted that a disease is "simply anything the medical profession agrees to call a disease." By that standard, alcohol dependence has been a disease for some time. However, with the refinement of diagnostic criteria there is now far clearer guidance in identifying those who suffer from it.

RESOURCES AND FURTHER READING

The recommended readings on this resource list might appear sorely out of date. But assembling this list, we deliberately chose the primary, original sources for the major historical pieces of work discussed. Because this chapter reviews the evolution of the disease framework as well as approaches to diagnosis, there is considerable value in examining the original articles. Beyond allowing the authors to speak for themselves, these older classic works offer instructive insights into the views of alcoholism that then prevailed.

American Psychiatric Association: *Diagnostic and statistical manual,* ed. 3, Washington DC: APA, 1980.

American Psychiatric Association: *Diagnostic and Statistical Manual,* ed .3 (revised), Washington DC: APA, 1987.

American Psychiatric Association: *Diagnostic and statistical manual,* ed. 4, Washington DC: APA, 1994.

Brower KJ, Blow FC, Beresford TP: Treatment implications of chemical dependency models: An integrative approach, *Journal of Substance Abuse Treatment* 6(3):147-157, 1989.

    Five basic models of chemical dependency and their treatment implications are described. The moral model, although disdained by most treatment professionals, actually finds expression in over half the steps of Alcoholics Anonymous. The learning model, albeit the center of the controlled-drinking controversy, is also utilized by most abstinence-oriented programs. The disease model, which enjoys current popularity, sometimes ignores the presence of coexisting disorders. The self-medication model, which tends to regard chemical dependency as a symptom, can draw needed attention to coexisting disorders. The social model emphasizes the importance of environmental and interpersonal influences in treatment, although the substance abuser may endorse it as a justification to adopt a victim's role. A sixth model, the dual diagnosis model, is presented as an example of how two of the basic models can be integrated both to expand the treatment focus and to increase treatment leverage. Whereas the five basic models are characterized by a singular, organizing treatment focus, the dual diagnosis model is viewed as an example of a multifocused, integrative model. It is concluded that effective therapy requires (1) flexibility in combining elements of different models in order to individualize treatment plans for substance abusers, and (2) careful assessment of both the therapist's and the substance abuser's beliefs about treatment models in order to ensure a treatment match based on a healthy alliance.

Cottler LB: Comparing DSM-III-R and ICD-10 substance use disorders, *Addiction* 88(5):689-696.

At present the *DSM-III-R* is nearing its final stages of metamorphosis into *DSM-IV*. A series of field trials has been completed, which has focused attention on the coverage of the different systems, the impact of social and legal problems on crossing the diagnostic threshold, the importance of subtyping by tolerance and withdrawal, the exclusionary diagnosis of abuse, the duration criterion, and other nosological comparisons. The focus of this article is the comparison of rates between *DSM-III, III-R,* and both the old and new ICD-10 diagnostic systems, using data from the *DSM-IV* Substance Use Disorders Field Trials. Especially noteworthy is the inclusion of African Americans, females, and a population with a range of diagnoses and use patterns. Comparisons of *DSM-III, III-R,* and ICD-10 substance-use diagnoses among alcohol, nicotine, cannabis, and cocaine users indicate considerable agreement for dependence but fewer similarities between systems for abuse and harmful use. These findings suggest that the dependence criteria may be more stable than those chosen to represent abuse and harmful use. More work needs to be done to evaluate the differences and similarities of the diagnostic systems.

Criteria Committee, National Council on Alcoholism: Criteria for the diagnosis of alcoholism, *American Journal of Psychiatry* 129(2):41-49, 1972.

Hasin DS, Grant B, Endicott J: The natural history of alcohol abuse: Implications for definitions of alcohol use disorders, *American Journal of Psychiatry* 147(11):1537-1541.

Is the *DSM-III-R* category of alcohol abuse validly differentiated from the DSM-III-R category of alcohol dependence, or is abuse primarily a mild, prodromal condition that typically deteriorates into dependence? A four-year longitudinal epidemiologic study of male drinkers provided data to answer this question. The study used identical questions at baseline and follow-up. At follow-up, 70% of the subjects who were initially classified as alcohol abusers were still abusers or were classified as remitted. This contrasted significantly with outcome in the subjects who initially reported alcohol dependence. Although additional research is needed, these results indicate that alcohol abuse often has a course distinct from that of alcohol dependence (Author abstract).

Jellinek EM: Phases of alcohol addiction, *Quarterly Journal of Studies on Alcohol* 13:673-684, 1952.

This work sets forth the natural history and the progression of the disease of alcoholism, based upon a survey of 2,000 early AA members, each of whom identified the order of symptom appearance. This study has continued to influence current views of the course of alcoholism.

Jellinek EM: *The disease concept of alcoholism,* New Haven, CT: 1960, Hill House Press.

This work synthesizes research conducted by E.M. Jellinek, including his discussion of the conditions under which alcoholism might be viewed as a disease.

Peele S: Can alcoholism and other drug addiction problems be treated away or is the current treatment binge doing more harm than good? *Journal of Psychoactive Drugs* 20(4):375-383, 1988.

This essay challenges those who question the disease concept and the current treatment of alcoholism. The historical origins of the current views of alcoholism and its treatment are described. The author cites considerable literature, which fails to support the efficacy of these popular treatment approaches. His conclusion is that the treatment system is ineffective for those needing care and does nothing to address the epidemiology of alcohol–substance abuse problems. Simultaneously noted is a growing intolerance for alternative views. (Author abstract.)

Rinaldi RC, Steindler EM, Wilford BB, Goodwin D: Clarification and standardization of substance abuse terminology, *Journal of the American Medical Association* 259(4):555-557, 1988.

A four-stage Delphi survey of substance abuse experts was conducted to help achieve greater clarity and uniformity in terminology associated with alcohol and other drug-related problems. This multidisciplinary group of experts was asked to reach a consensus on alcohol and other drug-related terms and definitions. Results produced a list of 50 substance abuse terms deemed important, along with the most agreed-on definition for each term. (Author abstract.)

Vaillant GE: *The natural history of alcoholism,* Cambridge, MA: 1983, Harvard University Press.

A longitudinal prospective study of adult development involving two cohorts provided the opportunity to examine the natural history of alcoholism. The significant findings were as follows: (1) There was a lack of support for the theory of an "alcoholic personality." The presumed "predisposing personality factors," or emotional problems, result from drinking in actuality. (2) The major predictors of alcoholism are a positive family history, being raised in a culture whose norms proscribe childhood alcohol use, prescribe heavy adult alcohol use, and accept intoxication. (3) In respect to diagnosis, by the time individuals have experienced four lifetime problems from use, typically they will meet any diagnostic criteria for alcoholism. (4) However, treatment was not initiated until the occurrence of 8 to 11 lifetime problems. (5) After alcohol dependence is established, the two most common eventual outcomes are recovery or death: over the 30-year follow-up, nonproblematic drinking continually declined. (6) Successful recovery is associated with four factors: developing a vital interest that can replace the role of drinking; external reminders that drinking is painful; increased sources of unambivalently offered social support; and the presence of a source of inspiration, hope, and enhanced self-esteem.

Woody G, Schuckit M, Weinrieb R, Yu E: A review of the substance use disorder section of the DSM-IV, *Psychiatric Clinics of North America* 16(1):21-32, 1993.

In 1988 the Board of Trustees of the American Psychiatric Association (APA) appointed a Task Force on DSM-IV to revise the Diagnostic and Statistical Manual (DSM) to be compatible with the World Health Organization's (WHO) International Classification of Diseases, tenth edition. The Substance Use Disorders work group was formed to assist in the effort. A three-step process included literature reviews on selected topics, reanalysis of several preexisting data sets, and conduct of field trials in America and Europe to determine the best way to diagnose abuse and dependence. Reports from the work group suggested significant alterations to DSM-IV in several areas: the optimal criteria for abuse, modifications in the criteria for dependence, diagnostic guidelines for dealing with psychiatric syndromes in individuals with substance use disorders, further scrutiny for diagnostic criteria for remission, the need to define severity more clearly, reorganization in the notation of some substance use disorders, handling of nicotine withdrawal, and inclusion/exclusion of *alcohol idiosyncratic intoxication.* In addition, other reports suggested no change for DSM-IV with regard to inclusion of caffeine abuse and dependence, highlighting anabolic steroid dependence, relevance of protracted abstinence syndromes (withdrawal), a new subtype of dependence based on familial pattern of the disorder, and combination of amphetamines and cocaine into a large category, "Stimulants." (Author abstract.)

Four Factors Associated with Recovery (see Vaillant, G.E.)

1. A Vital Interest
How would you like to see my collection of Campbell soup labels.

2. External Reminders
It looks lousy on the lawn—but it reminds me that I can't drink.

3. Unambivalent Social Support
We all like you even though you're wierd.

4. A Source of Hope and Inspiration
HIGHER POWER

Etiology of alcohol dependence

What is man, when you come to think upon him, but a minutely set, ingenious machine for turning, with infinite artfulness, the red wine of Shiraz into urine?

ISAK DINESEN, 1934

What are the causes of alcohol dependence? As more knowledge is gained, the answers become more complex. It may be useful to make a comparison to the clearly less severe common cold. Once you have "it," there isn't much question. The sneezing, the runny nose, the stuffed-up feeling, the cold tablet manufacturers describe so well, leave little doubt. But why you? Because "it" was going around. Your resistance was down. Others in the family have "it." You became chilled when caught in the rain. You forgot your vitamin C. Everyone has a pet theory and usually chalks it up to a number of factors working in combination against you. Some chance factor does seem to be involved. There are times when we do not catch colds that are going around. Explaining the phenomenon cannot be done with precision. It is more a matter of figuring out the odds and probabilities as the possible contributing factors are considered.

The public health field has developed a systematic way of tackling this problem of disease, its causes, and the risks of contracting it. First, they look at the *agent,* the "thing" that causes the disease. Next, they consider the *host*, the person who has the illness, to find characteristics that may have made him a likely target. Finally, the *environment* is examined, the setting in which the agent and host come together. A thorough look at these three aspects ensures that no major influences are overlooked.

PUBLIC HEALTH MODEL

Alcohol dependence qualifies as a public health problem. It is the third leading cause of death in the United States. It afflicts one out of every ten adults. It touches the lives of one out of every eight children. The response to alcohol dependence is unfortunately pale compared to its impact.

From the public health viewpoint, the first sphere to be examined as a possible cause is the agent. For alcohol dependence the agent is the substance, alcohol. This is such an obvious fact that it might seem silly to dwell on it. No one can be alcohol-dependent without an exposure to alcohol. The substance must be used before the possibility of dependence exists. Alcohol is an addictive substance. With sufficient quantities over long enough time, the body undergoes physical changes. When this has occurred and the substance is withdrawn, there is a physiological response, withdrawal. For alcohol there is a well-defined set of symptoms that accompanies cessation of drinking in an addicted person. Any person can be addicted to alcohol but to use this fact alone to explain alcohol dependence represents untidy thinking. That alcohol is addicting does not explain why anyone would drink enough to reach the point

78

of addiction. Temperance literature tries to paint a picture of an evil demon in the bottle. Take a sip, and he's got you. This may appear humorous to those whose alcohol use is casual and unproblematic. It is obvious that drinking need not lead inevitably to a life of drunkenness. Let us look at the action of the drug itself. What invites its use and makes it a candidate for use sufficient to cause addition?

THE AGENT

We take any number of substances into our bodies—from meats to sweets, as solids or liquids. Although everyone overeats occasionally, to consider habitual overeating as a form of "substance" abuse, or the associated craving as just as powerful as that associated with drugs, is a very recent concept. A physiological basis for this has not been identified. However, in the case of alcohol, the physiological effects themselves suggest some of the reasons it is such a likely candidate for heavy chronic use. First, alcohol is a depressant drug. One of its first effects is on the central nervous system, the "higher" centers related to judgment, inhibition, and the like. What is more important is what this feels like, how it is experienced. With mild intoxication comes relaxation, a more carefree feeling. It is generally experienced as a plus, a high. Preexisting tensions are relieved. A good mood can be accentuated. Alcohol is experienced as changing mood for the better. This capacity of alcohol is one factor to remember in trying to understand use sufficient for addiction.

A common expression is "I sure could use a drink now." It may be said after a hard day at work, after a round of good physical exercise, or after a period of chaos and emotional stress when the wobbly knees are setting in. This expression certainly includes the awareness that alcohol can influence our emotional state. Equally as important is the word *now*. There is a recognition that the effects are immediate. Not only does alcohol make a difference, it does so very rapidly. If alcohol had a delayed reaction time, say 3 days, or 3 weeks, or even 3 hours, it wouldn't be a useful method to alter our feelings. The unpredictability of people's lives makes drinking now for what may happen later seem silly. So its speed in altering emotional states is another characteristic of the drug alcohol that enhances its likelihood for overuse.

Alcohol has another characteristic common to all depressant drugs. With mild inebriation, behavior is less inhibited; there are feelings of relaxation. However, at the same time there is a gradual increase of psychomotor activity. While feeling the initial glow, the drinker is unaware of this. As the warm glow subsides, the increased psychomotor activity will become apparent, often experienced as a wound-up and edgy feeling similar to that caused by too many cups of coffee or caffeinated soft drinks. The increase in psychomotor activity builds up gradually and extends *beyond* the feeling of well-

*Candy is dandy
But liquor is quicker.*
OGDEN NASH

The peculiar charm of alcohol lies in the sense of careless well-being and bodily comfort which it creates. It unburdens the individual of his cares and fears. Under such conditions it is easy to laugh or to weep, to love or to hate, not wisely but too well.

DR. HAVEN EMERSON
Alcohol and Man

being. Since it is delayed and its onset masked, the drinker is not very likely to recognize the feeling as a product of the alcohol use. Instead, the reasonable perception is to view this edginess as the "normal" self. In fact, it is more probable that the drinker is feeling less serene or calm than earlier, before the first sip. What would be the rational thing to do? Have another drink! It is quite possible that many people, including those not dependent upon alcohol, have a second or third drink to get rid of the very feelings created by the earlier ones.

There is one nasty catch to the physiological phenomenon just described. The agitation phase that accompanies alcohol consumption extends considerably beyond the relaxed initial experience. A second drink will only temporarily cover the edginess of the first drink. The second drink, with its own edginess coming on behind, will combine with that left over from the first. Were this to continue, a point would be reached when the accumulated tensions and increased psychomotor activity could no longer be masked by adding more alcohol. Normally, people are wholly unaware of this phenomenon because it is interrupted after two or three drinks. They have set their limit. They have dinner and go on to other activities. They go to bed.

These particular characteristics of alcohol do not alone account for the phenomenon of alcohol dependence. They are certainly responsible for the possibility of its occurrence. As other factors are examined we can see how an interaction may work.

THE HOST—GENETIC FACTORS

The belief that alcoholism runs in families has long been a part of the folk wisdom. In your childhood, possibly, a great aunt explained away the town drunk with "He's his father's son." No further comment was necessary. The obvious truth was clear: that many of life's misfortunes are the result of "bad" genes. Just such an inadequate understanding of genetics, supported by warped theological views, led to statutes that authorized the sterilization of the feebleminded, the hopelessly insane, and the chronically drunk.

In the face of new knowledge, such an approach has fallen into disrepute. It is now clear that heredity is not as simple as it seemed. Each individual, at the point of conception, receives a unique set of genetic material. This material is like a set of internal "instructions" that guide the individual's growth and development. In many instances, the genetic endowment simply sets down limits, or predispositions. The final outcome will depend on the life situation and environment in which the person finds, or places, him- or herself. Thus some people tend to be slim and some tend to put on weight easily. Such a *tendency* is probably genetic. Whether people are fat, thin, or just right depends on them.

Nature versus nurture

What are the facts about the role of heredity in alcohol dependence? Actually, alcohol dependence does run in families. The child of an alcohol-dependent parent is more likely to become similarly alcohol-troubled. One study tracing family trees found that 50% of the descendants of alcoholics were themselves also alcoholic. Though that figure is a bit higher than other similar studies, it is a dramatic example of the typical finding that suggests that the off-spring of those who are alcohol-dependent have a four-times-greater risk of developing the disease.

Yet something running in families is not proof that it is inherited. After all, speaking French runs in families—in France. Identifying the role of home life, that is, separating nature from nurture, is a complex but necessary job. Certainly, an alcohol-dependent, actively drinking parent would be expected to have an impact on a growing child. It is not unreasonable to expect that inherent in the family lies the soil of addiction. Yet again, the simple fact that this sounds reasonable does not make it true.

The most current hypothesis is that heredity does play a significant role in the development of alcohol dependence in some people. Research to determine which people, and by which mechanisms, is exploding and much has been learned since the early 1970s. If heredity is a factor, there must be some basic biochemical differences between those who are prone to develop alcohol dependence and those who are not.

The observations of those working in the area of alcohol rehabilitation and treatment lend support to the view of a constitutional vulnerability. Some clients encountered will report a major alcohol problem very early in life, often by the time of adolescence, that progressed rapidly in the absence of any unique identifiable psychological stress. Similarly, at AA meetings the remark may be heard, "I was an alcoholic from my first drink." Usually this means that for seemingly idiosyncratic reasons the speaker never drank "normally" as did peers but used, and was affected by, alcohol differently. Interestingly, back in 1940, Jellinek recognized a possible hereditary factor and suggested a distinguishable "familial" type of alcoholism.

Twin and adoption studies

Methods of scientific investigation using an experimental model are not possible in the task of separating nature and nurture. We can't ask some families to raise children one way and other families to raise their children differently so that the differences might be determined! Human research requires locating individuals with particular life experiences or characteristics and then comparing them to those with other backgrounds. Twin studies and adoption studies

Drunkards beget drunkards.
PLUTARCH

are the two classical methods for doing this. Donald Goodwin is a clinician-researcher who has worked extensively on the topic of alcoholism and heredity. Many of his (and others') studies have used data from Scandinavia, because these countries keep very complete records of marriages, births, and so on. This makes tracing families easier.

One early study was based on a large sample of twins. In each set, *one* twin was alcoholic. The researchers determined whether the twins were identical or fraternal. Then they interviewed the twin of the known alcoholic. The prediction: if alcoholism has a hereditary basis, the other twin of identical sets would be more likely also to be alcoholic than if he were fraternal. This assumption was made because identical twins share the same genetic material. That proved to be the case. However, the hereditary endowment does not act to totally dictate the development of alcoholism because not all the identical twins were both alcoholic. It was further discovered that an apparent predisposition exists toward having, or being spared, the social deterioration associated with alcoholism. If both twins were alcoholic, the best predictor of the other twin's life situation was not how much or how long he had been drinking. The life situation of the first twin was more reliable. So there appears to be a hereditary predisposition both to alcoholism and the social problems associated with it.

An adoption study conducted by Goodwin, using Danish subjects, further supports the influence of heredity. He traced children born to an alcoholic parent. These children had been adopted by the age of 6 weeks. He compared them to adopted children of nonalcoholic biological parents. The adoptive families of both groups were essentially the same. He discovered that those who had a biological parent who was alcoholic were themselves more likely to develop alcoholism in adulthood. Thus alcoholism cannot be attributed simply to the home environment.

The subjects of the above studies were men. Work is now being conducted with female adoptees. The results have been less conclusive. Perhaps this is because the sample sizes were smaller. Also, the past strong cultural prohibitions against women drinking heavily may have served as a cultural "protection" against developing alcoholism.

Further studies have helped separate the relative influence of genetic makeup and home environment. These studies have used half-siblings. Of the half-siblings, one had an alcoholic parent, the other did not. Thus one of the children had a biological predisposition while the other did not. These half-brothers and half-sisters were raised together in the same home. In some cases both were reared in a nonalcoholic family. In other cases, both grew up in a home with an alcoholic parent. As expected, those with genetic background positive for alcoholism were themselves more likely to develop alcoholism as adults. Of equal significance, being reared in

Heredity. The heredity of form and the heredity of mental traits and character are unquestioned. Inebriety belongs to the same class, and has been recognized as hereditary for all ages. On one of the monuments of Egypt there is a drawing of a drunkard father and several drunken children, and the grouping conveys the idea that the inebriety of the parent was the direct cause of the children's disgrace.

SPOONER, WALTER, W.
The Cyclopaedia of Temperance and Prohibition, 1891.

a home with an active alcoholic did not further increase the chances of developing alcoholism. This was true for both the biologically at-risk children and their half-brothers and half-sisters who did not have a biological predisposition. This has been confirmed by other studies. Growing up in a home with an alcoholic parent does not add to the risk of developing alcoholism. Such findings provide strong support for the importance of the genetic predisposition in some cases of alcoholism.

Studies of nonalcoholic blood relatives

These studies are sometimes referred to as studies of persons at high risk. They are similar to the genetic marker studies. Any genetic difference between those biologically prone to alcohol dependence and those who are not will be manifested in some biochemical differences. Efforts are underway to see what factors may distinguish between these two groups. The major hypotheses are that there are differences in the way our bodies handle alcohol and how our brains experience its effects. The differences could conceivably be differences of metabolism, or differences in response to chronic exposure to ethanol, or possibly a unique response to a single dose. For example, those at high risk may experience greater pleasure and those at low risk more discomfort.

What does the research to date show?

- There does seem to be a difference in metabolism. In one study, a group of presently nonalcoholic young men with an alcoholic father or brother showed greater acetaldehyde levels during alcohol metabolism than another similar group who did not have an alcoholic family member. Much higher levels of acetaldehyde often accompany drinking in Orientals. These higher levels produce a disulfiram-like reaction, which discourages alcohol consumption and thereby provides protection against the development of alcoholism. Paradoxically though, with a modest increase of acetaldehyde, the addiction process may be facilitated.

- Another preliminary study has looked at how alcohol's effects are experienced. Again these have used young men who exhibit no symptoms of alcohol dependence but who have an alcoholic blood relative. Those having an alcohol-dependent family member describe a lesser response to a single dose of alcohol than those with no alcoholic blood relative. To translate this—those with a family history of alcoholism didn't feel as "high" as did those who had no family history of alcohol dependence. If feeling alcohol's effects is a significant part of drinking, then those with a family history will need to drink more than their peers. This may increase their risks for dependence.

- Other researchers have determined that those with a family history of alcoholism have greater muscle relaxation with a single dose of alcohol than those without such a family background.

After drinking, those at "high risk" also have been reported to have more brain alpha-wave activity, as measured by electroencephalogram (EEG). Such brain waves are associated with feelings of relaxation.

- High-risk subjects, those with a family history of alcohol dependence, perform less well on portions of standard neuropsychological tests that measure a variety of different cognitive functions. This finding is noteworthy because it long has been recognized that alcoholics do poorly on some of these tests, such as a test for abstracting ability. Their diminished performance had always been presumed to be the result of brain damage from heavy drinking. Now the question has to be whether or not this condition predates the dependence.

- And finally, related animal and human research has suggested that some alcoholics may have genetically decreased CNS levels of naturally occurring opiate activity. These opiates, normally present in the brain, are believed to mediate many pleasurable and rewarding experiences. A deficiency in natural opiate activity has been posed as the basis for craving in alcoholics.

It is known that alcohol and some of its genetically determined by-products can stimulate endogenous opiate receptors. (These are catecholamine-like metabolites. Therefore they resemble naturally occurring neurotransmitters, specifically the alkaloid tetrahychoisoquinolones.) Such activation is highly reinforcing and thereby may constitute an important biochemical basis not only for craving but for the disease of alcoholism, as well.

Most research initially discussed the differences described above as deficiencies, as something "missing" or "lacking." It is now being recognized that what is inherited may not necessarily be a deficiency but might, paradoxically, be a "strength." In other words, some people might inherit an ability to handle alcohol "too well." They may be more immune to negative physical consequences of drinking such as nausea and hangovers, or be able to function better than the average person when alcohol is ingested. If so, those who are alcoholism-prone are deprived of the very cues that may keep drinking in check for others.

Familial versus nonfamilial alcoholism

Given the strong evidence for the role of a genetic factor in some cases of alcohol dependence, researchers increasingly are suggesting that we begin to think in terms of two types of alcoholism. The types are *familial* and *nonfamilial* and are suspected to have some differences. The familial form is believed to be characterized by a positive family history of alcohol dependence, an earlier age of onset, and more "destructive" symptoms. This necessitates and leads to treatment at a relatively young age. This form involves no increased likelihood of other psychiatric illness. On the other hand, the nonfamilial type is seen as having a later onset. It is also characterized by less virulent symptoms.

Genetic marker studies

Another group of studies are known by the shorthand title of "genetic marker" studies. In such investigations, attempts are made to link alcohol dependence to any traits that are known to be inherited. This would establish a genetic basis for the disease. Some of the early possibilities that were studied included, for example, blood types. It is known that blood type is inherited; the genes controlling this also may be responsible for other characteristics.

Genetics research is growing increasingly sophisticated. What was virtually unimaginable a decade ago is now a reality. It is possible for researchers to examine genes in a much more direct fashion. As part of this revolution, there is a massive national research program underway called the "Human Genome Project." The goal of this effort is to create a map of all genetic material. For the field of biology, this is a challenge similar to that of space explorations and the dream of walking on the moon. The task of identifying the function of individual genes is especially important in light of another major advance. Techniques have been developed which allow the altering of defective portions of genes. People now speak of "gene therapy" or "genetic engineering." This provides the potential for treating illnesses which are known to be caused by a specific genetic abnormality. It is more than treatment as we usually think about it, because the source of the disease is totally removed.

In respect to alcoholism, a study was published in 1990 that seemed to point to a major breakthrough in the understanding of alcoholism's genetic basis. The research involved an examination of genetic material in the brain tissue of persons with alcoholism and comparing it to genes in the brain tissue of nonalcoholics. Of particular interest was a gene that is associated with the brain's receptors for dopamine, a neurotransmitter. Dopamine is one of the neurochemicals in the brain that is involved with the sensation of pleasure. The receptor is the site where this neurochemical acts. The particular gene is known as D_2.

It was found that there are two different forms of this gene. Different forms of a gene are called alleles. As a point for comparison, think of the gene for eye color as having different alleles. One allele corresponds to brown eyes, another to blue eyes, and so on. The researchers discovered that there were two forms of the dopamine receptor gene. In the shorthand that geneticists use, these gene variations are referred to as A1 and A2. Of special interest was whether or not alcoholism was associated with a particular form of the gene. Indeed that was found to be so. Among those with alcoholism, 69% had the A1 allele. Only 20% of those without alcoholism had that version. The finding that the association of alcoholism with one of the versions of the gene was not 100% positive does not mean that the gene has no role in the origins of alcoholism. What this kind of association suggests is that the A1 gene may act to increase the susceptibility to alcoholism. Its presence does not make alcohol dependence inevitable. Likewise, its absence doesn't provide immunity.

The above finding led to a flurry of further research. The results of later studies have not been as clear-cut. In any case, the genetic basis for alcoholism is most likely the result of a number of genes, many of which may function independently. Thus our genetic make-up may well determine our susceptibility not simply to alcohol addiction but also to organ damage associated with heavy drinking or the severity of withdrawal.

Animal studies

A very different avenue of research involves animal studies. These studies cannot be directly generalized to humans. However, work with chimps, baboons, or even rats can shed light on the promising areas for human investigation and provide clues.

Some of the more curious studies involve rats. Different strains of rats were given a choice of water or water spiked with alcohol of differing concentrations. Inevitably, they sampled each and usually opted for plain water. They would drink the alcohol-water solution only when it was the sole liquid available. Several strains of rats were important exceptions. They preferred alcohol and water solutions of around 5%, which translates to 10-proof. These "drinking rats" could be inbred to produce offspring that preferred even higher alcohol concentrations. The tentative conclusion is that they are different biochemically from their water-drinking counterparts. Interestingly, even "drinking rats" very rarely choose to drink to intoxication. Although a taste for alcohol may exist, they do not go on to become alcoholic. Dogs are apparently different. They will drink to intoxication more frequently. They will even indulge in several days of "heavy" drinking, but they stop spontaneously. Despite the fact that the dogs seem to experience what the experimenters interpret as a hangover, or mild withdrawal, the animals abstain. Unless the dogs were binge drinkers, it would appear that alcoholism is a human problem.

THE HOST—PSYCHOLOGICAL FACTORS

It is important to note at the outset of this section, that in the past, psychological factors were seen as the most important predictors and/or precursors of future alcohol dependence. Today such a view is largely discounted. Those who develop the disease do not have a higher rate of psychological problems than the general population. What had long been considered an "alcoholic personality" is in fact a constellation of the symptoms of the illness, not the preexisting personality. While recognized in the treatment and scientific community, this fact has not yet become part of the fund of general knowledge. Many people still assume some psychological explanation for alcoholism. To understand this widely held belief, it is necessary to look at how the perspective developed.

Research on alcoholism stopped during prohibition. "No alcohol=no problem" was the short-lived attitude. Much of what we now take for "fact" was established only recently. Until 1953, the DTs was thought to be caused by malnutrition, not by alcohol withdrawal. It was only in 1973 that fetal alcohol syndrome was described in the scientific literature in the United States. Until 1976, it was thought that cirrhosis of the liver was due wholly to malnutrition. Given how little was known about the basic medical facts, it is not surprising that people looked to psychological explanations to understand the origins of alcoholism.

Efforts to explain alcoholism centered upon exploring psychological predispositions. The theorists were using all the facts available to them at the time. Furthermore, to look at behavior "psychologically" was a popular, up-to-date approach from the late 1930s through the 1960s. Our present almost unthinking acceptance of psychological factors as the significant determinants of behavior represents a revolution in defining human behavior that began little more than 100 years ago. The credit for this revolution goes to Dr. Sigmund Freud. A testimony to his influence is our common daily use of words such as "unconscious," "neurotic," "repressed," "anxious," and "Freudian slip" in describing behavior. Although Freud might not consider our usage proper, these words have been added to our vocabularies.

No nation is drunken where wine is cheap; and none sober where the dearness of wine substitutes ardent spirits as the common beverage.

THOMAS JEFFERSON

Psychological needs

It is now generally recognized that our behavior is at least partially determined by factors of which we are unaware. What are these factors? Our grade school geography classes usually focused on food, clothing, and shelter as the three basic human needs. But there are emotional needs, just as real and important, if people are to survive healthy and happy. What do we need in this realm? Baruch, in her book *New Ways of Discipline: You and Your Child Today* (published in 1949, so now hardly new!) puts it this way:

> What are the emotional foods that every human being must have regardless of age? What are the basic emotional requirements that must come to every small infant, to every growing child, to every adult?
>
> In the first place, there must be affection and a lot of it. Real, down-to-earth, sincere, loving. The kind that carries the conviction through body warmth, through touch, through the good mellow ring of the voice, through the fond look that says as clearly as words, "I love you because you are you."

Closely allied with being loved should come the sure knowledge of belonging, of being wanted, the glow of knowing oneself to be a part of some bigger whole. Our town, our school, our work, our family—all bring the sound of togetherness, of being united with others, not isolated or alone.

Every human being also needs to have the nourishment of pleasure that comes through the senses. Color, balanced form and beauty to meet the eye, harmonious sounds to meet the ear. The heady enjoyment of touch and taste and smell. And finally, the realization that the pleasurable sensations of sex can be right and fine and a part of the spirit as well as the body.

Everyone must feel that he is capable of achievement. He needs to develop the ultimate conviction, strong within him, that he can do things, that he is adequate to meet life's demands. He needs also the satisfaction of knowing that he can gain from others recognition for what he does.

And most important, each and every one of us must have acceptance and understanding. We need desperately to be able to share our thoughts and feelings with some other person, or several, who really understand. . . . We yearn for the deep relief of knowing that we can be ourselves with honest freedom, secure in the knowledge that says, "This person is with me. He accepts how I feel!"*

If these needs are not satisfactorily met, the adult is not whole. A useful notion in assessing what has happened is to think of the unmet needs as "holes." Everybody has some holes. They vary in number, size, and pattern. What is true for all is that holes are painful. Attempts are made to cover up, patch over, or camouflage our holes so we can feel more whole, less vulnerable, and more presentable.

Psychological approaches

Historically, the various psychological approaches that emerged essentially were all attempts to categorize the nature of the "holes," their origins, and why alcohol is used to cover them up. Although seemingly logical enough at the time, there was a major flaw. The people being studied were already alcoholics. The idea that an "alcoholic personality" might be a result of the disorder rather than an underlying cause was unheard of. One of the strengths of George Vaillant's work in the 1980s was that he began not with alcoholics but with individuals *before* their development of alcoholism. In effect, he studied large samples of people over time, beginning in late adolescence. Some of these people later developed alcoholism, and others did not. Thus he was able to see what actually were the predictors of the disease.

MAYbe we should put some "StoPleak" in his next drink.

*From Baruch D: *New ways of discipline: You and your child today,* New York: McGraw-Hill, 1949.

Theories of personality used in the past to understand alcoholism

Among the theories of personality that shaped our earlier thinking, the first was the *psychoanalytical,* based on the work of Sigmund Freud. Freud himself never devoted attention to alcoholism. However, his followers did apply aspects of his theory to the disease. It is impossible to present briefly the whole of Freud's work. He recognized that psychological development is related to physical growth. He identified stages of development, each with its particular, peculiar hurdles that a child must overcome on the way to being a healthy adult. Tripping over one of the hurdles, he felt, led to difficulties in adulthood.

Some of the events of childhood are especially painful, difficult, and anxiety-producing. They may persist unrelieved by the environment. This makes the child feel incompetent, resulting in a "hole." The child seeks unique ways to patch over the holes. However, the existence of the hole shapes future behavior. It may grow larger, requiring more patchwork. The hole may render the child more vulnerable to future stress and lead to new holes.

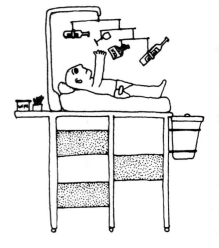

The concept of oral fixation was used in applying *psychoanalytic* theory to alcoholism. This meant the holes began in earliest childhood. Observe infants and see how very pleasurable and satisfying nursing and sucking are. Almost any "dis-ease" or discomfort can be soothed this way. Individuals whose most secure life experiences were associated with this period will tend to resort to similar behaviors in times of stress. These people will also, as adults, tend to have the psychological characteristics of that life period. The major psychological characteristics of the oral period are infants' egocentricity and inability to delay having their needs met. They're hungry when they're hungry, be it a convenient time from mother's viewpoint or not. And they're oblivious to other people except as they fit into their world. Thus alcoholics, according to this theory, were likely to be individuals who never fully matured beyond infancy. They were stuck with childlike views of the world and childlike ways of dealing with it. They were easily frustrated, inpatient, demanding, wanting what they wanted when they wanted it. They had little trust that people could help meet their needs. They were anxious and felt very vulnerable to the world. According to this theory, nursing a drink seemed an appropriate way of handling discomforts. Alcohol was doubly attractive because it worked quickly: bottled magic.

Another psychoanalytic concept, applied to male alcoholics, was that of latent homosexuality. (It needs to be pointed out that, like alcoholism, homosexuality is far better understood today. It is no longer considered a "disease." Being gay or lesbian is no longer seen as caused by psychological problems. Sexual identification is seen as genetically established. One does not choose to be homosexual any more than one chooses to be six feet tall.) Nonetheless the earlier thinking was that the origins of alcoholism were rooted in the oedi-

pal period, which corresponds to the preschool, kindergarten age. According to Freud, an inevitable part of every little boy's growing up is a fantasy love affair with his mother. There is an accompanying desire to get Dad out of the picture. Given the reality of Dad's size, he has a clear advantage in the situation. The little boy eventually gives up and settles on being like Dad, rather than taking his place. Through this identification process, the little boy assumes a male role. Several possible hitches can occur. Maybe the father is absent, or the father is not a very attractive model. In such instances, the child will not grow to manhood with a sense of himself as a healthy, whole male. As an adult he may turn to alcohol to instill a sense of masculinity. Or he may like drinking because it provides a socially acceptable format for male companionship.

Other personality theorists focused on different characteristics. Adler latched onto the *feelings of dependency*. He saw the roots of alcoholism as being planted in the first 5 years of life. He thought firstborn children were most likely to become either alcoholic or suicidal. In this view the dynamics of both are essentially the same. The firstborn is displaced or dethroned by the next child. He loses a position in which both parents pampered him, and feels less important. If the parents are unable to reassure him, he has increased feelings of inferiority and pessimism. The feelings of inferiority, or the longing for a sense of power, require strong proofs of superiority for satisfaction. When new problems arise, arousing anxiety, the person seeks a sense of *feeling superior* rather than really overcoming difficulties. Theoretically, then, drinking as a solution is, to the alcoholic, intelligent. Alcohol does temporarily reduce the awareness of anxiety and gives relief from the inferiority feelings. Without the relief of alcohol, the inferiority feelings and anxiety could build up and lead to the ultimate escape of suicide.

Another psychological approach to alcoholism attempted to define the alcoholic personality. The hope was to identify common characteristics by looking at groups of alcoholics. Currently such attempts have been largely abandoned. Because active alcoholics were studied, what appeared to be the "alcoholic personality" was in fact a set of symptoms for alcoholism. The behavior being studied was either drugged or behavior essential to continue the drugged state. Although an alcoholic personality exists, it is unrelated to the prealcoholic personality.

In 1960, William and Joan McCord published *Origins of Alcoholism*. Their studies used extensive data collected on 255 boys throughout their childhoods. What they found negated many of the psychoanalytic theories. Oral tendencies, latent homosexuality, and strong maternal encouragement of dependency were not, in fact, predictors of alcoholism. From their analysis, a consistent, statistically significant picture emerged. The typical alcoholic, as a child, underwent a variety of experiences that heightened inner stress.

This stress produced the paradoxical effect of intensifying both his need for love and his strong desire to repress this need. The conflict produced a distorted self-image. McCord and McCord examined "the personality of alcoholics, both in childhood and in adulthood. In childhood, the alcoholics appeared to be highly masculine, extraverted, aggressive, 'lone-wolfish'—all manifestations. . . . of their denial of the need to be loved. An analysis of the personality of adult alcoholics leads to the conclusions that the disorder itself produces some rather striking behavioral changes." The contribution of McCord and McCord highlighted the complexity of the social and psychological interactions.

On the heels of the McCords' research was the emergence in the 1960s of what was called the *human potential,* or *personal growth movement.* In essence it was devoted not to "curing" mental illness but applying the expertise of psychology and psychiatry to assist "normal" people to function better (whatever that meant to them). Tied in with this was the emergence of new psychological or personality theories. The primary question became "What is going on *now*, and how can the individual-client change?" The previously pressing question "What are the origins of the sickness or dysfunction?" was less important. Transactional Analysis, popularly known as TA, and Reality Therapy emerged. Both made a big splash in lay circles as well as in the professional community. Both were used to address the problem of alcoholism.

A short-lived approach of the late sixties (when else!) was popularized by a book *Games Alcoholics Play* by Claude Steiner. This applied TA to alcoholism and the alcoholic. The thesis was that the origins of alcoholism lay in alcoholics' childhood conditions and their responses to them. For example, the child found himself in a predicament with parents. When he behaved in a way that felt good or made sense to him, he ran into problems. He discovered the real him wasn't okay. To overcome this and become okay, he adopted a life-style or script for himself. In the script, he attempted to respond so as to counterbalance the message that said "You're not okay." For the alcoholic, the dominant script theme, according to Steiner, was "Don't think." This originated in a home where there were clear disparities between what was going on and what the parents said was happening. An observant child picks this up. If he pointed it out, he got a "You just do what I say," or "You just mind your own business," or "Don't get sassy." To survive, he is seen as needing to find mechanisms for tuning out, turning off. As an adult, being an alcoholic is a fine way to continue the "Don't think" script.

William Glasser is associated with the development of an approach known as *reality therapy.* Its thesis is that besides obvious, inborn biological needs, all humans have two basic needs: to love and be loved, and to feel that we are worthwhile to ourselves and others. Failure to fill these needs leads to pain. A possible solution to

dealing with such pain is the route to addiction—the use of some substance or behavior that, while it continues, completely removes the pain.

Learning theories

The other major class of psychological theories that have been used to explain alcoholism came from a very different branch of psychology. These are the *learning* theories, which look at behavior quite differently. They see behavior as a result of learning motivated by an individual's attempt to minimize unpleasantness and maximize pleasure. What is pleasant is a very individual thing. A child might misbehave and be "punished," but the punishment, for that child, might be a reward and more pleasant than being ignored. Thus what is pleasant or rewarding is very much a factor of the environment.

In applying learning theory to alcoholism, the idea is that alcoholic drinking has a reward system. Alcohol, or its effects, are sufficiently reinforcing to cause continuation of drinking by the individual. Behavior most easily learned is that with immediate, positive results. The warm glow and feeling of well-being associated with the first sips are more reinforcing than the negative morning-after hangover. This theory would hold that anyone could become alcoholic if the drinking were sufficiently reinforced. Vernon Johnson, founder of a highly successful treatment program and author of the book *I'll Quit Tomorrow* gave great emphasis to the importance of learning in explaining drinking. He noted that those who use alcohol have learned from their first drink that alcohol is exceedingly trustworthy. It works every time and it does good things. This learning is highly successful, being sufficient to set up a lifetime relationship with alcohol. The relationship may alter gradually over time, finally becoming a destructive one, but the original positive reinforcement keeps the person seeking the "good old days" and minimizing the destructive elements. Seen in this light, alcoholic people are not so far distant from people who remain in what are now unsatisfactory marriages, jobs, or living situations out of habit or some hope that the original zest will return.

All the aforementioned theories were formulated in the "salad days" of psychology and alcohol studies. The first modern efforts to understand the causes of alcoholism focused exclusively on psychological factors. These early efforts assumed that physiological factors or environmental factors were irrelevant. A growing understanding of alcohol as a drug and the mounting evidence of biological influences led those in the alcohol field to seriously question the importance of psychological factors in causing alcoholism. Clearly, psychological theories could no longer be considered as the single, definitive explanation of alcoholism.

With the publication in 1983 of *The Natural History of
Alcoholism,* the debate was finally settled. In that work Vaillant, in
effect, showed that psychological factors were at most of minimal
consequence as a cause of alcoholism. His research reported on the
follow-up of two very different groups: members of Harvard
University's Grant Study, and an inner-city sample. In both groups,
those who developed alcoholism were not distinguishable from their
colleagues along psychological lines. Again it was a family history of
alcoholism that was the most potent predictor, in combination with
an individual's cultural background and the norms associated with
alcohol use.

Current thinking

Psychology is the study of behavior. Within the field of psychology, it is recognized that a number of different influences must be
considered in explaining behavior. This general approach is applied
to alcoholism as well. Research directed to explaining the "whole
ball of wax" using only personality or psychological explanations has
been abandoned. Instead research is being directed to understanding how individuals, given their particular genetic make-up, interact
with their environment. Some of the specific areas being studied
are, for example, the role of expectations. How does what we believe
about alcohol determine our response? What are the different
sources of information which give rise to our beliefs, and how do
these change? As we think about possible approaches to prevention,
answers to such questions are particularly helpful. It is also recognized that there are differences between individuals in *tempera-
ment*, a concept similar to but different from personality. Whether
one is shy or outgoing, adventuresome or cautious, in part seems to
be a biological given. How do these innate predispositions influence
drinking habits, and interact with other factors? Because of the
apparent multiple factors that interact to cause alcoholism, one of
modern psychology's major contributions is its effort to understand
these interactions.

THE ENVIRONMENT—SOCIOLOGICAL FACTORS
An alternative cultural view

One approach has not received the attention we believe it
deserves. It fits neatly into neither the sociological nor the psychological approach to the etiology of alcoholism. It was advanced in a
provocative paper by the late Gregory Bateson, a maverick anthro-
pologist-sociologist. One of his many concerns was how people
process information, drawing on their culture and their own style of
thinking. An essay published in 1972, "The Cybernetics of 'Self': A
Theory of Alcoholism," offers some intriguing ideas as to why alco-

holism may be reaching epidemic proportions in Western cultures. It certainly provides an interesting hypothesis on why abandoning alcohol is so difficult for the alcoholic.

Bateson points out that Western and Eastern cultures differ significantly in the way they view the world. Western societies focus on the individual. The tendency of Eastern cultures is to consider the individual in terms of the group or in terms of one's relationships. To point out this difference, consider how you might respond to the question "Who is that?" The "Western" way to answer is to respond with the person's name, "That's Joe Schmoe." The "Eastern" response might be "That's my neighbor's oldest son." The latter answer highlights the relationship of several persons.

One of the results of Westerners' zeroing in on the individual is an inflation of the sense of "I." We think of ourselves as wholly separable and independent. Also we may not recognize the relationships of ourselves to other persons and things and the effects of our interactions. According to Bateson, this can lead to problems. One example he cites is our relationship to the physical environment. If nothing else, the ecology movement has taught us that the old rallying cry of "man against nature" does not make sense. We cannot beat nature. We only win—that is, survive—if we allow nature to win some rounds too. To put it differently, we are now starting to see ourselves as a part of nature.

How does this fit in with alcohol? The same kind of thinking is evident. The individual who drinks expects, and is expected, to be the master of alcohol. If problems develop, the individual can count on hearing "control your drinking," "use willpower." The person is supposed to fight the booze and win. Now there's a challenge. Who can stand losing to a "thing?" So the person tries different tactics to gain the upper hand. Even if the individual quits drinking for a while, the competition is on: me versus it. To prove who's in charge, sooner or later the drinker will have "just one." If disaster doesn't strike then, the challenge continues to have "just one more." Sooner or later. . . .

Bateson asserted that successful recovery requires a change of world view by the person in trouble with alcohol. The Western tendency to see the self (the I) as separate and distinct from, and often in combat with, alcohol (or anything else) has to be abandoned. The alcoholic must learn the paradox of winning through losing, the limitations of the I and its interdependence with the rest of the world. He continues with examples of the numerous ways in which AA fosters just this change of orientation.

A truism seems to be that the more we learn about a given topic, the more we know we don't know. As research methods become increasingly more sophisticated, the flaws in older studies come to light. Cultural and subcultural differences are at best difficult to tease out. With television, jet travel, etc., differences are less clearcut than they were. However, historically the differences in rates of alcoholism from culture to culture were substantial enough to provoke study and research. As genetic and psychological approaches fall short of fully explaining the phenomenon of alcoholism so do cultural differences. But a review of past studies is useful in considering the ways in which broad cultural attitudes seemingly contribute to high rates of alcoholism, or, conversely, to identify those attitudes that promote moderate use.

Statistically, the odds on becoming an alcoholic have in the past varied significantly from country to country. Studies in epidemiology once showed that the Irish, French, Chileans, and Americans had a high incidence of alcoholism. The Italians, Jews, Chinese, and Portuguese had substantially lower rates. The difference seemed to lie with the country's habits and customs. Indeed whether someone drinks at all depends as much on culture as it does on individual characteristics.

Culture includes the unwritten rules and beliefs by which a group of people live. Social customs set the ground rules for behavior. The rules are learned from earliest childhood and are followed later, often without a thought. Many times such social customs account for the things we do "just because. . . . "The specific expectations for behavior differ from nation to nation, and between separate groups within a nation. Differences can be tied to religion, sex, age, or social class. The ground rules apply to drinking habits as much as to other customs. Cultures vary in attitudes toward alcohol use as they differ in the sports they like or what they eat for breakfast.

CULTURAL ORIENTATION'S EFFECTS ON ALCOHOLISM RATES

Several distinctive drinking patterns and attitudes toward alcohol use have been identified. Which orientation predominates in a culture or a cultural subgroup was, and in certain cases still is, thought to be influential in determining that group's rate of alcoholism. One such attitude toward drinking is total *abstinence*, as with the Muslims or Mormons. With drinking forbidden, the chances of alcoholism are exceedingly slim. Expectedly, the group as a whole has a very low rate of alcoholism. There is an interesting twist we'll get to later about what happens when members leave the group.

Another cultural attitude toward alcohol promotes *ritual* use. Drinking is primarily connected to religious practice, ceremonies, and special occasions. Any heavy drinking in other contexts would be frowned on. When drinking is tied to social occasions, with the emphasis on social solidarity and camaraderie, it is termed *convivial use*. Finally, there is *utilitarian use*. The society "allows" people to drink for their own personal reasons—to meet their own needs, for example, to relax, to forget, or to chase a hangover. Rates of alcoholism are highest where utilitarian use is dominant.

Differences among nations are growing less marked with technological developments such as television, jet planes, and increased

travel. Italy has adopted the cocktail party; America is on France's wine kick. Nonetheless, a look at some of the differences between the traditional French and Italian drinking habits shows that cultural attitudes toward the use of alcohol can influence the rate of alcoholism. Both France and Italy are wine-producing countries—France first in the world, Italy second. Both earn a substantial part of their revenue from the production and distribution of wine. Yet the incidence of alcohol addiction in Italy a generation ago was less than one fifth that of France.

Traditionally in France there were no controls on excessive drinking. Indeed there was no such thing as excessive drinking. Wine was publicly advertised as good for the health—creating gaiety, optimism, and self-assurance. It was seen as a useful or indispensable part of daily life. Drinking in France was a matter of social obligation; a refusal to drink was met with ridicule, suspicion, and contempt. It was not uncommon for a Frenchman to have a little wine with breakfast, to drink small amounts all morning, to have half a bottle with lunch, to sip all afternoon, to have another half bottle with dinner, and to nip until bedtime, consuming 2 liters or more a day. Frenchmen did get drunk. On this schedule, drunkenness would not always show up in drunken behavior. The body, however, was never entirely free of alcohol. Even people who never showed open drunkenness could have withdrawal symptoms and even DTs when they abstained. The "habit," and the social atmosphere that permitted it, seemed to be facilitating factors in the high rate of alcoholism in France.

Italy, on the other hand, which had the second highest wine consumption in the world, consumed only half of what was consumed in France. Italy had a low rate of alcoholism on a world scale. The average Italian didn't drink all day but only with noon and evening meals. One liter a day was the accepted amount, and anything over that was considered excessive. There was no social pressure for

drinking as in France. As Jellinek said, "In France, drinking is a
must. In Italy it is a matter of choice." Drunkenness, even mild
intoxication, was considered a terrible thing, unacceptable even on
holidays or festive occasions. A guy with a reputation for boozing
would have had a hard time getting along in Italy. He would have
had trouble finding a wife. Both she and her parents would have
hesitated to consent to a marriage with such a man. His social life
would have been hindered, his business put in jeopardy; he would
have been cut off from the social interaction necessary for advance-
ment.

Jews historically have had a low rate of alcoholism. Jewish drinking patterns were similar to the Italians', bolstered by the restraint
of religion. The Irish were more like the French and had a high incidence of alcoholism for many of the same reasons. The Irish had
ambivalent feelings toward alcohol and drunkenness, which tended
to produce tension and uneasiness. Drinking among the Irish (and
other groups with high rates) was largely convivial on the surface;
yet purely utilitarian drinking—often lonely, quick, and sneaky—was
a tolerated pattern.

What, then, are the specific factors that account for the differences? These are obviously not based on abstinence. Among the
Italians and Jews, many used alcohol abundantly and yet they had a
low incidence of alcoholism. While the attitudes in these cultures
have changed over the years, some factors that do affect the rates of
alcoholism still seem to be found in certain groups. Low rates of
alcoholism are found in cultures in which the children are gradually introduced to alcohol in diluted small amounts, on special occasions, within a strong, well-integrated family group. Parents who
drink a small or moderate amount with meals, who are consistent in
their behavior and their attitudes, set a healthy example. There is
strong disapproval of intoxication. It is neither socially acceptable,
stylish, funny, nor tolerated. A positive acceptance of moderate,
nondisruptive drinking and a well-established consensus on when,
where, and how to drink create freedom from anxiety. Drinking is
not viewed as a sign of manhood and virility, and abstinence is
socially acceptable. It is no more rude to say no to liquor than to coffee. Liquor is viewed as an ordinary thing. No moral importance is
attached to drinking or not drinking; it is neither a virtue nor a sin.
In addition, alcohol is not seen as the primary focus for an activity;
it accompanies rather than dominates or controls.

High rates of alcoholism tend to be associated with the reverse of
the above patterns. Wherever there has been little agreement on
how to drink and *how not* to drink, alcoholism rates go up. In the
absence of clear, widely agreed upon rules, whether one is behaving
or misbehaving is uncertain. Ambivalence, confusion, and guilt easily can be associated with drinking. Those feelings further compound the problem. Individuals who move from one culture to

*"Man comes from dust and ends in
dust" (Holy Day Musaf prayer)—
and in between, let's have a drink.*
YIDDISH PROVERB

another are especially vulnerable. Their guidelines may be conflicting, and they are caught without standards to follow. For this reason, individuals who belong to groups that promote abstinence similarly run a very high risk of alcoholism if they do drink.

Studies have provided insights into what the broad determinants are for differing rates of alcoholism. In many cases they describe traditional practices of specific groups that have changed in the intervening years. For example, a report by the French National Institute of Agriculture Reform and the National Office of Table Wines shows that French drinking patterns have changed dramatically. Drinking is no longer seen as a part of everyday nourishment but has become a source of pleasure. These changes are being attributed to automation and television. The workers in a Renault factory are not going to be sipping wine throughout the day as was the custom of their grandfathers who were manual laborers. The bistro no longer serves as the hub of social life, and the practice of stopping by after work has declined with television. The French, just like their American counterparts, head home to an evening by the tube—the news, the Monday-night soccer match, the late movies.

Just as cultural differences between groups are becoming less marked, so too it cannot be assumed that every member of a specific group follows the group norms. Being Jewish is no protection against alcoholism. The historically low rates of alcoholism among Jews may lead to under-recognition and greater stigmatization of those who are alcoholic.

Norms associated with alcohol problems. A review of the literature on alcohol problems reinforces the above observations. The following norms and drinking practices have been identified as predictive of the occurrence of problems from alcohol use: (1) solitary drinking; (2) overpermissive norms of drinking; (3) lack of specific drinking norms; (4) tolerance of drunkenness; (5) adverse social behavior tolerated when drinking; (6) utilitarian use of alcohol to reduce tension and anxiety; (7) lack of ritualized and/or ceremonial use of alcohol; (8) alcohol use apart from family and social functions of close friends; (9) alcohol use separated from overall eating patterns; (10) lack of child socialization into drinking patterns; (11) drinking with strangers, which increases violence; (12) drinking pursued as recreation; (13) drinking concentrated in young males; and (14) a cultural milieu that stresses individualism, self-reliance, and high achievement.

The influence of cultural subgroups. Beyond the influence of broad-based cultural factors, there has been recent interest in the relative influence of cultural subgroups such as family or peers, as well as the characteristics of the immediate drinking situation. Not surprisingly, much of this research has focused upon adolescents and the factors that promote or protect against alcohol use and abuse. Some of these studies have resulted in some interesting findings. However, although considerable research is being conducted, each study is fairly circumscribed and specific. This body of research has yet to be integrated into a theoretical approach to the influences of the smaller social systems in which we live.

For example, among the research findings of interest, in a group of people drinking, the heaviest drinker sets the pace for the others. Thus, how much an individual drinks on a particular occasion is likely to be influenced by the amount consumed by others in the group. Another is that adolescent alcohol use increases with perceived access to alcohol and the perceived lack of degree of adult supervision. If one were to extrapolate from the broad cultural norms, one might reasonably suspect that when alcohol use is introduced in the home, this would provide a protective factor. Recent research has not supported that assumption. To the contrary, adolescents who are introduced to alcohol in the home are more likely than other adolescents to use alcohol in unsupervised settings. The authors note that further research is required to examine whether later unsupervised use is an across-the-board phenomenon or associated with different ways in which alcohol use is introduced. Having a glass of wine with a family meal may be quite different than a father and son both having a beer while watching a televised football game, or an adolescent being allowed to help himself to the cold beer in the fridge.

Effect of legal sanctions and approaches

The focus thus far has been on the unwritten rules that govern drinking behavior and influence the rates of alcoholism. How about the rules incorporated into law, which govern use and availability? What impact do they have on the rates of alcoholism? Though their impact is less than the factors just discussed, which permeate all of daily life, they do make a considerable difference. Think back to this nation's experience of Prohibition. On one level Prohibition can only be described as a fiasco. It did not abolish all problems associated with alcohol use. Moreover, research on alcohol problems was abandoned; those with alcoholism were further ostracized. On the other hand, with the lowering of consumption there was a marked reduction in the rate of alcoholism. Death from cirrhosis during Prohibition declined. Nonetheless, few would maintain that Prohibition was a successful experiment. What is clear is that laws, if they are to work, must reflect how people want people to behave.

Short of Prohibition, there are significant ways society can influence the use of alcohol. Among these are cost of alcoholic beverages, regulations on advertising, and legislation on when and where alcohol may be sold. Evidence from other countries, as well as our own experience with Prohibition, strongly suggests that the rate of alcoholism is related to per capita consumption. So banning advertising, increasing taxes, and other measures calculated to reduce sales can be expected to achieve a lower rate of alcoholism. Beyond laws governing consumption, sales, and pricing, the legal arena influences alcohol use in other ways.

The Last Straw
New Hampshire's budget woes have not yet set the masses marching in the streets.
Warning that our schoolchildren will be deprived have not done it.
Warnings that a student's costs for attending the University of New Hampshire will rise have not done it.
Warnings that there will be less treatment for the mentally ill have not done it.
Warnings that there will be reduced counseling services for the troubled have not done it.
Warnings that there will not be enough manpower to ensure pure water supplies have not done it.
Warnings that law enforcement officials may not be able to hold down the crime rate have not done it.
But now you better batten down the hatches and keep your riot shields handy.
This week there was a headline that said, "LIQUOR STORES THREATENED BY BUDGET."
That'll do it.

Editorial that appeared in *The Valley News*, Lebanon, New Hampshire, in September 1977, after the New Hampshire legislature and governor had failed to adopt a budget for the state.

The late 1980s and early 1990s: a decade of change

In terms of social policy, in our country, we can not expect to have all of the above possible approaches implemented in to as one piece of legislation. American society tackles public concerns in a more incremental fashion. However, a variety of steps have been taken that reflect efforts to moderate drinking patterns.

One of the initial steps, resulting from governmental activity, was to establish a uniform drinking age. The legal drinking age nation-wide is now 21 years. For the most part, in the United States, the laws regulating alcohol use have been set by the states. The blood alcohol level defining legal intoxication has not been universally the same. There are now efforts underway to set .05 as the legal standard for impairment. At its 1989 meeting, the policy-setting body of the American Medical Association, the House of Delegates, passed a resolution favoring the .05 level and instructed the Association to lobby for its adoption. States may vary as well on when, where, and what a citizen may drink within its borders. And some states even vary from county to county—Texas, for example. Laws range from dry, to beer only, to anything at all but only in private clubs, to sitting down but not walking with drink in hand, ad infinitum.

The gap between states is beginning to close in response to federal actions and changes in public perceptions. The uniform increase of the drinking age to 21 years was championed by many, in the hope that it would be an effective measure to reduce alcohol-related highway fatalities among young people. But it was resisted too on several grounds. Some cited the fact that the age of majority is 18 years; college campuses, despite the recognition of problem drinking on campus, were concerned about living with a law that was so out of sync with the behavior of its students. Ultimately the states' passage was in no small part prompted by a federal "incentive"—the conditional tying of federal highway funds to the states' enactment of a 21-year-old drinking age.

There have been other governmental initiatives which would have been highly improbable a decade ago, such as the requirement that alcohol beverages have warning labels. This was accomplished despite the presence of a highly organized and well-financed alcohol beverage industry lobby. Such steps require broad public support rather than advocacy by a small, highly vocal minority.

In respect to drinking and driving, changes have been dramatic. The activity of grass-roots organizations such as MADD (Mothers against Drunk Driving) and its derivative SADD (Students . . .) were substantial. The lobbying for stricter penalties for drinking and driving offenses has, for the most part, been successful. The concept of the "designated driver" clearly has taken hold. Advertising campaigns to combat drinking and driving are now commonplace, at least at holiday times. All of this has had an impact. Driving fatalities attributable to alcohol have declined.

The legal system also has both spurred and reflected changes in society. One major influence has been the issue of legal liability and the suits that can be filed for compensation when death or injury occur as a result of drinking. There long have been Dram Shop laws, which hold a tavern owner or bar keeper liable for serving an obviously intoxicated customer. Until several years ago these were rarely invoked. This is no longer the case. Liability also has been extended to hosts or to those who might allow an intoxicated person to use their car. The issue of liability, particularly in light of higher legal drinking ages, has prompted college campuses to pay attention to issues of alcohol use.

Concern about liability also has touched the workplace. It has prompted business establishments largely to abandon parties where the alcohol flows freely, particularly on company time. If drinking takes place at work-sponsored activities, during the time for which an employee is being paid, any alcohol-impaired employee injured on the way home is a candidate for workmen's compensation. In addition the company can anticipate a lawsuit. Other changes in business practices resulted from a "small" change in the Internal Revenue Code. The three-martini lunch went by the boards when the IRS no longer allowed companies to write off the purchase of alcohol as a legitimate business cost. This is a good example of how social change occurs. Small changes such as alteration of the tax code affect behavior, which in turn modifies perceptions or allows alternative views to be expressed. The "three-martini lunch" not only does not qualify as a business expense. It no longer is viewed as a requisite for doing business and, in many quarters, is concerned inappropriate.

As changes have been prompted by governmental action, they have been reinforced and mirrored by the actions of private groups who also have the capacity to influence patterns of alcohol use. For example, in professional sports, drunken fans were long seen as an inevitable part of the game! Drinking in the stands was spurred by beer sales at the concession stand, a not-insignificant source of revenue. Over the past several years, professional teams have begun to sharply curtail drinking. In some instances drinking has been entirely banned. In both professional and college stadiums there are now blocks of "family" seats, where no alcohol consumption is allowed. In collegiate sports in 1990, the NCAA set limits on the amount of advertising by beer companies during the television broadcasts of its games.

Presumably some relationship exists between the changing attitudes and policies toward alcohol use and the intensive efforts in the arena of drug problems. In 1988, the federal government passed legislation, The Omnibus Anti-Drug Abuse Act, which became the foundation of the "war on drugs." The Anti-Drug Abuse Act incorporated steps to decrease the availability of drugs. This, borrowing from economic jargon, is the "supply side"; and efforts directed

We're drinking my friend,
To the end of a brief episode,
Make it one for my baby
And one more for the road,

JOHNNY MERCER
"One' For My Baby'

ALE-GATOR

toward reducing the use of drugs, thus reducing the markets, is the "demand-side." It was in the context of this initiative that then–First Lady, Nancy Reagan, launched a public drug prevention campaign with the slogan, "Just say No." The major target was illicit psychoactive substances, primarily cocaine and its variant crack, and, to a lesser degree, other psychoactive substances such as heroin, the amphetamines, and the designer drugs.

With the above legislation as the backdrop for social policy, the federal government also uses its regulatory powers to promote changes in society. The federal goals of the "Drug-free Campus" and the "Drug-free Workplace" by the year 1995 are being encouraged through education and also through linking institutions' receipt of federal funds to their mounting prevention programs. Though questioned by unions and those concerned about civil liberties and intrusion on privacy, drug screening in the workplace is being implemented for both current employees and job applicants.

A concern about anti-drug initiatives has been that they largely ignored the substances most widely associated with addiction in our society—alcohol, nicotine, and prescription drugs. Many in the alcohol and public health fields are appalled by the lack of attention alcohol is receiving despite the fact that its associated problems dramatically overshadow those associated with illicit drug use. There are those too who remember the public's response to the "counterculture" of the '60s, when psychoactive drug use and experimentation was accepted by a large segment of the adolescent and young adult population. Alcohol was then viewed as far more benign than other drugs. The refrain of parents when confronted with an adolescent's drinking was purportedly a relieved, "Well at least he isn't on drugs." As a means of reminding everyone that alcohol is a drug, the federal Office of Substance Abuse Prevention adopted the terminology of "alcohol and *other* drug use" rather than the phrase "alcohol and substance abuse." That is now being expanded to "alcohol, tobacco, and other drug use."

Attitudes toward alcohol use continue to be varied. In some quarters, it remains manly and sophisticated to drink. In others, drinking is felt to be unnecessary. In some, it is seen as outright decadence. Despite the considerable changes in laws and public policy, our contradictory and ambiguous views toward alcohol remain embodied in our liquor laws. Regardless of concern about adolescent use, the law implies that on that magical twenty-first birthday, individuals are treated as if they suddenly know how to handle alcohol appropriately. As the rhetoric of "Just say No" is applied to alcohol, as it has been in federally funded campus prevention efforts, it skirts the issue of alcohol's legal status for those 21 and over; there's no mention of when or under what circumstances it is okay to "say Yes."

As a society, we long have attempted to "have our booze and drink it too." We want alcohol without the associated problems. Because that is not possible, the question has been, what compromises are we willing to make? What inconveniences and costs are we willing to assume? Will we accept further steps, for example, a ban on package sales after 10:00 PM on the assumption that folks who want to buy alcohol at that hour don't need it? Will we allocate a reasonable share of the alcohol tax dollar to help the inevitable percentage who get into trouble with the drug? Will treatment of alcohol and other drug problems be incorporated into or left out of health care reform? Comments which have arisen in the discussion of mandating alcohol and other drug treatment as part of a basic health-care plan have been instructive. In light of concern about cost, the question is raised as to why those who don't need such benefits should be forced to purchase the coverage and be required through their insurance payments to subsidize treatment of others. This reflects a "we" versus "they" attitude. It suggests a belief that those in with alcohol and/or other drug problems brought their difficulties on themselves. For all the discussion of addictions representing a disease, seemingly just below the surface continues to lurk the perception of addictions as immoral, "bad" behavior. How addiction coverage fares under health care reform may be the most telling statement of how far we have or have not come in our national understanding of this public health issue.

Nonetheless, America since the mid-1980s has moved further towards a consensus, at least about the behaviors deemed unacceptable with respect to drinking. But, with alcohol widely available everywhere, until agreement emerges on *appropriate* as well as inappropriate use, American society will continue to be a fertile breeding ground for alcoholism.

RESOURCES AND FURTHER READING

These references may appear dated. However, we have selected the original primary sources for inclusion—the articles in which the ideas or findings set forth were first introduced in the scientific literature.

Anthenelli RM, Schuckit MA: Genetic studies of alcoholism (review), *International Journal of the Addictions* 25(1):81-94, 1991.

> This paper reviews recent developments in the evaluation of genetic factors in alcoholism. After presenting the results of family, twin, and adoption studies, the authors turn to investigations focusing on children of alcoholics. An emphasis is placed on the finding of a decreased intensity of reaction to alcohol in sons and daughters of alcoholics. The potential implications of these findings are discussed. (Author abstract.)

Bales R: Cultural differences in rates of alcoholism, *Quarterly Journal of Studies on Alcohol* 6:489-499, 1946.

> It has long been recognized that in considering the origins of alcohol problems and alcoholism, one must look not only at the individual but also at society. Countries were recognized as having different rates of alcoholism. Bales describes four dif-

ferent cultural orientations toward drinking and their role in influencing the culture's rate of alcoholism. The effects of a cultural orientation toward alcohol or other drug use continue to influence the understanding of the origins of alcohol and other drug problems, and thereby influence public policy and program development.

Bateson G: The cybernetics of "self": A theory of alcoholism, *American Journal of Psychiatry* 34:1-18, 1971.

Fraser M and Kohlert N: Substance abuse and public policy, *Social Services Review* 62(1):103-126, 1988.

This article assesses the American effort to control and eradicate substance abuse and drug trafficking. Five drug control strategies—foreign crop eradication, border interdiction, deterrence, treatment, and prevention—are evaluated. In each area the basic programs and their effectiveness are described. The authors conclude that U.S. policy is misdirected and dominated by long-standing and insupportable beliefs about the effectiveness of supply-side intervention such as eradication and interdiction.

Goodwin DW: Is alcoholism hereditary? *Archives of General Psychiatry* 25:545-549, 1971.

This article presents the first studies that demonstrated the role of heredity in some cases of alcohol dependence. Although it has been observed for a long time that alcoholism runs in families, the task of separating the influences of nature vs. nurture is still difficult.

Johnson V: *I'll Quit Tomorrow* (rev ed), New York: 1980, Harper & Row.

This work introduced the technique of "the intervention," a method to initiate treatment. The use of "interventions" promoted earlier treatment and prompted care for those previously seen as either "unready" or "inaccessible." The adoption of this clinical approach dispelled the myth that a patient's apparent motivation to cease use is a significant factor in determining treatment outcome, thus revolutionizing alcohol treatment, and, by example, drug abuse treatment as well. This work also introduced the concept of "enabling," i.e., the interactions of the family of the alcoholic that unwittingly support the continuation of drinking or drug use. Efforts to counter these behaviors, tied to the framework of the "intervention," offer the family a constructive role beyond "detachment with love," the primary orientation of Al-Anon, the self-help group for family members.

McCord W and McCord J: Some current theories of alcoholism: A longitudinal evaluation, *Quarterly Journal of Studies on Alcohol* 20:727-749, 1959.

A significant research dilemma in efforts to ascertain the influence of emotional and personality factors on the origins of alcohol or other drug dependence is that the individuals most easily studied are already alcohol- or drug-dependent. In that case the research requires efforts to define retrospectively the premorbid personality. The preferred methodology is a longitudinal prospective study to allow comparisons between those who do and those who do not become alcoholic or drug-dependent and to allow a clear assessment of personality before the emergence of symptoms. The McCords' study was the first to use such a longitudinal, prospective research design. The subjects had been closely studied many years earlier and initially recruited as part of a research project to explore the origins and precursors of juvenile delinquency.

Murray JB: Alcoholism: Etiologies proposed and therapeutic approaches tried, *Genetic, Social, and General Psychology Monographs* 115(1):81-121, 1989.

Alcohol, probably the most popular mood-altering drug, has frightening consequences when abused. Genetic factors and sociocultural influences contribute to alcoholic behavior. Study of endocrines, neurotransmitters, and neuropeptides may reveal biological markers to help identify those at risk for alcoholism. Drinking patterns often are based on the expectation of alcohol's mood-altering quality. The focus of treatment has expanded to include not only drinking behavior but also emotional, social, and vocational adjustment. Controlled drinking has proved effective for some alcohol abusers, so that complete abstinence is no longer the sole goal of therapy. Behavioral, marital, group and individual, and outpatient and inpatient therapy, with drugs as adjuncts, all help some alcoholics; but none is a cure for all. Answers still lag behind questions, but researchers have registered some advances that challenge therapists to enlarge therapeutic approaches to fit the multifaceted picture of alcoholism.

NIAAA: The genetics of alcoholism, *Alcohol Alert* No. 18, October, 1992.

NIAAA, Department of Health and Human Services: *6th Special Report to the U.S. Congress on Alcohol and Health,* Washington DC: U.S. Government Printing Office, 1987.

NIAAA, Department of Health and Human Services: *7th Special Report to the U.S. Congress on Alcohol and Health,* Washington DC: U.S. Government Printing Office, 1990.

NIAAA, Department of Health and Human Services: *8th Special Report to the U.S. Congress on Alcohol and Health,* Washington DC: U.S. Government Printing Office, 1994.

Pittman DJ, White HR, eds: *Society, culture, and drinking patterns reexamined,* New Brunswick NJ: Rutgers Center of Alcohol Studies, 1991.

> This volume represents a revision or sequel to a classic work "Society, Culture and Drinking Patterns," by Pittman and Snyder, which was first published in 1962. It is a compilation of primary materials, and chapters prepared especially for this volume, by those whose work has defined the field. Thus it has assembled the thinking on use and abuse of alcohol, from the range of social science research. The book is intended to consider the social and cultural influences which shape drinking practices, and which alongside individualistic and genetic based factors contribute to alcoholism. There are forty chapters. These are organized into five major sections. The first section sets forth an anthropological approach to drinking. The second provides current observations of alcohol use, both patterns of use and socialization processes related to use. The third focuses upon social structure, subcultures, and drinking patterns, considered by age, religion, race and ethnicity, and drinking institutions. The fourth section deals with the genesis and patterns of alcohol problems. This includes definitions, concepts of the phenomena, the pro- and anti-disease positions, the natural history, etiology, and relation of alcohol problems to social institutions—the family, economic and legal structures. The final section is directed to social movements which have arisen in response to these phenomena and the systems of control. This section considers the AA group, the adult children of alcoholics movement, medicalization of alcohol-related problems, and societal values, including the rise of what has been described as the "new" temperance movement.

Schuckit MA: Reaction to alcohol as a predictor of alcoholism, *Clinical Neuropharmacology* 15(1):305-306, 1992.

> Alcoholism is a genetically influenced disorder. However, unlike Huntington's disease, the development of alcohol dependence requires the interaction between relatively strong environmental influences and genetic factors. The hereditary forces in this disorder are complex, probably representing either polygenic forces and/or incomplete penetrance of a dominant inheritance pattern. Thus, it is not likely that there is a single major gene that is a potent contributor to the alcoholism risk in the great majority of alcoholics. As a consequence of these complex factors, a search is under way for more easily identified trait markers of an alcoholism vulnerability. Ideally, these traits will be relatively easily measured attributes of an individual which are linked to specific genes that contribute to the alcoholism vulnerability which would always be expressed, even if environmental events such as life-long abstinence preclude the expression of alcoholism itself. To date, several potentially important markers of risk have been studied, with most efforts focusing on children of alcoholics. One important lead relates to a lower amplitude of the P3 wave of the Event-Related Potential (ERP) in the substantial minority of sons

of alcoholic fathers. Other investigations are evaluating the pattern of lower frequency waves (e.g., alpha and beta) on the background cortical EEG (3). Several other more preliminary studies point to the potential relevance of a number of blood proteins as potential trait markers of the alcoholism risk, including activity level of adenylate cyclase and monoamine oxidase. (Author abstract.)

Thomasson HR, Li TK: How alcohol and aldehyde dehydrogenase genes modify alcohol drinking, alcohol flushing, and the risk of alcoholism, *Alcohol Health and Research World* 17(2):167-172, 1993.

The alcohol-related flushing experienced by many Asian people may further understanding of the genetic and the metabolic components of alcoholism. In this research report, the authors discuss the inheritance of variant forms of two enzymes involved in alcohol metabolism and the role these enzymes play in alcohol-related flushing. Public Domain.

Vaillant G: *The Natural History of Alcoholism*, Cambridge, MA: 1983 Harvard University Press.

A longitudinal prospective study of adult development, involving two cohorts, provided the opportunity to examine the natural history of alcoholism. The significant findings are as follows: (1) There was a lack of support for the theory of an "alcoholic personality." The presumed "predisposing personality factors" or emotional problems, in actuality result from drinking. (2) The major predictors of alcoholism are a positive family history and being raised in a culture whose norms proscribe childhood alcohol use, prescribe heavy adult alcohol use, and accept intoxication. (3) In respect to diagnosis, by the time individuals have experienced 4 lifetime problems from use, typically they will meet any diagnostic criteria for alcoholism. (4) However, treatment was not initiated until the occurrence of 8 to 11 lifetime problems. (5) After alcohol dependence is established, the two most common eventual outcomes are recovery or death: over the 30-year follow-up, nonproblematic drinking continually declined. (6) Successful recovery is associated with four factors: developing a vital interest that can replace the role of drinking, external reminders that drinking is painful, increased sources of unambivalently offered social support, and the presence of a source of inspiration, hope, and enhanced self-esteem.

Medical complications

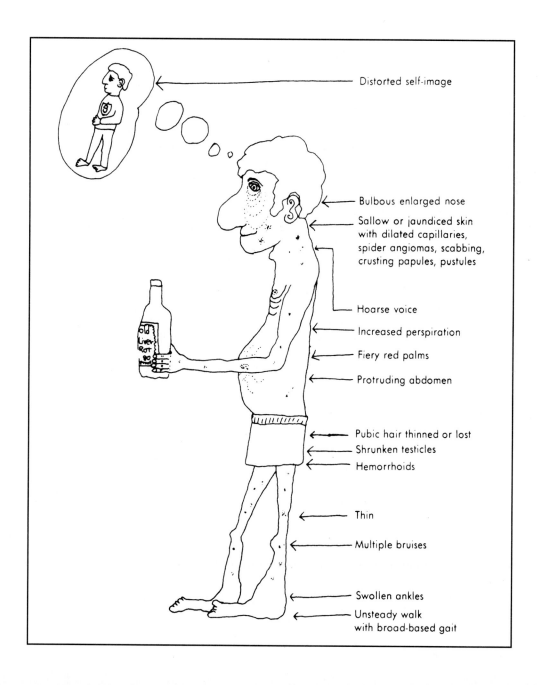

Distorted self-image

Bulbous enlarged nose

Sallow or jaundiced skin
with dilated capillaries,
spider angiomas, scabbing,
crusting papules, pustules

Hoarse voice

Increased perspiration

Fiery red palms

Protruding abdomen

Pubic hair thinned or lost

Shrunken testicles

Hemorrhoids

Thin

Multiple bruises

Swollen ankles

Unsteady walk
with broad-based gait

Part I
Advice for the moderate drinker

It probably comes as no great surprise to most people that excessive use of alcohol over a long period can lead to serious problems. What is unfortunately less recognized and appreciated is that, even in moderate amounts, alcohol use can present medical risks. There is no set "dose" of alcohol that reliably can be considered "safe" for people in general or for a single individual throughout his or her life.

Contraindications to moderate use

For some people, in some circumstances, at particular times, what is usually considered moderate alcohol use is too much. The most striking example is the caution against alcohol use during pregnancy. (This will be discussed in further detail in Chapter 7.) It is becoming more widely appreciated that drinking during pregnancy can cause abnormalities in the infant, a condition called *fetal alcohol syndrome* or *fetal alcohol effects*. The woman wishing to conceive should be thoughtful about her drinking. Since many pregnancies are not confirmed until the middle of the first trimester, it is possible that she might ingest harmful levels of alcohol before being aware of her pregnancy. There are other possible adverse consequences of alcohol use during pregnancy. Moderate alcohol use has been linked to an increase in spontaneous abortions. Drinking 1 to 2 drinks per day, for a total of one ounce of alcohol per day, doubles the risk of spontaneous abortions during the second trimester. Nursing mothers, too, are advised to refrain from alcohol use because alcohol can pass through breast milk to the infant. Though maternal alcohol use while nursing does not affect mental development, infants whose mothers consumed one or more drinks per day have been found to have slower rates of motor development.

Even relatively modest alcohol use can create problems for those with cardiac and circulatory problems, e.g., coronary artery disease and/or congestive heart failure, as well as hypertension. High blood pressure in up to 10% of all cases is believed to be the direct result of alcohol use. For those with established hypertension, alcohol use can make management and adequate control of blood pressure more difficult. Moderate drinking also has been found to elevate the level of certain blood fats in individuals with *Type IV hyperlipoproteinemia*.

Others for whom moderate drinking may be unwise may include those with seizure disorders, particular kinds of hyperlipoproteinemias, diabetes mellitus, gout, osteoporosis, and various skin conditions, including psoriasis, as well as those with gastric and duodenal ulcers. The ways in which alcohol may aggravate these conditions are discussed in Part II.

Although none of these medical conditions may constitute an absolute contraindication, all fall into the category of *relative contraindications*. A glass of wine with meals once or twice a week may present no problem, but several drinks before dinner plus wine with the meal, or an evening on the town, are ill-advised. As a general rule, those being treated for any medical condition ought to inquire about the need to modify temporarily what may be very moderate drinking. In addition to the possibility of alcohol complicating a medical condition, there is the possibility of interactions with medications prescribed to treat them.

Alcohol-drug interactions

Alcohol-drug interactions may be the area in which the moderate drinker is potentially most vulnerable to problems arising from alcohol use. Alcohol is a drug. When alcohol is taken in combination with prescribed or over-the-counter medications, there can be undesirable and quite possibly dangerous alcohol-drug interactions. Though these interactions can vary from individual to individual, they depend primarily on the amount of alcohol and type of medication consumed, as well as the person's drinking history. The moderate drinker who has not developed tolerance will have a very different response than the habitual heavier drinker. In fact, the consequences may be far more serious.

Wine is at the head of all medicines.

TALMUD: BABA BATHRA, 58B

The basis of alcohol-drug interactions. Two basic mechanisms can explain virtually all alcohol-drug interactions. One is that the presence of alcohol alters the liver's ability to metabolize other drugs. In the moderate drinker, the MEOS system, which metabolizes a variety of other drugs as well as alcohol (see Chapter 2), may be significantly inhibited, or slowed down, in the presence of alcohol. Therefore drugs ordinarily metabolized by the liver's MEOS system will not be removed as rapidly or completely as usual. The result is that these medications will then be present in the body in higher-than-expected levels. This can result in unexpected toxic effects.

On the other hand, for those with a long history of heavy drinking, alcohol has the opposite effect on the MEOS system. The MEOS action is enhanced, or speeded up, through a process known as *enzyme induction*. Thus certain drugs will be removed, or metabolized, more quickly. The medication is removed more rapidly, so its levels in the body will be lower than expected or desired. The net effect is that the individual will very likely not be receiving the intended therapeutic effects of a given dose of the drug. To compensate for this, it may be necessary to increase the dose of the drug administered to achieve the intended therapeutic effect.

The other major source of difficulty results from so-called additive effects. Alcohol is a CNS depressant. Other medications may also depress CNS functions. When two depressant drugs are present simultaneously, their combined effects often may be far greater than would be expected with the sum of the two. It is also important to be aware that drugs and alcohol are not metabolized instantaneously. Recall that it takes the body approximately 1 hour to handle one drink (whether the drink is a 12-ounce bottle of beer or one mixed drink with a shot of 80-proof liquor). Therefore if someone has had several drinks, an hour or two later alcohol will still be in the system. As long as alcohol remains in the body, potential exists for significant additive effects, even though the other depressant drugs are taken several hours later, or vice versa.

Common interactions of medications and alcohol. Many of the potential interactions of alcohol with some commonly prescribed medications are outlined in Table 3. These include the general types of interactions described and a variety of others not specifically discussed. Please note that the chart is *not* all-inclusive. If a drug is not listed, don't assume that it has no interaction with alcohol. Anyone who uses alcohol and is taking other medications is advised to ask his or her physician or pharmacist specifically about potential alcohol-drug and drug-drug interactions.

Problems associated with drinking and intoxication

A boxcar filled with beer derailed near White River Junction, Vermont, a few winters ago. It was successfully attacked by looters on bobsleds and snowmobiles.

BOSTON GLOBE

Accidents and injury. Along with alcohol-drug interactions the other common medical problem associated with alcohol use is accidents and injuries. These are more likely to occur during an intoxicated state because of the nature of alcohol-induced impairment. Judgment is impaired, placing individuals in situations that invite danger. Diminished judgment, along with decreased reaction and response time and poorer motor skills, leads to a lessened ability to cope with whatever occurs. In addition to injuries being more common with intoxication, their severity has also been found to rise with the level of impairment.

AIDS. In the minds of the general public as well as health care and alcohol-substance abuse professionals, AIDS is clearly linked with those who use drugs intravenously, a group for whom AIDS is becoming virtually endemic. The dramatic rise of AIDS among intravenous drug users is not based primarily on the pharmacological properties of the drugs but the route of administration. Among intravenous drug users, HIV infection is readily transmitted by the common and dangerous practice of sharing needles. Given the multiple problems associated with chronic drug use, this group is not easily touched by informational and preventative efforts.

As part of the increasing research on AIDS, the relationship of alcohol use and AIDS is now being examined. The ability of chronic alcohol use to suppress the immune system (as described later) has been clearly established. The effect of acute use among those who drink moderately is just now becoming evident. Pilot experiments with healthy volunteers suggest that a single administration

TABLE 3

The interaction effects of alcohol with other drugs

Type of drug	Generic name	Trade name	Interaction effect with alcohol
Analgesics Nonnarcotic	Salicylates	(Products containing aspirin) Bayer Aspirin Bufferin Alka-Seltzer	Heavy concurrent use of alcohol with analgesics can increase the potential for GI bleeding. Special caution should be exercised by individuals with ulcers. Buffering of salicylates reduces possibility of this interaction.
Narcotic	Codeine Morphine Opium Oxycodone Propoxyphene Pentazocine Meperidine	Pantopon Parepectolin (paregoric) Percodan Darvon Darvon-N Talwin Demerol Tylox	The combination of narcotic analgesics and alcohol interact to reduce functioning of the CNS and can lead to loss of effective breathing function and respiratory arrest: death may result.
Antianginal	Nitroglycerin Isosorbide dinitrate	Nitrosat Isordil, Sorbitrate	Alcohol in combination with antianginal drugs may cause the blood pressure to lower—creating a potentially dangerous situation.
Antibiotics Antiinfective agents	Furazolidone Metronidazole Nitrofurantoin	Furoxone Flagyl Cyantin Macrodantin	Certain antibiotics, especially those taken for urinary tract infections and *Trichomonas* infections, have been known to produce disulfiram-like reactions (nausea, vomiting, headaches, hypotension) when combined with alcohol.
Anticoagulants	Warfarin sodium Acenocoumarol Coumarin derivatives	Coumadin, Panwarfin Sintrom Dicumarol	With chronic alcohol use, the anticoagulant effect of these drugs is inhibited. With acute alcohol use the anticoagulant effect is enhanced: hemorrhaging could result.
Anticonvulsants	Phenytoin Carbamazepine Primidone Phenobarbital	Dilantin Tegretol Mysoline Luminal	Chronic heavy drinking can reduce the effectiveness of anticonvulsant drugs to the extent that seizures previously controlled by these drugs can occur if the dosage is not adjusted appropriately. Enhanced CNS depression may occur with concurrent use of alcohol.
Antidiabetic agents Hypoglycemics	Chlorpropamide Acetohexamide Tolbutamide Tolazamide Insulin	Diabinese Dymelor Orinase Tolinase Iletin	The interaction of alcohol and either insulin or oral antidiabetic agents may be severe and unpredictable. The interaction may induce hypoglycemia or hyperglycemia; also disulfiram-like reactions may occur.

Continued.

TABLE 3

The interaction effects of alcohol with other drugs—cont'd

Type of drug	Generic name	Trade name	Interaction effect with alcohol
Antidepressants Tricyclics	Nortriptyline Amitriptyline Desipramine Doxepin Imipramine	Aventyl Elavil, Endep Pertofrane Sinequan Tofranil	Enhanced CNS depression may occur with concurrent use of alcohol and antidepressant drugs. Alcohol itself can cause or exacerbate clinical states of depression.
Monoamine oxidase inhibitors (MAOI)	Pargyline Isocarboxazid Phenelzine Tranylcypromine	Eutonyl Marplan Nardil Parnate	Alcoholic beverages (such as beer and wines) contain tyramine, which will interact with an MAOI to produce a hypertensive hyperpyrexic crisis. Concomitant use of alcohol with MAOIs may result in enhanced CNS depression.
Antihistamines	(For example) Chlorpheniramine Diphenhydramine	(Many cold & allergy remedies) Coricidin Allerest Benadryl	The interaction of alcohol and these drugs enhances CNS depression.
Antihypertensive agents	Rauwolfia preparations Reserpine Guanethidine Hydralazine Pargyline Methyldopa	Rauwiloid Serpasil Ismelin Apresoline Eutonyl Aldomet	Alcohol, in moderate dosage, will increase the blood pressure-lowering effects of these drugs, and can produce postural hypotension. Additionally, an increased CNS-depressant effect may be seen with the rauwolfia alkaloids and methyldopa. Alcohol itself causes hypertension and may counteract the therapeutic effect of antihypertensive agents.
Antimalarials	Quinacrine	Atabrine	A disulfiram-like reaction and severe CNS toxicity may result if antimalarial drugs are combined with alcohol.
CNS depressants Barbiturate sedative hypnotics	Phenobarbital Pentobarbital Secobarbital Butabarbital Amobarbital	Luminal Nembutal Seconal Butisol Amytal	Since alcohol is a depressant, the combination of alcohol and other depressants interact to further reduce CNS functioning. It is extremely dangerous to mix barbiturates and alcohol. What would be a nondangerous dosage of either drug by itself can interact in the body to the point of coma or fatal respiratory arrest. Many accidental deaths of this nature have been reported. A similar danger exists in mixing the nonbarbiturate hypnotics with alcohol.

Category	Drug	Trade name	Interaction
Nonbarbiturate sedative hypnotics	Methaqualone Glutethimide Bromides Flurazepam Chloral hydrate	Quaalude Doriden Neurosine Dalmane Noctec	Disulfiram-like reactions have been reported with alcohol use in the presence of chloral hydrates.
Tranquilizers (major)	Thioridazine Chlorpromazine Trifluoperazine Haloperidol	Mellaril Thorazine Stelazine Haldol	The major tranquilizers interact with alcohol to enhance CNS depression, resulting in impairment of voluntary movement such as walking or hand coordination; larger doses can be fatal. Increases incidence and severity of extrapyramidal side effects of these drugs.
Tranquilizers (minor)	Diazepam Meprobamate Chlordiazepoxide Oxazepam Lorazepam Alprazolam	Valium Equanil Miltown Librium Serax Ativan Xanax	The minor tranquilizers depress CNS functioning. Serious interactions can occur when using these drugs and alcohol.
CNS stimulants	Caffeine Amphetamines Methlyphenidate Dextroamphetamine Methamphetamine	(in coffee and cola) Vanquish Benzedrine Ritalin Dexedrine Desoxyn Ritalin	The stimulant effect of these drugs can reverse the depressant effect of alcohol drugs on the CNS, resulting in a false sense of security. They do not help the intoxicated person gain control over coordination or psychomotor activity.
Disulfiram (anti-alcohol preparation)	Disulfiram	Antabuse	Severe CNS toxicity follows ingestion of even small amounts of alcohol. Effects can include headache, nausea, vomiting, convulsions, rapid fall in blood pressure, unconsciousness, and—with sufficiently high doses—death.
Diuretics (also antihypertensive)	Hydrochlorothiazide Chlorothiazide Furosemide Quinethazone	Hydrodiuril, Esidrix Diuril Lasix Hydromax	Interaction of diuretics and alcohol enhances the blood pressure—lowering the effects of the diuretic; could possibly precipitate hypotension.

equivalent to 0.7 to 3.1 liters of beer (that converts to the range of two to eight 12-ounce cans) has an impact on the immune system. Furthermore, these effects extend for up to 4 days after ingestion. The question this raises is whether casual alcohol consumption can increase either the vulnerability to infection or enhance the progression of latent HIV infection. On behavioral grounds alone, there is a link between intoxication and an increased risk of HIV infection. With intoxication, sexual activity is likely to be more casual and less considered, involve sexual partners determined by their "availability" rather than their being associated with an ongoing close emotional relationship, and be less likely to involve contraception or safer sex practices to reduce the risk of sexually transmitted disease, including HIV infection.

Unexpected and sudden natural deaths. The association between intoxication and unnatural causes of death such as accident, suicide, and homicide has been described in Chapter 1. Equally as significant is the recent finding of the high prevalence of positive BACs among people who have died suddenly and unexpectedly from natural causes. This finding is based upon the determination of the blood alcohol concentration as part of medicolegal autopsies conducted for all natural out-of-hospital deaths occurring during a 1-year period in a large Finnish metropolitan area. For this group of sudden and unexpected deaths, 36% of males and 15% of females had positive blood alcohol levels. The blood alcohol concentration for approximately half of these men and women was 0.15 or greater. Acute consumption of alcohol in nonalcoholics was certified as being a significant contributor in 23% of male and 8% of female sudden, unexpected deaths. For men, acute alcohol use was a contributing factor for 11% of deaths from coronary artery disease, 40% of other heart disease, and 7% for all other diseases. For both sexes the most vulnerable people are those in middle age.

Alcohol use and exercise

With the increasing interest in fitness and exercise, what are the recommendations for drinking in relation to sports and exercise? Alcohol can affect performance and be the source of potential problems if used immediately before, during, or immediately after exercise. Athletes who release pregame tension with a "few beers" before competition to take care of the jitters may slow reaction time and impair coordination, thus reducing their optimal performance. Before competition, endurance athletes sometimes "carbohydrate load," i.e., eat extra carbohydrates to increase the glycogen stored in muscles that serves as a source of energy. They may include beer as part of their pregame meal. However, beer is a poor source of carbohydrates compared to juices or soda. As for calories, two thirds of the calories in beer come from the alcohol. These calories are therefore used as heat and are not available for energy. Besides being a

Hey, the coach said no alcohol for 24 hours prior to performance.

You mean he was talking about the game! I thought he was talking about when we get together with the cheerleaders after the game.

poor source of carbohydrates, the alcohol can affect heat tolerance and lead to dehydration because of alcohol's inhibition of antidiuretic hormone. Athletes who consume alcohol before a performance are at risk for significant fluid loss. Hence the recommendation of sports physicians is not to consume alcohol for 24 hours before performance.

Part II
Medical complications of chronic heavy alcohol use

Alcoholism is one of the most common chronic diseases. The prevalence is 7% in the population at large. Untreated, its natural history is a predictable, gradually progressive downhill course. The observable early symptoms and manifestations of the primary disease alcoholism are largely behavioral and *non*physical. Later in its course, alcoholism causes a wide variety of medical complications in a multitude of different organ systems. These are associated with a host of different physical signs and symptoms.

It is important to emphasize the distinction between the primary disease alcoholism and its later secondary medical complications. Alcoholism, the disease, is one of the most highly treatable of chronic illnesses. If recognized and treated early—that means before major medical complications have occurred—it may be entirely arrested. Treated individuals can function quite normally. Their only long-term disability is that they cannot use alcohol. Its complications on the other hand, may be irreversible and may have a fatal outcome if the underlying alcoholism is untreated.

This section focuses on the later secondary medical complications of alcoholism. Because nearly every organ system is affected, an acquaintance with the medical complications of chronic heavy alcohol use is equivalent to familiarity with an exceedingly broad cross section of disease. In the past, in view of the protean and multi-system manifestations of both tuberculosis and syphilis, it was said, "to know TB or syphilis is to know medicine." The same can now be said of alcoholism, "to know alcoholism is to know medicine."

We will now touch briefly, in a systems-oriented fashion, on most of the major alcohol-related problems. First, however, let us examine a composite picture of a person afflicted with the visible signs of chronic alcoholism.

Visible signs and symptoms of chronic heavy drinking

Statistically, the typical alcoholic is male; thus we will use "he." However, women alcoholics can and do show virtually all the same signs of chronic heavy alcohol use except those involving the reproductive organs. Bearing in mind that any given alcoholic may have

There is this to be said in favor of drinking, that it takes the drunkard first out of society, then out of the world.
EMERSON, 1866

There are more old drunkards than old physicians.
RABELAIS

It's not the fluid that bothers me, Doc. It's the two live goldfish I swallowed last Time I was drunk.

Many a man keeps on drinking till he hasn't a coat to either his back or his stomach.

GEORGE D. PRENTICE

many or only a few of these visible manifestations, let us examine a hypothetical chronic drinker who has them all.

He is a typically thin, but occasionally somewhat bloated-appearing, middle-aged individual. Hyperpigmented, sallow, or jaundiced skin accentuates his wasted, chronically fatigued, and weakened overall appearance. He walks haltingly and unsteadily with a broad-based gait (ataxia). Multiple bruises are evident. He perspires heavily. His voice is hoarse and croaking, punctuated by occasional hiccups, and he carries an odor of alcohol on his breath.

His abdomen protrudes, and closer examination of it reveals the *caput medusae*—a prominent superficial abdominal vein pattern. There is marked ankle swelling, and he has hemorrhoids. His breasts may be enlarged; his testicles may be shrunken; and his chest, axillary, and/or public hair is entirely lost or thinned. Inspection of the skin reveals dilated capillaries and acne-like lesions. His nose is enlarged and bulbous. There is scabbing and crusting secondary to generalized itching. On the upper half of his body he has "spider angiomas." There are small red skin lesions that blanch with light pressure applied to their centers and spread into a spidery pattern with release of pressure. His palms may be a fiery red (liver palms). He may have "paper money" skin, so called because tiny capillaries, appearing much like the tiny red-colored fibers in a new dollar bill, are distinctly visible. In colder climates, there may be evidence of repeated frostbite. The fingernails are likely to be affected. They may have either transverse white-colored bands (Muehrcke's lines) or transverse furrows, or they may be totally opaque without half-moons showing at the base of the nail. He may well have difficulty fully extending the third, fourth, and fifth fingers because of a flexion deformity called *Dupuytren's contracture*. A swelling of the parotid glands in the cheeks, giving him the appearance of having the mumps, is known as "chipmunk facies." Finally, a close look at the whites of his eyes reveals small blood vessels with a corkscrew shape.

Now, with this as an external picture, let us look inside the body at the underlying diseased organ systems.

GASTROINTESTINAL SYSTEM

Alcohol affects the gastrointestinal (GI) system in a variety of ways. This system is the route by which alcohol enters the body and is absorbed. It is where the first steps of metabolism take place. Moderate amounts of alcohol can disturb and alter the normal functioning of this system. Moreover, chronic heavy use of alcohol can raise havoc. Alcohol can have both direct and indirect effects. Direct effects are *any changes that occur in response to the presence of alcohol.* Indirect effects would be *whatever occurs next, as a consequence* of the initial, direct impact.

Irritation, bleeding, and malabsorption

Chronic use of alcohol, as does any alcohol use, stimulates the stomach lining's secretion of hydrochloric acid and irritates the gut's lining. It also inhibits the muscular contractions called peristalsis that pass food along the intestines. In combination, these effects can lead to a generalized irritation of the mucous membrane lining the gut, especially in the stomach. Chronic heavy drinkers may also complain of frequent belching, loss of appetite, alternating diarrhea and constipation, morning nausea, and vomiting.

Irritation, rather than being found throughout the GI system, more often is localized to particular portions of it. For instance, if the esophagus is irritated, esophagitis results—experienced as midchest pain and pain when swallowing. Acute and chronic stomach irritation by alcohol result in gastritis, which involves inflammation, abdominal pain, and maybe even bleeding. Chronic alcohol use can certainly aggravate, if not indeed causing ulcers of the stomach or duodenum (the first section of the small intestine). Bleeding can occur at any of the irritated sites. This represents a potentially serious medical problem. Bleeding from the GI tract can be either slow or massive. Either way, it is serious. Frequently, for reasons to be discussed later in this chapter, the alcoholic's blood clots less rapidly. So the body's built-in defenses to reduce bleeding are weakened. Surgery may be required to stop the bleeding in some cases.

In addition to the causes of GI bleeding just mentioned, there are several other causes. The irritation of the stomach lining, not unexpectedly, upsets the stomach. With that can come prolonged violent nausea, vomiting, and retching. This may be so severe as to cause mechanical tears in the esophageal lining and bring on massive bleeding. Another cause of massive and often fatal upper GI bleeding is ruptured, dilated veins along the esophagus (esophageal varices). The distention and dilation of these veins occurs as a result of chronic liver disease and cirrhosis.

Chronic irritation of the esophagus by a combination of long-standing heavy alcohol consumption and cigarette smoking significantly increases the risk of developing esophageal cancer. The result of chronic excessive use of alcohol on small intestinal function can lead to abnormal absorption of a variety of foodstuffs, vitamins, and other nutrients. Although no specific diseases of the large intestine are caused by alcohol use, diarrhea frequently occurs. Hemorrhoids, also a by-product of liver disease and cirrhosis, are common in alcoholics.

Pancreatitis

Alcohol is frequently the culprit in acute inflammation of the pancreas. This is known as *acute pancreatitis*. The pancreas is a gland tucked away behind the stomach and small intestine. It makes

Pouring to achieve a large "head" on the beer enhances the bouquet and allows less carbonation to reach the stomach.

THE DOCTOR SAID Alcohol WAS MAKING MY blood too thin— SO NOW I add a little CORN STARCH TO each drink to help thicken it up.

A drunkard is like a whiskey bottle, all neck and belly and no head.
AUSTIN O'MALLEY

digestive juices that are needed to break down starches, fat, and proteins. These juices are secreted into the duodenum through the pancreatic duct, in response to alcohol as well as other foodstuffs. They are alkaline and thus are important in neutralizing the acid contents of the stomach, thereby helping to protect the intestinal lining. The pancreas also houses the islets of Langerhans, which secrete the hormone insulin, needed to regulate sugar levels in the blood.

Currently there are two major theories as to how alcohol causes acute pancreatitis. The first, which is less favored, suggests that the pancreatic duct opening into the duodenum can become swollen if the small intestine is irritated by alcohol. As it swells, pancreatic digestive juices cannot pass through it freely; they are obstructed or "stopped up." In addition, it has been suggested that bile from the bile duct, which opens into the pancreatic duct, may "back up" into the pancreatic duct and enter the pancreas itself. The pancreas then becomes inflamed. Because the bile and digestive juices cannot freely escape, in effect, autodigestion occurs.

The second theory holds that some of the excess fats in the bloodstream caused by excessive drinking are deposited in the pancreas. These fats are then digested by pancreatic enzymes, whose usual task is breaking down dietary fats. In turn the products of this process, free fatty acids, cause cell injury in the pancreas, which results in further release of fat-digesting enzymes, thus creating a vicious cycle.

The symptoms of acute pancreatitis include nausea, vomiting, occasional diarrhea, and the severe upper abdominal pain radiating straight through the back. Chronic inflammation of the pancreas can lead to calcification, visible on abdominal x-ray films. This is a relapsing illness almost always associated with long-standing alcohol use. Diabetes can result from decreased capacity of the pancreas to produce and release insulin as a result of chronic cell damage.

Liver disease

The liver is a fascinating organ. You recall that it is the liver enzyme, alcohol dehydrogenase (ADH), that begins the process of breaking down alcohol. The liver is also responsible for a host of other tasks. It breaks down wastes and toxic substances. It manufactures essential blood components, including clotting factors. It stores certain vitamins such as B_{12}, which is essential for red blood cells. It helps regulate the blood sugar level, a very critical task because that is the only food the brain can use. Liver disease occurs because the presence of alcohol disturbs the metabolic machinery of the liver. Metabolizing alcohol is always a very high-priority liver function. Therefore whenever alcohol is present, the liver is "distracted" from other normal and necessary functions. For the heavy drinker, this can be a good part of the time.

As you may know, liver disease is one of the physical illnesses most commonly associated with alcoholism. Three major forms of liver disease are associated with heavy alcohol use. The first is *acute fatty liver*. This condition may develop in anyone who has been drinking heavily, even for relatively brief periods of time. Fatty liver gets its name from the deposits of fat that build up in normal liver cells. This occurs because of a decrease in breakdown of fatty acids and an increase in the manufacture of fats by the liver. The latter is a result of the "distracting" metabolic effects of alcohol (see Chapter 2). Acute fatty liver occurs whenever 30% to 50% or more of the dietary calories are in the form of alcohol. This is true even if the diet is otherwise adequate. Acute fatty liver is a reversible condition if alcohol use is stopped.

Alcoholic hepatitis is a more serious form of liver disease that often follows a severe or prolonged bout of heavy drinking. Although more commonly seen in alcoholics, hepatitis, like acute fatty liver, may occur in nonalcoholics as well. In hepatitis, there is actual inflammation of the liver and variable damage to liver cells. One may also find associated evidence of acute fatty liver changes. Frequently, liver metabolism is seriously disturbed. Jaundice is a usual sign of hepatitis. Jaundice refers to the yellowish cast of the skin and the whites of the eyes. The yellow color comes from the pigment found in bile, a digestive juice made by the liver. The bile is being handled improperly, and therefore excessive amounts circulate in the bloodstream. Other symptoms of alcoholic hepatitis may include weakness, tiring easily, loss of appetite, occasional nausea and vomiting, low-grade fever, mild weight loss, increasing ascites, dark urine, and light stools.

In some patients, hepatitis is completely reversible with abstinence from alcohol. In others, it may be fatal or go on to become a smoldering chronic disease. Among patients who stop drinking, only one in five will go on to develop alcoholic cirrhosis. But 50% to 80% of those who continue drinking will develop cirrhosis. For many, alcoholic hepatitis is clearly a forerunner of *alcoholic cirrhosis*. But it is thought that alcoholic cirrhosis can also appear without the prior occurrence of alcoholic hepatitis.

Cirrhosis of the liver is a condition in which there is widespread destruction of liver cells. These cells are replaced by nonfunctioning scar tissue. In fact, the word *cirrhosis* simply means *scarring*. There are many different types and causes of cirrhosis. However, in the United States, long-term heavy alcohol use is the cause in the majority (80%) of cases. It is estimated that about one in ten long-term heavy drinkers will eventually develop alcoholic cirrhosis. Given the nature of the disease, it is accompanied by very serious and often relatively irreversible metabolic and physiological abnormalities, which is very bad news. In fact, more than half of the patients who continue to drink after a diagnosis of alcoholic cirrhosis are dead within 5 years.

In alcoholic cirrhosis the liver is simply unable to perform its work properly. Toxic substances, normally removed by the liver, circulate in the bloodstream, creating problems elsewhere in the body. This is particularly true of the brain, as we shall see later. The liver normally handles the majority of the blood from the intestinal tract as it returns to the heart. The cirrhotic liver, now a mass of scar tissue, is unable to handle the usual blood flow. The blood, unable to move through the portal vein (the route from the blood vessels around the intestines to the liver), is forced to seek alternative return routes to the heart. This leads to pressure and "backup" in these alternative vessels. It is this pressure that causes the veins in the esophagus to become enlarged, producing esophageal varices and inviting hemorrhaging. The same pressure accounts for hemorrhoids and the *caput medusae*.

Another phenomenon associated with cirrhosis is *ascites*. Caused by back pressure, the tissue fluid "weeps" directly from the liver into the abdominal cavity. This fluid would normally be taken up and transported back to the heart by the hepatic veins and lymph system. Large amounts of fluid can collect and distend the abdomen; a woman, for example, can look very pregnant. If you were to gently tap the side of a person with ascites, you would see a wavelike motion in response, as fluid sloshes around.

Another result of alcoholic liver disease is diminished ability of the liver to store glycogen, the body's storage form of sugar. There is also less ability to produce glucose from other nutrients such as proteins. Then this can lead to low blood sugar levels (see Chapter 2). This is an important fact when it comes to treating an alcoholic diabetic: insulin also lowers the blood sugar. Another situation in which this is important is in treating apparent coma in any alcoholic. Insufficient amounts of blood sugar may cause coma, essentially because the brain does not have enough of a fuel supply to function. Intravenous glucose may be necessary to prevent irreversible brain damage. On the other hand, alcohol and alcoholic liver damage may lead to states of diabetes-like, higher than normal–blood glucose levels. This occurs in large part both because of the effects of liver disease and the effects of alcohol on the range of hormones that regulate glucose.

Hepatic coma (hepatic encephalopathy) can be one result of cirrhosis. In this case, the damage comes from toxins circulating in the bloodstream. In essence, the brain is "poisoned" by these wastes and its ability to function is seriously impaired, leading to coma. Cancer of the liver is also a complication of long-standing cirrhosis. Another source of bad news is that as many of 50% of those with cirrhosis will also have pancreatitis. So these persons have two serious medical conditions. Still other complications may include GI bleeding, salt and water retention, and kidney failure. The main elements of treatment for cirrhosis are abstinence from alcohol, multivitamins, a nutritionally balanced adequate diet, and bed rest. Even with such treatment, the prognosis for cirrhosis is not good, and many of the complications just described may occur.

The different forms of alcohol-related liver disease result from specific changes in liver cells. Unfortunately, there is no neat and consistent relationship between a specific liver abnormality and the particular constellation of symptoms that develops. Although laboratory tests indicate liver damage, they cannot pinpoint the kind of alcohol-related liver disease. Therefore some authorities believe a liver biopsy, which involves direct examination of a liver tissue sample, is essential to evaluate the situation properly.

Until the early-to-mid-1970s it was not recognized that the liver damage common in alcoholism was a *direct* result of the alcohol. Rather, it was believed that the damage was caused by poor nutrition. It has since become clear that alcohol itself plays a major, direct role. Even in the presence of adequate nutrition, liver damage can occur when excessive amounts of alcohol are consumed.

IT'S A MARTini SANDwich - A 5ᵗʰ of gin and an empty vermouth bottle. His doctor Told him to eat more and drink less.

HEMATOLOGICAL SYSTEM

The blood, known as the *hematological system,* is the body's major transportation network. The blood carries oxygen to tissues. It takes up waste products of cell metabolism and carts them off to the lungs and kidneys for removal. It carries nutrients, minerals, and hormones to the cells. The blood also protects the body through the anti-infection agents it carries. Although the blood looks like a liquid, it contains "formed elements" (solid components). These formed elements include red blood cells, white blood cells, and platelets. They are all suspended in the serum, the fluid or liquid part of the blood. Each of the formed elements of the blood is profoundly affected by alcohol abuse. Whenever there is a disturbance of these essential blood ingredients, problems arise.

Red blood cells

Let us begin with the red blood cells. The most common problem here is anemia—too few red blood cells. *Anemia* is a general term like *fever.* It simply means *insufficient function or amounts.* Logically, one can imagine this coming about in a number of ways. Too few red blood cells can be manufactured if there is a shortage of nutrients to produce them. Even if they are adequately produced, they can be defective. Or they can be lost, for example, through bleeding. Or they actually can be destroyed. Alcohol contributes to anemia in each of these ways.

How does alcohol abuse relate to the first situation, inadequate production? The most likely culprit here is inadequate nutrition. Red blood cells cannot be manufactured if the bone marrow does not have the necessary ingredients. Iron is a key ingredient. Alcohol,

I Know I'm anemic Doc - but it's OK - I always drink my V-8 with my Bloody Marys.

or some of its metabolic products like acetaldehyde, are thought to interfere with the bone marrow's ability to use iron in making hemoglobin, which is the oxygen-carrying part of the blood. Even if there is enough iron in the system, it "just passes on by." On the other hand, a poor diet, not uncommon among alcoholics, may mean an insufficient iron intake. Chronic GI bleeding may also result from chronic alcohol abuse. If so, the iron in the red blood cells is lost and not available for recycling. This type of anemia is called *iron deficiency anemia.* Another variety, *sideroblastic anemia,* is also related to nutritional deficiencies. This comes from too little pyridoxal phosphate (a substance that facilitates the production of vitamin B_6 related cofactor). This substance is also needed by the bone marrow cells to produce hemoglobin.

These first two varieties of anemia account for the inadequate production of red blood cells. Another variety, *megaloblastic anemia,* is also related to nutritional deficiencies. There is too little folate. This happens because folate is not in the diet in sufficient quantities, and/or the small intestine is unable to absorb it properly because of other effects of chronic alcohol abuse. What results then is defective red blood cell production. Without this vitamin, red blood cells cannot mature. They are released from the bone marrow in primitive, less functional forms that are larger than normal. Chronic loss of blood from the gut—GI bleeding—can result in anemia. Here the bone marrow simply cannot make enough new cells to keep up with those that are lost. The body normally destroys and "recycles" old red blood cells through a process called *hemolysis.* Abnormally rapid hemolysis may occur in alcoholics. The life span of red cells can be shortened by up to 50%. One abnormal cause of hemolysis is hypersplenism, which results from chronic liver disease. The spleen, enlarged and not working properly, destroys perfectly good red blood cells as well as the old worn-out ones. Toxic factors in the blood serum are also thought to be responsible for three other varieties of hemolysis. Stomatocytosis is a transient, relatively benign form of anemia related to binge drinking and unrelated to severe alcoholic liver disease. *Spur cell anemia,* on the other hand, is associated with severe, often end-stage, chronic alcoholic liver disease. The name comes from the shape of the red cell, which, when looked at under the microscope, has jagged protrusions. *Zieve's syndrome* is the simultaneous occurrence in an alcoholic patient of jaundice, transient hemolytic anemia, elevated cholesterol levels, and acute fatty liver disease without enlargement of the spleen.

In France, other changes in red blood cells have been reported in those who drink at least 2 to 3 quarts of wine each day. These are changes typically seen with lead poisoning. (Lead, even in low concentrations, can mean trouble.) Excessive intake of wine in France is thought to be a significant source of dietary lead. In the United States, there are periodic reports of lead poisoning connected with alcohol use, but the circumstances are different. The beverage has not been wine but moonshine. In these cases, old car radiators were used in the distilling process.

White blood cells

On to the effects of alcohol on white blood cells. These cells are one of the body's main defenses against infection. The chronic use of alcohol affects white cells. This contributes to the increased susceptibility to and frequency of severe infections, especially respiratory tract infections, in alcoholics. Alcohol has a direct toxic effect on the white blood cell reserves. This leads to a reduced number of two types of white cells that fight infection (granulocytes and T lymphocytes). *Chemotaxis,* or white cell mobilization, is diminished by alcohol. In other words, although the white cells' ability to kill the bacteria is not affected, they have difficulty reaching the site of infection in adequate numbers. Alcohol also interferes with white cell adherence to bacteria, which is one of the body's defensive inflammatory reactions. Possibly this occurs because under the influence of alcohol, white cells may have a diminished ability to ingest bacteria.

Platelets

Alcoholics are frequently subject to bleeding disorders. They bruise easily. Bleeding can occur in the GI tract, the nose, and the gums. This is largely explained by the effect of alcohol on decreasing the number of platelets. Platelets are a major component of the body's clotting system and act like a patch on a leak. Alcohol has a direct toxic effect on bone marrow's production of platelets. Thus, one out of every four alcoholic patients will have abnormally low platelet counts. Within 1 to 3 days of stopping drinking, the count will begin to rise. Recall that severe liver disease can cause hypersplenism. This can cause abnormally rapid destruction of platelets, as well as red blood cells, thereby contributing to the low platelet counts seen in alcoholics.

Clotting factors and DIC

When the liver's metabolic processes are disrupted by the effects of chronic alcohol use, there is often a decrease in the production of some of the necessary serum-clotting factors. One thing to bear in mind is that there are 13 to 15 such substances needed to make a clot. Of these, five are liver produced; hence liver disease may in this way frequently lead to bleeding problems in alcoholics.

Severe liver damage can also contribute to the occurrence of *disseminated intravascular coagulation (DIC)*. This is a life-threatening state of diffuse, abnormally accelerated coagulation. It consumes large quantities of clotting factors, as well as platelets, and leads to dangerously lowered amounts of both, which can, in turn, result in excessive and uncontrolled bleeding.

Alcohol and the immune system

Another area of research is examining ways in which the immune system may be altered by alcohol. Actually, there are two different immune systems. One is associated with *circulating immune factors,* such as complement and immunoglobulins, in the blood system. The other is associated with antibodies attached to individual cells. Changes in both systems can occur with chronic alcohol use. The ability of serum (the unformed elements of the blood) to kill gram-negative bacteria is impaired by alcohol. This may be related to the diseased liver's lowered ability to produce complement, an important agent in the body's inflammatory response. Many immune and defensive responses depend on complement's presence.

Although not clearly established, the effects of alcohol on B lymphocytes may lead to decreased production of circulating antibodies, which normally fight bacterial infections. Alcohol has also been shown to decrease the numbers of T lymphocytes, which mediate cellular *immunity.* Moreover, it inhibits their responsiveness to stimuli that activate their functioning. These changes probably account in large part for the alcoholic's increased susceptibility to infection.

Research has suggested that alcohol-induced changes in some white cells, together with changes in the cell-based immune system, may lead to an increased production of certain types of fibrous tissues. It is just such fibrous tissues that are characteristic of cirrhosis. A current question is whether the scar tissue of cirrhosis can be attributed at least in part to white cell changes and alterations in the cells' immune response that are induced by chronic alcohol use.

Even though the hematological complications of chronic heavy alcohol use are many and potentially quite serious, they are in general totally reversible after abstinence. But the liver disease that caused them may be so severe as to preclude this. The speed with which they reverse is often dependent upon improvement in the underlying liver disease. But the reversal can be enhanced in many instances by administering the deficient substances, such as folate, pyridoxine, and iron, in addition to restoring a fully adequate diet.

CARDIOVASCULAR SYSTEM

A specific form of heart muscle disease is thought to result from long-term heavy alcohol use. Known in the past as *alcoholic car-*

diomyopathy, it is now referred to as *alcoholic heart muscle disease* (AHMD). This occurs in a clinically apparent form in 2% of alcoholics. However, it is estimated that 80% have similar though less severe, and therefore subclinical forms of alcohol-related heart muscle disease. When clinically apparent, AHMD is a severe condition with low-output heart failure, shortness of breath with the least exertion, and dramatic enlargement of the heart. Low-output failure refers to the heart's inability to pump the volume of blood necessary to meet the body's usual, normal demands. Most commonly, AHMD occurs in middle-aged men who have been drinking heavily for 10 or more years. It often responds well to discontinuing alcohol, plus long-term bed rest. As some have noted, "Abstinence makes the heart grow stronger." Other standard medical treatment for congestive heart failure is also helpful as adjuncts in the treatment of AHMD.

Another form of alcoholic heart disease, with high-output congestive heart failure, is known as *beriberi heart disease.* High-output heart failure is a form of secondary heart failure. It occurs when an otherwise normal heart fails because it can't keep up with the abnormally high rate of output being demanded by the body. For reasons that are unclear in this case, it results from a deficiency of vitamin B_1, thiamine. It may respond dramatically to correction of the thiamine deficiency and replacement of thiamine in the diet. As an aside a rather unusual and specific type of severe cardiac disease occurred a few years ago among drinkers of a particular type of Canadian beer. It was found to be caused not by alcohol per se but rather by the noxious effects of small amounts of cobalt. The cobalt had been added to the beer to maintain its "head." These cases occurred in the mid to late 1960s and had a mortality rate of 50% to 60%. Fortunately, the cause was identified, and presumably cobalt-induced heart disease will no longer occur. An earlier similar epidemic of congestive heart failure because of arsenic-contaminated beer occurred around the turn of the century in England.

A variety of *abnormalities in cardiac rhythm* have been associated with alcohol. In fact, nearly the entire spectrum of such abnormalities may be caused by acute and chronic alcohol intake. Arrhythmias, as they are called, may affect either the upper (atrial) or lower (ventricular) portions of the heart. The upper chambers of the heart are like the primers to the lower part, which acts as the pump. Thus ventricular rhythm irregularities involving the pumping action tend to be more serious. Atrial fibrillation and atrial flutter occur in the upper heart muscles and produce an ineffective atrial beat that diminishes the priming of the ventricular beat to follow. Another alcohol-induced irregular rhythm in the upper part of the heart is *paroxysmal atrial tachycardia.* This involves a different and more rapid than usual heartbeat. Alcohol also causes an increase in the frequency of premature ventricular contractions. These, along with atrial flutter and fibrillation, are the most common alcohol-induced arrhythmias. There are also irregular or in-between contractions of the lower part of the heart. These can create a very dangerous condition. If the irregular contractions occur in a particular pattern, which may be induced by alcohol, they can cause sudden death. In fact, studies have shown an increased incidence of sudden death in alcoholic populations. Another effect is *sinus tachycardia with palpitations*. This is thought to occur because of the effects of alcohol and its metabolite, acetaldehyde, in releasing norepinephrine. The sinus node is the normal pacemaker of the heart. Its rate of firing can be greatly increased by the amount of circulating epinephrine and norepinephrine.

Recently there have been reports of a new alcohol-induced, arrhythmia-related syndrome. It goes by the name *holiday heart syndrome*. As you might expect from the name, arrhythmias occur after heavy alcohol intake, around holidays and on Mondays after weekend binges. The syndrome involves palpitations and arrhythmias but no evidence of cardiomyopathy or congestive heart failure. The signs and symptoms clear completely after a few days of abstinence.

Even in moderate amounts, alcohol exacerbates certain abnormalities of blood fats in individuals with *Type IV hyperlipoproteinemia* but not in normal persons who don't have this condition. Alcohol elevates fat levels of a particular kind believed to increase the rate of development of arteriosclerosis (hardening of the arteries). The coronary arteries thus become increasingly occluded, or blocked, making premature heart attacks more likely. Even small amounts of alcohol can significantly affect this disorder in individuals at risk.

Alcohol is well known for causing dilation of peripheral superficial blood vessels and capillaries. It does not seem to have a similarly predictable effect on the coronary arterial blood vessels and the blood flow through them. Therefore, despite its use in treating angina in the past, currently this is not considered helpful. Recent studies indicate that in persons with angina, alcohol decreases exercise tolerance. In conjunction with vigorous exercise or physical activity, alcohol use by persons with angina may be especially dangerous.

Perhaps somewhat surprisingly, findings of recent research suggest that moderate amounts of alcohol (two or fewer drinks per day) may provide a protective effect against the occurrence of heart attacks in people without blood fat abnormalities. Such reports suggest that one cocktail per day has roughly the same effect on serum cholesterol as the average lipid-lowering diet or regular vigorous exercise. It leads to increased level of HDL cholesterol and decreased levels of LDL cholesterol. Higher and lower levels of these substances, respectively, are associated with lower risks of heart attacks. So moderate daily use of alcohol may be desirable from your heart's point of view.

In recent research a definite link was shown between heavy drinking and *hypertension*. Heavy drinkers had both elevated systolic and diastolic blood pressures. This was true even when weight, age, serum cholesterol level, and smoking were controlled. Although this relationship seems well established, the specific role alcohol plays in the development of atherosclerosis (the process by which hardening of the arteries occurs) is much less clear, especially in view of the multiple and complex interaction of factors causing this condition.

GENITOURINARY SYSTEM
Urinary tract

Almost uniquely, the kidneys are not commonly directly affected by alcohol in major ways. What happens in the kidneys generally is the result of disordered function elsewhere in the body. For example, alcohol promotes the production of urine through its ability to inhibit the production and output of antidiuretic hormone by the hypothalamic-pituitary region of the brain. The blood goes to the kidney for filtering, and water and wastes are separated from it and excreted through the bladder. Normally, in this process, antidiuretic hormone allows water to be reabsorbed by the kidney to maintain the body's fluid balance. When the hormone levels are suppressed, the kidney's capacity to reabsorb water is diminished. Instead, it is excreted from the body. Alcohol only inhibits this hormone's production when the blood alcohol level is rising. This is so after as little as 2 ounces of pure alcohol. When the blood alcohol level is steady, or falling, there is no such effect. In fact, the opposite may be true; body fluids may be retained. Alcohol can lead to acute urinary retention and recurrence and exacerbation of urinary tract infections and/or prostatitis. This is due to its ability to cause spasm and congestion in diseased prostate glands as well as in the tissues around previously existing urethral strictures.

It has recently been found that patients with alcoholic cirrhosis occasionally have abnormalities involving the glomeruli in their kidneys. The glomeruli are tiny structures at the extreme "upstream end" of the kidney's major functional unit, the nephron. They act as a sieve or a filter, collecting cells, serum proteins, and other elements to return to the general circulation. There are two main types of glomerular abnormality. The first, a variety of *glomerulosclerosis,* is the more common and rarely causes significant problems. The second, *cirrhotic glomerulonephritis,* fortunately far less common, interferes with the filtration process and elimination of the wastes produced by the kidney. Cirrhosis may cause additional troubles. It can cause retention of sodium, which may play a significant role in the ascites and edema of cirrhosis, abnormal handling of other ions, and an inability to excrete excess water normally. The causes of all these functional renal abnormalities, not fully understood, are complex and very likely caused by a number of factors in combination.

A nearly fatal but fortunately uncommon consequence of chronic alcohol use is the *hepatorenal syndrome*. This is thought to be caused by a toxic serum factor or factors secondary to severe liver disease. These factors cause shifts in kidney blood flow and impede its being effectively filtered by the kidney. Unless the underlying liver disease is somehow reversed, irreversible kidney failure can occur. Interestingly, there appears to be nothing intrinsically wrong with the kidneys themselves. They can be transplanted into a patient without underlying liver disease and perform normally. Likewise, liver transplantation in such patients will restore normal kidney function. Thus the kidney failure is thought to be due to some circulating toxic factor or factors presumably resulting from the associated liver disease.

Reproductive system

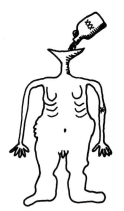

Chronic heavy alcohol use affects the reproductive system in both men and women. In women, there may be skipped menstrual periods; in men, diminished libido, impotence, and occasionally sterility may result. In addition to its many other functions, the liver plays an important role in the balance of sex hormones. So when the liver is impaired, an imbalance of sex hormones results.

Both male and female sex hormones are normally present in both sexes, only in different proportions. The increased levels of female hormones in alcoholic men, caused by the decreased liver metabolism of these hormones, can lead to "feminization" of features. Breasts can enlarge, testicles shrink, and a loss or thinning of body hair can occur. Sex-hormone alterations in males also result from alcohol's direct action on the testes, decreasing the production of testosterone, a male sex hormone. Ingestion of alcohol also may speed up the liver's metabolism of testosterone, thereby decreasing its levels. Testosterone levels may be lowered in other ways, such as by alcohol's direct inhibiting effect on the various brain centers involved in the production and release of luteinizing hormone (LH), which in turn prompts the release of testosterone. Thus when alcohol diminishes LH levels, the net effect is decreased testosterone levels. This brain-mediated hormonal effect of alcohol is a direct one, independent of any liver or nutritional problems.

Sex-hormone alterations in women are not as completely understood. In part, this is because the female reproductive system, located within the body, is less accessible to study and research. However, it is also because the effects of the use of alcohol by women as a distinct area of inquiry is a fairly recent development. Nonetheless, there is some evidence that alcohol may have direct toxic effects on both the ovaries and the pituitary. These are likely to play a role in the menstrual and fertility changes in female alcoholics.

Finally, although sexual interests and pursuits may be heightened by alcohol's release of inhibitions, ability to perform sexually can be impaired. For example, in men there may be either relative or absolute impotency, despite alcohol-fueled increased desire. Centuries ago Shakespeare in *Macbeth* (Act II, Scene 1) described these paradoxical effects of alcohol:

Macduff: What three things does drink especially provoke?

Porter: Merry, sir, nose-painting, sleep, and urine. Lechery, sir, it provokes, and unprovokes; it provokes the desire, but it takes away the performance.

Abstinence from alcohol, improvement in liver disease, and an adequate diet will reverse, though often not completely, the alcohol-induced changes in sexual and reproductive functions. Some males may also benefit from testosterone replacement.

ALCOHOL AND PREGNANCY
Fetal alcohol syndrome

Since 1971, considerable attention has been directed toward the effects of chronic alcohol use during pregnancy. At that time, a researcher reported his observations of infants born to alcoholic mothers. The constellation of features observed has since been termed *fetal alcohol syndrome*. Alcohol can pass through the placenta to the developing fetus and interfere with prenatal development. At birth, infants with fetal alcohol syndrome are smaller than normal, both in weight and length. The head size is smaller, probably related to arrested brain growth. These infants also have a "dysmorphic facial appearance," that is, they are strange looking, appearing "different," although the difference is not easily described. Changes include an overall small head, flat cheeks, small eyes, and a thin upper lip. At birth the infants are jittery and tremulous. Whether this jitteriness is the result of nervous system impairment from the long-term exposure to alcohol and/or mini-withdrawal is unclear. There have been reports of newborn infants having the odor of alcohol on their breath. Cardiac problems and retardation are also associated with the fetal alcohol syndrome in almost half of the cases (46%). In recent reports, FAS in combination with Fetal Alcohol Effects has been established as the leading cause of retardation in the United States—and the most preventable one. (See Chapter 6 for further discussion of the effects of maternal alcoholism on children.)

Fetal alcohol effects

It is now well established that a mother does not have to be an alcoholic to expose her unborn baby to the risks of alcohol during pregnancy. Nor do alcohol's effects on the fetus have to occur as the

Wine prepares the heart for love, unless you take too much.

OVID

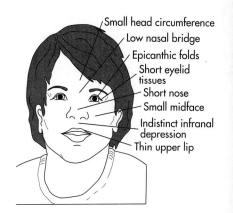

Small head circumference
Low nasal bridge
Epicanthic folds
Short eyelid tissues
Short nose
Small midface
Indistinct infranal depression
Thin upper lip

Facial effects of FAS.

full-blown fetal alcohol syndrome. They can occur with variable degrees of severity. When less severe, they are referred to as *fetal alcohol effects*.

Perhaps even more worrisome than the classical fetal alcohol syndrome are the reports documenting the adverse effects on the unborn baby of the mother's drinking more than two drinks (1 ounce of pure alcohol) on even a single occasion. As little as two drinks a day may lead to an increased risk of abnormalities. This two-drink figure is not a numerical average but refers to the amount of alcohol consumed on any one day. As the amount of alcohol consumed on any given day rises, the risk also increases:

Less than two drinks	Very little risk
Two to four drinks	10% risk of abnormalities
Ten drinks	50% risk of abnormalities
Over ten drinks	75% risk of abnormalities

Clearly, fetal alcohol effects are not restricted to the children of women who are alcoholics. Not unexpectedly, given similar findings with other drugs, the teratogenic effects of alcohol are greater in the first three months of pregnancy than they are in the fourth through ninth months. Based on this information, the NIAAA issued a health warning in the summer of 1977, advising expectant mothers not to have more than two drinks a day. In 1981 a much stronger warning was issued. The U.S. Surgeon General (the nation's highest public health official) advised that women wishing to become pregnant, as well as women who are pregnant, consume *no* alcohol.

How alcohol interferes with normal prenatal growth is not fully understood. Research with animals suggests that alcohol crosses the placenta freely and diffuses throughout fetal tissues in much the same fashion as it does in adults. As a toxin, alcohol disrupts the normal growth sequence; the developing fetus cannot later "make up" for these disruptions. The particular abnormalities seen are directly related to the critical development that was occurring when alcohol was present.

Preliminary research suggests, too, that the alcohol level of some of the fetal tissues may be higher than that of the mother. If this is in fact the case, the reason has not been clearly identified. One would predict that the alcohol, because it can pass freely through the placenta to the fetus, should be able to exit just as easily. Therefore both mother and fetus would be expected to have equivalent blood alcohol levels. Case reports of women who drank alcohol during labor, and in whom blood alcohol level studies were done, indicate that the newborn baby's blood alcohol and tissue alcohol levels do not drop as fast as the mother's. The reason presumably is that the infant has an immature liver. Newborns do not have the fully developed enzyme systems (alcohol dehydrogenase) necessary to metabolize and eliminate alcohol as rapidly as their mothers do.

Heredity. There are on record many instances of inebriety in children conceived soon after marriage (when the parents drank wine), although children born to the same parents later in life (when the parents abstained) were temperate. If the parent is intoxicated at the time of conception, the child is likely to be a victim to insanity, inebriety and idiosy. Mothers who indulge in intoxicants freely before the birth and during the lactation of their children impart to them impulses toward inebriety. . . .

SPOONER, WALTER, W.
The Cyclopaedia of Temperance and Prohibition, 1891.

Thus for a given maternal blood alcohol level, the fetus may have a somewhat higher blood and tissue alcohol concentration for a longer period of time than the mother.

With the passage of time since FAS and FAE were first recognized, there has been the opportunity to follow into adolescence and young adulthood those affected. The nature and extent of impairments found to be associated with FAS and FAE can only be characterized as devastating. Retardation is a common part of the picture. In a large group of FAS/FAE individuals, it was found that the average IQs of FAS and FAE patients were 68 and 73 respectively. Typically 100 is thought of as average. The range of IQ extended from 20 (severely retarded) to 105 (the normal range.) No FAS patient had an IQ of 90 or greater at follow-up. Thus there is some variation, and it is impossible to predict the severity of intellectual deficits. But what is evident is that both FAE as well as FAS individuals are at very high risk for diminished intellectual and adaptive functioning. In the study the average chronological age was 16.5 years, but in terms of general functioning and ability to get along in the world, the general level of functioning was 7.5 years. Impulsiveness, lack of social inhibition, and social naiveté are often problems. People with FAS can behave in a way that causes them problems because behavior is inappropriate and potentially dangerous or invites being exploited by others. Inappropriate sexual behavior is common. What as children or preteens may have been seen as others as their being very "friendly" and often involves touching and being physically close to others becomes socially less acceptable. Of all those studied, 95% had been in special education classes at some point during their school experience.

Most significantly with age there is *no general improvement*—in IQ, achievement, or ability to cope with everyday tasks. Of the group, only 5% lived alone and none were fully self-sufficient. The special needs of children with FAS/FAE persist through life. This means that some kind of protective services and special structure are necessary for many children with FAS/FAE throughout their life.

RESPIRATORY SYSTEM

Alcohol affects the respiratory rate. Low-to-moderate doses of alcohol increase the respiration rate. Presumably this is due to the direct action of the respiration center in the brain. In larger, anesthetic, and/or toxic doses, the respiration rate is decreased. This latter effect may contribute to respiratory insufficiency in persons with chronic obstructive pulmonary disease.

In the past, it was thought that alcohol for the most part spared the lungs as far as the direct harmful effects were concerned. This is apparently not the case. Recently such effects have been recognized and investigated. There is interference with a variety of important pulmonary cellular defenses—both mechanical and metabolic.

Normal cilia pushing dust out bronchial tree

drunk cilia with hangovers

This can be an important contribution to chronic airflow obstruction and possibly can produce bronchospasm in some individuals. The direct effects of alcohol on the lungs may have significant consequences for those with emphysema, chronic obstructive pulmonary disease, chronic bronchitis, and asthma.

There also are a variety of noxious effects that occur in an indirect fashion. The combination of stuporousness, or unconsciousness, and vomiting as the results of alcohol use can lead to aspiration of mouth and nose secretions or gastric contents. This can lead to bacterial infections. Because of an alcoholic's diminished defenses against infection, pulmonary infections, especially with pneumococci and gram-negative bacteria, seem to occur more frequently and severely than in nonalcoholics. Also because of the alcoholic's diminished defenses against infection, there is a higher incidence of tuberculosis. Thus any alcoholic with a newly positive skin test for tuberculosis should be considered for treatment to prevent possible active infection with tuberculosis bacteria.

ENDOCRINE SYSTEM

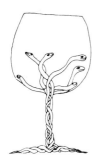

The endocrine system is composed of the glands of the body and their secretions, the hormones. Hormones can be thought of as chemical messengers, released by the glands into the bloodstream. They are vital in regulating countless body processes. There is a very complex and involved interaction between hormonal activity and body functioning.

Alcohol can affect the endocrine system in three major ways. Although there are many glands, the pituitary gland, located in the brain, can be thought of as the "master gland." Many of its hormonal secretions are involved in regulating other glands. One way that alcohol can affect the endocrine system is by altering the function of the pituitary. If this happens, other glands are unable to function properly because they are not receiving the proper "hormonal instructions." Alcohol can affect other glands directly. Despite their receiving the correct instructions from the pituitary, alcohol can impede their ability to respond. Finally, interference with the endocrine system can develop as a result of liver damage. One of the functions of the liver is to break down and metabolize hormones, thereby removing them from the system. Liver disease diminishes this capacity and hormonal imbalances can result.

Several hormonal changes have already been mentioned. As described, the level of testosterone, the male sex hormone, is lowered by alcohol in a number of different ways. First, it is lowered by the direct action of alcohol on the testes, and second, through alcohol's action on the pituitary and its subsequent failure to secrete LH, the hormone that stimulates the testes' secretion of testosterone. Another factor is that the liver's clearance of testosterone may be increased in the alcoholic. Finally, malnutrition, which frequently occurs in alcoholics, may inhibit the hypothalamic-pituitary-testicular axis at all levels.

Serious liver disease reduces the liver's ability to break down another of the pituitary's hormones, melanocyte-stimulating hormone (MSH). This may result in increased levels of MSH, which leads to a deepening of skin pigmentation and frequently a "dirty tan" skin color.

The adrenal glands are also affected by alcohol. The adrenal glands produce several hormones and thus serve multiple functions. One function known to us all comes from the release of adrenaline (epinephrine) when we are frightened or fearful. This charge of adrenaline, with its rapid heartbeat and sweating, makes up the "fight-or-flight" response. Heavy intake of or withdrawal from alcohol prompts increased discharge of catecholamines by the adrenals. This may be partly responsible for the rapid heartbeat and hypertension during withdrawal. Another adrenal hormone, aldosterone, which plays a major role in regulating the body's salt and water levels, is increased with both heavy use and in withdrawal. Increased aldosterone levels often lead to significant and potentially serious salt and water imbalances visible clinically as swelling (edema). Increased aldosterone level is frequently seen in cirrhosis with ascites. This is thought to be, in part, the cause of the peripheral edema that is often seen with this condition. In some alcoholics the adrenals secrete excess cortisol. The excess cortisol causes a condition clinically indistinguishable from Cushing's disease, except that it clears rapidly with abstinence from alcohol.

Animal research is raising several interesting questions about alcohol's effects on the endocrine system. In animals, heavy drinking increases the levels of norepinephrine in the heart. The question is being asked might increased levels of norepinephrine contribute to the development of alcoholic heart muscle disease?

As noted earlier, carbohydrate metabolism, ordinarily regulated by the hormone insulin, can be adversely affected by chronic alcohol intake. Heavy drinking may lead to abnormally high levels of glucose similar to those seen in diabetics. This condition is referred to as *hyperglycemia*. Usually all that is needed to correct this is abstinence from alcohol and an improved, well-balanced diet. Long-term excessive alcohol intake as well as short-term heavy drinking binges can, on the other hand, lead to low blood sugar levels, known as *hypoglycemia*. This disturbance in endocrine function has two causes. First, because of poor diet and liver dysfunction, there is decreased glycogen, the body's stored form of glucose usually available for conversion into circulating glucose. Second, there is a diminished ability by the liver to produce glucose on its own by converting amino acids into glucose, a process known as *glucogenesis*. Hypoglycemia can cause coma. If prolonged, irreversible brain damage can result. This is a medical emergency and must be treated as rapidly as possible.

The increased NADH to NAD$^+$ ratio is also a major function in causing two dangerous forms of metabolic acidosis frequently seen in alcoholics. The first is known as *alcoholic ketoacidosis*. It occurs when the altered ratio leads to the production not of carbon dioxide and water, as alcohol is metabolized, but of ketones, which are organic acids. The second, *lactic acidosis,* also occurs because of the altered ratio of NADH to NAD$^+$. In this case, there is an increased production of lactate. Both types of acidosis are dangerous and must be treated with intravenous fluids and sodium bicarbonate.

Another area of research is whether alcohol's effect on the endocrine system might contribute to the development of different types of cancer. Heavy drinkers are known to have a higher incidence of skin, thyroid, and breast cancers. Recall that the pituitary gland is the master control gland. It influences the activity of various other glandular tissues through the hormones it secretes. Alcohol inhibits the breakdown of pituitary MSH. It may also play a role in the release of hormones that promote thyroid activity and milk production by the breast. These three hormones have one thing in common: they affect their target tissues—the skin, thyroid gland, and breast—by causing these tissues to increase their metabolic activity. So, the pieces may be falling into place. Cancer, simply put, occurs when there is uncontrolled or abnormal cellular metabolic activity and growth. It is possible that alcohol's presence over long periods of time produces so many hormonal messages to the skin, thyroid, and breast tissues that in certain patients, in some as yet undetermined fashion, tumors may be produced.

SKIN

Chronic alcohol use affects the skin directly and indirectly. Its most pronounced direct effect is dilation of the vessels of the skin. A variety of pathological effects on other systems are recognized through the condition of the skin. For example, a chronic flushed appearance, itching, jaundice, thinning of the skin, changes in hair distribution, the presence of spider angiomas, a grayish cast to the skin, and fingernail changes *all* reflect significant liver dysfunction. Bruising, paleness, and skin infections may reflect major abnormalities in the hematological system.

Skin changes may suggest the presence of nutritional deficiencies in alcoholism. These include vitamin B, especially niacin—the deficiency of which causes pellagra—vitamin C, and zinc deficiencies. Skin manifestations often may reflect the chaotic life circumstances of many alcoholics. There may be evidence of accidents, such as bruises, abrasions, lacerations, and multiple old scars. In colder climates, there may be evidence of frostbite. Nicotine stains and/or cigarette burns may be present. Heavy and chronic alcohol use, among other causes, will precipitate or aggravate a condition

called *rosacea* in predisposed persons. This condition includes
flushing and inflammation, especially of the nose and middle portion of the face. Particularly striking is the excessive growth of the
subcutaneous tissue of the nose, a condition called *rhinophyma* or
"rum nose." Another skin condition associated with chronic alcoholism and alcoholic liver disease is *porphyria cutanea tarda*. This
includes increased pigmentation, hair growth, and blistering in sun-
exposed areas. It has been thought by some that there may be a
causal link between major primary skin diseases, such as psoriasis,
eczema, and scleroderma, and alcoholism. Others feel that it is
more likely that these conditions are simply much harder to manage
and therefore seem to be more severe in alcoholics because of concurrent medical problems, nutritional inadequacy, and poor treatment compliance often seen.

MUSCULOSKELETAL SYSTEM

Chronic alcohol use affects the skeletal system in three major
ways. First, there are at least four different types of arthritis that are
linked to heavy alcohol use. *Gouty arthritis* results from increased
uric acid levels. These levels can be increased in two ways. One is
as a result of the increased levels of organic acids that accompany
the altered ratio of NADH to NAD^+. In this instance the kidneys
try unsuccessfully to secrete both uric acid and as well as these
acids. Thus, excess amounts of uric acid accumulate. Another
comes from lead-contaminated "moonshine." The lead damages
the kidneys and leads to increased uric acid levels. In both cases,
abstinence and specific treatment for gouty arthritis may prove
beneficial. Arthritis occurs too in conjunction with *alcoholic pancreatitis*. This is believed to be caused by the direct or indirect damage to joints by the enzymes that are circulating in the bloodstream
as the result of damage to the pancreas. *Degenerative arthritis,* also
known as *osteoarthritis*, occurs more frequently with chronic heavy
alcohol use. This probably comes from the higher frequency of falls,
injuries, and fractures in alcoholics. *Septic arthritis* (infection in
the joint space) also is seen more frequently in those who drink
heavily. This is probably a result of several factors. Osteoarthritis,
which is more common in alcoholics, causes a roughened joint surface where bloodborne infectious agents may be more likely to set-
tle. Alcoholics are likely to have a higher incidence of blood-borne
bacterial infections for a number of reasons, including more frequent infections of all types, more frequent injuries, and less attention to hygiene. In general the alcoholic's defenses against such
infections are diminished.

Osteoporosis, a generalized thinning or demineralization of the
bones occurring especially in the elderly, is accelerated by heavy
alcohol use. This condition can lead to a 25% decrease in bone
mass, which in turn frequently leads to fractures. Fractures of the

hip (especially the neck of the femur), the wrist, the upper arm bone or humerus, and the vertebral bodies in the spinal column are most common. Rib fractures are also quite common in heavy drinkers, but they are probably caused by an increased frequency of falls and trauma rather than by changes in the bone. There are many possible causes of osteoporosis in alcoholics. They include alcohol-induced loss of calcium and/or magnesium through the kidneys, decreased absorption of calcium and/or vitamin D by the small intestine because of the effects of chronic alcohol use, and the demineralizing effects of adrenal corticosteriod hormones, the release of which is stimulated by alcohol.

Aseptic necrosis, or bone death, especially of the head of the femur, caused by inadequate blood supply to that region, is another condition especially frequent in alcoholic men. In fact, as many as 50% of those with this condition (of whom two thirds are men) have a history of heavy alcohol use. Deformity of the hip joint often results in and can lead to severe arthritis, which can be disabling and may eventually require total hip joint replacement. The cause is unknown but is postulated to be fat deposits, which are thought to be caused by pancreatitis or alcohol-induced abnormalities in the liver's metabolism of fats (see Chapter 2). These deposits lodge in the small arterial vessels supplying the femoral head and cut off essential nutrition and oxygen to that area.

NERVOUS SYSTEM

The central nervous system (CNS), of all the major organ systems, is perhaps most widely and profoundly affected by the effects of acute and chronic alcohol use. The major acute effect of alcohol on the CNS is that of a depressant. The common misconception that alcohol is a stimulant comes from the fact that its depressant action disinhibits many higher cortical functions. It does this in a somewhat paradoxical fashion. Through the depressant effects of alcohol, parts of the brain are released from their normal inhibitory restraints. Thus behavior that would ordinarily be "censured" can occur. Acute alcohol intoxication, in fact, induces a mild delirium. Thinking becomes fuzzy; and orientation, recent memory, and other higher mental functions are altered. An electroencephalogram (EEG) taken when someone is high would show a diffuse slowing of normal brain waves associated with this mild state of delirium. These acute effects are, of course, completely reversible.

Dependence, tolerance, and withdrawal

Chronic alcohol use can lead both to psychological dependence and physical dependence (the preferred phrase for addiction). Physical dependence is marked by the development of tolerance and withdrawal symptoms. What is tolerance? It refers to changes that occur as a result of repeated exposure to alcohol. There are changes in how the body handles the alcohol (metabolic tolerance) and changes in alcohol's impact on the nervous system (functional or behavioral tolerance). With the development of tolerance, there is both an increased rate of metabolism of alcohol and a decrease in behavioral impairment for a particular blood alcohol level. The non-tolerant individual will have a relatively constant and predictable amount of impairment for a given dose of alcohol.

As tolerance develops, the person requires increasing amounts of alcohol to get the effects previously produced by lower doses. Tolerance represents the nervous system's ability to adapt and function more or less normally despite the presence of alcohol. This adaptation occurs rapidly. For example, if the blood alcohol levels are raised slowly, virtually no signs of intoxication may be seen. The reason or reasons are unclear. The best guess is that long-term alcohol use produces subtle shifts or adjustments in nerve metabolism. Furthermore, even if the dose of alcohol leading initially to high blood alcohol levels is held constant, the blood alcohol level may fall somewhat and clinical evidence of intoxication may decrease. The basis for this metabolic tolerance has not been established. Chronic heavy drinkers often experience a sharp drop in tolerance well along in their drinking careers. Rather than being able to drink more, with only a drink or two they become intoxicated. This phenomenon is referred to as *reverse tolerance*. The reason for this drop in tolerance is thought to be related, in part, to the decreased ability of a diseased liver to metabolize alcohol. Recent research has also shown that some individuals are initially more tolerant to the intoxicating effects of alcohol than others. This inherent tolerance to the effects of alcohol turns out to be a major risk factor for the eventual development of alcoholism.

The most dramatic effects on the central nervous system are those associated with the abrupt cessation of alcohol intake, that is, the symptoms of acute withdrawal. Withdrawal is commonly considered to be the product of a long career of heavy drinking. However, a hangover on the "morning after" is in fact evidence of withdrawal. The hangover headache is most likely related to changes in the blood vessels and probably has nothing to do with the brain. The brain itself has no pain receptors. So any headache pain must be from the nerves of the surrounding lining, skin, vessels, muscles, or bones.

As classically considered, the individual who has regularly abused alcohol—that is, developed tolerance—will have withdrawal symptoms whenever there is a *relative* absence of alcohol. This means that although the person may still be drinking, the amount consumed is less than usual and therefore the blood alcohol level is lowered. The symptoms can include intention tremors (the shakes when he tries to do something), which are rapid and coarse, involving the head, tongue, and limbs. These will more likely be worse in the morning, assuming that the last drink was the night before and the blood alcohol level has dropped since then.

The withdrawal syndrome is the nervous system's response to the lack of alcohol. If the chronic alcohol drinker does not consume more alcohol, he is likely to develop other symptoms of withdrawal. It is thought to be a sort of rebound effect. In the absence of alcohol and its chronic suppressant effects, certain regions of the brain become overactive. The severity of the symptoms of withdrawal can vary widely, depending on the length of time of heavy drinking and the amount of alcohol consumed, plus individual differences in people. Symptoms of withdrawal can include tremulousness, agitation, seizures, and hallucinations. These will be discussed in detail later in this chapter.

Alcohol idiosyncratic intoxication (pathological intoxication)

Aside from withdrawal symptoms, other important CNS disorders are related to alcohol use. A relatively unusual manifestation is a condition previously called *pathological intoxication,* it was later classified as *alcoholic idiosyncratic intoxication.* (This category, however, has been dropped from DSM-IV.) Some susceptible persons, for reasons unknown, have a dramatic change of personality when they drink even small amounts of alcohol. It is a transient psychotic state with a very rapid onset. The individual becomes confused and disoriented; may have visual hallucinations; and may be very aggressive, anxious, impulsive, and enraged. In this state the person may carry out senseless, violent acts against others or himself. The state can last for only a few minutes or for several hours. Then the person lapses into a profound sleep and has amnesia for the episode. Were he to be interviewed later, he might be very docile, not at all the madman he was during the episode. Most likely he would report, "I don't know what happened; I just went bananas." It is unclear whether there is a relationship between this syndrome and other organic impulse disorders.

Organic brain disease

Chronic alcohol use can also lead to varying degrees of dementia or organic brain disease. The particular type of brain disease, its name and associated impairment, is determined by the portion of the brain involved. *Wernicke's syndrome* and *Korsakoff's psychosis* are two such syndromes closely tied to alcoholism. Sometimes they are discussed as two separate disorders. Other times people lump them together as the *Wernicke-Korsakoff syndrome.* Both are caused by nutritional deficiencies, especially thiamine, a B vitamin, in combination with whatever toxic effects alcohol has on nerve tissue. In addition, recent evidence suggests that a genetic factor in the form of an inherited lack of an enzyme (transketolase) may play an important role in the development of Wernicke-Korsakoff syndrome.

The difference in terms of pathology is that Wernicke's syndrome involves injury to the midbrain, cerebellum, and areas near the third and fourth ventricles of the brain, whereas Korsakoff's psychosis results from damage to areas of the brain important to memory function (the diencephalon, hypothalamus, and hippocampal formation) and is often associated with damage to peripheral nerve tissue as well. Prognostically, Wernicke's syndrome has a brighter picture. When recognized and treated early, it often responds very rapidly to thiamine therapy. Korsakoff's psychosis is much slower and less likely to improve. Someone with Korsakoff's psychosis will probably require nursing home or custodial care.

Clinically, a person with Wernicke's syndrome is apt to be confused, delirious, and apprehensive. There is a characteristic dysfunction called *nystagmus* and/or paralysis of the eye muscles that control eye movements. Nystagmus and other eye signs are often one of the first symptoms to appear and later, with treatment, to disappear. Difficulty with walking (ataxia) and balance are a typical part of Wernicke's syndrome. Both are caused by peripheral nerve damage or cerebellar damage.

Korsakoff's psychosis presents a somewhat different picture. There is severe memory loss and confabulation. Confabulation—that is, making up tales, talking fluently without regard to facts—is the hallmark. It occurs in an individual who is otherwise alert, responsive, and able to attend to and comprehend the written and spoken word. In other words, the memory impairment is greatly out of proportion to other cognitive dysfunctions. Because of the severe damage to areas of the brain crucial to memory, the person simply cannot process and store new information. In order to fill in the memory gaps, he makes up stories. These are not deliberate lies: trickery would require more memory and intent than someone with Korsakoff's psychosis could muster. For example, were you to ask someone with this disorder if he had met you before, the response might be a long, involved story about the last time the two of you had been together. It would be pure fantasy. This is the phenomenon of confabulation. Memory both for things that happened recently as well as long ago is variably but often severely impaired. Things simply are not stored for recall, and the person cannot remember events even 5 minutes after they occurred. With Korsakoff's psychosis, ataxia may also be present. Ataxia causes a characteristic awkward gait, with feet spread apart to assist in walking. Korsakoff's psychosis and Wernicke's syndrome can both have a sudden, rapid onset. However, it is not infrequently the case that Korsakoff's psychosis follows a bout of delirium tremens (the DTs).

Cerebral atrophy (generalized loss of brain tissue) often can occur in chronic alcoholism. Most typically this is seen in people in their 50s and 60s. Another name for this disorder is *alcoholic dementia.* A variety of factors common in alcoholics most likely combine to cause this condition. Treatment of these diseases includes administration of thiamine, a well-balanced diet, and discontinuation of alcohol. This treatment is more successful in reversing the signs and symptoms of Wernicke's syndrome. Only about 20% of persons with Korsakoff's psychosis recover completely. The recovery process is slow, taking perhaps from 6 months to 1 year. The mortality rate of the combined disorder is approximately 15%. The dementia associated with cerebral atrophy is irreversible. However, with abstinence and adequate nutrition it is probably likely to stabilize and not progress further.

Alcoholic cerebellar degeneration is a late complication of chronic alcohol use and nutritional deficiencies. It is more likely to occur in men, usually only after 10 to 20 years of heavy drinking. In such cases, patients gradually develop a slow, broad-based, lurching gait, as if they were about to fall over. This results from the fact that the cerebellum, the area of the brain that is damaged, is what coordinates complex motor activity. There is no associated cognitive or mental dysfunction because the portions of the brain governing such activities are not affected. But signs of peripheral neuropathy and malnutrition may be present.

Two forms of organic brain dysfunction are a direct result of severe alcoholic liver disease. These are known as acute and chronic *portosystemic encephalopathy (PSE).* They are caused by the diseased liver's diminished ability to prevent naturally occurring toxic substances from getting into the general body circulation (e.g., ammonia and glutamine, which are normally confined to the portal circulation). This raises havoc with the central nervous system. In both acute and chronic forms of PSE there may be cognitive and memory disturbances, changes in levels of consciousness—the extreme being so-called *hepatic coma*—a flaplike tremor, and a foul, musty odor to the breath. In the acute form, which is much less frequent, there is no evidence of chronic liver disease that is typically present in the chronic form. Along with abstinence from alcohol to enable the liver to normalize as much as possible, aggressive, multipronged medical management is aimed at reducing the body's production of toxic nitrogen-containing substances. A particularly severe variant of chronic PSE is known as *chronic hepatocerebral disease.* This is a complication of long-standing liver disease in which the brain is adversely affected by toxins chronically circulating in the bloodstream. As a result, the brain has areas of cell death and a proliferation of scarlike CNS cells. Mirroring these, there is a corresponding loss of function, with dementia, ataxia, speech impairment (dysarthria), and sometimes bizarre movements. Scarred or damaged brain tissue cannot be repaired, so any such losses are permanent. Patients with this condition often require chronic care facilities.

Two final organic brain diseases, which are quite obscure but serious, are also related to alcohol abuse and nutritional deficien-

In some Cases
a flap-like Tremor
and a foul breath
does not indicate
Porto Systemic
encephalopathy.
It indicates you
are examining a seal.

cies. First, *central pontine myelinolysis* involves a part of the brain-stem known as the *pons*. This disease can vary in intensity from being unapparent to fatal over a 2- to 3-week period. The pons controls respiration, among other things. As it degenerates, coma and finally death occur from respiratory paralysis. Second, *Marchiafava-Bignami disease,* also exceedingly uncommon, involves the nerve tracts connecting the frontal areas on the two sides of the brain. Their degeneration leads to diminished language and motor skills, gait disorders, incontinence, seizures, dementia, hallucinations, and frequently eventual death.

A term one sometimes hears in discussion of alcohol's chronic effects on the central nervous system is "wet brain." There is no specific medical condition that goes by this name. Probably it developed colloquially among lay people to encompass the variety of nonreversible organic brain syndromes that cause significant mental impairment and diminished physical capacity such that those affected require nursing home care.

Nerve and muscle tissue damage

Nerve tissue other than the brain tissue can be damaged by chronic alcohol use. The most common disturbance is *alcoholic polyneuropathy* from nutritional deficiencies. This has a gradual onset and progresses slowly. Recovery is equally slow and generally

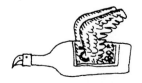

incomplete, taking weeks to months with discontinuation of alcohol, plus appropriate vitamins. Most commonly the distal nerves (those farthest from the body trunk) are affected first. The damage to these nerves seems to be caused primarily by nutritional deficiencies, though direct toxic effects of alcohol may be involved. Typically, someone with polyneuropathy will have a painful burning of the soles of the feet, yet an absence of normal sensation. Because there is sensory impairment, the Individual isn't getting feedback to the brain to tell him how this body is positioned. This loss of position sense may lead to a slapping style of walk because he's unsure of where his feet and legs are in relation to the ground.

Muscle damage often accompanies nerve damage. In turn, muscle tissue is usually wasted in the areas affected by nerve damage. Muscles are improperly nourished in some fashion if there is surrounding nerve damage. Other forms of muscle damage and degeneration have been reported even in the absence of neuropathy. One form involves acute muscle pain, swelling, and destruction of muscle tissue in the aftermath of acute binges and is referred to as acute *alcoholic myopathy*. Another form seen in chronic heavy drinkers is *chronic alcoholic myopathy* and involves the proximal muscles (those nearer the body trunk). Yet another type of muscle damage may result when a person is intoxicated, passes out, and lies in the same position for a long time. With constant pressure of body weight on the same muscles, pressure *necrosis* can result, leading to muscle degeneration, which like any other myopathy means that certain muscle proteins (myoglobins) are released into the bloodstream. If these muscle protein levels are too high, kidney failure can occur. Potassium is also a product of such muscle tissue breakdown. An increase in the level of potassium can disturb mineral balance throughout the body. For reasons that are currently unclear, alcoholics are known to be very prone to muscle cramps.

Finally, an entity known as *alcohol-tobacco amblyopia* (dimness of vision) is another nervous system disorder. As the name implies, it is associated with chronic, excessive drinking and smoking. It is characterized by slow onset of blurred, dim vision with pain behind the eye. There is difficulty reading, intolerance of bright light, and loss of central color vision. Although blind spots can occur eventually, total blindness is uncommon. The cause is thought to be a vitamin deficiency coupled with the toxic effects of alcohol. Treatment includes B-complex vitamins, plus abstinence, and is usually effective in reversing the eye symptoms. Typically, recovery is slow and only partial.

Subdural hematoma

An indirect result of chronic alcoholism is the increased frequency of subdural hematomas. These can be the result of falling down and striking the head, being assaulted, or being in an auto accident, all of which are more frequent occurrences when an individual is intoxicated. Any such injury to the head can cause tearing of the vessels of the brain lining, the dura, with bleeding as a result. The skull is a rigid box, so any bleeding inside this closed space exerts pressure on the brain. The bleeding can be very serious, even life threatening, and often is not recognized. Signs and symptoms can vary widely, although fluctuating states of consciousness (i.e., drifting in and out of consciousness) are often associated with this. Treatment involves removal of the blood clot.

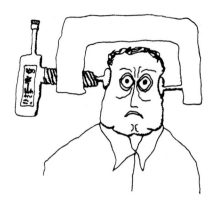

Miscellaneous CNS disturbances

Other neurological conditions occur with increased frequency in alcoholics. These include bacterial meningitis, seizures following head trauma, and concussive syndrome. Strokes (cerebrovascular accidents) and brain hemorrhages seem to occur with increased frequency during acute alcohol intoxication. Whether this is also true in cases of chronic alcoholism has yet to be proven.

NEUROPSYCHOLOGICAL IMPAIRMENT

Personality change has long been regarded as an aspect of chronic alcohol use. Historically this was chalked up to serious underlying psychological problems. Then the emphasis shifted to viewing the "alcoholic personality" as a lifestyle the alcoholic developed to rationalize his alcoholic problems and to protect his right to drink. There was little systematic research to explore a physiological basis, if any, and to correlate it to personality changes. This is now changing. Neuropsychological research, using psychometric tests, has uncovered specific impairments associated with alcohol abuse.

Overall intellectual deterioration is not seen until very late in the course of alcoholism. The IQ of most alcoholics, especially verbal IQ, remains relatively intact and normal. Nonetheless, there are other specific deficits, including decreased ability to solve problems, a lessened ability to perform complex psychomotor tasks, a decreased ability to use abstract concepts, and memory impairment. Drinking history is the major factor determining severity of impairments. How much alcohol has been consumed and for how long are the questions to be asked. These deficits tend to improve with abstinence. The first 2 to 3 weeks bring the most dramatic improvement. After that, improvement is gradual for the next 6 months to 1 year. It is important to realize that the improvement, though considerable, is not necessarily complete.

The areas of the brain that seem to be the most affected are the frontal lobes and the right hemisphere. This may help to explain the profound personality changes associated with chronic alcohol use. In fact, some of the behaviors accompanying alcoholism, such as "inability to abstain" and "loss of control," may partially be a product of organ-

ic brain dysfunctions. Most of this impaired functioning is subtle, not readily apparent. In fact, many of those in the clinical studies documenting neuropsychological impairment seemed "normal." They often were described as "young, intelligent, and looking much like any other citizen." That should alert us to the possibility that such alcohol-related brain damage may be more widespread than previously thought.

MISCELLANEOUS EFFECTS

Alcohol is also related to a variety of other signs, symptoms, and conditions that do not fit neatly into a discussion of a particular organ system.

Hodgkin's disease is a form of lymphatic cancer that, although certainly very serious, is becoming more and more treatable. Many persons with Hodgkin's disease who drink may experience pain in the regions affected by the disease. Alcohol abuse may also be associated with *Dercum's disease,* which is characterized by symmetrical and painful deposits of fat around the body and limbs.

An interesting property of alcohol is its ability to alleviate dramatically the tremor in persons with *familial tremor.* As suggested by the name, this condition runs in families. It may occur in relatively young persons, through it is more common in the elderly. The cause is unknown. To account for the heavier-than-expected drinking seen in many patients with this condition, it has been hypothesized that they might be medicating themselves by drinking, thereby inviting alcoholism. Fortunately, other drugs are as effective as alcohol for this condition and are much safer.

Alcohol abuse is associated with a variety of metabolic disorders, including the following:

- *Hyperuricemia,* that is, elevated uric acid levels in the blood, causing a number of medical complications.
- *Diminished potassium levels* (hypokalemia) caused by excess mineral-regulating hormone (aldosterone), associated with cirrhosis and ascites.
- *Decreased magnesium levels* in the blood, probably from the direct effect of alcohol on the kidneys' handling of magnesium along with decreased oral intake and increased loss through the GI system.
- *Metabolic acidosis,* an increase of hydrogen ion concentration in the blood from altered liver metabolic functioning.
- *Decreased levels of calcium and phosphate* are seen frequently in alcoholics. Neither the cause nor clinical significance of these is well understood.

Described here are the many medical complications frequently associated with chronic heavy drinking and/or alcoholism. It is important, however, to realize that health problems can arise from any alcohol use. One does not have to be an alcoholic or problem drinker. Increasingly, alcohol use is being considered a risk factor for the development of a variety of illnesses. The earlier general notion that alcohol poses a health hazard "only if you really drink a lot" is going by the wayside.

SLEEP AND SLEEP DISTURBANCES IN ALCOHOLICS

Many people say they can't sleep unless they have a drink or two before bedtime "to relax." Actually, alcohol interferes with sound sleep. To understand this, let's look at how people sleep, how alcohol affects normal sleep, and what can be done for clients who cannot sleep after they have stopped drinking.

Scientists have studied sleep by recording brain waves of sleeping subjects on an EEG. Everyone sleeps in basically the same way. There are four stages of sleep: stage 1, stage 2, delta, and REM. Each stage has characteristic brain-wave patterns. These stages occur in a fairly predictable sequence throughout the night.

Sleep patterns

Before we can fall asleep, we need to relax. This is a fairly individualized affair—what might relax one person would stimulate someone else. Some relax best in a dark, quiet bedroom; others need a loudspeaker blasting rock music before they can let go. In either case, as soon as one becomes drowsy, the brain will show alpha waves. Next comes the transition period, a time when one is half asleep and half awake. This is called *stage 1*. One still feels awake but does not attend to input from the environment. Brief dream fragments or images may occur at this time. Stage 1 sleep lasts anywhere from 2 to 10 minutes in normal sleepers, but it can last all night in some recovering alcoholics. Finally, there comes the real thing—sleep. The average, nondreaming sleep is called *stage 2*, and we spend about 50% to 60% of our sleep in this stage. Stage 2 is a medium deep and restful sleep, and the first episode of it will last about 20 to 45 minutes.

Gradually, sleep deepens until we are in the most sound sleep of the night—*delta sleep*. The length of time one spends in delta sleep depends on age, ranging from up to several hours in children to little or none in older age groups. Delta sleep is mainly concentrated in the early part of the night and rarely occurs after approximately the first 3 hours of sleep. After delta sleep, we return to stage 2 sleep for awhile. Then, about 60 to 90 minutes after falling asleep, the most exciting sleep begins. This is rapid eye movement, *REM sleep*. The brain waves now resemble a waking pattern. The eyes are moving rapidly under closed eyelids, but the body is completely relaxed (in fact, paralyzed) and asleep. During REM sleep we dream. The first dream of the night lasts about 5 minutes. Following it, there is a return to stage 2, possibly some delta sleep again, but it is not quite as deep as the first time. The second dream sleep of the night occurs about 3 hours after sleep onset and lasts about 10 minutes.

The cycle of alternating nondreaming (stage 2) and dreaming (REM) sleep continues throughout the night. Dreams occur about every 90 minutes. As the night goes on, nondreaming sleep becomes shorter, and dreaming (REM) sleep becomes longer. You can see that we are guaranteed about four dreams in 6 hours of sleep. In fact, you dream for about 20% of an average night. During dreaming, part of the brain is awake, part is not. For example, the long-range memory part of the brain does not function during dreaming. So, to remember a dream, you have to wake up from it and think about the dream immediately after you awaken. (Because dreaming is a light state of sleep, one often wakes up from it.) Someone who reports dreaming a lot either is not sleeping very well, and therefore wakes up a lot, or thinks about the dreams a lot just after waking. Someone who claims never to dream is probably a reasonably sound sleeper, with few awakenings. That person probably also jumps right out of bed upon waking and therefore forgets the dreams. Someone who claims to be dreaming "more" lately has either become more interested in himself and things more about his dreams or is waking up more because he has developed poorer sleep.

Sleep seems to be good for both body and mind. Stage 2 and especially delta sleep are thought to be mainly body-recovery sleep. When this sleep functions well, the body feels refreshed on awakening in the morning. Dreaming sleep, on the other hand, has something to do with our psychological recovery. People do not go crazy if they are deprived of dreams, as was originally believed, but they lose some psychological stability. Someone who is usually very reliable, stable, and punctual may become irresponsible, irritable, and impulsive if deprived of REM sleep. As to the amount of sleep someone needs, the old 7 to 8 hours rule is useless. It depends on the individual. Some people do perfectly well with only 2 or 3 hours; 12 hours are necessary for others.

Sleep disturbances

Why do we need sleep? Take it away and see what happens! Despite what most of us think, an occasional sleepless night is not all that devastating. Although you might feel awful and irritable, total loss of sleep for one or two nights has surprisingly little effect on normal performance and functioning. Two exceptions are very boring tasks, such as watching radar blips or driving long distances, and very creative tasks, such as writing an essay. These are affected by even one night of very little sleep. On the other hand, for most jobs of average interest and difficulty, if one really tries to do so, one can draw on one's reserves and "rally" to the task even after two to four totally sleepless nights.

Three brain systems regulate the state of our existence: the awake or arousal system (the reticular activating system), the sleep system, and the REM (dreaming) system. There is a continual struggle among the three, each trying to dominate the other two. The three different systems have different anatomical bases in the brain and apparently run on different neurochemicals. If you influence these neurochemicals, you disturb the balance among the three systems. Alcohol does disturb these neurochemicals.

It is not too difficult to disturb the balance between the waking and the sleeping systems for a few days. Stress and stimulants, such as coffee and Dexedrine, will strengthen the waking system; sleeping pills will help the sleeping system. However, after just a few days or weeks, the brain chemistry compensates for the imbalance, and the chemicals become ineffective. Therefore after just 1 month on sleeping pills, an insomniac's sleep will be as poor as ever. There is even some evidence that the continued use of sleeping pills in itself causes poor sleep. Furthermore, when the sleeping pill is withdrawn, sleep will become extremely poor for a few days or weeks because the brain's chemical balance is now disturbed in the opposite direction. Many people stay on sleeping pills for decades even though the pills do not really help them because of this "rebound insomnia" when they try to sleep without drugs. Because one sleeps so poorly for awhile when withdrawing from the chronic use of sleeping pills, caution should be used. Go slowly, cutting down on the use of sleeping pills in very gradual doses over a period of weeks. Abrupt withdrawal from some sleeping pills can be dangerous and even cause seizures. In addition, practically all sleeping pills, contrary to advertising, suppress dreaming sleep. After stopping the pills, the dreaming sleep increases in proportion to its former suppression. It then can occupy from 40% to 50% of the night. Dreaming sleep, too, takes 10 days or so to get back to normal. During these days there is very little time for deep sleep because dreaming takes up most of the night..

You feel exhausted in the morning because you had very little time for body recovery. Nonetheless, people who have taken heavy doses of sleeping pills for a long time often sleep better after being withdrawn than they did while taking them. It is all right to take a sleeping pill on rare occasions, say before an important interview, or after three to four nights of very poor sleep. However, it rarely makes any sense to take sleeping pills regularly for more than a week or two.

Insomnia

Insomnia can be based on either an overly active waking system or a weak sleeping system. On rare occasions insomnia can have an organic or genetic basis. Some people have a defective sleep system from birth. However, most insomnias are based on psychological factors. Any stress, depression, or tension will naturally arouse the waking system. When this is the case, the cure obviously involves helping the person deal with the psychological stress.

Surprisingly, poor sleep is often little more than a bad habit! Say you went through a stressful life situation a few years back and, quite naturally, couldn't sleep for a few nights because of it. Being very tired during the day after a few bad nights, you needed sleep more and more. So you tried harder and harder to get to sleep; but the harder you tried, the less you could fall asleep. Soon a vicious cycle developed. Everything surrounding sleep became emotionally charged with immense frustration, and the frustration alone kept you awake.

How can this cycle be broken? The treatment is simple and effective, provided you stick with it. The first step is to recognize you are misusing the bed by lying in it awake and frustrated. The specific rules for treatment are as follows:

1. Whenever you can't fall asleep relatively quickly, get up because you are misusing the bed. You can do your "frustrating" somewhere else, but not in the bedroom.
2. As soon as you are tired enough and think you might fall asleep quickly, go to bed. If you can't fall asleep quickly, get up again. This step is to be repeated as often as necessary, until you fall asleep quickly.
3. No matter how little sleep you get on a given night, you have to get up in the morning at the usual time.
4. No daytime naps!

If you stick to this regimen for a few weeks, the body again becomes used to falling asleep quickly. Therapists trained in this type of behavioral treatment may be of considerable help and support.

Shortening the time spent in bed is also crucial to many insomniacs. Because they haven't slept during the night, many insomniacs stay in bed for half the morning. They want to catch a few daytime naps, or they feel too tired and sick after not sleeping to get up. Pretty soon they lie in bed routinely for 12, 14, even 20 hours. They sleep their days away while complaining of insomnia. It is important that one maintain a regular day/night rhythm, with at least 14 to 16 hours out of bed, even if the nights are marred by insomnia. In some individuals, undiagnosed medical disorders or physical disturbances during sleep may give rise to insomnia. If insomnia problems persist for months or years, it is a good idea to consult with a doctor or a specialist in sleep disorders.

Alcohol's effects on sleep

How does alcohol affect sleep? Many find that a nightcap "fogs up" an overly active waking system. No question, some people can fall asleep faster with a drink. However, alcohol depresses REM (dreaming) sleep and causes more awakenings later at night. The drinker frequently wakes many times throughout the night, which results in a lack of recovery during sleep. These effects continue in chronic drinkers. In addition, the pressure to dream becomes stronger the longer it is suppressed. The dreaming sleep system will finally demand its due. Thus after a binge there is a tremendous recovery need for dreaming. It is thought that part of the DTs and the hallucinations of alcohol withdrawal can be explained by a lack of sleep (many awakenings) and a pressure to dream (lack of REM). The great fragmentation of sleep and lack of delta and REM sleep in chronic alcoholics is a serious problem. Even though they think they sleep well, there is little or no recovery value in it. This very poor sleep makes people want to sleep longer in the morning and during the day, which adds to the usual problem of coping.

Another sleep problem of real concern to alcoholics is that of *sleep apnea*. This is a relatively common breathing disturbance in which a person's air passages become obstructed during sleep. It is especially common in older individuals and those who are overweight. Alcohol markedly worsens sleep apnea and puts the affected individual at serious risk for medical complications that can be life-threatening. Frequent, loud snoring is often a good indicator of this problem.

What happens to sleep when the booze is taken away from a chronic alcoholic? First, there is the rebound of dreaming. Increased dreaming can last up to 10 days before subsiding. Often there are nightmares because dreaming is so intense. The sleep fragmentation lasts longer. A loss of delta sleep can go on for as long as 2 years after drinking ceases. Sober alcoholics, as a group, still have more sleep disturbances than nonalcoholics. We don't know why. It could be due to some chronic damage to the nervous system during binges, as has been produced in alcoholic rats, or it could be that some alcoholics were poor sleepers to start with. In any case, it appears that the longer one can stay on the wagon, the more sleep will improve.

BLACKOUTS

Having covered a multitude of physical disorders associated with alcohol abuse, it would seem that there is nothing left to go wrong! Yet there remains one more phenomenon associated with alcohol use that is highly distinctive: *the blackout*. Contrary to what the name may imply, it does not mean passing out or losing consciousness. Nor does it mean psychological blocking out of events, or repression. A blackout is an amnesia-like period that is often associated with heavy drinking. Someone who is or has been drinking may appear to be perfectly normal. He or she seems to function quite normally with the task at hand. Yet later, the person has no memo-

ry of what transpired. A better term might be *blank out*. The blank spaces in the memory may be total or partial. A person who has been drinking and who experiences a "blank out" will not be able to recall how the party ended, how he got home, how he landed the 747, how he did open-heart surgery, or how the important decisions were made at a business lunch. As you can imagine, this spotty memory can cause severe distress and anxiety, to say nothing of being dangerous in certain circumstances.

What causes blackouts? The exact mechanisms are not fully understood; but, apparently, during a blackout, memory function is severely and selectively impaired by alcohol, while virtually all other spheres of affect—cognition, behavior, and brain function—remain relatively intact. Up to one third of alcoholics report never having had a blackout. Some alcoholics have blackouts frequently, whereas others only have them occasionally. Recent research indicates that blackouts occur in nonalcoholics who have drunk more heavily than they usually do and to the point of intoxication. However, blackouts have usually been associated with alcoholism that is at a fairly advanced stage. And thus they are thought to be generally, although nonspecifically, dose dependent and dose related. As a general rule, the greater the severity of the alcoholism (the heavier the drinking and the greater the number of years over which is has occurred), the more likely the occurrence of blackouts. There is also a positive relationship between the occurrence of blackouts and the extent and duration of alcohol consumption during any given drinking episode. Several other factors correlate with the occurrence of blackouts in alcoholics: poor diet, high tolerance, a previous head injury, and the tendency to gulp drinks.

The current research findings on blackouts differ in significant respects from the frequently quoted work of Jellinek done in the 1950s. Recall that in describing the phases of alcohol addiction (Chapter 3), Jellinek focused on blackouts as heralding the onset of the prodromal phase. Thus he suggested that they were an early manifestation of the disease or denoted those persons who had a high risk of later developing it. He felt that blackouts had a high degree of specificity in predicting eventual alcoholism. Other studies done recently have found that 30% to 40% of young- to middle-aged, light-to-moderate (social) drinkers have had at least one alcohol-induced blackout. Typically, it occurred on one of the few occasions when they were truly inebriated. In fact, among these individuals, blackouts seem to be more frequent among those who generally are light drinkers.

How are the disparities between the old and new research findings reconciled? One possibility is that individuals vary in their "susceptibility" to blackouts. Accordingly, those people who experience the blackout-producing effect of alcohol may find it so frightening and unpleasant that they will be strongly motivated to drink in moderation. Others, possibly with a genetic predisposition to alcoholism,

We were to do more business after dinner; but after dinner is after dinner—an old saying and a true, 'much drinking, little thinking'.

JONATHAN SWIFT, 1768

may have a naturally high "tolerance" to blackouts. Consequently, they will not experience them until relatively late in their drinking careers, after the disease of alcoholism has been established. In effect, those who become alcoholics, not having experienced blackouts earlier, may have been deprived of an important physiological warning signal.

What is evident, despite the still limited research, is that for some reason, in some people, alcohol selectively interferes with the mechanisms of memory. Memory is one of the many functions of the brain, a complex process that in general is still poorly understood. We can recall and report what happened to us 5 minutes ago. Similarly, many events of yesterday or a week ago can be recalled. In some cases, our memories can extend back many years or even decades. Psychological and neuropsychological research has identified different types of memory, categorizing them into immediate, short-term (recent), and long-term memory. Memory of whatever type involves the brain's capacity to receive, process, and store information. According to one popular theory of memory function, the brain has at least two different kinds of "filing systems" for information. Immediate memory is stored for very short periods electrochemically. Long-term memory involves a biochemical storage system that is relatively stable over long periods. Short-term, or recent, memory is a way station somewhere between these two that is thought to involve the process of conversion of electrochemical brain activity into stable neuronal, probably protein macromolecules. It is hypothesized that this is the point at which alcohol exerts its influence to impair memory function. It is suspected that this occurs because alcohol interferes with the metabolic production of proteins by certain neuronal cells. This in turn inhibits the brain's ability to move short-term memory into longer-term storage. Although alcohol interferes with the "conversion process," it does not seem to interfere directly with the electrochemical basis of immediate memory (events occurring during the blackout itself) or for events from before the blackout (those already stored in long-term memory banks as stable protein macromolecules). This could account for the seemingly normal appearance and function of the person in a blackout, even with respect to relatively complicated tasks.

The amnesia that occurs during a blackout is typically one of two types. It may be sudden in onset, complete, and permanent, or it can lack a definite onset and be something that the person is unaware of until he is reminded of or spontaneously recalls the forgotten event. In the latter instance recall is usually dim and incomplete. Interestingly, in such cases recall may be enhanced by the use of alcohol. This facilitation of recall by alcohol is thought to reflect the phenomenon of state-dependent learning, in which whatever has been learned is best recalled when the person is in the same state or condition that existed at the time of the original learning.

In conclusion, there has been discussion of blackouts being employed as a defense in criminal proceedings. Although a novel approach, it would appear that there is no evidence to support the contention that a blackout alters judgment or behavior at the time of its occurrence. The only deficiency appears to be in later recalling what occurred during the blackout. Of course, having no memory of an event would make it difficult to prepare a case or decide from one's own knowledge whether to plead guilty or innocent. It is hoped that more will be learned about blackouts. Research is difficult because it depends almost entirely on anecdotal self-report. Thus far, no one has found a predictable way to produce blackouts experimentally. Nor can one know for sure when a spontaneous blackout is occurring. Thus to date it has not been possible to use new, highly sophisticated neurological diagnostic techniques that might help us understand the neurophysiological basis of blackouts.

WITHDRAWAL

Alcohol is an addictive drug. When taken in sufficient quantities, the body, particularly the CNS, becomes adapted or accustomed to its presence. Drinking as much as a quart of liquor daily for 1 week can create a state of physical dependence. After physical dependence has been established, if consumption is curtailed there will be symptoms. Taken together, these symptoms constitute the so-called *abstinence or withdrawal syndrome.* One sure way to terminate an abstinence syndrome is to administer more of the addictive drug.

One aspect of physical dependence, a term that is replacing addiction, is that tolerance develops. Over the long haul, increasing amounts of the drug for which tolerance has been established are necessary to achieve the same effect and to continue to ward off withdrawal symptoms. The withdrawal symptoms for any drug are generally the reverse of the effects induced by the drug itself. Alcohol is a depressant. Therefore the alcohol abstinence syndrome is characterized by symptoms that are indicative of an activated state. A hangover, a kind of mini-withdrawal, testifies to this. The well-known symptoms of jumpiness, edginess, irritability, and hyperactivity are the exact opposite of alcohol's depressant qualities.

The physiological basis of withdrawal is hypothesized to be related to alcohol's depressant effects on the CNS. With regular heavy use of alcohol, the activity of the CNS is chronically depressed. With abstinence, this chronic depressant effect is removed. There follows a "rebound" hyperactivity. An area of the CNS particularly affected is the *reticular activating system,* which modulates or "oversees" the general level of CNS arousal and activity. The duration of the withdrawal syndrome is determined by the time required for this "rebound" overactivity to be played out and a normal baseline level of neurophysiological functioning to be reestablished. Studies of

CNS activity with EEGs during heavy drinking, abstinence, and withdrawal support this.

Not everyone physically dependent on alcohol who stops drinking has the same symptoms. In part, the severity of the withdrawal state will be a function of how long someone has been drinking and how much. Another big factor is the drinker's physical health plus his unique physiological characteristics. Therefore accurately predicting the difficulties with withdrawal is impossible. Despite the phrase *abstinence syndrome,* withdrawal can occur even while someone continues to drink. The key factor is a *relative lowering* of the blood alcohol level. Thus *relative abstinence* is the condition that triggers withdrawal. This phenomenon often prompts the alcoholic's morning drink. He is treating his withdrawal symptoms.

Withdrawal syndromes

Four different major withdrawal syndromes have been described in conjunction with alcohol. Although they can be distinguished for the purpose of discussion, clinically the distinctions are not so neat. In reality, these syndromes blend together.

The earliest and most common sign of alcohol withdrawal is a generalized state of *hyperarousal.* This can include anxiety, irritability, insomnia, loss of appetite, rapid heartbeat (tachycardia), and tremulousness. Avoiding this state often is what motivates the actively drinking alcoholic to have a morning or midday drink. Recall that with increasing tolerance, increasing amounts of an addictive drug are necessary to ward off withdrawal symptoms and only a relatively lowered blood alcohol concentration (BAC) is necessary to induce withdrawal. An alcoholic who is used to drinking heavily in the evenings is eventually going to find himself feeling shaky the next morning. The BAC will have fallen from the level of the night before. A drink, by raising the BAC, will take this discomfort and edginess away. With time, further boosts of booze during the course of the day may be necessary to maintain a BAC sufficient to prevent the shakes. As tends to be the case with all addicting drugs, progressively increasing amounts of alcohol will be consumed, not for their positive effects but as a means of avoiding withdrawal symptoms.

If the physically dependent person abstains completely, there will be a marked increase of symptoms. The appearance is one of stimulation. The alcoholic will startle easily, feel irritable, and in general be "revved up" in a very unpleasant way. He will have a fast pulse, increased temperature, elevated blood pressure, sweating, dilated pupils, a flushed face, and trouble sleeping. Usually these symptoms subside over 2 or 3 days. The shakes will disappear, and the vital signs will return to normal. However, feeling awful, being irritable, and having difficulty sleeping can persist for 2 to 3 weeks or even longer. Although the judicious use of medication (benzodiazepines) may

I figure when I can't pop the pop top it's time to stop.

make the withdrawal process more tolerable by lessening the severity of symptoms, this acute withdrawal syndrome by itself often does not require medical treatment. But it is important that the person not be left alone and be carefully observed for signs of incipient DTs. When the acute stage passes, the probability of developing DTs is greatly lowered. However, if the acute symptoms do not resolve or if they should worsen, beware. Be sure the person is evaluated by a physician because such symptoms indicate that the progression to DTs is likely.

Another syndrome of alcoholic withdrawal is *alcoholic hallucinosis*. This condition occurs in some 25% of those withdrawing from alcohol. It is usually seen early, within the first 24 hours of withdrawal. It includes true hallucinations, both auditory and visual. It also includes illusions, the misperception or misinterpretation of real environmental stimuli. However, the individual with hallucinosis is oriented to person, place, and time. Very bad nightmares often accompany this withdrawal syndrome. It is believed that the nightmares may be due to REM rebound following the release from alcohol's long suppression of dreaming sleep. This rebound effect usually clears by the end of the first week of withdrawal. In a small number of cases, however, a chronic and persistent form of the syndrome may develop and continue for weeks to months. Acute alcoholic hallucinosis is not dangerous in itself and does not necessarily require specific medical treatment. It is important, however, to recognize it as a common withdrawal phenomenon and not be misled into thinking that the hallucinations are necessarily indicative of an underlying primary psychiatric disorder.

The chronic form of alcoholic hallucinosis accompanying alcohol withdrawal is often thought of as a separate syndrome. It is characterized primarily by persistent, frightening auditory hallucinations. Usually the hallucinations have a distinctly paranoid flavor and are of voices familiar to the patient, often of relatives or acquaintances. In the early stages they are threatening, demeaning, or arouse guilt. Because they are true hallucinations, the person believes they are real and acts on them as if they were. This can lead to the person harming himself or others. When the hallucinations persist over time, they become less frightening and may be tolerated with greater equanimity. (Some patients with chronic hallucinosis may develop a schizophrenia-like condition and require treatment with antipsychotic medications.) However, in most instances alcoholic hallucinosis does not indicate an underlying psychiatric problem but simply represents the CNS's response to the absence of alcohol. Appropriate treatment entails observing someone in an environment in which he will be safe, plus possible use of mild sedation. Alcoholic hallucinosis, unless very severe, probably should not be treated with antipsychotic medications during the first 2 to 4 days of withdrawal. During that period there is an increased risk for seizures, and such drugs are known to lower the seizure threshold.

Convulsive seizures, sometimes referred to as "rum fits," also occur in association with acute alcohol withdrawal. These seizures are almost always generalized, grand mal, major motor seizures, in which the eyes roll back in the head, the body muscles contract and the relax and extend rhythmically and violently, and there is loss of consciousness. In fact, they are so typical that the occurrence of any other type of seizure should raise concern about causes other than simply alcohol withdrawal. After the seizure, which lasts a minute or two, the person may be stuporous and groggy for as long as 6 to 8 hours. Although very frightening to watch, convulsive seizures in and of themselves are not dangerous. Any treatment during a seizure is limited to protecting the person's airway and to preventing injury, by placing a pillow under the head. A serious complication of a single, isolated seizure is the development of status epilepticus, in which seizures follow one another with virtually no intervening seizure-free periods. Usually only one or two seizures occur with acute alcohol withdrawal. Status epilepticus is very uncommon and, if present, also suggests causes other than alcohol withdrawal. The only long-term treatment of alcohol withdrawal seizures is to prevent them through abstinence. Unless a person in withdrawal has a history of prior seizures, anticonvulsant drugs are not routinely prescribed. If they are used for seizures clearly attributable to acute alcohol withdrawal, they should be discontinued before discharge, because further seizures would not be expected after withdrawal. It is critical, though, to rule out any other possible cause of the seizures and not merely to assume that alcohol withdrawal is responsible. Infections, electrolyte disturbances, and falls with associated head trauma or subdural hematoma, to which the alcoholic is prone, can be causes. Seizures are most likely to occur between 12 and 48 hours after stopping alcohol use, but they can occur up to 1 week after the last drink. Alcohol withdrawal seizures indicate a moderate-to-severe withdrawal problem. One third of all persons who have seizures are said to go on to develop DTs.

Withdrawal seizures are also thought to be caused by "rebound" CNS hyperexcitability. Alcohol has an anticonvulsant effect acutely in that it raises the seizure threshold. With abstinence, however, the seizure threshold is correspondingly lowered. (This has been postulated as the basis for the increased seizures in epileptics who drink, because these seizures tend to occur the morning after, when the blood alcohol level has fallen.)

Delirium tremens (DTs) is the most serious form of alcohol withdrawal syndrome. In the past, mortality rates as high as 15% to 20% were reported. As many as 1 of every 5 persons who went into DTs died. Even with modern treatment, there is a 1% to 2% mortality rate. The name indicates the two major components of this withdrawal state. Either of these components can predominate.

Epilepsy. This fearful disease is one of the maladies to which the excessive drinker is subject. It is most frequent among absinthe drinkers. In its early stages alcoholic epilepsy is comparatively easy of cure. It is cured spontaneously sometimes by simple total abstinence from alcohol.

SPOONER, WALTER, W.
The Cyclopaedia of Temperance and Prohibition, 1891.

Delirium refers to hallucinations, confusion, and disorientation. Tremens refers to the heightened autonomic nervous activity, marked tremulousness and agitation, fast pulse, elevated blood pressure, and fever. Someone who eventually goes on to develop the DTs will initially have all the symptoms first described with early withdrawal. However, instead of clearing by the second or third day, the symptoms continue and, in fact, get worse. In addition to increased shakiness, profuse sweating, fast pulse, hypertension, and fever, there are mounting periods of confusion and anxiety attacks. In full-blown DTs, there are delusions and hallucinations, generally visual and tactile. The terrifying nature of the hallucinations and delusions is captured by the slang phrase for DTs, "the horrors." Seeing bugs on the walls and feeling insects crawling all over the body naturally heighten the anxiety and emotional responses. In this physical and emotional state of heightened agitation, infections, respiratory problems, fluid loss, and physical exhaustion create further difficulties. These complications contribute substantially to the mortality rate. The acute phase of DTs can last from 1 day to 1 week. In 15% of cases it is over in 25 hours; in 80%, within 3 days. The person will then often fall into a profound sleep and, on awakening, feel better though still weak. Usually he or she will have little memory of what has happened.

Since there is no specific cure for DTs, treatment is aimed at providing supportive medical care while it runs its course. Vital signs are monitored closely to spot any developing problems. Efforts are made to reduce the agitation, conserve energy, and prevent exhaustion. This involves administering sedatives. Despite arguments to the contrary, there is no clear-cut single regimen that is obviously superior. Amounts and type of medications will be determined by the patient's physical condition. One of the concerns will be liver function. The liver, possibly damaged by alcohol, is the organ needed to metabolize virtually any drug given. If the liver is not up to the task, drugs will not be as speedily removed from the body, a situation that can lead to further problems. The benzodiazepines (Ativan, Librium, Valium, Serax) are often the first choice. They seem at least as effective as other agents, they have a wider margin of safety and less toxicity than some of the alternative drugs, and they contribute a significant anticonvulsant effect as well. The specific benzodiazepine chosen will depend upon a number of pharmacological considerations. As symptoms abate, the dose is decreased gradually over time to avoid cumulative unwanted sedation. Paraldehyde, an old, time-tested, and effective agent, has in recent years become less popular. Paraldehyde is metabolized by the liver and consequently must be used with care when significant liver disease is present. It also must be carefully stored in sealed brown bottles to prevent its breakdown into acetaldehyde. Last, it imparts an objectionable odor to the breath that is unavoidable because it is extensively excreted by the lungs. The major tranquilizers, or antipsychotic agents, are also somewhat less desirable. Although they have sedative properties, they also lower the seizure threshold, which is already a problem for withdrawing alcoholics. Whatever medication is used, the purpose is to diminish the severity of the acute symptoms accompanying the DTs, not to introduce long-term drug treatment for the alcoholism.

Although predictions cannot be made about who will go into DTs, those who fit the following description are the most likely candidates. A daily drinker who has consumed over a fifth a day or more for at least a week prior to abstinence and who has been a heavy drinker for 10 years or more is statistically very susceptible. The occurrence of withdrawal seizures, or the persistence and worsening rather than improving over time of the acute early withdrawal symptoms, should indicate that the DTs are more likely to occur. If in a prior period of acute abstinence the person had convulsions, extreme agitation, marked confusion, disorientation, or DTs, he or she is also more likely to have them again. Another ominous sign is recent abuse of other sedatives, especially barbiturates, which also have potentially very serious withdrawal syndromes much like those seen with alcohol. Abuse of multiple drugs complicates withdrawal management. If there is evidence of physical dependence on more than one drug, generally simultaneous withdrawal will not be attempted. Serial withdrawal is the preferred approach.

Late withdrawal phenomena

In those who received high doses of benzodiazepines as treatment for the symptoms of acute alcohol withdrawal, the very same symptoms, including seizures, may reappear 2 to 3 weeks after withdrawal from alcohol when the benzodiazepines are discontinued. This is more likely to occur if high doses were required acutely and if they were stopped abruptly. Probably, this represents a separate sedative-hypnotic withdrawal syndrome caused by discontinuing the benzodiazepines and is not a delayed or reemergence of alcohol withdrawal. It can be treated by reintroducing the benzodiazepines and then discontinuing them more gradually. Another late withdrawal phenomenon is known as *protracted abstinence syndrome*. This is characterized by the persistence over a variable but prolonged period (several weeks to months) of symptoms suggestive of the acute stages of alcohol withdrawal. These can include variable cognitive and memory disturbances, anxiety and irritability, insomnia, tremulousness, depressive symptoms, and an intense desire to drink. Unfortunately alcohol provides prompt relief for this persistent and often intensely uncomfortable state. This may account in part for relapse among some treated alcoholics.

Delirium Tremens. Delirium tremens, or mania a potu, is a nervous disorder caused by the habitual use of alcoholic stimulants, and in regard to its pathological tendency may be defined as nature's ultimate protest against the continuance of the alcohol vice. The first remonstrance comes in the form of nausea, langor and sick headache—symptoms familiar in the experience of every incipient toper. Loss of appetite and general disinclination to active exercise are the penalties of intemperance in its more advanced stages of development, and those injunctions remaining unheeded, nature's ultimatum is expressed in the incomparable distress of nervous delirium

SPOONER, WALTER, W.
The Cyclopaedia of Temperance and Prohibition, 1891.

Some cautions

Not all those who experience withdrawal symptoms intend to! Withdrawal will occur by itself in a physically dependent person whenever a drug is reduced or terminated. So circumstances may play their part and catch some people unaware. Addicted individuals who enter hospitals for surgery, thereby having to curtail their usual consumption, may, to their surgeon's (and even their own) amazement, develop acute withdrawal symptoms. Another possibility is the family vacation. When the secretly drinking housewife, who has been denying a problem, intends to just "sweat it out," she can wind up with more than she bargained for.

Any clinician working with active alcoholics is going to work with people who do want to loosen their grip. Giving up alcohol can be tough on the body as well as the emotions. In making any assessment, the therapist will have to be concerned about the real possibility of physical dependence and the likelihood of withdrawal. In all cases, medical evaluation is good practice. Withdrawal needs to be medically supervised and carefully monitored. However, not every withdrawing patient requires hospitalization. In fact, the vast majority of patients—in some studies 90% or more—who do not have serious medical complications can be safely and effectively withdrawn on an outpatient basis.

Planning has to include arrangements for care during the process of physical withdrawal. No person should be alone. Family members need to know what to be alert for so that the necessary medical treatment can be sought when and if indicated. A simple rule of thumb is that if there is any significant likelihood of serious withdrawal, seek hospitalization. Virtually every alcoholic has stopped drinking for a day or so, so he or she has some sense of what happened then. Any client with a history of previous difficulty during withdrawal is at increased risk in the future. Even when there is not a history of prior difficulty during withdrawal, if current symptoms are worse, seek medical treatment immediately. At every step along the way it is imperative that alcohol dependent persons receive lots of TLC. They need repeated reassurance and support. They need their questions answered and all procedures explained. Anything that can be done to reduce anxiety and fear is vitally important. Surprisingly such support may often help clients through alcohol withdrawal without the use of sedative-hypnotic medications.

RESOURCES AND FURTHER READINGS

Adler RA: Clinically important effects of alcohol on endocrine function (review), *Journal of Clinical Endocrinology and Metabolism* 74(5):957-960, 1992.

The purpose of this review is to highlight those effects of alcohol use and abuse that cause clinical abnormalities of endocrine function. Many other effects of ethanol are of interest but are beyond the scope of this review. There are both direct and indirect effects of alcohol. Acute and chronic alcohol ingestion may have separate effects, and alcohol withdrawal may change endocrine function. Secondary complications such as liver disease, malnutrition, and other medical illnesses commonly found in alcoholics may also have endocrine consequences. (Author abstract.)

Al-Jarallah KF, Shehab DK, and Buchanan WW: Rheumatic complications of alcohol abuse (review), *Seminars in Arthritis and Rheumatism* 22(3):162-171, 1992.

The purpose of this report is to review rheumatic complications associated with alcoholism. Data were collected by an English-language literature search using MEDLINE (1966 to December 1991) and references from identified articles. Studies in humans, including case reports of joint disease and allied disorders associated with alcoholism, were reviewed. According to the data identified, alcoholism is associated with many rheumatic problems, including neuropathic arthropathy, hyperuricemia with gouty arthritis, septic arthritis, and joint hypermobility. Osteoporosis, osteonecrosis, and myopathy also are common. Several other rare musculoskeletal complications have been described. Early recognition of these problems is important for management. Further studies are needed to examine the effect of alcohol on connective tissue components in joints. (Author abstract.)

Anthenelli RM, Klein JL, Tsuang JW and others: The prognostic importance of blackouts in young men, *Journal of Studies on Alcohol* 55(3):290-295, 1994.

In order to test the commonly held perception that blackouts are an early sign of alcoholism, the authors evaluated a sample of 230 nonalcoholic young men longitudinally over an 8- to 12-year follow-up period. Consistent with the literature, blackouts were a common occurrence in this cohort, with 26% of the men reporting blackouts by their early twenties and 30% of the subjects experiencing blackouts over the approximately 10-year follow-up. Alcohol-related amnestic episodes were associated with the quantity and frequency of drinking, and men with blackouts (especially four or more) were more likely to have other problems related to their heavy drinking. Although few alcoholics will report not having had such amnestic spells, blackouts are not sensitive indicators of the risk for developing alcoholism. The data suggest that blackouts should be viewed as an important warning sign of problem drinking but not as a "hallmark" of alcoholism. (Author abstract.)

Arria AM, Van Thiel DH: The epidemiology of alcohol-related chronic disease, *Alcohol Health and Research World* 16(3):209-216, 1992.

The authors examine the epidemiological data linking alcohol use to various types of chronic disease. They discuss the potential for alcohol to interact with a person's diet, smoking, and environment to induce or exacerbate neurologic disorders, cardiovascular disease, and certain types of cancer. Public domain.

Ashery RS: Issues in AIDS training for substance abuse workers, *Journal of Substance Abuse Treatment* 9(1):15-19, 1992.

Workers in drug treatment programs need specialized training concerning acquired immune deficiency syndrome (AIDS) to meet the demands of their expanding roles. Initially, the treatment community failed to anticipate training needs fully, but now, comprehensive and systematic AIDS training programs must be developed. This article discusses the five steps in developing and implementing such programs: (a) assessment and information gathering, (b) curriculum development, (c) training of instructors, (d) training delivery, and (e) evaluation. (Author abstract.)

Blot WJ: Alcohol and cancer, *Cancer Research* 52(7):2119-2123, 1992.

Although ethanol has generally not been found to induce cancer in experimental animals, the consumption of alcoholic beverages has been linked to increased risks of several cancers in humans. Risks of oral, pharyngeal, laryngeal, esophageal, and liver cancer are elevated among drinkers, typically in proportion to the amount consumed. Evidence associating colorectal and breast cancer with alcohol drinking is suggestive but awaits confirmation. All types of alcoholic beverages seem to be implicated, pointing to an etiological role for ethanol or its metabolites. The mechanisms, however, by which alcohol induces cancer in humans are not clear. This review summarizes epidemiological studies of alcohol and cancer, focusing primarily on characteristics of the association that may provide clues to causal pathways. (Author abstract.)

Conigrave KM, Saunders JB, Reznik RB, and others: Prediction of alcohol related harm by laboratory test results, *Clinical Chemistry* 39(11):2266-2270, 1993.

The authors examined the value of laboratory markers of excessive alcohol (ethanol) intake as predictors of mortality, morbidity, and health-care utilization in a cohort of 330 patients attending an acute ambulatory care service. Among men, all four markers examined, glutamyltransferase (GGT) and aspartate aminotransferase (AST) activities, high-density lipoprotein cholesterol (HDL-C), and mean corpuscular volume (MCV) were predictive of medical sequelae and health-care utilization over a 3-year period. In contrast, social problems were more closely related to the amount of alcohol consumption at initial assessment than to any biological marker. Serum GGT and AST activities and MCV were predictive of medical sequelae in women. The predictive value of GGT was an independent risk factor and did not merely reflect recent alcohol intake or the presence of chronic liver disease. The authors conclude that these readily available laboratory tests provide important prognostic information and should be an integral part of the assessment of persons with hazardous alcohol consumption. (Author abstract.)

Delin CR, Lee TH: Drinking and the brain: current evidence (review), *Alcohol and Alcoholism* 27(2):117-126, 1992.

There is no question, as accumulating evidence reveals, that alcohol in excess negatively affects the brain and neuropsychological functioning, both immediately and in the long term. The important question for social drinkers, however, is whether moderate amounts of alcohol can have deleterious effects on the brain or performance in either the medium or long term. It has been proposed that there is a continuum of negative consequences with light drinkers at one end and chronic alcoholics at the other end. Three levels of study of this hypothesis are distinguished: behavioral, structural, and cellular. Research into effects at these three levels is reviewed both for alcoholics and for social drinkers. A further hypothesis relates to the possibility that cognitive functioning is impaired even after blood alcohol concentration has returned to zero. It is concluded that while neither the continuity hypothesis nor a 'hangover' hypothesis is supported by current evidence, considerably more research is needed. (Author abstract.)

Devgun MS: The effects and consequences of alcohol use and abuse: a review (review), *Journal of Biological Education* 26(2):143-147, 1992.

This article discusses some broad-ranging and sobering aspects of alcohol in relation to body; these include a summary on the physiology and biochemistry of alcohol metabolism. The consequences on health, social, financial, and professional status are outlined. The impact of the economics of alcohol sale in the United Kingdom and the efforts taken to counteract misuse of alcohol by health education groups are also reviewed. Awareness of the amount of alcohol consumed and the resultant blood alcohol concentration is presented; this is then illustrated in a practical exercise as an aid to understanding the alcohol that we all like to drink and enjoy from time to time. (Author abstract.)

Gentilello LM, Cobean RA, Walker AP, and others. Acute ethanol intoxication increases the risk of infection following penetrating abdominal trauma, *Journal of Trauma* 34(5):669-675, 1993.

Acute alcohol (ETOH) intoxication as a risk factor for infection in trauma victims to our knowledge has not been previously reported. To determine if ETOH intoxication increases infection risk, the authors examined data from 365 patients with penetrating abdominal trauma who were enrolled in a multi-center antibiotic study. Ninety-four patients sustained an injury to a hollow viscus. To separate acute from chronic ETOH effects, infections were divided into two categories: (1) trauma-related infections caused by bacterial contamination at the time of injury, while blood alcohol level (BAL) was elevated and (2) nosocomial infections caused by bacteria acquired during hospital stay, after BAL had normalized. A BAL greater than or equal to 200 mg/dL was associated with a 2.6-fold increase in trauma-related infections. There was no association between BAL and subsequent nosocomial infection. Since infection rates for intoxicated patients were not higher after BAL had normalized, acute rather than chronic effects of ETOH appear to be responsible. (Author abstract.)

Griffiths HJ, Parantainen H, and Olson P: Alcohol and bone disorders, *Alcohol Health and Research World* 17(4):299-304, 1993.

The effects of alcohol consumption on bone often go unrecognized. According to the authors, alcoholism may lead to several specific bone disorders. Alcohol also causes fractures indirectly as a result of an increased number of motor vehicle crashes and falls. A complex combination of alcohol-related metabolic bone disorders can result in loss of bone mineral. The factors that promote this combination of disorders in alcoholics include dietary deficiencies, impaired vitamin D metabolism, and hormonal imbalances. Death of bone tissue in alcoholics is caused by factors that decrease the blood supply to a portion of a bone. Alcoholic bone disease can lead to pain, deformity, and fractures. Alcoholics should be screened regularly for vitamin D deficiency and bone loss. Public domain.

Higgins EM, du Vivier AWP: Alcohol and the skin, *Alcohol and Alcoholism* 27(6):595-602, 1992.

The cutaneous stigmata of chronic alcoholic liver disease have been well recognized since the nineteenth century. However, it is now clear that the skin may be affected as an early feature of alcohol misuse. In particular, psoriasis, discoid eczema, and superficial infections are more common in heavy drinkers. Awareness of these early associations can alert physicians to patients at risk of future complications of alcoholism. Great advances have been made in the understanding of the physiological and pathological effects of ethanol. The implications of these changes in the skin are discussed with reference to both the new and established cutaneous signs of alcohol misuse. (Author abstract.)

Jurkovich GJ, Rivara FP, Gurney JG, and others. The effect of acute alcohol intoxication and chronic alcohol abuse on outcome from trauma, *Journal of the American Medical Association* 270(1):51-56, 1993.

Objective: To determine the effect of acute alcohol intoxication and chronic alcohol abuse on morbidity and mortality from trauma. Design: Prospective cohort study. Patients: Blunt or penetrating trauma patients at least 18 years of age admitted to one trauma center or dying at the injury scene. Main outcome measures: Mortality, complications (infection, pneumonia, respiratory failure, or multiple organ failure), and length of hospital stay. Results: Acute intoxication had no effect on risk of dying at the injury scene, within the first 24 hours of hospitalization, after the first 24 hours, or overall. Acute intoxication also did not increase the risk of complications and was associated with shorter lengths of stay. Patients with both biochemical and behavioral evidence of chronic alcohol abuse had a twofold increased risk of complications, particularly pneumonia and any infection, compared with those with no evidence of chronic alcohol abuse. Conclusions: Chronic, but not acute, alcohol abuse adversely affects outcome from trauma. Attention to the problem of chronic alcohol abuse appears to be warranted. (Author abstract.)

Lange WR, White N, Robinson N: Medical complications of substance abuse, *Postgraduate Medicine* 92(3):205+, 1992.

Substance abuse is involved in many instances of intentional and unintentional injury. It can also cause medical complications that affect various organ systems—among them the cardiac, vascular, neurologic, pulmonary, gastrointestinal, immunological, and reproductive systems. Even though there is pressure to create a new medical specialty to specifically address substance abuse issues, the truth is that any physician, regardless of specialty, may encounter patients with substance abuse problems. Alcoholism and drug abuse, with their associated psychosocial and clinical ramifications and complications, cut across all specialty fields. Consequently, all physicians need to be familiar with the spectrum of clinical problems associated with substance abuse and comfortable with addressing these problems prudently and promptly. (Author abstract)

Lehman LB, Pilich A, Andrews N: Neurological disorders resulting from alcoholism, *Alcohol Health and Research World* 17(4):305-309, 1993.

Severe neurological disorders, from chronic memory and muscle control to acute blackouts and seizures, have been associated with chronic heavy drinking. The authors review both chronic and acute effects of alcohol on the nervous system, the cause of such effects, and the resulting symptoms. Public domain.

Lieber CS: *Medical and Nutritional Complications of Alcoholism: Mechanisms and Management,* New York: Plenum Publishing Corporation, 1992.

This work with 18 chapters and 17 different contributors in addition to the author provides a review of the major medical complications associated with alcoholism, as well as the pathophysiological basis and approaches to clinical management. Individual chapters deal with metabolism; acetaldehyde and acetate; hormonal influences on metabolism; lipid disorders including fatty liver, hyperlipemia, and atherosclerosis; effects of ethanol on amino acid and protein metabolism; interactions of alcohol and other drugs; the liver; immunological reactions resulting from liver disease; the hematological system; the digestive system; the pancreas; the cardiovascular system; effects on skeletal muscle, the central nervous system, the kidney. It also discusses carcinogenic effects; fetal alcohol syndrome; nutritional problems associated with alcoholism; and biological markers of alcoholism.

Litten RZ, Allen JP: Pharmacotherapies for alcoholism: Promising agents and clinical issues, *Alcohol: Clinical & Experimental Research* 15(4):620-633, 1991.

The past 10 years have witnessed important advances in research on pharmacotherapy for alcoholism. Promising drugs are discussed under six headings: agents to treat alcohol withdrawal, anticraving agents, agents that make drinking an aversive experience, agents to alleviate concomitant psychiatric problems, agents to treat concurrent drug abuse, and amethystic ("sobering-up") agents. Research on the drug classes is summarized, and clinical issues surrounding specific agents and alcoholism pharmacotherapy in general are discussed. Finally, long-range therapeutic implications of recent findings on the actions of alcohol on basic mechanisms of the brain are offered. (Author abstract.)

Marsano L: Alcohol and malnutrition, *Alcohol Health and Research World* 17(4):284-291, 1993.

The human body uses alcohol as a source of calories. At high blood alcohol levels and in alcoholics, however, the body uses the calories from alcohol less efficiently than it does those from food sources. The author describes alcohol's relationship with malnutrition and use of such nutrients as carbohydrates, proteins, lipids, and vitamins. The author also discusses alcohol's deleterious effects on portions of the digestive system and gives a summary of clinical methods for assessing a person's nutritional status. Public domain.

Mendenhall CL: Immunity, malnutrition, and alcohol, *Alcohol Health and Research World* 16(1):23-28, 1992.

Nutrition influences all aspects of the immune system, and malnutrition—in particular, protein energy malnutrition—has been found both to suppress and to stimulate certain immune responses. Alcoholism is associated with poor nutrition, and in severe cases, with malnutrition. The author discusses the complex and poorly understood relationships among nutrition, alcoholism, and functioning of the immune system. Public domain.

Moushmoush B, Abi-Mansour P: Alcohol and the heart (review), *Archives of Internal Medicine* 151(1):36-42, 1991.

The toxic effects of chronic alcohol abuse on cerebral and hepatic function have long been recognized. Moreover, it is clear that the habitual consumption of large amounts of alcohol has a variety of deleterious effects on the cardiovascular system. This review considers the evidence about the long-term effects of alcohol on the cardiovascular system with particular reference to its effects on the myocardium, arrhythmias, blood pressure, coronary artery disease, and alcohol-induced congenital heart disease. Such disorders are often caused by a combination of the toxic effects of ethanol or its metabolites and genetic predisposition. Gender, intensity and duration of alcohol abuse, and metabolic and nutritional factors probably play important roles. Research on alcoholism offers hope that it may soon be possible to identify those individuals at risk for alcoholism and provide them with more effective therapy. Meanwhile, reducing or stopping the consumption of alcohol could prevent its deleterious complications. (Author abstract.)

National Institute on Alcohol Abuse and Alcoholism: *Eighth Special Report to the U.S. Congress on Alcohol and Health,* Rockville MD: National Institute on Alcohol Abuse and Alcoholism, 1993.

This most recent in a series of reports by NIAAA, first published in 1971, provides current documentation of progress in understanding the effects of alcohol on health. A valuable reference tool, the report contains a wealth of current data, statistical information displayed in numerous tables and charts, and summaries of the major topics of current interest: epidemiology, genetics and environmental influences, neurosciences, medical consequences, fetal alcohol syndrome and other effects on pregnancy outcome, social consequences, diagnosis and assessment, prevention, early and minimal intervention, and treatment. Each chapter has an extensive bibliography.

Nelson S, Shellito J, Mason C, and others: Alcohol and bacterial pneumonia, *Alcohol Health and Research World* 16(1):73-80, 1992.

Bacterial pneumonia is typically the outcome of an acquired imbalance resulting from a failure of the immune system to destroy or rid itself of invading pathogens. The authors discuss the body's highly integrated system of defense mechanisms against pathogens and how alcohol can cause aspects of this system to fail. Public domain.

Parsons OA, Nixon SJ: Neurobehavioral sequelae of alcoholism, *Neurologic Clinic* 11(1):205-218, 1993.

The purpose of this article is to discuss the current state of knowledge concerning the neuropsychological (cognitive-perceptual-intellectual) changes found in alcoholics subsequent to detoxification and withdrawal. These changes range from clearly diagnosable organic mental syndromes, such as the amnestic (Korsakoff's) syndrome and alcoholic dementia, through what Grant et al have proposed calling the intermediate duration (subacute) organic mental disorder of alcoholism, to essentially no discernible residual neuropsychological impairment. It has been estimated that approximately 10% of treated alcoholics fall into the organic mental syndrome group. Of the remaining 90%, estimates are that as many as 50% to 85% will manifest mild-to-moderate impairment in some aspect of neuropsychological functioning. The discussion of the neuropsychological findings in these two groups is oriented around answering the following questions: (1) Which mental functions are affected and how severe is the impairment? (2) Which neuropsychological model best fits the pattern of impairment? (3) What are the determinants of the impairment? and (4) What is the course of recovery? (Author abstract.)

Romelsjo A, Karlsson G, Henningsohn L, and others: The prevalence of alcohol-related mortality in both sexes: variation between indicators, *American Journal of Public Health* 83(6):838-844, 1993.

The purpose of this study is to analyze the prevalence of alcohol-related mortality—according to various indicators—in both sexes in Stockholm, Sweden. A study of alcohol involvement at death was undertaken for all 668 deceased persons aged

15 through 54 years in 1987 in Stockholm. Death certificates, autopsy information, police records, and information about earlier conviction were analyzed. When different measures of estimation were compared, there were great differences in the prevalence of alcohol involvement. According to the death certificates, 9.2% of the males and 11.2% of the females had alcoholism, alcohol intoxication, pancreatitis, or liver cirrhosis as underlying cause of death. When all accessible information was used, potential alcohol involvement was found in 57.5% of the male and in 32.2% of the female deaths. There was a marked association between earlier drunken driving and alcohol involvement. After reevaluation of the diagnoses with autopsy findings, the number of cases with cardiac enlargement and suspected cardiomyopathy increased from 10 to 62. The results point to the serious underdiagnosis of alcohol involvement in death certificates and the misclassification of important causes of death (i.e., liver cirrhosis and cardiac disease); they also call for increased efforts regarding prevention. (Author abstract.)

Rubino FA: Neurologic complications of alcoholism, *Psychiatric Clinics of North America* 15(2):359-372, 1992.

Alcohol is still the most abused drug today and may affect the peripheral, central, and autonomic nervous systems in many ways. There are several pathophysiological mechanisms that include direct effects through intoxication, withdrawal effects, secondary effects from nutritional problems and systemic diseases, and, of course, syndromes of unknown etiology. The alcoholic is also susceptible to trauma to both the central and peripheral nervous systems. In many of the clinical entities, multiple factors play a role. (Author abstract.)

Saunders JB, Aasland OG, Amundsen A, and others: Alcohol consumption and related problems among primary health care patients: WHO collaborative project on early detection of persons with harmful alcohol consumption, *Addiction* 88(3):349-362, 1993.

This WHO collaborative project is the first phase of a program of work aimed at developing techniques for early identification and treatment of persons with hazardous and harmful alcohol consumption. The aim of the present study is to determine the prevalence of hazardous and harmful alcohol use among patients attending primary health care facilities in several countries and to examine the correlates of drinking behavior and alcohol-related problems in these culturally diverse populations. The broader purpose is to determine whether there is justification for developing alcohol screening instruments for cross-national use. One thousand, eight hundred and eighty-eight subjects in Australia, Bulgaria, Kenya, Mexico, Norway, and USA underwent a comprehensive assessment of their medical history, alcohol intake, drinking practices, and any physical or psychosocial problems related to alcohol. After nondrinkers and known alcoholics had been excluded, 18% of subjects had a hazardous level of alcohol intake and 23% had experienced at least one alcohol-related problem in the previous year. Intrascale reliability coefficients were uniformly high for the drinking behavior (dependence) and adverse psychological reactions scales and moderately high for the alcohol-related problems scales. There were strong correlations between the various alcohol-specific scales and between these scales and measures of alcohol intake. Although the prevalence of hazardous and harmful alcohol consumption varied from country to country, there was a high degree of commonality in the structure and correlates of drinking behavior and alcohol-related problems. These findings strengthen the case for developing international screening instruments for hazardous and harmful alcohol consumption. (Author abstract.)

Smart RG, Mann RE: Alcohol and the epidemiology of liver cirrhosis, *Alcohol Health and Research World* 16(3):217-222, 1992.

Studies show that alcohol can produce cirrhosis in the absence of dietary deficiencies and that the prevalence of cirrhosis is related to the duration of heavy drinking. The authors review the data on rates of cirrhosis and the relationship of cirrhosis to alcohol consumption and diet, as well as trends in cirrhosis rates. The authors suggest various explanations for the recent decline in cirrhosis rates and discuss other important questions that remain. Public domain.

Steinmetz G: Fetal alcohol syndrome, *National Geographic* 181(Feb.):36-39.

Zuckerman B, Breshnahan K: Developmental and behavioral consequences of prenatal drug and alcohol exposure, *Pediatric Clinics of North America* 38(6):1387-1406, 1991.

This article summarizes what is known about the effects of cocaine, opiates, marijuana, and alcohol on neonatal and postnatal growth and development. The development of a child affected by prenatal exposure to drugs and alcohol is best understood through a multifactorial model consisting of interrelated prenatal and postnatal factors. The article also describes the prenatal effects of drugs and alcohol on the newborn, especially on central nervous system functioning, which is seen as creating a biological vulnerability that renders a child more vulnerable to the effects of poor caretaking. (Author abstract.)

The behavior of alcohol dependence

There are some striking similarities in the behavioral "look" of those with alcohol dependence. This is true whether the person is male or female, age 17 or 70. From these similarities a general profile can be drawn, although it will not apply totally to all. This profile would cause signal bells to ring when seen by someone familiar with the disease. Indeed, it was the recognition of similarities that in part prompted the futile pursuit for "the alcoholic personality."

A BEHAVIORAL COMPOSITE

Those who are alcohol dependent create confusion for those around them by constantly sending out mixed messages. "Come closer, understand. Don't you dare question me!" The moods and behavior of alcoholics can be very volatile: jubilant and expansive, then secretive, angry, suspicious, laughing or crying. Tense, worried, confused, she quickly changes to a relaxed "Everything's fine." Anxious over unpaid bills one day, the alcoholic is financially irresponsible the next. He buys expensive toys for the kids, while the rent goes unpaid. She may be easygoing or fight like a caged tiger over a "slight." His telling unnecessary lies and having them come to light is not uncommon.

A considerable amount of time is spent justifying and explaining why she does things. She is constantly minimizing any unpleasant consequences of drinking. He is hard to keep on the track. There is always a list of complaints about any number of people, places, and things. "If only ..." She considers herself the victim of fate and of a large number of people who are "out to get" her. He has thousands of reasons why he *really* needs and deserves a drink. She will be exuberant over a minor success only to decline rapidly into an "I'm a failure because of ..." routine. He's elusive and is almost never where he said he'd be when he said he'd be there. She's absolutely *rigid* about her schedule, especially her drinking times.

The mood swings are phenomenal! The circular arguments never quite make sense to a sober person. The denial can cause a lot of hand-throwing-up. Now and then the thought surfaces in the drinker's awareness that he or she might have a psychiatric problem. Those around the drinker also can wonder if that is where the problem lies. She is a perfectionist at some times and a slob at others. Though occasionally cooperative, he's often a stone wall. Her life is full of broken commitments, promises, and dates that she often doesn't remember making.

Most of all, the behavior denotes guilt. Extreme defensiveness accompanies alcohol-dependent drinking. This seems to be one of the key behaviors that is picked up on early and seen, but not understood, by others. "Wonder why Andy's so touchy? What a short

Woe unto them that rise up early in the morning, that they may follow strong drink.

ISAIAH 5:11

168

fuse!" Certainly, at times behavior that can only be described as that of a drunken slob is obvious, but often the really heavy drinking is secretive and carefully hidden.

It would be easier to pin down the problem if the behaviors described only occurred with a drink in hand. This is rarely the case. The behaviors are sometimes more pronounced when the alcoholic is "on the wagon," or working very hard at controlling his drinking. The confusion, anger, frustration, and depression are omnipresent until a radical change occurs in the relationship with alcohol.

HOW, IF NOT WHY

The preceding profile is a fair description of the behavior that accompanies alcohol dependence. This behavior is part of the disease syndrome, which develops slowly. The many changes in personality occur gradually, making them less discernible to the alcoholic or those around him or her. So the slow, insidious personality change is almost immune to recognition as it occurs.

Despite the fact that a host of physical problems have long been known to accompany long-term heavy drinking, medical researchers are only beginning to get clues to the physiological basis for the behavior seen (see Chapter 5). Current neurological and physiological research do not yet come close to providing an adequate explanation for this well-known behavioral phenomenon. Despite the inability to provide the exact cause of personality changes, how the transformation occurs can be described. Vernon Johnson, in *I'll Quit Tomorrow,* has developed a four-step process that accurately captures the personality changes occurring in the alcohol-dependent person. His explanation in effect describes what emerging alcohol dependence feels like from "the inside out." Becoming familiar with these stages will be helpful in dealing with those with alcohol dependence or alcohol abuse, as well as those whose use of any drug is a growing problem.

Alcohol, or other drug dependence for that matter, requires the use of alcohol or other drugs—an obvious fact. Another obvious fact: for whatever reasons, drinking or drug taking becomes an important activity in the life of the problem drinker or budding drug user. The individual develops a *relationship* with alcohol or another drug of choice. The relationship, with all that word implies, is as real and important a bond as the bond with friends, a spouse, or the long-time family pet. Accordingly, energy is expended to maintain the relationship. The bond may be thought of as a love affair. Long after the good times, the pleasure, and the thrill are gone, all kinds of mental gymnastics are used to maintain the myth that it's still great.

How does this progression occur? The first step is quite simple. The individual destined for later trouble is seemingly no different than anyone else. For anyone who uses alcohol, the first important experience is to *learn the mood swing.* This learning has a physiological basis. Alcohol is a drug with acute effects. It makes us feel good. At any time, our moods could be plotted on a graph representing a continuum. One end represents pain and the other end represents euphoria. Before drinking, if our mood falls in the middle or normal range, the effect of the drink is to shift our mood toward the euphoric end. When the effects of the alcohol wear off, we're back where we started.

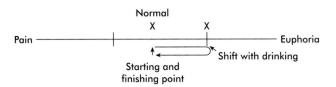

Anyone who drinks learns this pharmacological effect of alcohol. As importantly, we learn that it happens consistently. Alcohol the drug can be depended upon. If you reflect back on the discussion of alcohol's acute effects in Chapter 2, you'll recall that a number of things make this learning potent. You do not have to wait very long to experience what alcohol does. The effects of the drug can be felt almost immediately. For the new drinker, who has not acquired any tolerance to alcohol's effects, the change can be dramatic.

The second stage in the developmental process is termed *seeking the mood swing*. This happens after someone learns that alcohol can be counted on to enhance or improve mood. Now drinking can have a particular purpose. Anyone who drinks occasionally does so to make things better. Whatever the occasion—an especially hard day at work, a family reunion, celebrating a promotion, or recovery from a trying day of hassling kids—the expectation is that alcohol will do something nice. In essence, the person has a contract with alcohol. True to its promise, alcohol keeps its side of the bargain. Furthermore, by altering the dose, the person can control the degree of mood change. Still there are no problems. Nothing up to this point suggests that alcohol use can be anything but pleasurable.

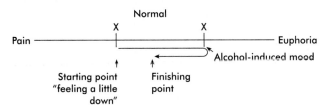

Who hath woe? Who hath sorrow? Who hath contentions? Who hath babbling? Who hath wounds without cause? Who hath redness of eyes? They that tarry long at the wine.

PROVERBS 28:31-32

Somewhere along the line, predictably, most people who use alcohol will have a negative drinking experience. This may happen early in someone's drinking career. The unpleasant event can be the discomfort of a hangover, "the morning after," or it can be the sensation of closing one's eyes and feeling the world begin to spin. It may also be *not* the physical aftermath of intoxication but the behavior that took place then. What occurred when drinking can make the person squirm at its recollection. At any rate, most people are quite clear that alcohol was the significant factor. They tell themselves, "Never again," and that's that. Possibly described as "sadder but wiser" as a result of what has happened, they alter their pattern of use in the future and markedly reduce the risk of future problems resulting from alcohol use.

For a significant minority of drinkers, the above scenario has a different outcome. These are the people for whom alcohol use becomes an emerging problem. In Johnson's schema, these people have crossed a thin and still undefined line that separates the second and third stages. The third phase is *harmful dependence.* Suddenly alcohol's use has a boomerang effect. Alcohol, which previously had only a beneficial, positive effect, now has some negative consequences. Sketched out on the pain-euphoria continuum: initially the mood changes in the desired direction and achieves the drinker's purpose. But then something new occurs. The mood swings back, "dropping off" the person with less comfortable feelings than prior to the drinking.

Wine in excess keeps neither secrets nor promises.

CERVANTES,
Don Quixote

One of the disadvantages of wine is that it makes a man mistake words for thoughts.

SAMUEL JOHNSON

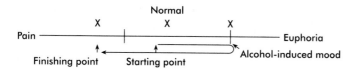

This difference has important consequences. From this point, to continue drinking in the same fashion will exact *emotional costs.* For whatever reasons, unwilling to abandon the use of alcohol as a means of altering their moods, some are willing to pay the price and accept whatever the negative consequences may be. This decision to accept the consequences isn't a conscious one. Emotionally, they remain "loyal" to their relationship with the drug. It is here that denial enters the picture and there is an altering of priorities which is needed to maintain the relationship with alcohol.

The most significant costs are psychological. Drinking behavior and its consequences are inconsistent with fundamental values and self-image. To deal with this contradiction, continued drinking will require the alcoholic person to make personality adjustments. The normal, run-of-the-mill psychological devices will be used to distort reality just enough to explain away the costs. These psychological defenses are the same ones each of us uses virtually daily to some degree. If I'm walking down the street, say hello to a friend, and get no response, my feelings are momentarily hurt. Almost automatically I tell myself, "She must not have seen or heard me." So I shut off the hurt feelings with an explanation that may or may not be true. I seize an explanation that allows me to turn off the unpleasant feelings the situation has evoked. Another time, if I'm ill-tempered, a

What is said when drunk has been thought out beforehand.
-Flemish Proverb

complete grouch, and behaving in a fashion that I don't really like, I become uncomfortable with myself. In such circumstances I could say, "Yep, I sure am being a real pain in the neck to anyone near me." More likely the internal conversation will come out: "I've not been myself. The pressure of work must have gotten to me." In this way, we all attempt to control our discomfort and maintain psychic harmony. In doing so, we often overlook the obvious and adjust our experience just enough to take off the painful, rough emotional edges.

The budding problem drinker, too, uses these kinds of defenses to maintain harmony and equilibrium in the relationship with alcohol. One way to accomplish this and "explain away" the costs is to suppress emotions. As negative emotions arise, the individual strives to keep them at bay. "I just won't think about it." So the fellow who made a fool of himself at last night's party tries to ignore the whole thing. "Heavens, these things happen sometimes. There's no sense in worrying about it." However, pretending emotions aren't there doesn't make them disappear. They simply crop up somewhere else. Because suppression doesn't work totally, other psychological devices need to be used. Rationalization is a common device—seizing an explanation that inevitably stays clear of alcohol itself. "I really got bombed last night because Harry was mixing such stiff ones." Here projection is at work as well. The reason for whatever occurred and the emotional discomfort was that the drinks were *stiff*, and it's Harry's fault! No responsibility is accepted by the drinker or blame laid on alcohol.

A number of rationalizations are so frequently used that they might almost qualify as warning signals of alcoholism. For example: "I can't be alcoholic because I never drink in the morning. *I'm* too young, too old, too smart, etc. I can quit *whenever* I want to. *Everyone* I know drinks the same way I do. I *only* drink beer. I only drink wine spritzers. I *never* miss work. Casual drinkers would never consider such explanations necessary.

Several factors allow such distortions to go unchallenged. One is attributable to the action of the drug. Alcohol warps perceptions. The only firsthand memory anyone will have of a drinking event is the one that was laid down in a drugged state. So if someone under a haze of alcohol perceives herself as being clever and witty, sobering up in the morning is not going to be sufficient to make her realize that she was loud, coarse, and vulgar. This "rosy memory" is termed by Johnson "euphoric recall." Until recently with more public awareness of alcohol problems, it was unlikely that other people would take it upon themselves to let the drinker know what really transpired. There might not be any problems if these distortions were only occasional—but they aren't. And what proves to be even more destructive is that with continued heavy drinking, the discrepancy becomes greater and greater between what the individual *expects* to happen and what *does* happen. Proportionately, the need for further distortion to explain this discrepancy grows.

Drinking is supposed to improve the mood, but as dependence emerges, more and more frequently the opposite proves to be the case. To illustrate this on the mood continuum, after a drinking occasion the emotional state is one of greater discomfort than it was before the drinking. As alcohol's effects wear off, the individual is finding himself being dropped off further down toward the pain end of the spectrum. The result of alcohol use is not an enhanced but a diminished sense of well being.

A vicious cycle is developing. The psychological mechanisms used to minimize the discomfort simultaneously prevent a recognition of what is really happening. None of the defenses, even in combination, are completely foolproof. At times, individuals feel remorse about their behavior. At those times it doesn't matter where the blame lies—on Harry, on oneself, on alcohol—any way you cut it, the drinker regrets what's happening. So a negative self-image develops.

For the most part, the drinker truly believes the reality created by the projections and rationalizations. Understandably, this begins to erode relationships with others. There are continual hassles over whose version of an event is accurate. This introduces additional tensions and problems arise with friends, family, and co-workers. Self-esteem shrinks. The load of negative feelings expands. Ironically, there is more and more reliance on the old relationship with alcohol. Drinking is deliberately structured into life patterns. Drinking is anticipated. The possibilities of drinking may well determine which invitations are accepted, where business lunches are held, and other activities. Gradually, *all* leisure time is set up to include drinking.

*Boundless intemperance
In nature is a tyranny; it hath been
Th'untimely emptying of the happy
throne
And fall of many kings.*

SHAKESPEARE,
Macbeth

The stage is set for the last developmental phase in the emergence of clear-cut alcohol dependence. The alcoholic individual now *drinks to feel normal.* This is often wholly unappreciated by those for whom drinking is not a problem. Others assume, erroneously, that the alcohol-dependent person is drinking to feel "good" and have "fun." By this point the idea of drinking to feel euphoric has long since gone. Alcohol has become essential *just* to achieve a normal feeling state.

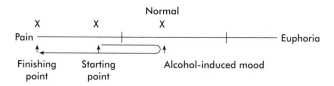

In addition to offering a normal feeling state, alcohol may assist "normal" functioning in other respects. Psychologists have documented the phenomenon of "state-dependent learning." Things learned in a particular context are most readily recalled under similar circumstances. Thus things learned when sober are best recalled later in a sober state. Similarly, information learned while drinking will also be more available for recall later when the person is again (or still) consuming alcohol. Thus the heavy drinker may have a repertoire of behavior, coping mechanisms, social skills, even information that, if learned during drinking, is less accessible when sober. In fact, drinking may be necessary to tap a reservoir of knowledge. This fact is what sometimes explains the inability to find liquor stashes that were hidden when drinking. Another way in which alcohol may be essential to "normalize" function is to ward off withdrawal symptoms if the drinker has become physically dependent.

Memory distortions are not uncommon at this point. Blackouts may mean the absence of memory for some events. Repression is a psychological mechanism that also blocks out memory. Further havoc continues to be raised by "euphoric recall." The memories are only of the good times and the sense of relief associated with drinking. The problems and difficulties seemingly don't penetrate. The same kind of progression can be seen in the use of other drugs. Some are more quickly addicting than others, and in some cases the progression is less gradual. With illegal substances there are also the extra problems of cost and assuring a steady supply, as well as the ever-present danger of contaminants and varying levels of potency. These factors exacerbate deterioration and may make the problems more apparent.

If God wanted us high, He would have given us wings.

ARSENIO HALL

DETERIORATING FUNCTIONING

Because of transformation of thinking, distorted view of reality, and ebbing self-esteem, the alcohol-dependent person's functioning deteriorates. Each of us is expected to fulfill various roles in life. For each slot in which we find ourselves, there is an accompanying set of expectations about appropriate behavior. Some of the typical roles are parent, spouse, employee, citizen, friend. Others may be more transient, such as scout leader, committee chairman, patient, or Sunday school teacher. No matter what the role, with alcohol dependence performance suffers. There are expectations that others have of us in a particular role. The alcohol-dependent individual does not reliably meet them. Behavior is inconsistent. The individual is undependable—sometimes doing what is expected and doing it beautifully; the next time, "no show" followed by the flimsiest excuse. To add insult to injury, he or she gets furious at others for being disappointed, annoyed, or not understanding.

This unreliable behavior has a profound impact on the people around the alcoholic. Since these people have the normal insecurities of all humans, they think it might or must be their fault. Unwittingly, they accept the rationalizations and projections. Some find themselves confused and often feel left out. They sense and fear the loss of an important relationship, one that has been nourishing to them. In turn, *their* usual behavior becomes distorted. Now, in addition to whatever problems are directly attributable to alcohol, interpersonal relationships are impaired. This fuels the tension.

FAMILY AND FRIENDS

Let us focus briefly on the family, close relationships, and friends. Applying behavioral learning terms, the alcoholic person has those people in his or her life on a variable interval–reinforcement schedule. There they are, busily trying to accommodate. Everyone feels that somehow if they behave differently, do the "right thing," the alcoholic will respond. One time they're harsh, the next time they try an "understanding" approach. Then another time they might try to ignore the situation. But nothing works. The alcoholic does not respond in any predictable way to their behavior. If he happens to be a "good boy," or she's been a "perfect lady" on occasion, it really has no connection to what the family has or has not done. The others, in fact, are accommodating themselves to the alcoholic individual. Never sure why some times go better, they persist in trying—and trying some more. Meanwhile, the inconsistency and unpredictability remain.

Eventually the family or partner, as well as close friends, give up and try to live around the situation. Alternately the drinker is ignored or driving them crazy. Yet, out of love and loyalty, all too long others provide protection from the consequences of the drinking. This dynamic is often described as "enabling behavior" and will be elaborated on in Chapter 7. In a marriage or relationship, if one partner has a major alcohol problem, the other gradually assumes the accustomed functions of the drinking partner. If a wife is alcoholic, the husband may develop contingency plans for supper in case it isn't ready that night. If a husband is alcoholic, the wife may be the one who definitely plans to attend Little League games or school conferences. If the husband is up to it, fine, if not, a ready excuse is hauled out. This leads to resentments in both partners. The spouse carrying the load feels burdened; the drinker feels deprived and ashamed.

With alcohol dependence present, you can count on sexual problems in the primary relationship. In American society, concern over sexual performance seems to be the national pastime. Sexual functioning is not merely a physical activity, it also has strong psychological components. How someone feels about himself or herself and a partner is bound to show up in the bedroom. Any alcohol use can disturb physiological capacity for sex. Shakespeare said it most succinctly: alcohol provokes the desire but takes away the performance. In the male, alcohol interferes with erection—popularly referred to as "brewer's droop." The psychological realm has as strong an impact. Satisfying sexual relationships require an emotional relationship, a bond of love and affection. In a relationship with alcohol as the third member, neither partner is able to trust that bond. There are doubts on both sides. Problems result in many ways. Intoxication invites revulsion and rejection. Any qualities of love have, for the moment, been washed away by booze. Intercourse also can become a weapon. One of the partners can try the old tactic

*Wine makes a man better pleased
with himself; I do not say that it
makes him more pleasing to others.*

SAMUEL JOHNSON

used in the ancient Greek play, *Lysistrata,* of emotional blackmail: refusing sex unless the partner changes his or her behavior. On the other hand, both partners can approach intercourse as the magic panacea. If they can still make love, they can minimize the importance of everything else lacking in the relationship. Sexual fears and anxiety, which are rampant in the total population, are compounded in the alcoholic relationship.

FRIENDSHIPS

In the earlier stages of problem drinking, friends, especially close ones, make the same kind of excuses for the drinker that family members make. But as time goes on, and problems mount as drinking behavior worsens, friendships disappear in inverse relationship to their closeness. In the later stages of alcoholism there may be "drinking buddies" but few true friends. The reasons are fairly obvious. Casual acquaintances are unlikely to be interested in becoming friends after a few examples of erratic behavior. It's simply not worth it. Close friends who have begun to see the alcohol problem emerging will probably try to help by talking to the drinker. In the early stages of an alcohol problem this may well be effective in prompting treatment. However, the defenses grow in magnitude to the problem. Later in the development of alcoholism, the common response is telling the friend to mind her or his own business, thus immobilizing the friend. The drinker's relationship to the bottle takes precedence over all others.

The exceptions only highlight the problem. One type of friend who may remain a companion is one who also drinks as the drinker does and can be counted on to share the sherry luncheons or the six packs on the way home from work. Another kind of friend who will remain in loose touch, ready to lend a hand when needed, is a recovering alcoholic who has gone through much the same process. This person knows the friendship cannot be maintained or profitably cultivated while the drinking continues. But she will often stay in touch, poised to be of assistance and support should the drinker show evidence of wishing to face the problem and stop. When faced with an alcohol problem in someone close to them, recovering individuals, or treatment professionals for that matter, often don't have an edge on anyone else. Their special expertise or personal experience matters little as the dynamics of the family or friendship persist. Maybe because they are more aware than others of the dangers associated with abusive or alcoholic drinking, their desire to have things be "anything but" may be very strong.

WORK

Often, although the alcoholic is deeply mired in deteriorating social and family relationships and suffering physical problems, he or she still may be able to function at work. The work arena seems to be the last part of the drinker's life to be affected. The job is often the status symbol for both the alcoholic employee and the partner. With families more and more dependent upon two paychecks for economic stability, maintaining the income of both members is necessary. He or she might think or say: "There's nothing wrong with me. I'm still bringing in a good paycheck!" The partner is likely to make excuses to the other's boss on his or her behalf to protect the family livelihood.

Intervention at the workplace is, of course, possible at even the earliest signs. Much effort is being made to alert employers to the early signs of alcohol and other drug-use problems and to acquaint them with rehabilitation possibilities. The employer is in a unique position to effect treatment at a relatively early stage. A recommendation that someone go for treatment may well be a precipitating factor in a recovery. The fact that the employer sees the problem and calls a spade a spade can go far in breaking down the denial system. Keeping a job may be sufficient motivation for an employee to face the problem. Employee assistance programs and their impact on earlier intervention and treatment are described further in Chapter 8.

Those in serious trouble with alcohol generally believe that their public cover-up is successful. The behavior of those about them often does little to challenge this misconception. Too often their deteriorating functioning is covered up by other workers. Absences with the "flu" are ignored, and a gradual decline in their work is put down to "problems at home" or some other such excuse. Most people, finding that it is not easy to confront someone with a drinking problem, wait until ignoring it is no longer possible. Over 20 years ago a study found that persons other than family members had noticed drinking problems on an average of 7 years before the alcoholics first sought help. Vaillant's work confirmed this too. Although four or more alcohol-related problems were virtually sufficient to guarantee a diagnosis of alcohol dependence, it wasn't, in fact, until 11 separate such incidents had occurred that people entered treatment.

Often alcohol-impaired persons have no idea how obvious their difficulties are to so many other people. When they are finally confronted, it can be a great shock to find out how much of their behavior that they thought was hidden was, in fact, observed. The rationalization and denial systems actually convinced the active alcoholic that *no one* on the job or in the community knew about the drinking problem.

The behavior that accompanies alcoholism causes pain and confusion for all—the individual and those around him or her. Unfortunately, most of the family's and friends' efforts to alter the situation don't work. Regardless of good will, alcohol dependence rarely responds to the more common maneuvers of concerned people. Affecting these destructive patterns takes a special knowledge of the dynamics of the disease, its effects on others, and treatment approaches, with clinical skills of a disinterested, but not an uninterested, participant.

RESOURCES AND FURTHER READING

Johnson V: *I'll Quit Tomorrow,* revised edition, New York: Harper & Row, 1983.
> In this chapter we have attempted to convey what alcohol dependence feels like for the individual with the disease and for those whose lives are closely touched by it. Tackling the scientific writings, with their reports of controlled studies, tables of data, and reams of footnotes, is unlikely to be a useful avenue for further exploration. Instead we suggest you turn to literature. An autobiography of someone with alcoholism might provide more insight into and understanding of the behavior and feelings that characterize the disease. Consider the plays of Eugene O'Neill. *Long Day's Journey into Night* powerfully captures the family beset by addiction.
>
> Identify a recovering individual with whom you can just talk. Don't consider this a formal interview; consider it a conversation initiated by an interested person who wants to know what another's life was like. Take as a guide the conversation you might have with a close friend who has returned from that long-anticipated trip of a lifetime. Through your questioning and listening, by asking her to "relive" the trip, you imagine being a companion on the adventure.
>
> Attend open meetings of AA or related self-help groups. As members tell their "stories," as they speak about "what it was like," the behavior and the emotional life of active alcoholism are powerfully conveyed.

Schuckit MA, Smith TL, Anthenelli R, and others: Clinical course of alcoholism in 636 male inpatients, *American Journal of Psychiatry* 150(5):786-792, 1993.
> Objective: This study was undertaken to determine the relative order of appearance of symptoms in alcohol dependence. Method: The age at which 21 alcohol-related major life events first occurred was investigated in 636 male alcohol-dependent impatients through a standardized, structured personal interview with each subject and at least one resource person. Results: A general pattern of first occurrence of these events was observed. Heavy drinking escalated further when the subjects were in their late 20s, followed by evidence of interference with functioning in multiple life areas in the early 30s, a subsequent perception of loss of control, and then an intensification of social and job-related problems, along with evidence of deterioration in body systems, in the mid- to late 30s. similar patterns of problems emerged when the alcoholic subjects were divided into subgroups based on onset of alcohol dependence before or after age 30, presence or absence of a family history of alcoholism, and presence or absence of additional psychiatric disorders. Conclusions: These data indicate that there is a typical progression of events related to alcohol dependence. This information can be useful for clinicians in their work with patients and for teachers and researchers as well. (Author abstract.)

von Knorring AL, Annotation: Children of alcoholics (review), *Journal of Child Psychology and Psychiatry* 32(3):411-421, 1991.
> This review of the literature focuses upon the areas of alcohol-related birth defects, home and social environments, psychopathology, somatic problems, and cognitive functioning. (Author's abstract.)

Effects of alcohol problems on the family

·FAMILY PORTRAIT·

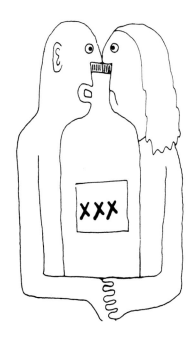

Alcoholism is often called a "family illness." This refers to the tremendous impact those with active alcohol dependence have upon those around them. There is no way the family members can escape or ignore the alcoholic member. The majority of the impairments symptomatic of alcohol dependence are behavioral. So in the day-to-day interactions of family life, the family members are confronted with the behaviors symptomatic of alcoholism, although the behaviors initially may appear to have little connection to the drinking. Over time, the family can become as functionally impaired as the member with alcoholism.

One of the major developments in the alcohol field during the 1980s was the vastly increased attention to the plight of the family. This is evidenced particularly by involvement of families in alcohol treatment. In addition, there has been a major increase in efforts to reach out to family members, even if the alcohol-dependent person is not in treatment. In the early 1980s a review of two books purporting to be comprehensive works on alcoholism noted the scanty attention paid to the impact of active alcoholism on the family. The reviewer plaintively asked, "Why is so much written about the effects of alcoholism upon a patient's liver enzymes and so little written about the effects of parental alcoholism on the children?" Fortunately that question no longer has the same ring of truth to it.

Certainly no family member ever caused alcoholism. Yet the family may, despite its best intentions, behave in a way that allows the continuation of drinking. They may protect the alcoholic member, make excuses, buy into the alibis, help establish the "cover-up." They might call the employer, pretending the absenteeism is due to "the flu." Other facilitating behavior can include covering a bad check or retaining a good lawyer to beat a DWI charge. The alcoholic's actions are bound to increase the family's anxiety level. This in turn may provoke more alcoholic drinking to relieve the alcoholic's own anxiety, which raises the family's anxiety even higher. The higher the anxiety, the more the family members react by doing more of what they were already doing, and then the alcoholic drinks more because of the higher anxiety, ad infinitum. The anxiety escalates on both sides until some crisis occurs. The family is no better able to cope with the disease in its midst than is the impaired member.

There is far more variety in family life today than there was several generations ago. Families today come in many forms. They range from the traditional family, statistically described as husband, wife, 2.2 children, and a dog, to single parent families, unmarried couples, same-sex gay couples, as well as "blended" families, with children from prior marriages or relationships. Variations on the traditional theme inevitably introduce new twists for families. Nonetheless, when it comes to coping with an alcohol problem,

If I were a college student, I would dedicate myself, without fanaticism, but with firm courage and flaming enthusiasm, to the noble cause of Total Abstinence, in order to stop the use of Drink, which has been the great curse to the human family.

JOSEPH HENRY CROOKER,

1914

180

there seem to be very similar dynamics and issues to be faced, whatever the family structure.

THE FAMILY'S RESPONSE

Joan Jackson, in a classic monograph published in 1954, "Alcoholism and the Family," was the first to describe the stages that occur as a family comes to grips with alcoholism. Her research was conducted through her attending meetings and speaking with members of a group known as the *AA Auxiliary*. Later, the Auxiliary became what we know as *Al-Anon Family Groups*. Given the time in which her research was conducted, the stages she identified are based upon the family in which the husband and father was the alcoholic. However, with appropriate translation, the stages she set forth have come to be viewed as describing any family with an alcoholic member. The six stages Jackson sketched out are described below in the order in which they typically unfold.

Denial

Occasional episodes of excessive drinking at first are explained away by both partners. Early in the emergence of alcoholism, drinking because of tiredness, worry, nervousness, or a bad day is not unbelievable. The assumption is that the episode is an isolated instance and therefore no problem. If the couple is part of a group in which heavy drinking is acceptable, this provides a handy cover for developing dependency. A cocktail before dinner easily becomes two or three, and wine with the meal and brandy afterward also pass without much notice.

Attempts to eliminate the problem

Here the alcoholic's partner recognizes that the drinking is not normal and tries to pressure him or her to quit, be more careful, or cut down. "If you only pulled yourself together," or "If you only used a little willpower," or "If you really love me, you won't do this any more." Simultaneously, the alcoholic's partner tries to hide the problem from the outside and keep up a good front. At the same time the alcoholic probably sneaks drinks, or drinks outside the home, in an attempt to hide the amount he or she is drinking. Children in the family may start having problems in response to the family stress.

Years after Jackson's article, in *I'll Quit Tomorrow*, Vernon Johnson pointed out that these early attempts to eliminate the problem may be successful. In such cases, formal treatment or AA involvement is unlikely. Indeed, it may not be needed. Historically, the danger for families at this point was that they might enter some general counseling—whether with clergy, psychologist, or social worker—that failed to address the problem drinking head on. In such cases, cou-

I get no kick from champagne,
Mere alcohol doesn't thrill me at
all,
So tell me why should it be true
that I get a kick out of you?

COLE PORTER (1934)
'I Get a Kick Out of You'

ples or individual therapy easily became a part of the denial. It could be a way for the alcoholic to continue drinking and for both partners to pretend to be doing something about it. Helping professionals are far more knowledgeable about substance abuse today, so the chances of alcohol problems going undetected are less likely.

Disorganization and chaos

The family equilibrium has now broken down. The alcoholic's spouse can no longer pretend everything is okay and spends most of the time going from crisis to crisis. Financial troubles are common. Under real stress, possibly questioning his or her own emotional health, the spouse may seek outside help. In general, women are more likely than men to use outside assistance. Too often spouses may seek help from friends who know no more than they do about what to do. Similarly, they may seek out a member of the clergy who has no training in dealing with alcoholism. Or they may turn to the family physician, who might wish to prescribe some "nerve" pills when confronted by their distraught condition. If at this stage the nonalcoholic partner seeks assistance from alcohol professionals and/or becomes involved with Al-Anon, the process will take a different course altogether.

Reorganization in spite of the problem

The spouse's coping abilities have been strengthened. He or she gradually assumes the larger share of responsibility for the family unit. This may mean getting a job or taking over the finances. The major focus of energy is no longer directed toward getting the alcoholic partner to "shape up." Instead, the spouse takes charge. The spouse fosters family life, despite the alcoholism. It has been recognized that the degree to which a stable family life can be established and maintained, even if the alcoholic remains in the home, can have important implications for the welfare of children in the family. Children fare far better in families in which the family rituals are maintained, whether these are celebrations such as Christmas, birthdays, and family vacations, or other things "we always do together."

Efforts to escape

Separation or divorce may be attempted. If the family unit remains intact, the family continues living around the alcoholic member.

Family reorganization

In the case of separation, family reorganization occurs without the alcoholic partner and parent. If the alcoholic achieves sobriety, a reconciliation may take place. Either path will require both partners to realign roles and make new adjustments.

As mentioned, Jackson's formulations are focused on the family in which the husband is alcoholic. An interesting difference is found in marriage outcomes depending on which partner has the alcohol problem. Among alcoholics, the female alcoholic is much more likely to be divorced than is the male alcoholic. In the past, those trying to account for this difference speculated that women who marry alcoholics have unconscious, neurotic needs to be married to weak, inadequate males. The implication was that because of this need, they stayed married and got psychological strokes for doing so. That view no longer has much credence. The more current view is that, in large measure, nonalcoholic wives remain married to their alcoholic husbands because they are debilitated by stress.

Research on marriage has identified some reasons why partners choose each other. For all persons, it is generally recognized that finding one's "true love" and the choice of a marriage partner is not a random event. People tend to select marriage partners with similarities to their parents. Many women who marry alcoholic men are daughters of alcoholics. For them, a situation that appears to us as stressful and painful may simply be what they expect in a marriage. Those involved in alcohol treatment are struck by the fact that some women marry or live with a succession of alcoholics.

Given economic realities, it is not unexpected that the nonalcoholic wife stays in her marriage longer than the nonalcoholic husband. She may well feel a need for the husband's financial support to maintain the family. Indeed, following a divorce, the economic situation for the majority of women and their children declines. On the other side, men in general are less likely to seek outside help for any kind of problem—no matter what kind. Therefore the husband of a female alcoholic may see no alternative to divorce to save himself, as well as the children.

Of course not all families experience these stages in the textbook fashion. Some families may get bogged down in different stages. Some never move beyond denial. Some seem trapped in an endless cycle of chaos and crisis. And some go through a painful succession of attempts to escape from the situation, reconciliations, followed by later attempts again to escape. Our understanding of the factors that account for these differences is limited. One factor that may make a difference is when the problem drinking emerges. Those who have studied alcoholic marriages suggest that wives most able to help themselves and their families are those who were married before their husbands became problem drinkers.

THE FAMILY SYSTEM

The most common approach to the alcoholic family is to view the family as a system. Central to this view is the belief that changes in any part of the system (any family member) affect all of the others.

The other members, in response, also make changes in an attempt to maintain the family equilibrium. The metaphor that captures this close interdependence is that of a circus family specializing in a high-wire balancing act. All members of the act climb up to the top of the tent. In turn, they step out on the thin wire to begin an intricate set of maneuvers to build a human pyramid high above the audience. Timing and balance are critical; the mutual interdependence is obvious. Each is sensitive to even the tiniest movement of the others. All of the family members in the performance continually adjust and readjust their balance, which is necessary to maintain the routine. If only one fails to do the expected, the entire routine fails.

In essence, families with an impaired member function in a very similar fashion. The alcoholic's behavior begins to invade the family routine. Everyone attempts to compensate, with the goal of restoring the equilibrium to the family. Most families make precarious, and usually unhealthy, adjustments to the presence of drinking. They expend energy to maintain the status quo, "the familiar and known." The family's behavior is designed to avoid doing anything which might further upset the delicate balance that prevails, which to their minds would prompt further deterioration of the family's situation. And, after having adjusted to a problem, the family would be required to make significant readjustments if the impaired member were to seek treatment.

In terms of the kinds of accommodations that families make, there can be a range of responses. At one extreme the drinking alcoholic is almost like a boarder in the family's household. The family isolates and walls off the alcoholic. They expect little. They give little. In this way, they maintain some stability and continuity for themselves. At the other extreme the entire family life is constantly alcohol-centered, responding to the crisis of the moment. In addition, families can vacillate between patterns of accommodating the alcoholic, depending on whether the alcoholic is drinking or on the wagon.

In looking at the way in which family members accommodate the alcoholic member, Vernon Johnson noted that many of their behaviors have a very unexpected result. While attempting to live with and around the alcoholism and to reduce the level of pain for themselves, the family's behavior often unwittingly "allows" the drinking to continue. This is occurring whenever the family's actions protect the alcoholic member from the drinking's consequences. By removing the costs that result from drinking, the family takes away the major impetus for change. This phenomenon Johnson termed *enabling*. Enabling behavior can be "white lies," the explanations provided to others that take the alcoholic off the hook. Enabling can consist of "overlooking," or not commenting upon, the most outrageous behavior. Often it entails active intervention on the alcoholic's behalf. It is happening whenever the spouse scurries around to raise bail money and then follows up with a call to the local newspaper requesting that the arrest be kept out of the paper. It is happening when parents cover the cost of an adolescent son's car repairs plus the added insurance premiums resulting from a DWI. Enabling can be cleaning up your college roommate when she comes in drunk and throws up on herself, the rug, the bed, and *your* sweater that she was wearing.

Ironically, while sparing the alcoholic from experiencing the consequences and thus the associated pain, the family members absorb the pain themselves. The behavior considered as enabling may be viewed as necessary because: "I care," "At least it buys peace," "I just can't take any more," "I'm afraid of what will happen to me (to the children) if I don't," "Someone has to assume some responsibility," and on and on. Nonetheless, it usually involves actions that are distasteful or feel wrong. Enabling behaviors can evoke twinges of guilt, anger, despair, frustration, and shame. Returning to the concept of the family system, the enabler and alcoholic are in an escalating equilibrium, the behavior of each reinforcing and maintaining the other, while also raising the costs and the emotional consequences for both.

The costs to family members are not limited to their psychological health, self-esteem, or identity. The consequences can be measured, too, in greater levels of physical illness, especially of stress-related illnesses. Family members are, for example, more vulnerable to gastrointestinal disease, migraine headaches, hypertension, anxiety, and depression. A comparison of health-care costs for family units both before and after alcoholism treatment of a family member bears this out. Before treatment of the alcoholic member, others in the family had significantly more medical problems than did the general population. After treatment, this difference disappeared. The members of the family with active alcoholism also are more likely to be touched by domestic violence.

Codependency

A term that increasingly has been used to describe the effects on family members touched by alcoholism is *codependency. Codependent* is the term used for the affected individual. While widely used, there is no single definition for these terms. Sometimes they are used as a label, simply as a shorthand means to refer to family members. In other instances, codependency is viewed as a clinical diagnosis with a set of specific symptoms. Timmen Cermak M.D. has been one of the leading advocates for the use of codependency as a clinical diagnostic category. He views it as a type of personality disorder. Using the diagnostic schema of DSM-III, Cermak has suggested that the following criteria be used to make the diagnosis:

1. Continued investment of one's self-esteem in the ability to control oneself and others in the face of serious adverse consequences

2. Assumption of responsibility for meeting others' needs to the exclusion of one's own
3. Anxiety and boundary distortions with respect to intimacy and separation
4. Enmeshment in relationships with personality disordered, chemically dependent, other codependent, and/or impulse disordered individuals
5. Three or more of the following:
   - excessive reliance on denial
   - constriction of emotions
   - depression
   - hypervigilance
   - compulsions
   - anxiety
   - substance abuse
   - being the victim of past or current physical or sexual abuse
   - stress-related medical illnesses
   - remaining in a primary relationship with an active substance abuser for at least 2 years without seeking help

A word of caution. The widespread adoption of "codependency" and "codependent" terminology has been the source of increasing discomfort for many in the alcohol and substance abuse fields. No one would dispute the effects of alcohol dependence on family members or the fact that these family members are statistically more likely to encounter many problems in greater numbers than their counterparts in the general population. However, to award labels indiscriminately and to presume that every family member shares the constellation of symptoms of codependency is a grave disservice to clients. Assumptions based simply on family status cannot substitute for a careful assessment and evaluation. There is the danger too that the strengths of families and family members are overlooked when one assumes pathology.

The research on families touched by alcoholism is growing geometrically. Among the issues being examined, for example, are the factors that are associated with differing levels of family dysfunction, the factors that are associated with stable recoveries in families following treatment, and the indications for different types of family treatment. The evidence suggests that all families are not affected by alcohol dependence in a uniform manner. As such research continues we will be better able to substitute facts for hypotheses and suppositions. The same is true with respect to children in the family.

CHILDREN OF ALCOHOLICS
Children in the home

It is estimated that in the United States, one of every eight children under the age of 18 is growing up in a family with parental alcoholism. These children deserve special attention. In an atmosphere of conflict, tension, and uncertainty, their needs for warmth, security, and even physical care may be inadequately met. In a family where adult roles are inconsistently and inadequately filled, children lack good models to form their own identities. It is more likely that such children will have a harder time than their peers as they enter into relationships outside the home, at school, or with playmates. A troubled child may be the signal of an alcohol problem in a family. Although alcoholics represent only 7% of the American population, their children account for approximately 20% of all referrals to child guidance clinics.

It cannot be emphasized too strongly how much remains unknown about the impact of alcoholism on children. In the following discussion of children's coping styles and the impact that continues into adulthood, it must be emphasized that the conclusions that this is not based on unbiased scientific research. Much of what is now being attributed to children of alcoholics has originated in self-help groups of adults who grew up in alcoholic homes. Or the information has come from children of alcoholics who have sought treatment. Although their wounds are real, one must ask how far one can safely generalize from their experiences. They may represent a minority of children of alcoholics. Or they may be speaking primarily for another generation—when alcoholism treatment was less common, when family treatment was unheard of, and when alcoholism was more of a stigma.

Without question, growing up with an alcoholic parent is far from ideal. At the same time, the experiences of children in alcoholic families vary greatly. There are different patterns of drinking and different behaviors associated with drinking. Children are various ages, as are their parents, when the drinking problem becomes apparent, or when loss of control occurs. Furthermore, there are differences in the coping styles of the non-alcoholic parent, which can moderate the impact of the drinking on family life. All these factors influence how a parent's drinking affects the child. The specific problems of particular children will vary. Furthermore, a child's own natural resilience may be buttressed by the nurturing of extended family, scout leaders, coaches, teachers and neighbors, or parents of peers. Thus a child's experience may be less impoverished than it might appear. Furthermore, many of the problems encountered are not exclusive to the alcoholic home. Many of the characteristics attributed to alcoholic families may be generally true of any dysfunctional family. Nonetheless, in thinking of children it is hard not to think in terms of the dramatic.

Take 5 minutes to imagine what life might be like for a child with an alcoholic parent.

As a preschooler. What is it like to lie in bed listening to your parents fight? Or to have Daddy disappear for periods of time unexpectedly? Or to be spanked really hard and sent away from dinner just because your milk

spilled? Or to have a succession of sitters because Mommy works two jobs? Or to get lots of attention one moment and be in the way the next instant?

As an elementary schoolchild. What is it like when your mom forgets to pack a lunch? Or to wait and wait after soccer practice for a ride, long after the other kids have been picked up? Or for Dad to cancel out on the cub scout hike because he is sick? Or not to be allowed to bring friends home to play? Or to have your friends' moms not let them ride in your car? Or to be scared to tell your mom you need a white shirt to be a pilgrim in the class Thanksgiving play?

As an adolescent. What is it like if you can't participate in school functions because you must get home to care for your younger brothers and sisters? Or if the money you made mowing lawns is missing from your room? Or if your dad's name is regularly featured in the court column? Or if your mother asks you to telephone her boss because she has a black eye from falling down? Or if there's no one from your family to come to the athletic awards banquet?

In considering the impact of such behaviors, it is helpful to consider the normal developmental tasks which confront children of different ages and consider how these may be impeded by a parental alcohol problem. Those who have studied the process of emotional development see very early childhood as the period in life in which the major emotional tasks center on developing a sense of security and an ability to trust the environment. At the same time a sense of one's ability to interact with others to have basic needs met should be learned. For the child of an alcohol-dependent parent, these basic conditions may not be met. For preadolescent children a major emotional task is developing a sense of autonomy and an ability to use rules to cope with life events. For adolescents, the emotional tasks center around separation from the family and developing the ability to function independently in the world.

The problems may have begun before birth. As discussed in Chapter 5, maternal alcohol use can influence fetal development. At its most extreme, this is expressed as *fetal alcohol syndrome*. In addition to the direct impact of the drug, behaviors associated with alcoholism may affect fetal development. Physical trauma, including falls, malnutrition, or abnormalities of glucose metabolism, are not uncommon in alcoholics. Any of these could have an impact on a developing baby.

The emotional state of the expectant mother probably influences fetal development. It certainly has an influence on the course of labor and delivery. The emotional state of the alcoholic expectant mother might differ dramatically from that of a normal, healthy, nonalcoholic expectant mother and may be a source of problems.

An alcoholic expectant father may exert some indirect prenatal influences. If he is abusive or provides little emotional and financial support, this could cause anxiety in the mother. Lack of support and consequent anxiety during pregnancy are associated with more difficult deliveries. In a similar vein, stress at certain times during pregnancy increases fetal activity. This, in turn, is linked to colicky babies.

No specific data are available on labor and delivery for either female alcoholics or wives of male alcoholics. Increased maternal anxiety may precipitate problems of labor and delivery. Furthermore, these difficulties are related to developmental disorders in children.

Another crucial time in any infant's life comes shortly after delivery. The very early interactions between mother and infant are important influences in the mother-child relationship. Medications that may be required for a difficult delivery can make the bonding more difficult. Both the mother and the infant, under the effects of the medication, are less able to respond to each other.

A new mother needs emotional and physical support to help her deal with the presence of the baby in her life. At a minimum, the baby requires food, warmth, physical comfort, and consistency of response from the mother. In the case of a family with an active alcoholic, one cannot automatically assume that everything is going smoothly.

Children's coping styles

Some children of alcoholics may be having quite apparent and obvious problems. Yet, given the potential for a chaotic environment in the alcoholic family, it is sometimes striking how well children cope with alcoholism. Drawing on a family systems approach to the alcoholic family, family therapists have identified several distinctive coping styles that children adopt.

One of these coping styles is to be the *responsible one*. This role usually falls to the only child or the oldest child, especially the oldest daughter. The child may assume considerable responsibility not only for himself or herself but also for younger brothers and sisters— taking over chores and keeping track of what needs to be done. In general, this child compensates as much as possible for the instability and inconsistency introduced by the parental alcoholism. Another coping response is that of the *adjuster*. This child doesn't take on the responsibilities of managing. Instead the child follows directions and easily accommodates to whatever comes along. This child is remarkable for how much he or she takes in stride. The third style is to be the *placater*. This role involves managing not the physical affairs, as the responsible one does, but the emotional affairs. This child is ever attuned to being concerned and sensitive to others. It may include being sympathetic to the alcoholic and

Darlene is mother's little helper. I don't know how I'd survive without her.

THe family Scapegoat

alternately to the nonalcoholic parent, always trying to soothe ruffled feathers.

What these roles have in common is that each in its own way is an attempt to survive, a coping strategy. These roles also can provide the child with support and approval from persons outside the home. For example, the *responsible one* probably is a good student, Mommy's little helper, and gets praise for both. The danger to a child is becoming frozen in these roles. These roles can become a lifetime pattern. What is helpful in childhood can be detrimental for an adult. The *responsible one* can become an adult who needs always to be on top of things, in control, destined to the stress of attempting to be a lifetime superachiever. The *flexible one* (the adjuster) may be so tentative, so unable to trust, as to be unable to make the long-term commitments that are required to succeed in a career or intimate adult personal relationships, such as spouse or parent. Likely as not, the *adjuster* adults are so attuned to accommodating others that they allow themselves to be manipulated. An ever-present option for the adult *adjuster* is to marry someone with a problem, such as an alcoholic, which allows the continuation of the adjuster role. The adult *placaters* are continually caring for others, often at the price of being unaware of their own needs or being unable to meet them. This can lead to large measures of guilt and anger, neither of which a placater can handle easily.

A different but similar typology of the roles that children adopt in response to parental alcoholism includes *the family hero, the lost child, the family mascot,* and *the scapegoat.* The first three have much in common with the three styles just discussed: the responsible one, the adapter, and the placater. The specific labels are less important than the fact that children develop coping styles in response to the family stress of alcoholism. Most of these coping styles may not elicit external attention or invite intervention. The exception is the *scapegoat,* who is the one most likely to be in trouble in school or with the authorities. This is the one who, usually acting angry and deviant, may be the only child clearly seen as having a problem. If the child is a teenager, the trouble may take the form of drug or alcohol abuse. (This is discussed in the section on adolescents in Chapter 10.) Frequently, through the attention focused on this child by outsiders or the family, the family alcohol problem may first surface. Of course, initially the family will see the child as the central problem. And the scapegoat's behavior takes the focus off the parental alcohol problem. Having a common problem to tackle may help keep a fragile family intact. Often the family may create the myth that the drinking is the parent's coping response to the child's behavior. Alternately, the child may be held responsible for aggravating the parent's drinking.

In adulthood, these coping styles can be translated into skills. The placater's sensitivity and ability to be sympathetic and understanding may be assets in helping professions such as social work, psychiatry, and counseling. So too the responsible ones may have acquired skills that can serve them in good stead, through their diligence as students and their continued sense of responsibility. The challenge for both is to appreciate the origins and be attuned to the pitfalls.

Adult children of alcoholics

Over the past decade, there was a rapid rise in attention to another population of family members, the *adult children of alcoholics*. On the heels of a self-help movement that arose for adult children, treatment programs began to pay more attention to this group. Presumably because attention and help for the alcoholic is such a recent phenomenon, these now adult children reared in homes with parental alcoholism received no help as children in dealing with this, no matter what the fate of the alcoholic parent. Whether the alcoholic parent died from the disease, or left the home, or recovered, these children, in adult life, see themselves and are seen as experiencing difficulties that developed from their experiences in an alcoholic family.

The attention to adult children of alcoholics as a population with special problems and special needs grew out of self-help groups. The earliest and in some instances most widely cited writings are not based on research data. Instead they are based on anecdotal evidence and observations of those involved in self-help, who viewed their problems in adulthood as related to their childhood experiences in a home with alcoholism. This literature has set forth a set of characteristics seen as common to adult children. The characteristics include fear of losing control, fear of feelings, fear of conflict, an overdeveloped sense of responsibility, feelings of guilt when standing up for oneself, an inability to relax, let go, or have fun, harsh self-criticism, living in a world of denial, difficulties with intimate relationships, living life from the stance of a victim, the tendency to be more comfortable with chaos than security, the tendency to confuse love and pity, the tendency under pressure to assume a black-and-white perspective, suffering under a backlog of delayed grief, a tendency to react rather than to act, and an ability to survive. While not based on research, these characteristics still have the ring of truth for those who are still coming to grips with a childhood in an alcoholic family. They are felt to offer a useful framework for addressing this legacy. Going from an assumed set of common characteristics, some have suggested that this adult behavior pattern should be considered a variant of the psychiatric disorder—Post–Traumatic Stress Disorder (PTSD). While popularly associated with problems experienced by some Vietnam veterans, PTSD is recognized as a disorder that may occur following any severe trauma, be it rape, incest, a natural disaster, or armed conflicts.

While the self-help movement may have been the first to identify adult children of alcoholics as a group with special concerns, there has been a growing body of research. For example, Claudia Black compared adults raised in an alcoholic home to adults raised in a nonalcoholic home as to their perceptions of violence, sexual abuse, communication in their childhood homes, and interpersonal differences experienced as adults. The adults raised in alcoholic families reported (1) significantly less use of interpersonal resources as a child, (2) significantly more family disruptions characterized by a higher divorce rate and premature parental and sibling death, (3) more emotional and psychological problems in adulthood, (4) more physical and sexual abuse as children, and (5) they became alcoholic and married alcoholics more frequently than adults raised in nonalcoholic families.

A study by Emily Werner that has not received the attention it deserves compared the offspring of alcoholics who did and those who did not develop serious coping problems by age 18. The study examined the characteristics of the children and the caregiving environment in which they were raised. Those studied were members of a multiracial cohort of approximately 700 children born in 1955 on the Hawaiian island of Kauai. Follow-up studies were conducted at ages 1, 2, 10, and 18. Of this entire group, approximately 14% had either a mother or father who had alcoholism. Children of alcoholics who did not develop serious coping problems by age 18 were distinguished from those who did, in terms of their personal characteristics and their early environment. Those without serious problems had a belief in taking care of themselves, an orientation toward achievement, a positive self-concept, and an internal locus of control (meaning their behavior was prompted more by their own feelings and beliefs than its being a response to others). In terms of the environment, in the first 2 years of life they received a high level of attention from the primary-care giver and experienced fewer stressful events that disrupted the family unit. Thus Werner found it was not the presence or absence of alcoholism per se that predicted difficulties, but the interaction of the child and the environment. Werner also identified some differences depending upon the sex of the alcoholic parent and the child. Boys had higher rates of psychosocial problems in childhood and adolescence than did girls Also, the children of alcoholic mothers had higher rates of problems in childhood and adolescence than did offspring of alcoholic fathers.

It cannot be assumed that all children who grew up or are now growing up in an alcoholic home share a single set of personality characteristics. Nor can it be assumed that all problems encountered in adult life can be attributed to being a child of an alcoholic. But the adult-children-of-alcoholics framework may well be useful to those suffering from problems, of whatever origins, who need to find some way out of an impasse and make needed changes.

Genetic vulnerability

Another way in which the child of an alcoholic is vulnerable to alcoholism is in terms of genetic endowment. Children of alcoholics are considered at risk for development of the disease in an approximate 4:1 ratio to those without an alcoholic parent. Research has suggested that the gender of the child is a significant factor influencing later life problems. Boys of alcoholic parents are more likely to suffer from attention deficit disorders with hyperactivity than are children of nonalcoholic parents. On the other hands, girls are more likely than their brothers to encounter eating disorders or depression in later life.

ALCOHOLISM IN OTHER FAMILY MEMBERS

Alcoholism is obviously not limited only to the parental generation. It may occur in adolescents, or it may occur in grandparents. The effects on the family are still powerful, though possibly less dramatic. Adolescent alcohol problems and alcoholism among the elderly are discussed in Chapter 10. However, it is important to realize that regardless of the particular family member affected, the effects of alcoholism are not limited to the alcoholic alone. The response of the family will resemble the stages described by Jackson. The problems are now seen as requiring intervention. Also they are increasingly the focus of prevention efforts. In addition, family issues are now a central part of any alcohol treatment. Treatment approaches to the alcoholic family are discussed in Chapter 9.

RESOURCES AND FURTHER READING

Beidler RJ: Adult children of alcoholics: Is it really a separate field of study? *Drugs and Society* 3(3/4):133-141, 1989.

> This article reviews the nature of the literature on children of alcoholics, comparing and contrasting that which is research based and that which is intuitive and largely anecdotal. The central question addressed by this review is whether there is a discrete set of characteristics that warrant the consideration of adult children of alcoholics as a separate field of study.

Black C, Bucky SF, and Wilder-Padilla S: The interpersonal and emotional consequences of being an adult child of an alcoholic, *International Journal of the Addictions* 21(2):213-231, 1986.

> The purpose of this study was to compare adults raised in an alcoholic home (N ;eq 409) with adults raised in a nonalcoholic home (N ;eq 179) as to their perceptions of alcohol-related differences in the home, violence, sexual abuse, communication, and interpersonal differences experienced as adults. The adults who were raised in alcoholic families (1) reported significantly less utilization of interpersonal resources as children, (2) had significantly more family disruptions, characterized by a higher divorce rate and premature parental and sibling death, (3) reported more emotional and psychological problems in adulthood, (4) experienced more physical and sexual abuse as children, and (5) more frequently became alcoholic and married alcoholics than adults raised in nonalcoholic families (Author abstract).

Brown S: *Treating adult children of alcoholics: A developmental perspective,* New York, John Wiley & Sons, 1988.

This work offers a theoretical foundation for understanding and treating children of alcoholics. In three parts, following a literature review, it discusses (1) the alcoholic family, addressing family environment and patterns of common interaction, (2) the impact of parental alcoholism on individual development in terms of defenses, attachments, and identity formation, and (3) the recovery process with attention to core issues, therapeutic tasks, and the process or stages in recovery.

Brown SA: Life events of adolescents in relation to personal and parental substance abuse, *American Journal of Psychiatry* 146(4):484-489, 1989.

The author examined the life events reported by 138 adolescents in relation to their own and their parents' alcohol and/or drug use. The 62 adolescents who were substance abusers reported more negative events involving deviance and emotional distress and evaluated the life events they experienced as less desirable than did the 76 nonabusing adolescents. The substance-abusing adolescents and the 31 nonabusing adolescents with substance-abusing parents experienced comparable numbers of stressful life experiences; however, the type and qualitative features of the events differed. Adolescents with substance abuse in only one family generation experienced more emotional distress than those with substance use patterns consistent across generations (Author abstract).

Cermak TL: *Diagnosing and treating co-dependence: A guide for professionals who work with chemical dependents, their spouses and children,* Minneapolis: Johnson Institute Books, 1986.

The author, a clinician involved early in the treatment of those living with an alcoholic spouse or parent, describes these dysfunctions as a syndrome, which he terms "codependency" and conceptualizes as a disease entity consistent with DSM-III diagnostic criteria. Using a DSM-III–like schema, criteria for diagnosis of codependency are presented and treatment approaches described.

Gorney B: Domestic violence and chemical dependency: Duel problems, dual interventions, *Journal of Psychoactive Drugs* 21(2):229-238, 1989.

This article addresses the link between domestic violence and chemical dependency. Both are extremely prevalent and pose serious threats to individuals, families, communities, and society at large. The commonly observed association between substance abuse and violent interactions traditionally has been explained as a cause and effect. It is assumed that intoxication causes violence, and this viewpoint has traditionally dominated research on the subject as well as treatment methodology. This interpretation may lead treatment providers to assume that once abstinence from alcohol and other drugs is achieved, violence will also disappear. Researchers in the field of domestic violence argue that violence occurs both when substance abuse is present and when it is absent. This article addresses the need to assess and treat both problem areas concurrently. In addition to providing assessment and treatment guidelines, the author describes the scope of the problem, etiological issues, and factors that may serve as barriers to treatment providers in identifying violence as a problem in chemically dependent relationship systems (Author abstract).

Jackson JK: The adjustment of the family to the crisis of alcoholism, *Quarterly Journal of Studies on Alcohol* 15(4):562-586, 1954.

Through a study of members of the "AA Auxiliary," the predecessor for what became Al-Anon, the author identifies a seven-step progression in a family's adjustment to the presence of an alcoholic member. This progression continues to inform discussions of alcoholism's effects on the family. The stages are denial, to efforts to eliminate the problem, followed by disorganization, efforts to reorganize despite the problem, efforts to escape the problem, which may entail a dissolution of the marriage, and leading either to reorganization of part of the family or recovery and reorganization of the whole family.

Johnson V: *I'll Quit Tomorrow,* (rev ed), New York: Harper & Row, 1980.

This work introduces the technique of "the intervention," a method to initiate treatment. The use of "interventions" promotes earlier treatment and prompts care for those previously seen as either "unready" or "inaccessible." The adoption of this clinical approach dispelled the myth that a patient's apparent motivation to cease use is a significant factor in determining treatment outcome, thus revolutionizing alcohol treatment and, by example, drug abuse treatment as well. This work also introduces the concept of "enabling," i.e., the interactions of the family and the alcoholic that unwittingly support the continuation of drinking or drug use. Efforts to counter these behaviors, tied to the framework of the "intervention," offer the family a constructive role beyond "detachment with love," the primary orientation of Al-Anon, the self-help group for family members.

Jones CL, Battjes RJ, editors: *Etiology of drug abuse: Implications for prevention, NIDA research monograph 56,* Rockville, MD: National Institute on Drug Abuse, 1985.

This monograph defines the "state of the art" in prevention research in respect to drug abuse. Contributors are those conducting research funded by National Institute on Drug Abuse (NIDA). The work is divided into two major sections. The first is "Childhood and the Transition to Adolescence," which includes discussion of familial antecedents of adolescent drug use from a developmental perspective, the development of health orientation among children and the implications for substance use prevention; predictors of adolescent substance abuse; and research strategies to identify developmental vulnerabilities for drug abuse. The second section, "Transition to Young Adulthood," addresses recent historical changes that may relate to issues of etiology and prevention; age of onset of drug use as a factor in subsequent problems; patterns of use of legal, illegal, and medically prescribed psychotropic drugs during later adolescence; prevention of adolescent drug abuse drawing upon etiological, developmental, behavioral, and environmental models; and discussion of pressing research questions. Federal Publication No ADM 85-1335.

Pilat JM, Jones JW: Identification of children of alcoholics: Two empirical studies, *Alcohol Health and Research World* 9(2):26-36, 1985.

This paper presents the CAST (Children of Alcoholics Screening Test): a thirty-item yes-or-no questionnaire, which summarizes the validation and reliability studies conducted. The authors then describe its use in two settings. The first identified children of alcoholics in a classroom setting (10th, 11th, and 12th grade students). According to the CAST, 27% were children of alcoholics. The second study used the CAST to identify children of alcoholics among those enrolled in a course on alcoholism and family dynamics. The students consisted of experienced professional clinicians, social work and family therapy students, and other helping professionals. The CAST identified 28.4% of the experienced therapists, 25.5% of the students, and 46.2% of other helping professionals as children of alcoholics.

Rivinus TM, editor: *Children of chemically dependent parents: Multiperspectives from the cutting edge,* New York: Brunner/Mazel, 1991. (chapter refs.)

This edited work with 21 contributors has three goals. The first is to bridge the literature of the self-help movements and academic communities, the second is to focus upon the particular problems of younger children within families with substance abuse problems, and the third is to integrate the basic science, clinical, and research findings with public policy and public health prevention efforts. The work is organized into four sections. The first is devoted to "academic" perspectives. It reviews the biological and genetic research and reviews the major theoretical approaches with special attention to developmental considerations. The second deals with issues of psychiatric perspectives relevant to diagnosis, namely the relationship between codependence and narcissism, and chronic trauma disorders of childhood. The third section is devoted to treatment considerations. The final section centers on issues related to public policy.

Roosa MW, Sandler L: Risk status of adolescent children of problem drinking parents, *American Journal of Community Psychology* 16(2):225-239, 1988.

> These studies assessed the risk status of children of untreated alcoholics. In study one, a cross-sectional survey of 208 high school students identified 18% as having serious concern about their parents' drinking. In study two, 32 children of problem-drinking parents and 39 others who participated in self-help groups were surveyed. Children of problem-drinking parents were more at risk for depression, low self-esteem, and heavy drinking than their peers in the general high school population. Within self-help groups, however, children's symptomatology was not related to their parents' drinking status. The results support the need for preventive intervention for children of problem-drinking parents and for developing strategies for improving the participation rate of such children in the intervention programs that are available (Author abstract).

Werner EE: Resilient offspring of alcoholics: A longitudinal study from birth to age 18, *Journal of Studies on Alcohol* 47(1):34-40, 1986.

> This study focuses on child characteristics and on the qualities of the caregiving environment that differentiated between offspring of alcoholics who did and those who did not develop serious coping problems by age 18. The 49 subjects (22 male) are members of a multiracial cohort of 698 children, born in 1955, on the Hawaiian island of Kauai. Follow-up studies were conducted at ages 1, 2, 10, and 18. In this group, males and the offspring of alcoholic mothers had higher rates of psychosocial problems in childhood and adolescence than females and the offspring of alcoholic fathers. Children of alcoholics who developed no serious coping problems by age 18 differed from those who did in characteristics of temperament, communication skills, self-concept, and locus of control. They also had experienced fewer stressful life events disrupting their family unit in the first 2 years of life. Results of the study support a transactional model of human development and demonstrate bidirectionality of child care–giver effects (Author abstract).
>
> Note: There is concern that the dysfunctions associated with being a child of an alcoholic are being overdiagnosed and too often are ascribed on the basis of family history rather than upon clinical evaluation. Another trend of concern is the tendency to generalize from the body of work on children of alcoholics, much based upon lay efforts, to the larger field of children of dysfunctional families. This study provides an invaluable context for any consideration of the effects of alcohol problems upon children, and the study from which it was derived (Werner EE, Smith RS: *Vulnerable but invincible: A longitudinal study of resilient children and youth,* New York: McGraw-Hill, 1982) similarly offers a context for consideration of the impact of dysfunctional families upon child development.

Woititz J: *Adult children of alcoholics,* Hollywood FL: Health Communications, Inc., 1983.

> One of the first popular handbooks on the topic and widely read in both the counselor and lay communities, it has been the source of many of the precepts that have influenced both professional treatment and self-help approaches.

Wood BL: *Children of alcoholics: The struggle for self and intimacy in adult life,* New York: New York University Press, 1987.

> In a field that primarily addresses adult children of alcoholics descriptively, this work provides a theoretical perspective to support clinical practice with children of alcoholics. The book reviews the writings of major contributors to the work on adult children, draws upon the author's clinical practice, and integrates this with the theoretical perspectives provided by object relations theorists and self psychology. The author draws upon the discussions of problems with identity, intimacy, and self-esteem characteristically seen in adult children of alcoholics.

Woodside M: Research on children of alcoholics: Past and future, *British Journal of Addiction* 83(7): 785-792, 1988.

There are 28.6 million children of alcoholics in the United States—one out of every eight Americans. Many of them suffer negative physical, mental, and emotional consequences as a result of parental alcoholism. Research investigations of their health status, cognitive abilities, and adaptive behaviors confirm these problems, although notable impediments to research efforts presently exist. Among the fruitful areas for future study are investigations that explore levels of vulnerability and risk factors for children of alcoholics in combination with genetic and psychosocial factors. Other recommendations for study, as well as the major activities of the Children of Alcoholics Foundation to promote and disseminate research findings and new data, are described (Author abstract).

Evaluation and treatment overview

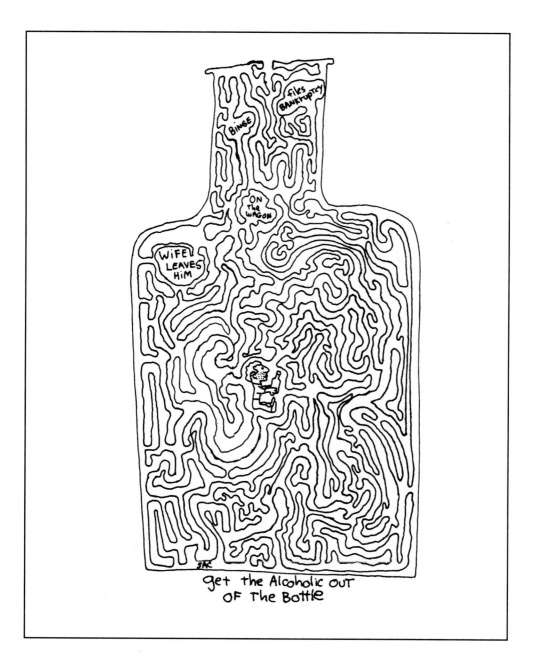

As muse or creative companion, alcohol can be devastating. In memoriam to some of those who did battle with this two-faced spirit:
John Barrymore
John Berryman
Lillian Roth
U.S. Grant
O. Henry (William Sydney Porter)
Eugene O'Neill
Stephen Crane
Hart Crane
F. Scott Fitzgerald
Edna St. Vincent Millay
Jack London
Ernest Hemingway
Dylan Thomas
Diana Barrymore
Isadora Duncan
Sinclair Lewis
Kenneth Roberts
Judy Garland
Joseph McCarthy
Robert Benchley
Edgar Allen Poe
Jim Thorpe
Charles Jackson
Dame May Whitty
Sarah Churchill
Jackson Pollock
W.C. Fields
Audie Murphy
Henri de Toulouse-Lautrec
Baudelaire
Brendan Behan
Ring Lardner
Robert Lowell
Jimi Hendrix
Alexander the Great

When one is acutely aware of alcohol problems and alcoholism, the question arises, "How can they be treated?" Perhaps your question is more personal, "How can I help?" As a prelude to this, it is essential to consider how people recover and what treatment or intervention is about.

At this juncture in earlier editions we (1) made a principled plea for early intervention, (2) backed that up with the reminder that this approach is indicated for any chronic disease process, then (3) acknowledged that this represented an ideal, which unfortunately was infrequently reflected in actual practice, and (4) proceeded to zero in on treatment of alcoholism. There was virtually no mention of evaluation, diagnostic assessment, or treatment approaches to other problems associated with alcohol use. Indeed, even 5 to 10 years ago many alcohol clinicians had very little need for or opportunity to use those skills. The diagnosis of alcoholism or what is now termed *alcohol dependence,* for all practical purposes, had occurred before the client's arrival in the alcohol clinician's office. Very few individuals came into contact with alcohol or drug treatment facilities by mistake. The chief practical use for informing an alcohol or substance abuse professionals of diagnostic criteria was to enable them to educate other human service professionals, thereby facilitating referrals of those with alcohol dependence who were going undetected. This information was also helpful in providing client education. Similarly, the major role of the alcohol use history was in developing treatment plans, rather than it being a prerequisite for diagnosis.

In days past, those who by today's classification are alcohol abusers, if they became clients in the alcohol treatment system, were treated as "early-stage alcoholics." Accordingly, they were provided the standard treatment for alcoholism. Their life situations often were reminiscent of the typical alcoholism client's circumstances 10 to 20 years before treatment. Remember, an average of 7 years elapsed from the point of the disease being clearly present to the point of entering treatment. That fact was used to "sell" the diagnosis and attempt to lead the client to accept it, hopefully with gratitude! Alcohol treatment professionals obviously recognized that such individuals were different from the usual client. It was recognized that providing full-blown alcoholism treatment might be a bit drastic. However, it was viewed as the prudent, cautious approach. Even if the diagnosis of alcoholism were incorrect, initiating treatment seemed preferable to the alternative, which would be allowing alcoholism to go unaddressed and presumably progress. The two choices were then perceived as either loss of drinking "privileges" or potential loss of life. Equally important was the fact that, at the time, the clinician could offer the problem drinker no other treatment options.

The situation now is dramatically different. Those with alcohol dependency continue to represent the majority of clients seen by alcohol treatment facilities. At the same time, there is an ever increasing proportion of referrals for other alcohol-related problems. One can no longer assume that arrival at an alcohol treatment program is a clear indicator of alcoholism. The problem may be alcohol abuse. The referral may have followed on the heels of an incident caused by alcohol use. There are self-referrals of individuals who are concerned about a family member, a friend, or their own alcohol use. Similarly, alcohol treatment personnel are called upon more and more by other helping professionals—school counselors, social workers, physicians, clergy—to provide consultation.

With clients now reflecting the spectrum of alcohol problems, there is increasing demand upon alcohol therapists to provide a thoughtful assessment and to match clients to appropriate treatment. Other pressures come into play and also demand assessment and treatment planning skills. A significant pressure is economic. Insurance companies, state regulatory agencies, as well as clients, their families, and employers no longer automatically accept without question 28-day residential or inpatient care as the treatment of choice. The realization that there are options has become apparent. Alcohol treatment programs advertise on TV. While the numbers of treatment programs may recently have been shrinking due to changes in insurance coverage, nonetheless individuals have a wider range of services to choose from in almost every community compared to the previous generation. Also, a growing number of treated and recovering people have opinions on the strengths and weaknesses of various programs. In this climate, assessment, evaluation, and diagnostic skills become more central.

THEORETICAL PERSPECTIVES

It may have been far simpler when the major and exclusive concern of the alcohol clinician was alcoholism. Knowing how to treat the person sitting in the office was rarely a difficulty. The real challenge and major frustration was in getting those who needed care across the threshold. As the clinical concerns broaden to encompass a range of alcohol problems, life becomes more complicated for the clinician. The remarks presented here are intended to provide a framework and offer orientation.

If treatment programs are oriented primarily toward treating alcoholism, ironically, that orientation serves as a set of blinders preventing recognition of other alcohol problems. This is reminiscent of the old adage, "If the only tool you have is a hammer, every problem tends to look like a nail!" In thinking about alcoholism, we naturally think of its progression in terms of moving from alcohol use, to alcohol problems, to alcohol abuse, to alcoholism. In this framework, severity depends upon where the client falls on that continu-

um. This thinking contains some pitfalls. The necessity for action or intervention is understandably associated with what is perceived as the seriousness of the situation. Thus the person with the alcohol problem may be seen as being in less danger. Although it is true that there may be less danger in respect to the alcoho*lism,* that is only half of the picture.

PROBLEMS OF ALCOHOL USE

Alcohol problems are not restricted to alcoholism. Nor are they restricted to alcohol use at intoxicating levels. For example, the danger of alcohol use by the individual who is depressed is not alcoholism—it is suicidal thoughts being "loosened" by the impaired state and diminished capacity. Therefore those who are in treatment for depression should be counseled to abstain from alcohol.

Adolescents provide some of the most dramatic examples of the dangers of alcohol use. For teenagers, the primary danger of alcohol use isn't dependence, although it certainly does occur. The leading causes of death in this age group are accidents, suicide, and homicide, all of which are clearly linked to alcohol use. The net and tragic result is that the age group from 16 to 24 years is the only group in our country with a declining life expectancy. Alcohol use may also have more subtle dangers for adolescents, such as impeding emotional and social maturation. In addition, there are the problems related to sexuality, unwanted pregnancies, and HIV infection.

Any drinker is at some risk for alcohol problems. Alcohol is a potent pharmacological agent. Negative consequences can follow on the heels of a single drinking episode. These would represent problems of acute use. Negative consequences can also result from the pattern of use. This represents a chronic problem. Evaluation and assessment needs to explore both possibilities.

What is a "safe" dose of alcohol or a low-risk pattern of alcohol use? This varies from individual to individual. What is judicious use similarly varies for a single individual throughout his or her life span. For the pregnant women, no alcohol is the safest alternative. Alcohol use is a health issue in the broadest sense. The alcohol treatment professional is unlikely to see an individual until some problem becomes evident. Therefore much of the burden of prevention and identification of individuals at risk falls to those outside the alcohol field.

Another pitfall can occur when conceptualizing all alcohol problems in terms of the progression of the disease of alcoholism. It is the temptation to treat all alcohol problems as emerging dependence. That means offering alcoholism treatment. This can cause clients to balk or bolt. At the same time, it sets up barriers when dealing with other professionals. Such an approach can give the impression of alcohol clinicians being "technicians," not therapists, always ready to apply their treatment formula indiscriminately.

Chronic disease framework

In considering the spectrum of alcohol problems, the model for
managing chronic disease is very useful. It offers an approach that
ensures that acute problems are effectively addressed. At the same
time, it ensures that alcohol dependence will not develop unnoticed.
All acute problems are seen as requiring attention in their own right
and as potential warnings of a possible long-term problem. The following example may help.

In respect to general medical management of any chronic disease, among the most significant actions are those taken *before* the
clear onset of the full-blown disease process. Take heart disease, for
example. A young man comes into his physician's office. He is overweight, both smokes and drinks, consumes a cholesterol-laden diet,
never exercises, and has a family history of men who die before the
age of 50 of coronary disease. From his physician's perspective, he is
a walking time-bomb. To feel comfortable intervening the physician
does not have to be convinced that this individual will be true to his
genes. It is sufficient to know that statistically this individual is at
risk. Even if the client is wholly asymptomatic, that is, has no elevation of blood pressure, the physician will feel perfectly comfortable
urging rather drastic changes to reduce risk. (These changes for our
hypothetical young man are equivalent to the changes associated
with abstinence.) If the physician were really on top of it, he would
refer this client to several groups, load him down with pamphlets,
and through continuing contacts monitor compliance and provide
encouragement and support. We would hold up *this* model with
respect to the optimal management of alcohol problems. In this
framework, the most relevant question is no longer, "Is this person
alcoholic?" The central question instead becomes, "If this person
continues with the current alcohol use pattern is he at risk for
developing alcoholism or other alcohol-related problems?"

Using the framework of chronic disease, many of the questions
that now plague caregivers are circumvented. In the discussion that
follows, we are going to act as if alcohol problems, alcohol abuse, or
alcohol dependence is a condition like heart disease. As a chronic
disease, alcoholism has well-demonstrated warning signs. It develops slowly over time. For this reason, it would probably be impossible ever to pinpoint an exact time at which a nonalcoholic "turns"
alcoholic. No one wakes up in the morning having come down with
a case of alcoholism overnight! Remember, the time when it is most
critical to act is before the disease process is firmly established,
when the individual is in that "gray" area. So it is useful to think in
terms of whether someone is *developing* alcohol dependence. If so,
then intervention is appropriate.

Such an approach makes it clear that any alcohol problem is sufficiently serious to warrant continuing attention. It has become
widely recognized that alcoholism isn't "cured" and that ongoing

efforts will be needed to maintain sobriety. Similarly, alcohol problems shouldn't be assumed to be "fixed" by a single encounter with a clinician or participation in an alcohol education class. An ongoing relationship is appropriately established to monitor the client's status. Over time, there needs to be the opportunity to assess the efforts to moderate risks and alter dangerous drinking patterns. If these efforts prove to be unsuccessful, then further intervention is going to be required.

The changes that are taking place with respect to treatment of alcohol problems, as well as the public definition of what constitutes an alcohol problem, are almost as dramatic as the changes that have occurred over the last 25 years regarding tobacco use. We may well be on the brink of a similar revolution with alcohol use. Questions about smoking are now a standard part of any medical history. Probably very few smokers are unaware that smoking may cause or aggravate medical problems. A smoker who sees a physician expects to be asked questions about smoking and awaits the associated comments that smoking is ill-advised. Beyond that there is the increasing likelihood that a referral will be made to a smoking cessation program. Also the attitudes of the general public have changed. There is now a vocal anti-smoking lobby that does not wish to put up with secondhand smoke; there are also the concerned family members and friends of smokers, who are more frequently expressing their concerns directly to the smoker, and regulation of smoking in public places has become the norm. Restaurants generally must provide you nonsmoking accommodations and more and more are smoke free. The White House is a nonsmoking building, not to mention hospitals. Beyond protecting nonsmokers, these regulations certainly cramp a smoker's style and prompt him or her to consider the inconvenience as well as the problems which result from smoking.

If one reflects upon what has occurred in the decade with respect to alcohol use, one cannot help but notice some striking changes. The general public's attitudes toward the use of alcohol have shifted significantly. Alcohol is more commonly viewed as a drug. Drunkenness is far less tolerated and has become socially unacceptable in more and more circles and circumstances. The possibility that an intoxicated person puts others in jeopardy is now an issue of public concern. Reinforcing this is a heightened interest of the general population in a variety of efforts to promote health, such as proper diet, exercise, or other self-care measures. This has provided a moderating influence upon alcohol use. So along with less red meat, fewer animal fats, jogging, and Jane Fonda's workout, there's more Perrier water. Coupled with all this are the improvements that have taken place in the professional training of physicians, clergy, nurses, social workers, and teachers about alcohol, alcohol problems, and alcoholism, compared to the previous generation.

At the same time, there is still some way to go. In the abstract, a person can be well informed about alcohol problems, but when they pop up in real life, it can be a different matter. All too often, along with the realization that there is a possible alcohol problem comes a lot of hand-wringing and waiting. The family, friends, physician, clergy—all those involved—can be immobilized. They can often wait until the possible problem has progressed to the point where it is unequivocally and unquestionably the real thing.

Also problematic is that the professional treatment community has not yet reached a clear consensus as to what constitutes appropriate treatment for those who are in trouble with alcohol but who are not alcohol dependent. This should not be a surprise. The alcohol field has not had the similar collective experience in approaching alcohol problems that it has had with alcoholism. The legacy of some of the nontraditional approaches to treatment of alcohol dependence may make clinicians squeamish. We refer to the efforts to teach controlled drinking to clients with alcoholism, an approach that has been discredited. However, what was ineffective with that population in many instances is exactly the approach called for in the treatment of alcohol abuse, when abstinence is not an essential goal in treatment. There are those in specialized niches of the alcohol field who are acquiring considerable experience in dealing with alcohol problems. This is true particularly of the drinking and driving programs and of efforts on the college campus. Such programs can be looked to as a guide for the future.

SCREENING AND EVALUATION

The ability to intervene in an alcohol problem depends upon two obvious factors. First, it requires the problem to be identified. Second, it requires an adequate evaluation to determine the nature of the problem. Alcohol problems have many guises beyond also being quite common. Consequently, screening for alcohol problems needs to be routine in any counseling or health-care setting.

Screening instruments

Several very easily administered screening tests have been shown to be effective in identifying those with a high likelihood of having alcoholism or other alcohol problems. As their name indicates, they are *screening* instruments—not *diagnostic* instruments. They are intended to rapidly distinguish between those who are exceedingly likely to have a problem and those who are unlikely to have a problem. They do not provide sufficient information to allow formulation of a treatment plan. But if routinely administered, they can assist in identifying those whose alcohol use warrants closer scrutiny. In ensuring that those who don't "look" like people with alcohol problems don't go undetected, these tests may have less util-

CAGE

CUT DOWN

I'm cutting down—
I'm only getting
Two six-packs
tonite.

ANNOYED

Love me,
Love my
beer!
Goodbye!

GUILTY

I hope no one saw
me here last night.

EYE OPENER

I wonder if
the state liquor
store is open yet?

ity in a setting that deals exclusively with alcohol and/or drug problems. But they are basic tools to have in any human service worker's repertoire. They should be kept in mind by alcohol professionals for use in training others who may be less comfortable in discussing and less experienced in dealing with alcohol issues. Several screening tests are described below.

Cage. Since its introduction in 1970, the CAGE developed by Ewing and Rouse has become recognized as one of the most efficient and effective screening devices. The CAGE is both easy to administer as well as less intimidating than some of the other screening instruments. It consists of the following four questions:

"Have you ever felt you should **C**ut down on your drinking?"

"Have people **A**nnoyed you by criticizing your drinking?"

"Have you ever felt bad or **G**uilty about your drinking?"

"Have you ever had an **E**ye-Opener first thing in the morning to steady nerves or get rid of a hangover?"

Scoring two or three affirmative answers should create a high index of suspicion of the presence of alcoholism. Four positive responses are seen as equivalent to a diagnosis of alcohol dependence. The CAGE is not an instrument that is intended for use in screening for other alcohol problems (e.g. a score of a one or two does not indicate alcohol abuse).

For those concerned about being overly inclusive and thus falsely identifying as possibly alcoholic those who are not, the CAGE holds little danger. It is very reliable in providing an initial way of sorting those who may be alcoholic from those who are not. Only 20% of nonalcoholics will have a CAGE score of 1. As the number of positive responses increases, the nonalcoholic individuals who would be incorrectly identified drops markedly. For two positive responses, the proportion of nonalcoholics who would be falsely identified is 11%; for three positive responses, it drops to 1% of nonalcoholics being incorrectly classified, and for four positive responses, 0%.

Michigan Alcohol Screening Test (MAST). The MAST has become the other most widely used screening instrument. The original MAST, first published in 1971 by Selzer and associates, was a 25-item yes or no questionnaire. It was designed for use either within a structured interview or for self-administration. The questions touch on medical, interpersonal, and legal problems resulting from alcohol use. (There is a weighted scoring system, and question 7 is not scored.) Since its introduction, the reliability and validity of the MAST have been established in multiple populations.

Several variations have since been developed. The *Brief MAST* uses ten of the MAST items. The *Short MAST (SMAST)* was specifically created to be self-administered and uses 13 items found to be as effective as the entire MAST for screening. The MAST questions are outlined in the box.

MAST (Michigan Alcoholism Screening Test)

Points

2	(*<u>1</u>.)	Do you feel you are a normal drinker?
2	2.	Have you ever awakened the morning after some drinking the night before and found that you could not remember part of the evening before?
1	<u>3</u>.	Does your wife, husband (or parents) ever worry or complain about your drinking?
2	*4.	Can you stop drinking without a struggle after one or two drinks?
1	<u>5</u>.	Do you ever feel bad about your drinking?
2	(*<u>6</u>.)	Do friends or relatives think you are a normal drinker?
0	7.	Do you ever try to limit your drinking to certain times of the day or to certain places?
2	*<u>8</u>.	Are you always able to stop drinking when you want to?
5	(<u>9</u>.)	Have you ever attended a meeting of Alcoholics Anonymous (AA)?
1	10.	Have you gotten into fights when drinking?
2	<u>11</u>.	Has drinking ever created problems with you and your wife, husband?
2	12.	Has your wife, husband (or other family member) ever gone to anyone for help about your drinking?
2	(13.)	Have you ever lost friends or girlfriends/boyfriends because of your drinking?
2	(<u>14</u>.)	Have you ever gotten into trouble at work because of drinking?
2	15.	Have you ever lost a job because of drinking?
2	(<u>16</u>.)	Have you ever neglected your obligations, your family, or your work for 2 or more days in a row because you were drinking?
1	17.	Do you ever drink before noon?
2	18.	Have you ever been told you have liver trouble? Cirrhosis?
2	(19.)	Have you ever had delirium tremens (DTs), severe shaking, heard voices or seen things that weren't really there after heavy drinking?
5	(<u>20</u>.)	Have you ever gone to anyone for help about your drinking?
5	(<u>21</u>.)	Have you ever been in a hospital because of your drinking?
2	22.	Have you ever been a patient in a psychiatric hospital or on a psychiatric ward of a general hospital where drinking was part of the problem?
2	23.	Have you ever been seen at a psychiatric or mental health clinic, or gone to a doctor, social worker, or clergyman for help with an emotional problem in which drinking has played a part?
2	<u>24</u>.	Have you ever been arrested, even for a few hours, because of drunk behavior?
2	(<u>25</u>.)	Have you ever been arrested for drunk driving or driving after drinking?

*Negative responses are alcoholic responses.

( )Indicates questions included in the Brief MAST.

__Indicates questions included in the SMAST.

Scoring: A score of three points or less is considered nonalcoholic, four points is suggestive of alcoholism, a score of five points or more indicates alcoholism.

Trauma Index. Recognizing how commonly trauma is associated with excessive alcohol use, several Canadian researchers developed a five-question scale to identify early-stage problem drinkers, among both men and women, in an outpatient setting. The questions are as follows:

Since your 18th birthday, have you—
1. *had any fractures or dislocations to bones or joints?*
2. *been injured in a traffic accident?*
3. *had a head injury?*
4. *been injured in an assault or fight?*
5. *been injured after drinking?*

Two or more positive responses are indicative of excessive drinking or alcohol abuse. Though not as sensitive as the CAGE or the MAST, it will identify slightly over two thirds of problem drinkers.

For those with doubts

A word to those who are suspicious of screening instruments and their ability to detect a problem, especially given that prominent symptoms of alcohol dependence include minimizing, denial, repression, and distortions of memory and perception: The CAGE and the MAST have both been used extensively. The Trauma Index is a newer instrument. As part of the creation, development, and testing of such instruments, individual's responses are compared to the judgments of trained alcohol clinicians. The purpose of such screening instruments is after all to approximate the judgment that would be made by professionals were they to undertake a systematic evaluation. Indeed, for these instruments, those who answered the indicated number of questions positively were those whom the clinicians agreed had the syndrome (dependence or abuse) that the instruments were designed to detect.

If you remain leery, reflect back to the description of the behavior that is symptomatic of alcohol dependence in Chapter 6. The candor or absence of distortion is possibly not so unexpected. What the alcoholic client often strongly disagrees with is not the "facts," but their interpretation. Thus the alcohol-dependent individual might very readily acknowledge that a family member has expressed concern about drinking. What he or she would be likely to dispute is whether the concern is justified. The client may well provide the interviewer a very lengthy and unsolicited rebuttal of the family's concern and offer justifications for the drinking. In such situations, the interviewer needs to note the initial response to the question despite the explanation.

In using these screening instruments, common sense is in order. The purpose of these instruments is to rapidly and easily obtain a rough assessment of an alcohol problem. Err on the conservative side. One should be cautious in disregarding a score that is positive for the presence of an alcohol problem. But even when the score does not indicate alcoholism, if something does not ring true, follow up.

Follow-up questions

William Clark of Harvard Medical School, and formerly the Chief of Medicine at Cambridge City Hospital, has authored some of the best material on alcoholism diagnosis directed to physicians. Although his comments are concerned with the medical interview, they would be useful in any counseling situation. He has three basic rules: (1) Ask about the person, not about the alcohol. He is a firm believer in routinely using the CAGE questions. (2) Use the laboratory sparingly. That's easy for nonphysicians to follow! (3) Be prepared, ahead of time, with some follow-up questions for use when the CAGE is positive. He suggests a series of follow-up questions to get at the client's preoccupation with alcohol. To help remember them he has two mnemonics, HALT and BUMP.

Do you usually drink to get	**H**igh?
Do you sometimes drink	**A**lone?
Have you found yourself	**L**ooking forward to drinking?
Have you noticed an increased	**T**olerance for alcohol?
Do you have	**B**lackouts?
Have you found yourself using alcohol in an	**U**nplanned way?
Do you drink for	**M**edicinal reasons?
Do you work at	**P**rotecting your supply of alcohol?

Then to get at the common problems associated with alcohol use, Clark has a last series of questions:

Family history of alcohol problems
Alcoholics Anonymous attendance
Thoughts of having alcoholism
Attempts or thoughts of suicide
Legal problems
Driving while intoxicated
Tranquilizer or disulfiram use
The device for remembering this is FATAL DTs.

History of alcohol use

When routine screening provides evidence of an alcohol problem, then a more detailed alcohol use history is always indicated. Similarly, an alcohol use history should be an integral part of an interview with any troubled person, whether the person has come to a physician or hospital with a physical problem, or to a social worker, psychiatrist, psychologist, or clergy member concerning an emotional or life adjustment problem. The reasons for this should now

be clear. As we have previously noted, this is a drinking society; most people drink at least some alcohol. We have also noted that alcohol is a chemical and not as benign as previously thought. It simply cannot be ignored as a possible factor in whatever brings a person to a caregiver of any kind. Again, do not limit your attention to alcoholism alone. The purpose of the alcohol use history is simply to get as clear a picture of alcohol use as you would of other medical aspects, family situation, job difficulties, feelings, or whatever. It is part of the information-gathering process, which is later added up to give you an idea of what is going on in the person's life and how best to proceed.

Many sample drinking history forms are floating around—for physicians, nurses, and others. Our bias is that the attitude of the questioner is as important, if not more important, than the actual list of questions. If asking about drinking strikes you as an invasion of privacy, a waste of time, or of little use because the presenting problem is clearly not alcohol related, then you are going to be uncomfortable asking and will probably get unreliable answers from a now uncomfortable client. If your bias is the opposite and you see alcohol lurking in the corner of every problem, again discomfort and unreliable answers will probably be your lot. Somehow you need to begin with an objective stance. Alcohol might or might not be a factor, just as any other aspect of the client's life might or might not be of concern.

When to ask. It takes practice to take a reliable alcohol history. It also takes recognition of timing and a good look at what is in front of you. It may seem redundant to say, but an intoxicated or withdrawing client cannot give you good information. You wouldn't expect accurate information from someone going under anesthesia or coming out of it. Unfortunately, some of the forms we have seen are designed to be filled out on admission or intake with no recognition of this factor. Again, use your common sense. Try to ask the questions you need to at a time when the person is at least relatively comfortable both emotionally and physically. Ask them matter-of-factly, remembering that *your own drinking pattern is no yardstick for others.* For example, when someone responds to the question "How much do you usually drink on a typical occasion?" with "About four or five drinks or so," don't stare open mouthed.

What to ask. Basically, the information needed is what does the client drink, how much, how often, when, where, and is it, or has it caused, a problem in any area of life, including physical problems. These questions can be phrased in different ways. In general, however, we lean to a more informal approach than sitting there filling out a form as you ask the questions in order. Another issue that we consider to be as important as the above information, but that is not included on most forms, is the question of what the drinking does for the client. Questions such as "How do you feel when you drink?"

"What does alcohol do for you?" and "When do you most often want a drink?" can supply a lot of information.

How to ask. If the questions are asked conversationally along with other questions regarding general health, social aspects, and other use of drugs or medications, most people will answer them. The less threatened you are by the process, the more comfortable the individual being questioned will be.

Recording the data in the record

Alcohol use should be adequately described in the agency chart or medical record so that changes in drinking practices can be detected over time. If there is no evidence of alcohol being a problem, that, too, should be noted. Notes in the chart should include sufficient objective detail to provide meaningful data to other clinicians. Avoid one-word descriptions such as "socially" or "occasionally." If the agency does not have a prescribed format, it is suggested that the following be included for all clients: drinking pattern, problems related to alcohol use, expression of concern by family or friends, and the MAST or CAGE score.

WHAT NEXT?
Making a referral

Having identified an alcohol problem, the clinician who isn't primarily an alcohol or substance abuse professional is faced with referring the client to an alcohol facility. This may be either for further evaluation or for treatment. To accomplish this means keeping several things in mind. First, you cannot enthusiastically recommend the unfamiliar. Therefore you need to know about various facilities, their programs, and personnel. Second, in making any referral, there's always a danger of clients falling through the cracks. Therefore you need to be actively involved in the referral. Don't just give an agency name and phone number with instructions for the client to call. You make the appointment with a specific individual, at a specific time and inform the family. Third, if you've had an ongoing relationship with the client, a referral may feel like abandonment. If appropriate, continue the contact and let the client know that you are in this together.

In large measure the ability to effect a successful referral lies in your conveying a sense of concern and hope. It also depends upon assisting the client to see the difficulties in a new light, that there may be a disease causing these difficulties, and that it's not a question of who is at fault. In presenting the need for referral, remember that someone can absorb only so much information at one time. Consider for a moment the woman whose physician discovers a lump in her breast. The physician's next step is making a

referral to a surgeon for a biopsy and possibly to an oncologist. This is not the time to discuss the relative merits of radical mastectomy and/or chemotherapy in terms of 5-year survival. Nor is it the time to talk of side effects from chemotherapy. Such presentations would be likely to cause the woman to run because she abandons hope, or it might cause her to retreat into denial. The important messages to convey initially are (1) the situation is serious enough to warrant further investigation, (2) I'm referring you to someone I can trust, and (3) I'm in this with you. That same concern is what one is attempting to convey when making a referral for alcohol problems.

Evaluation in an alcohol treatment setting

For those working in a designated alcohol treatment program, the situation is a bit different. Here, the person may be referred or come in with a good idea that alcohol is a problem. The person may, however, want to prove that it isn't. Because of the alcohol treatment designation, the questions about alcohol can be more forthright and in depth. Consequently the responses may be more guarded—particularly responses to how much and how often. However, those are not the most helpful questions anyway. Remember the maxim, "Ask about the person, not about the drinking." Indeed, some suggest never asking these questions, at least in an initial encounter. The reason is that they are the questions most likely to trigger the client's defenses. It is probably *the* topic that has caused the most friction with family. If asked, the responses can range all the way from a gruff "a few and just socially" to a bragging "a whole case of beer whenever I feel like it." The prospective client will usually need to feel somewhat comfortable about seeing you before more candor is possible. And there is always the real possibility that the client doesn't *know* exactly how much or how often. The key thing for the clinician is to get as much reasonably reliable information as possible to develop appropriate treatment plans or initiate an appropriate referral. Information about quantity and frequency is not necessary to diagnose alcoholism. It can be useful in gauging the level of physical dependence and assessing possible withdrawal problems. However tolerance can be gleaned indirectly by other means, such as "How many drinks does it take to feel the effect?"

Another point to consider is that you do not always have to get all the history at one sitting. If a client comes to a treatment facility smelling of alcohol, clearly uncomfortable, and somewhat shaky, you need to know immediately how much alcohol has been consumed, for how long, and when the last drink was taken. You also need to know about other physical problems and what happened on other occasions when drinking was stopped. These questions are necessary to determine if the client needs immediate attention from a physician. If the client is not in crisis, the evaluation may occur over several outpatient visits.

One method of gathering information when a client is not in immediate physical difficulty is asking clients to review their drinking, beginning with the first drinking experience they remember. This chronological review gives the clinician a complete picture of the drinking pattern. It also can provide clients the opportunity of looking for the first time at their evolving drinking habits. It often helps them to see the shifts and changes that signaled or were part of an emerging problem and can thus be used as a therapeutic lever.

Initial interview. The initial interview is intended to get a general picture. As a result of the initial interview, the alcohol clinician will want to be able to answer the following questions:

1. What is the problem the client sees?
2. What does the client want?
3. What brings the client for help now?
4. What is going on in the individual's life, i.e., the "facts" of the family situation, social problems, medical problems, alcohol use—how much, for how long?
5. Is there a medical or psychiatric emergency?
6. What are the recommendations?

Certainly, much other information could be elicited. But the answers to the foregoing questions make up the essential core for making decisions about how to proceed.

Counseling is an art, not a science. No series of rules can be mechanically followed. However, one guideline is in order for an initial interview. It is especially apt in situations in which someone is first reaching out for help. *Don't let the interview end without adopting a definite plan for the next step.* Why? People with alcohol problems are ambivalent. They run hot and cold. They approach and back off from help. The person who comes in saying "I'm an alcoholic and want help" is very, very rare. You are more likely to meet the following: "I think I may have a problem with alcohol, sort of, but it's really my ___ that's getting to me." The concrete plan adopted at the close of the interview may be very simple. The plan may be nothing more than agreeing to meet a couple more times so that you can get a better idea of what's going on. Set a definite time. Leaving future meetings up in the air is like waving good-bye. It is not uncommon for the individual to try to get off the hook by flattering the therapist. "Gee you've really helped me. Why don't I call you if things don't improve? Why, I feel better already, just talking to you."

Despite your title of alcohol therapist, clients first coming to an agency are not coming to you to have you "do your treatment routine" on them. It is more likely that they want a clean bill of health.

They want to figure out why their drinking isn't "working" anymore. The only thing that may be clear is the presence of drinking. Clients are often unaware of its relationship to their problems in life. As they paint a picture of what is going on in their lives, the therapist will certainly see things the clients are missing or ignoring.

You can see that the client is alcohol dependent. In your opinion, the client may unquestionably need a rehabilitation facility. However, at the moment, the client is unable to use the treatment. First, it is necessary to make some connections—that is, get the arrows pointed in the right direction.

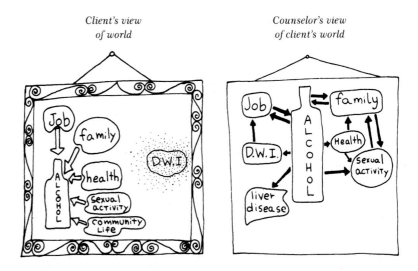

Family involvement. Participation of family in the evaluation is very desirable and becoming the norm. This is so vital that it's hard to imagine why family involvement was not always the case. In some instances family members may be the more reliable historians. Even if not, their perspective on the problem is essential. By including family members, the clinician can assess firsthand their needs and their ability to provide support, as well as engage them as partners in treatment.

Treatment planning. An evaluation may take one or more sessions. The goal of the evaluation is to develop a "recipe" or plan that will offer the client the optimal chance of getting those arrows pointed in the proper direction. The essential tasks of treatment will be discussed shortly. The treatment plan may use many of the treatment techniques to be discussed in Chapter 9. If the diagnosis is alcoholism, this can be provided on either an inpatient or outpatient basis. In deciding which of these to recommend, the following items should be considered.

Indications for inpatient care	Indications for outpatient care
• History of unsuccessful outpatient treatment	• First treatment attempt
• Potential withdrawal problems	• An intact and supportive family
• Medical problems	• An ability to use available supports
• Few social supports	• No medical complications
• A family that needs "time out"	• Recognition of the need for treatment
• Marked ambivalence about the need for treatment	• Little risk of serious withdrawal treatment

With managed care, and insurance oversight, longer-term inpatient care is pretty much a thing of the past. More than likely, if the indications are for inpatient care, it will be short term, and restricted mainly to handling withdrawal. This means that intensive outpatient treatment and aftercare is essential.

Treatment planning for those previously treated. A few comments are warranted in respect to treatment planning for the client who has been in treatment previously. A portion of the evaluation needs to focus on prior treatment. What was the treatment? Did the client have a period of stable sobriety? If so, what contributed to its maintenance? To what do the family and the client attribute the resumption of drinking? These perceptions may be insightful or way off base. However, they are important beliefs that will either need to be supported or challenged. If a stable sobriety was never achieved, what are their hypotheses as to what went wrong? Is there evidence to suggest a psychiatric disorder that has gone undiagnosed? Is there multiple drug use?

The client who has been through treatment a number of times and has not gained sobriety is often termed a "treatment failure." That is obviously a very loaded label for the client and the family (if they still are on the scene), as well as the treatment staff. It is never possible to predict when treatment will "take." Nonetheless simply one more exposure to the same treatment is probably not the best clinical decision. The comparison might be made to someone with an infection that does not respond to a particular drug. Simply increasing the dose probably won't work. One of the things treatment repeaters do have going for them is a knowledge of what doesn't work. To the extent possible, the client should be actively engaged in treatment planning and committing to it, for example, agreeing ahead of time to attend more AA meetings, seeking an AA sponsor, entering a halfway house after inpatient care, and continuing in aftercare.

One of the difficulties commonly encountered with these clients is that they show up in the midst of a serious crisis, for example, a medical illness requiring hospitalization or family turmoil or legal problems. This can lead to a situation in which the person, willing to comply (or at least not to resist), in essence finds himself or herself entered into a program. Although one may need to respond to the crisis, it is imperative to engage the client as soon as possible in planning treatment after the crisis is stabilized.

If someone comes to an agency with a history of multiple unsuccessful treatment attempts in that agency's program, the question needs to be asked if a referral to another facility might now be indicated. It is important this not be done as "punishment." Instead it should be a clinical decision based on the possibility that entry into treatment elsewhere may increase the odds in favor of a different outcome because that staff will not have been involved in the previous efforts and see the client as a "failure."

TREATMENT OF ALCOHOL PROBLEMS

If it is a small sacrifice to discontinue the use of wine, do it for the sake of others; if it is a great sacrifice, do it for your own sake.

S.J. MAY

Within the professional community there is reasonable consensus upon what constitutes the standard of treatment for alcohol dependence. However, at this point there are no universally accepted standards of care for the treatment of other types of alcohol problems. Nonetheless we are presenting some guidelines for your consideration. These we think can serve as a conservative approach until the time when a body of clinical experience with treatment of alcohol problems emerges, similar to that which has been acquired around alcoholism.

Alcohol incidents

By alcohol incidents, we refer to the negative consequence or consequences that result from an individual's drinking. It may be an accident, an altercation, or whatever. However, a thorough evaluation indicates no pattern of recurring problems to indicate abuse or alcoholism.

The *"Thou shall nots."* Don't presume that the incident has been enough to teach someone a lesson and guarantee that there will be no future difficulties. It's easy to assume that the embarrassment, guilt, discomfort, or anxiety that resulted was sufficient. It may even seem almost cruel to discuss it further. Others may mistakenly think the polite, kind thing to do is "just not mention it." Especially with younger people, who may be those most likely to experience an alcohol-related problem, the incident may be treated by peers as a joke. What is required? All those who may have contact—be it emergency room personnel, a school counselor, the police, or the family—all need to acknowledge the role of alcohol in what occurred. The actual or potential seriousness needs to be made clear. If you recall the progression of alcoholism in the framework set forth by Johnson (described in Chapter 6), the absence of feedback by others in the face of alcohol-related incidents is, in part, what allows a chronic alcohol problem to blossom. In fact, a second such incident should be a clear tip-off that a problem is emerging. One DWI "might" just happen, but a second should sound the warning signal that the person is continuing in a destructive pattern, despite prior negative consequences.

In the face of an incident involving alcohol, basic education is essential. This should not be cursory and superficial, but detailed. Alcohol has to be explained as a drug to the individual in light of what has occurred. What does BAC mean? How is it that alcohol can induce poor choices? What happens when someone chugs drinks? What are the mechanisms for alcohol-drug interactions?

The underlying message is that if people are going to use the drug alcohol, they need to be fully informed about it. Don't assume that people, however bright and sophisticated, are sufficiently knowledgeable about alcohol and its actions to figure out what the risks are. So the evaluation should also include an inventory of drinking practices, a review of settings in which drinking takes place, behaviors associated with drinking, plus family history of alcoholism or medical conditions that may be adversely influenced by alcohol use. The question to be answered is this: "Are there circumstances that are likely to place the individual at risk?" If so, specific steps should be discussed to address these. What might the person who is faced with being a passenger in a car with an intoxicated driver do? For the person who takes allergy medications, what are the implications for drinking? Identify potential problems and help the client think through—ahead of time—what should be done. Research undertaken about techniques for prevention of drug abuse came up with an interesting finding. One of the most successful techniques in reducing teenage drug use was to literally have the kids *practice* how to say no. Adequate information alone wasn't enough, nor were exhortations to "just say NO." They needed some practice doing it. What was required were tips for applying it. What is being suggested here is an extension of that. This is very important, too, in the event that future problems with alcohol use occur. If a problem were handled in the fashion suggested here, later it could be safely assumed that the individual, from that point on, was fully informed! A subsequent problem would indicate that a serious ongoing problem with alcohol is emerging and alcohol dependence is unfolding.

It is important that an alcohol incident not be treated as a "secret." It is suggested that the client's consent be secured to bring the situation to the attention of the client's family, friends, or spouse. The family needs to be informed in order to be aware and supportive of what is recommended. Although in an ideal world at least one follow-up visit might be scheduled just to check in with the individual, it is more likely that this will not happen. The family physician, often an untapped ally, *is* in a position to monitor how things are going in the future. The family physician is in a position to routinely inquire about alcohol use and therefore may be in the

best position to spot any future difficulties. Because one of the most useful factors in spotting an alcohol problem early is detecting changes that occur over time, getting the occurrence of an alcohol problem into the individual's medical record is important. A brief communication with the physician will accomplish that. For the person at risk for developing alcohol dependence, the signs and symptoms that should trigger a need for further evaluation should be understood by all.

Alcohol abuse

Unlike an alcohol incident that represents an acute problem, alcohol abuse is a chronic problem. It is defined as *a pattern of use that is physically hazardous or that interferes with the ability to fill major obligations, be it at home, work, or school, or causes major problems with others*. Practically speaking, alcohol abuse can be considered to be present when there is a pattern of alcohol problems and the sense that alcoholism is "just around the corner." Alcohol abuse may be present in an individual even if loss of control is unclear because there may have been no efforts to control or moderate alcohol use. If physical dependence and loss of control have not occurred, then moderation of drinking practices from a physiological standpoint is possible. However, depending upon the person's social situation and life circumstances, this may still represent a monumental feat. Consider the college student who is into the party scene. Changing drinking patterns will require marked changes in the student's circle of friends, daily routine, and choices of recreational activities. To achieve this magnitude of change will require the client be engaged in more than a supportive chat.

To our minds, to do this requires that the individual be engaged in some formal alcohol treatment, which involves alcohol education, individual counseling, and participation in a group with others in the same situation. Monitoring efforts to moderate alcohol use and avoid future problems is imperative. Through this process, in a number of cases, evidence may mount that there is loss of control or preoccupation with drinking. Therefore abstinence and alcoholism treatment are now needed. In essence, if efforts to address alcohol abuse are unsuccessful, the diagnosis of alcoholism can now be made.

TREATMENT OF ALCOHOL DEPENDENCE

Alcoholism treatment is nothing more (or less) than the interventions designed to short circuit the alcoholic process and provide an introduction to a sober, drug-free existence. Alcoholism is the third leading cause of death in the United States. It shouldn't be. In comparison to other chronic diseases, it is significantly more treatable. Virtually any alcoholic person who seeks assistance and is willing to actively participate in rehabilitation efforts can realistically expect to lead a happy, productive life. Sadly, the same may not be true for a victim of cancer, heart disease, or emphysema. The realization that alcoholism is treatable is becoming more widespread. The public efforts of prominent individuals who are recovering has contributed to this acceptance. Both professional treatment programs and AA are discovering that clients today are often younger and in the early or middle stages of alcoholism when they seek help. It is imperative for the helping professions to keep firmly in mind the hope that surrounds treatment.

Just as people initially become involved with alcohol for a variety of reasons, there is similar variety in what prompts treatment. For every person who wends the way into alcoholism, there is also an exit route. This exit is most easily accomplished with professional help. The role of the professional is to serve as a guide, to share knowledge of the terrain, to be a support as the alcoholic regains footing, and to provide encouragement. The therapist cannot make the trip for the alcoholic but can only point the way. The therapist's goal for treatment, the destination of the journey, is to assist the alcoholic individual in becoming comfortable and at ease in the world, able to handle life situations. This will require the alcoholic to stop drinking. In our experience, drinking alcoholics cannot be healthy, at peace with themselves, or alive in any way that makes sense to them. The question for the professional is never "How can I make him or her stop?" The only productive focus for the therapist is "How can I create an atmosphere in which he or she is better able to choose sobriety for himself or herself?"

In this discussion, abstinence is presumed to be required for the treatment of alcohol dependence. There was a time when researchers were actively exploring controlled drinking as an alternative (see Behavioral Approaches, Chapter 9). The optimism that was initially reported was met with skepticism by veteran alcohol treatment professionals. (The response of the recovering community was outrage!) When the fates of those treated by controlled drinking were examined, the sceptics were proven right. In virtually all cases, there was serious relapse and further alcohol problems. Vaillant, when questioned as to an alcoholic's ability to resume social drinking, uses the example of a motorist who decides to remove the spare tire from the car trunk. Disaster may not strike the next day, or the next week, or even within the month. But sooner or later. . . . In addition, the seriousness of the consequences cannot be predicted ahead of time. It may be only a flat tire in one's driveway, or it may be a blowout on a busy freeway during rush hour.

Abstinence as a requisite for recovery is viewed as having a solid physiological basis. Tolerance, once established, is maintained, even in the absence of further alcohol use. Were someone who has been abstinent for a considerable period to resume drinking, the person would very quickly be physically capable of drinking amounts consistent with the highest levels previously consumed. Drinking isn't resumed with a physiologically "clean slate." It may have taken a drinking career of 10 or more years for the alcohol-dependent person to reach consumption levels of a fifth a day. However, after tolerance has been established that level of drinking can be reinstated within literally *days*, even after a decade of sobriety. This "rapid reinstatement of tolerance," is recognized in medical circles as one of the hallmark signs of dependence, or what was formerly described as *addiction*. For those clients who ask "Is total abstinence really necessary?", one stock response is, "Your body will always remember you have alcoholism, even if you forget!"

Obstacles to treatment

If alcoholism is so highly treatable, what has been going wrong? Why aren't more people receiving help? The obstacles do require examination. Historically, one big handicap has been society's attitude toward alcohol and its use. Unfortunately, until recently, the chances of being treated for alcoholism were far too slim. Oh, you could count upon treatment for depression, gastritis, or cirrhosis but not for alcoholism. Despite all the public information and education, the notion remains lurking that talking about someone's drinking is in bad taste. It seems too private somehow, none of anyone's business. Most of us have a good feel for the taboo topics—sexual behavior or people's way of handling their children. The way someone drinks has long been a strong taboo. Ironically, as we have collectively become better informed, our reticence may be chalked up less to the topic's being in bad taste than to the fact that we feel as if we are making an accusation! If the behavior that evokes disapproval is not viewed as a symptom of alcoholism, it is perceived as wholly volitional. We have not yet reached the point where to comment on what is perceived as unwise, dangerous, or inappropriate alcohol use is a wholly neutral topic, much less a topic upon which we can universally assume anyone would welcome another's observations. The notion of alcoholism as a moral issue still remains a situation for which "willpower" is the presumed solution. The person with the alcohol problem believes that as firmly as anyone and expends considerable energy at trying not to drink so much.

Of course, an alcoholic has a stake in keeping the drinking and its associated problems off limits. Should the drinking behavior be discussed, the symptomatic rationalization combined with our cultural tendency to "psychologize" or analyze would spring another trap. The notion that someone drinks alcoholically *only* because he is an alcoholic sounds circular and simpleminded. Thus everyone scurries around to find the "real" cause. Alcoholism as a phenomenon, a fact of life, gets pushed aside and forgotten in the uproar.

Another obstacle is the confusion introduced for alcoholic individuals and their families by the behavioral symptoms of alcoholism.

One common characteristic of alcoholic behavior is the extreme variation, the lack of consistency—sometimes good mood, sometimes foul mood, sometimes sloshed, sometimes sober. This inconsistency prompts a host of explanations. Further, this very inconsistency allows the alcoholic, family, and friends to hope things will get better if left alone. It permits them to delay seeking assistance. It almost seems to be human nature to want—and wait—for things to improve on their own. Consider for a moment the simple toothache. If the toothache comes and goes, you probably will delay a trip to the dentist. After all, maybe it was something hot you ate. Maybe it was caused by something cold. On the other hand, if the pain is constant, if it is clearly getting worse, if you can remember wicked toothaches in the past, you'll probably call immediately for an emergency appointment with your dentist. The total time you are actually in pain in the latter case may be much less than what you would have put up with in the former example, but you are spurred into action because it doesn't appear it will improve by itself.

Unfortunately, even when alcoholism treatment is instituted, it can be seriously unbalanced, zeroing in on only some of the symptoms. When this happens, alcoholism treatment can end up resembling treatment for depression, cirrhosis, or just a "rest." These one-sided approaches have been major sources of habitual relapse and failure and frequently have given the impression that alcoholism treatment doesn't work.

Factors in successful treatment

Having alluded to failure and some sense of what to avoid, let us proceed to *success*. The likelihood of success is greatly enhanced if treatment is tailored to the characteristics of the disease being treated. The following factors, always present, should guide both the planning and process of treatment.

1. *Dysfunctional life patterns.* The individual's life has been centered around alcohol. If this is not immediately evident, it is because the particular client has done a better-than-average job of disguising the fact. Thus the clinician cannot expect a repertoire of healthy behaviors that come automatically. Treatment will help the individual build new behaviors, as well as rediscover and dust off behaviors from the past to replace the warped "alcoholic" responses. This at times is what makes residential treatment desirable. Besides cutting down the number of easy drinking opportunities, it provides some room to make a new, fresh beginning.

2. *Alcohol as a constant companion.* It is used to anticipate, get through, and then get over stressful times. Alcoholics, to their knowledge, do not have effective tools for handling problems. In planning treatment, be alert to what may be stressful for a particular client and provide supports. In the process, the

therapist can tap skills the client can turn to instead of the bottle.

3. *Psychological wounds.* Alcohol is both a best friend and a worst enemy. The prospect of life without alcohol seems either impossible or so unattractive as to be unworthwhile. The alcohol-dependent individual feels lost, fragile, vulnerable, fearful. No matter how well put together the client can appear or how much strength or potential the professional can see, the client by and large is unable to get beyond those feelings of impotence, nakedness, nothingness. Even when being firm and directive, the therapist has to have an awareness of this.

4. *Physical dysfunctions.* Chronic alcohol use takes it toll on the body. Even if spared the more obvious physical illnesses, other subtle disturbances of physical functioning are often present. Sleep disturbance can last up to 2 years. Similarly, a thought impairment would not be unusual on cessation of drinking. In the initial stage of recovery, difficulty in maintaining attention is commonplace. There will be diminution of adaptive abilities. During treatment, education about alcohol and its effects can help allay fears, remembering always that the most important ingredient in treatment is time away from the drug. Reminding the client of this and helping him or her see that improvement will come with more drug-free time is an important factor.

5. *Chronic nature of alcoholism.* A chronic disease requires continuing treatment and vigilance regarding the conditions that can prompt a relapse. This continued self-monitoring is essential to success in treatment.

6. *Deterioration in family function.* As described in Chapter 7, the family needs as much help as the alcoholic family member. Better outcomes result when they have a treatment program independent of the addicted member's treatment.

Recovery process

Recall how the progression of alcoholism can be sketched out. Similarly, recovery is a process that does not happen all at once. Gradually, in steps, the client becomes better able to manage his or her life. For the purpose of our discussion, we have distinguished three different phases: the preliminary or introductory phase, active initial treatment, and the continuing maintenance of recovery. There is no clear-cut beginning or end point. Yet each phase has its observable hallmarks.

Others, too, have sketched out the stages or progression of recovery. Stephanie Brown has titled these stages of recovery as (1) drinking, (2) the transition from drinking to abstinence, (3) the early stages of recovery, and (4) ongoing recovery. William Miller drew upon the stages associated with motivation and making behavioral changes to describe the process of recovery (see Chapter 9). The terminology may differ slightly, but the common denominators of these perspectives is to approach recovery as a dynamic process. It occurs over time and has the client address different tasks at different stages. The clinician needs to have a repertoire of skills to be able to intervene appropriately.

Preliminary or introductory phase. The preliminary or introductory phase begins when the problem of alcoholism comes to the foreground. This happens when those nagging suspicions that there is something wrong with the drinking are permitted to surface. On personal initiative, there might be some initial inquiries, which may be directed to friends and associates. "You know, Jane was really mad at me for getting a bit tipsy when we went out last Friday night. You were there. I don't see anything wrong with letting go after a long hard week, do you? She's always on my back about something these days." Often others may not recognize these queries as a disguised or tentative "cry for help."

Ideally the friend, co-worker, or colleague who is the recipient of these initial queries listens carefully and avoids the trap of offering false reassurance or reinforcing denial with a comment like "Oh, you're just imagining it." Ideally they will share the information that people can get in trouble with alcohol and that alcohol use can be a significant health problem. They will then urge the seeking of a professional opinion and do whatever they can to see the person gets there. The first overture may instead be made by a member of the clergy, family member, friend, or perceptive physician—someone who is sufficiently concerned to speak up and take the risk of being accused of meddling. Suspecting an alcohol problem, any one of them might request that an alcohol expert be sought to explore the possibility. On the other hand, a court may "sentence" an individual convicted of DWI to treatment. Increasingly common, too, is that the spouse may seek assistance as a result of the chaos of living with an alcoholic; or the employer may notice developing problems and attempt to intervene.

At this point the alcoholic is a fish nibbling at the bait. He moves close and backs off. He wants to know, but he doesn't. Sharing the societal view of the stigma against those with alcohol problems, he or she will do or say anything to avoid being labeled as one of "them." Of course the drinking causes problems, but he or she doesn't want or is scared to stop. What someone in this state really wants to learn is how to drink well. The hope is to drink without the accompanying problems. In getting in touch with an alcohol treatment professional, the chances are pretty good the individual wants the professional to teach him or her how to drink without the negative consequences. (This represents an impossible request, so avoid getting sucked into trying.)

What *can* the therapist do? The first step is to carefully evaluate the problem to assess its nature and severity. Following that, a tenta-

Do you really Think I drink like a fish?

tive treatment plan will be devised, possibly using outside expert opinions. These treatment recommendations will then be discussed with the client. This discussion will explain the recommendations, including any possible "risks" of treatment contrasted with the dangers of not initiating care. The assessment process for an alcohol problem or alcoholism, just like any other evaluation process, is intended initially to collect data. The clinician in a very general way will endeavor simply to get a clear picture of what is going on in the client's life.

In terms of the specifics, keep in mind that it is of the utmost importance to avoid getting into a defensive position. You need not be defensive as to the reason you can't be helpful in teaching the alcoholic how to drink successfully, since that might provoke the client to run away. There is, however, a mutual goal "to have things be okay." The therapist can buy into this without accepting the client's means of achieving it. The task of the therapy will be to assist the individual to see his or her behavior and its consequences accurately. As this occurs, the client will be confronted with the impossible nature of his or her request. The therapist will be most successful by being open, candid, and patient. Treatment is doomed if you are seduced into playing the "patsy" or if you try to seduce the client by being the "good guy, rescuer." Having a co-worker with whom to discuss cases and their frustrations can help keep the objectives in sight.

Alcoholism is a disease that requires the client to make a "self-diagnosis" for successful treatment to occur. Treatment, full steam ahead, cannot begin until the alcoholic client, inside himself or herself, attaches that label to cover all that is transpiring. A head, or intellectual, understanding does not suffice. It must come from the heart. The whole thing can be confusing. He certainly doesn't have to be happy about the diagnosis, he simply needs to know it's true. Then without hope of his own, he borrows the therapist's belief that things can change.

Active treatment phase. At this point of acknowledgment, seeing alcohol as the culprit, and with a desire to change, alcoholic clients by themselves are at a dead end. If they knew what to do, they would have done it. In essence, they turn the steering of their life over to the therapist. The clinician, in turn, must respond by providing clear, concrete, and simple stage directions. A rehabilitative regimen needs to be set forth. The environment must be simplified. The number of decisions to be confronted must be pared down. There is little ability to deal with anything more than "How am I going to get through this day (or hour) without a drink?" Effort needs to be centered on doing whatever is necessary to buy sober time. To quote the old maxim, "Nothing succeeds like success." A day sober turns on the light a little. It has become something that is possible. For the alcoholic this is an achievement. It does not guarantee continued sobriety, but it demonstrates the possibility. In the sober time, the individual in alcohol treatment is gaining skills. Behavior is discov-

ALCOHOL TREATMENT CENTER

OF COURSE I WANT YOU TO TREAT ME — I JUST DON'T WANT YOU TO TREATMENT me.

ered that can be of assistance in handling those events that previously would have prompted drinking.

Although we are not attempting to discuss specific techniques of treatment here, a mention of AA is nonetheless in order. The clinical experience of professionals in the alcoholism treatment field leads to the widespread view that clients who become involved in AA have a much better chance of recovery. This is not accidental. AA has combined the key ingredients essential for recovery. It provides support, and it embodies hope. It provides concrete suggestions without cajoling. It provides a haven, a place which ensures contact with sober alcoholics. Its slogans are the simple guideposts needed to reorder a life. And its purpose is never lost.

George Vaillant, in summarizing the four factors that his research identified as associated with recovery, noted that all four are embodied in AA affiliation. AA offers a source of hope; attendance at meetings and associations with members provide the needed external reminders to prevent the fading from memory of one's being alcoholic; it offers the opportunity for new relationships, where a clean slate is possible, relationships that aren't encumbered by the emotional baggage of the period of alcoholic drinking; and it offers support.

The necessity for a direct and uncluttered approach cannot be overstressed. In early alcohol treatment, clients are not capable of handling anything else. This is one of several reasons for the belief that alcoholism has to be the priority item on any treatment agenda. The only exceptions are life-threatening or serious medical problems. To work actively and successfully on a list of difficulties is overwhelming. Interestingly enough, when alcoholism treatment is undertaken, the other problems often fade. Furthermore, waiting to treat the alcoholism until some other matter is settled invites ambivalence. This waiting feeds the part of him that says, "Well, maybe it isn't so bad after all," or "I'll wait and see how it goes." Generally the matters are unsolvable because an actively drinking alcoholic has no inner resources to tackle anything. He or she is drugged.

Focusing on alcoholism as a priority, achieving the client's acceptance of this, and providing room and skills to experience sobriety make up the meat of therapy. As this takes place, the individual is able to assume responsibility for managing his or her life, using the tools acquired. With this, the working relationship between clinician and client shifts. They collaborate in a different way. The clinician may be alert to potential problematic situations, but the client increasingly takes responsibility for identifying them and selecting ways to deal with them. Rather than being a guide, the therapist is a resource, someone with whom the client can check things out. At this point, continuing treatment has begun.

Continuing treatment phase. The alcohol-dependent person learns, as do others with a chronic disease, the importance of

being able to identify situations and their responses to them that may signal a flare-up. With alcoholism, this entails maintaining a continuing awareness of the alcoholic status if sobriety is to continue. The individual certainly will not continue to see the therapist for a lifetime as a reminder of the need to be vigilant. However, each alcoholic will need to develop other alternatives to succeed in staying sober.

Why do I drink? This is the recurrent theme of many active alcoholics and those beginning active treatment. In our experience, focusing on this question, even when it seems most pressing to the client, is of little value. It takes the client off the hot seat. It looks to the past and to causes "out there." The more important question addresses the present moment: "What can be done now?" If there is a time to deal with the "whys," it comes during the continuing treatment phase. Don't misunderstand. Long hours spent studying what went wrong, way back, are never helpful. Rather, the reason can be discerned from the present, daily-life events, on those occasions when taking a drink is most tempting. Dealing with these situations can provide clients with a wealth of practical information about themselves for their immediate use. Dealing with the present is of vital importance. Newly recovering individuals, who have spent their recent lives in a drugged state, have had less experience than most of us in attending to the present. The automatic tendency is to analyze the past or worry about the future. The only part of life that any of us can hope to handle effectively is the present.

A client's hope for change often must be sparked by the clinician's belief in that possibility. Your attitudes about your clients and their potential for health exerts a powerful influence. This doesn't mean you cannot and will not become frustrated, impatient, or angry at times. Whether therapy can proceed depends on what you do with these feelings. You can only carry them so long before the discomfort becomes unbearable. Then you will either pretend they aren't there or unload them on the client. Either way your thinking can become "she can never change," "this guy is hopeless," or "she's just not ready." When that happens, therapy is not possible even if the people continue meeting. A better approach is to have a co-worker with whom you can discuss these feelings of impotence and frustration. Another aid for a therapist is involvement in Al-Anon. Either or both of these together makes it easier to say "I know this person can change, even if I can't imagine how it will happen. Certainly, stranger things have happened in the history of the world." At this point therapy can proceed. However, if an impasse in working with a particular client isn't broken through, the client should be referred to a co-worker.

Treatment is a process involving people. People have their ups and downs, good days, bad days. Some that you think will make it, won't. Some that you are sure don't have a chance will surprise you. There will be days when you will wonder why you ever got into this.

On others it will seem a pretty good thing to be doing. Remembering that it is an unpredictable process may help you keep your balance.

Common themes in treatment

Early in the recovery process, many clients have a tendency to become quite upset over very small matters. They look well, feel well, and sound well—but they really aren't quite there yet. This can be very trying for the clinician, the client, and the family as well. Remembering and reminding them of how sick they have recently been makes their upsets less threatening. The steps after any major illness seem slow and tedious. There are occasional setbacks; yet eventually all is well. It works that way with alcoholism, too. It is simply harder to accept because there are no bandages to remove, scars to point to, or clear signs of healing to check on. It cannot be emphasized enough that it *takes time*.

During this early phase of treatment, one point often overlooked is the client's inability to function on a simple daily basis. It is almost inconceivable to therapists (or anyone else for that matter) that a person who seems reasonably intelligent, looks fairly healthy after detoxification, and is over 21 can have problems with when to get up in the morning or what to do when he is up! Along with family, work, and social deterioration caused by alcohol dependence, the simple things have gotten messed up, too. He may have gargled, brushed his teeth, and chewed mints continually while drinking in an effort to cover up the smell of alcohol. He may, on the other hand, have skipped most mealtimes and eaten only sporadically with no thought to his nutritional needs. He may have thrown up with some regularity. Also, as we have seen in Chapter 5, his sleep is not likely to be normal. Getting dressed without trying to choke down some alcohol to quell the shakes may be a novel experience. It may have been years since he has performed the standard daily tasks in a totally drug-free state.

Clients are rather like Rip Van Winkles during the early weeks of their recovery. Everything they do is likely to feel strange. The face looking back at them from the mirror may even seem like a stranger's. They became used to the blurred perceptions they experienced while drinking. It is terribly disconcerting to find virtually every task one faces as a whole new thing. Whereas it used to take 2 very careful days to prepare Thanksgiving dinner, it now requires only a few hours. The accompanying wine for the cook, trips back to the store for forgotten items (and by the way, a little more booze), the self-pity over *having* to do it, the naps necessary to combat the fatigue of the ordeal, the incredible energy devoted to controlling the drinking enough to get everything done—all these steps are eliminated.

The newly sober individual is continually being faced with the novelty of time—either having too much time or not having enough time. He or she also may panic over the problem of what to do next. Many clients will need help scheduling their time. After years of getting by on the bottle, they have to regain a sense of how much time it really takes to accomplish some tasks. The individual may plan to paint the entire house in 2 days or, conversely, decide that he or she can't possibly fit a dental appointment, a luncheon engagement, and a sales call into one day. She may believe that it is all she can manage to stop by the bank on the way to work and pick up a loaf of bread and the dry cleaning on the way home. Tomorrow she intends to make new living room drapes in time for that evening's dinner party!

The perception of time is as distorted as other areas of perception. Reassurance that this is a common state of affairs, along with assistance in setting realistic daily goals, is greatly needed. This is one reason newcomers to AA find the slogans "Keep it simple" and "First things first" so helpful.

Clients may not mention their dilemmas over time and schedules to you. They may feel ashamed about such helplessness over simple things. However, a gentle question from you may open the floodgates. This provides the opportunity to help bring order out of chaos. You can offer some much-needed guidance in re-mastering the details of daily living. All too often they wail "I don't know! The house was a mess. . . . The kids were a mess. . . . I was a mess. . . . I just couldn't handle it, so I drank!"

Another aspect of reorienting the client to reality involves the misperception of events. The faulty memories caused by the drugged state will have to be reexamined. One cannot always wait for some sudden insight to clear things up. For example, he is talking to you about difficulties he has had with his wife. He remembers her as a nagging bitch, on his back about a "few little drinks." You might remind him that on the occasion in question, he was picked up for driving while impaired with a blood alcohol content of 0.20— clearly not a few drinks. Then go on to point out that because he has misperceived the amount he was drinking to such an extent, he may have misperceived his wife's behavior. The opportunity is there, if indicated, to educate the client briefly on the distortions produced by the drug or alcohol and to suggest that sober observations of his wife's behavior are more valid. You might instead suggest a couples' meeting, but keep clearly in front the issue of the alcohol use.

Different strokes for different folks. Another easy trap to fall into is to expect the same course of recovery to occur for most clients. They don't get sick at the same rate, and neither do they get well at the same rate. One will be up and at 'em and lookin' good in very short order; another will seem to be stuck, barely hanging on, forever; and there will be those in between. What is difficult for one is a breeze for another. Don't assume that you know what is going to be a problem for any one particular person. We have tried to point out some of the more common difficulties, but there are lots of surprises around still. There are simply no formulas or easy prescriptions that will work every time. There is no substitute for knowing a particular alcoholic individual and dealing with the one sitting before you.

Still later. At a point, after about 3 months, upon achieving some level of comfort with the new state of affairs, the focus of treatment can shift. The focus has been mainly on the mechanics of daily living. With that out of the way, or reasonably under control, the focus can move on to sorting out the client's stance in the world, feelings, and relationships. Though 3 months is a somewhat arbitrary designation, it is not wholly so. Recall the subacute withdrawal syndrome (see Chapter 5). The acute withdrawal period may pass within 5 days, but a longer period is required to regain the ability to concentrate, for example. Thus there is a physical basis for what the alcoholic client in early recovery can focus on productively. This does not mean that all the problems previously discussed are totally overcome or that work is not proceeding along some of the above paths. It simply means that other problems may now be surfacing. It is also at this point that some assessment should be made as to whether to refer the client to other professionals if the present caregiver is not equipped to handle this work. Some problems are fairly common, and one must be alert to them. Most basically require finding a balance between two extremes of behavior that are equally dangerous. John Wallace, a psychologist with long experience in the field, has compared these extremes to rocks and whirlpools that must be avoided in the recovery "voyage."

Denial. One of the first difficulties entails denial. The tendency for clinicians new to alcohol treatment, when faced with a massive rejection of reality, is to want to force these clients to face all the facts *right now*. The trouble with this approach is that self-knowledge is often bought at the price of anxiety, and anxiety is a drinking trigger. What to do? Provide lots of support to counteract the initial anxiety caused by the acceptance of the reality of the drinking itself. Then, gradually, keep supporting the small increments in awareness that occur in the sober experience.

It is always the temptation to take denial personally, to think the alcoholic client is "lying." Remind yourself that the person has adopted this defense as protection against the massive pain that would accompany facing the "cold, hard facts." Its function is to "deceive" or protect the self, not others. It is difficult, but very necessary, to remember that the denial of some particular issue is serving a useful purpose at the time, keeping overwhelming pain and anxiety at bay until more strength is available. The therapist must decide how much of either the client can tolerate. The therapeutic issue is whether the denial is still necessary or whether it has become counterproductive, blocking further progress.

Guilt. The presence of denial, the function of which is to protect against emotional pain, is evidence that the behavior is not congruent with the individual's core values and internal image. (The phrase used in psychotherapy for this phenomenon is *ego dystonic*, i.e., being out of harmony with one's "real" self.) So where there is denial, the issues of guilt and its fraternal twin, self-blame, cannot be far behind. It is clearly desirable to mitigate the degree of both. It is simultaneously necessary to avoid the pitfalls of their opposites, the rejection of social values and blaming others. Although excessive guilt leads to the guilt-drinking spiral, some degree of conscience and sense of responsibility is necessary to function in society. The therapist needs to be clear on this issue. The clinician must be able to point out unnecessary burdensome guilt on the one hand and yet allow honest guilt to be expressed. Dealing with both kinds of guilt appropriately is essential. On the blame issue, help is needed in accepting personal responsibility where necessary. Often, it can be helpful to point out that the disease itself, rather than oneself or others, may be the true cause of some of the difficulties, while gently reminding them that they are responsible for what happens now.

Compliance versus rebellion. Two other unhealthy extremes are often seen, particularly early in treatment: compliance and rebellion. In either case, strong confrontation is not a good strategy to choose. It seems simply to produce more of either. The compliant client becomes a more "model" client; the rebellious one says: "Aha! I was right. You are all against me," and then drinks. Moderation is again the key. The aim is to help clients to acknowledge their alcoholism and accept the facts of their situation.

Emotions. Emotions, and what to do about them, are another obstacle to be faced. Newly sober persons are likely to repress their feelings entirely. They do this to counteract their all too uncontrolled expression during the drinking experiences. Respect for this need to repress the emotions should prevail in the initial stages of recovery. But the eventual goal is to assist the client to recognize emotions and deal with them appropriately. Clients need to learn (or relearn) that feelings need not be repressed altogether, or conversely, wildly acted out. Instead, a recognition and acceptance of them can lead to better solutions. These are by no means the only examples of extremes for which you need to be alert. The therapist needs to be wary when dealing with any extreme behavior or reaction to avoid having the client plunge into the opposite danger. Some of these problems are continuing ones and may require different tactics at different stages in the recovery process.

Dependency and intimacy. Many articles, and indeed whole books, have been written about dependency and alcoholism. Historically, the alcoholic individual was depicted as a particularly dependent type emotionally who had resolved conflicts inappropriately by using alcohol. This is basically another variant of the earlier mistake of confusing the symptoms of alcoholism for the personality before the onset of alcoholism. Nonetheless, it is crucial to address issues of dependency treatment. One long-term worker in the field, Dr. LeClair Bissel, has summed up the whole of treatment as "the task of helping people to become dependent upon people rather than booze." Be alert during treatment of the client's characteristic "all or none" approach. There is the vacillation between stubborn independence and indiscriminate dependence. During the early months of recovery the individual may need to poll everyone he or she knows to make a decision on some seemingly inconsequential matter; but when a major decision comes along, no advice is solicited. As individuals discover their need for others, this can lead to discomfort and confusion. On one hand, there is the potentially mistaken notion that turning to others is evidence of some weakness, a voice within says, "I should be able to." On the other hand, with little recent history of good judgment and having little reason to trust one's own capacities and feeling there may not be much margin for error, one can see a tendency to turn to others for almost everything. One of the long-term tasks of recovery is not only to recognize the need for dependence, but to become more discriminating in handling it. The basic questions the client will be addressing in this process are "Whom *should I and can* I be dependent on?" "For *what?*' "At what *cost?*" "For what *gain?*"

Closely tied to the issue of dependency is that of intimacy. Intimacy is the capacity for closeness, for allowing oneself to be vulnerable to another. One of the tasks in early recovery is becoming reacquainted with oneself while simultaneously growing emotionally. To be rediscovering oneself while also establishing relationships with others is not an insignificant undertaking. One of the features of AA that contributes to recovery is that it provides a community in which the traditions of the fellowship provide safeguards and limits for all its members as the issues of dependency and intimacy in relationships get sorted out. It is also a setting in which one discovers that people are all interdependent to some degree.

Left to their own devices, recovering alcoholics seem to have an uncanny capacity for finding persons with whom they forge destructive relationships. There are always those around who would rescue them and be willing to assume the role of their perpetual caretakers.

Another issue may well be encountered by single persons or those caught in unhappy marriages. It is not uncommon for them to find themselves "suddenly" involved in an affair or an extramarital relationship. With a little bit of sobriety, they are very ripe to fall in love. This may have several roots. They may be questioning their sexuality, and the attentions of another may well provide some affirmation of attractiveness. Also possible is that with sobriety comes a sense of being alive again. There is the reawakening of a host of feelings that have long been dormant, including sexual feelings. In this sense, it may be like the bloom and intensity of adolescence. A romantic involvement may follow very naturally. Unfortunately, it can lead to disaster if followed with abandon. A counselor needs to be alert to this general possibility, as well as the possibility of being the object of the crush.

Getting stuck. Speaking of dependency, anyone working with alcohol-troubled people is bound to hear this remark some time: "Sending someone to AA just creates another dependency." The implication of this is that you are simply moving the dependency from the bottle to AA and ducking the real issue. That the dependency shifts from alcohol to AA or a clinician or treatment program for the newcomer is probably true. We view that as a plus. We also think no one should get stuck there. By "there," we mean in a life that is just as alcohol-centered as before. The only difference is that the focus is on "not drinking" instead of "how to continue drinking." Granted, physical health is less threatened, traumatic events are less frequent, and maybe even job and family stability have been established. Nonetheless, it is a recovery rut (maybe even a trench!).

The fact that some do get stuck is unfortunately true. Many factors probably account for the "stuckness." One might be an "I never had it so good, so I won't rock the boat" feeling, a real fear of letting go of the life preserver even when safely ashore. Another factor is that some people in recovery, particularly those who began drinking as teenagers, have spent the bulk of their adult lives as active alcoholics. Therefore they have no baseline of adult healthy behaviors to return to. They are confronted with gaining sobriety, growing up, and functioning as adults simultaneously. This is a tall order that can be overwhelming. To make the task more manageable, it may well be tempting for these people to keep their world narrowed down to recovery. The only thing they now feel really competent to do, the only area where they have had support and a positive sense of self, is in getting sober. Giving up the status of "newcomer" to be replaced by that of "sober, responsible adult" may be scary, so a relapse or drinking episode may ensue. They then can justify and ensure that they can keep doing the only thing they feel they do well, which is being a client, an AA newcomer, and a recovering alcoholic.

Another factor that may cause the newcomer to get stuck could be that some clinicians (and some AA members) are better equipped to deal with the crisis period of getting sober than with the later issues of growth and true freedom. Time constraints are too often the cause of the clinician's inability to encourage the "letting go," or stretching, phase. They are often overwhelmed with the numbers of clients truly in crisis. They simply have no time or energy to put out for the clients who are "getting along okay." Those who are not content with their clients' just getting by could aid the process by referring them to different types of therapy and groups that deal with specific and related issues. The adjunctive treatments are not substitutes for alcoholism therapy. Instead they supplement whatever has worked thus far—whether it is AA, individual therapy, or some other regimen.

The professional who works with clients on a long-term basis should beware of getting stuck in back-patting behavior. The phrase, "Well, I didn't do much today, but at least I stayed sober," is okay once in awhile. When it becomes a client's standard refrain over a long period, it should be questioned as a satisfactory lifestyle. Those who work around treatment programs affiliated with larger agencies are all too aware of groups of alcohol clients who hang around endlessly, drinking coffee, talking to others in similar circumstances, and clearly going nowhere. For instance, for some who may have suffered brain damage and thus have serious limitations, this may be the best that can be hoped for. However, we suspect that many are there simply because they are not being helped and encouraged to proceed any further. These are the recovering individuals most clearly visible to the health-care professionals; thus they may be one reason for the low expectations professionals have for the recovery process. They don't see the ones who are busy, involved, highly functioning individuals. Our contention is that professionals can increase the number of the latter and "unstick" more and more if they are sensitive to this issue.

Relapse. Any individual with a chronic disease is subject to relapse. For those with alcohol dependence, relapse means the resumption of drinking. Why? The reasons are numerous. For the newly sober person it may boil down to a gross underestimation of the seriousness and severity of the disease. For these individuals, there has been a failure to really come to grips with their own impotence to deal with it single-handedly. Hence, while perhaps going through the motions of treatment, there may be a lingering notion that although others in recovery may need to do this or that, somehow they are exempt. This may show up in very simple ways, such as the failure to address the little things that are likely to make drinking easier than not drinking. "Hell, I've always ridden home in the bar car; after 20 years that's where my friends are." "What would people say if _____." "There's a lot going on in my life; getting to the couples group simply isn't possible on a regular basis." If families and close friends are not well informed about treatment and are not willing themselves to make adjustments, they can unwittingly support and even invite this dangerous behavior.

For the recovering individual with more substantial sobriety, relapse is commonly tied to two things. Relapse may be triggered by the recovery rut already described. On the other hand, if things have been going well in the recovering alcoholic's life, there is the trap of considering alcohol dependence to be a closed chapter.

As an aside, probably as a response to this danger, one sometimes hears alcohol treatment professionals, AA members, or those well acquainted with alcoholism stating a preference for the phrase "recover*ing* alcoholic," rather than "recover*ed*." The use of *recovering* serves as a reminder that one is not cured of alcoholism. From a medical standpoint, this is quite accurate. The evidence points strongly to biological changes that occur during the course of heavy drinking. Even with long-term abstinence, in this respect there is no return to the "normal" or prealcoholic state. The body's biological memory of alcoholism remains intact, even if the recovering individual has "forgotten." The addiction can be rapidly reinstated. The alcohol-dependent individual who resumes drinking may very quickly, in weeks or even days, be drinking quantities equal to amounts prior to abstinence.

The inclusion in treatment of specific relapse prevention efforts will be discussed in greater detail in Chapter 9. An observation frequently made when considering the treatment of addictions is reminiscent of Mark Twain's comment about having stopped smoking—he'd done it many times. The more difficult task for clients is not necessarily in stopping the drinking or substance use, but in *maintaining* abstinence. Treatment programs have begun to address the issue of relapse in a new way. In the past the temptation for treatment professionals, as they contemplated relapse, was simply to add more and more components to the original treatment regimen, as if engaged in a search for the missing ingredient. The popular view now is that the maintenance of sobriety entails different tasks for the client than those necessary for ceasing initial use and that one can teach skills that will enhance a client's ability to maintain sobriety.

It is recommended that management of a relapse, should one occur, be discussed and incorporated into the continuing treatment plan. After all, relapse is not an unheard of occurrence. It is far better for the client, family, and clinician to openly discuss how it shall be handled ahead of time. In the midst of the crisis of relapse, neither the family nor the client can do their most creative and clear-headed problem solving. Also, having gotten this taboo subject out in the open, it may be easier for all to attend to the work at hand, rather than worry about "what if." Any plan for responding to a relapse should be very explicit and concrete; for example, the family will contact the therapist, the client will agree to do A, B, and C.

Although one can look ahead in the abstract, it is during ongoing therapy that the clinician needs to be alert to possible signals of impending relapse. This can then be dealt with in individual sessions. Of course, part of the real meat of educational efforts is teaching clients to become aware of danger signals. If a drinking episode occurs, it does not have to be the end of the world, but neither should it be taken lightly. Whether it is one drink or an evening, a weekend, or a month of drinking, the individual needs to be immediately reinvolved with a treatment center, a clinician, or—if active or previously active in AA—an AA member, or do several of these things. The important thing is not to sit back and do nothing. It is critical that a drinking cycle not be allowed to develop. Active intervention is needed to prevent this. If the client is still involved in treatment with you at the time of relapse, it is a clear sign that more help is needed. If treatment is being provided on an outpatient basis while the individual continues to hold down a job and handle all the usual obligations, the drinking episode clearly shows that this approach is not working. A residential inpatient experience that allows, and indeed forces, the client to direct his or her full attention and energy to treatment may well be what is needed.

Some may instead have "played" at treatment, seen a therapist a few times, and decided things were under control. Fully resolved not to drink again, they then terminated formal treatment. However, willpower and determination, even with a dash of counseling, did not accomplish what they had intended; so the answer is to make a commitment and become engaged in more substantive care.

Seasoned clinicians often say that the most dangerous thing for a recovering alcoholic is a "successful drink." By this they refer to the recovering individual who has a drink, does not mention it to anyone, and suffers no apparent ill effects. It wasn't such a big deal. A couple of evenings later it isn't a big deal either. Almost inevitably, if this continues, the individual is drinking regularly, drinking more, and on the threshold of being reunited with all the problems and consequences of active alcoholism. The danger, of course, is that the longer the drinking continues, the less able the alcoholic is to recognize the need for help or to reach out for it. Someone who has had a difficult withdrawal in the past may also be terrified of the prospect of stopping again. It may be wise for you to make an agreement with the client that if he or she has a drink—or a near encounter—this has to be discussed.

With some substantial sobriety, reentry into treatment after relapse may be especially difficult. Among a host of other feelings there is embarrassment, remorse, guilt, and a sense of letting others down. Recognition that alcoholism is a chronic disease and that it can involve relapses may ease this. However, refrain from giving the impression that relapse is inevitable. Following a relapse, it is necessary to look closely at what led up to it, what facilitated its occurrence. The client can gain some valuable information about what is critical to maintaining his or her own sobriety. That is another reason it is so important to deal with a relapse openly. The clinician must also be sensitive to the issues that a relapse may evoke in the family.

For the moment—and we emphasize *the moment*—the family also may be thrown back into functioning just as it did during the old days of active drinking. The old emotions of hurt, anger, righteous indignation, and the attitude of "to hell with it all" may spring up as strongly as before. This is true even if—especially if—the family's functioning has vastly changed and improved. All of that progress suddenly evaporates. There also may be the old embarrassment, guilt, and wish to pretend it isn't so.

Growth. It is important that you maintain contact with your clients for an extended period to help reduce the likelihood of relapse. The client's best insurance against relapse is continuing to grow. So don't be casual with follow-up care. Concluding sessions are as important as all the earlier ones. By taking it seriously, you

It would take 14,931,430 six-packs of 12-oz cans to float a battleship.

NATHAN COBB
Boston Globe

communicate this to your clients as well. Although your contacts may be less frequent, and possibly appointment times will be less than a full hour, don't allow the follow-up visits to become an empty ritual. Greeting clients with a "Hi, how are you?" and "You're looking great," and then escorting them to the door is not a very therapeutic style. If things are not going well, the client hasn't been given much opportunity to tell you! Be alert to the fact that clients may be reluctant to talk about difficult times. They may feel they should be able to handle it alone, or they may feel they are letting you down. But the opportunity provided by follow-up sessions may allow continuing therapeutic work to be done.

It isn't as if you don't know the person you are seeing! Be sure to bring up issues that have been problematic in the past, such as job or family issues. Find out how things are going now. If there were particular concerns the last time you met, be sure to find out how things turned out. Identifying successes is every bit as important as identifying difficulties. Notes made in the clinical record may be especially important to help you keep track of what has been discussed and to identify any recurrent themes. Be sure to review your notes before seeing a client; it's easy to lose track of what happened, when, and sometimes even with whom.

Pay attention to the things that are known to be stress points for the client. These may include job changes, even when it's a promotion; entrances and exits from the family, whether it's a birth, death, divorce, or the children leaving home for the military, college or even kindergarten; illness in the family; changes in economic circumstances, from retirement, a family member's entering or leaving the work force or taking a second job to winning the lottery. Don't forget holidays. These supposedly joyous occasions are also stressful for most individuals. Preholiday tension is often followed by postholiday blues.

The reason for emphasizing considerable treatment over a fairly long period is simple. The people most successful in treating alcoholism are those who recognize that anywhere from 18 to 36 months are necessary to be well launched in a stable and functional recovery pattern. It might be said that recovery requires becoming "weller than well." To maintain sobriety and avoid developing alternate harmful dependencies, the client needs to learn a range of healthy alternative behaviors to deal with tensions arising from problems that accompany living. Nonaddicted members of society may quite safely alleviate such tensions with a drink or two. Because living, problems, and tensions go hand in hand, being truly helpful implies helping the client become healthier than might be necessary for the general population.

RESOURCES AND FURTHER READING
Screening

Ewing JA: Detecting alcoholism, the CAGE questionnaire, *Journal of the American Medical Association* 252(14):1905-1907, 1984.

Selzer ML: The Michigan Alcoholism Screening test: the quest for a new diagnostic instrument, *American Journal of Psychiatry* 127(12):1653-1658, 1971.

Skinner HA and others: Identification of alcohol abuse using laboratory tests and a history of trauma, *Annals of Internal Medicine* 101(6):847-851, 1984.

Assessment

Clark WD: Alcoholism: Blocks to diagnosis and treatment, *American Journal of Medicine* (71):275, 1981.

Clark WD: The medical interview: Focus on alcohol problems, *Hospital Practice* 20(11):59-68, 1985.

Krampen G: Motivation in the treatment of alcoholism, *Addictive Behaviors* 14(2):197-200, 1989.

The study replicates work conducted 30 years ago on alcoholics' motivations for going into treatment and their relationship to treatment outcome. The results confirmed earlier findings that "threatened" loss of job, spouse, or driver's license, plus a subjective discomfort, are positively related to treatment outcome. However, if the person has already sustained such a loss, the alcoholic's prognosis is not favorable. (Author abstract.)

Magruder-Habib K, Durand AM, and Frey KA: Alcohol abuse and alcoholism in primary health care settings (review), *Journal of Family Practice* 32(4):406-413, 1991.

Alcohol problems are common in primary-care patients, yet they are often not detected and treated. Methods for improving the detection and diagnosis of alcohol problems in the primary-care setting are reviewed in terms of pertinent history, physical examination, and laboratory findings. Screening instruments, such as the CAGE questionnaire and the Michigan Alcoholism Screening Test, are recommended for routine use by primary-care physicians. Such instruments have been shown to have higher sensitivity than laboratory tests alone. Although less is known about intervention and management, earlier intervention with innovative (less costly) management techniques may be both efficacious and acceptable to the patient. (Author abstract.)

McLellan TA: *Guide to the addiction severity index: Background, administration and field testing results,* Rockville MD: National Institute on Drug Abuse, 1988.

This monograph reviews the Addiction Severity Index (ASI), which is a structured interview designed for administration by a trained technician and takes approximately 45 minutes to administer. It is suitable for clients who abuse alcohol or other substances and is designed for both male and female clients. The interview collects objective and subjective information in seven problem areas—alcohol use, medical condition, drug use, employment support, illegal activity, family/social relations, and psychiatric function. From this, a 10-point rating of severity is obtained for each problem area. The ASI is suited for research purposes, diagnostic screening, and/or assessing changes at intervals of a month or longer. The monograph describes the background of the ASI and the impetus for its development. Also, it describes the design of the ASI and the studies to establish reliability and validity, reviews its strengths and limitations, and provides instructions for administration. Appendixes include a copy of the ASI, instructions for scoring, plus instructions for computer coding and data entry.

Miller WR: Motivation for treatment: A review with special emphasis on alcoholism, *Psychological Bulletin* 98(1):84-107, 1985.

Motivation is often regarded as a client attribute related to maladaptive defense mechanisms and is used to explain unfavorable treatment outcome. This article provides an integrative review of research relating motivational variables and interventions to treatment entry, compliance, and outcome; special focus is on alcoholism and other addictive behaviors. Empirical evidence is considered regarding motivational interventions including advice, feedback, goal setting, role playing, modeling, contingencies, continuity of care, voluntary choice, and modification of behavior attractiveness. Beyond these specific interventions, nonspecific aspects of motivation are reviewed including client characteristics (stress, self-esteem, locus

INDIVIDUAL COUNSELING

Earlier we defined treatment as all the interventions intended to short-circuit the alcoholism process and to introduce the individual to effective sobriety. This could be put in equation form as follows:

Treatment = individual counseling + family therapy + family education + client education + group therapy + medical care + AA + Al-Anon + Antabuse + vocational counseling + activities therapy + spiritual counseling. . . .

As can be seen, individual counseling is only a small part of the many things that treatment involves. So what is it? A very simple way to think of individual counseling is as the time, place, and space in which the rest of the treatment is organized, planned, and processed. One-to-one counseling is a series of interviews. During these sessions the therapist and client work together to define problems, explore possible solutions, and identify resources, with the therapist providing support, encouragement, and feedback to the client as he or she takes action.

One of the difficulties in thinking about, discussing, or writing about counseling is knowing where to begin. It can seem a bit overwhelming. One of the problems is that most of us have never seen a real counselor at work. We have all seen police officers, telephone line workers, carpenters, or teachers busy on the job. So we have some sense of what is involved and can imagine what it would be like. The clinician's job is different. It is private and not readily observable. Unfortunately, most of our ideas come from books or television. It doesn't take too much television viewing to get some notion that a good counselor is almost a magician, relying on uncanny instincts to divine the darkest, deepest secrets of the client's mind. You can't help thinking the therapist must have a T-shirt with a big letter S underneath the button-down collar. Television does an excellent job of teaching us that things are not always as they seem. Yet, remember, in real life they often—indeed, usually—are. Everyone is quite adept at figuring out what is going on.

ITS SUPERCOUNSELOR!
HE'S STRONGER THAN A DOUBLE MARTINI.

Observation

An alcohol counselor's first task is to observe the client.

Each day we process vast amounts of information without much thought. Our behavior is almost automatic. Without the benefit of a clock, we can make a reasonable estimate of the time. When shopping, we can, without too much trouble, distinguish the clerk from fellow customers. Sometimes, though, we cannot find a person who seems to be the clerk. Take a couple of minutes to think about the clues you use in separating the clerk from the customer. One of the clues might be dress. Clerks may wear a special outfit, such as smock, apron, or shirt with the store's logo. In colder weather, customers off the street will be wearing or carrying their coats. Another

Selzer ML: The Michigan Alcoholism Screening test: the quest for a new diagnostic instrument, *American Journal of Psychiatry* 127(12):1653-1658, 1971.

Skinner HA and others: Identification of alcohol abuse using laboratory tests and a history of trauma, *Annals of Internal Medicine* 101(6):847-851, 1984.

Assessment

Clark WD: Alcoholism: Blocks to diagnosis and treatment, *American Journal of Medicine* (71):275, 1981.

Clark WD: The medical interview: Focus on alcohol problems, *Hospital Practice* 20(11):59-68, 1985.

Krampen G: Motivation in the treatment of alcoholism, *Addictive Behaviors* 14(2):197-200, 1989.

> The study replicates work conducted 30 years ago on alcoholics' motivations for going into treatment and their relationship to treatment outcome. The results confirmed earlier findings that "threatened" loss of job, spouse, or driver's license, plus a subjective discomfort, are positively related to treatment outcome. However, if the person has already sustained such a loss, the alcoholic's prognosis is not favorable. (Author abstract.)

Magruder-Habib K, Durand AM, and Frey KA: Alcohol abuse and alcoholism in primary health care settings (review), *Journal of Family Practice* 32(4):406-413, 1991.

> Alcohol problems are common in primary-care patients, yet they are often not detected and treated. Methods for improving the detection and diagnosis of alcohol problems in the primary-care setting are reviewed in terms of pertinent history, physical examination, and laboratory findings. Screening instruments, such as the CAGE questionnaire and the Michigan Alcoholism Screening Test, are recommended for routine use by primary-care physicians. Such instruments have been shown to have higher sensitivity than laboratory tests alone. Although less is known about intervention and management, earlier intervention with innovative (less costly) management techniques may be both efficacious and acceptable to the patient. (Author abstract.)

McLellan TA: *Guide to the addiction severity index: Background, administration and field testing results,* Rockville MD: National Institute on Drug Abuse, 1988.

> This monograph reviews the Addiction Severity Index (ASI), which is a structured interview designed for administration by a trained technician and takes approximately 45 minutes to administer. It is suitable for clients who abuse alcohol or other substances and is designed for both male and female clients. The interview collects objective and subjective information in seven problem areas—alcohol use, medical condition, drug use, employment support, illegal activity, family/social relations, and psychiatric function. From this, a 10-point rating of severity is obtained for each problem area. The ASI is suited for research purposes, diagnostic screening, and/or assessing changes at intervals of a month or longer. The monograph describes the background of the ASI and the impetus for its development. Also, it describes the design of the ASI and the studies to establish reliability and validity, reviews its strengths and limitations, and provides instructions for administration. Appendixes include a copy of the ASI, instructions for scoring, plus instructions for computer coding and data entry.

Miller WR: Motivation for treatment: A review with special emphasis on alcoholism, *Psychological Bulletin* 98(1):84-107, 1985.

> Motivation is often regarded as a client attribute related to maladaptive defense mechanisms and is used to explain unfavorable treatment outcome. This article provides an integrative review of research relating motivational variables and interventions to treatment entry, compliance, and outcome; special focus is on alcoholism and other addictive behaviors. Empirical evidence is considered regarding motivational interventions including advice, feedback, goal setting, role playing, modeling, contingencies, continuity of care, voluntary choice, and modification of behavior attractiveness. Beyond these specific interventions, nonspecific aspects of motivation are reviewed including client characteristics (stress, self-esteem, locus

of control, severity, conceptual level), environmental variables, and therapist characteristics (hostility, expectancy, empathy). (Author abstract.)

Miller WR, Benefield RG, and Tonigan JS: Enhancing motivation for change in problem drinking: A controlled comparison of two therapist styles, *Journal of Consulting and Clinical Psychology* 61(3):455-461, 1993.

To investigate the impact of counselor style, a two-session motivational check-up was offered to 42 problem drinkers (18 women and 24 men) who were randomly assigned to three groups: (A) immediate check-up with directive-confrontational counseling, (B) immediate check-up with client-centered counseling, or (C) delayed check-up (waiting-list control). Overall, the intervention resulted in a 57% reduction in drinking within 6 weeks, which was maintained at 1 year. Clients receiving immediate check-up showed significant reduction in drinking relative to controls. The two counseling styles were discriminable on therapist behaviors coded from audiotapes. The directive-confrontational style yielded significantly more resistance from clients, which in turn predicted poorer outcomes at 1 year. Therapist styles did not differ in overall impact on drinking, but a single therapist behavior was predictive ($r = .65$) of 1-year outcome such that the more the therapist confronted, the more the client drank. (Author abstract.)

NIAAA, Department of Health and Human Services: *7th Special Report to the U.S. Congress on Alcohol and Health,* Washington DC: U.S. Government Printing Office, 1990.

These two chapters address early and minimal intervention and treatment. For both subjects, most current research findings are reviewed and summarized, including many topics that go beyond the scope of this book, such as studies of treatment outcome and efforts to match patients to treatment.

NIAAA, Department of Health and Human Services: *8th Special Report to the U.S. Congress on Alcohol and Health,* Washington DC: U.S. Government Printing Office, 1994.

This is the most recent update of work on alcohol problems and their treatment.

Clinical care

Keene J, Raynor P: Addiction as a "soul sickness": The influence of client and therapist beliefs, *Addiction Research* 1(1):77-87, 1993.

The aim of this research was to carry out a small scale intensive study, describing the progress of clients through a Minnesota treatment program. It is intended to give an insight into the process of treatment and change and maintenance of change and to provide an understanding of individual and interpersonal processes taking place at the Centre. The ethnographic data gathered from Centre staff and 40 clients as they passed through the treatment process allowed the examination of possible variables influencing different outcomes, giving an indication of why particular individuals "succeeded" in treatment while others "failed." This study found a relationship between the beliefs and theories of client and therapist on the one hand and successful outcome on the other. (Author abstract.)

Rohrer GE, Thomas M, and Yasenchak AB: Client perceptions of the ideal addictions counselor, *International Journal of the Addictions* 27(6):727-733, 1992.

Addicted persons in a residential treatment center rated the traits which they felt were the most positive and negative in a counselor. Lists of traits were developed by having one group of clients make a list, in their own words, of positive and negative traits. These traits were compiled into lists from which other groups of clients rated the top 10 positive and the top 10 negative counselor traits. Profiles were developed for eight subgroups (Males, Females, Black Clients, White Clients, Alcoholics, Cocaine Addicts, Younger Clients: 18-23 years old, and Older Clients: 43+ years). Significant differences were found in the type of counselor preferred by various groups within the sample. The data suggest that addicted persons, while using colorful and imprecise language, have definite preferences and aversions toward certain counselor traits. These findings should be useful to counselors, as well as those involved in training programs. (Author abstract.)

Treatment techniques and approaches

INDIVIDUAL COUNSELING

Earlier we defined treatment as all the interventions intended to short-circuit the alcoholism process and to introduce the individual to effective sobriety. This could be put in equation form as follows:

Treatment = individual counseling + family therapy + family education + client education + group therapy + medical care + AA + Al-Anon + Antabuse + vocational counseling + activities therapy + spiritual counseling. . . .

As can be seen, individual counseling is only a small part of the many things that treatment involves. So what is it? A very simple way to think of individual counseling is as the time, place, and space in which the rest of the treatment is organized, planned, and processed. One-to-one counseling is a series of interviews. During these sessions the therapist and client work together to define problems, explore possible solutions, and identify resources, with the therapist providing support, encouragement, and feedback to the client as he or she takes action.

One of the difficulties in thinking about, discussing, or writing about counseling is knowing where to begin. It can seem a bit overwhelming. One of the problems is that most of us have never seen a real counselor at work. We have all seen police officers, telephone line workers, carpenters, or teachers busy on the job. So we have some sense of what is involved and can imagine what it would be like. The clinician's job is different. It is private and not readily observable. Unfortunately, most of our ideas come from books or television. It doesn't take too much television viewing to get some notion that a good counselor is almost a magician, relying on uncanny instincts to divine the darkest, deepest secrets of the client's mind. You can't help thinking the therapist must have a T-shirt with a big letter S underneath the button-down collar. Television does an excellent job of teaching us that things are not always as they seem. Yet, remember, in real life they often—indeed, usually—are. Everyone is quite adept at figuring out what is going on.

Observation

Each day we process vast amounts of information without much thought. Our behavior is almost automatic. Without the benefit of a clock, we can make a reasonable estimate of the time. When shopping, we can, without too much trouble, distinguish the clerk from fellow customers. Sometimes, though, we cannot find a person who seems to be the clerk. Take a couple of minutes to think about the clues you use in separating the clerk from the customer. One of the clues might be dress. Clerks may wear a special outfit, such as smock, apron, or shirt with the store's logo. In colder weather, customers off the street will be wearing or carrying their coats. Another clue is behavior. The clerks stand behind counters and cash registers, the customers in front. Customers stroll about casually looking at merchandise, whereas clerks systematically arrange displays. Another clue might be the person's companions. Clerks are usually alone, not hauling their children or browsing with a friend. Although we have all had some experience of guessing incorrectly, it rarely happens. In essence, this is "the good guys wear white hats" principle. A person's appearance provides us with useful, reliable information about them. Before a word of conversation is spoken, our observations provide us with some basic data to guide our interactions.

We hope that you are convinced everyone has observational powers. Usually, people simply do not think about these skills. The only difference between the clinician and others is that the therapist will cultivate these observational capacities, listen carefully, and attend to "how" something is said and not merely "what" is said. The counselor will ask: "What is the client's mood?" "Is the mood appropriate to what is being said?" "What kinds of shifts take place during the interview?" "What nonverbal clues, or signs, does the client give to portray how she feels?" So, in a counseling session, from time to time, momentarily tune out the words and take a good look. What do you "see?" Reverse that. Turn off the picture and focus on the sound.

One important thing to note is that the questions you ask yourself (or the client) are not "why" questions. They are "what" and "how" questions that attempt to determine what is going on. Strangely enough, in alcohol treatment, successful outcomes can occur without *ever* tackling a "why." Ignoring what or how issues, however, may mean you'll never even get into the ball park.

So what is the importance of observation? It provides data for making hypotheses. A question continually before the therapist is: "What's going on with this person?" What you see provides clues. You do not pretend to be a mind reader. Despite occasional lapses, you do not equate observations, or hunches, with ultimate truth. Your observations, coupled with your knowledge of alcohol and its impact upon people, suggest where attention might be focused. An example: a client whose coloring is poor and who has a distended abdomen and a number of bruises will alert the counselor to the possibility of serious medical problems. The client may try to explain this all away by "just having tripped over the phone cord," but the therapist will urge the client to see a physician.

You do your work by observing, listening, and asking the client (and yourself) questions to gain a picture of the client's situation. The image of a picture being sketched and painted is quite apt to capture the therapeutic process. The space above is the canvas. The total area includes everything that is going on in the individual's life. As the client speaks with the therapist, this space is filled in. Now the therapist is getting a picture of the client's situation. Not only do

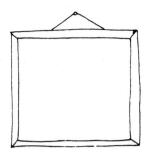

you have the "facts" as the client sees them, but also you can see the client, and his or her mood and feelings and get a sense of what the world and picture *feels* like to the client as well. As this happens, the space gets filled in and begins to look like this:

You have a notion of the various areas that make up the client's life: family, physical health, work, economic situation, community life, how the person feels about himself/herself, and so on. You are also aware of how alcohol may affect these areas. As you find it necessary, you will guide the conversation to ensure that you have a total picture of the client's life. You are also aware that if the client is having a problem, it means that the pieces are not fitting together in a way that feels comfortable. Maybe some parts have very rough edges. Maybe one part is exerting undue influence on the others. So you also attempt to see the relationship and interaction between the parts.

Confrontation

Confrontation is a technique used by the therapist to help the client make the essential connections. Confrontation does *not* equal attack. According to *Webster's,* to confront means "to cause to meet: bring face to face." Several examples of what therapists may do to bring clients face to face with the consequences of their behavior are to have a family meeting so that the family's concerns can be presented; to make a referral to a physician for treatment and consultation about the "stomach problems"; or to make a referral to an alcohol discussion and educational group. The therapist endeavors to structure situations in which the client is brought face to face with facts.

Feedback

In assisting the client to "see" what is going on, the therapist's observation skills pay off. A common feature of alcohol dependence is a markedly warped perception of reality. The ability of the therapist to provide accurate feedback to the client, giving specific descriptions of behavior and of what the client is doing, is very valuable. The alcohol-dependent person has lost the ability for self-assessment. It is quite likely that any feedback from family members has also been warped and laced with threats so that it has become useless. In the counseling session, it may go like this: "Well, you say things are going fine. Yet as I look at you, I see you fidgeting in your chair, your voice is quivering, and your eyes are cast down toward the floor. For me, that doesn't go along with someone who's feeling fine." *Period*. The therapist simply reports the observations. There is no deep interpretation. There is no attempt to ferret out unconscious dynamics. The client is not labeled a "liar." Your willingness and ability to simply describe what you see is a potent therapeutic weapon. The client can begin to learn how he or she comes across, how others see him. Thus your use of observation serves to educate the client about himself.

Education

In addition to self-awareness, the client also needs education about alcohol, the drug, and the disease of alcoholism. Provide facts and data. A host of pamphlets are available from state alcohol agencies, insurance companies, and AA. Everybody likes to understand what is happening to them. This is becoming increasingly apparent in all areas of medicine. Some institutions have hired client educators. Client education sessions on diabetes, heart disease, cancer, and care of newborns are becoming commonplace. Education about alcohol problems is important for two reasons. The first is to help instill new attitudes toward alcoholism, that it is a disease, it has recognizable signs, and that it is treatable. The hope is to elicit the client's support in helping to manage and treat the problem.

The other reason for education is to help the client handle feelings of guilt and low self-esteem. The chances are pretty good that the client's behavior has been looked at as downright crazy—and not just to others; it has also been inexplicable to the alcoholic individual. The fact that he or she has been denying a problem confirms this. There is no need to deny something unless it is so painful and so inconsistent with values that it cannot be tolerated. Learning facts about alcohol and alcoholism can be a big relief. Suddenly, things make sense. All the bizarre behavior becomes understandable, at least for an active alcoholic. That makes a significant difference. Successful recovery appears to be related to a client's acceptance of this framework of disease as the basis for what has been

occurring. Energy can be applied to figuring out how one can live around the illness, live successfully, now. The individual is relieved of the need to hash around back there, in the past, to uncover causes, to figure out what went wrong. There is no need to dwell on the pattern of harmful, senseless behavior; it becomes merely a symptom, one that the individual isn't doomed to reexperience if efforts are made to maintain sobriety.

Self-disclosure

At this juncture it seems appropriate to add some cautionary word about the technique of self-disclosure. And make no mistake about it, we consider this to be a *counseling technique*. As such, it requires the same thoughtful evaluation of its usefulness as any other counseling tool. It is important to recognize that "self-disclosure" is not limited to sharing information of one's own problems with alcoholism. Self-disclosure in counseling or therapy refers to sharing not only the facts of one's life but also one's feelings and values as well. This is in contrast to the style of the early psychoanalyst, who never revealed information about himself nor in any way presented himself as an individual to his clients. Counselors are self-disclosing when they express empathy or when they note that the client's concerns are those with which other clients have also struggled.

This phrase does, however, have special meaning in the alcohol and substance abuse field. The clinician may also be a recovering alcoholic in private life, and as one, he or she may have participated in AA when self-disclosure was appropriate. In a professional individual counseling or group therapy session the need for self-disclosure may not always be clear-cut.

Particularly at the early stages of the client's treatment or in the assessment process, it may seem only natural to allay some of the client's nervousness or resistance with the news that you, as a clinician, have "been there," know just how he or she feels, and furthermore can testify to the possibility of a successful recovery. What seems natural may, however, be totally inappropriate or even counter-therapeutic. Therapists need to remember that their professionalism is important to the client, particularly in the early days of treatment. That professionalism is comforting! The patient in an intensive cardiac care unit is interested in the physician's medical assessment of his condition, the physician's treatment recommendations, and the probable outcome. That patient is not interested in hearing the physician's personal story of her own heart attack.

This is not to imply that self-disclosure shouldn't ever be used or that it is ineffective. But we see the technique too often used as a matter of course without proper thought given to the possible ramifications of it in a particular instance. Because we do see it as a very powerful clinical tool, we recommend that great care be taken to see

that it is used at the best possible time for the best possible reason—the benefit of the client. It should never be used to make the therapist feel more comfortable by getting "everything out in the open" or as a substitute for professional skills.

When is self-disclosure therapeutic? There may be times when the behavior that has resulted from alcoholism creates an overwhelming sense of worthlessness, isolation, and pervasive hopelessness. In such circumstances, self-disclosure may be useful. It may provide a desperately needed human connection, helping to relieve feelings of utter despair, spark just a glimmer of hope and a recognition that maybe, just maybe, things can be different. In a group setting, it may be preferable that such efforts to reach out come from group members. But there are times, certainly in individual sessions, when this falls to the clinician.

Client responsibility

The therapist expects the client to assume responsibility for his or her actions. You do not accept the client's view of himself as either a pawn of fate or a helpless victim. An ironic twist is present. You make it clear that you see the client as an adult who is accountable for his or her choices. Simultaneously, you are aware that those dependent upon alcohol, when drinking, abdicate control to a drug. By definition, an alcoholic cannot be responsible for what transpires after even one or two drinks. Therefore being responsible ultimately means that the attempt to manage alcohol use must be abandoned. Here again, facts about the drug, alcohol, and the disease of alcohol dependence are important. A large chunk of the client's work will be to examine the facts of his or her own life in light of this information.

The alcoholic's need to have an alibi, to rationalize, and to otherwise explain away the obvious varies. But the therapist consistently holds up the mirror of reality, playing the client's story back to him. The therapist shares his or her observations, and in this way the client is enabled to move toward the first step of recovery—acknowledging the inability to control alcohol.

A word of caution

One word of caution to newcomers to the field: active alcoholics are sometimes described as manipulative or "con artists." Appreciate that they've had to be. To continue drinking alcoholically, in spite of the consequences, has required their adopting behaviors and perceptions of the world that could make their drinking feel and appear rational. These patterns do not disappear with the first prod, push, or pull toward treatment. Old habits die hard. With alcohol dependence, the habit of protecting the right to drink (even to death) is a long-standing one. When a client discovers that you

I've heard him renounce wine a hundred times a day, but then it has been between as many glasses.
DOUGLAS JERROLD

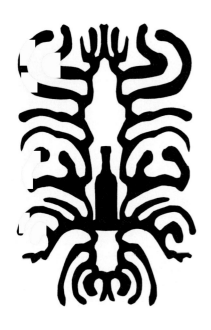

are probably not going to hand out a simple "three-step way to drink socially" and thus allow the drinking to continue, all considerable cunning can rise up in defense.

> "Gee, you've really helped me to see exactly what I have to do. I'll do _____ and _____ and everything will be just fine. Thanks so much. You've made my life so much better already."

> "Both my parents were alcoholics. I even had a grandfather who was. But you know, I really don't drink like that at all! It only started when Johnny had that awful operation, and I spent hours at the hospital, and then my husband was called away to South America, and I needed *something* to help me over those awful times. But my husband's due home next week, and I'm just sure that now that I know all the facts you've given me, I'll just stop by myself, and everything will be just fine! Thank you so much."

> "I can't imagine why my wife says what she does about my drinking. She must really be down on me, or jealous, or something. After all, I only have a couple of beers with the guys after work."

> "Did you hear about that new research they've been doing? You know, the stuff that talks about having a dog helps. I bet if I just get a dog and take something for my nerves (after all, my nerves are the *real* problem), I'll be just fine!"

Many individuals can be far more inventive than these examples show. Add tears, or a charming smile, or bruises from a beating. If they're not at the moment falling down, slobbering, throwing up, or slurring their words, it is hard not to believe them. There they sit—full of confidence, hopeful, and very friendly. After all, this isn't a charade for your benefit. The active alcoholic is desperately trying to hold on to the picture they paint. Experience has shown that at some point, you will either see, hear from, or hear about these people, and their situations will have gone downhill. They don't know how familiar their stories are—to themselves, the stories are unique. These people are not lying; they are simply trying to hang on to the only help they feel they have—the bottle.

Also, always keep in mind that the purpose of the "con" is *not* to deceive you. The client is trying above all to maintain his or her own self-deception. You may be able to help him or her loosen the grip by not allowing these pat replies to go unchallenged.

Motivation

A significant contribution of learning psychologists active in the alcohol and substance abuse fields has been in clarifying the concept of motivation. In the past, motivation was seen as a characteristic of a client, as a "something" that was either absent or present. "Motivated" clients were perceived as having good outcomes; conversely, treatment failures were often chalked up to a client's "lack of motivation." William Miller, drawing upon work done in other fields, has introduced into the alcohol and substance abuse treatment a very different view of motivation. In his formulation, motivation is a dynamic process with discrete stages that parallel the stages occurring whenever anyone makes significant life changes. Specific clinical interventions are either well suited or to be avoided, depending upon where the client is in the change process. The stages outlined by Miller are as follows:

- *Precontemplation.* This is the point when the individual is not even considering change. There is no perceived need to. Instead, a problem is recognized by someone else, such as family member, physician, clergy, or co-worker. In this stage, the important clinical task is to help the individual gain awareness of the dangers involved in his or her present behaviors.
- *Contemplation.* Now the individual is more ambivalent. There is a mixture of favoring and resisting change. As change is considered, the person perceives both pluses and minuses. In this stage if confronted with arguments on one side, the client's likely response is to defend the opposite side. So it is helpful for the clinician to address both the negative effects of the alcohol use, the features the client considers pluses, and the potential benefits of change.
- *Determination.* In this phase, there is less ambivalence. The client often "sounds" different and can acknowledge a situation warranting change. Efforts are actively being made to consider alternatives. For the patient at this stage, rapid, immediate intervention is important. If too much time passes, the individual reverts to the stage of contemplation. Thus a potential opportunity for change has been lost. In this stage the client needs the professional's assistance in selecting an optimal strategy for making changes, plus the client needs lots of support for the resolve to follow through.
- *Action.* At this point the client is engaged in implementing a plan, which often may be formal treatment. At this point, the clinical task is providing assistance and direction as the client carries out the plan.
- *Maintenance.* When significant changes in behavior have been made, then maintenance of the change is what becomes important. The individual can't simply rest on his or her laurels. Maintenance of change is seen as being sustained by continuing action. Interestingly, the process of making change is in and of itself reinforcing. It encourages the desire to make other needed changes and demonstrates that change is possible.
- *Relapse.* Here the individual reverts back to the previous behavioral pattern. If relapse occurs, then it is necessary to once again go through the stage of initiating change, again

starting with contemplation. Now we return to the discussion of individual counseling.

Problem identification and problem solving

In therapy, problem identification and problem solving constitute a recurring process. No matter what the problem, two kinds of forces are always at work: some factors help perpetuate the problem; other factors encourage change. These can be sketched out in a diagram, as shown on the next page. Suppose the problem is: "I don't like my job." The line going across represents the current situation. The arrows pointing upward stand for the factors that ease or lighten the problem. The arrows pointing downward represent the factors aggravating the problem.

If the individual's goal is to be more content at work, this might happen in several ways. The positive forces can be strengthened or others added, or attempts can be made to diminish the negative ones. A similar sketch might be made for alcoholic drinking. This kind of chart can help you decide what factors might be tackled to disturb the present equilibrium.

Left to his or her own devices, the alcoholic individual would piddle along for years. The fact that he is sitting in front of you indicates that something has happened to jiggle the equilibrium. This can be a force for change. Take advantage of it. Jiggle the equilibrium further. In the illustration just given, to take away the family denial or co-worker cover-up would blow the whole act. It is becoming widely acknowledged that for the clinician to precipitate such a crisis is the most helpful thing to do.

The therapeutic relationship

Whole volumes have been written on the nature and components of the therapeutic relationship. This book cannot even begin to summarize what has been set forth. Some of the attributes of the helping relationship were alluded to at the beginning of the previous chapter on treatment. The therapist is a guide. The therapist cannot do the work, but only can attempt to bring the client's attention to the work that needs to be done. The therapist may provide some "how to" suggestions but will proportionally provide more support as the client does the actual work.

Although an exposition of the therapeutic relationship is beyond the scope of this book, several items are common points of confusion for newcomers. First, whatever the peculiar thing is that is the client-clinician relationship, it is not a friendship. It is not based on liking one another. The value of the therapist to the client is paradoxically that he is not a friend; the therapist does not need or exact anything from the client. Indeed, if that sneaks into the equation, then the potential value of the therapist has accordingly been diminished. Beyond being someone with a knowledge of alcohol and its effects, the therapist is someone who can be trusted to be candid and open and who strives for objectivity. She or he can be counted upon to say what needs to be said and trusted to hear the difficult things a client must say without scolding or judging. Although it may initially sound demeaning, in point of fact the therapist is most effective with clients when the relationship is "just part of the job."

With the client-therapist relationship outside the realm of friendship, several potentially difficult situations for the clinician are more easily avoided. Some predictably difficult situations are what to do when the client becomes angry, threatens to drop out of counseling, claims you are taking someone else's side, or insists that you don't care or understand. It's very tempting and ever so easy to experience such situations as personally (and undeservedly) directed toward you. So first, take a deep breath. Second, remind yourself it isn't you who's being attacked. This is not an occasion for either reminding the client of "everything you've done for him," or just how experienced you are, even if the client doesn't appreciate it. As quietly and calmly as possible, discuss what's going on, which includes acknowledging the feelings the client is experiencing. Resist trying to make the patient feel "better" or talk him or her out of those feelings. Expression of negative emotion is something to be anticipated. Indeed, if it never occurs, it may mean that the therapist is sending signals that it is not permitted. Allowing negative feelings to be expressed doesn't mean being a sponge for everything, or not setting limits, or not stating a different perspective if you have one. One of the most important lessons the client may need to learn during treatment is that negative emotions can be expressed and the

world doesn't fall apart. Nor will others immediately try to placate or run away.

The other side of the "emotions coin" can present a different trap. It is difficult not to respond to: "You are so wonderful," "You are the only person who really understands," or "You are the only person I can say this to." Beyond the danger of inflating the therapist's ego, there is the danger for the client that all the power is invested in the therapist. In the process of treatment, it is important that the client experience, and take credit for, the therapeutic work that is being done. So, for example, in responding to "You are the only person who really understands," a gentle reminder of the client's share of the work is appropriate. You might ask if there are other relationships, too, in which the client wishes to be able to share more and then help decide how to attempt to do that.

Administrative tasks

Now to sound a very different note. An inevitable and necessary part of a therapist's work is administrative—writing notes in the chart, contacting agencies or counselors for previous records, dictating discharge summaries, contacting the referring party or others to whom a client will be referred. This is often perceived as a pain in the neck and the portion of one's job most likely to get short shrift. However, attending to these details is an important part of good clinical care. Treatment is almost never a solo act, but a team effort. How effectively the team functions often depends on the clinical personnel who orchestrate and coordinate the various efforts.

The client's chart or medical record is one very important vehicle for communicating information. This is especially true in a residential facility, with multiple staff working different shifts. There are often questions as to what should and shouldn't go in a chart. To handle things that should be noted but are particularly sensitive, some agencies have adopted a set of confidential files, separate from the main record. Although not wishing to take lightly the concern for confidentiality, it can be a red herring. In thinking about what to include in the chart, ask yourself "What do others need to know to respond therapeutically?" Rarely does this have anything to do with "deep dark secrets." More often it has to do with the everyday nuts and bolts—worrying over a date for discharge, preoccupation with an upcoming court appearance, or a strained family meeting. The chart is not the place for verbatim accounts of individual sessions. But notation of any general themes, plus any modification of treatment plans, is needed.

In addition to charting, it will also fall to the client's primary therapist to present cases at team planning meetings. On such occasions, a little preliminary thought helps: Are there special questions you have that you'd like to discuss with others? Along with these formal routes of communication, there are also informal channels. Take the opportunity to brief others. Beyond orchestrating the activities of the treatment team, it falls to the primary therapist to be a liaison, and sometimes an advocate, with external groups such as employers, welfare workers, and the courts. In these situations, you must have the client's permission before acting. Also, it is important not to do for clients what they can do for themselves. Generally, it is more therapeutic to do a lot of hand holding as clients take care of business, rather than doing it yourself in the interest of efficiency.

GROUP WORK

Group therapy has become an increasingly popular form of treatment for a range of problems, including alcohol abuse. (Of course, with AA dating back to 1935, recovering has been occurring in groups long before group therapy became popular or alcohol treatment was even known.) Why the popularity of group treatment methods? The first response often is: "It's cheaper," or "It's more efficient; more people can be seen." These statements may be true, but a more fundamental reason exists. Group therapy works, and it works very well with alcoholics. Some of the reasons for this can be found in the characteristics of the illness, plus normal human nature.

Of course I have friends — Jack Daniels, Chivas Regal, Kahlua

For better or worse, people find themselves part of a group. And whatever being human means, it does involve other people. We think in terms of our family, our neighborhood, our school, our club, our town, or our church. On the job, at home, on the playground, wherever, it is in group experiences where we feel left out or, conversely, experience a sense of belonging. Through our contacts with others, we feel okay or not okay. As we interact, we find ourselves sharing our successes or hiding our supposed failures. Through groups we get pats on the head or a kick in the pants. There is no avoiding the reality that other people play a big part in our lives. Just as politicians take opinion polls to see how they're doing with the populace, so do each of us run our surveys. The kinds of questions we ask ourselves about our relationships are: "Do I belong?", "Do I matter to others?", "Can I trust them?", "Am I liked?", "Do I like them?" To be at ease and comfortable in the world, the answers have to come up more ayes than nays. The active alcoholic doesn't fare so well when taking this poll. For the myriad reasons discussed before, the alcoholic's relationships with other people are poor. Isolated and isolating, rejecting and rejected, helpless and refusing aid—with such a warped view of the world, they are oblivious to the fact that their drinking has been causing the trouble. When one is wed to the bottle, other bonds cannot be formed. Attempts to make it in the world sober will require reestablishing real human contacts. Thus groups, the setting in which life must be lived, become an ideal setting for treatment.

When you ask one friend to dine,
Give him your best wine!
When you ask two,
The second best will do!

LONGFELLOW

Group as therapy

Being a part of group can do some powerful therapeutic things. The active alcoholic is afraid of people "out there." The phrase "tiger land" has been used by alcoholics to describe the world. That's a fairly telling phrase! Through group treatment, ideally the client will *reexperience* the world differently. The whole thing need not be a jungle—other people can be a source of safety and strength.

Another bonus from a group experience is derived from individuals' opportunities to become *reacquainted* with themselves. A group provides a chance to learn who they are, their capabilities, their impact on and importance to others. Interacting candidly and openly provides an opportunity to adjust and correct their mental pictures of themselves. They get feedback. Group treatment of those in a similar situation reduces the sense of *isolation*. Those with active alcoholism tend to view themselves *very* negatively and have an overwhelming sense of shame over their behavior. Coming together with others proves that one is not uniquely awful.

Yet mere confession is not therapeutic. Something else must happen for healing to occur. Just as absolution occurs in the context of a church, in a group that functions therapeutically, the members act as priests to one another. Members hear one another's confession and say, in essence: "You are forgiven, go and sin no more."* That is to say, group members can see one another apart from the behavior that accompanies alcoholism. They can also often see a potential that is unknown to the individual. This is readily verified in our own lives. Solutions to other people's problems are so obvious, but not so solutions to our own. Members of the group can see that people need not be destined to continue their old behaviors. Old "sins" need not be repeated. Thus they *instill hope* in one another.

Interestingly enough, one often finds that people are more gentle with others than they are with themselves. In this regard, the group experience has a beneficial boomerang effect. In the process of being kind and understanding of others, the members are in turn forced to accord themselves similar treatment.

What has been discussed is the potential benefit that can be gleaned from a group exposure. How this group experience takes place can vary widely. Group therapy comes in many styles and can occur in many contexts. Being a resident in a halfway house puts one in a group, just as the person who participates in outpatient

---

*A short lesson in linguistics: the word *sin* is derived from a Greek word meaning "to miss the target." It is used in archery. A person standing next to the target would call back to the archer so that the archer could readjust his aim. It does not imply evil, or bad, as is so often assumed.

group therapy. Group therapy means the use of *any* group experience to promote change in the members. Under the direction of a skilled leader, the power of the group processes is harnessed for therapeutic purposes.

Group work with those with alcohol problems

In contemplating group work for those with alcohol problems, the leader will need to consider several basic issues. What is the purpose of the group? What are the goals for the individual members? Where will the group meet? How often? What will the rules be? The first question is the key. The purpose of the group should be clear in the leader's mind. There are many possible legitimate purposes. Experience shows that not all can be met simultaneously. It is far better to have different types of groups available, with members participating in several, than to lump everything into one group and accomplish nothing. Some of the more common groups are educational, self-awareness, problem solving, and activity or resocialization.

Educational groups attempt to impart factual information about alcohol, its effects, and alcoholism. There is a complex relationship between knowledge, feelings, and behavior. Correct facts and information do not stop serious problematic drinking, but they can be important in breaking down denial, which protects the drinking. Information provides an invaluable framework for understanding what has happened and what treatment is about. In an educational group, clients acquire some cognitive tools to participate more successfully in their own treatment. Educational groups may be organized around a lecture, film, or presentation by a specialist in the alcohol field, followed by a group discussion. Topics such as a description of AA and how it works, alcohol's effects on the body, and the recovery process may be included.

Self-awareness and support groups are intended to assist their members to grapple seriously with the role of alcohol in their lives. The group function is to support abstinence and to identify the characteristic ways in which people sabotage themselves. In these groups, the emphasis is on the here and now. The participants are expected to deal with feelings as well as facts. The goal is not for members to achieve an intellectual understanding of why things have or are occurring. Rather, the goal is to have members discover how they feel and learn how feelings are translated into behavior. Then they choose how they would prefer to behave and try it on for size.

A problem-solving group is directed at tackling specific problems or stressful areas in the group members' lives. Either discussion, role play, or a combination may be used. For example, how to say no to an offer to have a beer, how to handle an upcoming job interview, or how to get through the upcoming holidays could be appropriate subjects. The goal is to develop an awareness of potential stressful

That is a treacherous friend against whom you must always be on your guard. Such a friend is wine.

C.N. BOVEE

situations, identify the old habitual response patterns, recognize how these patterns have created problems, and then try new behaviors. These sessions thus provide practice for more effective coping behaviors.

Activity groups are those least likely to resemble the stereotype of group therapy. In these groups an activity or project is undertaken, such as a ward or client government meeting or a planning session for a picnic. The emphasis is on more than the apparent task. The task is also a sample of real life. Thus it provides an arena for the clients to identify areas of strength and weakness in interpersonal relationships. Here, too, is a safe place to practice new behaviors.

Group functions

No matter what the kind of group, a number of functions will have to be performed. For any group to work effectively, there are some essential tasks, regardless of the goal. Initially the leader may have to be primarily responsible for filling these roles:

- Initiating—suggesting ideas for the group to consider, getting the ball rolling
- Elaborating or clarifying—clearing up confusions, giving examples, expanding on contributions of group members
- Summarizing—pulling together loose ends, restating ideas
- Facilitating—encouraging others' participation by asking questions, showing interest
- Expressing group feelings—recognizing moods and relationships within the group
- Giving feedback—sharing responses to what is happening in the group
- Seeking feedback—asking for others' responses about what you are doing

As time goes on, the leader does need to teach the group members to share the responsibility for these functions.

Different types of group therapy can be useful at different times during recovery. During the course of an inpatient stay, a client might well attend an educational group, a problem-solving group, and a self-awareness group. In addition, the person could attend outside AA meetings. In this example, the client would be participating in four different types of groups. On discharge from the residence, the person would return for weekly group sessions as part of follow-up, and with his or her spouse and they might join a couples group. None of these group experiences is intended to substitute for AA. The most effective treatment plans will prescribe AA plus alcohol-related group therapy. They are no more mutually exclusive than is AA or group therapy occurring simultaneously with medical treatment of cirrhosis.

I've actually got 7 personalities but only one of us is an alcoholic.

Groups as a diversion

For a while group experiences, for the general population, became something of a fad. There was a bandwagon phenomenon—marathon, encounter, TA, gestalt, sensitivity, EST. These and many other forms were seemingly offered everywhere: schools, churches, on the job, by women's clubs, at community centers. There was a whirlwind of activity around the use of groups for "personal growth." While these variants of groups directed to personal growth may sound a bit dated and passée, the group phenomena remains, having simply changed focus. Groups directed at personal growth have seemingly been supplanted by an ever burgeoning number of self-help groups, many of them modeled after Alcoholics Anonymous. There is now Adult Children of Alcoholics (ACA or ACOA), Overeaters Anonymous (OA), Narcotics Anonymous (NA), Cocaine Anonymous (CA), plus less well known but similarly constituted groups for victims of incest, rape, and child abuse codependency; those with sexual addictions; plus those who have been batterers or have engaged in or are concerned about their potential for child abuse.

The emphasis placed on groups here does not imply that those with a serious drinking problem should ride the group therapy circuit. On the contrary, those seeking and requiring *alcohol* treatment in a group *not* restricted to those with alcoholism are likely to waste their own and other people's time. As was stated earlier, until one has taken some step to combat the alcohol problem, there is little likelihood of working on other problems successfully. Inevitably, the still drinking alcoholic member will raise havoc in a nonalcohol focused group. Our prediction is that the alcoholic group member will have others running in circles figuring out the whys, get gobs of sympathy, and remain unchanged. Eventually others in the group will wear out, end up treating the alcoholic member just as the family does, and experience all the same frustrations as the family. However, in a group with others in trouble with alcohol and a leader familiar with the dynamics of alcohol dependence or alcohol abuse, it's a different story. The opportunity to divert others' attention from the role of alcohol is diminished to virtually zero because everyone knows the game thoroughly. The agenda, in this latter instance, clearly is how to break out of that pattern.

Historically, and for too long, all too often the family members of those being treated for alcohol problems have been shortchanged. In the past, if a family member contacted a treatment agency about an alcohol problem in the family, what was likely to happen? He or she may have been told to have the troubled person call on his or her own behalf, or have heard a sympathetic "Yes, it's awful," or have been told to call Al-Anon. It was unusual that families or family members were invited to come in as clients in their own right. In

Sunday night I go to a parent support group. Monday night I have my NA meeting. Tuesday night is my Overeaters Anonymous meeting. Wednesday night is my children of alcoholics group. Thursday there's a single mother's support group. Friday is my emotions anonymous group. And Saturday nights I stay home and watch television. I love Saturday nights.

instances in which the alcohol-troubled person was seeking help, the family may have been called in by a clinician only to provide some background information and was then subsequently ignored. Any further attention family members got came only if a problem arose or if the counselor believed that the spouse or family wasn't being supportive. Treatment efforts did not routinely take into account the problems the spouses faced and their own, independent need for treatment.

Although these events may still occur, nonetheless very few in the alcohol field would claim that the approach is adequate. By definition, alcohol treatment that ignores the family has come to be seen as second-rate care! Although larger treatment programs now have staff whose specialty is family work, every clinician needs to have some basic understanding of the issues that confront families and develop some basic skills for working with family members.

Members of the family do need treatment as much as the alcohol-dependent person. More and more often they are coming to this conclusion themselves and seeking help. Clinicians are likely to find that more and more of their clients are, in fact, family members.

WORKING WITH FAMILIES

The most important thing the clinician needs to keep in mind is that the client being treated is the person in the office—in this case, the family. The big temptation, and what was once seen as the appropriate stance, was to try treating the alcoholic family member in absentia. This may be the family member's wish, too. But it would be futile to attempt it.

What does the family need? One important need is for education about alcohol, the drug, the problems that evolve with chronic heavy use, and the disease, alcoholism. The family also needs education on how the symptoms of the disease affect the family. By families we include not only the traditional family, but the many new forms of family life. "Home" was described by the poet Robert Frost as the place where, "when you go there, they have to let you in!" Calling upon this definition, "family" includes all those in the home.

Another area in which assistance is required is in sorting out the family's behavior to see how it fits into or even perpetuates the drinking. They need also to sort out their feelings and realistically come to grips with the true dimensions of the problem and the toll being exacted from them. Accompanying all this is the need to examine their options for problem solving. Most importantly the family members require support to live their own lives *despite the alcoholism* in their midst. Paradoxically, by doing this, the actual chances of short-circuiting the alcoholism process are enhanced.

Family assessment

Just as all those with alcohol dependence do not display the identical symptoms or have the same degree of chronicity and extent of impairment, the same is true of family members. In the assessment process, many of the same questions the therapist asks in dealing with the alcoholic individual should be considered. What has caused the family member to seek help now? What is the family's understanding of the problem? What supports do they have? What is the economic, social, and family situation like? What coping devices do they use? What are their fears? What do they want from you? Where the clinician goes in working with the family will depend on the answers to these questions. Treatment plans for family might include individual counseling, support groups, Al-Anon, or being seen in a general social service agency.

You will notice that we have been speaking interchangeably about families and family members. Contact with a helping person is typically made by a single individual. Efforts to include the other members of the family or the alcohol-troubled member usually fall to the clinician. In some cases, all it takes is the suggestion. In other cases the family member who made the contact may resist. This resistance may result from a sense of isolation or that no one else in the family cares, or it may instead be fear of the other family members' disapproval for having "spilled the beans" about the family's secret. Although the ideal might be having the family member approach the others, as the therapist, you (with the client's permission) can contact other family members to ask them to come in for at least one session. Almost universally others will come in at least once (and this includes the alcoholic member), if you tell them you are interested in their views of what is happening.

Robert's father is willing to drive us here, but he won't come inside. He prefers to stay in the car with his bottle of bourbon.

Family intervention

The initial focus has to be working with the family members on their own problems. Nonetheless, the indisputable fact is that the alcohol dependence is a central problem and that the family would like to see the alcoholic member receive help. It is important to recognize that, ineffective as their efforts may have been, still much of a family's energy has gone into "helping." Now, as a result of education about the disease, plus after assistance with sorting out their own situation, they in essence have become equipped to act more effectively in relation to the alcoholic family member. At the very least the family has been helped to abandon its protective, and though unintended, its nonetheless enabling behavior.

However, more is possible. In the early 1970s, a time when it was believed that treatment could not be successful unless the alcoholic individual had "hit bottom" and was requesting help, a clinical technique was introduced by the Johnson Institute in Minneapolis that proved otherwise. This clinical approach is known as an "intervention." It consists of involving the family and other significant people in the person's life to promote the alcohol dependent member's entry into treatment. This intervention technique and its supporting rationale were first described in *I'll Quit Tomorrow*.

The introduction of the "intervention" dramatically changed the treatment field. It forced clinicians, the recovering community—all concerned about those with alcoholism—to rethink some of the earlier assumptions about what was necessary for successful outcomes. Family and clinicians no longer had to sit around helplessly, waiting and praying for some magic insight to promote the request for help. Whether described as "raising the bottom," "early intervention," or "confrontation," clinicians now had a therapeutic tool that could help move sick people into care.

Since the introduction of intervention, it has become increasingly apparent that successful treatment can occur in a number of situations in which the entry into treatment might be considered "coercive." Among the programs with the best treatment outcomes are those in which the stakes are quite clear—EAP (or Employee Assistance Programs), programs conducted by the military, court-mandated treatment, or treatment offered by professions where there is close monitoring in post-treatment, such as among airline pilots, physicians, and nurses. In such instances, while the individual may not be highly motivated to enter treatment, entry into care is clearly preferable to the alternative. To use the framework for motivation described earlier, external circumstances often play a role in sparking change. With hindsight we now can see that the treatment field's historical mistake was in not recognizing that ambivalence is a part of the change process and, thus, expecting alcoholic individuals to be further along in the process of making change before we were ready (or knew how) to extend professional assistance.

The ingredients of intervention

The intervention process involves a meeting of family, other concerned persons, and the alcoholic individual, conducted under the direction of a trained clinician. The scenario entails each individual present, in turn, presenting to the alcoholic person a list of specific incidents related to drinking that have caused concern. Each person also expresses the hope that the person will enter treatment. To be effective, these facts must be conveyed in an atmosphere of genuine concern for the alcohol-dependent person. The intended effect of this is that the alcoholic person can more accurately see the fundamental nature of the problem and why external assistance is needed. By providing the painful facts, the intervention process attempts to cut through the denial and can be viewed as precipitating a crisis.

The therapist who is involved in family work is well advised to become skilled in conducting interventions, either by attending workshops or by "apprenticing" to someone trained in this technique. We should be clear that conducting an intervention is *not* something you do on the spur of the moment. It is not something to be done impromptu, just because you happen to have the family together. Nor is it something you describe to the family and suggest they do on their own after supper some evening.

The effectiveness of intervention depends on the participants' ability to voice a genuine concern and describe incidents that have caused concern in an objective, straightforward manner. This takes briefing and preparation. Typically, this will entail several meetings with the family. The family members must become knowledgeable about the disease that confronts them so that the behaviors that previously were seen as designed to "get them" can be seen for what they are, symptoms. The preparation will usually involve a rehearsal during which each participant goes through the things he or she would like to convey to the alcoholic family member. The participants also need to discuss what treatment options are to be presented, and the actions they will take if the person does not seek help. Is the spouse ready to ask for a separation? Is the grown daughter ready to say she will not be comfortable allowing Mom to baby-sit for the grandchildren anymore? Are the parents ready to make continuation of college tuition payments contingent upon their son's entering treatment? Beyond preparing the participants, a successful intervention also requires that the therapist be supportive to *all* present, equally, and deflect the alcoholic member's anxiety and fears, which may surface as anger.

Family treatment in conjunction with alcohol treatment

By whatever process and point at which individuals enter formal treatment, involvement of the family is critical. The family should be included as early as possible. Family involvement is far from being elective or a nice touch; it is vital to securing an adequate database for treatment planning.

Say alcoholism is clearly evident—having progressed to the stage it is diagnosable even by the parking lot attendant. In such circumstances, the family may be the only reliable source of even the most basic information, such as how much alcohol is being consumed, past medical history, and prior alcohol treatment. The individual's judgment may be so severely impaired that realistically others will need to make the decision about admission for treatment.

The family members' views of what the problem is, their understanding of alcoholism as a disease, their ability to provide support, and their willingness to engage in the treatment will have a bearing on the treatment plans for the individual. The family may be in pure chaos, at a point at which concern for the alcohol-dependent member is lost under feelings of anger and frustration. In this case inpatient care may be far preferable to outpatient treatment. On the other hand, the family may have already been involved in treatment for themselves and thus able to be supportive and to marshal its collective resources.

Many alcohol and substance abuse clinicians find themselves with clients referred from other sources. To point out the obvious, for them the individual and his or her family are new patients. Even the best crafted letter of referral or prior telephone contact only imparts basic information. This initial database will need to be supplemented by working with the patient and family to develop further treatment plans. Even more importantly, while a medical record or chart can be used to pass along a client from one clinician to another, therapists cannot pass along or be the recipient of a therapeutic relationship. Each clinician needs to establish this for himself or herself.

For these reasons a family meeting is becoming a routine part of the intake and assessment process. At this time, the clinician will seek the family members' view of what is happening. In initial contacts with the family you don't go into a family therapy routine. It is data collecting time. For a newly involved clinician, the task is to understand how the family sees and deals with the alcoholism in its midst. In joint meetings, be prepared to provide the structure and lay the ground rules. For example, explain that people often see things differently and that you want to know from each of those present what has been going on. If need be, reassure them that everyone gets equal time, but no interruptions, please.

During the individual's treatment the family may become involved in regularly scheduled family counseling sessions or participate in a special group for family members or couples, in addition to attending Al-Anon. Some residential treatment programs are beginning to hold "family weekends." In these programs the families of patients are in residence and participate in a specially structured program of education, group discussion, and family counseling.

Family issues

Entry into treatment, especially residential treatment, may impose very real immediate problems for a family. The spouse may be concerned about even more unpaid bills, problems of child care, fears of yet more broken promises, and so on. In the face of these immediate concerns, long-range benefits may offer little consolation. Attention must be paid to helping the family deal with the nitty-gritty details of everyday living. Just as the alcoholic individual in early treatment requires a lot of structure and guidance, so does the family.

Another issue for the family will be to develop realistic expectations for treatment. On one hand, they may think everything will be rosy, that their troubles are over. On the other, they may be exceedingly pessimistic. Probably they will initially bounce back and forth between these two extremes.

The family at some point will need to have the alcoholic member "really hear" what it has been like for them at the emotional level. If there has been an intervention, it stressed objective factual recounting of events and being sympathetic to the alcoholic member. Although a presentation of the family's emotional reality may not be apropos at the time of the intervention, it must take place at some point. If the family is to be reintegrated into a functioning unit, it is going to require that both "sides" gain some appreciation of what the disease has felt like for the other. How this occurs will vary. Within some family weekend programs there may be a session specifically devoted to "feelings," led by skilled family therapists. These sessions can be highly charged, "tell-it-like-it-is" cathartic sessions. To do this successfully requires considerable skill on the therapist's part, as well as a structure that provides a lot of support for the family members. For the alcoholic individual, the pain and remorse and shame of his or her drinking can be devastating. For the family, witnessing the remorse and shame can, in turn, invoke guilt and remorse in themselves. These responses must be addressed; a session cannot be stopped with the participants left in those emotional states. More commonly this material will be dealt with over time, in "smaller doses." It may occur within family sessions and frequently also within the context of working in the AA program.* Again, the important issue is that you recognize this as a family task that must be dealt with in some way at some time. Otherwise, the family has a closet full of "secrets" or "skeletons" that will haunt them, come between them, and interfere with their regaining a healthy new balance.

Suggestions for working with families during treatment

The data gathering completed, the task turns to helping the family make the readjustments necessary to reestablish a new balance. Here are some concrete suggestions for dealing with alcoholic families at this treatment stage. You are the most objective person present; therefore it is up to you to evaluate and guide the process.

Concentrate on the interaction, not on the content. Don't become the referee in a family digression.

Teach them how to check things out. People tend to guess at other peoples' meanings and motivations. They then respond as though the guesses were accurate. This causes all kinds of confusion

Actually, in working with your family, my training as an alcohol counselor is less helpful than my experience as a hockey referee.

---

*Dealing with the effects of the alcoholic's drinking on the family may be part of taking an inventory (Step 4) and part of making amends (Step 8). See the Twelve Steps of AA later on in this chapter.

and misunderstandings and can lead to mutual recriminations. The therapist needs to put a stop to these mind-reading games and point out what is going on.

Be alert to "scapegoating." A common human tendency is to lay it all on George. This is true whatever the problem. The alcoholic family tends to blame the drinker for all the family's troubles, thereby neatly avoiding any responsibility for their own actions. Help them see this as a no-no.

Stress acceptance of each person's right to his or her own feelings. Any good therapy stresses acceptance of each person's right to his or her own feelings. One reason for this is that good feelings get blocked by unexpressed bad feelings. One of the tasks of a therapist is to bring out the family's strengths. The focus has been on the problems for so long that they have lost sight of the good points.

Be alert to avoidance transactions. This includes such things as digressing to Christmas 3 years ago in the midst of a heated discussion of Dad's drinking. It is up to you to point this out to them and get them back on the track. In a similar vein, it may fall to you to "speak the unspeakable," to bring out in the open the obvious, but unmentioned, facts.

Guide them into problem-solving techniques as options. You can do this by making these patterns clear to the family. You can help them begin to use these techniques in therapy, with an eye to teaching them to use them on their own.

After some success, when things seem to be going better, there may be some resistance to continuing therapy. The family fears a setback and wants to stop while they're ahead. Simply point this out to them. They can try for something better or terminate. If they terminate, leave the door open for a return later.

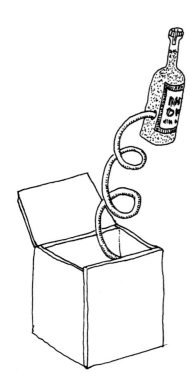

Things to keep in mind when working with families

Pregnancy. You may recall some of the particular family problems that relate to pregnancy and the presence of young children in the family. A few specific words should be said about these potential problematic areas. The first is contraceptive counseling. Pregnancy is not a cure for alcohol problems in either partner. In a couple in which one or both partners are actively drinking, they should be advised to make provisions for the prevention of pregnancy until abstinence is well established. It is important to remember that birth control methods adequate for a sober couple may be inadequate when alcoholism is present. Methods that require planning or delay of gratification are likely to fail. Rhythm, foam, diaphragms, or prophylactics are not wise choices if one partner is actively drinking. A woman who is actively drinking is not advised to use the pill. So the alternatives are few: the pill for the partner of an active male alcoholic, a condom for the partner of a sexually active female alcoholic. In the event of an unwanted pregnancy, the possibilities of placement or therapeutic abortion represent two difficult options that may need to be considered. At the moment, no amniotic fluid assay test exists that can establish the presence of fetal alcohol syndrome.

Should pregnancy occur and a decision be made to have the baby, intensive intervention is required. If the expectant mother has alcoholism, every effort should be made to initiate treatment and get her to stop drinking. Regular prenatal care is also important. Counseling and supporting both parents if alcohol is present is essential to handle the stresses that accompany any pregnancy. If the prospective father is alcohol dependent, it is important to provide additional supports for the mother.

Pregnancy is always a stress for any couple or family system. Contraceptive counseling should also be considered for persons in early recovery. At that point, the family unit is busy coping with sobriety and establishing a solid recovery.

Children in the family. A few words on behalf of older children in the family are in order. In many cases, children's problems are related to their parents' stress. Children may easily become weapons in parental battles. With alcohol dependence, children may think their behavior is causing the drinking. A child needs to be told that this is not the case. In instances where the clinician knows that physical or severe emotional abuse has occurred, child welfare authorities must be notified. In working with the family, additional parenting persons may be brought into the picture. Going to a nursery school or day-care center may help the child from a chaotic home.

What cannot be emphasized too strongly is that children must not be "forgotten" or left out of treatment. Sometimes parents consider a child too young to understand or feel the children need to be "protected." What this can easily lead to is the child's feeling even more isolated, vulnerable, and frightened. Children in family sessions tend to define an appropriate level of participation for themselves. Sometimes the presence of children is problematic for adults not because they won't understand, but because of their uncanny ability to see things exactly as they are: for example, without self-consciousness the child may say what the rest are only hinting at or may ask the most provocative questions. Along the same line, while a parent is actively drinking, the inevitable concerns and questions of the child must be addressed. Children may not need all the details, but the pretense by adults that everything is okay is destructive.

When initially involving the family, consider the children's needs in building a treatment plan. Many child welfare agencies or mental health centers conduct group sessions for children around issues of concern to children, such as a death in the family, divorce, or alcohol–substance abuse problems. Usually these groups are set up for children of roughly the same age and run for a set period, such as 6 weeks. The goal is to provide basic information, support, and the chance to express feelings the child is uncomfortable with or cannot bring up at home. The subliminal message of such groups is that the parents' problems are not the child's fault, and talking about it is okay. In family sessions, you can make the message clear too. You can provide time for the child to ask questions and also provide children with pamphlets that may be helpful for them.

Occasionally a child may seem to be "doing well." In fact, the child may reject efforts by others to be involved in alcohol discussions or treatment efforts. If the parent who is alcohol dependent is actively drinking, the resistance on the child's part may be part of the child's way of coping. Seeing you may be perceived by the child as taking sides; it may force the child to look at things he or she is trying to pretend are not there. Resistance also may surface to joining the family treatment during early sobriety for many of the same reasons. Listen to the child's objections for clues to his or her concerns. What is important here is not to let a child's assertion that "everything is fine" pass without some additional questioning.

On the other hand, beware of embarking on a witch hunt to ferret out the unspoken problems of children. Children cannot be expected to function as adults. While they can be amazingly insightful at times, don't presume that those who do not voice "the unspeakable" are therefore "hiding" something. It is important to appreciate the defenses that children do have. Defenses are never to be viewed as "good" or "bad" but as fostering or impeding functioning. Children's defenses may be quite important for them. In dealing with children, if you've any questions or are concerned you are in danger of getting in over your head, feel free to seek advice from a child therapist.

Recovery and the family. A common mistake when working with the family is to assume that once the drinking stops, things will get better. Yet when the alcohol-dependent member stops drinking, the family again faces a crisis and time of transition. Such crises can lead to growth and positive changes, but not automatically or inevitably. For the family who has lived with alcoholism, there has been a long period of storing up anger and of mistrust and miscommunication. This may have been the children's only experience of family life. At times children who previously were well behaved may begin acting out when a parent becomes sober. Children may feel that earlier their parent loved alcohol more than them and that now their parent loves AA more. The parent may have stopped drinking, but in the children's eyes they're still in second place.

Recovering families have a number of tasks to accomplish before they return to healthy functioning. They must strengthen generational boundaries. They must resume age- and sex-appropriate roles in the family. They must learn to communicate in direct and forthright ways with one another. They must learn to trust one another. And finally they must learn to express both anger and love appropriately. It might be expected, if one considers the family as a unit, that there are stages or patterns of a family's recovery from alcoholism. This has not yet been adequately studied. No one has developed a "valley chart" that plots family disintegration and recovery. Those professionals who have had considerable involvement with families of recovering alcoholics have noticed and are now beginning to discuss some common themes of the family's recovery.

One observation suggests that the family unit may experience growth pains that parallel those facing the alcoholic individual. It has long been a part of folk wisdom that the alcoholic individual's psychological and emotional growth ceases when the heavy drinking begins. So when sobriety comes, the individual is going to have to face some growing up issues that the drinking prevented attending to. In the family system, what may be the equivalent of this Rip Van Winkle experience? Consider an example of a family in which the father is the alcohol-dependent individual whose heavy drinking occurred during his children's adolescence and whose recovery begins just as the children are entering adulthood. If he was basically "out of it" during their teenage years, they grew up as best they could, without very much fathering from him. When he "comes to," they are no longer children but adults. In effect, he was deprived of an important chunk of family life. There may be regrets. There may be unrealistic expectations on the father's part about his present relationship with his children. There may be inappropriate attempts by him to "make it up" and regain the missing part. Depending on the situation, his therapist may need to help him grieve. There may be the need to help him recognize that his expectations are not in keeping with his children's adult status. He may be able to find other outlets to experience a parenting role or reestablish and enjoy appropriate contacts with his children.

Divorce or separation. Vaillant, in examining the course of recovery from alcoholism, found that quite commonly those men who recovered "acquired a new love object." Among several other factors, one which differentiated those who recovered from those who did not was having found someone to love and be loved by. This "someone" had not been part of his life during the period of active alcoholism. This cannot be used as evidence that family treatment is not warranted because there has been too much water over the dam, too much pain, and too much guilt. The men he studied were those who were treated before the time in which family involvement in treatment was commonplace. So who knows what the outcome would have been had attention been directed to family members as well. Early intervention was not the rule then either. His sample consisted of men with long-established cases of alcoholism. However, it does serve to remind us of an important fact. Not all families will come through alcohol treatment intact. Divorce is not uncommon in our society. Even if alcoholic individuals had a divorce rate similar to that of nonalcoholics, it would still mean a substantial number of divorces. Therefore, for some families, the work of family counseling will be to achieve a separation with the

least pain possible and in the least destructive manner for both partners and their children.

Issues of family relationships are not important just for the client whose family is intact. For those who enter treatment divorced and/or estranged from their families, the task during the early treatment phase will be to help them make it without family supports. Their family members may well have come to the conclusion long ago that cutting off contacts was necessary for their welfare. Even if contacted at the point of treatment, they may refuse to have anything to do with the client and his or her treatment. However, with many months or years of sobriety, the issue of broken family ties may emerge. Recovering individuals may desire a restoration of family contacts and have the emotional and personal stability to attempt it, be it with parents, siblings, or their own children. If the client remains in follow-up treatment at this point, the clinician ought to be alert to his or her attempts to reconcile with the family. If the individual is successful, it will still involve stress; very likely many old wounds will be opened. If the attempt is unsuccessful, the therapist will be able to provide support and help the person adjust to the reality of those unfulfilled hopes. As family treatment becomes an integral part of treatment for alcoholism, the hope is that fewer families will experience a total disruption of communications in the face of alcoholism. It is hoped that a more widespread knowledge of the symptoms of alcoholism may facilitate reconciliation of previously estranged families.

Al-Anon

Long before alcoholism was widely accepted as a disease, much less one that also affected family members, wives of the early members of AA recognized disturbances in their own behavior. They also encountered problems living with their alcoholic spouses whether they were sober or still drinking. They saw that a structured program based on self-knowledge, reparation of wrongs, and growth in a supportive group helped promote recovery from their disorder, so why not a similar program for spouses and other family members?

In its earliest days, what became Al-Anon was known instead as the *AA Auxiliary.* Then in the mid-1950s, Al-Anon was officially formed and soon became a thriving program in its own right. The founders were quick to recognize that patterns of scapegoating the alcoholic person and trying to manipulate the drinking were nonproductive. Instead, they based their program on the premise that the only person you can change or control is yourself. Family members in Al-Anon are encouraged to explore and adopt patterns of living that can nourish them, regardless of the actions of the alcoholic.

Using the Twelve Steps of AA (described in detail on pp. 270-272) as a starting point, the program also incorporated the AA slogans and meeting formats. The major difference is in Al-Anon members' powerlessness being over others' alcohol use rather than over their own personal alcohol use. Effort is directed at gaining an understanding of their habitual responses to situations that are dysfunctional and evoke pain and substituting behaviors that will promote health and well-being. They are encouraged to accept responsibility for themselves by abandoning their focus upon the alcoholic family member as "the problem." Instead, they can see by shared example the effectiveness of changing themselves, of "detaching with love" from the drinker.

Although no promises are made that this will have an impact on a still-drinking alcoholic, there are many examples of just such an outcome. At the very least, when family members stop the behaviors that tend to perpetuate the drinking, not only will their lives be better, but the odds are increased for a breakthrough in the pervasive denial characteristic of alcohol dependence.

Many people have found support and hope in the Al-Anon program for personal change and growth through education about the disease and its impact on families coupled with the sharing of experiences with others who have lived with the shame and grief that the family experiences when living with the disease of alcoholism.

Alateen

Alateen is an outgrowth of Al-Anon set up for teenagers with an alcoholic parent. Their problems are different from those of the partner of the alcoholic, and they need a group specifically to deal with these problems. Under the sponsorship of an adult Al-Anon or AA member, they are taught to deal with their problems in much the same manner as the other programs teach.

Even with the currently more widespread information about alcoholism, alcoholics and their families still feel stigmatized. Most of them feel completely alone. It is such a hush-hush issue that anyone experiencing it thinks they are unique in their suffering. The statistics mean little if your friends and neighbors never mention it and seem "normal" to you. It is very painful to have a problem about which you are afraid to talk because of the shame of being "different." One of the greatest benefits of both Al-Anon and Alateen is the lessening of this shame and isolation. Hard as it may be to attend the first meeting, once there, people find many others who share their problems and pain. This can begin a healing process.

Although Al-Anon or Alateen can be a tremendous assistance to the family, you need to point out what they are *not* designed to do. Frequently confusion is introduced because all family treatment efforts may be erroneously referred to as "Al-Anon." Al-Anon is a self-help group. It is not a professional therapeutic program whose members are trained family therapists, any more than AA members are professional clinicians. However, Al-Anon participation can nicely complement other family treatment efforts. Referral to Al-Anon or

Alateen is widely recommended as a part of the treatment regimen for families.

ALCOHOLICS ANONYMOUS

Volumes have been written about the phenomenon of AA. It has been investigated, explained, challenged, and defended by lay people, newspapers, writers, magazines, psychologists, psychiatrists, physicians, sociologists, anthropologists, and clergy. Each has brought a set of underlying assumptions and a particular vocabulary and professional or lay framework to the task. The variety of material on the subject reminds one of trying to force mercury into a certain-sized, perfectly round ball.

In this brief discussion, we certainly have a few underlying assumptions. One is that "experience is the best teacher." This text will be relatively unhelpful compared to attending some AA meetings and watching and talking with people in the process of recovery actively using the AA program. Another assumption is that AA works for a variety of people caught up in the disease and for this reason deserves attention. Alcoholics Anonymous has been described as "the single most effective treatment for alcoholism." The exact whys and hows of its workings are not of paramount importance, but some understanding of it is necessary to genuinely recommend it. Presenting AA with such statements as "AA worked for me; it's the only way," or, conversely, "I've done all I can for you, you might as well try AA," might not be the most helpful approach.

History

Alcoholics Anonymous began in 1935 in Akron, Ohio, with the meeting of two alcoholics. One, Bill W., had a spiritual experience that was the major precipitating event in beginning his abstinence. On a business trip to Akron after about a year of sobriety, he was overtaken by a strong desire to drink. He hit upon the idea of seeking out and talking with another suffering alcoholic as an alternative to taking that first drink. He made contact with some people who led him to Dr. Bob, and the whole thing began with their first meeting. The fascinating story of AA's origins and early history is told in *AA Comes of Age*. The idea of alcoholics helping each other spread slowly in geometric fashion until 1939. At that point, a group of about a hundred sober members realized they had something to offer the thus far "hopeless alcoholics." They wrote and published the book *Alcoholics Anonymous*, generally known as the *Big Book*. It was based on a retrospective view of what they had done that had kept them sober. The past tense is used almost entirely in the Big Book. It was compiled by a group of people who, over time, working together, had found something that worked. Their task was to present this in a useful framework to others who might try it for themselves. This

story is also covered in *AA Comes of Age*. However, it was in 1941 that AA became widely known as the result of an article published in a widely read national magazine, *The Saturday Evening Post.** The geometric growth rapidly advanced, and in 1992 there were an estimated 2,048,954 million active members worldwide.

Goals

Alcoholics Anonymous stresses abstinence and contends that nothing can really happen until "the cork is in the bottle." Many other helping professionals tend to agree. A drugged person—and an alcoholic person is drugged—simply cannot comprehend, or use successfully, other forms of treatment. First, the drug has to go. The goals of each individual within AA vary widely: simple abstinence to adopting a whole new way of life are the ends of the continuum. Individuals' personal goals may also change over time. That any one organization can accommodate such diversity is in itself something of a miracle. AA now includes many people with multiple addictions, to alcohol and other drugs. With more younger people entering the program, drug use of some kind often accompanies the alcohol. References to alcohol in the following sections do not exclude the use of other substances.

In AA, the words *sober* and *dry* denote quite different states. A dry person is simply not drinking at the moment. *Sobriety* means a more basic, all-pervasive change in the person. Sobriety does not come as quickly as dryness and requires a desire for, and an attempt to work toward, a contented, productive life without reliance on mood-altering drugs. The Twelve Steps provide a framework for achieving this state.

Here we wish to mention the important advice the newcomer receives about getting a sponsor. The sponsor is a person with substantial sobriety and one with whom the newcomer feels comfortable. "Comfortable" does not mean primarily being of similar backgrounds, social class, or ethnic membership, although that may be important. It refers to someone the newcomer respects and therefore can speak with and most importantly listen to and hear. The role of the sponsor is to be a mentor and a guide and assist the newcomer in working the program. Much of this occurs outside of the context of meetings. The sponsor is a person who will keep a close eye on the newcomer, leading him or her through difficult times and helping out in situations that are best dealt with outside the context of meetings. Sponsors can also help the newcomer focus on the basic principles and not get sidetracked by extraneous, secondary

I drink when I have occasion, and sometimes when I have no occasion.
—Cervantes

---

*Reading this article by Jack Alexander is highly recommended. Its graphic depiction of what confronted the early members of AA and what the disease of alcoholism was like in that era, when it was viewed paradoxically as the result of human failing and a terminal condition, is a useful point of reference for anyone in the field.

issues. The sponsor is one of the most valuable resources a new-comer can have.

The Twelve Steps

The Twelve Steps function as the therapeutic framework of AA. They were not devised by a group of social scientists, nor are they derived from a theoretical view of alcoholism. The Twelve Steps of AA grew out of the practical experience of the earliest members, based on what they had *done* to gain sobriety. They do, indeed, require action. AA is not a passive process.

The initial undrugged view of the devastation can, and often does, drive the dry alcoholic back to the bottle. However, the Twelve Steps of AA, as experienced by its sober members, offer hope for another road out of the maze.

Step 1 "We admitted we were powerless over alcohol—that our lives had become unmanageable," acknowledges the true culprit, alcohol, and the scope of the problem, the whole life. **Step 2,** "Came to believe that a Power greater than ourselves could restore us to sanity," recognizes the insanity of the drinking behavior and allows for the gradual reliance on some external agent (e.g., God, some other spiritual concept, the AA group, the therapist, or a combination) to aid an about-face. **Step 3,** "Made a decision to turn our will and our lives over to the care of God as we understood Him," enables the person to let go of the previous life preserver, the bottle, and accept an outside influence to provide direction. It has now become clear that as a life preserver, the bottle was a dud, but free floating cannot go on forever either. The search outside the self for direction has now begun.

Step 4, "Made a searching and fearless moral inventory of ourselves," allows a close look at the basic errors in perceiving the world and at behaviors that were part of the drinking debacle. It is the Step that begins the process of teaching alcohol-dependent people about their own responsibility during the drinking days. This Step also includes space for the positive attributes that can be enhanced in the sober state. An inventory is, after all, a balance sheet. **Step 5,** "Admitted to God, to ourselves, and to another human being the exact nature of our wrongs," provides a method of cleaning the slate, admitting just how painful and destructive it all was, and getting the guilt-provoking behavior out in the open instead of destructively "bottled up."

Steps 6 and 7, "Were entirely ready to have God remove all these defects of character," and "Humbly asked Him to remove our short-comings," continue the "mopping-up" process. Step 6 makes the alcoholic individual aware of his or her tendency to cling to old behaviors, even unhealthy ones. Step 7 takes care of the fear of repeated errors, again instilling hope that personality change is possible. (Remember, at this stage in the process, the recently sober person is likely to be very short on self-esteem.)

Steps 8 and 9 are a clear guide to sorting out actual injury done to others and deciding how best to deal with it. Step 8 is "Made a list of all persons we had harmed and became willing to make amends to them all." Step 9 is "Made direct amends to such people wherever possible, except when to do so would injure them or others." They serve other purposes, too. First, they get the person out of the "bag" of blaming others for life's difficulties. To make an amend, that is to attempt to atone for a wrong committed, does not require the forgiveness of the receiver. The recovering person's part is to make the effort to apologize, pay back money, or do whatever is necessary to try to balance the scales, whatever the response of the person to whom the amend is being made. This attempt offers a possibility for repairing presently strained relationships and hope of alleviating some of the overwhelming guilt that is common with initial sobriety. These Steps clearly relate to the importance of acknowledging and owning up to events that have occurred, whether they took place in an impaired state or as part of the disease.

Steps 10 to 12 promote the maintenance of sobriety and the continuation of the change process that has already begun. Step 10, "Continued to take personal inventory and when we were wrong promptly admitted it," ensures that the alcoholic person need not slip back from the hard-won gains. Diligence in focusing on one's own behavior and not excusing it keeps the record straight. Step 11, "Sought through prayer and meditation to improve our conscious contact with God as we understood Him, praying only for knowledge of His will for us and the power to carry that out," fosters continued spiritual development. Finally, Step 12, "Having had a spiritual awakening as a result of these Steps, we tried to carry this message to alcoholics and to practice these principles in all our affairs," points the way to sharing the process with others. This is one of the vital keys Bill W. discovered to maintain his sobriety. It also implies that a continued practice of the new principles is vital to the sober life.

A word must be said here about "Two Steppers." This phrase is used to describe a few individuals in AA who come in, admit they are alcoholics, dry out, and set out to rescue others. However, it is often said in AA that "you can't give away what you don't have." This refers to a quality of sobriety that comes after some long and serious effort applying all the Twelve Steps to one's life. It is interesting to note that "carrying the message" is not mentioned until Step 12. Once that point is reached however, it is important that the member reach out and to others, repaying a debt so to speak, and also in the process experience feelings of being of use again.

No AA member who is serious about the program and sober for some time would ever imply that the Steps are a one-shot deal. They are an ongoing process that evolves over time—a great deal of it—

into ever-widening applications. When approached with serious intent, the Steps enable a great change in the individual. That they are effective is testified to not only by great numbers of recovering alcoholics, but also by their adoption as a basis for such organizations as Overeaters Anonymous, Narcotics Anonymous, and Gamblers Anonymous. These other fellowships simply substitute their own addiction for the word *alcohol* in Step 1.

A therapist, counselor, or friend should be alert to the balance required in this process of "working the Program." The newcomer who wants to tackle all Twelve Steps the first week should be counseled with one of AA's slogans: "Easy does it." The member hopelessly anguished by Step 4, for instance, could be advised that perfection is not the goal and a stab at it the first time through is quite sufficient. The agnostic having difficulty with "the God bit" can be told about using the group or anything else suitable for the time being. After all, the spiritual awakening doesn't turn up until Step 12 either.

The Twelve Traditions

Organization. AA has very little structure as an organization. It describes itself as a fellowship and functions around the Twelve Steps and Twelve Traditions. The Twelve Traditions cover the organization as a whole, setting forth the purpose of the fellowship, which is to carry its message to the still-suffering alcoholic. They also define principles of conduct; for example, that AA does not affiliate with other groups, nor lend its name; that it should not be organized and should remain forever nonprofessional. Individual AA groups are autonomous and decline outside contributions. Thus all care has been taken not to obscure or lose sight of the organization's purpose. The individual groups function in accord with these principles. Their focus is on sobriety, anonymity, and individual application of "the program," which includes meetings, attempting to work the Twelve Steps, and service to other alcoholics.

Anonymity. Before discussing the meetings, a special word about anonymity. Alcoholics Anonymous' Tradition 12 reads as follows: "Anonymity is the spiritual foundation of all our traditions ever reminding us to place principles before personalities." This concept evolved out of the growth pains of the organization. Early members admit candidly that fear of exposure of their problem was their *original* motivation for remaining anonymous: the need "to hide from public distrust and contempt." However, the principle of anonymity, which was introduced into the fellowship on the basis of fear, soon demonstrated evidence of its value on a totally different level.

This same evolutionary process tends to occur for most individual members of AA. At first, the promise of anonymity is viewed as a safeguard against exposure. The stigma attached to alcoholism has not yet disappeared. Added to this are the alcohol-dependent person's own guilt, sense of failure, and low self-esteem. It is vital to maintain this promise to encourage fearful newcomers to try out the program while assuring them of complete confidentiality. As individuals gain sobriety, fear gives way to the deeper understanding revealed in the practice. To be simply Joe or Mary, one alcoholic among many, has a therapeutic value.

In practice, anonymity takes the form of first names only during the meetings, not identifying oneself through the media as a member of AA, and being careful not to reveal anyone else's attendance at meetings. Some meetings end with the reminder that who you see here and what is said here, stays here. It is important to AA to be able to continue its healing mission to suffering alcoholics that this principle of anonymity be respected.

Meetings plus

There are open meetings (open to any spouses, friends, interested parties, etc.) and closed meetings (with only professed alcoholics attending the latter). Both types can be speaker or discussion meetings. Speaker meetings have one to three speakers who tell what it was like drinking (for the purpose of allowing newcomers to identify), what happened to change this, and what their sober life is now like. A discussion meeting is usually smaller. The leader may or may not tell his story briefly as just described (or "qualify" in AA jargon). The focus of the meeting is a discussion of a particular Step, topic, or problem with alcohol, with the leader taking the role of facilitator.

Attendance at meetings is not all there is to AA. The AA meeting might be like a patient's visit to a doctor's office. The office visit doesn't constitute the whole of therapy. It is a good start, but how closely the patient follows the advice and recommendations and acts on what is prescribed makes the difference. Sitting in the doctor's office doesn't do it. So too with AA. The person who is seriously trying to use AA as a means of achieving sobriety will be doing a lot more than attending meetings. Those successful in AA will spend time talking to and being with other more experienced members. Part of this time will be spent getting practical tips on how to maintain sobriety. Time and effort go into learning and substituting other behaviors for the all-pervasive drinking behavior. Alcoholics Anonymous contacts will also be a valuable resource for relaxation. It is a place a newly recovering alcoholic will feel accepted. It is also a space in which the drinking possibilities are greatly minimized. A new member of AA may spend a couple of hours a day phoning, having coffee with, or being in the company of other AA members. Although it is strongly recommended that new members seek sponsors, they will be in touch with a larger circle of people. Frequent contact with AA members is encouraged, not only to pass on useful information but also to make it easier for the new members to reach out in times of stress, when picking up a drink would be so easy and

instinctive. The new member's contacting a fellow AA member when a crunch time comes makes the difference in many cases between recovery and relapse.

Slogans

Slowly the new member's life is being restructured around not drinking, and usually the slogans are the basis for this: "One day at a time," "Easy does it," "Keep it simple," "Live and let live," "Let go and let God," to name a few. Although they can sound trite and somewhat corny, remember the description of the confused, guilt-ridden, anxious product of alcohol dependence. Anyone in such a condition can greatly benefit from a simple, organized, easily understood schedule of priorities. A kind of behavior modification is taking place so that a growth process may begin. Some new members feel so overwhelmed by the idea of a day without a drink that their sponsor and/or others will help them literally plan every step of the first few weeks. They keep in almost hourly touch with older members. Phone calls at any hour of the day or night are encouraged as a way to relieve anxiety.

Resistances

Some alcoholic individuals and their families may be quite resistant to AA. A therapist often finds they may agree to anything, as long as it isn't AA. This resistance probably has a number of sources. It may be based on erroneous information and myths about AA. Quite likely it is embarrassment, plain and simple. The client may have been notorious at office parties, a regular in the newspaper column for drinking and driving offenses, or almost single-handedly keeping the neighborhood general store solvent with beer purchases, but heaven forbid should the individual be seen entering a building where an AA meeting is held! Also, going to an AA meeting represents, if not a public admission, at least a private one that alcohol is a problem. Seeing a therapist, even one clearly specializing in alcohol and substance abuse, may allow the alcoholic client multiple interpretations, at least for a while. Going to AA is clear-cut, not open to ambiguity and in that respect is a big step. In dealing with this resistance, education is useful. Also required is a certain quiet insistence that going at least for a reasonable "experimental" period is expected of the client, so he or she can get firsthand knowledge.

Sometimes clients will have had some limited prior exposure to AA, which they use as the basis for their objections. Commonly this is coupled with the similarly "negative" experiences of their best drinking buddies, who also agree AA doesn't work. Usually these clients say they "tried it once," but it wasn't for them, and they didn't like it. Any examination of what was going on in their lives generally reveals, at best, a very halfhearted "try." More importantly, liking or not liking AA is not an issue. Usually we care little if people like any other prescribed treatments as long as the treatment produces positive results. No one *likes* braces or casts on broken limbs or hospital stays for any reason, but they are accepted as necessary to produce a desired result. Feel free to point out that it is the results that are important.

The alcoholic may have found some professionals who will support his or her resistance. If the alcoholic remains in treatment with such a person, consider getting in touch with that professional. Possibly the alcoholic is misinterpreting what has been said. If not, you need to do a bit of informal education, explaining why you think AA is indicated and dispelling misconceptions.

Professional resistance toward AA is certainly far less than it once was, but it has not wholly disappeared. Some professionals both in the general helping professions as well as in the alcohol-substance abuse field do, at times, show resistance to expecting their clients to use AA. At times one gets the sense that AA is not considered to be "real" treatment, or it is considered less sophisticated. Why these feelings? Although we're not sure, our suspicion is that a number of reasons lie behind such attitudes. One reason is that anyone who deals with alcohol-troubled people will periodically lose touch with what the disease of alcoholism is really like. The literal hell that is the life of the active alcoholic is forgotten. Those people are who AA is for. Yet at times, we forget that the primary purpose of AA is to help people to escape their hell. Then we begin to act as if AA were supposed to do other things, for example, be a psychologically-oriented therapy group or handle marital problems.

Another point of possible professional resistance is that we sometimes take our resistive clients' objections too seriously. We unwittingly buy their criticisms of AA. We accept their not "liking" AA as a valid reason for their not going. But we do not expect them to "like" to see their physicians or "like" to use other forms of treatment! With alcohol problems being addressed at earlier and earlier stages, there may be the tendency for those helping professionals outside of the substance abuse field to consider that AA involvement is only for those whose disease has been long-standing, and who have many highly visible problems that resulted from drinking. In other words, some people's alcohol dependence isn't yet "bad enough" to warrant prescribing AA.

Another point of friction seems to be that AA does not build termination into the program. Although more could be said about this, for now it is sufficient to remember that any chronic disease is terminated only by death. For chronic illnesses, even when the disease is under control, regular check-ups are routine practice. Finally, professionals sometimes have mistakenly gotten the impression that AA, as an organization, holds AA to be incompatible with other therapies. This is not true. Nothing in the AA program would support this premise. Certainly, an occasional client will give this impression in which case as a therapist, you can help clear up this misconception.

Against diseases the strongest fence is the defensive virtue, abstinence.

ROBERT HERRICK

View of recovery. One thing assumed in AA is that recovery is a serious, lifelong venture. Safety does not exist, and some kind of long-term support is necessary. This seems to be the case, and a lot of experience supports the assumption. Alcoholics, like all of us, have selective memories and are inclined, after varying periods of dryness, to remember only the relief of drinking and not its consequent problems. Some kind of reminder of reality seems to be necessary. Any alcoholic with long-term sobriety will be able to tell about the sudden desire to drink popping up out of nowhere. Those who do not succumb are grateful, for the most part, to some aspect of their AA life as the key to their stability returning. No one knows exactly why these moments occur, but one thing is certain: they are personally frightening and upsetting. They can reduce the reasonably well-adjusted recovering alcoholic to a state very like that first panic-ridden dryness. The feelings could be compared to the feelings after a particularly vivid nightmare. Whatever the reason for the phenomenon, these unexpected urges to drink do spring up. This is one reason continued participation in AA is suggested. Another is the emphasis (somewhat underplayed from time to time) on a continued growth in sobriety. Certainly, groups will rally around newcomers with a beginner's focus and help them learn the basics. In discussion meetings with a group of veterans, however, the focus will be on personal growth within the context of the Twelve Steps. Alcoholics Anonymous may advertise itself as a "simple program for complicated people," but an understanding of it is far from a simple matter. It involves people, and people are multifaceted. Its simplicity is deceptive and on the order of "Love thy neighbor as thyself." Simple, and yet learning to do so could easily take a lifetime. In closing, we again strongly urge you to attend a variety of AA meetings; also speak at some length with veteran members. So much has been written about AA—in some respects it is so understandable an approach—that people assume they know what it's about without firsthand knowledge. Just as you would visit treatment programs or community agencies to see personally what they are about, so, too, go to AA.

Referral

A few words are in order about making an effective referral to AA. Simply telling someone to go probably won't work in most cases. The clinician needs to play a more active role in the referral. Alcoholics Anonymous is a self-help group. What AA can do and offer is by far best explained *and* demonstrated by its members. The clinician can assist by making arrangements for a client to speak to a member of AA or can arrange for the client to be taken to a meeting. Helping professionals, whether dealing exclusively with addiction or not, often have a list of AA members who have agreed to do this. Even if the clinician is an AA member, a separate AA contact is advisable. It is less confusing to the client if AA is seen as distinct from, although compatible with, other therapy. The therapist need not defend, proselytize, or try to sell AA. Alcoholics Anonymous speaks eloquently for itself. You do your part well when you persuade clients to attend, listen with an open mind, and stay long enough to make their own assessments.

A standard part of many treatment programs is an introduction and orientation to AA. This would seem to be very important because treatment programs are an ever-growing source of referrals to AA. Many residential treatment programs include AA meetings on the grounds or transport clients to outside meetings. It is not unusual for presentations on AA to be included in an educational series or references made to AA either in individual counseling or group therapy. Some programs encourage, indeed some push, clients to work on Steps 1 through 5 while they are actively involved in treatment. The hope is that this will give clients added insight into AA and increase the chances of their continuing involvement.

By their being a growing source of referrals to AA, treatment programs are challenged in several respects. Although wishing to be supportive of AA, treatment programs need to respect the boundaries between AA and treatment, which AA has long acknowledged. One challenge to treatment programs is to help clients distinguish between formal treatment and AA. Nowhere may this be more important than in terms of aftercare. It must be pointed out that attending a treatment program's alumni group is not the same as going to AA. Nor for that matter is a chat with a sponsor necessarily a substitute for an aftercare session. Conversely, having a therapist should not be allowed to be seen as a substitute for having an AA sponsor. Another challenge to programs is not to appropriate AA through overly lengthy intellectual presentations on the nature of AA or using the language of AA and its slogans to mislead clients into thinking such discussions and their treatment *is* AA. There is a danger of clients becoming pseudosophisticates in respect to AA. They can use the jargon properly, make reference to the slogans and the Steps, but have very limited firsthand experience of the Fellowship.

AA membership

Since 1968 the General Service Office of AA has conducted a triennial survey of its members. The most recent survey, conducted in 1992, provides some interesting information. The age range of members is from 12 to 85. Men in AA outnumber women by about 2 to 1 ratio: 65% of the members are men and 35% women. The number of younger members represent 19% of all AA members. Among this younger group, there are more women, 43%, and there is more addiction to other drugs. Although 38% of all members report the use of other substances this is particularly seen in younger people. Multisubstance use is the pattern for 79% of those

under age 21 and 60% of those under age 31. In respect to their introduction to AA, 43% credit a rehab facility or professional for their affiliation with AA. Of all those coming into AA, about 30% acknowledge a treatment program for the referral. That represents an increase of almost 60% since 1977.

AA members clearly do not find counseling incompatible with AA involvement. Two thirds of the members report some professional assistance before their joining AA. Of those, 8 out of every 10 members said this played a part in directing them to AA. Furthermore, after their joining AA over half of the members report having received some other type of counseling help. Almost 90% credit this with playing an important role in their recovery.

In terms of length of sobriety, 35% of members have been sober over 5 years, 34% have been sober between 1 and 5 years, and 31% represent newcomers, those sober less than 1 year.

OTHER SELF-HELP GROUPS

In addition to AA, there are a wide variety of other self-help groups. For the most part, these are 12-Step programs modeled after AA. These include, for example, Narcotics Anonymous, Cocaine Anonymous, or Overeaters Anonymous. Very recently a new self-help group has emerged for those with alcoholism, Rational Recovery. It is not a 12-Step program and in fact developed as an alternative to AA. While AA members refer to *Alcoholics Anonymous,* one of its key publications, as the "Big Book", as a point of contrast, Rational Recovery terms its counterpart publication as "The Little Book."

Rational Recovery specifically rejects what are seen as the spiritual and religious overtones of AA. Thus it appears to attract those who have been turned off by AA and particularly those who have a more "intellectual" orientation and those uncomfortable with the spiritual aspects of the AA program. Inasmuch as Rational Recovery is a relatively new program, it is too early to discuss its effectiveness. However, it appears that of those who become involved, the proportion achieving sobriety approximates the proportion who become sober through AA.

For the counselor, whether to refer a client to AA versus Rational Recovery may not be the big issue it might appear at first glance. Setting aside whatever biases the clinician may have, there appear to be a number of reasons to select AA over any other self-help alternative groups. It does have the established track record, it is available in virtually every community, and thereby it can assure a client access to a group no matter what. On the other hand, if a client tries AA and even after a reasonable exposure, vigorously resists and is having problems making a connection, then a referral to Rational Recovery is warranted. Whatever the biases of the counselor, if it works, it works. Keeping that goal in mind is important. What is important is the destination, not necessarily the route!

SPIRITUAL COUNSELING

There is increasing effort to educate and inform clergy members about alcohol abuse and alcoholism. The focus of the effort is to equip pastors, priests, rabbis, ministers, and chaplains who come into contact with alcoholic individuals or their families to assist in early identification of the disease and to facilitate the entry into appropriate treatment.

Presumably the merits of this effort are self-evident. There is plenty of room in the alcohol field for many different kinds of care providers. This section on spiritual counseling is not about this educational outreach to clergy members. Instead, we wish to discuss the contribution that clergy members, priests, or rabbis may make to the recovery process in their pastoral roles. Those with alcoholism may have a need for pastoring, "shepherding," or spiritual counseling, as do other members of the population. In fact, their needs in this area may be especially acute. Attention to these needs is a critical part of recovery.

It is not easy to discuss spiritual matters. Medical, social work, psychology, or rehabilitation textbooks do not include chapters on spiritual issues as they affect prospective clients and patients. The split between spirituality and the "rest of life" has been virtually total. In our society, that means for many it has become an either/or choice. Because defining crisply what we mean by spiritual issues is not easy, let us begin by stating what it is not. By *spiritual* we do not mean the organized religions and churches. Religions can be thought of as organized groups and institutions that have arisen to meet spiritual needs. The spiritual concern is more basic than religion, however. In our view, the fact that civilizations have developed religions throughout history is evidence of a spiritual side to human beings. There are also experiences, difficult to describe, that hint at another dimension different from but as real as our physical nature. They might be called "intimations of immortality," and they occur among sufficient numbers of people to give more evidence for the spiritual nature of humankind.

Over the past decade there was a renewed interest in spiritual concerns in contemporary America. Whether it has been transcendental meditation, Eastern gurus, the Moral Majority, fundamentalism, mysticism, the golden era of television evangelists, or the more traditional Judeo-Christian Western religions, people have been flocking in. They are attempting to follow these teachings and precepts in the hope of filling a void in their lives. It is being recognized that "the bottom line" may not be adequately calculated in terms of status, education, career, or material wealth. The culturally defined

It is hard to believe in God, but it is far harder to disbelieve in Him.
EMERSON

evidence of achievement and having "made it" can still leave some-one feeling that there is something missing. This "something" is thought by many to be of a spiritual nature. This missing piece has even been described as a "God-shaped hole."

Sociologists have observed that the apparent renewed interest in religion and increased church attendance in the mainline denomi-nations can be explained by sheer demographics. It may not be attributable to a societal perception of a spiritual vacuum. Church attendance historically is always lowest among adolescents and young adults. Consequently with the "baby boomers" now entering middle age, this large segment of the population has reached the age where religious interests have always arisen. These two viewpoints are not mutually exclusive. With maturity and some life experi-ences, a part of adult development is to reassess values, reexamine one's priorities in life, and redefine what *is* important. An offhand comment seems to capture this well: "No one on a death bed ever expressed regret that he or she hadn't spent more time on work!"

Alcoholism as a spiritual search

How do spiritual concerns fit in with alcohol use and the disease of alcoholism? First, it is worth reflecting on the fact that *the* word most commonly used for alcohol is "spirits." This is surely no acci-dent. Indeed, consider how alcohol is used. It is often used in the hope it will provide that missing something or at least turn off a gnawing ache. From bottled spirits, a drinker may seek a solution to life's problems, a release from pain, an escape from circumstances. For awhile it may do the job, but eventually it fails. To use spiritual language, you can even think of alcoholism as a pilgrimage that dead-ends. Alcohol can be thought of as a false god, or, to para-phrase the New Testament, that alcohol is not "living water."

If this is the case and alcohol use has been prompted in part by spiritual thirst, the thirst remains even though alcoholic drinking ceases. Part of the recovery process must be aimed at quenching the thirst. Alcoholics Anonymous has recognized this fact. It speaks of alcoholism as a threefold disease with physical, mental, and spiritual components. Part of the AA program is intended to help members by focusing on their spiritual needs. It is also worth noting that AA makes a clear distinction between spiritual growth and religion.

Assistance from the clergy

How can the clergy be of assistance? Ideally, the clergy are soci-ety's designated "experts" on spiritual matters. Notice we say ideal-ly. In real life, clergy are human beings, too. The realities of religious institutions may have forced some to be fund raisers, social direc-tors, community consciences, almost everything but spiritual mentors. Yet there are those out there who do, and maybe many more who long to, act as spiritual counselors and advisors. One way the clergy may be of potential assistance is to help those seeking recovery deal with "sin" and feelings of guilt, worthlessness, and hopelessness. Many of those with alcoholism, along with the public at large, are walking around as adults with virtually the same notions of God they had as 5-year-olds. He has a white beard, sits on a throne on a cloud, checks up on everything you do, keeps a ledger of your behavior, and punishes you if you aren't "good." This is certainly a caricature but also probably very close to the way a lot of people really feel if they think about it.

Those just getting sober feel remorseful, guilt-ridden, worthless, endowed with a host of negative qualities, and devoid of good. In their minds, they certainly do not fit the picture of someone God would like to befriend or hang around with. On the contrary, they probably believe that if God isn't punishing them He ought to be! So these persons may need some real assistance in updating their concept of God. There's a good chance some of their ideas will have to be revised. There's the idea that the church, and therefore (to them) God, is only for the "good" people. A glance at the New Testament and Christian traditions doesn't support this view, even if some parishes or congregations may act that way. Jesus of Nazareth didn't exactly travel with the "in crowd." He was found in the company of fishermen, prostitutes, lepers, and tax collectors. Or consider the Judaic tradition as reflected in the Torah or Old Testament. The chosen of God were constantly whining, complaining, going astray, and breaking as much of the Law as they followed. Nonetheless, God refused to give up on them. Virtually all spiritual traditions have taken human frailty as the given. Whether a new perspective on God or a Higher Power leads to reinvolvement with a church, assists in affiliation with AA, or helps lessen the burden of guilt doesn't matter. Whichever it does, it is a key factor in recovery.

Again, to use spiritual language, recovery from alcoholism involves a "conversion experience." The meaning of conversion is very simple, "to turn around" or "to transform." Comparing the sober life with the previous drinking certainly testifies to such a transformation. A conversion experience doesn't necessarily imply blinding lights, visions, or a dramatic turning point—although it might. Indeed, if it does involve a startling experience of some nature, the newly sober individual will need some substantial aid in understanding and assimilating this experience.

Carl Jung

It is interesting to note that an eminent psychiatrist recognized this spiritual dimension of alcoholism and recovery over 50 years ago, in the days when alcoholism was considered hopeless by the medical profession. The physician was Carl Jung. Roland H. had

been through the treatment route for alcoholism before seeking out Jung in 1931. He admired Jung greatly, saw him as the court of last resort, and remained in therapy with him for about a year. Shortly after terminating therapy, Roland lapsed back into drinking. Because of this unfortunate development, he returned to Jung. On his return, Jung told Roland his condition was hopeless as far as psychiatry and medicine of that day were concerned. Very desperate and willing to grab at any straw, Roland asked if there was any hope at all. Jung replied that there might be, provided Roland could have a spiritual or religious experience—a genuine conversion experience. Although comparatively rare, this had been known to lead to recovery from alcoholism. So Jung advised Roland to place himself in a religious atmosphere and hope (pray) for the best. The "best" in fact occurred. The details of the story can be found in an exchange of letters between Bill W. and Jung, published in the AA magazine, *The Grapevine.*

In recounting this story many years later, Jung observed that unrecognized spiritual needs can lead people into great difficulty and distress. Either "real religious insight or the protective wall of human community is essential to protect man from this." In talking specifically of Roland H., Jung wrote: "His craving for alcohol was the equivalent, on a low level, of the spiritual thirst of our being for wholeness, expressed in medieval language; the union with God."

Such concepts are foreign in contemporary American society; we no longer have even the vocabulary to consider such a question. You would be hard pressed to find drinkers who would equate the use of alcohol with a search of God! Heaven only knows they are too sophisticated, too contemporary, too scientific for that. Yet an objective examination of their use of alcohol may reveal otherwise. Alcohol is viewed as a magical potion, with the drinker expecting it to do the miraculous. The problem is that for a time indeed it does, alleviating shyness, awkwardness, or simply by turning off painful feelings. The backlash occurs later as we have seen.

Clinician's role

If convinced that a spiritual dimension may be touched by both alcoholism and recovery, what do you as a therapist do? First, we recommend cultivating some members of the clergy in your area. It seems that many communities have at least one member of the clergy who has stumbled into the alcohol field—and we do mean stumbled. It was often not a deliberate, intellectual decision. It may have occurred through a troubled parishioner who has gotten well or one whom the clergy member couldn't tolerate watching drink him or herself to death any longer and so blundered through an intervention. The pastor may have aided a parishioner with alcoholism and finds more and more showing up on his/her doorstep for help. Or the clergy may themselves be in recovery and thus drawn into helping others. At any rate, this is the one you want. If you cannot find him or her, find one with whom you are comfortable talking about spiritual or religious issues. That means one with whom you don't feel silly or awkward and, equally important, who doesn't squirm in his or her seat either at talk of spiritual issues. (Mention of God and religion can make people, including some clergy, as uncomfortable as talk of drinking can!)

Once you find a resource person, it is an easy matter to provide your client with an opportunity to talk with that person. One way to make the contact is simply to suggest that the client sit down and talk with Joe Smith, who happens to be a Catholic priest, or a rabbi, or something else. It may also be worth pointing out to the client that the topic of concern is important and that the individual mentioned may be helpful in sorting it out. Set up the appointment, and let the clergy member take it from there. Some residential programs include a clergy member as a resource person. This person may simply be available to counsel with clients or may take part in the formal program, for example, by providing a lecture in the educational series. What is important is that the presence and availability of this person gives the message to clients that matters of the spirit are indeed important and not silly.

How do you recognize the person for whom spiritual counseling may be useful? First, let us assume you have found a clergy member who doesn't wag a finger, deliver hellfire and brimstone lectures, or pass out religious tracts at the drop of a hat. Rather, you have found a warm, caring, accepting, and supportive individual. A chat with someone like that isn't going to hurt anyone. So don't worry about inappropriate referrals. Nonetheless, for some clients the contact may be particularly meaningful. Among these are individuals who have a spiritual or religious background and are not experiencing it as a source of support, but rather as a condemnation. Others may, in their course of sobriety, be conscientiously attempting to 'work the program' but have some problem that is hanging them up. Another group who may experience difficulty are Jewish alcoholics. "Everyone knows Jews don't become alcoholics." This presents a problem for those who do. It has been said that there is double the amount of denial and consequent guilt for them. Because the Jewish religion is practiced within the context of a community, there may also be a doubled sense of estrangement. A contact with a rabbi may be very important. It is worth pointing out that someone can be culturally or ethnically Jewish but not have been religiously Jewish. The intrusion of an alcohol problem may well provide the push to the Jewish alcoholic to explore his or her spiritual heritage. Other groups, for example, for whom spiritual issues may be of particular importance are Native Americans and Afro-Americans. They too may need special help in reconnecting with their spiritual heritage and incorporating it into their recovery. The clinician is advised to be sensitive to this as well as supportive.

yes I am a Jewish alcoholic. Nobody thought Jews were alcoholics. that's how I got away with it for so long.

The clinician, as an individual, may or may not consider spiritual issues personally important. What the caregiver needs is an awareness of the possibility (even probability) of this dimension's importance to a client, as well as a willingness to provide the client with a referral to an appropriate individual.

ACTIVITIES THERAPY

Activities therapy has been a mainstay of inpatient psychiatric treatment for a long time. It includes recreational and occupational therapy. To those unfamiliar with this field, the activities that are encompassed may look like "recreation" or "free time" or diversionary activities, not *real* treatment. For the activities therapist, the event, such as a picnic—with the associated menu planning, food preparation, set up and clean up afterwards—is of far less importance than the process.

Recall that the alcohol-dependent person's repertoire of social skills has been depleted. Plus, it may have been a long time since there have been social interactions without alcohol, or tasks completed, and responsibilities assumed and fulfilled. In addition, many clients have come to think of drinking not only as part of relaxation or leisure time. They think that alcohol is necessary to get some "time out" from responsibilities, to let them "turn off" tensions, or necessary to "get into" some diversions. Then, too, during treatment, the client can spend only so many hours a day in individual counseling, or group therapy sessions, or listening to lectures and films. Activities therapy programs can be the forum in which the client has the opportunity, with support and guidance, to try out some of the new behaviors that may have been discussed elsewhere and will be necessary in sobriety. Activities therapy may be the portion of the therapeutic program that will most closely approximate real life.

A common dilemma for those in recovery is how to fill the time that they used to spend drinking. A part of the activity therapist's task will be to identify past interests or activities that can be reawakened and resumed, not only to fill time but also to provide a sense of accomplishment and belonging. The activities therapist will be sensitive to the client's limitations. The person who used to have a half-acre garden and is now going to make up for lost time by plowing up another half acre can be cautioned to take it easy. One or two tomato plants plus a few lettuce and radish plants may be the place to start.

One of the more imaginative adaptations of activities therapy in alcohol treatment has been the use of Outward Bound programs. Outward Bound grew out of the British Merchant Navy in the Second World War. It was discovered that among the merchant marines who were stranded at sea, those who survived were not the youngest and most physically fit but their older "life-seasoned" comrades. From that observation, an attempt was made to provide a training experience that incorporated physically challenging and psychologically demanding tasks to demonstrate to people their capacities.

Outward Bound was introduced in the United States in 1961. Since that time, its programs have been conducted in a range of settings from rehabilitation programs for the physically handicapped to training for corporate executives. The programs can be a day, several days, or a week in length.

Typically, an Outward Bound experience combines both group exercises, such as a group being given the task of getting all of its members over a 10-foot wall, with individual activities, such as rock climbing. Within alcohol treatment programs, Outward Bound has been made available to individual clients and clients with their families, and it has been used particularly with adolescents. The staff often includes a professional alcohol clinician, as well as the Outward Bound instructors. Integral to Outward Bound is discussing and processing what transpires during a particular exercise. Alcoholics Anonymous adages such as "One step (day) at a time," or "Easy does it," might be the topic of a group meeting. These take on a new meaning to someone who has been involved in scaling a cliff or negotiating a ropes course 20 feet off the ground.

A few words about fun

A family beset by alcoholism usually has lived a lopsided life. There's probably been little time, energy, or capacity for anything except crisis management or holding one's breath waiting for the next incident. Any sense of fun or true recreation has long since disappeared in a sea of alcohol. Despite what they may claim, being drunk is not *fun* for active alcoholics and neither are the clenched-teeth efforts to control drinking. Witnessing either of these behaviors is no fun either. Even small children in the home where alcoholism is present may have become so inhibited by the tension or so hypervigilant that there is too little opportunity for true play.

I really don't care about the beer, it's just that the peanuts make me sooooo thirsty.

A common complaint from an alcoholic nearing or entering treatment is "Everyone drinks! How can I have any fun if I'm the only one who isn't!" Lots of others in recovery seem to manage, however. Despite the fact that this is often a last gasp effort to discount the need for treatment, it does point to a real problem down the line—how to have fun without alcohol, or for some, how to have fun at all. What is the clinician to say? There may be little to be said at the point the question is raised, when the more significant question is "Is life fun *now?*" But it is an issue that has to be taken seriously.

In planning treatment whether inpatient program or outpatient care, it needs to be addressed. "Fun" ultimately is not what we do but how we experience what we do. It is not an event but an experience. The word recreation thus may be more apt to capture the phenomena. It flows from the activities in life that refresh us, renew us, and offer us the sorely needed counterpoint to the hectic, busy lives we live. One person's recreation is another's work. Recreation can encompass active pursuits, such as swimming, a brisk walk, or a pick-up game of softball on the empty neighborhood lot. Recreation can be individual, a private activity with some solitary time for reading a book, writing a letter, gardening, or puttering in the basement workshop. Recreation may be group activity. It can be spontaneous or it may be planned. Were one to attempt to define an essential characteristic of recreation, it is being wholly engaged. When we are living in the present, we can neither worry about tomorrow nor relive yesterday.

Initial treatment, whether in a residential or an outpatient setting, is going to be highly regimented and entail a well-structured schedule. The idea is not to schedule assigned time slots in which clients are instructed "to have fun." They would be at a total loss. To relax or "have fun" does not usually occur on command either. For those in recovery, it is a capacity that will need to be evoked and rediscovered. For many, the initial moments of relaxation may go unrecognized. They may be quite unspectacular moments. A game of cards, a conversation, or going to a movie—recreation can encompass anything that pushes alcohol from the foreground and turns off preoccupation with oneself and one's plight. It is important to assist clients to recognize these moments and not discount the enjoyment. It is more important too, to incorporate events that up the odds of these moments occurring. During later recovery, recreation is no less an issue. At this point it may be considered as a part of the task that confronts us all. It can be put under the rubric of "taking care of ourselves." Recreation is a necessary self-indulgence.

Activities that center around fitness and sports are becoming a more important element in many individuals' taking care of themselves. Within treatment programs, efforts to address general fitness and well-being are now more common. In residential settings, without conscious effort to have it be otherwise, the day would be filled almost exclusively with sedentary activities. The link between emotional well-being and physical well-being is being appreciated. The treatment of alcohol or substance abuse can simultaneously address larger issues of general well-being, without diverting attention from the focus of alcohol or substance abuse as the paramount concern.

The self-care focus prompted many treatment programs to be "smoke free," to not allow smoking, and to promote or require smoking cessation as well as abstinence from alcohol use. The case for not allowing nicotine use can be made on many grounds—(1) smoking is viewed as a health issue and medical concern, as serious as chronic alcohol use, (2) smoking is seen as a behavior that often accompanies drinking so that if not discontinued it will be a ready cue to take a drink, (3) nicotine is viewed as a drug as, or more, addictive than alcohol or other substances, or (4) all of the above. As a practical point, the physical and emotional discomfort of withdrawal from alcohol is not compounded by the simultaneous withdrawal of nicotine. Residential programs that have initiated such policies have reported a relatively infrequent number of client complaints in respect to also giving up nicotine.

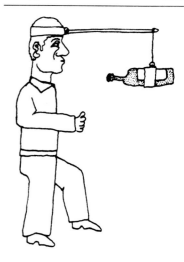

BEHAVIORAL THERAPY

The terms *behavioral therapy* and *behavior modification* have been bandied about by many, some of whom are poorly informed about them. Unfortunately, in too many facilities the terms have been used so casually and imprecisely that what is being discussed is not really behavior modification at all. Here we would like to give you a brief rundown of the pertinent factors and to point out some things that have muddied the waters.

Early approaches

Obviously, any therapy has behavior modification as its goal. However, behavioral therapy is the clinical application of the principles psychologists have discovered about how people learn. The basic idea is that if a behavior can be learned, it can also be unlearned, or changed. This can be done in several ways. To put it very simply, one way is to introduce new and competing behavior in place of the old or unwanted behavior. By using learning principles, the new behavior is reinforced, meaning the person experiences positive results and the old behavior is in effect "squeezed out." Another technique is to negatively reinforce, or punish, the unwanted behavior; therefore it becomes less frequent. Recall the discussion of Johnson's model for the development of drinking behavior in Chapter 6. That explanation was based on learning principles. People *learn* what alcohol can do; alcohol can be counted on in anyone's early drinking career to have dependable consequences. Therefore drinking is reinforced and the behavior continues.

Behavioral therapy is a field of psychology that developed in the early 1950s. Its techniques have been applied to the treatment of alcoholism. However, the early behavioral approaches fared no better than did other psychological approaches, which were unable to offer by themselves a full explanation of alcoholism nor alone were sufficient to guide treatment.

Historically, one of the first behavioral methods to be used in alcohol treatment was *aversion therapy*. Electric shock and chemicals were the things primarily used. The alcoholic person would be given something to drink, and as he swallowed the alcohol, a shock would be applied. Alternatively, a drug similar to disulfiram would induce sickness. The procedure was repeated periodically until it was felt that the drinking was so thoroughly associated with unpleasantness in the subject's mind that the person would be unlikely to continue drinking alcohol. Although short-term success was ensured, those results were not maintained over the long haul. As one author noted in reviewing behavioral approaches toward alcoholism, "Historically there have been many fads in the treatment of alcoholism. Behavioral therapists have also been guilty of this faddism in the form of aversion therapy. There has been an awareness on the part of behavioral therapists that this rather naive approach to a complex clinical problem such as alcoholism is unwarranted." Aversion therapy of this form is used very rarely now.

As the field became more sophisticated, it became clear that an effective behavioral treatment program could not be based on a single behavioral technique. One cannot expect all clients to be successfully treated by the routine application of the same procedure. Just as not all clients are given the same kind and dose of a medication, neither can they be given the same behavioral treatment. Thus efforts were then made to devise total alcohol treatment programs based on a variety of behavioral techniques. One behaviorally oriented program received considerable attention and generated much controversy. It centered on efforts by behavioral psychologists in the early 1970s to teach controlled drinking as the treatment for alcohol dependence. Linda and Mark Sobell are the researchers most closely identified with this. The initial reports were quite positive. Controlled drinking as an alternative to abstinence seemed to be further supported by several studies that followed up on individuals who had been similarly treated for alcoholism. Though the programs the clients had been involved in were generally abstinence oriented, a portion of these clients (although nowhere near a majority) were reported to have returned to moderate drinking without problems.

The optimism about controlled drinking as an alternative to abstinence could not be sustained. A group of researchers very painstakingly tracked down the subjects of the Sobells' study to see how they had fared over the long haul. Of the original group, only one was described as continuing as a moderate drinker. All of the others had serious problems and relapses, and four had died of alcohol-related problems. Similarly, Vaillant's work suggested that once an addictive state has been established, a return to moderate, controlled drinking is very rare. If one follows people over time as he did, the proportion who can maintain a controlled drinking pattern declines. It must also be noted that "controlled" drinking is not to be confused with "social" drinking. Most social drinkers do not need to invest considerable attention and energy to maintain a moderate level of alcohol use.

Ironically, while controlled drinking did not prove to have been a viable goal for treatment of alcohol dependence, many of the approaches used have subsequently been adopted in treating a different population of persons, those whose diagnosis is alcohol abuse. Abstinence may not be a requisite treatment goal for those with a diagnosis of alcohol abuse. Without question, they need to moderate their drinking practices, to reduce the likelihood of acute problems that arise with intoxication and to reduce the risk of future dependence. By way of example, the approaches introduced initially in efforts to teach "controlled" drinking to alcoholic patients have been used with college student groups, such as fraternities or dormitory groups, to reduce dangerous drinking practices.

At this point, designing alcoholism treatment programs exclusively on behavioral methods has largely been abandoned. What has now become far more commonplace is the use of behavioral methods to treat particular aspects of an alcohol problem in the context of a multi-pronged clinical approach.

Behavioral techniques

In recovery, the client is likely to face a multitude of problems. One of these may be a high level of anxiety. It can be of a temporary nature, the initial discomfort with the nondrinking life, or more chronic if one is the "nervous" type. Whether temporary or chronic, it is a darned uncomfortable state, and the alcoholic client has a *very* low tolerance for it. Those dependent upon alcohol have become accustomed to using alcohol for the quick, if temporary, relief of anxiety. What is later remembered (and longed for) is the almost instant relief of a large swig of booze. When alcohol or drugs are no longer an option, the recovering individual has the problem of how to deal with anxiety. Many simply "sweat it out"; others relapse.

Some positive things can be done to alleviate their anxiety. One is *relaxation therapy*. It is based on the fact that if the body and breathing are relaxed, it is impossible to *feel* anxious. The mind rejects the paradox of a relaxed body and a "tense" mind. Working with this fact, some techniques have evolved to counter anxiety with relaxation. Generally, the therapist vocally guides a person through a progressive tensing and relaxing of the various body parts. The relaxing can start with the toes and work up or with the scalp and work down. The process involves first tensing the muscles, then relaxing them at the direction of the therapist. These directions are generally given in a modulated, soft voice. When the client is quite relaxed, it is suggested a soothing picture be held in his or her mind. The client is then given a tape of the process to take home, with instructions on its use, as an aid in learning the relaxation. With practice, the relaxed state is achieved more easily and quickly. In some cases, the client may finally learn to totally relax with just the thought of the "picture." Once thoroughly learned, the relaxation response can be substituted for anxiety at will. This response can be used by the recovering alcoholic to deal with those situations in which taking a drink might be almost second nature.

Another behavioral approach to deal with anxiety, *systematic desensitization,* builds upon the relaxation response. This technique has been found quite useful in treating people with phobias. This is an appropriate approach for recovering alcoholics who may feel panic at the mere thought of a particular situation. We mean real panic, such that even the idea gets them so tense that the temptation to drink may be overwhelming.

In this process, with the aid of a therapist the individual in his imagination approaches the situation that leads to anxiety. As the anxiety builds up, the person is directed to use relaxation techniques that have been taught. Gradually, going step by step, relaxation is used to turn off the anxiety, and eventually the situation itself becomes much less anxiety provoking. In alcohol treatment, this approach has been used for persons whose drinking has been partially prompted by stressful, anxiety-producing situations. Given another option, they are better equipped to avoid drinking when such situations arise.

Assertiveness training, another technique that has evolved from behavioral methods, is sometimes used in alcoholism treatment. One of the more common applications is to help recovering alcoholics learn how to say "no" comfortably to a drink in social situations or say "no" to other things that might threaten sobriety.

Record keeping is another tool borrowed from behavioral psychology. Not uncommonly, in recovery, some clients report finding themselves, with some regularity, "suddenly" in the midst of some kind of troubling situation (e.g., an argument with a spouse), with no idea as to what led up to it. There may instead be periods of inexplicable despondency. Often there is a pattern, but the key elements may not be apparent. Keeping a personal log or diary of one's daily routine sometimes is used to help identify the precursors that lead up to difficult moments. Recovery requires all kinds of readjustments to routines. By keeping a daily log, over time, one may have a far better sense of what areas need attention.

Relapse prevention is one of the major contributions of behavioral psychology. Relapse prevention encompasses, in combination, many of the approaches just outlined. Relapse prevention efforts have increasingly become a standard component of care. In the past the alcohol field tended to avoid any mention of relapse in working with clients. The topic was taboo, as if in acknowledging relapse as a possibility, one were either giving permission to clients to resume drinking or implying that a resumption of drinking was inevitable. However, largely through the efforts of learning psychologists in combination with a growing understanding of alcohol dependence as a chronic disease, the potential for relapse is being openly and effectively addressed.

MEDITATION

Meditation is frequently suggested as an aid in achieving and maintaining sobriety. Any number of approaches are available to those wishing to try it, and many treatment centers include an introduction to one or more of these methods. Although meditation has different results depending on the type practiced, the process of reaching a meditative state is somewhat similar to relaxation. A fairly relaxed state is necessary before meditation can begin. Some schools of meditation use techniques quite similar to relaxation methods as a lead-in to the meditation period. In yoga, physical exercises are coupled with suggested ideas as a precursor. Studies have shown that altered physiological states accompany meditation or deep relaxation. Altered breathing patterns and different brain-wave patterns are examples. These changes are independent of the type of meditation practiced. The real physical response in part accounts for the feelings of well-being after meditation periods. Those who practice meditation find it, on the whole, a rewarding experience. Many also find in the experience some form of inspiration or spiritual help. Several highly advertised schools of meditation are receiving attention these days. You might investigate those that are available for clients who express an interest in meditation.

A word of caution is needed here. Alcoholics tend to go overboard. Meditation should never be a substitute for their other prescribed treatment. Also, there are extremists in every area of life, and meditation is no exception to exploitation. That is why some personal knowledge of what is available, who is using it, and how it affects those who do use it is necessary before advising your alcoholic client to try it. Meditation is only helpful if it alleviates anxiety and allows the recovering client to continue learning how to function better in the world.

DISULFIRAM (ANTABUSE)

In the late 1940s, through a series of accidents, a group of Danish scientists discovered that the drug disulfiram, which they were testing for other purposes, lead to a marked reaction when alcohol was ingested by a person exposed to it. Disulfiram alters the metabolism of alcohol by blocking out an enzyme necessary for the breakdown of acetaldehyde, an intermediate product of alcohol metabolism. Acetaldehyde is normally present in the body in small amounts, in somewhat larger ones when alcohol is ingested, and in toxic amounts when alcohol is taken into the body after disulfiram medication.

This adverse physical reaction is characterized by throbbing in the head and neck, flushing, breathing difficulty, nausea, vomiting, sweating, tachycardia (rapid heartbeat), weakness, and vertigo. The intensity of the reaction can vary from person to person and varies also with the amount of disulfiram present and the amount of alcohol taken in. Disulfiram is excreted slowly from the body, so the possibility of a reaction is present for 4 to 5 days after the last dose and in some cases longer. Because of this reaction, Antabuse (the trade name for disulfiram) has been widely used in the treatment of alcoholism.

Prescription, administration, and use

Over the years since disulfiram's discovery, trial and error and research have led to some suggestions for its prescription, administration, and use in alcohol treatment. Disulfiram is not a cure for alcoholism. At best, it can only postpone the drink. If the recovering client chooses to use disulfiram as an adjunct to AA, psychotherapy, group therapy, and so forth, it can be most useful in helping not take the impulsive drink. Because it stays in the system for such a long time, whatever caused the impulsive desire for a drink can be examined. It possibly could be worked through during the 5-day grace period to forestall the need for the drink entirely.

Anyone who wishes to use it should be allowed to do so, provided they are physically and mentally able. The client should first be thoroughly examined by a physician to determine physical status. Some conditions contraindicate disulfiram usage. There is still some debate as to the need for such caution with lower doses, but only the client's physician can decide this point. In some cases, physicians consider the risks of a disulfiram reaction not as dire as continued drinking certainly would be. There are those who suggest that administration should usually be supervised for at least a short time. Preferably the spouse should *not* be the one expected to do this. Rather this can be done through a visit to an outpatient clinic or an employee health clinic. Disulfiram should be used in combination with other supportive therapies.

The client taking disulfiram must be thoroughly informed of the dangers of a possible reaction. A variety of substances (such as cough syrup, wine sauces, paint fumes) that contain some alcohol can cause a reaction. Clients taking disulfiram should be provided a list of such substances. Carrying a card or wearing a "Med-Alert disk" stating they are taking disulfiram may be wise. Some medications given to accident victims or in emergency situations could cause a disulfiram reaction compounding whatever else is wrong. There is no way to be able to tell if an unconscious person has been taking disulfiram without such a warning.

A client who wishes to use disulfiram often begins taking the drug in a hospital setting after primary detoxification. Generally, one tablet (0.5 gm) daily for 5 days is given, then half a tablet daily thereafter. During the initial 5 days the client is carefully monitored for side effects. Once the client is receiving the maintenance dose, the client can continue for as long as it is beneficial.

Disulfiram can free the client from the constant battle against the bottle. When someone decides to take the pill on a given day, that person has made one choice that will postpone that drink for at least 4 or 5 days. If continuing to take it daily, that fourth or fifth day is always well out ahead. This allows time to begin acquiring or relearning behaviors other than drinking behaviors, and the habits of sobriety can take hold.

Disulfiram has been described as a crutch (which is not really out of place when one's legs are impaired). Instead, one might think of it as buying sober time until the alcohol dependent person's "legs" are steadier and other healthy supports are found. The supports may be available already, but the individual has to be able to use them successfully. Until then, these supports would fit him no better than a basketball player's crutch would fit a 10-year-old boy!

Medications containing alcohol

Alcohol, in one or another of its many forms, was for centuries virtually *the* pharmacological agent available to physicians. In the twentieth century, alcohol has had rather limited medicinal uses. Now, in addition to being used externally as an antiseptic (e.g., to wash the skin before giving an injection or taking a blood sample— *except*—when this sample is being obtained to measure blood alcohol levels), its only other major use is as an "inert" medium or carrier for liquid medications. Alcohol is an almost universal ingredient of cough medicines and liquid cold preparations sold over the counter or by prescription (see Table 9-1).

Moreover, the percentage of alcohol in these preparations can be substantial. NyQuil, for example, contains 25% alcohol. That's 50 proof! Alcohol is also an ingredient in a variety of other kinds of commonly used liquid medications (see Table 9-2).

Recovering alcoholics in general are well advised to avoid alcohol-containing preparations. For those taking disulfiram, it is imperative. Some preparations available for coughs and colds do not contain alcohol. These are listed in Table 9-3.

However, some of these contain substances also having psychoactive properties. Although using such agents will avoid the danger of disulfiram reactions, recovering alcoholics may wish to carefully monitor their exposure to the effects of any such drugs by carefully measuring the medication, taking it only at specified intervals, or settling for hot lemonade with honey and consoling themselves that this cold, too, shall pass.

In conclusion, all of the aforementioned therapies can be used together or in almost any combination that is deemed by the counselor to suit the situation of the client. They can be considered as a set of tools, which the therapist in combination with other treatment staff use as appropriate to the circumstances in any particular combination, to get the job done.

TABLE 9-1

Some alcohol-containing preparations for coughs, colds, and congestion

Drug	Manufacturer	Percentage of alcohol
Actol Expectorant	Beecham Labs	12.5
Ambenyl Expectorant	Parke-Davis	5.0
Calcidrine Syrup	Abbott	6.0
Chlor-Trimeton Syrup	Schering	7.0
Citra Forte Syrup	Boyle	2.0
Coryban-D Syrup	Pfipharmecs	7.5
Demazin Syrup	Schering	7.5
Dilaudid Cough Syrup	Knoll	5.0
Dimetane Elixir	Robins	3.0
Dimetane Expectorant	Robins	3.5
Dimetane Expectorant-DC	Robins	3.5
Dimetapp Elixir	Robins	2.3
Hycotuss Expectorant and Syrup	Endo	10.0
Lufylin-GG	Mallinckrodt	17.0
Novahistine DH	Dow Pharmaceuticals	5.0
Novahistine DMX	Dow Pharmaceuticals	10.0
Novahistine Elixir	Dow Pharmaceuticals	5.0
Novahistine Expectorant	Dow Pharmaceuticals	7.5
NyQuil Cough Syrup	Vicks	25.0
Ornacol Liquid	Smith Kline & French	8.0
Periactin Syrup	Merck Sharp & Dohme	5.0
Pertussin 8-Hour Syrup	Cheeseborough-Ponds	9.5
Phenergan Expectorant, Plain	Wyeth	7.0
Phenergan Expectorant, Codeine	Wyeth	7.0
Phenergan Expectorant VC, Plain	Wyeth	7.0
Phenergan Expectorant VC, Codeine	Wyeth	7.0
Phenergan Expectorant, Pediatric	Wyeth	7.0
Phenergan Syrup Fortis (25 mg)	Wyeth	1.5
Polaramine Expectorant	Schering	7.2
Quibron Elixir	Mead Johnson	15.0
Robitussin	Robins	3.5
Robitussin A-C	Robins	3.5
Robitussin-PE and DM	Robins	1.4
Robitussin-CF	Robins	4.75
Rondec-DM	Ross	0.6
Theo-Organidin Elixir	Wampole	15.0
Triaminic Expectorant	Dorsey	5.0
Triaminic Expectorant DH	Dorsey	5.0
Tussar-2 Syrup	Armour	5.0
Tussar SF Syrup	Armour	12.0
Tussi-Organidin	Wampole	15.0
Tuss-Ornade	Smith Kline & French	7.5
Tylenol Elixir	McNeil	7.0
Tylenol Elixir with Codeine	McNeil	7.0
Tylenol Drops	McNeil	7.0
Vicks Formula 44	Vicks	10.0

TABLE 9-2

Other commonly used drugs containing alcohol

Drug	Manufacturer	Percentage of alcohol
Alurate Elixir	Roche	20.0
Anaspaz-PB Liquid	Ascher	15.0
Aromatic Elixir	Circle	22.0
Asbron Elixir	Dorsey	15.0
Atarax Syrup	Roerig	0.5
Belladonna, Tincture of	Purepac	67.0
Benadryl Elixir	Parke-Davis	14.0
Bentyl-Phenobarbital syrup	Merrell-National	19.0
Carbrital Elixir	Parke-Davis	18.0
Cas-Evac	Parke-Davis	18.0
Choledyl Elixir	Warner/Chilcott	20.0
Decadron Elixir	Merck Sharp & Dohme	5.0
Dexedrine Elixir	Smith Kline & French	10.0
Donnagel	Robins	3.8
Donnagel-PG	Robins	5.0
Donnatal Elixir	Robins	23.0
Dramamine Liquid	Searle Labs	5.0
Elixophylin	Cooper	20.0
Elixophyllin-KI	Cooper	10.0
Feosol Elixir	Smith Kline & French	5.0
Gevrabon	Lederle	18.0
Ipecac Syrup	Lilly	2.0
Isuprel Comp. Elixir	Winthrop	19.0
Kaochlor S-F	Warren-Teed	5.0
Kaon Elixir	Warren-Teed	5.0
Kay Ciel	Cooper	4.0
Kay Ciel Elixir	Cooper	4.0
Marax Syrup	Roerig	5.0
Mellaril Concentrate	Sandoz	3.0
Minocin Syrup	Lederle	5.0
Modane Liquid	Warren-Teed	5.0
Nembutal Elixir	Abbott	18.0
Paregoric Tincture		45.0
Parelixir	Purdue Frederick	18.0
Parepectolin	Rorer	0.69
Propadrine Elixir	Merck Sharp & Dohme	16.0
Serpasil Elixir	CIBA	12.0
Tedral Elixir	Warner/Chilcott	15.0
Temaril Syrup	Smith Kline & French	5.7
Theolixir (Elixir Theophylline)	Ulmer	20.0
Valadol	Squibb	9.0
Vita-Metrazol Elixir	Knoll	15.0

TABLE 9-3

Some nonalcoholic preparations for coughs, colds, and congestion

Drug	Manufacturer
Actifed-C Expectorant	Burroughs Wellcome
Actifed Syrup	Burroughs Wellcome
Hycodan Syrup	Eaton Labs.
Ipsatol Syrup	Key
Omni-Tuss	Pennwalt
Orthoxicol Syrup	Upjohn
Sudafed Syrup	Burroughs Wellcome
Triaminic Syrup	Dorsey
Triaminicol Syrup	Dorsey
Tussionex Suspension	Pennwalt

RESOURCES AND FURTHER READING

Aguilar TE, Munson WW: Leisure education and counseling as intervention components in drug and alcohol treatment for adolescents, *Journal of Alcohol and Drug Education* 37(3):23-34, 1992.

The purpose of this paper is to illustrate the association between substance abuse and leisure experiences and to present a rationale for leisure interventions designed to remediate this social and behavioral problem. Leisure education and counseling is suggested for inclusion in broad-based prevention or intervention strategies for substance abuse. Recommendations are provided for strengthening leisure education and counseling programs by including suggestions for theory, content, format, and duration. (Author abstract.)

Brisbane FL, editor: Treating the alcoholic: A social work challenge, *Social Casework* 70(6):323-392 (entire issue), 1989.

The theme of this special issue, alcoholism, was selected by the editor in response to the large numbers of dysfunctional families alcoholism produces, the inadequate attention that has been paid to treatment, and the historic failure of the profession to assess and treat alcoholism. The contributors include practitioners, academics and researchers, and program administrators from the alcohol field. The topics addressed include a biopsychosocial model of alcoholism, dual diagnosis and clinical implications, family systems treatment models, interventions with special client populations, i.e., adolescents, women, and black males, and training for social workers.

Carroll S: Spirituality and purpose in life in alcoholism recovery, *Journal of Studies on Alcohol* 54(3):297-301, 1993.

This study examines the relationship between spirituality and recovery from alcoholism. Spirituality is defined as the extent of practice of Alcoholics Anonymous Steps 11 and 12 and is measured by a Step Questionnaire developed by the researcher. Step 11 suggests prayer and meditation, and Step 12 suggests assistance of other alcoholics. Expressed degree of purpose in life is also seen as a reflection of spirituality. It was postulated that the extent to which Steps 11 and 12 were practiced would be positively correlated with the extent of purpose in life reported by 100 Alcoholics Anonymous members. The major findings affirm this. The findings suggest that a sense of purpose in life increases with continuing sobriety and practice of the spiritual principles of Alcoholics Anonymous. Copyright 1993, Alcohol Research Documentation, Inc. Used with permission.

Carruthers CP: Leisure and alcohol expectancies, *Journal of Leisure Research* 25(3):229-244, 1993.

This article presents the results of a study investigating the ways in which individuals expect drinking to affect their leisure experiences and the relationship of these expectancies to alcohol consumption patterns. Data were obtained from a community sample of 144 adults who completed a mail questionnaire. Results suggest that individuals expect alcohol to affect their leisure experience in three ways: 1) facilitate disengagement from responsibilities and tensions, 2) increase self-assurance and acceptance, and 3) heighten engagement in the immediate experience. The strength of these expectancies has utility in predicting frequency and quantity of alcohol consumption. In addition, the ways in which individuals expect that alcohol consumption will affect their leisure experiences is dependent on the leisure context. These results provide preliminary insight into the complex relationship between alcohol consumption and leisure. (Author abstract.)

Chappel JN: Long-term recovery from alcoholism, *Psychiatric Clinics of North America* 16(1):177-187, 1993.

This article provides data to show that alcoholism can be treated successfully and that long-term recovery lasting for decades can be achieved. The evidence is contained in the database accumulated by Alcoholics Anonymous (AA), the membership survey. Described are the membership survey, stable aspects of Alcoholics Anonymous, and changing aspects of Alcoholics Anonymous. AA has demonstrated success in steadily increasing membership, with no loss of the proportion of those with over 5 years of sobriety. It has been recognized as effective long-term treatment for alcoholism by psychiatrists and psychoanalysts experienced in the treatment of addictions. Suggestions are given for the uses psychiatrists can make of the membership survey data and knowledge from AA.

Galanter M, Egelko S, and Edwards H: Rational recovery: Alternative to AA for addiction, *American Journal of Drug and Alcohol Abuse* 19(4):499-510, 1993.

Rational Recovery (RR) is a new self-help movement for substance abusers, with a cognitive orientation. It has been suggested as an alternative to Alcoholics Anonymous. This study was designed to examine the nature of RR and its impact on those who join. A national sample of 433 substance-abusing people attending 63 established RR groups was evaluated, using codable self-report questionnaires completed at RR meetings. Members were mostly men with college experience who had previously attended AA. Among recruits who attended their first RR meeting in the last month, 38% were abstinent in the last month. Among members who had joined 3 or more months before, 73% were abstinent in the last month; they had attended an average of 4.1 RR meetings in that month and carried out exercises at home based on Rational Emotive Therapy. Among those who joined 6 or more months before, 58% reported at least 6 months of abstinence. Among members with a history of heavy cocaine use, the portion reporting abstinence in the last month was not significantly different from those who had never used cocaine. The minority of members who were engaged for 3 months were still drinking, though, and did so on an average of 9.9 days in the last month. RR succeeded in engaging substance abusers and promoting abstinence among many of them while presenting a cognitive orientation that is different from the spiritual one of AA. Its utility in substance abuse treatment warrants further assessment. (Author abstract.)

Gelderloos P, Walton KG, Orme-Johnson DW, and others: Effectiveness of the Transcendental Meditation program in preventing and treating substance misuse: A review, *International Journal of the Addictions* 26(3):293-325, 1991.

This article reviews 24 studies on the benefits of Transcendental Meditation (TM) in treating and preventing misuse of chemical substances. Studies cover noninstitutionalized users, participants in treatment programs, and prisoners with histories of heavy use. All the studies showed positive effects of the TM program. Some of the survey-type studies were unable to exclude the possibility of self-selection or responder biases. These and other studies indicate the program simultaneously addresses several factors underlying chemical dependence, providing not only immediate relief from distress but also other areas of psychophysiological health. (Author abstract.)

Gorney B: Domestic violence and chemical dependency: Dual problems, dual interventions, *Journal of Psychoactive Drugs* 21(2):229-238, 1989.

This article addresses the link between domestic violence and chemical dependency. Both are extremely prevalent and pose serious threats to individuals, families, communities, and society at large. The commonly observed association between substance abuse and violent interactions has traditionally been explained as a cause-effect. It is assumed that intoxication causes violence, and this viewpoint has traditionally dominated research on the subject as well as treatment methodology. This interpretation may lead treatment providers to assume that once abstinence from alcohol and other drugs is achieved, violence will also disappear. Researchers in the field of domestic violence argue that violence occurs both when substance abuse is present *and* absent. This article addresses the need to assess and treat both problem areas concurrently. In addition to providing assessment and treatment guidelines, the article describes the scope of the problem, etiological issues, and factors that may serve as barriers to treatment providers in identifying violence as a problem in chemically dependent relationship systems. (Author abstract)

Hester RK, Miller WR, editors: *Handbook of alcoholism treatment approaches,* Elmsford NY: Pergamon Press, 1989.

This multiauthored handbook discusses evaluation and motivation, primary treatment approaches, other types of intervention, and matching individuals with interventions. It is written with a behavioral learning perspective. While much of the subject matter is similar to other general works, its unique features are (1) the discussion of motivation for change and using the natural process for initiating change to engage the client into treatment, and (2) interventions based upon behavioral approaches, e.g., relapse prevention, social skills training, and anxiety and stress management.

Howard MO, Elkins RL, Rimmele C, and others: Chemical aversion treatment of alcohol dependence, *Drug and Alcohol Dependence* 29(2):107-143, 1991.

Developments in the application of chemical aversion therapy to the treatment of alcohol dependence are discussed. Historical factors leading to the early use of chemical aversion therapies are delineated, and the theoretical underpinnings of chemical aversion interventions are evaluated. Ethical and procedural considerations are addressed, and an assessment of the efficacy of the therapy is attempted. Future research activities that would lead to refinement of chemical aversion therapy protocols are highlighted. The effectiveness of chemical aversion treatment of alcohol dependence is discussed vis-a-vis production of conditioned alcohol-aversion and treatment outcome. (Author abstract.)

Marron JT: The Twelve Steps: A pathway to recovery, *Primary Care* 20(1):107-119, 1993.

The primary-care physician can have a pivotal role in promoting recovery in alcohol- and other drug-dependent patients. The clinician's attitudes toward self-help, 12-Step programs that the patient may be using could have a significant impact on the outcome of the usually fragile early recovery program that the patient is developing. The fellowship of Alcoholics Anonymous (AA) is described. The manner in which it may complement other treatment is discussed.

Miller WR, Benefield RG, and Tonigan JS: Enhancing motivation for change in problem drinking: A controlled comparison of two therapist styles, *Journal of Consulting and Clinical Psychology* 61(3):455-461, 1993.

To investigate the impact of counselor style, a two-session motivational check-up was offered to 42 problem drinkers (18 women and 24 men) who were randomly assigned to 3 groups: (a) immediate check-up with directive-confrontational counseling, (b) immediate check-up with client-centered counseling, or (c) delayed check-up (waiting-list control). Overall, the intervention resulted in a 57% reduction in drinking within 6 weeks, which was maintained at 1 year. Clients receiving immediate check-up showed significant reduction in drinking relative to controls. The two counseling styles were discriminable on therapist behaviors coded from audiotapes. The directive-confrontational style yielded significantly more resistance from clients, which in turn predicted poorer outcomes at 1 year. Therapist styles did not differ in overall impact on drinking, but a single therapist's behavior was predictive (r = .65) of 1-year outcome such that the more the therapist confronted, the more the client drank. (Author abstract.)

Miller WR, Kurtz E: Models of alcoholism used in treatment: Contrasting AA and other perspectives with which it is often confused, *Journal of Studies on Alcohol* 55(2):159-166, 1994.

Current popular and professional conceptions of alcoholism in the United States blend four models that differ in their emphases and implications and contain mutually contradictory beliefs. Elements of moral-volitional, personality, and dispositional disease models have been confused with, and mistakenly attributed to, the essential spiritual views of Alcoholics Anonymous (AA). An original AA model can be distinguished from prior and subsequent beliefs with which it has been added. Clarity regarding the essential elements of an AA understanding of alcoholism is important both for clinicians and for those who would undertake research on AA. (Author abstract.)

O'Brien RY: Spirituality in treatment programs for addicts, *Journal of Ministry in Addiction & Recovery* 1(1):69-76, 1994.

The dichotomy of the sacred and secular that pervades much of society has a deleterious effect upon recovery from addiction when members of a treatment staff are timid and tenuous about the spiritual dimension of recover. Spirituality is the experience of the transcendent in the recovery process, and it cannot be either forced or fabricated. The first three Steps in the 12-step program provide a solid foundation for incorporating spirituality into recovery without committing to a particular theological or ecclesiastical bias. (Author abstract)

Olitzky KM, Copans SA: *Twelve Jewish steps to recovery,* Woodstock, VT: Jewish Lights Publishing, 1991.

A personal guide to turning from alcohol and other addictions, Twelve-Step programs of Alcoholics Anonymous and Narcotics Anonymous are interpreted from the perspective of Judaism. Each of the steps is interpreted using biblical stories, history, prayers, and discussion. Resource organizations, a glossary of important words, and selected readings are included.

Pendery ML, Maltzman IM, West LJ: Controlled drinking by alcoholics? New findings and a reevaluation of a major affirmative study, *Science* 217(4555):169-175, 1982.

Controlled drinking has recently become a controversial alternative to abstinence as an appropriate treatment goal for alcoholics. In this study we reexamine the evidence underlying a widely cited report by Sobell and Sobell of successful controlled drinking by a substantial proportion of gamma (physically dependent) alcoholic subjects in a behavior therapy experiment. A review of the evidence, including official records and new interviews, reveals that most subjects trained to do controlled drinking failed from the outset to drink safely. The majority were hospitalized for alcoholism treatment within a year after their discharge from the research project. A 10-year follow-up (extended through 1981) of the original 20 experimental subjects shows that only one, who apparently had not experienced physical withdrawal symptoms, maintained a pattern of controlled drinking; eight continued to drink excessively—regularly or intermittently—despite repeated damaging consequences; six abandoned their effort to engage in controlled drinking and became abstinent; four died from alcohol-related causes; and one, certified about a year after discharge from the research project as gravely disabled because of drinking, was missing.* (Author abstract.)

Peteet JR: A closer look at the role of a spiritual approach in addictions treatment, *Journal of Substance Abuse Treatment* 10(3):263-267, 1993.

12-Step Programs such as AA's play a major role in addictions treatment, and their members are increasingly accepting of psychotherapy and medication. However, many clinicians question the role of an approach defined by these Programs as spiritual. This paper explores the nature, indications, and limitations of a spiritual approach to addiction and the implications for collaboration with mental-health professionals. It suggests that 12-Step Programs not only provide accessible group support and a clear ideology regarding addiction but address individuals' needs for identity, integrity, an inner life, and interdependence within a larger social and moral or spiritual context. It examines the ways in which the religious connotations of the Program remain an obstacle for many patients and clinicians. Clarification of the different needs met by modalities such as AA can improve the specificity and the comprehensiveness of treatment for patients with substance use disorders. (Author abstract.)

Room R, Greenfield T: Alcoholics Anonymous, other 12-step movements and psychotherapy in the US population, 1990, *Addiction* 88(4):555-562, 1993.

Based on the 1990 US National Alcohol Survey, this note provides the first available comprehensive findings on self-reported use of a variety of sources of personal support and counseling for alcohol and other problems. Respondents were queried about lifetime attendance and number of times they went to identified sources of help in the prior year. Twelve-step groups included Alcoholics Anonymous, Al-Anon, Adult Children of Alcoholics, and other nonalcohol-oriented groups like Gamblers Anonymous, Narcotics Anonymous, and Overeaters Anonymous; additional questions inquired about support or therapy groups and individual counseling for non-alcohol problems. Of the US adult population, 9% have been to an AA meeting at some time, 3.6% in the prior year, only about one third of these for problems of their own. About half these percentages, mostly women, have attended Al-Anon. Of the same population, 13.3% indicate ever attending a 12-step meeting (including nonalcohol-oriented groups), 5.3% in the last year. During the prior year a further 2.1% used other support/therapy groups and 5.5% sought individual counseling/therapy for personal problems other than alcohol. In contrast to this high reported use, only 4.9% (ever) and 2.3% (12 months) reported going to anyone, including AA, for a problem (of their own) related to drinking. (Authors' abstract.)

Rousso J: Psychotherapy with the recovering alcoholic, *Alcoholism Treatment Quarterly* 9(3/4):201-206, 1992.

This article discusses in detail psychotherapeutic approaches in working with alcoholic patients in recovery. It stresses the principles of patience and acceptance on the part of the therapist. It stresses ways to help alcoholics recognize and deal with feelings that have so long been buried under the influence of alcohol. (Author abstract.)

Smart RG, Mann RE: Recent liver cirrhosis declines: Estimates of the impact of alcohol abuse treatment and Alcoholics Anonymous, *Addiction* 88(2):193-198, 1993.

This paper examines the proposition that increased treatment for alcohol abuse and Alcoholics Anonymous (AA) membership can account for a large part of the recent declines in cirrhosis mortality and morbidity. Data on treatment and AA

---

*This article and the one by the Sobells represent one of the most significant, strident, and continuing controversies in the alcohol-drug field, i.e., whether "controlled drinking" (or drug use) is a suitable alternative to abstinence as a treatment goal. See *Journal of Studies on Alcohol* 50(5):465-486, 1989, containing an article on the topic, an editorial note, and two invited responses.

membership in the USA between 1979 and 1987 and in Ontario between 1975 and 1986 are used, together with estimates of cirrhosis risk and the likely impact of treatment and AA membership. The results show that increased treatment levels and AA membership could account for all of the reductions in cirrhosis deaths and hospital admissions in Ontario. In the USA, all of the deaths and about 40% of the admissions could be accounted for by these factors. (Authors' abstract.)

Smith DE, Buxton ME, Bilal R, and others: Cultural points of resistance to the 12 step recovery process, *Journal of Psychoactive Drugs* 25(1):97-108, 1993.

This article addresses some of the key issues in developing culturally relevant approaches to drug abuse treatment and recovery, using the Haight Ashbury Free Clinics (HAFC)/Glide African-American Extended Family Program as a positive example of effective cultural adaptability within recovery. Cultural points of resistance to the recovery process are also addressed, including the perception that 12-Step fellowships are exclusive and confused with religion, involve confusion over surrender versus powerlessness, and raise concerns about low self-esteem, dysfunctional family structure, communication difficulties, and institutionalized and internalized racism. The authors also focus on professional resistance in other countries, where different treatment approaches and philosophies block the acceptance of a recovery concept in general and the 12-Step process in particular. In explicating these issues, addiction is presented as a multicultural problem in need of multicultural solutions. The challenge is to adapt the process of recovery to all cultures and races, to counter stereotypes on all sides, and to eliminate the perception that recovery only works for addicts from the White mainstream. (Author abstract.)

Snow MG, Prochaska JO, Rossi JS: Processes of change in Alcoholics Anonymous: Maintenance factors in long-term sobriety, *Journal of Studies on Alcohol* 55(3):362-371, 1994.

The change strategies associated with successful long-term sobriety remain an understudied area in addiction research. The following study recruited individuals in various stages of sobriety (range: 1 month to 27 years continuous abstinence). Subjects (N = 191) were surveyed on demographic, problem history, degree of self-utilization, current process of change use, and self-efficacy measures. Subjects were differentiated based on varying experience with AA, including exposure, frequency of meeting attendance, and degree of affiliation. Analyses included comparisons on demographic, problem history, process of change, and self-efficacy markers (i.e., self-change vs. self-help; differing levels of self-help utilization). Few differences were found between groups on demographic or self-efficacy indices, although there was a trend for past or current AA attendees and medium affiliates to report slightly greater alcohol use before quitting compared to self-changers or low affiliates. There was a consistent, positive relationship between the use of behaviorally oriented change processes and increased involvement with AA, with current attendees and high affiliates using these particular strategies more frequently than either self-changers, past attendees, or the low-to-medium affiliate groups. The utility of process analyses in helping map the pattern of successful addictive behavior change is discussed. (Author abstract.)

Sobell MB, Sobell LC: *Behavioral treatment of alcohol problems,* New York: Plenum Press, 1978.

The Sobells have been among the most prolific researchers in the behavioral quarter of the research-treatment community. This work includes a summary of a project involving a training regimen using behavioral paradigms that was reported successfully to replace addicted uncontrolled use with a pattern of "controlled drinking."

Special Issue on Alcoholics Anonymous: *Journal of Substance Abuse Treatment* 11(2):1-166, (entire issue) 1994.

The lead article is entitled "How AA works and why it's important for clinicians to understand." It notes that alcoholism is associated with tremendous suffering, psychological denial, and physical and emotional debilitation. Much of the suffering that plagues alcoholics is rooted in core problems with self-regulation involving self-governance, feeling life (affects), and self-care. Alcoholics Anonymous is effective because it is a sophisticated group psychology that effectively accesses, corrects, or repairs these core psychological vulnerabilities. The traditions of story-telling, honesty, openness, and willingness to examine ("take inventory") character defects allow people to express themselves who otherwise would not feel or speak or are deceitful (to self and others) and would deny vulnerability and limitation to openly admit to it. This article is followed by 10 other articles specifically related to aspects of AA with attention to the use of self-help groups by professionals and what helping professionals need to know to use these resources effectively.

Straussner SL: Intervention with maltreating parents who are drug and alcohol abusers. Ehrenkraz SM, and others: *Clinical social work with maltreated children and their families: An introduction to practice,* New York: New York University Press, 1989.

This chapter, directed to the nonspecialist in alcohol and substance abuse, provides an introduction to the relationship between substance abuse and the abuse and neglect of children. As background to that discussion, there is a brief overview of the various classes of drugs, the characteristics of those who abuse drugs and/or alcohol, and the relationship between drug and alcohol abuse and child maltreatment. The bulk of the chapter summarizes intervention techniques and strategies with parents and with children who have suffered abuse.

Thompson DL, Thompson JA: Working the 12 steps of Alcoholics Anonymous with a client: A counseling opportunity, *Alcoholism Treatment Quarterly* 10(1/2):49-61, 1993.

This paper describes problems that clients with alcoholism may experience once they have begun recovery in Alcoholics Anonymous: sponsorship, spirituality, and working the steps. Of special interest are those in AA who are also in therapy and the difficulties encountered engendered by misconceptions on the part of the client and counselor. A procedure is described by which the counselor can work the steps with the client as a foundation of counseling. (Author abstract.)

Tiebout HM: Surrender versus compliance in therapy, with special reference to alcoholism, *Quarterly Journal of Studies on Alcohol* 14:58-68, 1953.

In distinguishing between surrender and compliance, Tiebout addressed a concept that had special meaning for the early members of AA. Some of the points in his work have influenced professional treatment approaches and continue to leave their mark within the Fellowship, particularly what is perceived as necessary to follow the therapeutic regimen of AA. Surrender is distinguished from compliance and seen as an essential precursor for "acceptance." It takes place at the conscious level but more importantly the unconscious level, with a recognition of a fundamental inability to solve problems (handle alcohol) alone. This in turn provides the alcoholic with the motivation and ability to reach out for help and allows one to achieve psychological growth and change. In contrast "compliance" is viewed as a conscious or rational acceptance but unconscious resistance to the need for change, creating a state of tension, strain, and conflict and often blocking surrender.*

*Available as a monograph through the National Council on Alcohol and Other Drug Dependencies.

Walle AH: William James, legacy to Alcoholics Anonymous: An analysis and a critique, *Journal of Addictive Diseases* 11(3):91-99, 1992.

When evolving a philosophy and a "modus operandi" the pioneers of Alcoholics Anonymous made significant use of William James' Varieties of Religious Experience. Indeed, although AA carefully picked and chose various of James' ideas that seemed particularly relevant, James' imprint is clearly stamped upon AA philosophy and methodology. The author reviews James' work and explores what specific ideas were particularly relevant to AA's evolution as a self-help movement. The implications of this heritage will be explored. (Author abstract.)

Weber JA, McCormick P: Alateen members' and non-members' understanding of alcoholism, *Journal of Alcohol and Drug Education* 37(3):74-84, 1992.

In this study, Alateen and non-Alateen members were compared on their knowledge and understanding of alcoholism. The adolescent samples were also given the opportunity to openly discuss what their recommendations would be for a friend who was an alcoholic and what items they would like to see in an educational curriculum. Results indicated Alateen members understand alcoholism as a family disease, that family members are not responsible for an alcoholic's condition or behavior, and alcoholism is treatable. Alateen members suggested that an educational curriculum be designed with a message of successful treatment and hope for an alcoholic's condition, while non-Alateen members stressed the importance of understanding and gathering the facts about alcoholism. The significance of these findings are discussed in relation to developing an alcohol education curriculum. (Author abstract.)

White JR: Metachange in individuals recovering from substance dependence disorders, *Journal of Psychology and Christianity* 11(1):23-32, 1992. (30 refs.)

Recovery from substance dependence disorders is a dramatic life experience that involves a cognitive metachange. This metachange amounts to a reversal in how the recovering individual views the substance, world, self, and others. The discrepancy between this new view and that which was required to maintain active substance dependence produces an opportunity for increased capacity for paradoxical thought. A particular variety of paradoxical thought, the cognitive tendency to permit two superficially contradictory ideas to co-exist without resolution into conventionalized meaning, may be a prognostic indicator of, and a therapeutic adjunct to, recovery from substance-dependence disorders. Clinical guidelines are presented, and a case illustration involving a 54-year-old male recovering alcoholic is discussed. (Author abstract.)

Special populations

There may be remarkable similarities between the 15-year-old alcohol abuser, who also dabbles with cocaine, and the 72-year-old retired schoolteacher, who never drank anything stronger than sherry. But that should not blind us to the equally significant differences! In this chapter, we focus upon the distinctive characteristics of special populations, particularly adolescents, the elderly, women, and those in the workplace. Of course, there is no segment of the population untouched by alcohol problems. The chapter concludes with some suggested ways to identify the needs and issues of groups not discussed here. The groups selected for special attention here are those that cross-cut all segments of society.

Space does not allow equal discussion of even the major racial and ethnic groups and their particular needs nor other populations that may be of particular interest to individual readers, whether college students, gays and lesbians, or members of the military. Since we cannot adequately even begin to acquaint you with the characteristics and issues to bear in mind when working with clients from any particular ethnic, racial, or religious group, we must be content to urge you to speak with more experienced colleagues, as well as to turn to the ever-increasing body of literature on minority and high-risk groups, including Native Americans, Afro-Americans, Hispanics, migrant workers, and Asians. However, in thinking about the special considerations of the groups that are discussed, one of the hopes is to make you more sensitive to the characteristics of any client.

ADOLESCENTS

Adolescence is indeed a special period of life. It lies at the back door of childhood yet at the very doorstep of adulthood. At no comparable time in life do more physical and emotional changes take place in such a narrow span of time. *Adolescence* as a term is less

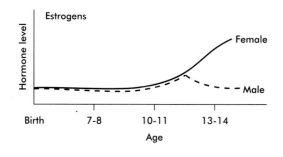

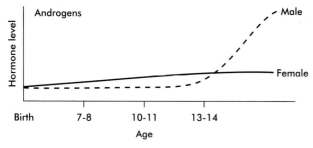

than 150 years old. Before that time, one grew straight from child-hood into adulthood. The needs of family and culture demanded earlier work and community responsibilities. Survival depended on it. With increasing industrialization, children left the factories and fields to spend more time in school, play, and idle time. Society became increasingly aware of the presence of teenagers as a group who had, and still have, fairly undefinable roles and rights. Most texts define adolescence as the period from 12 to 21 years of age. Physical and legal determinants would suggest otherwise. Physical changes indicative of the beginning of adolescence may begin as early as age 7 and not end until the mid-20s. Legal age differs between state and federal jurisdictions. Draft registration require-ments and voting privileges at 18 have clouded the definition.

Physical changes

The most striking aspect of adolescence is the rapid physical growth. These changes are mediated by the sex hormones. The rough charts above indicate that the first recognizable change in the male is caused by fat increase dictated by a small but gradual increase in estrogen. Every boy gains weight at the expense of height during these years. Some boys due to become tall and muscular men are quite chubby during these early adolescent years. To add insult to injury, the next body part to grow is the feet, then the thighs, making him appear short waisted and gawky. This slows, allowing the rest of the body to catch up. Androgen influence appears later, with pigment changes in the scrotal sac, then enlarge-ment of the testes, penis, the beginning of pubic hair, and early voice changes. The first nocturnal emission or "wet dream" may occur as

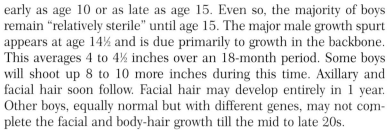

early as age 10 or as late as age 15. Even so, the majority of boys remain "relatively sterile" until age 15. The major male growth spurt appears at age 14½ and is due primarily to growth in the backbone. This averages 4 to 4½ inches over an 18-month period. Some boys will shoot up 8 to 10 more inches during this time. Axillary and facial hair soon follow. Facial hair may develop entirely in 1 year. Other boys, equally normal but with different genes, may not complete the facial and body-hair growth till the mid to late 20s.

We are indeed taller than our ancestors, which can be shown from historical evidence. Clothing, doorways, and furniture were made for shorter men and women. Better nutrition is mainly responsible for the changes seen.

A girl's first hormonal response is around age 7 or 8 with a normal vaginal discharge called leukorrhea. The feet then grow, but this is rarely as noticeable a change as in the male. A breast "button" begins about age 11 under the skin of one breast first, to be followed in weeks or months under the remaining breast. The breasts develop into adult breasts over a span of 4 to 5 years. Pubic hair begins approximately 6 months after the breast button stage. The hips widen, and the backbone gains 3 to 4 inches before she is ready for her menses. Although a critical body weight is not the only initiator, the body is influenced by this. If other criteria are met, such as developing breasts, pubic hair, widened hips, and growth spurt, a sample of American girls will begin their menses weighing from 100 to 105 pounds. Nutrition has a great deal to do with the menarche (first menses); girls in countries with poor nutritional standards begin their menses 2 to 3 years later. The mean age for menarche in the United States is 12. (Pilgrim girls, who suffered from many nutritional deprivations, often had menarche delayed until age 17.) A regular menstrual cycle is not established immediately. Quite commonly a girl will have anovulatory (no egg) periods for 6 to 18 months before having ovulatory periods. This change may bring an increased weight gain, breast tenderness, occasional emotional lability, and cramps at the midcycle. These are consequences of progesterone, a hormone secreted by the ovary at the time of ovulation. An adult pattern in ovulation will not be completed until the early 20s.

Until puberty, boys and girls are equally strong in muscle strength (if corrected for height and weight). Total body fat increases in girls by 50% from ages 12 to 18, whereas a similar decrease occurs in boys. Muscle cell size and number increase in boys; muscle cell size alone increases in girls. Internal organs, such as the heart, double in size. Blood pressure increases with demands of growth. Pulse rate decreases, and the ability to break down fatigue metabolites in muscle prepares the male, especially, for the role of hunter and runner that was so important for survival centuries ago.

Marked fatigue coupled with overwhelming strength is often difficult to fully appreciate. An adolescent may wolf down several quarts of milk, a full meal or two, play many hours of active sports,

and yet complain bitterly of severe fatigue at all times. This human metabolic furnace needs the food and rest as well as the drive to have the machine function and test itself out. These bodily inconsistencies often show in mood swings and unpredictable demands for self-satisfaction and physical expression.

The rapidity of these changes tends to produce almost a physiological confusion in many adolescents. Quite commonly, they become preoccupied with themselves. This can lead to an over-concern with their health. In some instances it is almost hypochondriacal. Adolescents may complain of things that to an adult appear very minor. The thing to remember is that their concern is very real and deep. Attention should be paid to their concerns. Remembering the rapid rate of physical changes that confront adolescents makes their preoccupation with their bodies understandable.

Characteristics

Adolescence characteristically is an extremely healthy time of life. In general, adolescents do not die off from the kinds of things that strike the rest of us, such as heart disease. The major causes of adolescent deaths are accidents, suicide, and homicide. Due to this healthiness, adults tend to assume that adolescents with problems are not really sick and thus do not give their complaints the attention they deserve. Furthermore, teens themselves may not perceive their health risk behaviors as dangerous or may be unable to articulate concerns that they may have. Another characteristic of adolescence is a truly tremendous need to conform to their peers. There is the need to dress alike, wear the same hairstyle, listen to the same music, and even think alike. A perpetual concern of the adolescent is that he or she is different. Although the sequence of physical development is the same, there is still variation in the age of onset and the rate of development. This can be a big concern for adolescents, whether the teenager is ahead, behind, or just on the norm. Worry about being different is a particular concern for the adolescent who may want or need professional help. The adolescent will not go unless it is "peer acceptable." Kids often stay away from caregivers out of fear. A big fear is that if they go, sure enough something really wrong will be found. This, to their minds, would officially certify them as different. They cannot tolerate that. They also fear that counselors will not respect confidentiality and will serve as parent surrogates rather than working with the teen in a true counselor-client relationship.

Also characteristic of adolescence is wildly fluctuating behavior. It frequently alternates between wild, agitated periods and times of quiescence. A flurry of even psychotic-type thinking is not uncommon. This does not mean that adolescents are psychotic for a time and then get over it. There are just some periods when their thinking really only makes sense to themselves and possibly to their friends. For example, if not selected for the play cast, he may be sure that he "proves" he will be a failure his entire life. If she is denied the use of the family car on Friday, she may overreact. With a perfectly straight face, she may accuse her parents of *never* letting her have the car, even as she stands there with the car keys ready to drive off.

Adolescence is very much a time of two steps forward and one step back, with an occasional jog to one side or the other. Despite the ups and downs, it is usually a continuing, if uneven, upward trip to maturity.

Another point of importance: in early adolescence, girls are developmentally ahead of boys. At the onset of puberty, girls are physically about 2 years ahead. This makes a difference in social functioning because social development takes place in tandem with physical development. This can cause problems in social interactions for boys and girls of the same age. Their ideas of what makes a good party or what is appropriate behavior may differ considerably. The girls may consider their male peers "total dweebs." The boys, aware of the girls' assessments, may be shaken up, while the girls feel dislocated, too. With the uneven development of boys and girls during early adolescence, girls may be a year ahead of boys. There is a catching-up period later, but in dealing with younger adolescents, keep this disparity in mind.

Developmental tasks. When does adolescence end? There are fairly clear-cut signs that mark the beginnings of the process. There is more to adolescence than just physical maturation. Defining the end can lead to philosophical discussions of "maturity." Doesn't everyone know a 45-year-old or 65-year old "adolescent?" There is more to assigning an end point than just considering a numerical age.

One way of thinking about the adolescent period is to assign to it four tasks. From this point of view, once the tasks have been reasonably accomplished, the person is launched into adulthood. These tasks are not tackled in any neat order or sequence. It is not like the consistent pattern of physical development. They are more like four interwoven themes, the dominant issues of adolescence.

The first task of adolescence is *acceptance of the biological role.* This means acquiring some degree of comfort with one's identity as either male or female. It is an intellectual effort that has nothing to do with sexuality or experimentation with sexuality.

The second task is the *struggle to become comfortable with one's sexuality.* This does not mean struggling with the question of "how to make out at the drive in!" It is the much more important question: "Who am I as a sexual person and how do I get along with those to whom I am actually or potentially sexually attracted?" Before adolescence, children are far more casual with each other. With adolescence, those days are over. Simply to walk by someone that one could be sexually attracted to and say "Hi" without blushing, giggling, or throwing up can be a problem. To become a person capable of sexual and emotional intimacy—able to carry on all manner of social and eventually sexual activities with another person—does not come easily. It is fraught with insecurity and considerable self-consciousness. If you force yourself to remember your own adolescence, some memories of awkwardness and uncertainty come to the fore. Thus there is the adolescent who does not ask for a date because of the anticipated no. Being dateless is much more tolerable than hearing a no.

The third task is the *choice of an occupational identity.* It becomes important to find an answer to "What am I going to do (be)?" There are usually several false starts to this one. Think of the 5-year-old who wants to be a fireman. He probably never will be, but he gets a lot of mileage for awhile just thinking he is. It is not so different for adolescents. It is not helpful to pooh-pooh the first ideas they come up with. Nor is handing over an inheritance and saying "Go ahead" recommended. They need some time to work it out in their heads. A fair amount of indecision, plus some real "crazy" ideas, are to be expected.

The fourth task is the *struggle toward independence..* This is a real conflict. There is the internal push to break away from home and parents and, at the same time, the desire to remain comfortably cared for. The conflict shows up in rebellion, because there are not many ways to feel independent when living at home, being fed, checked on, prodded, and examined by parents. Rebellion of some type is so common to this period of life that an adolescent who does not rebel in some fashion should be suspect.

Rebellion. Rebellion can be seen in such things as manner of dress and appearance. It is usually the opposite of what the parents' generation accepts. Little ways of testing out parents crop up in being late from a date, buying something without permission, or arguing with parents over just about anything. The kids are aware of their dependence, and they don't like it. There is even some shame over being in such a position. It is important that parents recognize the rebellion and respond to it. In the era of "Be friends with your kids," some well-meaning parents accepted any behavior from their kids. For example, if the kids, for the sake of rebellion, brought home some grass to smoke, their parents might just light up, too. Often the kids will do whatever they can just to get their parents angry. They are so often reminded by others of how much they look or act like their father or mother. They don't want that. *Adolescents want to be themselves.* They do not want to be carbon copies of their parents, whom they probably don't like much at the moment. Going out and drinking with the gang, doing something weird to their hair that Mom and Dad will hate, not cleaning their rooms, or helping the neighbors but not their parents are all fairly common ways of testing out and attempting to assert independence.

Hi, Dear, why don't you invite your friends in, and we can all sit around and smoke some joints.

Destructive rebellion can occur when the parents either do not recognize the rebellion or do not respond to it. It can take many forms, such as running out of the house after an argument and driving off at 80 or 90 miles per hour, getting really drunk, running away, or, for girls, getting pregnant despite frequent warnings from their perhaps over-restrictive parents to avoid all sexual activities.

There are many roadblocks to completion of these four basic tasks. One results from a social paradox. Adolescents are physically ready for adult roles long before our society allows it. Studies of other societies and cultures point this out. In some societies adolescence doesn't cover a decade or more. They leave school at earlier ages to go to work or into apprenticeships for example. Our society dictates instead that people stay in an adolescent position for a frightfully long time: junior high school, senior high school, college, graduate school. Another social paradox comes from the mixed messages. One the one hand, it's "Be heterosexual, get a date, " "Get a job," "Be grown up." One the other, it's "Be back by 1 AM," "Save the money for college," "Don't argue with me." The confusion of "Grow up, but stay under my control" can introduce tensions. Another roadblock can be posed by alcohol and drug use. Of all groups, adolescents are those most likely to be involved with drugs other than alcohol. In considering adolescents, it is imperative to think broadly, in terms of substance use and abuse, or chemical dependency, not just in terms of alcohol and alcoholism.

This has been a very brief overview of adolescence. There are many excellent books on the subject should you want a more in-depth study. For our purposes here, it will suffice as a context in which to consider alcohol use.

2 out of 8 AdolescenTS had 5 or more drinks in the last two weeks

Alcohol use

Alcohol use is common in adolescence. By 8th grade, 67% of teenagers have tried alcohol. By the 12th grade, the percentage increases to 81%.

But ociFer, I couldn't be drunk. I only had 7 beers, AND Then I had 2 cups of coffee and a cold shower.

Despite widespread alcohol use, adolescents tend to be uninformed about the effects of alcohol as a drug. Short on facts, adolescents tend more than adults to rely on myths. For example, beer, the overwhelming favorite beverage, is thought to be less intoxicating than distilled spirits. One study showed that 42% thought 5 to 7 cans of beer could be drunk in 2 hours without risk of intoxication. Seventy percent believed cold showers could sober someone up, and 62% thought coffee would do it. Also, adolescents minimize the consequences of drinking. Only 8% thought their driving ability would be "much worse" under the influence. They also do not consider their being in an accident a real possibility, much less one that might result in serious injury or death.

Adolescents use alcohol in many different ways, some of which are a normal part of the whole process. The "try it on" thread runs throughout adolescence. Alcohol is just one of the things to be tried. With drinking being a massive part of adult society, it is natural that the adolescent struggling toward adulthood will try it. Drinking is also attractive for either rebellious or risk-taking behavior. In addition, it can also serve to anesthetize the pain of adolescents who are isolated or subject to abuse by family or peers.

Adolescent alcohol problems

Not unexpectedly, accompanying adolescent drinking there are also alcohol problems. To cite just a few of the statistics from the ever-growing pile:

- In the 13 to 17 year age group, it is estimated that there are 3 million problem drinkers and over 300,000 teenage alcoholics.
- Drinking is a significant problem for between 10% and 20% of adolescents.
- 28% of high school seniors admit to drinking 5 or more drinks in a row in the past 2 weeks.
- 97% of drug-abusing adolescents also use alcohol.
- Over the last 20 years, life expectancy has increased for all age groups *except* ages 15 to 24. The three leading causes of death in this age group are accidents, suicide, and homicide, all closely linked to alcohol and drug use.
- The *leading cause of death* between ages 16 and 24 is driving while impaired.
- Drivers age 16 to 24 years constitute 17% of the population; they are involved in 48% of fatal accidents.
- Daily, 14 adolescents, age 15 to 19 years, die and 360 are injured in alcohol-related traffic accidents.

One way to understand the high incidence of problems with substance abuse in adolescence is in terms of the adolescent developmental tasks cited earlier. The first task mentioned was the acceptance of one's biological role. For women the onset of their menstrual cycle provides clear *biological* evidence of their transition into adulthood. For males the transition may be more difficult. But for both in contemporary America the question of how to know you are an adult is often difficult. For many adolescents, drinking serves as

EVERY DAY 14 ADolescents DiE IN Alcohol-Related Traffic Accidents

a rite of passage. Not only is it an adult activity, it is also one way to be "one of the crowd." Drinking can provide entry to a group of peers. Even as an adult, one is often encouraged to drink and given messages that not to drink is to be antisocial. For adolescents with their intolerance of differences and their increased vulnerability to following along with peers' behavior, not drinking at a party where others are drinking may be even harder than for adults.

The second developmental task mentioned was the struggle to become comfortable with one's sexuality. This can be threatening to many adolescents. Alcohol can be used to avoid intimacy or to seek intimacy without responsibility. It can also help avoid dealing with concerns or confusion related to sexual orientation. "I wasn't myself last night, I was really plastered" can be said by either boys or girls to disavow what happened the night before. The same is true in the sexual realm, as a means of experimenting without taking responsibility. In our society, being drunk has long provided a "way out." Often people are not held accountable for actions that occur when they are drunk. Thus getting drunk can often help adolescents express these increasingly powerful impulses, without really taking direct responsibility for their behavior. This can include not taking proper precautions as the rising number of AIDS cases among this group and the growing number of teenage pregnancies can testify. Very risky behavior, indeed.

Part of the task of attaining independence is learning to set limits for themselves, to develop self-control. For some adolescents, this is more difficult than for others. It is particularly difficult about issues like drinking where societal messages and alcohol advertising suggest that "having more than one" is appropriate adult behavior. In the process of learning self-control, adolescents react negatively to adults setting limits. If parents are too aggressive in forbidding alcohol use, it may backfire. Further confusing matters is that adolescent development is characterized by changes in patterns of thinking. Before the age of 12 to 13 years, adolescents generally adhere to concrete rules for behavior. From ages 13 to 15 years, adolescents are likely to question the justification of set rules. They feel that conventions are arbitrary, so rules supporting them are invalid. By the age of 16, most of them begin to realize that some rules are necessary.

Another important task mentioned earlier is the development of a sense of identity. Part of the task of gaining an independent identity involves experimentation in all realms. Adolescents may use alcohol for help in experimenting with different roles and identities. Closely connected to this experimentation is risk taking. Some of this risk taking involves physical danger. Adolescents are said to have a "sense of invulnerability." Unfortunately, alcohol can further increase this sense of invulnerability and lead to risk taking with dangerous consequences. It is not surprising, as mentioned earlier, that accidents are the leading cause of death for adolescents and that alcohol use and abuse is heavily implicated in fatal accidents from all causes.

As these adolescent developmental tasks are accomplished, the number of problem drinkers decreases. But for a significant proportion of problem drinkers, these problems will persist and grow worse. For far too many, the problem drinking may end in death or disability.

Signs of alcohol/substance use problems. Often the temptation is to disregard adolescent alcohol or drug problems as "just a stage," or a normal feature of adolescence. The criteria for diagnosing alcohol abuse in adolescents are the same as those for adults. It involves a pattern of pathological use and impairments in major life areas. Common signs of a possible substance use problem are listed below. These signs are not exclusively linked to substance use. Thus, if an evaluation rules out substance use, further exploration is required to identify and address the behaviors of concern.

School activities
- unexplained drop in grades
- unexplained drop in school performance
- irregular school attendance

Health indicators
- accidents
- frequent "flu" episodes, chronic cough, chest pains, "allergy symptoms"
- feelings of loneliness or depression
- being unable to fight off common infections, fatigue, loss of energy
- short-term memory impairment
- more than "the normal" adolescent mood changes, irritability, anger

Family relationships
- decreased interest in school or family social activities, sports, and hobbies
- not bringing friends home
- not returning home after school
- unaccounted for personal time
- failure to provide specific answers to questions about activities
- unexplained disappearance of possessions in the home
- verbal (or physical) mistreatment of younger siblings

Relationships with friends
- dropping old friends
- new group of friends
- attending parties where parents or adults are not present
- strange phone calls

Personal issues
- increased money or poor justification of how money was spent
- change in personal priorities
- wearing "druggie" clothing or jewelry

- possession of "drug" materials
- desire to be secretive or isolated

Indicators of a significant problem would include any "covering up" or lying about drug and alcohol use or about activities, losing time from school because of alcohol or drug use, being hospitalized or arrested because of drinking or drug-related behavior or truancy, plus alcohol or drug use. Alcohol or drug use at school generally indicates heavy use. One should be particularly alert to these signs and symptoms in children of alcoholics, who have a genetic predisposition and a parent for whom alcohol is a loaded issue.

The progression of a substance use problem in adolescents is similar to the progression seen in adults and described in Chapter 6. Table 10-1 summarizes the key features.

General considerations in working with adolescents. In working with an adolescent, it is wise to avoid obvious authority symbols, such as white laboratory coats, framed diplomas dripping off the walls, and a remote clinical attitude. Adolescents are probably already having some degree of difficulty with authority figures anyway, and they don't need you added to that list. Being somewhat informal in dress and setting can remove one barrier. On the other hand, spiked hair, playing CDs, and sitting on a floor cushion sucking on a "roach" when they arrive won't go down very well either. They want you to know about those things, but not be into them; unless, of course, you really are (even then, leave the roach at home). An attempt to fake out the adolescent will fail. They are a hard group to fool, and they place a high premium on honesty. Respect this and honestly be

TABLE 10-1

Natural history of substance use problems: signs and symptoms of adolescent substance use

Stage	Pattern of use	School	Peers	Family	Self
Experimentation	Occasional	◄——————————————— Few effects ———————————————►			
Regular use					
(Seeking the mood swing)	Weekends Occasional weekdays	Grades may become erratic	Hanging around drug using crowd	Some increase in family conflict	Changes in dress; choice of music; may be increased mood swings
Abuse					
(Preoccupation with use)	Occasional weekdays, e.g., before or after school	Decreased school performance	Avoids straight friends	Verbal and physical fights	Depression, stealing, fabrication, and misperception of events
Dependence					
(Use to feel normal or as a requisite for functioning)	Daily, instead of usual activities	May drop out or be expelled	Alienation from original friends; antisocial behavior, sexual acting out	Increased shame and conflict	Guilt, remorse, depression, anger, paranoia, physical deterioration

Modified from Kinney J: Alcohol use and its medical consequences. In Alcohol use, abuse, and dependence, Timonium, Md, 1989, Milner-Fenwick.

yourself. This means asking for a translation of their vocabulary if you are not familiar with the lingo.

Empathy rather than sympathy is the goal. This is true of all therapeutic relationships. Sympathy is feeling like the other person. Empathy is knowing how the person feels but not feeling like he or she does at the moment. For instance, it is simply not helpful to be depressed along with the person.

In general, three types of therapy are done with adolescents. One involves *manipulation of the environment*. This can include arranging for the father to spend more time with his child, getting the kid who hates Shakespeare into a different school program, or organizing a temporary placement for the child whose parents are nonsupportive at the time. These can be very valuable interventions.

Standard insight therapy—psychologically or psychiatrically oriented therapy—is not often used. Not many adolescents are ready for, or even could benefit from, this kind of therapy. The ones who can benefit from it tend to be "bright," advantaged young people, who seem more capable and older than their peers or their chronological age would suggest.

The most commonly productive therapy is what could be termed a *relational approach*. This requires time for you to become well acquainted and for the adolescent to feel comfortable with you. The counselor is a neutral person, available to the adolescent in a very different way than are parents or peers.

The issue of confidentiality always comes up. It can be a mistake to guarantee that "nothing you say will ever leave this room." The therapist does have the responsibility for others as well as the adolescent client. Given blanket protection, what happens when the kid announces he plans to rob the local deli or another says she plans to drive the family car off the road at the first opportunity? A different approach was suggested by Dr. Hugh MacNamee. His practice was to tell whomever he saw that though most of what they said would be held in confidence, if they told him anything that scared him about what they might do, that would be harmful to themselves or others, he was going to blow the whistle. He made it clear he would not do so without telling them; nonetheless, he would do it. In his experience, adolescents accept this, maybe even with relief. It may help to know that someone else is going to exert some control, especially if they are none too sure about their own inner controls at the moment.

In a similar vein, Dr. MacNamee would suggest keeping the adolescent posted on any contacts you have with others about him or her. If a parent calls, start off the next session by informing the adolescent, "Hey, your Dad called me, and he wanted. . . ." If a letter needs to be written to a school, probation officer, or someone else, share what you are writing with the adolescent. The chances are fairly good his or her fantasy about what you might say is worse than anything you would actually say, no matter what the problem.

Because trust is such an issue with adolescents, it is important that you be willing to say *to* them what you would say *about* them.

Although the aforementioned is a good general approach to the issue of confidentiality, you may need to be aware of other complicating factors. In particular, we refer to the legal issues of a child's right to care versus parental rights to be informed. There may be circumstances in which an adolescent has a legal right to be seen and treated without parental knowledge or consent. In any case, the ground rules you are following must be clear to the adolescent client.

Alcohol/drug assessment. Once the issue of confidentiality has been cleared up, it is important to take a family history. Ask about alcohol or drug problems, prescription or nonprescription. Include the grandparents, uncles, aunts, brothers and sisters, cousins, as well as the parents. Other important parts of the history include asking the adolescent how he spends his time. Ask him to describe a typical day. Ask what he and his friends do Saturday night. Ask about his peer group, about their ages, activities, and drug and alcohol use. Ask how they are seen and described by other groups in the high school, and then ask about his use of drugs and alcohol. Ask about parental relationships. Ask about sleep, appetite, depression, and the possibility of physical or sexual abuse. Also be able to discuss issues of sexuality and sexual orientation. It is also important to determine the adolescent's risk for HIV infection.

The fact that adolescent alcohol abuse can go on for as long as 6 years without being diagnosed is a tribute to the ability of these adolescents to hide their problems, to the ability of parents to avoid recognizing problems in their children, to the tendency of health providers not to address substance abuse and other sensitive issues, and to the ability of school systems to ignore or expel problem children. It is not unusual for parents to be actively protecting, rescuing, and taking care of a substance-abusing adolescent without realizing that this supports and prolongs the abuse. They make good on forged checks. They hire lawyers or pay to have legal charges dropped. They go to bat for them at school or blame school authorities for the problems. In our experience, parents must stop protecting these children and seek help for them instead.

When asking about drug and alcohol use, begin by asking about the first time they were drunk, how much they drink now, how often, if they have ever tried to stop or cut down. Ask about blackouts, legal problems, and school problems. Finally, don't assume that an adolescent is providing a wholly accurate history about drug and alcohol use. Denial is a central characteristic of adolescent alcohol or drug abuse. It is important to get information from parents and teachers whenever you are concerned about adolescent alcohol or drug problems.

Getting adolescents into treatment. Although occasionally adolescents will spontaneously request treatment, more often they come to treatment under some duress. In working with them, it is important to make it clear that your task is to help them and that you are not an agent of their parents, the law, or the school system. At the same time, part of helping them may involve an intervention, which entails confrontation and, as was mentioned earlier, total confidentiality cannot be assured.

In dealing with adolescents, the importance of working with the family cannot be overemphasized. The parents need to deal with their child's alcohol/substance abuse. And they must consider their own behaviors, which may have protected, covered up, excused, or even in part created the problem. When it is clear that there is a significant problem and all efforts to involve the adolescent in treatment have failed, the parents may need to seek legal help. Most states allow for parents to request state assistance if they feel they cannot enforce safe limits for their child. Although this is a very drastic and difficult step to take, it can be important when alcohol-abusing adolescents are acting in ways that endanger their lives. Probation can also be a way of mandating treatment for adolescents, but again this only works if the parents can stop protecting the adolescent from the consequences of his behavior.

Adolescent alcohol/substance abuse treatment. Once it has been determined that an adolescent needs treatment and the adolescent has agreed to treatment, it is important to proceed in a careful way. Because medical and psychiatric complications frequently accompany adolescent substance abuse, a thorough medical and psychiatric evaluation should precede or be an early part of any treatment plan. Treatment options include out-patient, residential, or hospital-based care and can involve individual, group, and family counseling, plus self-help groups such as AA or NA (Narcotics Anonymous). Halfway houses may also be helpful for adolescents who are not ready to return home from a hospital-based program but who no longer need the structure of a hospital.

There are very good alcohol/drug treatment programs for adolescents. There are those, on the other hand, that might most kindly be described as "nontraditional" or those less concerned with therapeutics than with turning a profit. Don't forget the standard questions before referring an adolescent to any program. "Does the program work?" "Is the program drug free?" "Is there a strong family component?" "Is there a strong therapeutic component?" "Is there a strong educational component?" "Is the adolescent involved in treatment planning?" "Is there a peer component?" "Are there provisions for aftercare?" "What are the costs and risks of treatment, including both financial cost and time cost?" "What beliefs are instilled?" "What are the staff's credentials, including training, experience, licensure, and certification?" "Is there a full range of services, including pediatric, psychiatric, educational, psychological, and alcohol counselors?" "Is there involvement with AA?" "How does the program feel when you visit it?" "Is the program accredited?" "If so, by whom?"

When referring an adolescent for treatment, it is important to remember that alcoholism and drug addiction are chronic diseases. Treatment does not end with discharge. The conceptual model to use is not that of an acute illness like appendicitis, where the offending tissue can be surgically removed and the problem will never recur. It is rather a chronic illness like asthma or arthritis, where ongoing monitoring is always essential and whereas some cases are mild and require only outpatient treatment, others may require hospitalization.

Adolescents and AA. For the adolescent with an alcohol/substance problem, how might AA be of use? The first thought might be that the adolescent would never identify with a group of predominantly 35- to 55-year olds. In many areas, that stereotype of the AA group does not necessarily hold true; there are now in some locales what are called "young people's groups." There the average age is the low- to mid-20s. Even if there are no young people's groups in your vicinity, age need not be a barrier to an adolescent's affiliating with AA. On the contrary, several features of AA might attract and intrigue the adolescent. It is a group of adults who will definitely not preach at him. Furthermore, given the collective life experiences within AA, the members are not likely to be shocked, outraged, or, for that matter, impressed by any of the adolescent's behavior. The members will generally treat the adolescent as an adult, presumably capable of making responsible choices, although cognizant that to do so isn't easy for anyone. There is within AA a ready assortment of potential surrogate parents, aunts, uncles, and grandparents. The intergenerational contact, possibly not available elsewhere to the adolescent, can be a plus. Also, AA remains sufficiently "unacceptable" so as not to be automatically written off by the adolescent wary of traditional, staid, "establishment," and "out-of-it" adult groups. Because being alcoholic or a drug abuser is still a stigmatized condition, the parents may be more uncomfortable than their children about AA attendance for adolescents. The therapist may need to help parents with this. In making a referral, the same guidelines outlined in the section on AA would apply. The adolescent is full of surprises, and his willingness to attend AA may well be another.

Adolescents and AIDs. A growing concern is the rapid increase of AIDS among young adults. This inevitably means that HIV was contracted during adolescence. Any discussion of adolescents and AIDS requires thinking about the role of the other "A"—alcohol. Alcohol is definitely involved in this equation for two reasons. First, there's the well known disinhibiting effect of alcohol and the impaired judgment that is a part of that.

when I'm sober I use safe sex. When I'm drunk, everything seems safe.

Sexual encounters are more likely when drinking. It is less likely that condoms will be used, increasing the risk of a variety of sexually transmitted diseases in addition to HIV. Sexual encounters are also more likely to be "casual," involving partners with little history and no on-going relationship. With the advent of AIDS the important message to be conveyed is that there is no longer, if there ever was, such a thing as "casual" sex. The stakes are higher and the costs are no longer simply psychological wounds.

The second important factor which has considerable significance in thinking about adolescents, alcohol and AIDS goes beyond simply altered judgment. It appears that one of the effects of alcohol, in anyone, not just in those who are alcohol dependent or who drink heavily, is to interfere temporarily with the immune system. Possibly for a day or two alcohol has seemingly "turned down the volume." Thus, the body's usually available means of fighting off infections and viruses are not up to par. Thus, this allows infections to gain a foothold which would otherwise not have happened.

Adolescent treatment and prevention programs need also to be involved in AIDS education. Some treatment programs, beyond including an educational component also discuss the issue of HIV testing; there are several who have adopted this as a routine part of their procedures. Beyond the fact that it really *does* matter if one is or is not HIV positive, these activities also serve to reinforce the point that HIV/AIDS is a real issue. It isn't something that can't or wouldn't touch an adolescent's life. These activities emphasize that it is the choices that adolescents make or don't make that have an impact on them.

Prevention

One important task for anyone working with adolescents is to be aware of the potential problems that virtually every adolescent will encounter with respect to alcohol and drugs. Even if adolescents are not currently into drugs or alcohol, anticipatory discussion can be very helpful. This means speaking with them as to how they can handle the situation when it inevitably does arise. Contacts with adolescents, for whatever reason, can be used. This might mean the school counselor who meets with the adolescent to discuss next year's course offerings. Or it may be the occasion of the mandatory physical examination required before participation in high school athletics. For the adolescent who is having a problem of some kind, an alcohol/drug history is imperative.

In many communities, there are also efforts underway through parent groups and groups of adolescents to support the development of healthy peer values and norms about alcohol/drug use. It is almost impossible to speak of adolescent alcohol or other drug use without hearing the phrase "peer pressure." Friends do have considerable influence. However, parents and adults do as well. The expectations of adults in the community has a big impact.

In thinking about prevention, one is not only trying to prevent use and abuse. The other goal is to prepare adolescents to deal with possible alcohol or other drug use emergencies. In fact, it may well fall to the kid who isn't drinking to be the one to do what needs to be done in such circumstances. This doesn't just mean figuring out alternative transportation. It is also important that they know how to respond to possible overdose, e.g., knowing the dangers of letting a really drunk kid "just sleep it off." Adolescents need to learn that when they are in the presence of drinking, they do need to be their "brother's —and sister's— keeper."

THE ELDERLY

Dishonor not the old: we shall all be numbered among them.

APOCRYPHA: BENSIRA 8:6

On one of the earliest television talk shows—that only the elderly will remember—Art Linkletter, the host, was interviewing children. The topics as you will see were a bit different then! The children came up with the following answers to a question he posed: "You can't play with toys anymore . . . the government pays for everything . . . you don't go to work . . . you wrinkle and shrink." The question was "What does it mean to grow old?" These responses contain many of the stereotypes our society attributes to the elderly. They also show that this negative picture develops from a very early age. There is a stigma about growing old. The notion is that for the elderly there is no play or fun, no money, no usefulness, and no attractiveness.

In considering the elderly, it is important to recognize that we all really are talking about ourselves. It is inevitable: we will all age; we will all become elderly. A participant at a geriatric conference reported being asked by a friend, "Give me the inside scoop, what can I do to keep from getting older?" The response the person received was simple: "Die now!" There is no other way to avoid aging. So, for those not yet elderly, in thinking about the older person, imagine yourself years in the future, because many of the circumstances will probably be the same.

It is now estimated that over 32 million persons are over age 65; this represents a larger percentage of the population than ever before. This is the group arbitrarily defined as the elderly or aged. Each day, 3000 people die and 4000 people reach their sixty-fifth birthdays, so there is a net gain of 1000 in the elderly population. The proportion of the population age 65 and over is the fastest growing segment of the population. Between 1900 and 1975, the proportion of the elderly increased seven-fold, while the total population hadn't quite tripled. Consequently, the problems of the elderly, including alcoholism, are become a growing concern for our society.

Coping styles

Despite the inevitability of aging and physical problems arising as the years pass, there is an important thing to keep in mind. It has been said many times and in many different ways that you are as young as you want to be. This is only possible, however, if a person has some strengths going for him. The best predictor of the future, specifically how someone will handle growing old, is how the individual has handled the previous years. Individuals who have demonstrated flexibility as they have gone through life will adapt best to the inevitable stresses that come with getting older. These are the people who will be able to feel young, regardless of the number of birthdays they have celebrated.

Interestingly, as people get older, they become less similar and more individual. The only thing that remains alike for this group is the problems they face. There is a reason for this. In going through life, people rely most heavily on the coping styles that seem to have served them well previously. With years and years of living, gradually individuals narrow down their responses. What looks, at first glance, like an egocentricity or eccentricity of old age is more likely a life-long behavior that has become one of the person's exclusive methods for dealing with stress. An example illustrating this point arose in the case of an elderly surgical patient for whom psychiatric consultation was requested. This man had a constant smile. In response to any question or statement by the nurse or doctors, he smiled, which was often felt to be wholly inappropriate. The treatment staff requested help in comprehending the patient's behavior. In the process of the psychiatric consultation, it became quite understandable. Friends, neighbors, and family of the man consistently described him as "good ole Joe, who always had a friendly word and a smile for everyone, the nicest man you'd ever want to meet." Now under the most fearful of situations, with many cognitive processes depleted, he was instinctively using his faithful, basic coping style. Very similarly, the person who goes through life with a pessimistic streak may become angry and sad in old age. People who have been fearful under stress may be timid and withdrawn in old age. On the other hand, people who have been very organized and always reliant on a definite schedule may try to handle everything by making lists in old age. What is true in each case is that the person has settled into a style that was present and successful in earlier life.

Major stresses

In working with the elderly, to understand what is evolving in an individual case, it is imperative for helping professionals to consider every possible piece of information. Integration of data from the social, medical, and emotional realm is essential for understanding what makes the elderly person tick to make an intelligent treatment plan. Four areas of stress should be considered in dealing with the elderly: social, psychological, biological or physical, and, unfortunately, iatrogenic—these are stresses caused by the helping professions as they serve (or inadequately serve) the elderly.

Social stresses. Social stresses can be summarized under the phenomenon of the national addiction to youth. Television commercials

highlight all types of products that can be used to disguise the process of aging. There is everything from hair colorings to dish detergents, which if used will make a mother's hands indistinguishable from her daughter's. Look around you. Who is being hired and who is being retired? Aging is equated with obsolescence and worthlessness. People who have been vital, contributing members of an organization suddenly find themselves with the title "honorary." It is often not an honor at all! It means these people have become figureheads; they have been replaced. The real work has been taken over by someone else—someone younger.

Next, let us consider social stresses resulting from the biases of the helping professions. Only two decades ago the National Institute of Mental Health spent a mere 1.1% of its budget for research on problems of the elderly. Only 1% of its budget for services went to provide care for the elderly. This is now changing, but it gives a graphic picture of the relative importance placed on this group of people in the recent past. The real issue is one of *attitude*. if one examines the dynamics behind this attitude, then one can see why there has been "disinterest" and "avoidance." Generally, the medical profession and other helping people, including family and friends, are overwhelmed by the multiplicity, chronicity, and confusing nature of the disorders of aging. Caregivers often feel helpless in dealing with the elderly and harbor self-doubts about whether they can contribute in a satisfactory manner that is also personally gratifying. To put it another way, most of us like to see results, to see things happen, to believe there is a "before" and "after" picture, in which the difference is clear. Also, it is important to feel that the part we have played, however big or small, has made a difference.

Helpers like it when someone puts out her hand and says "thank you." The elderly often say, "Don't bug me. I don't want help." If you consider who it is that voluntarily comes into most clinical agencies, it is not the elderly. Those elderly who do come have usually been coerced. Helpers do not like complainers. What do the elderly say? "This hurts; that hurts . . . you're not nice enough . . . you don't come soon enough . . . my old doctor was much better . . . do this, do that." Helpers like patients who receive maximum cures in the minimum of time. This certainly is not the elderly. There are more visits, more problems, more time. Helpers like patients who get well. How many of the elderly are cured? How can you take away their diabetes, their arthritis, the pain from the memory of a lost spouse? Helpers like patients who take their advice. With the elderly, you suggest A and they'll often do B.

These interactional dynamics are understandable but only aggravate the problem. They may rub the helper's instincts the wrong way. The result is that many potential caregivers decide they do not like working with the elderly, and it shows. Very few clinicians volunteer to take on elderly clients. If an elderly client comes into a helping agency, the chances are good that the person who sees the client may soon decide to transfer the case to someone more "appropriate" or refer the client to another agency.

Another factor that gets in the way of their receiving adequate care from helping people is that they *may resent the helper's youth, just as the helper fears their elderliness*. Also, the elderly generally dislike the dependent status that goes along with being a client or patient. It is the opposite of what they want, which is to be independent and secure and feel a sense of worth. Being in treatment implies that something is wrong with them. It also means that someone else is partially in charge and telling them how to run their lives.

Psychological stresses. The greatest psychological stress the elderly must face is *loss*. In the geriatric population losses are steady, predictable, and often come in bunches. And even if they do not, they are still numerous. What are the specific losses?

There is the loss that comes from the *illnesses* and *deaths* of family and friends. The older you get, statistically the more likely that those about you will begin to falter. So there are the obvious losses of supports and companionship. Not necessarily as obvious is that the deaths of others also lead to questioning about loss of self, anticipation of one's own death. This may sometimes be the source of anxiety attacks among the elderly.

There is the loss that comes from the geographical *separations of family*. This begins earlier in life, as children go to school and later leave home for college or the service and then eventually marry. For the elderly, this may be especially difficult, because 50% of all grandparents do not have grandchildren living close by. As new generations are being born, they are not accessible to the older generation whose lives are coming to a close.

There is the loss of *money* through earned income. Whether income is supplemented through pensions, social security, or savings, the elderly usually do not have as much money as they did earlier in their lives. Dollars do not only represent buying power; they also have symbolic values. Money represents power, stature, value, and independence. Lack of money has obvious implications in vital areas of self-esteem.

There are the losses that accompany *retirement:* loss of status, gratification, and often most important, identity. With retirement, you lose who you have been. This refers not only to retirement from a job; it includes retirement from anything—from being a mother, or a grandmother, or from just being a person who is capable of walking around the block. Often accompanying retirement is a loss of privacy. For married couples, retirement may mean more togetherness than they have had for years. Both spouses will have to change routines and habits and be forced to accommodate the presence of the other. The expectations may also be tremendous. Retirement, in most people's fantasies, is thought to usher in the "golden years" and provide the opportunity to do the things that have been put off. There may well be a letdown.

First I lost my hair. Then I lost my wife. My children have all moved away. My best friends have died, my vision is going, my hearing is going, and now you want me to give up alcohol. It's all I've got left.

Doc, I'm 86, and I don't care if whiskey kills me.

There is also the loss of *body functions and skills,* which may include a loss of attractiveness. Older people may develop body odors. They lose their teeth. They are more prone to infection. For women, the skin may become dry, including the skin of the vagina, which can lead to vaginal discharges and dyspareunia (painful intercourse). For men, there is general loss of muscle tone. Everything begins to stick out where it shouldn't. As physical problems arise, this may lead to loss of skills. The carpenter with arthritis or the tremors of Parkinson's disease will be unable to do the things that were formerly possible and rewarding.

The elderly may try to handle stress in a number of ways. One is the widely used defense of *denial.* In response to an observation that a client's hand is more swollen, he may well say, "Oh no, it's no different than it's always been." If a close friend is in the hospital and very seriously ill, she may dismiss the seriousness and claim it is "Just another of her spells, she'll be out, perky as ever, in a day or two."

Another common way of handling loss is by *somatization.* This means bringing the emotional content out in the open, but "saying" it in terms of it being the body that hurts. This is why so many of the elderly are labeled hypochrondriacal. When he says his knee hurts and he really cannot get up that day, what he also may be saying is that he hurts inside, emotionally. Because he may not get attention for emotional pains, having something wrong physically or "mechanically" is socially more acceptable.

Another way of handling loss is *restricting affect.* Instead of saying it does not exist, as with denial, there is a withdrawing. They become less involved, so they do not hear about the bad things happening. By being less a part of the world, they are less vulnerable.

Unfortunately, all these defenses boomerang and work against the elderly. How are love, affection, and concern expressed? Through words, behavior, and many nonverbal cues—a smile, a nod, a touch. After so many years of living, the elderly certainly know the signs of affection and caring as well as those of distancing and detachment. By withdrawing when they are fearful, they may well see others reciprocally withdrawing; the elderly may then be left without any source of affection, interest, or caring. This in turn they read as dislike, and they may feel their initial withdrawing was justified. Therefore one of the prime treatment techniques with the elderly is to reach out to them, literally. Smile, touch them, sit close to them. Attempt to reach through the barrier they may have erected with the "protective" psychological defenses mentioned.

The elderly frequently are hurt by what helping people instinctively say when reaching out to the aged. Statements like "you're lucky to be alive . . . quit worrying about things . . . grow old gracefully" are often misinterpreted by the elderly as someone telling them to ignore their losses, or that the person making such statements does not want to get close to them. The elderly's response is that they do not want to grow old gracefully, they do not want to be "easy to manage," they want to go out with a bang, leave a mark—they want to be individuals to the last day.

How about sex and the elderly? The most prevalent myth is that the elderly have no interest in sex. Physiologically, aging itself need not greatly affect sexual functioning. With advancing years, it takes a little longer to achieve an erection, a little more time to the point of ejaculation, orgasm is a little less intense, and a little more time is required before orgasms can be reexperienced. However, if the elderly are physically healthy, there is no reason why they should not be sexually active. The biggest factors influencing sexual activity in the elderly are the availability of a partner and social pressures. Among the elderly, when a partner dies, the survivor is often not encouraged to date or remarry. What is considered virility at age 25 is seen as lechery after age 65. Even when both partners are alive, if they are living in an institution or in the home of children, sexual activity may well be frowned upon or "not allowed."

Another loss is that of *sensation*. With aging, the senses become less acute. What this means is that the elderly are then deprived of accurate cues from their environment. This may be a big factor in the development of suspiciousness in older persons. Any paranoid elderly person should have hearing and vision evaluated. The most powerful loss, the loss no elderly person is prepared to understand or accept, is the loss of thinking ability. This loss may occur imperceptibly over time. It comes from the loss of cortical brain function. Suddenly a person who has been an accountant or a schoolteacher, for example, is adding 2+2, and it doesn't equal 4 every time. This is embarrassing and scary. Although they may be able to stand losing other things, to "lose one's mind" is the ultimate indignity.

The result of all or any of these losses is that self-respect, integrity, dignity, and self-esteem are threatened. The implication can be that usefulness is questioned and life is ebbing away. The feeling may well be that "my work is over."

Biological stresses. Of the elderly, only 5% are institutionalized in nursing homes, convalescent centers, or similar facilities. However, 45% of the elderly have some serious physical disability, such as heart disease, diabetes, lung disease, or arthritis. About 25% also have a significant functional psychological problem, with depression being the most prevalent. Understandably, as life expectancy increases and we live longer, there is more vulnerability to the natural course of disease. For this part of the population, receiving medical care and paying medical bills can mean additional big problems. The elderly have twice as many visits to a physician, their average hospital stay is three and a half times longer than for persons under age 65, and the hospital stay costs five times more than for the under-65 age group.

Depressive illness is very prevalent among the elderly. There may well be a physiological basis for this. The levels of neurochemicals (serotonin, monoamine oxidase, and norepinephrine) thought to be associated with depression change in the brain as people get older. These depressions, then, are not necessarily tied solely to situational events. However, because so many things are likely to be going on in the surrounding environment for the elderly, it is too easy to forget the potential benefits of judiciously prescribed antidepressants. Malnourishment, for instance, is all too common in the elderly. Nutritional deficiency can cause several syndromes that may look like depressions. Many physical ailments, such as thyroid dysfunctions, and illnesses caused by the disease processes themselves, manifest themselves as depression.

Depression in the elderly may not be the same as depression in younger persons, with tearfulness, inability to sleep, or loss of appetite. Some of the tips for recognizing depression in the elderly are an increased sensitivity to pain, refusing to get out of bed when physical problems don't require bed rest, poor concentration, a marked narrowing of coping style, and an upsurge of physical complaints. Often, the poor concentration leads to absent-mindedness and inattentiveness, which are misdiagnosed as defective memory and ultimately as "senility," while the depression goes unrecognized and untreated. Senility is really a useless clinical term. The proper term should be *dementia,* which means irreversible cognitive impairment. However, all cognitive impairment should be considered reversible (delirium) until proven otherwise. It should also be remembered that alcohol abuse, as well as sometimes creating problems itself, can, in patients with dementia, make the confusion worse. The elderly deserve an aggressive search for potentially treatable, reversible causes of organic brain syndromes by qualified medical personnel.

Suicide among the elderly is a very big problem. Of those who commit suicide, 25% are over age 65. The rate of suicide for those over 65 is 5 times that of the general population. After age 75, the rate is 8 times higher. In working with the elderly, a suicide evaluation should not be neglected because so many depressions are masked.

Alcoholism is also a big problem for the elderly. Dr. Robert Butler, formerly of the National Institute of Aging, estimates that 20% of the elderly have a significant alcohol problem. These problems are also ignored for many of the same reasons that sex in the elderly is dismissed. "That nice old lady drinks too much (or is interested in sex)!" "Never!" Some of the elderly have had a long history of alcohol use and abuse; they may have been alcoholics for a good long time, but with adequate medical care have somehow lived to old age. However, with the overall deterioration of physical functioning, the alcohol use may begin to take a heavier toll and become an increasingly difficult problem. Also, among the elderly are persons who do not have a prior history of alcohol abuse; their alcoholism is termed as *late onset.* The stresses of aging may have been too great or come too fast and at the wrong time. Or their bodies simply can't cope with drinking that in earlier years presented no problems.

A variety of changes associated with aging make the elderly more vulnerable to the acute effects of alcohol. Body water content declines and the body fat content increases with age. Between the ages of 20 and 70, there is 10% decrease in lean body mass. With a given amount of alcohol, these combined reductions lead to a higher blood alcohol level among the elderly. Furthermore, with aging there is diminished blood flow through the liver. This means that while the rate of metabolism is unaltered the alcohol is cleared more slowly. For any given amount, the peak blood alcohol level will be 20% higher for a 60 year old than a 20 year old. At age 90, the peak blood alcohol level is 50% higher. The elderly who may have some existing impairment in cognitive functioning have even greater sensitivity to alcohol. In addition to the increased acute effects of alcohol, a variety of other physical changes make the elderly more vulnerable to the medical consequences of use. By age 75, there is a 50% reduction in lung capacity; the kidneys work at only 45% of their earlier capacity, and heart function is reduced by 35%.

Iatrogenic stresses. Unfortunately, the medical problems of the elderly may be aggravated by the medical profession's insensitivities to the psychological and basic physiological changes in the elderly. All too often, medication is overprescribed in an attempt to keep behavior controlled rather than diagnosed. Too few clinicians take into account the dramatically altered way the elderly metabolize medications, which means that fewer medicines in combination and lowered doses of drugs are frequently required. There is also a tendency by everyone concerned to ignore the fact that alcohol, too, is a toxic drug. The combination of alcohol with other medications in light of the altered metabolism for both can create serious problems. Rarely is there any thought of whether the elderly patient can afford the medicine prescribed. Also the elderly person's ability to comply with directions for taking medications is overestimated.

A poignant example of the above was the case of an elderly woman who was discharged from the hospital with a number of medications. She had been admitted with severe congestive heart failure but had responded well to chemical treatment of hypertension and fluid retention. Within 2 weeks of her return home, her condition began to deteriorate, which was a source of dismay and consternation to her physicians. She was thought surely to be purposefully causing her ailments, and a psychiatrist, who was asked to consult on the case, decided to make a home visit. The woman knew which medications to take, when, and for what conditions. However, there was one problem. As she handed the bottle of capsules to the psychiatrist, with her crippled arthritic fingers, the "diagnosis" became obvious: the child-proof cap! She had been unable to open the bottles and therefore unable to take the medicine. This is a vivid

In the mornings I take one red pill, two blue pills, and a yellow pill with a green stripe.

At noon I take two red pills, one blue pill, and a little white capsule.

With dinner I take a big red capsule and two more blue pills.

Just before I go to bed I take three of the pink pills with a glass of cold water, and then I repeat these instructions four times, so I'll remember them in the morning.

reminder of the need to consider all the available information in assessing the problems of the elderly.

Alcohol and other drug problems

The elderly constitute the age group with the lowest rate of alcohol use. The majority of the elderly, 56% of men and 77% or women, are described as abstainers. Or they drink so infrequently that they have not had a drink in the past year. Among the elderly, there is less lifetime use, more have always been nondrinkers. Remember, the elderly grew up in a period in which drinking was less socially acceptable. Beyond those who have been life-long tee-totalers, there are also those who were drinkers but reduced their alcohol use as they get older. There is also the sad reality that those who may have been heavy drinkers in earlier life did not survive to old age, which would further lower the percentage of the elderly who report alcohol use. Finally, those with a history of long-term heavy drinking earlier in life are more likely to be institutionalized. Thus, they are not included in surveys. It is estimated that 20% of nursing home residents are have a past history of problem drinking.

The subgroup of the total elderly population with the highest risk for alcoholism is widowers over the age 65. Elderly widows do not have the same risk, with one exception—widows whose deceased husbands had been alcohol dependent and had been untreated. Alcohol problems emerged in these women as a response to pathological grief, which was the legacy of the alcoholic marriage.

Other drug use also represents a real problem for the elderly. Which group has the highest levels of deaths from drug interactions? It may come as a surprise, but it is not adolescents but the elderly. Of drug related deaths, 51% of are among the elderly, even though they are only 17% of the population. In large part, this is due to the physiological changes that accompany aging and affect drug metabolism. The risk of an adverse drug reaction in those 50 to 59 years old is 33% greater than for those in their forties. Above age 60 there is a further twofold to threefold increase. Diagnosis of adverse drug reactions is hampered because these drug reactions can resemble normal changes that often accompany the aging process. In addition to deaths, drug interactions are associated with other major medical problems, many of which require hospitalization. A large number of falls among the elderly are due to drug effects. Serious mental impairments, e.g., confusion, is a common drug-induced problem. Here too alcohol can be a part of the picture. Of the 10 most widely prescribed drugs, all can interact with alcohol. The same is true of half of the top 100 prescription drugs.

For the elderly, problems of alcohol cannot be considered apart from the problems associated with the use of medically prescribed and self-prescribed, over-the-counter medications or other home remedies. Concurrent use of drugs, even 10 or more hours apart,

My doctor said the combination of alcohol and my medicine could be dangerous, so I take my medicine during the week, and drink on the weekends.

can significantly change a drug's actions because of the changes in toxic effects or changes in absorption or metabolism. Adverse drug reactions are more common among the elderly, not only due to the effects of aging, but because they use significantly more drugs than the younger people, due mainly to the presence of multiple chronic illnesses.

Not uncommonly, the elderly are under the care of more than one physician, none of whom may be fully informed about the patient's drug regimen. Over-the-counter medications are also a big source of trouble for the elderly. For everyone, these are the usual, first responses in the event of an illness or a medical problem. Self-prescribed preparations are used much more extensively than pre-scription medications. The average American household has 17 different over-the-counter products. Among the elderly, use of such remedies is very widespread. These preparations are often used without their physician's knowledge. In response to the question of how they handle everyday health problems, 35% do not treat the problem, they simply ignore it. Another 35% report using an over-the-counter medication; 15% use prescription medications that they already have available in the home. There are 11% who use some other home remedy. Only 13% contact their doctor or dentist. (Dental problems are another significant health-care problem for the elderly.)

If the elderly take any action in response to a health-care prob-lem the odds are 2 to 1 that they will use an over-the-counter prepa-ration. They take seven times more over-the-counter drugs than any other age group. Having grown up in a generation with Carter's lit-tle liver pills, Doan's kidney pills, and the "spring tonic," they are accustomed to seeking out such preparations. For economic rea-sons, the elderly are less likely to have a regular family doctor. This provides an impetus to prescribe for themselves. With all of the chronic conditions that accompany aging there is a need to find preparations to ease discomfort.

It has been estimated that one third of all the elderly's expendi-tures for medications are for over-the-counter products. Daily, 40% to 60% of the elderly take some type of over-the-counter drug. Of those who use over-the-counter drugs daily, 80% are believed to simultaneously be using prescribed drugs, alcohol, or both. Virtually all the elderly use over-the-counter medications at some point. Some may often use six or more. One study of healthy elderly peo-ple identified 54% as regularly using over-the-counter drugs. Fifty percent of that group reported that they typically used analgesics, laxatives, or antacids between 4 to 6 times per week.

The number of over-the-counter preparations is growing. Furthermore, more potent medications that were previously dis-pensed as controlled substances have been reclassified, e.g., ibupro-fen, and thus are available for self-treatment. In addition an issue of growing importance is that health professionals are not the major sources of information about over-the-counter preparations. Among the elderly, advertising was identified as the primary source of information by 23% of those surveyed. Friends, relatives, and neighbors constitute the next largest group, accounting for 20%. The label on the product itself was noted by 13% as the source of information. Pharmacists were consulted as the source of information for 20%, and physicians were consulted by only 14%.

With more drugs being used, including alcohol, there is greater potential for adverse interactions. A study of hospitalized patients found that all patients taking more than eight drugs had a least one interacting pair of drugs in the therapeutic regimen. A setting in which drug mismanagement and over-medication can easily occur is in retirement and nursing homes.

Natural history. Alcohol problems make their initial appearance at different points in life. Some of the elderly have had a long history of alcohol use and abuse; they may have been alcoholics for a long time. Nonetheless, with adequate medical care, they have somehow lived to old age. However, with the overall deterioration of physical functioning, the alcohol use may begin to take a heavier toll and become an increasingly difficult problem. There may be those without a prior history of alcohol abuse. For them the stresses of aging may have been too great or come too fast and at the wrong time. They turned to alcohol as a coping mechanism. Reflecting these two different patterns, alcoholism among the elderly is commonly described either as early onset or late onset. Researchers have adopted different age cut-off points to distinguish these two varieties, cut-off points that fall anywhere between ages 40 to 60 years. Despite the differences in distinguishing between the two varieties, there is general agreement that of the elderly with alcohol dependence, 50% began drinking heavily before age 40; and for two thirds, heavy drinking appears before age 60. Thus the ratio of early onset to late onset is 2:1.

In terms of etiology, late-onset alcohol dependence is attributed to two possible factors. Problems from alcohol use may emerge in later life, without any changes in alcohol consumption nor in the face of any particular life stresses. Because of the normal aging process, for some what had previously been a non-problematic drinking pattern has now become too much. In addition, the elderly are subject to many social stresses. It is hypothesized this may lead to an increase in drinking. These include retirement, loss of a spouse, grief responses, economic hardships, social isolation, and changes in living situations.

The view that changing life circumstances may provoke alcohol problems in the elderly is largely speculative. Little is known about the relationship of alcohol use to the stresses that accompany life changes. The mushrooming of retirement communities has provided an interesting opportunity to examine some of these questions. It appears that at least in these settings, which offer their residents a variety of leisure activities such as golf, swimming, crafts classes, and discussion groups, social isolation is not tied to higher levels of alcohol use. To the contrary, the heaviest drinkers, defined as drinking at least two or more drinks per day, who constituted 20% of those studied, were also those who were socially more active. Since entering the community, one third of the individuals noted a change in drinking patterns. Of this one third, three fourths reduced their alcohol use. But that leaves one fourth who reported that their drinking had increased. One of the questions this raises is whether social activity in retirement communities may be tied to alcohol use and may facilitate or even promote heavier drinking by some individuals. At any age, alcohol may be used to cope with major life stresses. However, for the elderly, these stresses are predictable and more numerous. Furthermore, because of greater biological vulnerabilities, even modest alcohol use is less likely to serve as a non-problematic response, even in the short-term.

Treatment

For the clinician, the major reason to be aware of differences between early and late onset alcoholism is in relation to screening. For those with early onset alcoholism, the odds are greater that some of the usual social indicators of alcoholism can be elicited via past medical and social history. There is a greater probability of prior alcohol treatment. One treatment program found that slightly over one third of early onset patients had prior treatment. Even among those with late onset alcohol dependence, 17% had some prior treatment. For those with a past history of an identified alcohol problem, the danger is in misinterpreting an apparent reduction of intake in later life as a resolution of the past problem. It is always important to remember that few persons who had alcoholism treatment represent inaccurate diagnoses. Of those with a significant alcohol problem, the number who return to non-problematic social drinking is small. The odds of encountering such an individual in practice are also small. Thus any drinking by someone with a history of alcohol treatment should be of concern.

Alcohol problems among the elderly often have nonspecific presentations. This means that they might be symptoms of a variety of conditions. Many of the negative consequences that can indicate a potential alcohol and/or drug use problem among younger persons are not present among the elderly, such as job difficulties or family and legal problems. Alcohol-related medical consequences in a group with numerous physical ailments are not a specific indicator. Malnutrition, falls, other accidents, incontinence, mood swings, depression, confusion, less attention to self-care, and unexpected reaction to a prescribed medication, might indicate the presence of an alcohol problem. In terms of drinking patterns, daily drinking is more common than binge drinking for those with alcohol problems.

Whatever the variety of alcohol dependence present, intervention is important. All too often we are likely to dismiss the elderly with "What do they have to live for anyway . . . They have been drinking all these years; they'll never stop now . . . I don't want to be the one who asks them to give up the bottle." The *quality* of any amount of life left to any of us should be the paramount concern. We would not hesitate to assume that a 35-year-old man ought to get treated for his problem even though he could easily be killed in an auto accident next year. The elderly deserve just as much, if not more, consideration.

Screening. An alcohol and drug use history is imperative with elderly people. Screening among the elderly should try to identify alcohol dependence and alcohol use that may be medically hazardous, especially alcohol-drug and drug-drug interactions. The MAST, used to screen for alcohol dependence, is suitable for use with the elderly. However, the MAST will not identify medically hazardous drinking. This will need to be determined individually based on quantity and frequency of use in the context of the patient's medical status. Keep in mind that problems related to alcohol use are likely to occur with lower levels of consumption. "Modest" alcohol use may be implicated in both alcohol dependence and hazardous drinking. Although quantity and frequency may identify hazardous drinking, they do not identify alcohol dependence, which is a function of the patient's relationship with alcohol.

A set of routine suggested questions that address these significant issues include the following:

- Do you drink alcoholic beverages? How much and how often?
- Are you taking medication? How much and how often?
- What do you keep in your medicine cabinet?
- What typically happens when you have a drink?
- In what situations do you drink?

Obstacles to identification and intervention. As noted, there are many factors, individually or in combination, that can lead to a failure to recognize alcohol problems. One is the nature of the presentation marked by nonspecific features, described above, that differs from that of alcohol problems in younger people. Another is the tendency to attribute all problems to aging and presume some chronic process is at work that is not amenable to intervention. Another problem is that for the elderly health-care personnel and other caretakers may try to control behavior rather than diagnose its cause. Too often problems are assumed to be inevitable. The elderly, just like those who are younger, are also likely to be protected by family, friends, or helping people. Others often fail to see, or ignore what they suspect, or justify not intervening, because no one wants to take away "someone's last pleasure."

Although overlooking an apparent problem of alcohol use is not unique to situations involving the elderly, it may differ from what occurs in younger people in one important respect. Those persons closest to the elderly may actively facilitate the continuation of drinking. For example, a neighbor or housekeeper may ensure access to alcohol by purchasing it for the homebound person and thereby circumvent and sabotage others' efforts to intervene.

Detoxification and treatment. Detoxification protocols need to be adjusted in managing withdrawal. Generally, detoxification is better managed in a hospital than on an out-patient basis because of the client's medical condition. Although the general strategy is similar for managing withdrawal in younger patients, there are several special concerns. Routine use of benzodiazepines is contraindicated, because it might provoke confusion. It is generally recommended that their use be delayed and prescribed in response to specific signs and symptoms of withdrawal. Drugs with a short half-life are preferable to longer acting agents. Dosages can often be reduced by one half to two thirds.

The use of Antabuse (disulfiram) has been suggested by some as potentially useful. Careful consideration needs to be given to the risks and potential benefits. Among the elderly, the risks may be considerable. Physically they are more frail. Their metabolic ability to handle disulfiram is a factor. They may be less able to comply with the restrictions because of cognitive impairments. Their greater use of over-the counter preparations increases the probability of inadvertent drug reactions. A disulfiram reaction that might be uncomfortable for someone younger may represent a medical crisis and have a lethal outcome for someone who is elderly.

The elderly need the same type of rehabilitation services as younger persons—education, counseling, and involvement in self-help groups. Treatment programs typically incorporate the elderly in their general programs. Generally, the prognosis is as good for the elderly as it is for younger persons. Research in the 1980s showed that the elderly had comparable treatment outcomes to younger patients; this was interpreted as refuting the need for specially focused programs for older persons. However, more recent research has demonstrated that programs tailored to the elderly enhance outcome by reducing treatment drop-out, by increasing rates of aftercare, and by dealing with relapses that occurred, and therefore not losing these patients to treatment. If the elderly are incorporated into a general treatment program, in addition to the program's usual services, the elderly need more thorough medical evaluations and often require more extensive social services to ensure adequate and coordinated aftercare.

For too many of us, the issue of specialized versus standard programs is likely to be nothing more than an academic interest. Thus few programs have been developed for the elderly. However, with some creativity, some of the benefits of programs designed for the elderly can be achieved within standard programs. Matching

patients with clinicians who are knowledgeable about and comfortable in treating the elderly and who can work at a slower, gentler pace is important. Abrasive confrontation, which is used in some programs, is not likely to be effective with elderly persons. Programs that emphasize that style of group work may be poor choices for a referral. However, groups are important to the elderly in reducing the sense of isolation, enhancing communication skills providing a forum for problem solving, and dealing with denial. A particular element found to be important in working with the elderly is referred to as life review. Groups need to allow for the elderly person's reminiscence and processing of the past. It is important for all elderly persons to see their lives as a whole. For those in treatment for alcohol problems, incorporating this process in a way that does not diminish self-esteem or devalue the elderly person's life is important. This is not only important in formal alcohol treatment but in contacts with health-care and social-service professionals as well.

Prevention

Your middle age patient of today is some other clinician's elderly patient several years hence. Today's adolescent is establishing a framework for making independent decisions about self-care and health-care practices. These will have a bearing on life-long health habits. What kind of questions should any individual consider before he or she decides to take medication? What specific questions are important for the particular patient? Patients rarely consult their doctor before making such decisions. In fact, no doctor would want to be contacted on that basis! A resource available to everyone is the pharmacist. However, the pharmacist is an almost always available but under-utilized resource. One of his or her jobs is public education and information. Patients need instruction about the kind of questions to ask: "Are there any contraindications when using this product?", "If taking prescription medications is there a need for concern about interactions?", or "Are there any side effects?"

Practical treatment suggestions

1. If the elderly have some symptoms of psychological or physical problems, including a problem with alcohol, provide the same treatment you would for someone younger. Too often, problems of the elderly are dismissed under the assumption that the elderly are just complainers, senile, unlikely to benefit, will die soon anyway, or are incapable of appreciating help.
2. In making an evaluation of an older person, do a comprehensive assessment rather than just a symptom-oriented search. Pay attention to the person's social, financial, emotional, medical, cognitive, and self-care status. The latter is often overlooked. Is the person able to accomplish the daily activi-

ties required for well-being, such as preparing meals, getting groceries, or taking medications as prescribed?

3. Recent literature suggests that signs of alcohol abuse in the elderly may be less obvious. For example, DWI is an unlikely occurrence if the elderly no longer drive. Instead of accepting self-neglect, confusion, or repeated falls as the vicissitudes of aging, they should prompt questions about alcohol use, just as they would in a younger person.

4. Because many elderly persons are reluctant to seek or receive professional help, a family member is often the person to make the first contact. This will initially be your best source of information about the person. Be sure to find out the family's views of the situation, their ideas, and their fears. Whatever the problem, the chances are good that something can be done to improve the picture. Let the family know about the optimism. It often comes as a surprise to them that their elderly relative may get better.

5. Sometimes the family will appear to you as unhelpful, unsympathetic, or uncaring. This may infuriate and annoy you. Even if this happens, do not alienate the family. Whatever problems there may be with the family, it is possibly the only support system the client has.

6. In dealing with the elderly, remind yourself that you are working with survivors. The fact that they have made it even this far means they have some strengths. These people have stuck their necks out in the past and taken risks. Find out how they have done it, and see if you can help them replicate that. Also, try to raise their expectations that indeed they can "make it" again, just as they were able to before.

7. Use all the possible resources at your disposal. In many instances the elderly need to become reinvolved in the world around them. Meaningful contacts can come from a variety of people, not just from professional helpers. The janitor in the client's apartment building, a neighbor, or a crossing guard at the street corner may all be potential allies. If the person was once active in a church group, civic organization, or other community group, but has lost contact, get in touch with the organization. There is often a member who will visit or be able to assist in other ways. Many communities have senior citizen centers. They offer a wide range of resources, including social programs, Meals-on-Wheels, counseling on Social Security and Medicare, and transportation. If there is a single agency to cultivate, the Senior Citizen's Center would be the one.

We've started a singing group. We call it the Grateful Almost Dead.

8. In your interviews with the elderly, the importance of reaching out, showing interest, and having physical contact has already been mentioned. Also be active. Do not merely sit there and grunt from time to time. Your quietness may too easily be interpreted by them as distance and dislike. Another very

important thing to do is to provide cues to orient the elderly. Mention dates, day of the week, and current events. For anyone who has had any cognitive slippage, good cues from the environment are very helpful. In conversation with the elderly, don't stick with neutral topics like the weather all the time. Try to engage them in some topics of common interest to you both (such as gardening or baseball), as well as some controversial topic, something with some zip. This stimulates their egos, because it implies that you not only want their opinions, but you also want them to listen to yours.

9. If you give specific information to the client, write it down legibly. This makes it much easier for the client to comply. If family members are present, tell them the directions too. In thinking about compliance and what can be done to assist the elderly in participating in treatment, take some time to think about how your agency functions. What does it mean for an elderly person coming to see you? Are there long waits at several different offices on several different floors? Does it require navigating difficult stairs, elevators, and hallways in the process? Are there times of the day that make use of public transportation easier? Consider such factors, and make adjustments to make it much easier for your elderly clients. In specific terms, make every effort to do things in as uncomplicated, convenient, nonembarrassing, and economical a fashion as possible.

10. Separate sympathy and empathy. Sympathy is feeling sorry in company with someone. The elderly don't want that; it makes them feel like children. Empathy means you understand or want to understand. This is what they would like.

11. Be aware that you may be thought of and responded to as any number of important people in your client's long life. Also, you may alternately represent grandchild, child, parent, peer, and authority figure to them at various points in treatment, even within the same interview, and at the same time.

12. Have integrity with the elderly. Do not try to mislead or lie to them. They are too experienced with all the con games in life. If they ask you questions, give them straight answers. This, however, does not mean being brutal in the name of "honesty." For example, in speaking with a client you might well say, "Many other people I talk with have concerns about death, do you?" If the client responds, "No, I haven't thought much about it," you don't blurt out, "Well, you better think about it, you only have 6 months to live." That is *not* integrity.

13. In working with the elderly, set specific goals. Make sure that the initial ones are easily attainable. This means they can have some surefire positive experiences. With that under

their belts, they are more likely to take some risks and attempt other things.

14. Make home visits. Home visits are the key to working with this group. It may be the only thing that will break down their resistance and help them get treatment. Very few will seek help on their own initiative. So, if someone is not willing to come to your office, give him a call. Ask if you can make an appointment to see him at home. If the response you get is, "I don't want you to come," don't quit. Your next line is, "Well, if I'm ever in the area, I'd like to stop by." And try to do that. Bring some small token gift, such as notepaper or flowers. After your visit, you may well find his or her resistance has disappeared. The home visit can be vital in making an adequate assessment. Seeing the person in his or her own home, where security is at its peak, provides a much better picture of how the person is getting along, as well as the pluses and minuses of the environment. It also allows the client to be spontaneous in emotions and behavior. If you regularly make home visits, beware of making the person "stay in trouble" to see you. Don't just visit in a crisis. Instead, stop in to hear about successes. Your visits may be a real high point for the person, who may not like to think of losing this contact. Make a visit the day after the client's first day on a new volunteer job, for example.

15. Beware of arranging things for the elderly that will be seen as something trivial to occupy their time. If there is a crafts class, the point ought to be to teach them a skill, an art, not to keep them busy. Many of the elderly also have something they can teach others. The carpenter who is no longer steady enough to swing a hammer and drive a nail will be able to provide consultation to do-it-yourselfers who want to remodel their homes. The elderly have a richness of life experiences and much to contribute.

16. Thoroughly evaluate symptoms of memory loss, disorientation, and behavioral changes to uncover potentially treatable causes of organic brain syndrome. Have clients show you all their medicines, including over-the-counter types. Coordinate medical care to avoid duplication of prescriptions.

The task in working with the elderly is to assist them in rediscovering strengths, getting involved with people, and discovering life is worth living, at whatever age.

WOMEN

For far too long alcohol problems among women was a topic not much discussed. Alcoholism, heavy drinking, and problem drinking were thought to be problems of men. Accordingly a review of the sci-

entific literature between 1928 and 1970 found that only 28 studies of female alcoholics had been published in the English language. The traditional assumption as well was that when present, alcoholism is alcoholism, regardless of gender. For many years it was estimated that only 1 in every 7 alcoholics was a woman; then the ratio quoted became 1 in 4.

Differences in the drinking patterns of men and women today are far less marked than a generation ago. Younger women are more likely to have the same drinking patterns as their male peers than the drinking patterns of women in their mother's generation. Thus any protection provided in the past by the social prohibitions against women's drinking has been eroded. Accordingly, some authorities claim that the rates of alcohol dependence are similar for men and women, particularly among young age groups.

Alcohol dependence and alcohol problems among women has been an area of fast-growing inquiry. Much has been and is being written both in the scientific and popular literature about women and alcohol. Research is now being conducted on physiological differences between women and men. Similarly, the treatment community is becoming sensitive to factors that have a bearing on treatment approaches and access to care.

Despite the growing attention to women's alcohol problems, the available data are not easily synthesized. One difficulty is that much of the research conducted involves women who enter treatment. Whether these women are representative of women generally is unknown. Further complicating the situation is that women who are being studied seem to represent all of the possible combinations of alcohol and other substance use. Subjects of research studies range from women alcoholics to women with drug dependence to alcoholic women who use/or abuse /or are dependent on other substances to female substance users who drink/drink heavily/are alcohol dependent. Despite the sea of information, there is not always greater understanding.

Gender differences

Women do represent a growing percentage of drinkers. As noted among younger women the proportion of drinkers is beginning to approximate that of men. The only reason that men, as a group, are statistically more likely than women to be drinkers is due to the large number of abstainers among older women. These older women, born during prohibition or shortly thereafter, grew up in an earlier era in which women's drinking was less socially acceptable and far less common. The behavior of their granddaughters is quite different. In addition to age, there are other differences among women worth noting. White women drink more than women of color. More than half the women of Hispanic origin and a similar proportion from some Native American tribes are nondrinkers. Afro-American women are those with the highest proportion of abstainers. At the same time, Afro-American women are the group with the highest level of heavy drinkers. Compared to other women, there are more at either extreme.

Along with a greater number of women who drink, there is a corresponding increase in the number of women with alcohol problems and alcohol dependence. In what other ways do alcohol problems of women differ from those of men? The major differences that have been described are noted below, admittedly, in a very brief and cursory fashion.

- Apparently more women than men can point to a specific trigger for the onset of heavy drinking. This might be a divorce, an illness, death of a spouse, children leaving home, or some other stressful event. If a woman seeks help at such a point, both a careful alcohol use history and education about the potential risks of alcohol use are warranted. The danger of relying upon alcohol or other drugs is that the crisis can take on a long-term life of its own. The challenge to those dealing with a woman in the face of any of the above difficulties is in providing empathy rather than sympathy. Either overtly or covertly, the danger is often to imply that if that had happened to us, we would probably have responded in the same fashion. The current dangerous misuse of alcohol and drugs can become lost in the forest of other problems.
- Women's alcohol dependence is often described as "telescoped." This means the disease appears later and progresses more rapidly. The period of time between the onset of heavy drinking and entry into treatment is shorter among women too.
- Women are more susceptible to medical complications. For men, the presence of medical complications is tied to long term, regular heavy use. The several six packs a day over time will take their toll. For women, the situation may be different. Medical complications among women may be less a product of the amount usually consumed but tied to the frequency of heavy drinking occasions. Thus very heavy drinking once or twice a week may raise more havoc than if the same amount of booze were spread out over time. Women have particular susceptibility to liver disease. This may well be tied to the differences in the way men and women metabolize alcohol (see Chapter 2).
- Women with alcohol dependence consume significantly less alcohol than men, perhaps 45% less, but experience difficulties of similar magnitude.
- Women alcoholics tend to come into treatment earlier than men. The time between the onset of heavy drinking and a referral for treatment is likely to be shorter. This is believed to be due to higher rates of medical complications. Women too tend to exhaust the social supports and resources needed to

continue alcohol use. Also, women have a greater number of alcohol-induced problems than men, even when the length of drinking, the presence of psychiatric problems, and work status are taken into account. Men, however, outnumber women entering treatment by almost 4 to 1.

- In a marriage in which one spouse is alcoholic, when it is the woman, there is a significantly greater likelihood of divorce. If the wife has alcoholism, there is a nine-times greater chance of divorce than is found for male alcoholics. An important consequence is that the family and emotional support systems that are an asset in recovery are less likely to be present. Interestingly, *whatever* the woman's marital situation, it has been found that women entering treatment do not receive the solid support for that decision that men generally receive from family and friends.

- Women with alcohol and/or other drug problems are more likely than men to have a drug dependent partner.

- If the woman is unmarried or a divorced single parent, there are not only additional emotional demands but also economic burdens. Remember that in the aftermath of divorce, almost three quarters of women and their children are economically less well off, if not downright poverty stricken. Entry into treatment may stretch an already difficult financial situation.

- Women have higher rates of use of other drugs and also other drugs in combination with alcohol than do men. They are prescribed mood-altering drugs much more frequently than men. A sample of women alcoholics found that 70% had a past history of having been prescribed psychoactive drugs, a rate 1.5 times greater than for alcoholic men. Of the women prescribed psychoactive drugs, one half could recall at least one occasion of having used alcohol in combination with the medication; also, one half had been prescribed more than one category of drug. This suggests the need for a very careful drug use history, with a wary eye for multiple drug use and abuse.

- In respect to employment, women with alcohol dependence, just as women in general, are less likely than men to be employed. They also have fewer vocational skills and training.

- In terms of what prompts treatment and the perceptions of problems when entering care, women have been found to differ from men in several ways. Generally women report more depression, anxiety, sense of powerlessness, hopelessness, and guilt than men report. This is not the result of their having more psychiatric illness but is part of the female symptom pattern of alcohol dependence.

- Women entering treatment often have experienced recent episodes of violence.

- While reporting less support for entry into treatment, women, more than men, credit pressure from others as a major factor in their seeking treatment, whether from children, other relatives, co-workers, or their physician.
- More commonly women do not see either alcohol or drug use as their primary problem. Thus they were inclined to express concern about the ability of a substance abuse program to assist them. This also means that it is particularly important for treatment personnel to help them make the connection between their life problems and alcohol use.
- A concern unique to women is fear of losing custody of children.

Differences among women

Ethnicity would be expected to be an important basis for differences among women. However, very little research has been done in this area. Age has received more attention. The significant dividing line appears to be those who grew up either before or after the early 1970s, a period marked by dramatic social changes. Women who grew to adulthood after this time tend to differ from the older generation in several important ways. For one, they are much more likely to use multiple substances. Also, they started drinking at an earlier age, generally in their teens. Also among young women, eating disorders are more common, and there is a greater history of violence both as victim and perpetrator.

Natural history

In terms of the symptoms associated with alcohol problems, there are several notable differences between men and women. Women more frequently drink at home and drink alone. Women are still more likely to hide their drinking. Whether treated or untreated, women are more likely to encounter family disruption, with higher rates of divorce and separation. Generally, they have fewer social supports available and describe their primary relationships as being neither satisfactory nor supportive. Women are more likely than men to lose their jobs. Suicide attempts and depression are more common among women. Women in general are more vulnerable to affective disorders than men. This makes distinguishing the depression and despondency that accompany alcohol dependence from depression, the psychiatric illness, a real challenge with heavy alcohol use.

Medical complications from chronic, heavy drinking show up earlier and after less life-time consumption among women. Women also have more alcohol-induced problems. As was noted in the general discussion of etiology, when comparing countries, a cultural pattern of "utilitarian drinking" is associated with higher rates of alcoholism.

Interestingly this general rule is also significant in women's alcohol problems. Women who develop alcohol dependence in later life are those who earlier described their drinking as *purposeful*. That is, they drank with a specific purpose in mind, such as to relieve shyness, to get high, to be happy, or to get along better.

Treatment issues

Beyond the items already touched on that can influence the course of the disease process and when and how women are identified and diagnosed as alcoholic and are involved in treatment, there are also issues relevant to the treatment process itself.

Mothering and female sexuality are two aspects of self-esteem unique to women. If a woman has children, some of the questions she may well be asking herself include: "Am I a good mother?" "Can I be a good mother?" "Have I hurt my children?" "Can I ever cope with my children if I don't drink?" These may not be explicit in the therapy sessions, but they do cross her mind. They begin to be answered, hopefully positively, as she gains time in sobriety. Family meetings may also be one way she gains answers to these questions. However, in some cases where there has been child abuse or a child is having special difficulties, a referral to a children's agency, a family-service agency, or a mental health clinic may be important in dealing with these situations. One of the things any mother will need to learn if she is to regain her self-esteem as a mother is a sense of what the "normal" difficulties are in raising children.

In terms of her sexuality, there may be a number of potential questions. If she has had a divorce or an affair, she may well be wondering about her worth and attractiveness as a woman. Even if the marriage is intact, there may be sexual problems. On one hand, the sexual relationship may have almost disappeared as the drinking progressed. On the other, it may have been years since she has had sexual intercourse without benefit of a glass of wine or a couple of beers. Again, time in sobriety may well be the major therapeutic element. But couples' therapy and/or sexual counseling may be needed if marital problems are not resolved. In cases where the sexual problems preceded the active drinking, professional help is certainly recommended. Sobering up is not likely to take away the existing problem in some miraculous fashion. To let it fester is to invite even more problems.

What about single women or women caught in an unsatisfactory marriage? It is not uncommon for them to find themselves "suddenly" involved in an affair or an extramarital relationship. With a little bit of sobriety, they are very ripe to fall in love. This may have several roots. The woman may be questioning her femininity, and the attentions of a man may well provide some affirmation of her status as a woman. Also possible is that with sobriety comes a sense of being alive again. There is the reawakening of a host of feelings that have long been dormant, including sexual feelings. In this sense it may be like the bloom and intensity of adolescence. A romantic involvement may follow very naturally. Unfortunately, it can lead to disaster, if followed with abandon. This can be equally true for men.

We would caution male therapists working with women that if you are the first person in many years to accept her and if you have been making attempts to raise her self-esteem, she may mistake her gratitude for a personal emotional attachment to you. Your recognition of this "error" is imperative. If you provide contacts for her with other women in recovery, she may be better able to recognize this pitfall as well.

For women in treatment, children are another concern. If a woman has young children, long-term residential treatment may be very difficult to arrange. Many women have no husbands in the home, and extended family members do not always live down the street as was once the case. However, for that very reason, it may be all the more important for the woman to begin her recovery in a treatment center, where intense therapy may take place without the distractions of daily family life. Models of treatment to overcome this problem are being tried in many areas throughout the country. But in most places the usual facilities are still the only ones available. You will need to stretch your creativity to the limit to deal with this problem. Potentially, friends, extended family—even if they are called in from a distance—or a live-in sitter can be used. When in-patient treatment is warranted, there may be no way to allow her the optimum advantage of a 2- to 3-week stay in residential treatment. If this is the case, daily out-patient visits, intensive AA contact, or day treatment are possible options. Even if in-patient care can be arranged, you will be faced with her intense guilt over, and resistance to, leaving her children. There are no easy formulas, and the therapist is left to work out the best solution possible in each case.

Women and AA

The latest figures from the General Services Board of AA indicate that women continue to constitute a growing proportion of the new members coming into AA. It appears that whatever the differences between men and women with alcoholism, AA manages to achieve similar rates of success with both. It is as important to make a referral to AA for your female clients as for male clients. A few trips to local meetings should assure her that it is no longer the male stronghold it once was. In many communities, one will also find AA groups that are predominantly women. Being aware that alcoholism, alcohol problems, and treatment issues are not identical for men and women is important. The increasing body of literature on women and alcohol problems warrants attention.

Portrait of a man who stops in a bar for 3 drinks on his way home from work every night.

THE GREAT MAJESTO JUMPS 100 Feet into A Wet SPONGE

I know his secret. He wets the sponge with Cognac.

THE EMPLOYED

The majority of those who have alcoholism are members of the work force. A conservative estimate is that 8% of the nation's work force is adversely affected by the use of alcohol. As business and industry began to recognize the costs to them of employees with alcohol problems, there was a rapid development of special programs by employers to identify problems and initiate treatment. These work-based programs are generally termed either *employee assistance programs* or *occupational alcohol programs*.

Drinking has long been interwoven into work. Consider the office party, the company picnic, the wine and cheese reception, the martini lunches, the "drink date" to review business, the bar car on the commuter train, the old standby gift of a fifth for a business associate, a round of drinks to celebrate the closing of a business deal, or the construction crew stopping off for beers after work. Over the past several years the meshing of drinking and business has come under fire. First, the IRS decreed the martini lunch was not a legitimate business expense. Then the growing interest in physical fitness took its toll. Concern about liability when alcohol is a part of company-sponsored parties has come into play. Though recently receiving more attention, court cases addressing this go back to the mid-1970s.

Possibly most telling about the new attitudes is the very recent and growing discussion about the use of mandatory drug testing as a condition for initial hiring and continuing employment. This discussion has centered less on alcohol than on other drugs; however, alcohol no longer enjoys a status of being "okay," while all other drugs are seen as "bad." To our minds this is evidence of the growing recognition by businesses that substance use can and does interfere with performance and productivity and is therefore a legitimate concern. Nonetheless, for too long drinking in many work situations was not only accepted but expected. Whenever the alcohol use is tolerated, the potential for alcohol problems among susceptible individuals rises, more so if drinking is subtly encouraged.

Occupational high-risk factors

Although a job cannot be said to cause alcoholism, it can contribute to its development. Some of the factors that Trice and Roman, authorities in the area of occupational alcohol issues, have identified as job-based risk factors include:

- absence of clear goals (and absence of supervision)
- freedom to set work hours (isolation and low visibility)
- low structural visibility (e.g., salespeople away from the business place)
- being a "work horse," overly invested in one's job
- occupational obsolescence (especially common in scientific and technical fields)

- new work status
- required on-the-job drinking (e.g., salespeople drinking with clients)
- reduction of social controls (occurs on college campuses and other less structured settings)
- severe role stress
- competitive pressure
- presence of illegal drug users

The workplace cover-up

If bringing up the drinking practices and potential problems of a family member or close friend makes someone squirm, the idea of saying something to a co-worker is virtually unthinkable. Almost everyone accepts a separation between work and home or professional and private life. So until the alcohol problem flows into the work world, the worker's use of alcohol is considered no one else's business. That does not mean that no one sees a problem developing. Our suspicion is that someone with even a little savvy can often spot potentially dangerous drinking practices. The office scuttlebutt or work crew's bull sessions plus simple observation make it common knowledge who "really put it away this weekend," or the "poor devil who just got picked up for a DWI," or "you can always count on Sue to join in whenever anyone wants to stop for a drink after work."

Even if an employee does show some problems on the job, whether directly or indirectly related to alcohol use, co-workers may try to "help out" by doing extra work or at least by not blowing the whistle. Because employee assistance programs, if they are available, are based on identifying work deterioration, any attempt by co-workers to help cover up job problems makes spotting the alcohol problem all the more difficult. If a company does not have a program to help those employees with alcohol problems, odds for a cover-up by co-workers are even greater. Another important party in this concealment strategy is predictably the spouse, who usually doesn't want to do anything to threaten the paycheck.

In the past when the cover-ups no longer could hide a problem, the employee usually got fired; this may still happen in many companies. In such instances, the enterprise loses a formerly valuable and well-trained worker, statistically a costly "solution." The current thinking is that it is cheaper for a company to identify problems earlier and to use the job as leverage to get the employee into treatment and back to work.

There are two things that will be believed of a man whosoever, and or of them is that he has taken to drink.

BOOTH TARKINGTON

Employee assistance programs (EAPs)

Facts and experience suggest that the occupational environment may be one of the most efficient and economical means of providing an opportunity for early identification and treatment of alcoholism and alcohol-related problems.

Early intervention increases the chances for recovery for the following reasons:

- physical health has not deteriorated significantly
- financial resources are not as depleted
- emotional supports still exist in the family and community
- threat of job loss as leverage

Employee assistance programs (EAPs) are organized in a variety of ways, from an in-house counselor to contracts with outside groups for these services. Earlier programs were more narrowly restricted and focused upon alcohol and drugs alone. Now, these narrowly focused efforts have typically been replaced by what is known as the "broad brush" approach, that is, dealing with any of the many problems that may affect employees' performance.

The following are among the more common signs and symptoms that may point to a troubled employee and thereby help to identify the problem drinker or substance abuser:

- chronic absenteeism
- change in behavior
- physical signs
- spasmodic work pace
- lower quantity and quality of work
- partial absences
- avoiding supervisors and co-workers
- on-the-job drinking
- on-the-job accidents and lost time from off-the-job accidents

Training supervisors and others to recognize these signs is important so that early detection can occur. Training is also critical in helping employers to document and not diagnose. Where there have been broad educational efforts through information sessions, posters, pamphlets, and so forth, there has been an increase in peer or self-referrals. Such referrals may often make up the bulk of referrals to a program.

An important technique in dealing with those in the workplace is called either *intervention, constructive coercion,* or *confrontation.* The technique, based on the Johnson intervention model, is used in the work setting to motivate the individual to seek help to improve job performance and retain the job. In the context of a formal program, the procedure is to identify, document, and then confront the employee with the facts and an informal offer of referral for help.

Confrontation occurs within the company's normal evaluation and disciplinary procedures. A supervisor, manager, or union steward who notes certain behaviors and signs of deteriorating job performance documents them. If the confrontation is unsuccessful, the next phase would be a stepped-up disciplinary procedure, including a time limit and a formal referral with the "threat" of job loss if performance is not improved.

Portrait of a man
who thinks he's clever
when he's drunk

Implications for treatment

It is important for alcohol professionals to be knowledgeable about occupational programs. They can thereby better coordinate treatment efforts for the employed client.

Does the individual's employer have an EAP? If so, who is the clinician? What services are offered? For any client, it is important that you be aware of any work-related problems. If so, what is the current job status? Has a disciplinary procedure been instituted, or has the employee been informally warned and referred for treatment? In addition, to avoid future conflict, learn about any union involvement. Such information can help in formulating realistic treatment plans.

It is important to be sensitive to the policies and politics of the employed client's work setting. Without this knowledge and awareness, there is the danger of violating confidentiality or, conversely, of not taking full advantage of the opportunity to cooperate with the employer on the client's behalf. If there is a company policy, learn about it so that you can plan realistically and avoid treatment-work conflicts. The nature of the client's work and the potential impact of any medication, if prescribed, must be considered. A follow-up plan must consider the working person's hours and geographical location. The flexibility and accessibility of the treatment facility can be a key factor in successful rehabilitation. Evening office hours and early-morning and weekend appointments may have to be arranged so that treatment will not interfere with the job. On the other hand, if there is an EAP with clinical personnel, this may be the most appropriate site for follow-up and continuing care, after the initial intensive treatment.

You may also find that some individuals will have to be treated as outpatients even when inpatient services are more appropriate. The employee may not be able to take the time off or may not have adequate insurance coverage. Insurance companies who have been covering inpatient treatment are now attempting to change their policies to cover outpatient care exclusively or at least preferentially. They cite the fact that it is less expensive and that little or no evidence indicates that inpatient care provides better treatment outcomes. We must note here that these assumptions are based on data derived from group statistics. Both ends of the spectrum are lost to the statistical average. As we hope has become clear, all clients are not alike, and blanket assumptions regarding treatment are hazardous to a client's health.

Many larger companies are also becoming involved in managed health care plans. This means that there are designated providers, as in an HMO (Health Maintenance Organization), which either provides whatever medical care is needed or required to approve in advance a referral for treatment if the individual's medical coverage is to cover the associated medical care costs. The rationale for such arrangements is that unnecessary services will be eliminated and health-care dollars will be used more wisely. While notable in concept, in practice this arrangement has caused concern. With respect to alcohol and substance abuse services, there are several problems that have been identified. Some managed health-care systems have developed contracts with specific treatment agencies to provide all necessary services. Payment is often based on a per capita formula, with a set reimbursement paid for a diagnostic category, rather than reimbursements being made on the basis of actual costs incurred. Thus there is a clear incentive to limit services, for example to favor outpatient care over inpatient treatment, or to have outpatient treatment consist of a specified number of visits. This may work for the "average" client. However the average person in treatment is by analogy like the statistically average drinker we described in Chapter 1, virtually nonexistent. The provision of individualized treatment needed to ensure optimal care is sacrificed for indiscriminately delivering the statistically predetermined norm.

Occupational programs have made significant progress in demonstrating that the "human approach" is good business. Yet there is still a great deal to be done, and it can be better accomplished with cooperation among those involved in the occupational program field and alcohol clinicians.

OTHER SPECIAL POPULATIONS

When caring for clients, the fact is that the "average client" is virtually nonexistent. All kinds of factors have an impact, particularly racial and ethnic background, in combination with age and gender. These have an important impact in several ways. These factors, for example, determine what kinds of behavior are viewed as evidence of a problem, to whom people turn for help and under what circumstances, and their comfort in using professional care.

In this chapter, neither racial nor ethnic groups are discussed specifically. In the United States the major racial and ethnic groups are Afro-Americans, Hispanics, and Asians, as well as Native Americans. In addition, there are other client groups, which though their characteristics may be less dramatic are just as real, e.g., the Portuguese New England fisherman, the Vermont farmer, the client from the hills of Appalachia, or the blue collar worker from the midwest. Furthermore, even within a particular group there can be considerable diversity, as is true of Hispanics. Differences include geographical location, whether the individual is from California, Texas, Florida, or New York, whether the client is a recent immigrant or native-born, and if native-born, what generation.

For the clinician working with the member of an ethnic or racial group, one of the most useful pieces of information will be the client's relationship to his or her traditional culture as well as to the larger, dominant culture. This is sometimes referred to as *cultural orientation,* meaning what sets of rules an individual instinctively follows. The basic question is to what extent the client identifies with a traditional ethnic group and to what extent he or she thinks and is comfortable in functioning not as a member of a particular ethnic group but as part of the American "mainstream." Some of the terms used to describe these different orientations are "assimilated" as opposed to "non-assimilated," or bicultural. In brief, those individuals who are not assimilated think of themselves in terms of the values, rules of behavior of their group of origin. Those who are assimilated may or may not be familiar with the traditional ways; they are most comfortable functioning in the usual style of the dominant American culture. Those described as bicultural are able to function by the rules either of their native culture or the majority American culture.

In working with clients who are members of ethnic groups, a sense of their cultural orientation is important. The following chart indicates the different areas that might be considered.

Assessing cultural orientation

	Traditional culture or culture of origin	Majority culture
Social	• close friends from same ethnic background • leisure activities within ethnic community	• close friends not restricted to ethnic group • leisure not primarily within ethnic community
Language	• fluent in native language • uses primarily native language	• not fluent in native language
Spiritual/traditions	• familiar with and participates in ethnic ceremonies and celebrations	• unfamiliar with or does not participate in native festivities
Family	• defined by customs of the ethnic culture	• considers family the nuclear family unit, i.e. spouse, or parents and children

Becoming acquainted with a different culture

In working with clients who are members of any cultural group other than your own, it is important to become familiar with the values, practices, and ways of seeing the world that are part of that group. A useful place to start often is by considering the nature of your biases and the source of any preconceived notions.

Suggesting that a referral be made to a counselor or clinician who is also from the same ethnic or racial group as the client may be good advice. But it isn't always possible. At the very least it is important to know about the history and cultural traditions. In terms of alcohol problems, how are drinking problems defined? What are the behaviors that within the community would signal an alcohol problem? To whom do people tend to turn for help in time of trouble? Are there any particular biases against seeking professional care or getting help from an 'outsider?' Are there any particular customs that would make getting help more difficult? Be alert to any barriers caused by language. Therapists should be alert to and not be surprised to be watched closely for signs of prejudice or disinterest. As necessary, certainly acknowledge the limits and differences of your own experience and background. Wise advise that holds here as elsewhere is that "the patient is the best instructor," but it requires that you open yourself to learning.

RESOURCES AND FURTHER READING

Closser MH, Blow FC: Special populations: Women, ethnic minorities, and the elderly, *Psychiatric Clinics of North America* 16(1):199-209, 1993.

> The term special population has come to mean any of a number of subdivisions of populations. These may involve gender, race, psychiatric comorbidity, disability, or age and often involve finer distinctions among smaller groups. Failure to appreciate the importance of gender, culture, age-related, and other differences may contribute to existing barriers to treatment including lack of relevance, language, and treatment access problems. Research on treatment outcome in special populations is limited and impaired by problems with definition. This article discusses prevalence, the problems with identification, and issues in treatment of substance abuse, primarily among women, ethnic minorities, and the elderly, recognizing that these populations are not themselves homogeneous.

Ubell V, Sumberg D: Heterosexual therapists treating homosexual addicted clients, *Journal of Chemical Dependency Treatment* 5(1):19-33, 1992.

> Heterosexual therapists who are treating homosexual clients suffering from an addiction need to be accepting of and comfortable with homosexuality. This acceptance must include the awareness of the therapist's own internalized homophobic feelings and thoughts, as well as those of the clients. Equally important is the therapist's knowledge of addiction and the development of skills in aiding recovery. The authors discuss homosexuality and homophobia, consciousness raising for therapists, dealing with addiction, and family of origin issues. (Author abstract.)

Adolescents

Farrell M, Strang J: Substance use and misuse in childhood and adolescence (review). *Journal of Clinical Psychiatry* 32(1):109-128, 1991.

> Substance abuse has particular implications for the developing foetus in utero, for the child in the context of a family with an ongoing pattern of substance misuse, and for the teenager using a variety of substances. Additionally there are now forms of drug abuse that are related almost entirely to children and adolescents (notably volatile substance abuse). In many countries over the past decade the age of initiation into substance abuse has gradually reduced. This review assesses pertinent research developments in the field of substance abuse in the young and where relevant attempts to draw conclusions that are clinically applicable. The paucity of research is such that few data exist on many important areas within the substance abuse literature pertinent to the young. The review covers the areas of assessment, classification, epidemiology, biological factors, psychological factors, outcome, and treatment. (Author abstract.)

Farrow JA, Smith WR, Hurst MD, editors: *Adolescent drug and alcohol assessment instruments in current use: A critical comparison*, Seattle: State of Washington Division of Alcohol and Substance Abuse, 1993.

> This report evaluates the standardized assessment tools for adolescent drug and alcohol use. Information is presented that allows clinicians to choose which of the standardized assessment tools is best for their purposes. The instruments are judged for ease of administration and scoring, cost, and what exactly each is designed to measure. The instruments are organized into three broad categories: screening, mid-range assessment, and comprehensive assessment, based upon the time needed for administration and how many of the basic areas necessary for treatment are actually measured. A brief narrative describes each instrument with an evaluation of its psychometric properties. Tables summarize the descriptive

information and include ratings of how well the instrument meets criteria, such as ease of administration, reliability, validity, and norms.

Jurich AP, Polson CP: Family factors in the lives of drug users and abusers, *Adolescence* 20(77):143-159, 1985. (Review article.)

A review of the literature suggested nine family factors that had an impact upon drug use: parental absence, discipline, scapegoating, hypocritical morality, parent-child communication gap, parental divorce, mother-father conflicts, family breakup, and the use of "psychological crutches" to cope with stress.* In addition, data were collected on the closest family member to the drug-taking subject, the subject's perception of the most powerful family member, the family member who uses "psychological crutches," and situations where the most powerful member of the family used "psychological crutches." A paired analysis between drug users and drug abusers yielded significant differences on the use of two "psychological crutches" to cope with stressful situations: drugs and denial. Drug users were less likely to come from families where there was a communication gap and either laissez faire or authoritarian discipline. Drug abusers also came from families where the person whom they defined as most powerful tended to use "psychological crutches" to cope with stress. (Author abstract.)

McLellan AT, Dembo R: *Screening and assessment of alcohol- and other drug-abusing adolescents: Treatment improvement protocol (TIP). Series 3,* Rockville, MD: Center for Substance Abuse Treatment, 1993.

This treatment protocol focuses on two major areas. The first is strategies, procedures, and instruments that are appropriate for the initial detection of adolescent alcohol and/or other drug use or abuse. The second is comprehensive assessment of adolescent problems and subsequent treatment planning. It does not prescribe any particular screening or assessment tool. The specific topics covered include the preliminary screening of adolescents, comprehensive assessment of adolescents for referral and treatment, legal issues in the screening and assessment of adolescents, and screening and assessment of adolescents in juvenile justice systems. Six appendices are included providing sample instruments. Copyright 1994, Project Cork Institute.

Moore J, Campana J, Lam M, et al: Tobacco, alcohol, and other drug use among high school students: United States, 1991, *Morbidity and Morality Weekly Report* 41(37):698-703, 1992.

Patterns of tobacco, alcohol, and other drug use usually are established during youth, often persist into adulthood, contribute substantially to the leading causes of mortality and morbidity, and are associated with lower educational achievement and school dropout. This report presents selected data on current use of tobacco, alcohol, marijuana, cocaine, and steroid use among 9th-12th grade students from two components of the Youth Risk Behavior Surveillance System. Data are presented on current rates of tobacco, alcohol, and drug use by state. Copyright 1992, Project Cork Institute.

Morrison MA, Smith DE, Wilford BB, et al: At war in the fields of play: Current perspectives on the nature and treatment of adolescent chemical dependency, *Journal of Psychoactive Drugs* 25(4):321-330, 1993.

While the numbers of adolescents entering drug abuse treatment are not increasing dramatically, those adolescents entering treatment are getting sicker, according to clinical reports. Adolescents are entering treatment with multiple problems, including severe learning disorders, borderline personality disorders, multiple diagnoses of addiction, mental health, and physical problems (including HIV/AIDS), and issues arising from child abuse and incest. A case study in client-therapist interaction is presented, highlighting the concept of the wounded healer. The dis-

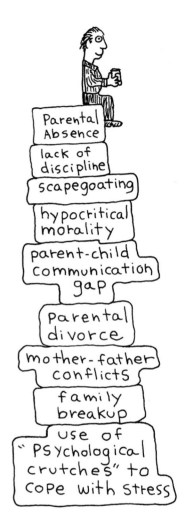

Parental Absence

lack of discipline

scapegoating

hypocritical morality

parent-child communication gap

parental divorce

mother-father conflicts

family breakup

use of "psychological crutches" to cope with stress

Psychological crutches are defined as means of coping with stress that relieve personal pain but sacrifice long-term coping and as behaviors that allow exoneration for responsibility for a situation and relieve the pressure created by a nonresponse.

ease model of addiction is discussed as it applies to adolescents, as is their need for habilitation, not rehabilitation. Current abuse trends and the drugs involved are also discussed. Multiple diagnoses, physiological disorders, HIV testing and counseling, surgical problems, and maternal/neonatal complications are reviewed. (Author abstract.)

Pandina RJ, Johnson: Familial drinking history as a predictor of alcohol and drug consumption among adolescent children, *Journal of Studies on Alcohol* 50(3):245-253, 1989.

Data concerning adolescent alcohol and drug using behavior, as well as the drinking patterns of their parents, were obtained from a sample of 1380 New Jersey youth born between 1961 and 1969. Initially tested between 1979 and 1981 at ages 12, 15 or 18, these subjects were retested between 1982 and 1984 (retest rate=95%). We wish to describe the early differences in patterns of alcohol and drug use between offspring of families exhibiting a positive history of alcoholism (FH+) and those without such backgrounds (FH-). FH+ subjects are compared to three other groups from varying parental backgrounds (heavy drinking nonalcoholic parents, high stress families, and symptom-free families) as regarding problem use. Several indicators of problem use (e.g., early onset of intoxication, frequent intoxication, escape drinking) were not found to be more prevalent among FH+ than FH- adolescents. Analyses indicate, however, that FH+ adolescents are more likely than FH- adolescents from symptom-free families to report experiencing problems/consequences related to both drinking and drug taking. (Author abstract.)

Schonberg SK: *Guidelines for the treatment of alcohol- and other drug-abusing adolescents: treatment improvement protocol (TIP). Series 4,* Rockville, MD: Center for Substance Abuse Treatment, 1993.

The panel that developed this protocol on adolescent alcohol and other drug (AOD) use and abuse problems was charged with producing guidelines to be used by governmental agencies and treatment providers in respect to the establishment, funding, operation, monitoring, and evaluation of treatment programs for AOD-abusing adolescents involved with the criminal and juvenile justice systems. This protocol has six major sections, covering the following topics: a comprehensive continuum of adolescent treatment options, out-patient treatment for adolescents, in-patient treatment for adolescents, adolescent AOD-abuse treatment in the juvenile justice system, legal and ethical issues in the treatment of substance-abusing adolescents, and cost models for adolescent treatment programs. It also includes an appendix of the major drugs of abuse.

Shifrin F, Solis M: Chemical dependency in gay and lesbian youth, *Journal of Chemical Dependency Treatment* 5(1):67-76, 1992.

The high incidence of chemical dependency among the adult lesbian and gay population has been noted by several authors. However, very little information exists concerning chemical dependency problems among gay youth. The lack of attention to this population reflects the assumption that the youth's homosexual or lesbian identity is a precursor to a normal heterosexual object choice or is a maladaptive pattern. Up until recently, the gay youth has had to face the denial of his or her heterosexually oriented family and educational systems, as well as exclusion from the adult lesbian and gay culture. In this article, the authors briefly describe the chemical dependency problems among a population of youths drawn from the Hetrick-Martin Institute and outline recommendations for treating these youths in both a gay-identified and a traditional treatment setting. (Author abstract.)

Swadi H: Alcohol abuse in adolescence: An update, *Archives of Disease in Childhood* 68(3):341-343, 1993.

Recent reports justify a more considered look at alcohol abuse among adolescents and the risks associated with it. First, studies show that teenagers are more likely to have casual sex and less likely to use condoms when they are under the influence of alcohol, thereby increasing the risk of HIV infection. Second, although adolescents are aware of their particular vulnerability to road trauma and drunk driving, in many countries road traffic accidents now account for more than half of male deaths among 15-19 year olds and the most important factor in these cases is alcohol. This article focuses on the influences of adolescents' attitudes to drinking and drinking patterns, the possible associated psychopathology, treatment issues, and prevention. (Author abstract.)

The elderly

Altpeter M, Campbell J: Alcoholism and aging: A user-friendly curriculum, *Substance Abuse (AMERSA)* 14(3):129-136, 1993.

Alcoholism has deleterious effects on older adults: it shortens life expectancy, causes and aggravates many physical health problems, destroys families and other relationships, impairs memory and other mental functions, and reduces the person's quality of life. It is estimated that 10% of the population 65 years and older are alcoholic and 50% of hospital admissions for this age group are alcohol-related, yet health-care professionals often do not recognize or understand alcoholism. Physical conditions, such as hypertension or insomnia, may be attributed to other etiologies: an unsteady gait or lack of muscle coordination may be viewed as part of the physical decline of aging, mood swings may be confused with depression, and a memory loss may be misperceived as dementia. Among health-care professionals who do recognize alcohol-related problems in older adults, there may exist confusion or ignorance regarding available services and access to these services.

Fitzgerald JL, Mulford HA: Elderly vs. younger problem drinker "treatment" and recovery experiences, *British Journal of Addiction* 87(9):1281-1291, 1992.

To address the question of whether or not elderly problem drinkers experience any treatment contact discrimination or recovery rate disadvantages, the programme use and recovery rate experiences of a representative sample of older and younger persons arrested for drinking and driving (DWI) in Iowa were compared. Subjects were interviewed by phone or mail shortly after their DWI arrest and then again approximately 12 months later. Younger persons (18-54 years old) were compared with elderly persons (55 and over and 65 and over). The elderly subjects were also dichotomized as early onset (at least one problem drinking indicator occurred before age 55) or late onset (all problem drinking indicators occurred at age 55 or later). The elderly were as likely as, or more likely than, their younger counterparts to make a treatment contact, to remain in treatment, and to recover. (Author abstract.)

Jennison KM: The impact of stressful life events and social support on drinking among older adults: A general population survey, *International Journal of Aging and Human Development* 35(2):99-123, 1992.

This article is an analysis of stressful life events, the buffering hypothesis, and alcohol use in a national sample of 1418 respondents 60 years of age and over. The results indicate that older adults who experience stressful losses are significantly more likely to drink excessively than those who have not experienced such losses or who have experienced them to a lesser extent. Increased drinking among older adults may therefore be a reaction to life circumstances in which alcohol represents an attempt to cope with traumatic loss, personal as well as within the kinship network. Supportive resources of spouse, family, friends, and church appear to have a stress-buffering effect that reduces the excessive-drinking response to life crisis. Data suggest, however, that older persons are vulnerable to the magnitude of losses experienced as they grow older and lose more of their family, friends, and peers. These stressors appear to seriously impact their drinking behavior and are not effectively buffered. Respondents report that drinking may increase during periods of prolonged exposure to emotionally depleting life change and loss, when supportive needs may exceed the capacities of personal and social support resources. (Author abstract.)

Liberto JG, Oslin DW, Ruskin PE: Alcoholism in older persons: A review of the literature, *Hospital and Community Psychiatry* 43(10):975-984, 1992.

Alcohol abuse and dependence in elderly persons is of growing social concern. The most consistent findings of cross-sectional and longitudinal studies are that the quantity and frequency of alcohol consumption is higher in elderly men than in elderly women, as is the prevalence of alcohol-related problems. Most studies show a decrease with age in consumption and alcohol-related problems among heavy drinkers. Longitudinal studies show no changes in consumption among light drinkers. Elderly persons with lower incomes consume less alcohol than those with higher incomes. Hospitalized and out-patient populations have more problem drinkers, and the elderly alcoholic is at greater risk for medical and psychiatric comorbidity. About one third to one half of elderly alcoholics experience the onset of problem drinking in middle or late life. Outcomes seem to be better for those who have late-onset drinking and may be improved for those treated in same-age rather than mixed-age groups. (Author abstract.)

Solomon K; Manepalli J, Ireland GA, et al: Alcoholism and prescription drug abuse in the elderly: St. Louis University grand rounds (review), *Journal of the American Geriatric Society* 41(1):57-69, 1993.

This article reviews the problem of alcoholism and prescription drug abuse in the elderly. Several case vignettes are presented. The pharmacology of alcohol and potentially addictive prescription medications are covered. The clinical presentations, the process of addiction, and the evaluation of the elderly are described. Common medical complications are reviewed, followed by a discussion of guidelines for the appropriate use of these drugs in the elderly. It concludes with a discussion of the treatment of patients with these disorders. (Author abstract.)

Thibault JM, Maly RC: Recognition and treatment of substance abuse in the elderly, *Primary Care* 20(1):155-165, 1993.

Elderly people do use substances to alter mood and states of awareness. Detection is difficult because presenting symptoms are often those that are commonly associated with aging itself. All patients who present with symptoms of self-neglect, falls, cognitive and affective impairment, and social withdrawal should be screened for substance abuse. The CAGE and MAST, although not perfect, can be used. When abuse is found, the elderly should be treated as aggressively as their younger counterparts, with slow, careful detoxification and the use of some form of group therapy, such as AA. Discussed are acknowledgment of a problem, difficulties in detecting substance abuse, age related physiological changes, substances most frequently abused by the elderly (alcohol, psychoactive prescription drugs), diagnosis, and treatment.

Women

Finkelstein N, Duncan SA, Derman L, et al: *Getting sober, getting well: A treatment guide for caregivers who work with women,* Cambridge, MA: CASPAR, 1990.

This treatment guide is based on the work of a women's program within a comprehensive alcoholism program, mental health system, and community hospital. It is a "hands-on" guide for trainers and caregivers who work with women and their families and friends. The guide addresses the similarities and differences of women in treatment. It is divided into two parts. Part One, Getting Sober, is organized into 10 sessions that cover the common ground of all treatment for alcoholic and drug abusing women from which more individualized treatment strategies can evolve, early intervention and counseling skills, physiology, prescription drug abuse, helping significant others in a woman's life, and providing models for enhancing women's treatment. Part Two, Getting Well, consists of 17 sessions that focus on the role of relationships in the lives of substance abusing women and the part they play in recovery. The "self-in relation" model based on the work of the Stone Center at Wellesley College is the organizing concept for women's psychological development and mental health. Major themes covered include violence, pregnancy, AIDS, eating disorders, and clinical activities for special populations: young women, women, of color, lesbians, disabled women, homeless women, older women, and women in the workplace. The sessions are structured with five parts: overview, staff training activities, client treatment activities, resources (books, pamphlets, organization lists) and reproducible handouts. (Available through Women's Alcoholism Program of CASPAR, 6 Camelia Ave., Cambridge, MA 02139.)

Gomberg ES: Women and alcohol: Use and abuse (review), *Journal of Nervous and Mental Disease* 181(4):211-219, 1993.

National surveys of the quantity/frequency of drinking, conducted over the last half century, show that the percentage of nonabstaining women has remained at about 60%. Although male/female differences in drinking are smaller than they were a generation ago, this appears to relate primarily to drinking by young adults. Study of social attitudes toward male and female intoxication has consistently indicated more disapproval of female intoxication. Alcoholism in women has a complex etiology that includes biological factors, positive family history, difficulties in impulse control, depression, and drinking by significant others in the social environment. Male/female differences in patterns and consequences of alcoholic behavior are summarized, as are differences among alcoholic women with earlier or later onset. (Author abstract.)

Hall JM: Lesbians and alcohol: Patterns and paradoxes in medical notions and lesbians' beliefs (review), *Journal of Psychoactive Drugs* 25(2):109-119, 1993.

There is growing awareness in the lesbian community about the prevalence of alcohol problems and the meanings and values attached to alcohol use are currently undergoing change. Little research has focused on lesbians' life experiences and alcohol use practices, although in earlier decades a number of medical theories linked lesbianism with alcohol problems as co-pathologies. More recent theories from the social sciences also linked lesbianism with alcohol problems, but on the basis of sociocultural dynamics and consequent negative self-images. This article compares and contrasts medical theories about lesbians and alcohol with lesbians' own ideas about alcohol use and alcohol problems. Mutually reinforcing themes in medical views and lesbians' experiences are identified. The analysis clarifies what is at stake in the current debates about alcohol, alcohol problems, and recovery experiences in the lesbian community and offers suggestions for research, theory, and practice regarding this significant health issue. (Author abstract.)

Lex BW: Some gender differences in alcohol and polysubstance users (review), *Health Psychology* 10(2):121-132, 1991.

Within the past 20 years, public and professional attention has focused on the legitimacy of research and treatment of substance abuse in women as a "special population." Recent efforts, however, have not as yet closed the gap in knowledge about factors promoting or perpetuating alcohol and other substance use problems in women. Materials that are presented in this article were selected to provide a broad spectrum of information about biological, psychological, and sociocultural aspects of substance abuse as it affects women. Data reported include findings from several studies conducted in our laboratories that have examined these effects. Overall, the discussion summarizes past knowledge, reviews current findings, points to unanswered questions, and concludes with a series of research recommendations that emerge from empirical data. (Author abstract.)

Roman PM.: *Women and alcohol use: A review of the research literature,* Rockville, MD: National Institute on Alcohol Abuse and Alcoholism, 1988.

This review of the research literature touches upon the social context of research in relation to women's issues, methodological problems, a review of epidemiology and social surveys, the biological features in relation to alcohol use, the psychological correlates of alcohol problems, and treatment. (ADM)88-1574.

Roth P, editor: *Alcohol and drug issues are women's issues. Volume One: A review of the issues,* Metuchen NJ: Women's Action Alliance and The Scarecrow Press, 1991.

Roth P, editor. *Alcohol and drug issues are women's issues. Volume Two: The model program guide.*

These two volumes review and summarize the major issues related to alcohol, drug use, women, and their lives. Volume One has 24 chapters and 30 contributors. Chapters are devoted to recent biomedical research pertinent to women, sociocultural phenomena, effects of alcohol and drug use during pregnancy, and special populations. The special population groups specifically discussed include those related to ethnicity and race, i.e., Native Americans, Asian Americans, lesbians, African Americans, Latinos. Also discussed are sexual orientation, relationships and status, i.e. as children, mothers, single parents, or being homeless. It concludes with a review of prevention and treatment approaches that are sensitive to women's needs. The second volume in the series is addressed to model programs. It covers the areas of initial planning, staffing, needs assessment, program content, staff development and training, a curriculum for participants, and evaluation. It also describes the experiences of six different women's service organizations, as case studies and examples. The final chapter provides a broad and annotated compendium of resources, ranging from audiovisual aids, to reading lists, to organizations and funding sources, both public and private, and materials such as protocols, and evaluation instruments.

The workplace

Ames GM: Alcohol-related movements and their effects on drinking policies in the American workplace: An historical review, *Journal of Drug Issues* 19(4):489-510, 1989.

This historical review of the influence of alcohol-related movements on drinking policies in the American workplace demonstrates that, in general, employers do not, or cannot, easily follow the trends of alcohol values in the larger culture. This paper identifies specific environmental pressures from within the workplace that have motivated various kinds of industries, during four historical eras, to incorporate, resist, influence, or bypass altogether, larger cultural pressures to control alcohol consumption of the American worker. A 200-year propensity for alcohol policies that focus on the individual rather than the work environment is analyzed and discussed. (Author abstract.)

French MT: The effects of alcohol and illicit drug use in the workplace: A review, *Journal of Employee Assistance Research* 2(1):1-22, 1993.

A large body of medical literature suggests that alcohol and illicit drug use adversely affect social, cognitive, and psychomotor functioning for many individuals. These adverse conditions are often linked to emotional and physical problems at home, in the classroom, and in the workplace. Recently, economists and other social scientists have begun to explore the labor market effects of substance use through statistical analyses of large national data sets and worksite-specific samples. Studies have found that substance use has a statistically significant effect on labor supply, absenteeism, retention, and various job performance measures. This paper critically reviews the literature on this impact and discusses the significance of the findings for employers, policymakers, and public health practitioners. (Author abstract.)

Special Issue: *Alcohol Health and Research World* 16(2):1-172, 1992.

This special issue is devoted to issues relevant to alcohol problems and the workplace. Separate articles are directed to client characteristics of those referred to EAPs, treatment outcome, differential rates of alcohol problems in different occupational groups, EAP administration and the supervisor's role, and also current initiatives and issues related to workplace drug testing.

Walsh JM; Gust SW, editors: *Workplace drug abuse policy: Considerations and experience in the business community*, Rockville, MD: Office of Workplace Initiatives, National Institute on Drug Abuse, 1989.

This monograph is based upon papers and discussions from the conference, "Interdisciplinary Approaches to the Problem of Drug Abuse in the Workplace," held in 1986, convened by the National Institute on Drug Abuse (NIDA) with the goal of developing a consensus on the need to address drug abuse in the workplace and to define the essential procedures. Chapters are authored by nationally recognized experts in the field. The volume reviews the issues related to drug abuse policy in the workplace, both the rationale and impetus for such policy, the legal and technical considerations, the human relations concerns, and then describes four successful programs. The concluding chapter presents the consensus statements on the major issues adopted by the conference to serve as guidelines for policy development.

Psychiatric considerations

In this chapter, we wish to focus upon psychiatric issues that are of importance for the alcohol clinician. These topics include suicide, the elements of the mental status examination, and the major categories of psychiatric illness. The classifications for mental illness are important on several counts. One is that many colleagues are from the mental health field, and it is useful to be comfortable with the terminology and issues with which they deal. Another is that alcohol problems will often mimic psychiatric conditions. Being informed about these conditions is vital when the task is determining if the behavior being observed or reported is a symptom of an alcohol problem or another mental illness. Of course, some clients will have a co-existing psychiatric problem in addition to alcohol dependence. This discussion also includes an overview of the most common types of medications used to treat psychiatric illness. Finally, the chapter also considers other drug use problems, which are common among those with alcohol problems.

SUICIDE EVALUATION AND PREVENTION

Alcohol use and suicide go together. Recall from Chapter 1 that in a substantial number of all suicide attempts, the individual had been drinking and that approximately 40% of all completed suicides are alcohol related. The suicide rate for alcoholics is 55 times that of the general population. Before we all are overwhelmed by these statistics, we should consider why suicide and alcohol are related and what we can do about them.

Types of suicide: completers, attempters, and threateners

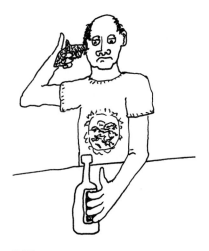

For practical purposes, there are several different groups to be considered when examining suicide. First are the completers, those who take their lives and *intended to*. Classically, these are lonely white men over 50 years of age or lonely teenagers. They use violent means such as a gun or hanging. Their methods are calculated and secretive. Second are those who succeed but *did not intend to*. These are the *attempters*. Classically they are white women, ages 20 to 40, often with interpersonal conflicts whose "method" is pills. The suicide attempt is often an impulsive response. Attempters die by mistake or as the result of miscalculation. For example, they lose track of dosage, or something goes wrong with their plans for rescue. The attempter's intent is not so much to die as to elicit a response from others. Emergency room psychology, which dismisses these clients with a firm kick in the pants, is inappropriate. Someone who is trying to gain attention by attempting suicide is in reality quite sick and deserves care. Third are the *threateners*. These are those individuals who use suicide as a lethal weapon: "If you leave me, I'll kill myself." They are often involved in a pathological relationship. These threateners usually do not follow through, but they are frightened and guilt ridden. In responding to them the therapist will attempt to challenge the threat and thereby remove the deadlock it has created.

Statistics and high-risk factors

The real statistic to keep in mind is that suicide is the second leading recorded cause of death in people under 18 or over 65 years of age. Sixty percent give some prior indication of their intent, thereby making suicide preventable. Typical indications might be "I have a friend . . . ," "What would you think if . . . ," or stockpiling drugs, or giving away possessions. New behaviors can be important cues. People doing things they have never done before may often indicate they have suddenly decided to commit suicide and are now at peace. Examples might be *suddenly* playing cards, dancing, or taking out the garbage when they have never made a practice of this before.

If present, certain high-risk factors should be identified. These include recent loss of a loved one or being single, widowed, and/or childless; living in urban areas; being unemployed, nonreligious, or "oppressed." High-risk emotional factors include anger plus hopelessness, broken or pathological family/friend communications, and isolation in a marriage or on-going relationship. Verbal high-risk cues take the form of both direct statements: "I'm going to kill myself," or indirect indications: "I won't be around to give you any more trouble." People entering *and* leaving a depression are especially vulnerable, as are those with chronic illnesses like arthritis, high blood pressure, ulcers, and malignancies.

Recall that 65% of all suicide attempts are related to alcohol. Several reasons explain this correlation. First, the chemical nature of alcohol tends to release certain brain areas from control. The guarding mechanisms are let down. Hidden thoughts and impulses are released. (You may have witnessed incidents such as the intoxicated guy calling the boss a bastard.) Second, because of the chemical action of alcohol, a state is created wherein the integrative capacity of the brain is diminished. It is a condition in which aspects of memory and concentration are lost. Third, when alcohol is used as a medicine, it is unfortunately a good one to initially produce a mood of relaxation and pseudo-stability. In this state, people may think things are just the way they should be. They feel cool, calm, and collected so that suicide at this point may seem relevant and a good idea: "I'll just jump. It's the rational solution." More alcohol acts as a true depressant with obvious potential consequences. Finally, alcohol may also bring out psychological weakness. It may place people on the edge of reality, tip the scales, lead to loose associations, bring out psychosis, disinhibit normal fears, and produce

voices saying: "The world is better off without you." In all these cases, alcohol acts as a catalyst, both physically and psychologically.

The most fertile ground for suicide is in cases of clinical depression. Most people who have the "blues" are not suicidal. They might think, "Gee, I wish I were dead, things are going so badly," or "I don't know how I'll make it. I might just drive off the road if things don't get better." Things usually do get better, however. On the other hand, clinical depression is characterized by a consistently low mood over a period of weeks, plus weight changes, sleep problems, and other physical symptoms. Pessimism is a symptom of the illness, just as fever is a symptom of the flu. Feelings of how bad things are are part of the depression. Depression, therefore, is bad enough alone, but combined with alcohol, it is a potent mix. "There is no way out." "I'm a bad person—the only way out is to kill myself."

How to ask

The therapist should *always* ask about suicide with any person who is depressed. The thing to remember is that we have never killed anybody by asking. We have certainly missed helping people we could have helped by not asking. There is no way to instigate a suicidal attempt by common-sense asking. It will come as a relief to your clients if you do ask them. Use your own emotional barometer to find out whether they are depressed or whether they are sad. Check yourself in an interview every so often. Block out the client for a moment and ask, "How am I feeling right now? Am I sad, angry, scared? What am I feeling?" It is probably a pretty good barometer of how the client is feeling. The client often says he feels great; check your own gut reactions and trust them.

Ask every client about suicide, but let rapport develop first. Do not just have the client come in and immediately ask him intimate questions like "How's your sex life?" or "Been hallucinating lately?" or "Feel like killing yourself?" The client will probably want to kill *you*. Let rapport develop, and later say, "Now we've talked about a lot of things these last 20 minutes. Have any of them ever gotten you to the point of feeling you couldn't go on any longer?" Don't leave it there; explain that when you say that, you mean suicide. Always say the word "suicide." Do not just ask clients if they ever thought of "throwing in the towel" or some other euphemism. They can take you pretty literally and might say, "Well, no. I dried myself pretty well this morning." You have to get yourself to say "suicide." Practice. It is not so easy to come right out and say it. The first few times it bombs, something like this, "Gee, we've talked about a lot of things. Have any of them ever gotten you to the point of thinking about committing s—s-ah—s-th—." It's almost the kind of thing you need to practice in front of a mirror. "Sui-i-cide. Suicide."

Clients may say, "Boy, you're kidding!" but it's not a hostile response. If anybody does say "Yes"—and he probably will tell you if

Hi dear. Ms. Jones called to say she'd relapsed and was going to kill herself, but when I said you were out of town on a fishing trip, she said she'd call back tomorrow.

he has been thinking about it—obtain as much information as you can. Then go on to say, "Well, when was the last time you thought of it?" "How about today?" Whenever the client was thinking of it last, find out what he was doing, how he thought about it, when he thought of it, and ascertain his plans for it as specifically as possible. In cases of most serious intent, the client will probably say, "Well, not only have I been thinking of it today, but I've been cleaning my gun, it's in my car, my car's outside." In other words, get *all* the data.

What to do

Try to diffuse the situation psychologically and in a practical way. For instance, offer alternatives. Say something like, "On the other hand, what specific reasons do you have for living?" Try to get to a positive thing. Start initiating reasons to live. The more seriously depressed the client, the fewer reasons will come to mind. Remember, that is part of the illness. The client will say, "nothing," and cry. At that point, try to reiterate things he or she told you earlier about him or herself that are reasons to live—a child, a spouse, a business. Provide the reason to live: "That child really needs you." If the client doesn't come up with anything, allow 60 seconds to think of something, even one reason, and then support that enthusiastically: "You're right. Tremendous!" Back the client up! Fill in the picture, and lead him or her into ways that can be acted upon practically. If it is a child, for example, ask where the child is now. How can the client as a parent be of help?

Another important thing is to make a referral, whenever possible, to a mental health clinic or mental health specialist. As a counselor, you have a key role in identifying potential suicides. You cannot expect yourself to single-handedly treat and manage the situation. Request a consultation for further evaluation. Possibly the person is in a real depression and needs medication or the supervision of an in-patient facility. So, call and make an appointment *before* the client leaves the office. In conjunction with the mental health clinic, a decision can be made about how quickly the person should be seen—immediately, later today, or tomorrow. If the client is already being seen by a therapist, contact the therapist. A therapist who is unaware of the situation will want to know and will also be able to provide guidance for you so that you are working together. Don't be afraid you are stepping on anyone's toes. Anybody contemplating suicide cannot have too many people in his or her corner.

Maybe here we can lay to rest any discomfort that arises from the philosophical debates on whether someone has a right to commit suicide. There is considerable discussion about the right to die. Looking at it from the practical side of the issue, anyone who thinks they do would just go ahead and do it. They wouldn't be in your office. Anyone who "happens" into a counselor's office, or phones, and acknowledges suicidal thoughts, directly or indirectly, is not there by chance. They are seeking help in settling their internal debate over life versus death. The counselor, as do other helping people, must come down clearly on the side of living. When depressed, a client cannot *rationally* make this decision. Once the depression clears, most clients are very pleased you prevented their action on suicide plans.

If a client has a weapon, ask that it be checked at the reception desk or elsewhere on the premises. If it is at home, ask that someone else take possession of it and notify you when that is done. *Never* let a client who is suicidal—and they usually improve during the interview—leave your office without your double-checking plans for the rest of the day. Be specific. Call home to make sure someone will be there if that is the expectation. Give the client chores and support. Get something for them to do. Have somebody there to watch the client around the clock and to give the attention he or she needs. Set up another appointment to see the person within 48 hours. Have them call you to check in later that day, or you call them. Be specific. Say, "I'd like to call you between 4 and 5," or at least "this afternoon." It is better not to give an exact time because that is often hard to meet. This kind of paternalism is needed at this time. The weaning of dependence and fostering of independence come later. Give reinforcements. "What do you like to do?" "What do you have to do?" "Do it and let me know how it goes."

In talking with a client the only times that you may foresee something going wrong are in the following three situations. It's simple logic, but it's also a trap.

1. If the client's theme is rejection and loss, for example, be careful you do not reject or put him or her off.

2. If you agree with the client about how bad things are, for example, the client says, "I am a worthless person. I beat my child," you may easily get into your own negative feelings about this. You might communicate "Well, you are right, that was a horrible thing to do." Do not crucify clients. Do not support their punitive guilt response.

3. Clients may say how bad they feel. You are tempted to say "I understand how badly you feel. I often feel that way myself." You're trying to sympathize and share the misery, but clients interpret this as permission to feel the way they do. You are getting away from the reasons the client has to live and are underscoring their pessimism. It is better to reinforce the reasons to live.

Other thoughts about evaluation and prevention come to mind. Get histories of previous suicide attempts. Anyone who has tried it once has a poor track record. A family history of suicide or other losses in childhood from divorce or illnesses or a history of childhood sexual abuse also increase the risk. For someone who has either attempted suicide or is thinking about it, reduce the isolation from family and friends. Hospitalization under close supervision may be needed if supports are lacking. Remove guns, ropes, pills, and so on. Have the client give you the weapon personally. Shake hands with the client as he or she leaves the office, and give "something of yourself" to take with them to put in wallet or pocket, such as a piece of paper with your name and phone number. Try to make sure the client does not have what would constitute a lethal dosage of medication. Any supply of tricyclic antidepressants greater than 1000 mg or a 5-day supply of meprobamate (Miltown) (8000 mg) can be lethal.

Now consider a special situation. If you happen to get involved in an emergency where someone is about to shoot himself, jump from a window ledge, or do something else rash, try to be calm. Keep your voice down. Do not ask philosophical questions, but ask practical questions: "What's your name?" "Where are you from?" Try to have a nonthreatening conversation. This is a grueling situation and can last for hours. Wear the person down. *Do not ever be a hero. Do not rush a person with a gun.* Stay alive to help the people who can be helped.

Trust your gut reactions. Don't feel that if you are unsuccessful, it is your fault. Don't ever forget that your job with suicidal clients is not to be God. Being God's helper is enough.

MENTAL STATUS EXAMINATION

The mental status examination is one of the techniques used by mental health professionals. Its purpose is to guide observation and assist the interviewer in gathering essential data about mental functioning. It consists of standard items, which are routinely covered, ensuring that nothing important is overlooked. The format also helps mental health workers record their findings in a fashion that is easily understood by their colleagues.

Three aspects of mental functioning are always included: mood and affect, thought processes, and cognitive functioning. Mood and affect refer to the dominant feeling state. They are deduced from the client's general appearance; what the client reports; and posture, body movements, and attitude toward the interviewer. Thought processes zero in on how the client presents his or her ideas. Are the thoughts ordered and organized, or does the client jump all over the place? Are his sentences logical? Is the content—what is discussed—sensible, or does it include delusions and bizarre ideas? Finally, cognitive functioning refers to intellectual functioning, memory, ability to concentrate, comprehension, and ability to abstract. This latter portion of the mental status examination involves asking specific questions, for example, about current events, definitions of words, or meanings of proverbs. The interviewer considers the individual's education, lifestyle, and occupation in making a judgment about the responses.

If the alcohol counselor can get some training in how to do a simple mental status examination, it can be helpful in spotting clients with particular problems. It can also greatly facilitate your communication with mental health workers. Just telling a psychiatrist or a psychiatric social worker that the person you are referring is "crazier than a bedbug" isn't very useful.

ALCOHOL PROBLEMS AND OTHER CO-OCURRING PSYCHIATRIC ILLNESS

Understanding the relationship between alcohol use and mood or behavior is one of the most challenging and essential components of anyone's work in the alcohol field. An effort to determine the relative contributions of addictive and nonaddictive psychiatric disorders to abnormal mental states is essential for several reasons. First, alcohol abuse is associated with other psychiatric conditions and can mask psychiatric disorders. Studies have shown the risk of having a problem with alcohol use increases 10 times if a person has schizophrenia or 15 times if a person has an antisocial personality disorder. Second, alcoholism and withdrawal from alcohol dependence can produce symptoms that resemble many other psychiatric disorders. For example, over one third of persons treated for alcohol disorders report a psychotic episode in the preceding 6 months. For this reason, psychiatry, perhaps more than any other medical discipline, must respect alcoholism as "the great mimicker." Psychoactive substance related disorders are the most common psychiatric disorders for people between the ages of 18 and 65. Because of this, it is imperative that all mental health workers include a thorough assessment of alcohol use for all people seeking mental health treatment. Furthermore, if alcohol abuse co-occurs with another psychiatric disorder, both disorders should be treated concurrently and aggressively.

In this text, we have placed considerable emphasis on the fact that psychological problems are not the cause of alcoholism per se. However, in trying to get that message across, it is important not to lose sight of the fact that an individual may have *both* alcohol dependence and another psychiatric condition. Whether alcoholism grows in the soil of some other psychiatric condition (sometimes termed *secondary* or *reactive alcoholism*) or whether it co-occurs with another psychiatric problem, when present, it develops a momentum of its own. On the other hand, the client's ability to establish and maintain sobriety may be dependent upon actively treating other psychiatric conditions as well. The clinician confronted by clients with dual diagnoses faces both diagnostic and treatment challenges, and all too frequently the client faces administrative and systemic barriers.

The next eight sections cover some of the major classes of psychiatric illness as they relate to alcohol use disorders.

Mood disorders

Mood and emotion are what you feel and how you show it. There are two extremes: people who are depressed and those who are manic, and people can fluctuate between these two extremes. This is called a *bipolar mood disorder.* People who are manic show characteristic behavior. Often they have grand schemes, which to others seem quite outlandish. Their conversation is very quick and pressured. Often they jump from topic to topic. If there were a conversation about the state of the union, a person when manic might say, "and, yes, Arkansas is a very pretty state. President Clinton was the governor of the state, and the governor of my car is out of kilter. The left tire is flat, out of air like a balloon Suzy got at the circus where she stained her best dress with cotton candy. . ." Although there is a logical connection between these thoughts, there is an inability to concentrate on any single thought. This pattern of thinking is termed "loose associations." One thought is immediately crowded out by the next. Someone who is manic may also be aggressive and irritable or feel themselves very attractive, sexually irresistible, or capable of superhuman performance. People when manic are perpetually in high gear, have difficulty sleeping, and may have trouble concentrating. Simply being in their company might well make you feel exhausted.

Depression, which is the other side of the mood coin and is far more common, has all the opposite characteristics. Rather than being hyped up, people when depressed grind to a halt. They find very little pleasure in most activities. Movements, speech, and thinking may be slowed down. Biological changes can accompany

depression and are called *vegetative symptoms*. These include disturbances of normal sleep patterns, constipation, slowed motor activity, and weight loss or gain. In extremes, the person with depression stops eating, is unable to rest, experiences a complete depletion of energy, and expends available motor energy in repeated, purposeless motions such as hand-wringing and pacing. Such depression is associated with a sense of self-reproach, irrational guilt, worthlessness, hopelessness, and loss of interest in life. In full force, these phenomena may culminate in suicidal thoughts, plans, or actions. Severe depression is a life-threatening disorder.

Most depression and mania are believed to have a biological basis. They are also episodic disorders. Between episodes, the mood states typically return to a normal state. This is not to imply that one simply sits back and waits for the manic or depressive episode to pass. With individuals who are significantly depressed, suicide is an ever-present possibility. Individuals when manic can incur phenomenal life problems that can wreak havoc for themselves as well as for their families. These conditions are highly treatable with medications (see the following section). Talking therapies may be helpful in less severe conditions but are of little use when someone's perception of reality and thought processes are seriously altered.

Alcohol use and alcoholism are intertwined with mood disorders in several ways. The most important one is that alcohol consumption can cause depressive symptoms in anyone. Alcohol can produce a toxic depression that embraces the full range of depression's symptoms including anorexia, insomnia, somatic complaints, suicidal thoughts, and despair. Experimental studies have demonstrated that heavy drinking can induce depressive symptoms in both alcoholics and nonalcoholics. Secondly, a temporary depression is frequently described as a feature of alcoholism that can remit with abstinence. Depending on the diagnostic criteria used, depression may be seen in over one half of those participating in alcohol rehabilitation. Women are more likely than men to present with symptoms of depression. Beyond the acute effects of the drug alcohol, chronic alcohol abusers often confront deteriorating social relations, loss of employment, associated trauma, and loss of health, which are factors also associated with depressed states.

As mentioned in the section on suicide, any alcohol use by someone in a depression is contraindicated. This is an additional concern for alcoholics. It is estimated that 7% to 21% of alcoholics commit suicide. Although suicidal behavior in general increases with alcohol consumption, active alcoholics attempt suicide far more often than nonalcoholics when drinking. Several factors contribute to this. Alcoholism may be an indicator of a suicide-prone individual; alcoholism itself can be considered a form of slow suicide. The loss of cognitive function resulting from alcohol abuse will create an increasing gap between personal expectations and actual performance, resulting in despair. The multiple losses mentioned before can compound a sense of hopelessness. In assessing an alcoholic's suicide potential, further risk factors to consider are the loss of a close interpersonal relationship within the previous 6 weeks, the presence of hopelessness, and negative attitudes toward the interviewer. The alcoholic with suicidal thoughts, above all, needs to be taken seriously whether he is inebriated or not. As an important aside, a reactive depression may also be seen in the family members of a substance abuser. Alcoholism is a family illness, and one out of three American families have direct contact with an alcoholic. These people may develop depression as their defenses are overwhelmed by the constant stress of dealing with emotional and physical abuse, economic instability, and their perceived impotence to change their loved one's behavior. Obviously, for most, referral to Al-Anon will be far more appropriate than the use of antidepressant medications.

Because depression is often a result of alcoholism, representing a reactive or secondary depression, usually the depressed symptoms seen in alcoholics do not require separate treatment. But research suggests that 10% to 15% of females and 5% of males seeking alcoholism treatment have a major affective disorder that *preceded* the alcohol abuse. In these instances, it is likely that the depression will not lift with abstinence and alcohol treatment. At the point of entry into treatment, it may be difficult to get the information needed to distinguish initially between an independent, primary depression and depression that results from alcoholism. The client may have difficulty providing an accurate chronology of events due to cognitive deficits that are a part of both alcoholism and depression. The most reliable information is often provided by family and friends.

The cause of depression for a person abusing alcohol may only become apparent over time. If the depressive symptoms lift with abstinence, then one can be confident that the affective disturbance was secondary to the alcohol abuse. If there are persistent depressed symptoms after several weeks of abstinence, then the clinician should consider the possibility of a co-occurring mood disorder and concurrent treatment for depression may be indicated. An extended period of sobriety before making the diagnosis of depression, though preferable, may not always be possible. On occasion, the clinician may be so impressed with the severity of depressive symptoms that waiting for several months cannot be justified. This is critically important, because without adequate concurrent treatment, these clients are likely to see themselves as treatment failures. For them, things have not gotten better with sobriety. Also, they may unwittingly be urged by AA friends or treatment personnel "to work the program harder." In fact, they have been giving it their all. All treatment for persons abusing alcohol must include education about depression, its biological basis, and why medications can be useful. Discomfort may surface around the use of medications, especially because many treatment programs caution clients about the dangers

of psychoactive drug use. Clients need to be reassured that the medications prescribed for depression have no addiction potential and are not associated with abuse. It is also important to keep in mind that several medical conditions (e.g., thyroid disease) can cause mood disorders as well.

Another association between mood disorders and alcohol use is that drinking can escalate during the period of mood disturbance. Research indicates that 20% to 60% of clients with bipolar disorders report excessive use of alcohol during the manic phases of their illness. It is unclear whether this is an effort to "self-medicate" their disturbing manic symptoms or whether it is a result of the poor judgment that is part of this phase of the illness. Regardless of why alcohol use increases, the consequences of the disinhibiting effects of alcohol, laid on top of the impaired judgment generally present are often disastrous. The focus of therapy for bipolar clients with alcohol abuse is two pronged. The primary disorder may require medication (lithium and/or antipsychotic agents); counseling and education are necessary to address alcohol use issues. In individuals with primary depression, 20% to 30% report increased alcohol intake during their mood disturbance. Here too this can complicate their treatment.

Disorders involving psychosis

Psychosis refers to a disintegration of thought processes frequently associated with disturbances in function. While psychosis as a symptom may be associated with a variety of psychiatric disorders, including substance related disorders, it is often prominent in schizophrenic disorders. Schizophrenia and other psychotic disorders are a group of chronic fluctuating disturbances that are among the most incapacitating of the mental disorders. They exact an enormous cost in human suffering and public and private resources. These disorders have a biochemical basis but are subject to environmental influences.

Schizophrenia occurs is about 1% of the general population. Schizophrenia is heterogenous in its presentation. Those with schizophrenia may have "positive" symptoms including hallucinations (a sensory perception with no corresponding stimulus), delusions (a fixed, false belief), or incoherence of thought with resultant disorganized speech. They may also have "negative" symptoms including shyness or withdrawal from social contacts, difficulty communicating, as well as a depressed mood. Attention and cognitive disturbances are frequently present. Attempts to communicate are very difficult because the person with schizophrenia may perceive reality very differently. The individual with schizophrenia often misinterprets environmental stimuli. This altered perception can be very subtle or very marked. Clients with schizophrenia may make connections between events that are not justified. For example, the client may hear a car backfire and see their landlord in the hallway and develop a concern that the landlord is "out to get me." If the client then hears imaginary voices saying "He'll shoot first, ask questions later," their sense of paranoia becomes even greater. The treatment of schizophrenic disorders as well as other psychotic disorders includes medications (see following section) as well as ongoing supportive counseling and other rehabilitative efforts.

Some conditions associated with alcohol abuse closely resemble psychotic disorders. One study found a history of psychotic symptoms in over 40% of alcoholics who sought treatment. One such condition that may be misdiagnosed and lead to the inappropriate use of antipsychotic medication is that of alcoholic hallucinosis. Although seen in less than 3% of chronic alcoholics, it is so easily confused with schizophrenia that it should be considered in all cases of acute psychosis. It is often part of withdrawal states, but it can occur in an actively drinking individual. Symptoms include auditory, tactile, or visual hallucinations. The person will typically develop delusions of a persecutory nature related to these hallucinations. Several features help to distinguish alcohol hallucinosis from schizophrenia. The client will have a history of heavy alcohol use. The majority of alcoholics with this condition will have their first episode after the age of 40, while schizophrenia typically appears earlier in life. The client usually has no family history of schizophrenia, but there may be a family history of alcoholism. Unlike schizophrenia, there is little evidence of a formal thought disorder, for example, loose associations and disorganization of thinking. The content of the hallucinations is fairly simple, unlike the less understandable or bizarre hallucinations of schizophrenia. In alcohol hallucinosis, the resolution of these symptoms is usually quick, occurring over the course of 1 to 6 days. Management should include hospitalization, close observation, some minor tranquilizers, and the limited use of antipsychotic medications. Wernicke-Korsakoff syndrome (see Chapter 5) also includes psychotic symptoms. This is an irreversible organic brain syndrome resulting from chronic alcohol abuse, which is characterized by prominent memory impairment and striking personality changes.

FORMAL THOUGHT DISORDER

Aside from the psychotic symptoms that may result from alcohol, estimates of the prevalence of alcohol use disorder co-occurring with schizophrenia range from 14% to 47%. This may occur with levels of alcohol consumption that would generally not be thought of as problematic in the general population. The combination of schizophrenia and alcohol abuse will often result in a rocky clinical course and a poor prognosis. Without specialized services, these individuals may have difficulty complying with any treatment plan. They will frequently not take medications as prescribed and may be unwilling or unable to follow recommendations for abstinence from alcohol. Efforts to end drinking in this population must be based on an assessment of what alcohol provides for the individual. If drinking is used to reduce anxiety around hallucinations, then increasing antipsychotic medication may be appropriate. If drinking is used to reduce uncomfortable side effects from anti-psychotic medication, then a reduction or substitution of medications may be necessary. If drinking represents their effort to achieve peer acceptance, then non-alcohol social alternatives should be developed. For these clients, the need for compliance with prescribed medication cannot be overemphasized. Abstinence for some persons with schizophrenia may be indicated because even moderate drinking may, for them, be disruptive, suggesting a vulnerability to the affects of alcohol.

For these patients, the standard alcohol regimen may be seen as threatening. Poor treatment outcomes in traditional alcohol treatment settings have been associated with the severity of psychiatric symptoms. Persons with schizophrenia tend to do poorly in group settings with lots of confrontation but can be treated quite effectively in less threatening groups. In recent demonstration projects, a phase model using engagement, persuasion, active treatment, and relapse prevention has been effective in achieving treatment goals. If AA is to be used as part of the treatment plan, then these persons must be thoroughly prepared for AA experiences after they have accepted the need for abstinence. The host group should be assessed in advance for receptiveness to the psychiatrically impaired. Specialized dual diagnosis self-help groups for this are ideal and are increasingly available in many regions.

Anxiety disorders

Anxiety disorders are relatively common and involve incapacitating nervousness, tension, apprehension, and fear. These symptoms may appear episodically and "out of the blue," as in panic attacks. The anxiety may be a fear of particular places or situations, as in agoraphobia, or it may be a symptom of fearing a specific object (e.g., spiders), which is called a *simple phobia*. For others it may take the form of unrelenting recurrent ideas (obsessions) or the need to perform repetitive rituals (compulsions). The anxious person may experience physical symptoms including diaphoresis (sweating), tremor, diarrhea, pallor, rapid pulse, shortness of breath, headache, or fatigue. In contrast to other mental disorders, which may also be associated with a significant amount of anxiety, the anxiety disorders do not involve major disturbances in mood, thought, or judgment. Care must be taken to rule out other medical problems or medications as the cause of anxiety symptoms.

The relationship of anxiety disorders to alcoholism remains controversial. As with mood disorders, the anxiety experienced may be independent of or secondary to alcoholism. Most clinicians know of clients who drink to control symptoms of panic or phobic disorders. This self-medication may well take on a life of its own, leading to alcohol abuse or dependence. There is a high prevalence of anxiety disorders in alcoholics in treatment. Several studies have reported the rate of associated anxiety disorders to be in a range between 22% and 44%. Investigators concede that the sequence of anxiety and drinking is highly variable between individuals.

Understanding the relationship of anxiety symptoms to the drinking behavior is essential. Abstinence alone may "cure" the anxious symptoms if they are the consequences of drinking. On the other hand, severe anxiety may increase the vulnerability of the dually diagnosed client to relapse. Treatment decisions must be based on a careful history of symptoms and observation of the individual following detoxification. If a co-occurring anxiety disorder is felt to be present, an integrated treatment plan might include the use of psychotherapy, behavioral therapy, or medications. Participation in safe supportive 12-step programs may also reduce symptoms from anxiety disorders. Antidepressants like imipramine (Tofranil) or phenelzine (Nardil) may be effective with certain anxiety disorders and have very little abuse potential. Benzodiazepines are often effective for the symptoms of anxiety, but because of their high abuse potential, they should be lower on the list of medication alternatives. Buspirone (BuSpar), with a good safety profile, not euphorigenic, and with few drug interactions, can be useful in treating an anxiety disorder in individuals with alcoholism. Cautious prescribing practices and a regular monitoring of clinical progress will minimize the risk of drug abuse and maximize the chances of successful recovery.

Personality disorders

Everyone has a unique set of personality traits that they exhibit in a range of social situations. When these traits are so rigid and maladaptive that they repeatedly interfere with a person's social or occupational functioning, they constitute a personality disorder. People with these disorders have the capacity "to get under everyone's skin." There are 10 different types of personality disorders described in DSM-IV, but the two most commonly associated with alcoholism are the antisocial and borderline types.

A person with an antisocial personality disorder is frequently in trouble, getting into fights, conning others for personal profit, committing crimes, and having problems with authority. Antisocial personality disorders appear to be inherited independent of the predisposition to develop alcoholism. Although these two disorders are *not* genetically linked together, those with antisocial personality disorder are at high risk for developing alcoholism. In addition, chronic alcohol consumption can lead to personality changes that closely resemble the antisocial personality. However, these behaviors may well disappear following abstinence. Studies have found that from 10% to 20% of men and about 5% to 10% of women in alcohol treatment

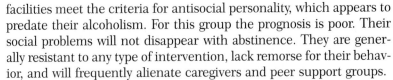

facilities meet the criteria for antisocial personality, which appears to predate their alcoholism. For this group the prognosis is poor. Their social problems will not disappear with abstinence. They are generally resistant to any type of intervention, lack remorse for their behavior, and will frequently alienate caregivers and peer support groups.

A person with a borderline personality disorder may act impulsively with multiple suicide attempts, exhibit inappropriate emotions such as intense anger or ingenuine affection, have feelings of emptiness or boredom, and have frequent mood swings. They also frequently use alcohol in chaotic and unpredictable patterns, and 13% to 28% of alcoholics seeking treatment have been given this diagnosis. It is again important to attempt to separate out the sequence of behavioral problems and alcohol abuse in developing appropriate treatment plans. People with this disorder also evoke strong negative feelings from their caregivers. All suicidal behavior, from threats to attempts, must be taken seriously. Treatment objectives include the creation of a safe and secure relationship and environment.

Attention-deficit/hyperactivity disorders

It has been recognized that some children are unable to remain attentive in situations where it is socially necessary to do so. This is often most apparent in school, but it can also be apparent in the home. In the past, these conditions were termed *hyperactivity* or *minimal brain dysfunction;* they are now known as *attention-deficit hyperactivity disorders (ADHD)*. Follow-up studies of children with ADHD have noted a tendency for the development of alcohol dependence in adulthood. The examination of alcoholics' childhoods also shows a higher incidence of ADHD. One hypothesis is that a subgroup of alcohol abusers begin to drink to stabilize areas of the brain that are "irritable" due to damage earlier in life. For them, alcohol can be considered self-medication. Alcohol may improve performance on cognitive tasks, allow better concentration, and offer a subjective sense of stability. Such a response to alcohol would be highly reinforcing and thereby increase the risk of addiction.

With adults, it is very difficult to sort out the cognitive impairment caused by alcohol from a preexisting, underlying deficit. Prolonged abstinence is once more desirable. On the other hand, these clients may be unable to achieve and maintain sobriety.

When confronted with an individual who has been through treatment several times and never been able to establish sobriety, take a careful childhood history. If there is evidence of difficulties in school or other problems suggesting ADHD, further evaluation and treatment with medication may be warranted. The medication prescribed in such cases may belong to the stimulant class; however, for such clients it has a paradoxical "calming" effect. In addition, the

signs of hyperactivity

Signs of living with hyperactivity

above data suggest it would be useful to discuss with parents of children currently diagnosed as having ADHD steps that might be taken
to reduce future risk of alcohol problems. Recent studies do not
support any conclusions that the use of medication in childhood
correlates with eventual substance abuse.

Organic mental disorders

A disorder is diagnosed as organic when it is caused by a known
defect in brain function. The causes can vary. For example, organic
mental disorders can result from trauma to the central nervous system, from a brain tumor, from a stroke, or from a variety of infections. These impairments in brain function limit the person's ability
to think and respond meaningfully to the environment. Usually
there are significant changes in cognitive function. Problems with
memory, an inability to concentrate, or a loss of intellectual capacity are common.

These disorders can represent permanent impairment, or they
can be completely reversible. Which of these outcomes occurs
depends mostly on whether there has been only temporary interference with the brain's function (e.g., through ingestion of drugs
or an active infection of the brain) or whether there has been permanent damage to brain tissue. Reversible organic mental disorders are referred to as *delirium*. Typically the onset of delirium is
rapid, and if the cause is identified and treated, the person may
return to his or her usual self within days. Another component of
delirium can be visual hallucinations, especially at night, which can
be particularly terrifying. *Dementia* generally refers to irreversible
organic brain syndromes. Usually these have a more gradual onset,
with there being a gradual deterioration of function over the course
of years. In addition to the limitations these disorders create for an
individual, an equally significant factor may be how the individual
perceives them. If the symptoms appear slowly, the individual may
be able to compensate, that is for the most part appear normal,
especially if in a familiar environment with no new problems to
solve. On the other hand, if the symptoms appear rapidly, the person may understandably be extremely upset. As the individual
experiences a reduction in thinking capacity, anxiety often results
and is very apparent.

The treatment of organic mental disorders attempts, when possible, to correct the underlying cause. If it is a tumor, surgery may
be indicated; if it is drug-induced, withdrawal of the toxic agent is
necessary. If permanent impairment is associated with organic mental disorders, rehabilitation measures will be initiated to assist the
person in coping with limitations. In relation to alcohol use, there
are a variety of organic mental disorders. Delirium may arise from
acute intoxication, which clearly impairs mental functioning, or it

may occur during withdrawal states, which can occur in the person physically dependent on alcohol.

Severe cognitive deficits in a chronic alcoholic may lead to the diagnosis of alcoholic dementia. This type of dementia develops insidiously and typically occurs during the drinker's fifth or sixth decade. The symptoms include a deteriorating memory and often dramatic personality changes. Mood swings are common; moods can swing from anger to euphoria. This condition is related to the widespread brain damage and actual shrinkage of brain tissue, which is apparent if the person has a CAT scan of the brain. With abstinence, there may be some recovery over the first 6 weeks. These improvements will be marked and be evident on a CAT scan. Abstinence, unfortunately, is difficult to achieve. The impairment in thinking doesn't allow the standard counseling and educational approaches to take hold. Generally some degree of dementia persists.

The elderly are particularly susceptible to mental disturbances caused by alcohol. Metabolism slows with age, leading to higher blood levels of alcohol with similar consumption in the geriatric population. Their increased use of prescribed medication also increases the likelihood of a medication/alcohol interaction, often leading to episodes of confusion. Among elderly patients seen in an emergency room, confusion was virtually three times more common for those with an alcohol problem. Older people have an apparent heightened sensitivity to all psychoactive compounds, leading to greater cognitive changes while drinking. Sometimes frank organic brain syndromes occur. As demographic changes result in a higher percentage of older people, practitioners will be increasingly challenged to identify alcohol-related cognitive deficits and not simply chalk them up to aging. The diagnosis is often missed in this population because the elderly tend to be protected by their friends and family. They may not meet strict DSM-IV criteria for alcohol abuse or alcohol dependence, but they still may be drinking pathologically.

Polysubstance dependence

Alcohol abuse among those who are primarily abusing other licit and illicit substances is frequently overlooked. In one study, 70% to 77% of clients entering treatment for benzodiazepine (minor tranquilizers) abuse also met criteria for alcohol abuse. Of opioid addicts in treatment, 20% to 35% were found to have alcohol-related problems. The danger here is that an alcohol problem is treated lightly and without any real alcohol assessment done or alcohol treatment provided. The cocaine abuser who routinely uses alcohol to offset the stimulant's effects may not be aware of a developing alcohol dependence. It is also necessary to look for other drug dependencies in those with identified alcohol problems. The rate of other drug abuse or dependence in treatment samples of alcoholics ranges from 12% to 43%.

Other addictive behaviors

The concept of addiction is now being extended to behaviors that do not involve substance abuse. These behaviors include gambling, running, and eating disorders. Some people refuse food intake because they believe they are too fat, although the scales say differently (anorexia). Others stuff themselves and vomit, over and over (bulimia.) Case reports of associations between eating disorders and alcohol abuse are increasing as recognition of each illness improves. A striking phenomenon is the frequency of referral for alcohol treatment of individuals who had eating disorders in earlier years. There appears to be a higher incidence of a positive family history for alcoholism in persons with anorexia, which also increases their risk for developing this dependency. Although prospective studies are needed, the potential risk of alcoholism among those with eating disorders should be recognized.

Clinical considerations

When confronted with a possible dual diagnosis of alcoholism and another psychiatric condition, alcoholism treatment personnel should consider consultation from a psychiatrist or mental health worker. Treating both conditions simultaneously is necessary and may require a delicate balancing act. Under any circumstances, extra support and education is essential. The client needs to appreciate that he is being treated for two very different conditions. Efforts to help the client integrate information from both treatment perspectives require thoughtful treatment planning.

Homelessness, alcohol use, and chronic mental illness

Although homelessness is not an illness, it represents a point where chronic mental illness intersects with alcohol problems. Alcohol dependence is one pathway toward homelessness. On the other hand, homelessness can be a condition that precedes increased alcohol abuse. Either way, alcohol-related problems within the homeless population are enormous. On any given night, over 600,000 people in this country are without adequate shelter, and about two fifths of them are affected by alcohol abuse. Certainly the "skid row bum," whose repeated detox and jail stints leave lasting impressions on providers, remains inextricably linked with homelessness in the popular consciousness. Historically, the "chronic public inebriate" frequently ended up on the streets. The odds for successful treatment then went down due to their social losses. Homeless persons with alcoholism have unique service and housing needs requiring creative responses.

The homeless alcohol abuser has been shown to be multiply disadvantaged with higher rates of physical, mental, and social problems than the non-alcohol abusing homeless person. The homeless

Eat not to fullness; drink not to elevation.

BENJAMIN FRANKLIN

alcohol abuser tends to be male, white, and elderly. They often have troubled marital and family histories, poorer employment records, and are more transient and socially isolated. They are frequently incarcerated for petty crimes and often are victims of violent attacks. As many as one half of alcohol abusing homeless persons have an additional psychiatric diagnosis. Homeless alcohol abusers are at high risk for neurologic impairment, heart disease and hypertension, chronic lung disease, liver disease, and trauma. These clinical features complicate engagement, intervention, and recovery.

Successful treatment of alcoholism depends on social and physical environments where sobriety is positively supported. These are hardly the conditions encountered in a street existence. Therefore the service needs of the homeless go beyond the provision of substance abuse treatment. Providing only detoxification and short-term in-patient care will reinforce the revolving door scenario that too often typifies homeless persons with alcoholism. Assistance and support for finding appropriate, affordable, and alcohol-free housing is the backbone of treatment for this special population. To accomplish even this basic goal, bridging the person's disaffiliation, distrust, and disenchantment is necessary. Overcoming these adverse motivational forces requires a great deal of clinical skill. It also requires a great deal of patience, since the homeless alcoholic will be among the most severe and chronically ill clients that a counselor is likely to encounter. The needs of the homeless alcohol abuser go beyond the capacity of any one provider. Clinicians will need to continue to form coalitions with advocates, politicians, and community resources to develop adequate service systems for this disadvantaged population.

MEDICATIONS

Alcoholism does not exist in a vacuum. Alcoholics, as do other people, have a variety of other problems, some physical, some psychiatric. They may be receiving treatment or treating themselves. The treatment may involve prescription or over-the-counter medications. The more one knows about medications in general, the more helpful one can be to a client. Those with alcohol dependence in particular tend to seek instant relief from the slightest mental or physical discomfort. The active alcoholic may welcome any chemical relief and is at risk for using some psychotropic medications in an addictive manner. The recovering person, on the other hand, may be so leery of *any* medication that he or she may refuse to use those medications that are very much needed. Thus some familiarity with the types of psychotropic medications and their appropriate use is important. They are not alike, either in terms of their actions or in their potential for abuse.

Taking a good medication history is imperative in dealing with clients with alcohol problems. Following are some of the questions you would want to have in mind: "What medications do you currently take?" "Is it prescribed, when was it prescribed, and by whom was it prescribed?" "Are you following the prescription?" "Do you take more or less or use a different schedule?" "Is the drug having the desired effects?" "What, if any, side effects exist?" "Do you have any medication allergies?" "What is your philosophy about medications?" "Have you ever abused medication in the past?" These questions can help identify abuse of current medications and prevent future abuse in vulnerable recovering alcoholics.

Tremendous confusion may arise from a communication gap between the patient and the prescribing physician. The physician prescribes a medication intended to have a specific effect on a particular patient. The patient is unclear about (and usually doesn't question) the need for medication. There may be limited access to the physician for follow-up calls. Only feedback from the patient enables the doctor to make adjustments, if necessary. The regimen for taking a drug is important, also. Often, as the patient begins to feel better, he or she stops or cuts the dose of prescribed drugs. One danger in this is that enough has been taken to relieve the symptoms but not enough to remove the underlying cause. Any client should be encouraged to consult with his physician *before* altering the way medications are taken. Because treatment requires good communication, you should help the client to ask questions about the treatment and the drugs involved. Also be sensitive to the problems that the cost of medications can present for some clients. Those without insurance can find the cost prohibitive. This may mean that they skimp on taking medicines as prescribed to make their supply last longer. Or they may put off having a prescription refilled on schedule, their budget simply can't be stretched that far, at that time.

Every drug has multiple simultaneous actions. Only a few of these effects are being sought when any drug is prescribed. These intended effects are the *therapeutic effects*. All other effects would be the side effects in that instance. In selecting a medication for a patient, the doctor seeks a drug with the maximum therapeutic impact and the fewest side effects. Ideally this should be a collaborative effort. Enough information must be exchanged to enable the client to give valid consent.

Psychotropic medications

The group of medications of particular interest in relation to alcohol are those with psychotropic effects. Any drug that influences behavior or mood falls into this category. Because of the abuse potential of some of them (particularly anti-anxiety medications) and their ability to mimic intoxicated states, these medications are of the greatest concern to the counselor. At the same time, they may be the most widely misunderstood. There is no denying that psychotropic medications are widely prescribed and sometimes over

prescribed. It ought to be noted though that the bulk of these mood-altering medications are not being prescribed by psychiatrists; rather they are prescribed by family physicians and other medical specialties. Because of their mood-altering properties, such medications may be candidates for abuse. "Down with drugs" is not apt to be an effective banner for an alcohol clinician, however. All psychotropic medications are not alike. Not all represent potential problems for clients.

A discussion of three major categories of psychotropic medications follows. Each has different actions and is prescribed for different reasons. These are the antipsychotic agents, the antidepressant agents, and the antianxiety agents.

Antipsychotic medications. The antipsychotic drugs are also called *neuroleptics* or *major tranquilizers*. These drugs relieve the symptoms of psychoses. In addition to the antipsychotic effect, they also have a tranquilizing and a sedative effect, calming behavior and inducing drowsiness. Antipsychotic medications have allowed many patients to live in the community rather than institutions. However, their potential for irreversible side effects mandates judicious use. Different medications in this group have differing side effects, making them either more or less sedating. The medication prescribed is selected on the basis of the client's constellation of symptoms. Thus a drug with greater sedative effects might well be selected for a person exhibiting manic or agitated behavior. Some antipsychotic drugs are currently available in a long-acting injectable form called decanoate. These shots can be useful in ensuring medication compliance in clients with a history of poor compliance.

The antipsychotic medications most frequently encountered are listed in Table 11-1.

TABLE 11-1

Commonly prescribed antipsychotic medications

Brand name	Generic name	Daily dose range (mg)
Thorazine	chlorpromazine	100-1000
Mellaril	thioridazine	30-800
Stelazine	trifluoperazine	2-30
Trilafon	perphenazine	2-64
Navane	thiothixene	6-60
Haldol	haloperidol	3-50
Haldol D	haloperidol Decanoate	30-200 (long-acting injection)
Prolixin	fluphenazine	2-64
Prolixin D	prolixin Decanoate	25-50 (long-acting injection)
Loxitane	loxapine	10-100
Moban	molindone	50-225
Clozaril	clozapine	25-450
Risperdal	risperidone	4-16

As with most medications, antipsychotic drugs interact with alcohol. A common effect of combining alcohol with sedating medications is *potentiation*. This implies that the two agents act in concert to exaggerate the sedative effects, which could cause problems. Alcohol can also increase brain chemicals that the neuroleptic agents are attempting to block, leading to reduced effectiveness. Another interaction worth noting is that alcohol has been reported to increase the likelihood of some side effects of neuroleptic agents.

Neuroleptic drugs are much less likely to be abused than the usual sedatives or antianxiety agents. They are not chemically similar to alcohol and are therefore not subject to cross-tolerance or addiction. The sensations they produce are generally not experienced as pleasurable and are therefore infrequently sought out. For these reasons, an antipsychotic agent may be prescribed, not to relieve psychotic symptoms, but for its sedative or tranquilizing properties. Several of the side effects caused by neuroleptic medications are unpleasant and require additional medication to reduce. The medications that can be used to reduce these unpleasant side effects include benztropine (Cogentin) and trihexiphenidyl (Artane). They can induce pleasurable mental changes and may be abused by clients.

Antidepressant medications. The antidepressants, another major class of psychotropic medications, are used to treat the biological component of depression. They must be taken at a high enough dose to achieve a therapeutic level. A period of regular use (often 2 to 4 weeks) is also necessary before these medications have their full effect. Therefore an initial complaint of patients is that the medicine isn't helping. Side effects vary according to the category of antidepressant. These are most pronounced when the person first begins taking the drug. The physician may choose to have the patient take the medication at a particular time of the day to minimize side effects. There are several different types of antidepressants, grouped according to their chemical properties, and how they act.

The SSRI's —the acronym for Selective Serotonin Reuptake Inhibitors—are the most commonly prescribed and most widely used antidepressant medications. In general, they have fewer side effects than the other categories of antidepressant medications. The most commonly encountered side effects include gastrointestinal symptoms, headache, insomnia, and agitation.

Tricyclics are the oldest category of commonly used antidepressants. Common side effects include dry mouth and constipation. A third category known as *monoamine oxidase inhibitors (MAOIs)* require additional dietary restrictions to avoid bad side effects. Drugs in the category have numerous other side effects as well. Buproprion is another commonly prescribed antidepressant. It is presently the only medication in its category and is chemically unrelated to the other antidepressants. Common side effects include agitation, dry mouth, insomnia, headache, gastrointestinal symptoms,

TABLE 11-2

Commonly prescribed antidepressant medications

Brand name	Generic name	Daily dose range (mg)
SSRIs		
Prozac	fluoxetine	20-80
Zoloft	sertraline	50-200
Paxil	paroxetine	20-50
Tricyclics		
Tofranil	imipramine	50-300
Elavil	amitriptyline	50-300
Aventyl/Pamelor	nortriptyline	50-150
Norpramin	desipramine	25-200
Sinequan	doxepin	25-300
MAOIs*		
Nardil	phenelzine	15-90
Parnate	tranylcypromine	30-60
Other Antidepressants		
Buproprion	wellbutrin	300-450
Asendin	amoxapine	150-600
Ludiomil	maprotline	75-300
Desyrel	trazadone	50-600

*Drinking alcoholic beverages with a high tyramine content (such as chianti wine, sherry, or beer) while taking MAOIs can possibly lead to severe hypertension, as well as increasing CNS depression.

and tremor. Other medications not included in the above-mentioned categories include trazadone, amoxapine, and maprotiline. Of these, only trazadone is used with any frequency and then more often for its side effect of sedation rather than its anti-depressant effect.

The most common antidepressants are listed in Table 11-2.

There is no clear evidence that antidepressant agents are addicting. However, overdoses of some of these medications (e.g., the tricyclics) can be lethal. Again, in combination with alcohol, problems can arise because of their additive effects.

Lithium carbonate is worth special mention. Unlike the antidepressants, lithium is a mood regulator. It can be helpful in either depression or mania and is a common medication used in controlling bipolar disorder. The dose is geared to body weight, and the level is monitored periodically through blood samples. Because lithium produces no pleasant effects it is unlikely to be abused by the client. The contrary behavior is the more common danger. Feeling greatly improved, those on lithium may decide it's no longer necessary. However, maintaining stability often depends upon continuation of the medication.

In addition to lithium, tegretol (Carbamazepine) and valproic acid are used in patients who cannot take lithium because of side effects, or they are taken in addition to lithium. Use of alcohol with either of these is contraindicated for two reasons. One is because of

TABLE 11-3

Commonly prescribed antianxiety medications*

Brand name	Generic name	Daily dose range (mg)
Librium	chlordiazepoxide	10-100
Valium	diazepam	6-40
Restoril	temazapam	7.5-30
Dalmane	flurazepam	15-30
Xanax	alprazolam	.75-4
Tranxene	clorazepate	7.5-60
Ativan	lorazepam	1-10
Serax	oxazepam	30-120
BuSpar	buspirone	15-60
Antarax/Vistaril	hydroxyzine	25-100

*We have grouped the antianxiety agents together for the purposes of this discussion. However, differences among them, based on their chemical composition, have significance if abuse occurs. These are elaborated on in the following section.

possible additive effects. Also, there is the possibility that either of them, on their own, can cause liver damage. This would be made worse by alcohol use.

Antianxiety medications. The final group of psychotropic medications are the antianxiety agents. The major action of these drugs is to promote tranquilization and sedation. Quite properly, alcohol can be included in any list of drugs in this class. The antianxiety agents are also called the *minor tranquilizers*. They have no antipsychotic or significant antidepressant properties and are very effective in the treatment of anxiety disorders. Short acting forms are frequently prescribed as sleeping aids. However, their high potential for abuse and dependence make them less likely to be the first medication prescribed for anxiety, especially in persons who have any history of abuse of alcohol or drugs. The most common antianxiety agents are listed in Table 11-3.

Medications in this class, along with barbiturates (now rarely prescribed), are those most likely to be troublesome for alcoholics. The potential for abuse of these antianxiety agents has become far more broadly recognized. Valium, Xanax, and Ativan are minor tranquilizers that have been widely associated with addiction syndromes. In the past, Quaalude, Placidyl—which interestingly are no longer available for prescription in this country—as well as Miltown and some barbiturates also caused major abuse/dependency problems. A more recently developed anti-anxiety medication, buspirone (BuSpar) has to date demonstrated little abuse potential. The same is true for hydroxyzine (Atarax, Vistaril).

Beyond problems of possible abuse, there are other dangers with the minor tranquilizers and alcohol. Taken in combination, alcohol and the minor tranquilizers potentiate one another. While most peo-

I'll trade you two valiums and a xanax for an ativan.

Every form of addiction is bad, no matter whether the narcotic be alcohol or morphine or idealism.

CARL GUSTAV JUNG

ple have heard of Karen Ann Quinlin, far fewer are aware that the cause of her irreversible coma was attributed to the combination of alcohol and Valium.

Because of their similar pharmacology, alcohol and the minor tranquilizers are virtually interchangeable. This phenomenon is the basis of cross-addiction and is the rationale for using minor tranquilizers in alcohol detoxification. It is their very interchangeability with alcohol that makes them very poor drugs for those with an alcohol problem, except for detoxification purposes.

On the whole, Americans are very casual about medications. Too often, prescriptions are not taken as directed, are saved up for the next illness, or shared with family and friends. Over-the-counter preparations are treated as candy. The fact that a prescription is not required does not render these preparations harmless. Some possible ingredients in over-the-counter drugs are antihistamines, stimulants, and of course, alcohol. These can cause difficulty if taken in combination with alcohol or may themselves be abused.

MULTIPLE SUBSTANCE USE AND ABUSE

Multiple substance abuse refers to simultaneous abuse of different mood-altering drugs, either one with another or in combination with that all-time favorite, alcohol. Sometimes it is referred to as polydrug use. Many who work in the alcohol field have come to believe that addiction is addiction regardless of the substance being abused. For these people the basic principles of treatment for drug abuse are very similar to those for alcohol treatment. Despite this view, the stereotype remains of drug abusers as being different from alcoholics and more difficult to help. Thus, there is a tendency among some who work with alcoholics to shy away from drug abusers or those who are cross addicted to drugs as well as alcohol. Nevertheless, those working with alcoholics must become more knowledgeable and comfortable in working with clients who are also involved with other drugs. The "pure" alcoholic is often hard to find. The most recent profile by AA of its members, conducted in 1990, revealed that 30% of those surveyed considered themselves addicted to drugs as well as alcohol. This was an increase of 7% from a similar survey 3 years earlier. Of AA members under 20 years of age, a whopping 76% said they were addicted to drugs as well, a 16% increase in just a 3-year period! Alcohol programs also report that the number of clients being seen who also abuse other drugs is increasing. Once again, the younger clients are more likely to use and abuse multiple substances.

The percent of the population who report use of different substances is summarized in Table 11-4. As is apparent, alcohol and nicotine, our legally available drugs are those which are most widely used. When other drugs are used, it is almost always accompanied by alcohol.

TABLE 11-4

Use of different psychoactive substances

Type of drug	Use reported during month before survey	
	Millions of people	% of Population
Alcohol	105.8	53.4
Nicotine (Tobacco)	57.1	28.8
Marijuana	11.6	5.9
Cocaine	5.8	4.1
Crack	.5	.2
Stimulants	1.7	.9
Analgesics*	1.1	.6
Tranquilizers*	1.2	.6
Inhalants	1.2	.6
Sedatives*	.8	.4
Hallucinogens	.8	.4

*non medical use.

Major classes of psychoactive substances

A complete listing of all the drugs of abuse and their effects is beyond the scope of this book. However, it is not necessary to be intimately familiar with every compound, if one is aware of the general classes into which psychoactive drugs or substances fall. Within each of the major classes there is similarity as to the drugs' effects and the problems that may be encountered with use. The major classes of "abuse-able" drugs are as follows:

Depressants

Examples: benzodiazepines (Librium, Valium, etc.), barbiturates, chloral hydrate, paraldehyde, meprobamate.

Action: not completely understood, in general produce a reversible depression of the central nervous system, some more selectively than others.

Desired effects: similar to alcohol; elation or excitement secondary to depression of inhibitions and judgment or reduction of anxiety.

Common problems: tolerance, physical dependence, respiratory depression with overdose.

Withdrawal syndromes: physical symptoms similar to alcohol withdrawal, including seizures; psychological withdrawal.

Stimulants

Examples: amphetamines (including Ice), cocaine (including Crack), methylphenidate (Ritalin).

Action: stimulation probably due to increased levels of norepineph-rine or dopamine in central nervous system.

Desired effects: increased alertness; feeling of well-being; euphoria; increased energy; decreased appetite; rapid onset of mood change with cocaine.

Common problems: tolerance, anxiety, confusion, irritability, psy-chosis, with cocaine delusions, some data indicating physical dependence.

Withdrawal syndromes: depression (possibly suicidal); loss of ability to enjoy ordinary pleasures.

Opiates

Examples: heroin, morphine, methadone, opium, codeine, Demerol, Percodan.

Action: affect central nervous system, probably by mimicking or blocking normally occurring opiate-like substances in the brain, thereby causing mood changes and mental clouding.

Desired effects: "the rush" (feeling of intense pleasure immediately following injection); state of mental and physical relaxation with decreased mental awareness and reduction of drives.

Common problems: production of tolerance and both physical and psychological dependence; death by overdose or as a result of injection.

Withdrawal syndromes: psychological (drug craving); physical symptoms (chills and sweats, abdominal pain, diarrhea, goose-flesh, crying).

Hallucinogens

Examples: LSD, mescaline, psilocybin, DMT.

Action: alteration of normal functioning of central and peripheral nervous systems, central nervous system excitement.

Desired effects: modification of perception of all sensory input (hal-lucinations, distortions); temporary modification of thought processes; claims of "special insights."

Common problems: acute anxiety and panic reactions, depression, flashbacks (post-LSD).

Withdrawal syndromes: generally believed not to occur.

Cannabinoids

Examples: marijuana, hashish, THC.

Action: acts on the brain as a foreign substance.

Desired effects: euphoria, detachment, modification of level of con-sciousness, relaxation, reported sexual arousal, altered percep-tions.

Common problems: psychomotor impairment; impairment in mem-ory, comprehension, thinking, learning, and general intellectual function; respiratory problems with prolonged use; reproductive system problems with prolonged use; paranoia and psychosis in large doses; possible long-term psychological impairment with chronic use.

Withdrawal syndromes: psychological dependence suggested, no physical withdrawal demonstrated.

Phencyclidine

Examples: Phencyclidine (PCP).

Action: nonspecific central nervous system depressant, anesthetic, psychedelic (multiple proposed actions on various neurotransmitters in central nervous system).

Desired effects: visual illusions and distorted perceptions; depersonalization; distortion of body image; hallucinations; feelings of strength, power, and invulnerability; claims of "special insights."

Common problems: feelings of severe anxiety, doom, or impending death; bizarre behavior; outbursts of hostility and excitement.

Withdrawal syndromes: potential for both psychological and physical withdrawal reported but not well documented.

Inhalants

Examples: aerosol sprays, paint, model cement, adhesives, gasoline, amyl nitrite, butyl nitrite, nitrous oxide, benzydrex inhalors, asthma inhalors.

Action: central nervous system depression, generally secondary to access through respiratory system.

Desired effects: immediate effects—euphoria, excitement (also often inexpensive and legal).

Common problems: impulsive and destructive behavior, slurred speech, ataxia, impaired judgment, development of tolerance, "Sudden Sniffing Death," possible long-term central nervous system damage and damage to multiple physical systems.

Withdrawal syndromes: psychologically documented; physical, not clinically established.

In respect to the drugs of abuse, there are clearly trends as to what is and is not popular, or "in," at any particular time. For example, the interest in psychedelics had waned; however use is now reported to be on the upswing. Cocaine use had become very widespread, along with a crystalline form, crack. But use is declining. At the same time, there is concern that heroin may be making a comeback.

Also apparently true is that drugs, though often touted as being nonaddictive when they are becoming popular, generally turn out not to be as benign as was thought. Current terminology refers to "recreational" drug use, which is the drug counterpart of "social drinking."

Controlled studies of the effects of "recreational" drug use are for the most part nonexistent. The problems that can accompany "casual use" are the same as for "casual use" of alcohol, for example, auto accidents from driving in an impaired state. Or there is the possibility that casual use may not remain casual. Any use of illicit substances invites its own special bag of other difficulties.

For the counselor, the importance of distinguishing between legal and illegal substances is less a matter of pharmacology than it is of "quality assurance." Inevitably, illicit drugs are pharmacologically of unknown strength and purity. And a safe, reliably available supply can never be ensured. Illicit drug use invites social and legal problems. For example, while the price of cocaine may be coming down, it remains a very expensive drug. Therefore large sums of money are spent for even "recreational" use. Heavy users may find themselves borrowing money, going into debt, stealing, or beginning to deal to support their own habits.

The observation has been made that for illicit drug users, some of the behaviors common in the later stages of alcoholism are present virtually from the beginning of drug use. From the onset of drug use, there is a need for the secretiveness, concern about supply, and feelings of guilt and apprehension.

Patterns of polydrug use

Different patterns of use may be identified. One pattern might be considered as "risk-taking" drug use, similar possibly to another generation's drag racing and "playing chicken" on the highway. This is particularly common among adolescents. They may try whatever is available, whether gleaned from the family medicine cabinet or a peer. From time to time, emergency rooms are confronted with sick adolescents who have ingested unknown drugs in unknown quantities.

Whether the other drug use is experimental, risk-taking, or recreational, alcohol is generally part of the picture. If one is in a situation in which drugs are being used, the beverage served is not likely to be root beer! And if supplies of other drugs are limited because of their cost or availability, if one wants some mood alteration, there is always the old standby, alcohol. Therefore if problems develop with drug use, it is not unlikely that alcohol will be one part of that picture. (See the section on adolescents in Chapter 10).

Some people use multiple drugs in an effort to *engineer moods*, to achieve different and particular feeling states. You name the mood, and they have a formula of drugs in combination to achieve it. This may mean uppers in the morning, downers to unwind later in the day, drugs to counteract fatigue, drugs to promote sleep, drugs to feel "better." Among those most likely to get into this drug use pattern are people with relatively easy access to drugs: nurses, physicians, pharmacists, and their spouses. This does not imply the medications are being stolen. Easy access can mean asking someone to write you a prescription as a favor. In all probability, this pattern of use starts out innocently. The aim is not to get high, but to cope. Accustomed to the use of medications often working at a pace beyond reasonable expectations, these professionals may try a little chemical assistance to get by. Despite their knowledge of pharmacology, before they know it, they are in trouble. The drugs are no longer something to be used in special situations; they are essential for functioning. Alcohol may well become a part of this picture. Alcohol workers are not immune. The clinician who relieves the incoming client of his booze and pills may very quickly acquire an impressive and tempting stash in his or her desk drawer.

Alcohol and other drug addiction

When alcohol is involved, polydrug abuse may not involve illicit drugs or fit the patterns just described. A portion of multiple drug abuse begins when people in the early stages of alcoholism start to ride "the doctor circuit" in search of a physical answer to their problems. Their complaints may be "nerves," "headaches," or "sensitive stomach." These people do not go to their physicians deliberately trying to obtain drugs. They truly want relief for their distress. If a careful alcohol history is not taken, their drinking may not initially appear to be different from that of other clients the physician treats. Quite possibly the budding alcoholic may openly tout alcohol as a godsend, given how he feels.

PHYSICIAN: How much do you drink?
PATIENT: Oh, not too much, mostly when I go out socially.
PHYSICIAN: How much is that, and how often?
PATIENT: Oh, not much, a couple of drinks at a party, occasionally a cocktail before dinner. But I tell you, these headaches have been murder. And I've sometimes said, I may not be a drinker, but I will be if they continue.
PHYSICIAN: They're that bad?

It all sounds straightforward. Our friend has tests done; nothing emerges to pin the headaches on. He is reporting stress at work, and eventually he walks out of the physician's office with a prescription for a minor tranquilizer. This fellow may be headed for trouble. There is an increasing sensitivity within the medical community to prescribing minor tranquilizers for vague, nonspecific problems. Despite the awareness of potential for abuse, a persistent client may often prevail.

Multiple drug use clearly has an impact on an individual's drinking career. Depending on the drugs involved, there can be difficulties of a more acute nature on any drinking occasion. The effects of multiple substances taken together may be additive or synergetic (an effect greater than the summed actions of the drugs), resulting in increased central nervous system depression. This can be a life-threatening situation.

In addition to physical problems, there are other potential difficulties for the active alcoholic. One is the use of other drugs to maintain and control the drinking. Though alcohol may be the drug of choice, somewhere along the line, the alcoholic may have learned the warning signs of alcoholism. By using pills, alcohol consumption may be maintained within what the drinker has decided are safe limits. What would *really* hit the spot would be a nice stiff drink— or six! Instead, the drinker settles for a capsule. He doesn't drink during the day, so he doesn't consider himself an alcoholic. Thus drug use can help the alcoholic keep alcohol use within "acceptable" limits. In the alcoholic's mind, then, his drinking career can be managed and extended.

Other drug use can prevent the reality of the alcohol problem from sinking in. The minor tranquilizers are also known as the *antianxiety agents*. Anxiety is what will eventually move the alcoholic into treatment. This happens when problems are such that he cannot explain them away or successfully drink them away—when the pain is no longer alcohol soluble. By turning off anxiety, the antianxiety agents can create a false sense of well-being. The individual using antianxiety agents will still intellectually know what is happening, but the emotional impact is blunted. In the mildly mulled state of minor tranquilization, it may seem much easier to the alcoholic simply to continue the life pattern as before, including the drinking. The active alcoholic has plenty to be anxious about. Although pills may help turn it off, they will be unable to alter the source of anxiety, which is the drinking and its consequences.

Withdrawal

Just as tolerance develops for alcohol, it can also develop for some other psychotropic medications. The list of abusable drugs mentioned earlier included a number of drugs that produce tolerance. These include barbiturates, sedatives, opiates, and minor tranquilizers. Just as with alcohol, as use continues, more of the substance is required to achieve the same desired effect. This is reinforced by the all-American viewpoint that discomfort is pointless when chemical comfort is only a swallow away. When tolerance develops, withdrawal symptoms may accompany abstinence.

Barbiturates have been around since the beginning of this century. Central nervous system depressants have an abstinence syndrome very similar to that of alcohol. At lower doses, withdrawal symptoms will most likely be limited to anxiety and tremulousness. At higher levels, more serious withdrawal symptoms may develop. These can include convulsions and a "DT-like" syndrome of delirium, disorientation, hallucinations, and severe agitation. Barbiturate withdrawal presents a medical situation as serious, and potentially as life threatening, as that accompanying alcohol withdrawal.

Minor tranquilizers can be subdivided into different groups depending on their chemical compositions. These differences are important when it comes to withdrawal and potential problems of abuse. Librium, Valium and Xanax belong to the subgroup known as the *benzodiazepines*. When drugs of this subgroup are abused, withdrawal symptoms may be present if use is abruptly stopped. Withdrawal symptoms can include anxiety, tremulousness, sweating, insomnia, nausea and vomiting, muscular weakness, confusion, psychosis, and possibly convulsions. A full-blown "DT-like" picture is generally *not* associated with the benzodiazepines. However, it is increasingly evident that physical dependence is not a casual issue. Even if the symptoms of physical withdrawal associated with these substances are not as dramatic as those of alcohol or barbiturates, getting off these medications is no easy matter. Withdrawal symptoms for these can be as dangerous as those associated with alcohol or barbiturates.

Polydrug use and abuse should be suspected when any drug, including alcohol, is being used. Younger people are at especially high risk for multiple drug abuse. When physical dependence on alcohol is combined with dependence on another drug, the problems of detoxification are increased. The task that then confronts the physician is sequential detoxification or withdrawal of one drug at a time. Medical management can be a very delicate process in these situations. It is critical for multiple dependencies to be identified when someone first enters treatment. If alcohol detoxification is not going smoothly, the first question to be asked is: "Are other drugs involved?"

Nicotine

The above discussion has focused primarily on prescribed medications and illicit or street drugs. Far and away the most commonly used substance along with alcohol is nicotine. One of the indicators of a possible alcohol problem is in fact smoking, because they so commonly do occur together.

For far too long, the alcohol treatment community ignored smoking. The thinking was that to ask clients to deal at the same time with more than one addiction was unreasonable. But then, they never got around to dealing with the issue of smoking later either. Another common defense was that smoking, unlike alcohol, did not make one life's unmanageable. That of course was to ignore the chronic medical problems that are an inevitable part of smoking. To walk into an alcohol treatment program was to walk into a space thick with smoke. Those days are over. There are undoubtedly a number of reasons. There is the anti-smoking lobby, the ever-increasing disapproval of smoking, the growing tendency to see addiction to whatever substances as not separate problems, clinics' and hospitals' becoming smoke-free environments, and the introduction of smoke-free meetings of AA. It has become apparent that in-patient treatment programs that expect patients to withdraw from tobacco/nicotine as well as alcohol or other drugs are not undermining treatment. If anything, it may help treatment, because of the long habit of drinking to signal a cigarette or vice versa. Unlike, addiction to alcohol, most of those who are nicotine dependent say they would like to stop smoking. What better time, especially for those who are in-patients, when one is in a controlled environment. Although smoking cessation has not been a standard part of alcohol treatment, it is rapidly moving in that direction.

RESOURCES AND FURTHER READING

Carr LA: The pharmacology of mood-altering drugs of abuse, *Primary Care* 20(1): 19-31, 1993.

The majority of psychoactive drugs that are likely to be abused appear to share several unique properties that contribute to drug dependence and overall abuse liability. These pharmacological phenomena include behavioral reinforcing effects, tolerance, and physical dependence. These terms are generally more useful than "addiction" or "habituation" in describing the characteristics of drug abuse because they are more easily defined and each is believed to have a specific biological basis. Experimental animal studies have clearly shown that drug dependence results from actions of exogenous chemicals on normal biologic mechanisms in the central nervous system. Drug classes discussed include alcohol and sedative-hypnotic drugs, inhalants, opiates, nicotine, psychotomimetic agents, amphetamines, phencyclidine, and marijuana. For each there is discussion of behavioral reinforcement, tolerance, physical dependence, pharmacokinetics, central nervous system effects, and mechanism of action and withdrawal.

Ciraulo DA, Sands BF, Shader RI: Clinical review of liability for benzodiazepine abuse among alcoholics, *American Journal of Psychiatry* 145:1501-1506, 1988.

The authors critically reviewed the literature on benzodiazepine use among alcoholics, psychiatric patients, and the general population to determine whether alcoholics have a greater liability for benzodiazepine abuse. Data suggest that the prevalence of benzodiazepine use among alcoholics is greater than in the general population but comparable to the prevalence in psychiatric patients. The liability for abuse may also be greater for alcoholics, but the substantial methodological deficiencies of existing studies preclude such a conclusion. Given the frequency of anxiety disorders and benzodiazepine use among alcoholics, the potential for benzodiazepine abuse among alcoholics is an important issue. The authors discuss clinical guidelines and strategies for future research. (Author abstract.)

Fujita B, Nikkel R: *Dual diagnosis training: A workshop for assessing and treating the client with both substance abuse and mental illness diagnoses. trainer's manual,* Salem, OR: Office of Alcohol and Substance Abuse, 1992.

This is one of three volumes that together comprise a training package on the subject of dual diagnosis. There are two participants' volumes, the first, Volume I, is directed toward providing mental health workers with substance abuse information. It was supplanted by Volume II, developed by the State of Oregon and directed toward providing information on psychopathology to substance abuse workers. This trainers manual accompanies these two volumes. It is recommended as an introductory course. This manual reviews goals and general considerations for trainers and then outlines the 3 days of training.

Helzer JE, Pryzbeck TR: The co-occurrence of alcoholism with other psychiatric disorders in the general population and its impact on treatment, *Journal of Studies on Alcohol* 49:219-224, 1988.

Jacobs MR, Fehr KOB: *Drugs and drug abuse: A reference text,* ed 2, Toronto: Addiction Research Foundation, 1987.

Drafted as a reference for judges and lawyers dealing with alcohol- and drug-related cases, this book is equally helpful to clinicians. Following an introductory chapter entitled "Understanding Drug Use" are chapters on the various classes of psychoactive agents, focusing upon the epidemiology, clinical manifestations of use, pharmacological properties, and the implications for treatment associated with each drug class.

Joseph AM, Nichol KL, Anderson H: Effect of treatment for nicotine dependence on alcohol and drug treatment outcomes. *Addictive Behavior* 18(6):635-644, 1993.

This study was designed to examine the effect of a policy banning smoking and a smoking-cessation intervention on alcohol and drug treatment outcomes. The authors compared long-term alcohol and drug treatment outcomes in two garoups hospitalized for substance use treatment, subjected to different smoking policies and cessation interventions in two periods. There were no significant differences between intervention and control groups in rates of "improvement" for alcohol, cocaine, or marijuana use or for these drugs combined. The findings suggest that concurrent intervention for nicotine dependence did not significantly harm treatment outcomes of patients using alcohol or marijuana as their drug of first choice. The intervention was associated with a small increase in self-reported smoking cessation. There is considerable interest in this patient population in smoking cessation after completion of treatment. (Author abstract.)

Krahn DD: The relationship of eating disorders and substance abuse (review), *Journal of Substance Abuse Treatment* 3(2): 239-253, 1991.

Initial interest in the relationship between eating disorders, which occur primarily in women, and substance abuse, which is much more frequent in men than women, stemmed from the observations of Crisp (1968), who noted that chronic anorexics who developed bulimic behavior often abused alcohol. More recently, cross-sectional studies of women with eating disorders have documented prevalences of alcohol and other substance abuse in these women that are much higher than those reported in the general female population. Conversely, women with substance abuse disorders report eating-disordered behavior more often than the general population. This article first presents a definition of eating disorders and then addresses (1) the rate of co-prevalence of eating disorders and substance abuse, (2) the mechanism of the co-prevalence of these disorders, (3) the clinical similarities of these disorders, and (4) future directions. (Author abstract.)

Landry MJ, Smith DE, Steinberg JR: Anxiety, depression, and substance use disorders: Diagnosis, treatment and prescribing practices (review), *Journal of Psychoactive Drugs* 23(4):397-416, 1991.

Attending physicians routinely encounter patients with signs and symptoms of anxiety and mood disorders, as well as psychoactive substance use and psychoactive substance-induced organic mental disorders. These symptoms may represent either primary disorders or pathology that is secondary to other disorders. This article describes some of the relationships between substance use disorders and symptoms of anxiety and depressive disorders. In addition, some patients with these disorders may have a concurrent substance use disorder or be at high risk for developing one. Routine treatment of anxiety disorders with psychoactive drugs can be successful in many patients but may lead to iatrogenic dependence in high-risk patients. Prescribing for high-risk patients should include a stepwise treatment protocol having three progressive levels: (1) conservative, nonpharmacological approaches; (2) nonpsychoactive pharmacotherapy, including the use of anxioselective agents, such as buspirone; and (3) psychoactive pharmacotherapy, such as the use of benzodiazepines. Proper prescribing practices for high-risk patients are described in terms of diagnosis, dosage, duration, discontinuation, dependence, and documentation. (Author abstract.)

Orleans CT, Hutchinson D: Tailoring nicotine addiction treatments for chemical dependency patients, *Journal of Substance Abuse Treatment* 10(2):197-208, 1993.

The growing scientific evidence for addressing nicotine addiction in chemical dependency (CD) treatment programs is reviewed. This evidence provided the impetus for a survey of smoking patterns and quitting motivation and barriers among CD patients to identify ways to tailor standard nicotine addiction treatment methods and goals to their needs. Major quitting barriers included the usual psychological and physical sequelae of tobacco abstinence in addition to being around other smokers. Surprisingly, very few patients expressed concerns that quitting smoking would threaten drug or alcohol sobriety. Treatment implications are discussed. In addition, a pilot four-session group treatment program is described. This program was geared to motivating smokers in "precontemplation" and "contemplation" stages of change to move ahead into the "action" stage (i.e., taking steps to quit). (Author abstract.)

Sees KL, Clark HW: When to begin smoking cessation in substance abusers, *Journal of Substance Abuse Treatment* 10(2):189-195, 1993.

During the past several years, there has been an increasing recognition and acceptance that the use of tobacco products often produces nicotine dependence and addiction. Despite this, the substance abuse treatment community has been slow to promote smoking cessation for patients who are in substance abuse treatment for another addiction. Dogma, although starting to change, persists that cigarette smoking pales in comparison to other addictions and should not be addressed at the time of initial treatment for another addiction. The research to date, reviewed in this article, does not support this view. Patients presenting for substance abuse treatment report high interest in stopping smoking, including interest in stopping when they initially present for substance abuse treatment. (Author abstract.)

Snow MG, Prochaska JO, Rossi JS: Stages of change for smoking cessation among former problem drinkers: A cross-sectional analysis, *Journal of Substance Abuse* 4(2):107-116, 1992.

Recent research suggests that problem drinkers are less successful in quitting smoking. Stages of change, decisional balance, and self-efficacy measures were used to assess readiness for smoking cessation in a cross-sectional sample of former problem drinkers who were current smokers. As expected, a very high percentage of recovering problem drinkers had been or currently were regular smokers. Distributions across the stages of change and relationships between stages and decisional balance in this problem drinker sample were found to be similar to results from more general smoking populations. Of those who had quit both smoking and alcohol, 62% quit drinking before or at the same time as smoking (53% before; 9% simultaneous). Those who quit drinking before or at the same time as smoking were characterized by a more problematic alcohol history. A stages-of-change perspective with this group is discussed. (Author abstract.)

Special Issue on Homelessness, *Alcohol Health and Research World* 11(3):1-91, Spring 1987.

Warner EA: Cocaine abuse (review), *Annals of Internal Medicine* 119(3):226-235, 1993.

Purpose: To discuss the forms of cocaine that are available and their methods of administration and to review the medical complications of cocaine abuse. Data sources: Pertinent articles were identified through a MEDLINE search of the English-language literature from 1986 to 1992 and through a manual search of bibliographies of all identified articles. Study Selection: All articles describing complications of cocaine use were either case reports, review articles, or small series. No controlled studies on the subject were available. Data Synthesis: A qualitative description of reported complications without the use of quantitative methods. Results: Multiple complications of cocaine use have been described and are often related to the method of administration of cocaine. Since the introduction of freebase and "crack" cocaine, new complications have been noted, and nearly all organ systems have been affected. Indirect complications, related to violent behavior and infectious diseases, are also important consequences of cocaine use. Conclusions: Adverse reactions to cocaine use should be considered in the differential diagnosis of various disorders, particularly ischemic events in young adults. The actual frequency of each complication is unknown. (Author abstract.)

Wilson GT: The addiction model of eating disorders: A critical analysis (review article), *Advances in Behavior Research and Therapy* 13(1):27-72, 1991.

Addiction is a poorly understood and widely misused concept. Far from providing an explanation of eating disorders, the concept is itself in need of explanation. Addiction is most commonly viewed as a disease, and it is this notion that has been applied uncritically to eating disorders in general and binge eating in particular. The associations between eating disorders and psychoactive substance abuse are reviewed. The evidence indicates a greater than expected rate of psychoactive substance abuse in patients with eating disorders and vice versa. Interpretation of these findings is obscured by a number of methodological problems, including inconsistent diagnostic criteria and assessment methods of questionable validity. Family studies show a similar co-occurrence but suffer from comparable shortcomings. Moreover, comorbidity rates between eating disorders and other psychiatric disorders are higher. Studies of clinical samples might simply reflect the well-known tendency for patients with multiple problems to seek treatment. Consistent with this view, the results of two community studies of eating disorder patients show no significant co-occurrence with substance abuse. (Author abstract.)

Woods JH, Katz JL, Winger G: Benzodiazepines: Use, abuse, and consequences (review), *Pharmacological Reviews* 44(2):151-347, 1992.

As a follow-up to their 1987 review of the liability for abuse and dependence of benzodiazepines, the authors present this current review, which is divided into six sections. Section I is the introduction. Section II considers studies of drug taking and drug seeking by animals and humans, what is commonly referred to as "psychological dependence." Section III considers research in animals and humans pertaining to the potential of the benzodiazepines to produce physiological dependence. Section IV reviews evidence pertaining to the ability of benzodiazepines to alter behavior in ways detrimental to the individual and/or to those around him or her. Section V considers epidemiological research pertaining to the use and misuse of the benzodiazepines. (Author abstract.)

Zimmerman RS, Warheit GJ, Ulbrich PM, et al: Auth JB. The relationship between alcohol use and attempts and success at smoking cessation, *Addictive Behavior* 15(3): 197-207, 1990.

This study assessed the relationship between alcohol use and smoking cessation in a general population sample (N=2115) of adults living in a county in north Florida. Nearly half of the sample had ever smoked. Of these, 44% had successfully quit; 34% had tried unsuccessfully to quit; 21% reported never having tried to quit. Using analyses that controlled for background factors, heavy drinkers were found to be less likely to attempt to quit smoking. And, if they had attempted to quit, they were less likely to succeed. Having quit drinking was very strongly related to success at smoking cessation. (Author abstract.)

Odds 'n ends

BEYOND COUNSELING

There are other topics we consider relevant for alcohol clinicians. Space considerations prevent us from doing little more than mentioning them here. Clinicians frequently discover that although their formal job description is centered around serving clients, there are often other expectations. Such duties fall into the general area of *indirect services*, an awkward phrase used to cover all the other things the clinician is often required to do. Public education, case consultation, and planning for community programs are just a few examples. These aspects of a therapist's work are vital to the overall success of alcohol treatment efforts.

Educational activities

Counselors are often called upon to participate in public and professional education programs. The former might include presentations to high school students or church groups or might require being a panelist on a radio or television talk show. The latter might take the form of in-service training for other professionals, supervision of trainees or students, or assisting with workshops.

Do's. In any educational endeavor, plan ahead—don't just "wing it." An effective presentation takes preparation. Find out from those organizing the program what they have in mind for a topic. You may wish to suggest an alternative. Who will be in the audience and what will be its size? How long are you expected to speak? Are there others on the program? In choosing a topic, consider what would be of interest; ask yourself "What kinds of questions are likely to be on the audience's mind?" Do not be overly ambitious and try to cover everything you think someone ought to know about alcohol. If your audience goes away understanding three or four major points, you can consider your presentation successful. Choose a subject about which you are more expert than your audience. A counselor might effectively talk about alcohol's effects on the body to a group of fifth or sixth graders. Any counselor who would attempt to lecture a group of doctors about medical complications is asking for trouble. However, you can share with physicians practical tips on how to interview an alcoholic or how to tell a patient about a suspected alcohol problem. On that topic, you are clearly the expert and able to provide them with information they can use and do not already have. Leave time for questions, and save some of your choice tidbits for a question-and-answer period.

Feel free to develop several basic spiels. Use films or videotapes. A film can be an excellent vehicle for stimulating conversation, but be sure it is appropriate. Three questions for sparking a discussion afterward are the following: "What kind of response did you (the audience) have?" "What new information did you learn?" and "What surprised you?"

when giving a talk, there is no substitute for genuine lack of preparation.

what about two quick double martinis?

If public speaking doesn't come easily, rather than trying hard to avoid such assignments or just struggling through with one eye on the clock, enroll in a public speaking course. A good place to look for such an offering is at a local community college or adult education program.

Feel free to borrow from colleagues. One of the things that marks effective speakers is having metaphors that somehow manage to capture the essence of a situation. By way of example, a colleague has a very effective response to the not uncommon question of "Can alcoholics drink again?" In responding to this, he uses the metaphor of someone's deciding to remove the spare tire from the trunk of the car. There may not be any problems the next day, the next week, or the next month. But sooner or later, ... When the inevitable happens, it may be merely an inconvenience or the circumstances might make it an absolute nightmare.

Dont's. Avoid crusading, "drunkalogs," or horror stories. These approaches may shock your audience and titillate them, but. And it is an important "but": most audiences will not identify with what you are saying. The presentation will be unconnected to their experience. Such an approach is likely to leave those in the audience with a "That's not me!" response. There seems to be a widespread tendency to share personal past history of one's own alcohol or other drug use, especially when speaking with teenagers. Perhaps the motivation is to establish credibility. Perhaps it is intended to demonstrate to teenagers that, even though an adult, the speaker is in tune with the teenagers' experience. Whatever the motive, we have strong biases against this approach. It is an approach that is out of touch with adolescents' psychology.

Preaching is preaching, whatever the guise. It's also a bit presumptuous. Does the speaker really think that his or her past history is *so* compelling that the recital of past problems should motivate others to change? Another danger is that what the speaker wishes to describe as problems are heard by those in the audience as escapades. There is the danger too that a degree of romanticism and bravado creeps into the telling. The speaker lived dangerously, at the edge, and beat the odds. Most importantly, it doesn't really go down with kids and accomplish what is intended. A middle school student, in response to a parental query as to what the mandatory drug education program was like, rolled his eyes, groaned, and recounted the "episode of the day," attributed to the educator's "friend." The educator, having grown up in the sixties, managed to produce a succession of "close" friends, each of whom had some experience with whatever the drug then being discussed happened to be. The student then summed up what they were learning, wryly commenting," I guess what we're really learning is that Mr. J. has some problems picking his friends." Whatever factual information was intended to be conveyed got lost. The general impression was that the sessions were contrived. The unfortunate effect too was to trivialize the subject.

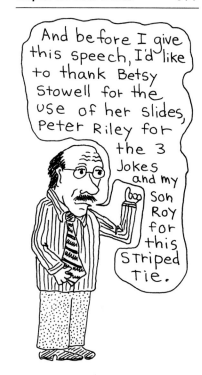

Finally, clinical vignettes as well are usually inappropriate with lay audiences. With professional audiences, if case material is used, great care must be taken to obscure identifying information. For either audience, avoid using jargon. Instead, look for everyday words to convey what you mean or use examples or metaphors that capture what you are trying to say.

Training others

Alcohol professionals have a special contribution to make in the training of other professionals. A common complaint of many substance abuse counselors is how ill-equipped other professional helpers may be to work with alcoholics. However, this situation is not likely to change unless and until the experts, such as counselors, begin to participate in education. So we would urge you to consider this a priority activity.

It is especially important to stick to your area of expertise. To our minds, your single unique skill is your ability to interact therapeutically with those with alcohol problems. Your specialized knowledge and experience is the most important thing you can share. Often this is most effectively communicated by examples of the kinds of questions you ask clients and the type of responses you make in return, rather than by lecturing. However, one trap you should avoid is giving the impression that what you do and know is a mystery that others could never hope to learn. This can come across to your students in subtle ways, through statements such as "Well, I've been there, so I know what it's like," or the offhanded comment that "If you really want to know what alcoholism's all about, what you have to do is (1) spend 2 weeks working on an alcohol unit, (2) go to at least 20 AA meetings, (3) talk firsthand to recovering alcoholics, (4) and so on." Any or all of these might be advisable and valuable educational experiences. However, you ought to be able also to explain in very concrete terms what experiences they might provide and *why* they are valuable.

A few words on supervision of trainees or students may be helpful. Do not be fooled by the notion that the arrival of a student or a trainee is going to ease your workload. It shouldn't. Doing a good job of supervision requires a big investment of your time and energy. Whether the student is with you for a single day, several weeks, or a semester, you will need to give some serious thought to what can be provided to ensure a valuable experience for the student. There are some basic questions you need to consider in planning a reasonable program. Do you want the trainee to acquire specific skills or just become "sensitized" to alcohol treatment techniques? What are the student's goals? What will prove most useful to the student later on? What is the student's background in terms of academic training and experience with alcoholism? The social worker trainee, the clergy member, the recovering alcoholic with 10 years of AA experience—

each is starting from a different point. Each has different strengths and weaknesses, different things to learn and unlearn. In planning the educational program, consider how you will incorporate the trainee. In what activities will the trainee participate? Generally, you will want to have the student at least "sample" a broad range of agency activity but also have a more in-depth continuing involvement in selected areas.

Probably the single most important thing is to allow the trainee ample time to discuss what goes on, either with you or with other staff. The idea is not to run a student ragged with a jam-packed schedule and no chance to sit down with anyone to talk about what has been observed. If a student is going to be joining you for an interview, be sure you set aside at least 10 to 15 minutes ahead of time as a pre-interview briefing. Also at the conclusion, spend some time reviewing the session and responding to questions. Do not expect that what the student is to learn is obvious.

Be sure to introduce or discuss with clients the presence of trainees. Clients do not need to be provided a student's resume nor be given a brochure describing in complete detail the nature of the training program. However, they do need to be told who the trainees are and to be reassured that they are working with the staff in a trainee capacity. Clients have every right to be uncomfortable and apprehensive at the thought either that the merely curious are passing through to observe them or that they are being used as guinea pigs. In our experience, most clients do not object to being involved with students if the situation is properly presented and if they recognize they have the *right* to say no.

Prevention programs

Prevention has been receiving ever more attention at the national, state, and local levels. Certainly, anyone involved in the alcohol field would like to see fewer people caught up in alcohol problems. However, the real interest in prevention appeared about a decade ago when the NIAAA first earmarked funds for prevention programs. More recently, with the creation of the Office of Substance Abuse Prevention at the federal level, there has been considerably more effort put forth in this direction.

Before commenting on some of the approaches, some background on prevention and its terminology may be useful. Activities directed at preventing the occurrence of disease have been the mainstay of all public health efforts. This is true whether it is the notion of vaccination to prevent smallpox, polio, or measles or efforts to ensure that the town water supply is uncontaminated so as to prevent cholera outbreaks. The emphasis and approaches to prevention within the alcohol field are probably more closely linked to prevention efforts as they developed in the community mental health movement in the 1950s and early 1960s. Attempts at primary, secondary, and tertiary prevention were first widely introduced in that context. What these three different kinds of prevention activity all have in common is that each is intended to reduce the total number of people who suffer from a disease. If you think about it for a moment, you will realize that it can be accomplished in only three ways. One way is to prevent the illness in the first place; thus no new cases develop. This is *primary* prevention. A second way is to identify and treat as quickly as possible those who contract the disease. By restoring to health those having the disease, you reduce the number of existing cases. This is *secondary* prevention. A third way is to initiate specific efforts to avoid relapse and maintain the health of those who have been treated. This is *tertiary* prevention.

Apply this framework to problems associated with alcohol. In respect to alcohol *dependence*, primary prevention efforts are activities directed at reducing the number of people who develop alcoholism. Secondary prevention is essentially early detection and intervention. Tertiary prevention efforts include follow-up care and continued monitoring after active intensive treatment to avoid relapse and reactivation of the disease. Prevention efforts can also be targeted at acute problems of alcohol use, which most frequently involve intoxication. Here, in theory, primary prevention is directed toward achieving moderate alcohol use. Secondary prevention would be the steps taken to prevent problems if intoxication occurs, and any efforts to avoid repetition of such situations in the future are tertiary prevention. However, within the context of current program policies at the federal level, the Office of Substance Abuse Prevention defines primary prevention as being achieved through abstinence.

When prevention efforts were first discussed and the earliest programs were conducted, the thinking about the task was not as crisp as it might have been. Not unexpectedly, there was a certain amount of just "muddling through." It was not fully appreciated that programs that may be effective for preventing acute problems could not be expected automatically to be effective in dealing with the problems of chronic use. Furthermore, the most successful programs at one level of prevention may not work well at another level. Not being especially clear as to exactly what it was that we were trying to prevent, people tended to lump all alcohol problems together. We've taken a step forward as these necessary distinctions are beginning to be made. Take as an example, SADD. This program may be effective in reducing the toll associated with teenage driving and alcohol use. However, it probably would not be a promising method by which to prevent alcoholism in teenagers now or as they grow to adulthood.

Until very recently, primary prevention of alcohol*ism* got the lion's share of discussion. Without question, it sounded like a very attractive and laudable goal. To question the idea was almost synonymous with bad-mouthing Mother and apple pie, but let us raise some questions. Any effort directed at preventing alcoholism has to make some assumptions about the causes. A brief review of the presentation in Chapter 4 on etiology reminds us that there is no simple, single cause of alcohol dependence. The best that can be said is that it results from a complex interaction between a drug, an individual (both biochemical and psychological makeup), and the person's culture. If you are designing a prevention program, which of these elements do you zero in on? Do you really know enough to do something that has a reasonable chance of making a difference, or are you going on the basis of hunches and common sense?

Much of the earliest prevention effort was conducted by agencies as part of their outreach efforts. It was generally directed at the single element that we have since come to recognize carries the least weight; that is, the individual's psychological makeup and functioning. Realistically this is probably the only point at which most agencies or individual clinicians have been equipped to intervene. A counseling center is not set up to do biomedical research to uncover the genetic basis of alcoholism, neither is the agency likely to be able to undertake a massive campaign to change U.S. drinking practices. These earliest programs targeted adolescents and took an educational approach, or endeavored to provide social alternatives, or attempted to build self-esteem or to teach drink refusal skills, or some combination of these approaches. The goal was to prevent teenage alcohol use.

There is ever-growing literature on prevention, including research on the impact of different prevention efforts. In general, this research suggests that prevention is less successful than what we might have hoped. For one reason, behavior changes that may occur immediately after participation in a program tend not to be very long lasting. Or, students learn the material and have more information, yet this doesn't get translated into changes in their behavior. Also, there are significant differences between kids' responses to such programs depending if they are or are not already involved with alcohol. None of these findings should probably surprise us. What it suggests is that any prevention effort cannot be a one shot deal but needs to be ongoing. Another finding worthy of note suggests that the hope of preventing all alcohol use is probably unrealistic. That should be no surprise. But what is clear is that anything that can be done to delay the onset of use is worth it. The later one starts to use alcohol, the lower the chances of the individual's having serious or long-term problems. In the drug field, there is debate about "gateway" drugs, that is, whether there are particular drugs that lead to the use of others. If there is a single major gateway drug, it appears to be nicotine. As is usually the case, alcohol and drug prevention efforts can't be separated, and what else is clear is that these efforts cannot afford to leave smoking out of the picture.

Prevention programs are becoming more sophisticated. We are now starting to see prevention efforts that combine legal approaches, public education, media campaigns, and outreach efforts targeted to specific high-risk groups. There is also greater attention being paid to the role of community organizations and what they can do to tackle alcohol and other drug problems in their neighborhoods. This may mean lobbying to try to reduce the number of retail outlets for package sales or to institute more police patrols. Much has been done as well to mobilize parents to respond collectively to alcohol problems of teens. A lot of what is being done is very basic but important. It may involve helping parents define their collective expectations, for example, around issues such as teenagers having parties without a parent or adults present, to parents allowing alcohol to be consumed in their homes, to organizing alcohol-free high school graduation parties. What these approaches are doing is making changes in the environment and changing attitudes toward alcohol use.

Even if prevention programs have a minimal impact on adolescent alcohol use, they may make a significant difference in other ways. Their presence may well promote secondary prevention, by changing the views, increasing the awareness of the potential dangers, and thereby increasing the likelihood of earlier intervention if a problem does occur.

THE REAL WORLD
Being a professional colleague

Historically the alcohol field developed outside of mainstream medicine and the other helping professions. Alcohol treatment programs initially developed for the very reason that those with alcoholism were excluded or poorly served by the traditional helping professions. The first alcohol treatment programs were often staffed by recovering people. The basic therapeutic program consisted of helping the client establish sobriety and attempting to orient him or her to the Fellowship of AA.

With the establishment of the NIAAA, alcohol treatment as we now know it began. Although no longer functioning in isolation, separate and outside the mainstream, some tensions need to be dealt with because of that history. Different professions in the field are just now learning to collaborate. Being the "new kid on the block," it may fall to the alcohol professionals to work a bit harder at this. One of the difficulties that may go unrecognized is problems in communication. Each profession has its own distinctive language (terminology and jargon) that often is not understood by the outsider. For example, a counselor reports to the client's physician that the client has "finally taken the First Step." The counselor shouldn't be surprised if the physician has no idea what he means. In such situations, it may be tempting to get a little testy, "Well, doggone it, doctors should know about AA," etc, etc. Of course they should, but they'll not learn if you don't use language they can understand.

Remember, you expect them to use language you can understand when discussing your client's medical condition. Return the favor.

Be sensitive also to the fact that many other professionals have a distorted view of alcohol treatment's effectiveness. In large part, this is because they never see the successes. However, those patients who come in again and again in crisis (though this may only be a very small minority of clients) are all too memorable. In fact, Vaillant found that as few as one half of 1% of all the clients at a detoxification center accounted for as many program admissions as did 50% of the clients who only entered once. Of the 5000 clients seen in a 78-month span, it seems that the 2500 who never returned were easily forgotten while the 25 who were admitted 60 times or more were always remembered. So encourage recovering clients to recontact the physician, social worker, or nurse who may have been instrumental in their entering treatment but who have no idea of the successful outcome.

Also make yourself available to other professionals for consultation. One of the surest ways to establish an ongoing working relationship with someone is to have been helpful in managing a difficult case. Consider offering to join a physician during an appointment with a person he thinks may be alcoholic. Or similarly, sit in with a member of the clergy. Your availability may make their task of referral far easier. They may be reluctant to make a referral to an alcohol treatment program because that would imply they had already made a definitive diagnosis. Alcohol clinicians should be sensitive to the fact that in "just making a referral," the counselor, physician, or clergy is being forced to deal with the alcoholic's denial, resistance, and ignorance of the disease. That's the hard part, especially for someone who doesn't do it day in and day out. So anything you can do at that stage will be very helpful.

Also, being a professional means being open to new ideas. One of the observations made of the alcohol field is that practitioners tend to keep using the "tried-and-true" rather than paying attention to new information. A recent article suggested that there are taboo topics, beliefs that govern how care is provided, that have not been validated by research, and furthermore are seemingly not even open to questioning. While something we may not like to hear, there is some truth to this observation. Whether the alcohol field is more guilty of such behavior than other fields is probably not an argument worth waging. And, to the extent these charges are true, there may be an historic explanation. When the alcohol field was founded, care was provided in a manner that contradicted what was then the accepted mainstream way of doing things. In fact, those who remember the early days of the field can recall when alcohol counselors often thought their job, in part, was to protect clients from the established professionals, who, however well-intentioned, didn't then have a very good track record. But that is now a very old battle, one that no longer needs to be fought. What is true is that it is always easier for any of us to continue doing what we have been doing. Don't our clients effectively remind us of this every day! Part of being a professional is evaluating new information and modifying our approaches based on what we learn.

Selecting a professional position

In seeking and selecting a position in the alcohol field, there are a number of points to consider. By analogy, accepting any employment is almost like entering into a marriage. When it works, it's marvelous, and when there's a "mismatch," it's quite the opposite. Many positions may have the title of "alcohol counselor" or "alcohol therapist," but there will be considerable variation among them, depending on the agency setting and its clientele. Beyond looking closely at the facility, it is equally important to look closely at yourself. Take a professional inventory. What are your clinical strengths and what are areas of lesser competence? What are you most comfortable doing and which things are more stressful? Is "routine" a comfort or is it likely to invite boredom? Because of the differences between people, one person's perfect job is another person's nightmare.

In considering agencies, you are your own best counsel. But at the same time, consult with colleagues and use the grapevine. What should you give thought to? Among the long list of things worth considering is: What is the work atmosphere like? Does the agency have a staff turnover or is it fairly stable? Why do people leave? Is there a sense of camaraderie? How do the various professionals on staff interact with one another? How does the alcohol counselor/therapist fit into the hierarchy? What are the opportunities for professional development, both formal and informal? How is clinical supervision handled? Does the agency support and encourage continuing education? Will the agency help cover costs of attending conferences and workshops? What are the routes for promotion? To what are promotions tied—formal credentials, experience, certification? Is the position part of a well-established program or a new venture just getting off the ground? What kind of security does the position provide? How much security do you want and need? Where do you want to be professionally 5 years from now; how will the position you are considering facilitate attaining that goal? What are the skills you would like to develop, and can they be learned in the position being considered?

Then there are always the nuts and bolts of personnel practices. Is the salary appropriate for the position and can you live on it? Are the benefits comparable with those for other professional staff? What are the hours? Is there "on call" or evening or weekend work? How many hours a week do comparable staff typically work? In both alcohol and human service agencies there is too often chronic

Of course, we're a bit understaffed at present - but once we get the grant we're applying for, we'll double our staff.

understaffing. So conscientious workers pitch in, work extra hours, and somehow never have the opportunity to take that time off later!

More and more alcohol clinicians are considering private practice. Whether this continues to be a realistic possibility with the changes that are taking place in health-care delivery remains to be seen. On the surface, private practice may seem a very attractive option. On the other hand, it can be very lonely. Those who are in private practice need to take specific steps to develop and maintain professional contracts. (This is in addition to developing referral sources to assure clients get the services they need, beyond those that you can offer.) More than any of us can appreciate is the extent to which our colleagues are responsible for helping us maintain our balance and are invaluable and needed resources for us. While its hard to set any minimum length of experience before setting up a private practice, this certainly is not the place for a newcomer to the field.

Being a professional

What it is. Alcohol counseling is a growing profession. The professional counselor has mastered a body of knowledge, has special skills, and has a code of ethics to guide in the work. Being a professional does not mean you have to know it all. Do yourself a favor right now. Give yourself permission to give up any pretense that it is otherwise. Feel free to ask questions, seek advice, request a consultation, say you don't know. Alcohol treatment requires diverse skills and talents. Treatment programs are staffed by people with different kinds and levels of training, for the very reason that no one person or specialty can do the job alone. Being a professional also means constantly looking at what you are doing, evaluating your efforts. There is always more than one approach. You cannot make sober people by grinding drunks through an alcohol treatment machine. Being open to trying new things is easier if you aren't stuck with the notion that you are supposed to be the big expert. And of course you will make mistakes—everyone does.

What it isn't. Overwhelming numbers of alcoholics need and ask for help out there. The tendency is to overburden yourself because of the obvious need. Spreading yourself too thin is a real problem and danger. One also needs to develop assertiveness to resist agency pressures to take on increasing responsibilities. In either instance it creates resentment, anger, frustration, and a distorted view of the world. "No one else seems to care! Somebody's got to do it." It's a trap. Unless you're an Atlas, you'll get mashed. Your personal life must be preserved, try to keep that in mind. Save your own space. Collapsing might give you a nice sense of martyrdom, but it won't help anybody. Better to be more realistic in assessing just what you can do productively, devoting your energy to a realistic number of clients, and giving your best. Keep a clear eye on your own needs for

time off, trips, and visits to people who have nothing to do with your work.

The people who live with you deserve some of your attention, too. It is hard to maintain a relationship with anyone if all you can manage is "What a day!", lapse into silence, and soon fall asleep. It is not going to be easy to handle, but some guidelines must be set in your own head to handle the calls that come after working hours. Some workers ruefully decide on unlisted home phone numbers. Drinking drunks and their upset families are notoriously inconsiderate. "Telephone-itis" sets in with a few drinks. You may decide you do want to be available at all hours. Whatever rules you set, however, try to be consistent. Take a good look at the effects on the important people in your life. Some compromise may be necessary between your "ideal therapist" and your own needs. Give it some thought. State your rules clearly to clients, preferably when they are sober, and then stick to them. If you said no calls when a client is drinking, then don't get caught listening to a "drunkalog" at 3 AM for fear he'll do something rash. Being inconsistent may be more dangerous in the long run. When you have had some experience, you will be able to tell when you must break your own rules. Then you can say that to your clients: "I did say I don't take home phone calls, but you do seem to be in a real bind."

You cannot take total responsibility for clients. Rarely does someone make it or not because of one incident. This does not mean that you should adopt a laissez-faire policy; however, just as you cannot take all the credit for a sober, happy alcoholic, neither can you shoulder all the blame when the client fails to remain sober.

Professional development

Part of the work life of any professional is properly directed, not to serving clients, developing programs, or promoting the broad interests of the alcohol field, but to nurturing the clinician's own professional growth. This can take many forms, for example, attending workshops, going to conferences, seeking consultation from colleagues, visiting other programs, or reading. It is important that you provide for your own continuing professional development.

It has been said that the "half-life" of medical and scientific knowledge is 8 years. This means that half of what will be known 8 years from now has not yet been discovered. On the other hand, half of what is now taken as fact will be out of date! Consequently, education must be a continuing process. What can so easily happen is that in the press of day-to-day work, you find you do not have enough time to keep up. Sadly, what can occur is that a clinician may have a resume with 10 years' job experience, but it is the first year's experience repeated nine more times. As with any specialty, the daily pressures make keeping current a real problem. Get on

NIAAA's mailing list, subscribe to a journal or two, and then make the time to read them. Area meetings of alcohol workers of all disciplines are also a way to keep up to date.

There is one final factor worth mentioning in respect to remaining current. One of the things that confronts the alcohol counselor is that much of the information that he or she needs to know comes from many different fields—from medicine, from psychology, from anthropology, from law, and so forth. Because of this keeping current isn't simply a matter of time. In many instances it means having access to an "interpreter", someone who can explain things in everyday language, in a way that you can understand. In turn, part of your work as needed becomes translating relevant information for clients. Beyond taking part in formal education programs, every alcohol clinician needs to have someone to whom they can turn, with whom they are comfortable saying, "Explain this to me."

Certification and licensure

If you plan to work as an alcohol and/or drug counselor, the issue of certification and licensure is important. In the past, certification by a counselor's association or licensure by a state board may have been primarily important for your own sense of professionalism. Now it is becoming virtually a necessity. More and more frequently, a clinician's being certified or licensed as an alcohol counselor is a hiring requirement. That agencies are establishing this as a requirement for employment is tied to regulations of insurance companies. More and more, insurance companies are paying attention to the credentials of those who provide care and making this one basis for reimbursement. In short, treatment agencies may no longer be able to bill for alcohol treatment provided by non-certified or non-licensed counselors. The same is true for counselors in private practice.

Certification or licensure are two different approaches to accomplish the same goal. They differ chiefly in terms of the type of group that is certifying that an individual has demonstrated a minimal level of competency, or training, and is therefore qualified to do a particular line of work. Certification is the term used when a special association or professional group confers the "seal of approval." Licensure is the term used when an officially designated state governmental body awards the credential. Certification or licensure is something that takes place at a state level. Each state has its own individual requirements. The very same thing is true of teachers, lawyers, nurses, social workers, as well oft times as barbers, beauticians, or some tradespeople, like plumbers or electricians. For professions, such as law, nursing, medicine, that have been around longer, there is generally reciprocity between states. In part, this is based on the fact that there are clear professional standards that have emerged over the years. Also, there is a national examination which all states use and recognize. In alcohol counseling there is much more variation between states, even though the areas assessed are similar. These areas are summarized in Table 12-1. The best way to find out the particular requirements for a state are to contact the State Office of Alcohol Programs, which will be able to provide the name and address of the certifying group.

ETHICS
Basic principles

Being a helping professional means being allied to a set of ethical standards. National groups and state counselor associations have adopted specific codes of ethics for their members. The principles that underlie these codes are the same as those for other helping professions. What these codes really are is a series of statements of the most basic rules you are striving to follow in working with clients. For counselors, ultimately the most basic tool you have to help others is yourself. Therefore, how you think about the responsibilities of working with others is vitally important. Ethical codes

TABLE 12-1

Overview of certification/licensure requirements

Certifying group	Varies by state, most commonly an alcohol counselors' association. Some states have more than one group offering certification.
Types of certification	States typically have different types of certification available. Distinctions may be made between alcohol and drug counselors. Some states offer an administrative or supervisory certificate as well as a clinician certificate. Levels of certification may distinguish more senior clinicians from those entering the field or those in training.
Requirements	Counseling experience Education/training Clinical supervision The biggest differences between states is in the time requirements for each; whether there is a formula for substituting formal educational programs for work experience; or to what extent the subject area of education and training is stipulated. Several states specify clinical competencies that must be covered, several require specific educational programs in the area of ethics. States may have additional special requirements, such as length of sobriety for those in recovery.
Testing	There is generally a written examination, a personal interview, as well as some "sample" of clinical work, whether preparation of a portfolio, making a case presentation, or providing a videotape of a clinical encounter.
Recertification	Length of certification ranges from 2 to 4 years. Recertification requires evidence of continuing education.

are intended to serve as guidelines. They have a history and have developed from experience.

Quite a few years ago, the graduation speaker for a group of counselor trainees at Dartmouth Medical School spoke on what constituted being a professional. The question raised was "How is a professional counselor different from the kindly neighbor, who one speaks to over the back yard fence?" The answer provided was that the professional counselor is able "to profess." That raised a few eyebrows, the meaning not being immediately obvious. What was being referred to as distinguishing the trained helping person from ordinary well intentioned people is that the professional is able to articulate what it is he or she does. The professional functions deliberately and thoughtfully. The professional doesn't rely on "seat of the pants" intuition or instinctive responses. The other important distinction is that the counselor has made a commitment to a set of beliefs as to how one interacts with clients. The counselor has an explicit set of ethical standards to guide helping behavior.

While a commonly used word, "ethics" nonetheless warrants a definition. One definition is that ethics encompasses the rules that define the "oughtness" of our behavior. Ethics is a statement of how we believe that we ought to behave. Those who study ethics have identified three basic principles that are germane to determining oughtness in respect to clinical work. If the clinician's behavior does not incorporate these values, there is considerable risk of doing harm. One such ethical principle for those in a helping relationship is a belief in a client's right to autonomy. Simply put, that refers to the belief that clients have the ultimate right to make the decisions that affect their lives. Another is the principle of *beneficence*. This represents a commitment to respect those in our care, compassion, a commitment to "doing good" and not behaving in a way that places our interests above those of the client. The third principle is that of *justice*. This too means being respectful. But it refers as well to behavior that promotes social justice, a self-imposed obligation both to be fair and to not discriminate in one's clinical work.

Even if a specific code of ethics for counselors did not exist and were not written down, these are basic ethical principles that are presumed by your other professional co-workers. What is required by those in helping professionals is above and beyond that which may be expected of others or expected of us in other situations. It also needs to pointed out as well that how these principles are put into practice is all too often neither clear-cut nor obvious. For example, consider the issue of autonomy. In respect to those who are alcohol dependent and drinking, one struggles with the question of whether a client is capable of acting in his or her own self-interest. If the principle of beneficence is also factored in, it may be felt that some degree of pressure or coercion to prompt treatment is warranted. Yet, there are limits to the degree of coercion and how it is exercised.

There are two ethical concerns that deserve special comment. One is confidentiality. The other is establishing and maintaining boundaries between what is personal and professional, between work and the rest of your life, and between your professional efforts and your personal AA participation.

Confidentiality

For the alcohol professional, as for anyone in the helping professions, confidentiality is a crucial issue. Most of us simply do not consider how much of our conversation includes discussion about other people. When we think about it, it can be quite a shock. It is especially difficult when we are really concerned about someone and are looking for aid and advice. There is only one place for this in a professional relationship with a client. That is with your supervisor or therapist co-workers. It is *never* okay to discuss a client with spouse, friends, even other alcohol workers from different facilities. Even without using names, enough usually slips out to make the client easily identified some time in the future. Unfortunately, this standard is not kept all the time. There are occasional slips by even the most conscientious workers. You will do it accidentally, and you will hear it from time to time. All you can do is try harder in the first instance and deliberately forget what you heard in the second. What your client shares with you is privileged information. That includes where he is and how he is doing. Even good news is his or hers alone to share.

If you are heading up an outreach office, rather than functioning within a hospital or mental health clinic, it is up to you to inform your secretary and other staff about confidentiality. The same is true for any volunteers working in the office. Of necessity they have some knowledge about the people being seen, at least who they are. It must be stressed that any information they acquire there is strictly private. You do not need to get huffy and deliver a lecture, but you should make the point very clearly and set some standards in the workplace.

There are federal regulations with respect to confidentiality of client information and records in alcohol and drug services. Information cannot be released to any outside party without the client's permission. This means friends, physician, employer, or another treatment facility. A treatment facility is not even allowed to say if anyone has ever been or is currently in treatment. Generally, one always has a client sign a statement agreeing to release information before anything written is sent out. This then becomes part of the client or medical record. Similarly, if you want to get information from another facility or party, you need to seek the client's permission and get a written release to forward to those from whom the information is being requested. The only exceptions to this are if the life of the client or someone else is at risk.

Setting boundaries

An ever important and ongoing dilemma is establishing appropriate boundaries in relationships with clients. This can turn up in many forms. But ultimately the question is doing what is required to maintain a professional relationship. One situation that may occasionally arise is when clients will show up with presents. While they are actively working with you, the general guideline is no gifts. This is especially true if something of real monetary value is offered. In such cases, it is important to discuss what is being said by the gift. Use your common sense, though; there are times when clearly the thing to do is accept graciously. (If you have a fantasy of an MG being delivered anonymously to your door, and it comes true . . . unfortunately, our experience doesn't cover that.)

Similarly, social engagements with a client alone or with the family are not recommended. It could be a "plot" to keep you friendly and avoid problems that have to be worked out. In the office time, deal with the invitation and gently refuse.

Helping professionals are expected to avoid romantic entanglements with clients. If a romantic inclination on the part of either client or counselor begins to show up, it should be worked out—and not in bed. This is the time to run, not walk, to an experienced coworker. It may be hard on our egos, but the fact is that people with problems are as confused about their emotions as everything else. They may be feeling so needy that they "love" anyone who seems to be hearing their cry. It really isn't you personally. If they had drawn Joe or Amy, then one of them would be the object of the misplaced emotion right now. So talk it over with a supervisor, guide, or mentor, not just a buddy. Then, *follow his or her advice.* It may have to be worked through with the client, or referral to another counselor may be necessary if it cannot. It is never acceptable to have a sexual relationship with a client.

The need to keep counseling and personal relationships separate does not only apply when the client is in actual treatment. It is also applicable afterward. This can be particularly difficult when the paths of a clinician and a former client intersect in other areas of life, such as if both were members of AA. However, as cruel as it may sound, former clients are forever off-limits.

These ethical standards are not arbitrary nonsense set up by a bunch of Puritans. They are protections designed to protect both you and the client before you from needless hurt. The hurts can be emotional or range all the way to messy court actions. Those who have walked the road before you have discovered what keeps upsets to a minimum, your sense of self-worth realistic, and your helpfulness at its optimum level.

Another ethical concern is how to keep your professional life and private life separate. Don't do a counseling number on your friends.

You are likely to end up with fewer of them if you do. It is just as inappropriate to turn friends or family into clients as it is to turn clients into friends. When you see a friend exhibiting behavior that you think indicates he or she is heading for trouble, it is hard not to fall into your professional role. Don't. Bite your tongue. A friend knows what business you're in. If that person wants help, he or she will ask. Should that day come, refer him to see someone else. And stay out of the picture. Counseling friends and relatives is another no-no. Vital objectivity is impossible. No matter how good you are with your clients, almost anyone else will be better equipped to work with your family or friends. If you are concerned about a close friend, then *you* see a counselor, as a client, to see whether you want to or can become part of an intervention process.

Considerably greater attention is now being paid to the ethical issues that arise in alcohol and other drug use counseling. This is the result of two factors. One is the field of medical ethics in general is becoming better established. Ethics committees in fact have been created in many institutions to help staff consider ethical dilemmas. The other factor is that alcohol and addictions are no longer on the outside, looking in, but have become a part of health and medical care. Thus the issues that are raised in other areas of medicine are now also being considered in respect to substance abuse clients. There are a number of ethical issues that have gotten particular attention. One of these arises around substance abusing pregnant women. The question becomes how one considers and balances the welfare of the unborn child and that of the mother? Another area in which there has been increasing discussion is around the question of organ transplants. Should alcohol dependent people be considered candidates for a liver transplant, given that the number of those who need liver transplants far exceeds the number of organs available?

Ethics also enters into the area of research. Anyone who works in a setting that conducts research needs to be familiar with the things that must be considered. Federal regulations that involve human subjects are very strict. Any research project that involves human subjects is required to take very careful steps to protect the subjects. First it must be demonstrated that the answers to the questions being raised require human research. Mice, rats, or baboons wouldn't do. With that established, virtually all institutions have a committee to review how the research is to be conducted. These committees are required to review the risks to those involved, to consider how it is proposed that subjects will be recruited, and the steps to be taken so that potential subjects understand what is entailed, what the risks are, and that no coercion is involved. This is not as straightforward as it sounds. Consider the situation in which the researcher is also the individual's counselor or doctor. There is an established relationship. Given the trust that is present, the client or patient may agree to virtually anything. It is not that they are being pressured, they are simply apt to comply with any request because *you* make it. They may not even really listen to your explanation but tend to do whatever you ask. On the other hand, they may not be wild about the idea. However, they are afraid of what the consequences might be if they say no. Will you be angry? Might you stop seeing them? These worries may seem unfounded to you, but they are very common. Another source of confusion is that clients and patients in general assume that any research will actually benefit them if they are involved. In some abstract way, all knowledge probably benefits all of us. But that isn't really the case with medical or research conducted in health-care settings. Such research is only justified when we truly don't know the answer. Is drug A more effective than drug B? Is the use of this counseling approach more effective than another? If the answer is clear—that means scientifically established, opposed to the answer being based on our hunches and impressions—then it is unethical to do research on that question. Occasionally one will see articles in the newspaper referring to some research project that has been discontinued early because it has become evident that one treatment being examined is superior to the alternative being considered.

Anyone who works in an organization that conducts research needs to think about this. Here is just a smattering of some of ethical questions being raised in the alcohol field related to research issues. Should it be permissible for researches to design a study that involves giving alcohol to alcoholics? What safeguards are needed to do this? What obligations are there to provide or at least offer treatment after the research is completed? What kinds of criteria might one feel are necessary to decide who could or could not be included in such a study?

Cases that raise ethical concerns do not have clear cut solutions. One can examine the case from different perspectives and possibly arrive at very different conclusions. To further complicate the situation, it is important to recognize that the course of action that different professions may deem ethical can differ. This is sometimes the source of unfortunate misunderstandings. It is most likely to come to the fore around cases that involve resistant clients. Counselors may well determine that terminating with a client who is in denial and for whom every reasonable effort has been made to intervene is the best and ethical course of action. To do otherwise may seem to the clinician to facilitate the continuation of drinking. One of the hard things that substance abuse clinicians have had to learn to say to clients is that "the way things are going, I don't see how I can help you." Counselors may fail to appreciate that this option may not be open to other professionals. The physician who is caring for a patient doesn't have the right to simply say I will not see you anymore. The person has a right to medical care, and the physician is ethically required to make a referral before terminating care. The issue is further compounded by the fact that the patient probably did not come to the physician for the alcohol problem in the first place but for some other condition. Counselors not understanding this have at times erroneously viewed physicians as enabling continued drinking because the doctor continued to provide medical care even if the patient refuses to deal with the alcohol or drug issue.

Hopefully, in your first years of counseling, you will have a supervisor to help you through such sticky wickets. Use him or her. The real pros are the ones who used all the help they could get when they needed it. That is how they got to be pros.

COUNSELORS WITH "TWO HATS"

Many workers in the alcohol field are themselves recovering alcoholics. Long before national attention was focused on alcoholism, private rehabilitation centers were operated and often staffed by sober alcoholics. In the course of recovery, many alcoholics find themselves working in many capacities, in many different types of facilities. We must say here that we do not believe that simply being a recovering alcoholic qualifies one as a professional. There is more to it than that. That view ignores the skill and special knowledge that many alcoholics working in the field have gained, on the job, and often without benefit of any formal training. They have had a harder row to hoe and deserve a lot of respect for sticking to it.

Being a recovering alcoholic has some advantages for a counselor, but it also has some clear disadvantages. Being a counselor may, at times, be most confusing for the recovering alcoholic who is also in AA. Doing AA Twelfth Step work and calling it counseling won't do, from the profession's or AA's point of view. Twelfth Step work is voluntary and has no business being used for bread earning. AA's traditions are clearly against this. AA is not opposed to its members working in the field of alcoholism, if they are qualified to do so. If you are an AA member and also an alcohol counselor, it is important to keep the dividing line in plain sight. The trade calls it "wearing two hats." There are some good AA pamphlets on the subject, and the AA monthly magazine, *The Grapevine,* publishes articles for two-hatters from time to time.

A particular bind for two-hat counselors comes if attending AA becomes tied to their jobs more than their own sobriety. They might easily find themselves sustaining clients at meetings and not being there for themselves. A way to avoid this is to find a meeting you can attend where you are less likely to see clients. On the occasions when clients do see you at meetings and bring up problems or questions about their treatment, gently tell them you will discuss it with them in the office. On the other hand if they are questioning some aspect of the AA meeting, introduce them to another member present.

It is too easy for both you and the clients to confuse AA with the other therapy. The client benefits from a clear distinction as much, if not more, than you. There is always the difficulty of keeping your priorities in order. You cannot counsel if you are drinking yourself. So, whatever you do to keep sober, whether is includes AA or not, keep doing it. Again, when so many people out there seem to need you, it is very difficult to keep from overextending. A recovering alcoholic simply cannot afford this. (If this description fits you, stop reading right now. Choose one thing to scratch off your schedule.) It is always easy to justify skimping on your own sober regimen because "I'm working with alcoholics all the time." Retire that excuse. Experience has shown it to be a counselor killer.

Another real problem is the temptation to discuss your job at AA meetings or discuss clients with other members. The AAs don't need to be bored by you any more than by a member who is a doctor describing the surgical removal of a gallbladder. Discussing your clients, even with another AA member, is a serious breach of confidentiality. This will be particularly hard, especially when a really concerned AA member asks you point-blank about someone. The other side of the coin is keeping the confidences gained at AA and not reporting to co-workers about what transpired with clients at an AA meeting. Hopefully, your non-alcoholic co-workers will not slip up and put you in a bind by asking. It is probably okay to talk with your AA sponsor about your job if it is giving you fits. However, it is important to stick with *you* and leave out work details and/or details about clients.

Watch out if feelings of superiority creep in toward other "plain" AA members or nonalcoholic colleagues. Recovery from alcoholism does not accord you magical insights. On the other hand, being a nonalcoholic is not a guaranteed route to knowing what is going on either. Keep your perspective as much as you're able. After all, you are all in the same boat, with different oars. To quote an unknown source: "It's amazing how much can be accomplished if no one cares who gets the credit."

Clinician impairment and relapse

Before proceeding further, it should be noted that the issue of impairment caused by alcohol and drug use is not solely a concern for the alcohol and substance abuse fields. While some professions have come further than others, virtually every professional group—physicians, nurses, social workers, psychologists—has recognized the problem and developed policies and programs to address it. These efforts are conducted under the auspices of an impaired professionals committee, which may be affiliated with the professional association or a state licensing board. The general thrust is to encourage reporting by concerned individuals, be it family members, colleagues, or patients; to initiate a non-prejudicial review, and where impairment is suspected, then endeavor to have the individual evaluated and, as indicated, provided treatment. In many of these instances, considerable leverage is provided by the obligation to report findings to licensing boards and the threat of disciplinary action if treatment is refused.

While every profession has members who are recovering alcoholics or drug-dependent individuals—as well as those who go untreated—the alcohol and substance abuse field is a special case, given its history. There would appear to be greater numbers of recovering people, and their recovery status is relevant to the work they perform. For those professionals who are recovering, we have alluded to a variety of situations that may spell potential trouble: burnout, inappropriate relationships with clients, slackening AA attendance, over-involvement with the job, and unrealistic expectations. For the clinician who is a recovering alcoholic, all of these can lead to a relapse. Becoming a professional in no way confers immunity to relapse. Unfortunately, this fact of life has not been very openly discussed by the alcohol counseling profession. It has been the profession's big taboo topic. On the occasions where it has occurred, the situation has too often been handled poorly. There is either a conspiracy of silence or a move to drive the counselor out of the field. The co-workers can very readily assume all the roles of "the family," and the counselor's co-workers can get caught up in functioning as "enablers."

What suggestions do we have? Ideally, the time to address the issue of possible relapse is at the time of hiring. To our minds, both the counselor and the agency have a mutual responsibility to be alert to possible danger signs, and they should agree to address them openly. This does not mean the recovering professional is always under surveillance. It simply is a means of publicly acknowledging that relapses can and do occur and that they are too serious to ignore. We would suggest that if a counselor relapses, it is his or her responsibility both to seek help and to inform the agency. The job status will be dependent on evaluating the counselor's ability to continue serving clients and to participate in treatment for himself or herself. The time to agree upon an arbitrator/consultant or referral is before relapse, not in the midst of it.

Some people favor an arbitrary ironclad rule: any drinking and you're out of your job. However, that seems to miss the point. There is the recovering professional, who buys a six-pack, has 1-2 beers, sees what is going on, picks up the phone, and calls for help. Another case is the person who "nips" off and on for weeks, who subsequently exhibits loss of control, and shows up at the office intoxicated. Though it is important not to treat the former case lightly, nonetheless the disease process has not been wholly reactivated as it has in the latter case. Interestingly, those we have known who have had a single drinking incident, as in the example given, have tended to take sick leave and enter a residential program. They have interpreted the drinking as a very serious sign that something in their life is out of balance, warranting serious attention. What *is* essential in any case is securing adequate treatment for the clinician and not jeopardizing the care of the clients.

If you are a clinician known to your clients as a recovering alcoholic, your relapse can have a profound effect on some of them. If you are off the job and enter treatment, you can count on the news rapidly becoming public knowledge. It is our belief that the agency and the co-workers dealing with your case load have a responsibility to inform your clients. Certainly, any details are a private matter, but that a relapse has occurred cannot be seen as none of their business.

A word to co-workers covering for a relapsed counselor: if you are the co-worker, be prepared to deal with clients' feelings of betrayal, hopelessness, anger, and fear. You will need to provide extra support. Be very clear about who is available to them in their counselor's absence. Also recognize that this can be a difficult painful experience for you and other co-workers, who may well share many of the client's feelings. Be prepared to call upon extra reinforcements in the form of consultation and supervision.

If you are a counselor who has relapsed and you return to work after a leave, there is no way you can avoid dealing with the fact of the relapse. How this is handled should be dealt with in supervision and with lots of input from more seasoned colleagues. You will be trying to walk along a difficult middle ground. On one hand, your clients do not need apologies, nor will they benefit from hearing all the details or in any way being put in the role of your therapist. Yet neither can it be glossed over, treated as no big deal and of no greater significance than your summer vacation. In short you have to, in your own counseling, come to grips with the drinking or relapse so that you do not find yourself working it out on the job with your clients.

A different but similar situation is posed by the clinician who enters the alcohol field as a nonalcoholic but who comes to recognize a budding alcohol problem. In the cases of which we are aware, the individuals were in very early stages of the disease. This raises interesting questions. Since there has been ample evidence of the wisdom of not having recovering alcoholics enter the field until sober a minimum of 2 years, how does the "2-years-of-sobriety-principle" apply in such situations? Does that automatically mean that those who have been good clinicians must exit from the field for the same length of time? To jump to that conclusion is premature. As a profession, we need to determine what the dynamics in this situation are, when an extended leave is needed and when it is not. In the meantime, common sense dictates that this situation needs to be carefully evaluated and monitored. Possibly a brief leave of absence might be indicated, although not necessarily because the counselor has to enter a residential program. A leave provides the

opportunity to work intensely on personal issues, which then reduces the risk that they will be dealt with inappropriately in sessions with clients. At the very least, it will be imperative that lots of clinical supervision be at work and that both a sponsor and a therapist for the counselor be an integral part of the recovery.

The foregoing may seem a very grim note on which to conclude this text. It is sobering, but it is reality, too. Maybe one of the hardest things to learn in becoming a clinician is how to take care of yourself. Like everything else, that takes a lot of practice too. One aspect of caring for yourself professionally as well as personally is to place yourself in the company of nurturing people.

For both of us the mention of nurturing cannot help but bring to mind faces of those who have been important to us. While a dedication at the conclusion of a book may seem most unusual, there are those we wish to thank. Their assistance is woven throughout this work.

For our colleagues and friends
Trevor Price, Mary Montgomery, Bernie Bergen,
George Vailliant, Sally Johnson, Ros Johnson, Charlie Miller

RESOURCES AND FURTHER READING
Issues of the profession

Anderson SC, Wiemer LE: Administrators' beliefs about the relative competence of recovering and non-recovering chemical dependency counselors, *Families in Society* 73(10):596-603, 1992.

> The authors review the literature on the relative competence of recovering and non-recovering counselors and report the findings of a study on the beliefs, preferences, and practices of administrators regarding these two groups. Most administrators believe that the two groups have no differences in effectiveness. Administrators are equally divided between preferring a balance of recovering and non-recovering counselors and having no preference. Implications for policy, practice, and research are discussed. (Author abstract.)

Banken JA, McGovern TF: Alcoholism and drug abuse counseling: State of the art consideration, *Alcoholism Treatment Quarterly* 9(2):29-53, 1992.

> Alcoholism and drug abuse counseling occupies a central place in the multidisciplinary, multifaceted, and multisituational responses to drug dependency issues. The origins and development of this profession/specialty are examined in the light of present realities and changes occurring within the profession itself and within the overall drug dependency field. A recent survey (1991) of professionals in the field identified such issues as primarily issues of professional identity and of credentialing; these issues are placed in an historical context. (Author abstract.)

Bell J: Treatment dependence: Preliminary description of yet another syndrome, *Br J Addict* 87(7):1049-1054, 1992.

> The last decade has witnessed an expansion of treatment services and research into alcoholism and addiction. As so often happens when attempting to find solutions to pressing individual and social problems, the solutions have come to acquire an importance of their own, obscuring the problems they were intended to solve. Many programs are characterized by stereotyped approaches to treatment, which seem more in line with the needs of the staff than with the problems of the clients. The hopes that treatment for addictions will solve some of the problems of contemporary society have given treatment a salience that cannot be justified in terms of results. Frustrated at the results of treatment, clinical staff intensify their efforts and attribute the shortcomings of treatment to a lack of client motivation. There are disconcerting parallels between these behaviors in clinicians and the

behavioral changes of the Alcohol Dependence Syndrome. The label 'treatment dependence syndrome' is proposed to characterize a pattern of individual and institutional behaviour that is both self-perpetuating and self-defeating. (Author abstract.)

Blume SB: *Confidentiality of patient records in alcoholism and drug treatment programs:* New York: American Medical Society on Alcoholism and Other Drug Dependencies and National Council on Alcoholism, 1987.

The pamphlet reviews the 1987 revisions of federal regulations governing confidentiality of alcohol and drug abuse patient records. It addresses the records covered by the regulations; types of communications covered; written informed consent; the application of consent to situations involving minors, incompetent, or deceased persons; types of information to be released with consent; and the security of records.

Chiauzzi EJ, Liljegren S: Taboo topics in addiction treatment: An empirical review of clinical folklore (review), *Journal of Substance Abuse Treatment* 10(3):303-316, 1993.

This article reviews 11 taboo topics, that is, research findings that question traditional assumptions and teachings of addiction treatment. These topics include (1) the lack of empirical support for the Minnesota Model, (2) questions about the necessity of Alcoholics Anonymous for maintaining abstinence, (3) the existence of spontaneous remission, (4) the detrimental aspects of labeling, (5) the value of addicted individuals' self-reports, (6) the lack of empirical support for the addictive personality concept, (7) cue exposure as an underutilized intervention, (8) the interactional nature of motivation, (9) the value of smoking cessation in early recovery, (10) the overuse of the addiction concept, and (11) the lack of empirical support for the disease concept of co-dependency. Misconceptions arise due to the lack of communication between disciplines and the experiential bias of current addiction treatment modalities. Emphasis is placed upon the importance of empiricism to advance the addiction field beyond faith and supposition. (Author abstract.)

Cooper MG: Treatment in the age of managed care, *Employee Assistance Quarterly* 9(2):83-97, 1993.

This article addresses issues introduced by managed care in health-care delivery and especially the impact on employee assistance professionals. It discusses the mutual and conflicting concerns about cost savings and quality assurance, abusers of treatment providers in terms of rumors of "finders fees", use of expensive in-patient care when out-patient community treatment may have been satisfactory, and abuses introduced by insurance companies. The challenges that confront the field—does treatment work, what is the definition of sobriety, treatment matching, use of review protocols—are also discussed.

DeJong CAJ, van den Brink W, Jansen JAM: Sex role stereotypes and clinical judgment: How therapists view their alcoholic patients, *Journal of Substance Abuse Treatment* 10(4):383-389, 1993.

In the course of a selection procedure for in-patient treatment in an addiction clinic, it was repeatedly noticed that the attitude of staff members toward male alcoholics was more confronting and critical as compared to a more empathic and supportive attitude toward female alcoholics. Two different processes may account for this phenomenon. First, male and female alcoholics may differ in their interpersonal behavior toward therapists, and subsequently these different behaviors evoke different attitudes and behaviors in therapists (interaction-hypothesis). Second, these different attitudes toward male and female patients may emerge from preconceived ideas among therapists about male and female alcoholics (stereotype-hypothesis). This study describes the stereotypes held by therapists regarding the interpersonal behavior of male and female alcoholics. Furthermore, it explores the influence of self-perceived interpersonal behavior of therapists on these stereotypes. The results suggest that the differences in attitude and behavior towards alcoholics are–at least partly–the result of different male and female alcoholic stereotypes held by therapists. These stereotypes were related to the self-perceived interpersonal behavior of the therapist. Pretreatment matching of patients and therapists should be based on interpersonal attitudes rather than on sex. (Author abstract.)

Garcia SA: Maternal drug abuse: Laws and ethics as agents of just balances and therapeutic interventions, *International Journal of the Addictions* 28(13):1311-1339, 1993.

Among the many pressing legal, psychosocial, and ethical issues surrounding perinatal chemical dependence is one of achieving balances between far-reaching rights claimed for the unborn and for children and those claimed by their mothers. In an attempt to achieve balances that are just and promote positive consequences' policies and laws have evolved that have pitted disparate individuals and groups against each other, most obviously mothers against their fetuses and children. Some such policies have had negative consequences, such as the further weakening of already at-risk families and the erosion of doctor/patient trust. This article asserts the ethical concepts and legal tenets must be combined to develop new paradigms designed to minimize conflict and to achieve just and therapeutic balances between the rights and needs of those involved. (Author abstract.)

Kalb M, Propper MS: The future of alcohology: Craft or science? *American Journal of Psychiatry* 133(6):641-645, 1976.

The authors discuss the problems that have resulted from the influx of professionals into the field of alcoholism, which has historically been dominated by paraprofessional workers. The interaction of the professional, who operates from a scientific model, with the paraprofessional whose model of treatment has followed craft lines, has created unique problems and tensions. A synergism has been created that has been detrimental rather than complementary. The authors suggest that the future of the alcohol field will have to be established along craft (paraprofessional) or scientific (professional) lines because the two models cannot profitably coexist. (Author abstract.)

Kurtz L: Cooperation and rivalry between helping professionals and members of AA, *Health and Social Work* 10(2):104-112, 1985.

Because Alcoholics Anonymous (AA) is an important resource for recovering alcoholics, most treatment centers want to work cooperatively with it. To identify factors that enhance this cooperation, the author surveyed AA members and professionals in the same communities and obtained a profile of their interactions, ideological similarities, and linking activities. (Author abstract.)

Lucey MR: Liver transplantation for alcoholic liver disease, *Bailliere's Clinical Gastroenterology* 7(3):717-727, 1993.

Alcoholic liver disease is the most common cause of cirrhosis in the USA and western Europe. In 1988, alcoholic-related liver cirrhosis accounted for 44% of the 26,572 deaths attributed to liver cirrhosis in the USA. By comparison, the total number of livers transplanted in the USA was 2512. Furthermore, the United Network for Organ Sharing (UNOS) estimated that nearly 1000 patients in North America were on liver transplant waiting lists by the end of 1990, and more than 100 patients per quarter were dying while on the waiting list. Thus if only a minority of alcoholic patients with end-stage liver disease were accepted for a liver transplantation, it is conceivable that they would overwhelm the available organ donor supply. For these reasons, the question whether liver transplants should be provided to those with alcoholic disease has become a topic of intense debate both within and without the medical community. (Author abstract.)

Marshall MJ, Marshall S: Treatment paternalism in chemical dependency counselors, *International Journal of the Addictions* 28(2):91-106, 1993.

This study investigated the degree of paternalism in the treatment philosophies of chemical dependency counselors in three categories of treatment center: adolescent-only, adult, and religious/minority. Counselors were shown picture arrays of either adolescent patients or adult patients and asked to choose a preferred treatment policy, either paternalistic or compensatory in nature. Results showed religious/minority counselors preferred a significantly greater paternalistic approach to all patients than did the adolescent-only and adult center counselors. The adolescent-only counselors responded more paternalistically to the adolescent patients than the adult patients, while the adult and religious/minority counselors did not respond significantly differently to either group. Copyright 1993, International Journal of the Addictions.

Modell JG, Glaser FB, Mountz JM: The ethics and safety of alcohol administration in the experimental setting to individuals who have chronic, severe alcohol problems, *Alcohol and Alcoholism* 28(2):189-197, 1993.

There is a popular belief that the experimental administration of alcohol to individuals who have chronic, severe alcohol problems (alcoholics) is inherently dangerous or unethical. This creates an environment in which researchers who desire to conduct a study involving the administration of alcohol to persons with severe alcohol problems must defend the relative safety and reasonableness of this practice when, in fact, scientific justification for not using this important methodological technique in alcohol research is lacking. The primary purpose of this manuscript is to present and discuss the safety, ethical, and practical considerations of research involving administration of alcohol to subjects who have had difficulty refraining from harmful alcohol use in the natural setting. It is concluded that there is no overriding reason why alcohol cannot, with due precaution, be safely and ethically administered in the experimental setting to human subjects who suffer from alcohol problems. (Author abstract.)

NAADAC Education and Research Foundation: *Salary and compensation study of Alcoholism and Drug Abuse Professionals, 1993,* Arlington, VA: NAADAC, 1993.

The study of alcoholism and drug abuse counselor salaries and incomes was commissioned by NAADAC's Education and Research Foundation to provide a national profile of the profession's compensation. The results also provide insight into several career pathways common to the profession and help to confirm or dispel many notions regarding compensation in a variety of occupations held by those trained as counselors. Information was gathered from 746 NAADAC members who completed a 4-page mailed questionnaire. This information is presented in 40 tables and covers some of the following areas: normal weekly hours and length of service in primary employment, earnings from primary employment for government employees compared with other professionals, respondents' years of experience and formal education, completed formal education and subject of highest degree earned by salaried respondents, and characteristics of employing organization.

Sayre LD: The parallel process in the addiction treatment staff system: An ethical perspective, *Alcoholism Treatment Quarterly* 9(2):65-75, 1992.

This article examines the manifestation of addictive family system dynamics in a parallel process among the addiction treatment staff system. Suggestions for using ethical principles and guidelines to erect appropriate staff system boundaries are given. Ethical principles and guidelines, training, and open staff discussion are presented as resources available to aid in the maintenance of healthy staff system functioning. (Author abstract.)

Shipko JS, Stout CE: A comparison of the personality characteristics between the recovering alcoholic and non-alcoholic counselor, *Alcoholism Treatment Quarterly* 9(3/4):207-214, 1992.

Graduate students in social work have been described as often being pessimistic about the treatment outcomes of alcoholics; such an attitude hinders treatment, diagnosis, and recovery for the patient. Within the field of alcoholism treatment, personality characteristics may exist that differentiate recovering alcoholic counselors from counselors who are non-alcoholic. In addition, the non-alcoholic counselors may use a treatment approach based on academic training and theory versus recovering alcoholic counselors who, in addition to theory and training, may tend to use their subjective experiences and participation in Alcoholics

Anonymous as a primary mode of alcoholism counseling. The combination of personality factors and of theoretical approaches may influence treatment outcome. (Author abstract.)

Wright N, McGovern T: Ethics for the alcoholism and drug abuse counselor, *The Counselor* 6(3):17-19, 1988.

This article discusses the revised and as of 1994, most recent Code of Ethics adopted by The NAADAC Board of Directors, July, 1987.

Prevention

Jones CL, Battjes RJ, editors: *Etiology of drug abuse: Implications for prevention. NIDA Research Monograph 56,* Rockville, MD: National Institute on Drug Abuse, 1985.

This monograph defines the "state of the art" in prevention research with respect to drug abuse. The contributors conducted investigations funded by NIDA research grants. The work is divided into two major sections. The first is "Childhood and the Transition to Adolescence," which includes discussion of familial antecedents of adolescent drug use from a developmental perspective; the development of health orientation among children and the implications for substance use prevention; predictors of adolescent substance abuse; and research strategies to identify developmental vulnerabilities for drug abuse. The second section, "Transition to Young Adulthood," addresses recent historical changes that may relate to issues of etiology and prevention; age of onset of drug use as a factor in subsequent problems; patterns of use of legal, nonlegal, and medically prescribed psychotropic drugs during later adolescence; prevention of adolescent drug abuse drawing upon etiological, developmental, behavioral, and environmental models; and discussion of the pressing research questions. (ADM)85-1335.

Moskowitz JM: The primary prevention of alcohol problems: A critical review of the literature, *Journal of Studies on Alcohol* 50(1):54-88, 1989.

The research evaluating the effects of programs and policies in reducing the incidence of alcohol problems is critically examined including: (1) policies affecting the physical, economic, and social availability of alcohol (e.g., minimum legal age, price, and advertising of alcohol), (2) formal social controls on alcohol-related behavior (e.g., drinking-driving laws), (3) primary prevention programs (e.g., school-based alcohol education), and (4) environmental safety measures (e.g., automobile airbags). The research generally supports the efficacy of three alcohol-specific policies: raising the minimum legal drinking age to 21, increasing alcohol taxes, and increasing the enforcement of drinking-driving laws. Also, research suggests that various environmental safety measures reduce the incidence of alcohol-related trauma. In contrast, little evidence currently exists to support the efficacy of primary prevention programs. However, a systems perspective of prevention suggests that prevention programs may become more efficacious after widespread adoption of prevention policies that lead to shifts in social norms regarding use of beverage alcohol. (Author abstract.)

U.S. Department of State, Bureau of International Narcotics Matters: *Building public awareness: A handbook for drug awareness campaigns,* Washington: U.S. Department of State, 1988.

This handbook, produced by the Department of State, was prepared to assist in public information campaigns to increase the awareness of the impact of drugs on society, viewed as a necessary antecedent for other prevention programming. It is organized into three parts. Part I, a planning guide, provides a rational, theoretical approach to communications, needs assessments, and targets and strategies. Part II focuses upon implementation, the creation of materials, pretesting, working with the media, working with organizations, and evaluation. The Appendixes, Part III, include sample materials, a glossary, and three well-selected articles, each with an extensive bibliography on the role of media, the use and effects of public service announcements, and a critical review of mass media and smoking cessation.

Publications

About AA: A newsletter for professional men and women

Alcoholics Anonymous is a self-help "fellowship of men and women who share their experience with each other and help others to recover from alcoholism." The newsletter reports AA activities and describes information about resources available through AA. Recent issues discussed AA in prisons and presented a demographic report of AA membership. Directed at health care providers, this single sheet letter is useful to anyone interested in AA programs.

(Contact: Alcoholics Anonymous, Box 459, Grand Central Station, New York, NY 10163. Quarterly. Free.)

The addiction letter: A resource exchange for professionals on preventing and treating alcoholism and drug abuse

The Letter includes practical information for professional counselors in signed articles, book reviews, abstracts of articles from current journals, and editorials. (Contact: Manisses Communications Group, Inc., P.O. Box 3357, Wayland Square, Providence, RI 02906-0357. Monthly.)

Al-Anon speaks out

This is a single sheet newsletter directed at community professionals. Issues have included articles about support by Al-Anon for adult children of alcoholics and a report of the first Al-Anon/Alateen survey.

(Contact: Al-Anon Family Group Headquarters, Inc., Box 182, Madison Square Station, New York, NY 10159-0182. Annual. Free.)

The Alcoholism Report: The Authoritative Newsletter for Professionals in the Field of Alcoholism

The Report provides current awareness services focusing on national activities with implications for alcoholism treatment. It includes extensive coverage of congressional and federal agency activities. The Report publishes news of proposed and enacted legislation, detailed descriptions of committee hearings, funding appropriations, and actions of national task forces. News briefs from treatment facilities, such as changes in leadership or programs, are included. Names, addresses, and phone numbers are provided for quick ordering of reports or to request further information.

(Contact: Manisses Communications Group, Inc., P.O. Box 3357, Wayland Square, Providence, RI 02906-0357. 401/831-6020. Monthly.)

NASADAD Alcohol and Drug Abuse Report

Two reports are published monthly. The Monthly Report focuses on current activities within the congressional and executive branches. The *Special Report* provides in-depth coverage of topics such as private health insurance for alcohol and drug dependency treatment services and prevention research in alcohol and drug abuse. The focus of both reports is on programs, rather than clinical care.

(Contact: National Association of State Alcohol and Drug Abuse Directors, 444 North Capitol Street, NW, Suite 530, Washington, DC, 20001. Semimonthly.)

The NACoA Network

The National Association for Children of Alcoholics is an advocacy organization offering publications, workshops, and conferences, which serves as a clearinghouse and lobbyist for the development of programs for this group. The NACoA Network offers news of the NACoA and contains articles of interest to children of alcoholics and treatment professionals.

(Contact: National Association for Children of Alcoholics, 31706 Coast Highway, Suite 201, South Laguna, CA, 92677. Quarterly.)

Of substance: A newsletter for the substance abuse treatment community
The Legal Action Center is a nonprofit, public interest organization that offers legal representation and counseling to ex-offenders, recovering alcohol and drug abusers, and to the programs and agencies assisting in their rehabilitation. Of Substance covers legal developments and issues in treatment. Included in the topics covered are reports on federal and state laws that protect recovering alcoholics from employment discrimination and also reports on issues of compliance with federal regulations governing confidentiality of records.
(Contact: Legal Action Center, P.O. Box 6825, Syracuse, NY 13217. Bimonthly.)

Prevention Pipeline
This bimonthly newsletter, published by the U.S. Center for Substance Abuse Prevention (CSAP), provides an update on activities in the substance abuse field. It is directed at a broad range of professionals including educators, researchers, information specialists, administrators and policymakers, and those planning and administering community programs. Issues offer updates on CSAPs program activities, reprints of articles, summaries of research findings, descriptions of new audiovisual and print materials, and a listing of alcohol and drug conferences. (Contact: National Clearinghouse for Alcohol and Drug Information, Dept. PP, P.O. Box 2345, Rockville, MD, 20852. Bimonthly.)

Index